*A History of*

*Modern British Adult Education*

## Roger Fieldhouse

### WITH ASSOCIATES

| | |
|---|---|
| Peter Baynes | Roseanne Benn |
| Walter Drews | John Field |
| Brian Groombridge | Mary Hamilton |
| John McIlroy | Harold Marks |
| Ian Martin | Naomi Sargant |

and research assistant
Vicky Fieldhouse

**NIACE**
THE NATIONAL ORGANISATION
FOR ADULT LEARNING

Published by the National Institute of Adult Continuing Education
(England and Wales)
21 De Montfort Street, Leicester LE1 7GE
Company registration no. 2603322
Charity registration no. 1002775

First published 1996
Reprinted 2000
© NIACE

CATALOGUING IN PUBLICATION DATA
A CIP record for this title is available from the British Library
ISBN 1 872941 66 4

Printed in Great Britain by Antony Rowe Ltd, Chippenham, Wilts

# Contents

# MODERN BRITISH ADULT EDUCATION

**Books are to be returned on or before
the last date below.**

LIBREX —

For my mother and father, both of whom have been lifelong learners in the autodidactic tradition. They gave me the best start in life: a happy childhood and a good education. The rest is my fault!

# Preface

We study history because of the desperate importance of the human past: what happened in the past ... governs the world we live in today, and created the many problems which beset us. ... To change the world, we have first to understand it.

(Arthur Marwick, *THES*, 25 November 1994)

This book will survey British adult education over the past two centuries, attempting to throw more light on the present and the future by critically analysing its historical development. A number of histories have been published over the years (e.g. Peers, 1958; Harrison, 1961; Kelly, 1962, 3rd edn 1992; Legge, 1982; Simon, 1990) but this book will concentrate less on description of the past and more on critical analysis. It does not seek to replace Thomas Kelly's invaluable *History of Adult Education in Great Britain from the Middle Ages to the Twentieth Century*, with its wealth of detailed information, but rather to build on it. Nor does it claim to be in any way the final word. As Arthur Marwick recently pointed out, 'All each individual historian produces is *contributions* to knowledge, tentative and fallible, which will be attacked, debated, qualified and amplified ...' (*ibid.*). This book will do no more than that. Its purpose is to contribute to a debate about the nature and significance of adult education in Britain by measuring its aims against achievements and comparing the rhetoric with the reality. It will attempt to calculate how influential adult education has been and what effect (if any) it has had on society. It will relate the historical development to the wider policy and ideological context within which it took place.

If we ask 'what is adult education?', it is rather like Pontius Pilot's question about truth – deceptively easy to answer. It is concerned with adult learning, of course. But whereas in the twentieth century this might be defined as education for people beyond compulsory schooling, no such definition can be applied to three-quarters of the nineteenth century, when there was no compulsory schooling. And even in the twentieth century, it has more frequently been applied to education for people above a certain age – 18 or 21. We shall use the term 'adult education' to apply loosely to education for adults beyond initial, normally full-time and (more recently) compulsory education: after the end of 'childhood'. And it is a term which embraces the many modern variations – community education, continuing education, lifelong education, and so on.

But what is 'education'? Is it teaching or learning?; didactic or self-directed?; face-to-face or at a distance?; formal or informal?; institutionalised or happening everywhere?; residential or non-residential?; state-funded or self-financing? Is it something that happens to (or is taken by) individuals or is it a collective activity? We shall attempt to embrace most of these formulations, but our coverage will necessarily be uneven. It will over-emphasise formal and institutionalised learning at the expense of the less-well-recorded autodidactic tradition. It is as well to recall, even if we do not reflect, the finding by Allen Tough that:

Only a small part of the iceberg shows above the water's surface. In adult learning or adult education that small highly visible tip of the iceberg is groups of people learning – in auditoriums, classrooms, workshops, or conferences. That is what adult educators have noticed and paid attention to over the years ... [But] if you look at one hundred learning projects, about 20 are planned by professionals and about 80 by the learner himself or herself or some amateur planner (Tough, 1983: 143–4).

The other major question the book will attempt to tackle is what purpose (if any) did this adult education serve? Was it predominantly for individual personal fulfilment or for social development? Did adult education help to produce a more active citizenship or a better informed and participatory democracy? Was its prime purpose to make good the inadequacies of schooling by offering those who had 'failed' a second chance? Or was it merely more education in adulthood for whoever wanted it? Was it primarily vocational in orientation? Was it a form of social control? Was it in reality a mixture of most or all of these functions, some of which became more important than others at different times and in different situations? These are the kinds of critical question that we will attempt to answer.

## Acknowlegements

For their generous assistance, I wish to acknowledge my gratitude to the following:

The (now defunct) UFC, the HEFCE and the University of Exeter for research grants which contributed enormously to the production of this book.

All my associates for their contributions. (It was tempting to write the whole book myself but any advantages there may have been in conformity of style would not have compensated for their greater expertise.)

Vicky Fieldhouse, my daughter, who was employed as a part-time research assistant. She unearthed and sifted through a mass of material and did a magnificent job in reducing it to useable proportions.

Rachel Hodge, who carried out a bibliographical search of historical sources for Chapter 6, and Anna Benn who undertook a similar task for Chapter 15.

Mel Doyle, Bernard Jennings and Jack Taylor for their helpful comments on drafts of Chapter 7; and Eileen Aird, Bill Conboy, Joe England, Keith Jackson, Mike Lieven, John Sheldon and R. Wildgust for their invaluable corrections to Chapter 9. (If I sometimes disagreed with their advice, I hope they will be forgiving.)

John Cain, Henry Cassirer, the late Edward Hutchinson, Meri Nokkala (Riuttu) and Naomi Sargant for much wise advice on the content of Chapter 14. A special debt regarding this chapter is also acknowledged to the writings of the late John Robinson (particularly for *Learning Across the Air*) and Asa Briggs (especially for his *History of British Broadcasting*).

Alan Tuckett and the staff at NIACE for the opportunity to consult the Institute's archives.

Christopher Feeney at NIACE, for his initial encouragement, for his patience as each deadline passed, and for all his editorial assistance.

Greta Tink, my secretary, who has assisted and supported me for many years, way beyond the call of duty.

My old friends and colleague Sheila and Tom Caldwell, for helping to find somewhere to work undisturbed on the final stages of this book in Espinas, France, during a lovely month of August 1995.

ROGER FIELDHOUSE
*University of Exeter*
November 1995

# 1

# Historical and Political Context

## Roger Fieldhouse

Some two hundred years ago the Vicar of Broughton Blean in Kent described the aims of Sunday Schools as being:

to furnish opportunities of instruction to the children of the poorer part of the parish, without interfering with any industry of the weekdays ... The children are to be taught to read and to be instructed in the plain duties of the Christian religion, with a particular view to their good and industrious behaviour in their future character of labourers and servants (Sylvester, 1970: 263).

A few years later, Tom Paine was complaining that despite Sunday Schools and other educational opportunities:

Many a youth, with good natural genius, who is apprenticed to a mechanical trade, such as a carpenter, joiner, millwright, shipwright, blacksmith, etc. is prevented getting forward the whole of his life, from the want of a little common education when a boy.

Paine therefore advocated a grant of 'four pounds a year for every child under fourteen years of age; enjoining the parents of such children to send them to school, to learn reading, writing and common arithmetic' (Paine, 1969: 263).

Tom Paine's radical proposal was not implemented. Nor was Samuel Whitbread's Bill, introduced to Parliament in 1807, for establishing parochial schools throughout England and Wales. But these proposals do illustrate the awakening interest in, and concern for, education, and also its perceived close links with industry and industriousness. The industrial revolution greatly stimulated this interest in education, not only for children, but also for the adult population who had not been adequately schooled in their childhood.

The industrial revolution wrought many changes to British society: the transformation from a predominantly rural to a largely urban society; the final demise of the domestic means of production; the destruction of many pre-industrial crafts; the gradual disappearance of the semi-independent, self-employed craftsman and labourer; the concentration of production in workshop, mill and factory; the mushrooming of sprawling industrial cities and the creation of teeming urban slums; the emergence of new industries such as cotton and engineering and new industrial infrastructures; rapid technological change; the creation of a vast amount of wealth; fundamental changes in the social structure; and the development of a collective optimism and arrogance which typified British attitudes to the rest of the world for much of the nineteenth century and enabled one small nation to stride across the continents, painting the atlas red with the blood and sweat of exploited peoples.

This new industrial environment engendered new ideas, new attitudes and many new needs. Not least of these was the need for a very different labourforce to that of pre-industrial society, to cope with the different working conditions and exhibiting a wholly different range of working practices and skills. But whether this warranted education for the industrial working class was a much debated topic. There was a widespread and very real fear that too much education would be tantamount to opening Pandora's box – all kinds of unwanted consequences would follow.

As Davies Giddy MP saw it, when opposing Samuel Whitbread's Parochial Schools Bill in the House of Commons in 1807, education for the labouring poor:

would be prejudicial to their morals and happiness; it would teach them to despise their lot in life instead of making them good servants in agriculture and other laborious employments ...; instead of teaching them subordination, it would render them fractious ... it would enable them to read seditious pamphlets, vicious books and publications against Christianity; it would render them insolent to their superiors, and in a few years [it would be] necessary to direct the strong arm of power against them (Hansard 1st series, ix, 1807: cols 798–9).

However, as the industrial revolution really got under way, there were many employers who wanted a more skilled workforce and were prepared to risk the political consequences. At the very least they could see the advantages of having employees who could read instructions, as Mr Portman, an Assistant Commissioner for the Royal Commission on Employment in Agriculture, recognised in 1867:

As the use of machinery ... is daily becoming more common it must surely be an advantage to the farmer to have in his employ men who at any rate are able to read the instructions which are necessary for the management of the various implements with the care of which they are entrusted (RC Report on Employment ... in Agriculture, H C, 1867–8: xvii).

At the same time many workers saw it as being to their advantage to acquire skills which would enable them to gain employment, or obtain more skilled or better paid jobs. As schools provided little such education until quite late in the century, many employers, employees and philanthropists shared an interest in promoting adult education. The mechanics' institutes and adult schools derived much patronage and participation from this mutual need.

Of almost equal importance to improving the labourforce was the widespread desire to understand the fundamental changes that were taking place. The sense of enquiry and the pursuit of greater knowledge, particularly about the scientific and technological innovations that were daily impacting on their lives, were important characteristics of the Victorians. Perhaps their sense of optimism and their faith in progress encouraged such inquisitiveness. It was all so exciting and worthwhile knowing. The numerous literary, philosophical and scientific societies, found in every town and many villages, epitomised this wish to understand, and thereby to control, the changing environment.

A third need which sprang from the industrial revolution and had a profound influence on education arose from the appalling living and working conditions that it engendered. Before very long it became all too apparent that in an urban, industrial economy, with an almost total division of labour and large-scale productive units completely outside the control of the workforce, it was patently beyond the powers of individuals either to cope with or to change the conditions without aid. Therefore, partly through a genuine sense of altruism and partly through fear of the growing power and political consciousness of the industrial working class, the British ruling class introduced a series of factory and mines Acts to provide some statutory controls over working conditions and hours of work, whilst an extensive range of Poor Laws and public health, housing, education and other legislation gradually brought improvements to living and social conditions.

There was a drift from the *laissez-faire*, self-help ethos which largely characterised the earlier part of the nineteenth century towards a comprehensive system of collectivist intervention by the end of the century and, in the twentieth century, to the growth of the welfare state and to the gradual adoption of a programme of municipalisation and nationalisation and government control of the economy, allowing greater centralised planning 'for the good of the nation'.

The growth of a state educational system, from the very first investment of public money in 1833, to the massive education machine of the twentieth century, was part of this ideological drift from self-help individualism to social collectivism. If recent governments have been attempting to reverse this trend a little, we should not underestimate the huge influence which this ideological evolution has had on all branches of education over the past 150 years. Obviously it affected mainly school-age education at first, but increasingly in the twentieth century it changed the nature of further, higher and adult education beyond the age of compulsory schooling also.

One of the factors which made education too important to leave to the whims of individualist self-help was the growing fear of foreign competition. By the late 1860s, Britain's apparently unassailable position as the leading industrial nation was beginning to look a little less secure. A number of European countries, particularly Germany, and the emerging United States of America were threatening to oust Britain from its comfortable industrial perch. As W.E. Forster, the Vice-President of the Council in charge of the Education Department, declared when introducing the 1870 Education Bill in the House of Commons:

Uneducated labourers – and many of our labourers are utterly uneducated – are, for the most part, unskilled labourers, and if we leave our work-folk any longer unskilled ... they will become over-matched in the competition of the world (Maclure, 1986: 104).

Thus by 1870, the need to improve Britain's international economic competitiveness was adding yet another impetus to the development of the education system. At first this was directed primarily at schooling, with the introduction of the School Boards and, 10 years later, compulsory education. But by the end of the 1880s the creation of the Technical Education

Committees under the newly established county councils placed training very much on the adult education agenda, where it has remained, to a greater or lesser degree, ever since.

Another aspect of collectivism which extended the role of education was the growing emphasis on 'the expert', first advanced by the Benthamites and later by the Fabians. They believed that adequate social welfare depended on the elimination of confusion, muddle and waste, and that this was best achieved by the replacement of British amateurism by a bureaucracy of experts who would be selected purely on merit. This meritocracy would be subject to ultimate public control through Parliament, but it was anticipated that it could be wholly disinterested and would administer the publicly owned industries and welfare state solely for the good of society as a whole.

To be able to carry out this important task, this meritocratic bureaucracy or Civil Service needed to be well educated (Greenaway, 1988). Although in practice many of these mandarins were recruited from a self-perpetuating, privately educated elite, the complexities of a modern industrial-collectivist state could not rely solely on such amateurism. It had to back it up with its own state-aided education system.

The extension of the male franchise after 1867 and the growing political involvement of organised labour, culminating in the formation of the Labour Representation Committee in 1900 (soon to become the Labour Party) was seen to be another reason for extending education. It was felt necessary 'to educate our new masters'. This was a task particularly suited to *adult* education. The 1908 Report on *Oxford and Working Class Education* reflects very much the perceived need to provide the working classes with 'the knowledge necessary to enable them to show foresight in their choice of political means' and to foster social harmony by helping them to become 'a more potent influence on the side of industrial peace' (Joint Committee ..., 1909: paras 77–8, 139). Moreover, this was more than a mere exercise in civic education. It was part of an elaborate plan to counter the growing influence of socialist and Marxist ideas which, around the turn of the century, were felt to be exerting an undesirable influence on the increasingly powerful and well-organised mass labour movement. During the 1890s a concerted effort had been made, with some success, to destroy the 'new unionism' but there were still fears about the political influence of the numerous small but vociferous socialist organisations and parties. 'New Liberalism' aimed to contain these socialist impulses and head off revolutionism by offering 'limited socialism' as an acceptable political alternative. The liberal social welfare reforms after 1906 formed a major part of this strategy. State aid for adult education following the 1908 Report was another, if small, part of this same strategy (Fieldhouse, 1987b).

Although this measure was very successful, it did not destroy the alternative strand of 'independent working-class education' which descended from the nineteenth-century autodidactic tradition and a whole complex of working-class organisations, to Ruskin College, the Plebs League and the National Council of Labour Colleges. This lived on as an influential, if declining force well into the twentieth century (*ibid.*, Simon, 1990).

The overt nationalism of the First World War was probably more effective than the Liberal social welfare reforms in stemming the tide of socialist ideas in Britain. However, the war created many new problems. In 1917 the coalition government established a Reconstruction Committee, and later a Ministry of Reconstruction, to plan how to tackle these problems after the war. The Reconstruction Committee set up a small Adult Education sub-committee under the chairmanship of A.L. Smith, the Master of Balliol. It saw the problems facing Britain as (a) international – the need to strengthen world peace and re-draw the map of Europe after the war; (b) imperial – the need to adjust to a new relationship between Britain and the dominions; and (c) domestic. The third category included political dilemmas such as the over-powerful Cabinet and the Second Chamber issue; economic problems revolving around the balance between nationalisation and private ownership; the industrial conflict of interests to be resolved between labour and capital; and social issues including the position of women and the 'two cankers of .... drink and prostitution' (Ministry of Reconstruction, 1919: 1–2). The Committee believed that 'the economic recovery of the nation' and 'the proper use of their responsibilities by millions of new voters' (including women for the first time) depended on the creation of a more intelligent public opinion. Therefore it concluded that 'adult education is a permanent national necessity, an inseparable aspect of citizenship' and that 'the opportunity for adult education should be spread uniformly and systematically over the whole community' (*ibid.*: 5). Thus the 1919 Report placed adult education very much centre stage in the affairs of the nation. It will be one of the tasks of this book to assess the extent to which it rose to that challenge.

A brief economic boom brought about by post-war reconstruction was followed by two decades of depression and high unemployment; the slow but steady decline of Britain's industrial base; its gradual displacement by finance capital and the City of London as the country's economic mainstay; two brief and less-than-glorious Labour governments interspersed by long periods of uninspired Conservative administration; the beginnings of public broadcasting; the 1926 General Strike; the hunger marches of the 1930s; the lengthening shadow of Fascism reaching across Europe; the failure of the League of Nations; the false hope and national guilt engendered by Munich; the rally to the flag again in the balmy autumn of 1939 followed by the Dunkirk spirit, Churchillian bulldog tenacity, the Blitz, the blackout and the blackmarket, and the fatal wartime haemorrhaging of Britain's fragile economy.

In 1944 the Coalition Government introduced a new Education Act. It laid upon the local education authorities the duty of securing efficient primary, secondary and further education in their areas. Further education was deemed to include full- and part-time education for people over compulsory school age and 'leisure-time occupation ... for any persons over compulsory school age who are able and willing to profit by the facilities provided for that purpose'. These were expected to include 'organized cultural training and recreation activities' (Education Act, 1944: clause 41).

The post-war Labour Government's education policy was geared to implementing the 1944 Act, and aimed to create greater equality of opportunities within a meritocratic society. It was not more socialistically egalitarian. Even Ellen Wilkinson, the Minister of Education (who as 'Red

Ellen' had participated in the hunger marches of the 1930s), wished only to reform the education system, not forge it into a tool for radical social change (Rubenstein, 1979: 161–2; Vernon, 1982: 202). Apart from the fierce debates about implementing the provisions in the 1944 Act to raise the school leaving age, the post-war Labour Government engaged in no serious thinking about education, and failed to provide any new ideas or inspiration. Its concentration on the 1944 Act led the Government and the Labour Party into 'thinking that we need not think about education so much' (Labour Party, 1952: 177). Moreover, the Government failed to implement the most innovative and far-reaching aspect of its further education plans – the provision of compulsory part-time education up to the age of 18 for all who left school, in new county colleges.

However, it has to be remembered that the Labour Government had to contend with intense post-war economic problems after 1945, aggravated by the replacement of the lend-lease arrangements with new interest-bearing loans by the American Government within weeks of Labour being elected. Dependence on financial aid under the Marshal Plan and the acute shortage of materials greatly limited the Government's options and forced it to cut back on its social programmes.

Progressive plans and expectations were dealt a further blow by the outbreak of the Cold War in 1947–8. Suddenly the over-riding need was seen to be to oppose the Soviet Union and contain communism. Social reconstruction was pushed into the background as the Government embarked on a programme of rearmament, including the development of nuclear weapons. At the same time, anti-communist crusades polarised political attitudes, making the ideological middle ground of the immediate post-war popular front period untenable. The high hopes for a new socialist society built on liberal foundations were shattered by the freezing intolerance of the Cold War.

Meanwhile, Britain began to divest itself of its anachronistic imperial responsibilities, which it could no longer afford. After many years of British procrastination, India gained its independence in 1947, and this was gradually followed by the reluctant but inevitable granting of independence to British colonies in Africa and elsewhere during the decade to follow.

At a more domestic level, the expansion of adult education suffered a serious check when the Ministry of Education was forced by economic circumstances to freeze its grants for 1952–3 and to threaten a 10 per cent reduction in the estimates for adult education for 1953–4. This led to the setting up of a committee to review the organisation and financing of adult education (the Ashby Committee) which issued its Report in 1954. Although the threatened cut was averted, nevertheless the crisis had exposed the real difficulty of meeting rising expectations with limited resources.

The underlying problem lay in the decline of Britain as a world economic power, indicated by the reduction in its share in world trade from 25 per cent in 1950 to 17 per cent in 1959 and 15 per cent by 1962 (Childs, 1986: 100). There were many reasons for this decline, most of them of long standing. They include Britain's over-commitment to military expenditure; the costly maintenance of the pound as a reserve currency; under-capitalisation in British industries and bad industrial relations, which led to inefficient industrial production. A low level of vocational training was also identified by the 1956 White Paper, *Technical Education,* which recommended a doubling of the number of workers given day-release by their employers (a measure that would have been unnecessary if the plans for compulsory part-time education up to the age of 18 had been implemented after the war).

However, there was one of Beveridge's unwanted giants which had been defeated during the war, and remained at bay for the best part of three decades after the war, and that was unemployment. Full employment had gradually led to an improvement in real earnings, and to growing prosperity by the later 1950s. This was enhanced by the extension of hire purchase and a reduction in the rate of purchase tax. The resultant extra demand for consumer goods helped to stimulate production in certain industries, while a fall in world food and raw-material prices made imports cheaper. Military expenditure was also reduced as a percentage of the gross national product, partly as a result of the Suez fiasco in 1956. All this helped to generate an unprecedented prosperity by the late 1950s - a boom in consumption and home ownership which led to Macmillan's famous claim in 1957 that 'most of our people have never had it so good', although even he recognised that there was a minority who were not enjoying this prosperity.

There was also, by the end of 13 years of Conservative government, an enormous balance-of-payments deficit and an increasing tendency to 'spend-now-and-pay-later'. Thus the 'never had it so good' boom was largely founded on credit and a stop-go economy. This brought problems and austerity measures later, but much of the 1960s was a period of optimism and 'joyful irreverence' (Marwick, 1982: 178). The 'swinging sixties' exuded a confident belief in increasing affluence and the imminent abolition of privilege, gross inequality and poverty. In the field of education this atmosphere produced a series of reports which advocated expansion, wider opportunities and greater equity. They included the Robbins Report on higher education and the Newsome Report on secondary education, both in 1963; the Plowden Report on primary education (1967); and the James Report on teacher training (1972). It also brought about the virtual elimination of the 11-plus selection and the replacement of the 1944 tripartite secondary education system by comprehensive schools; the establishment of polytechnics to end the universities' monopoly of higher education; and the creation of the Open University in 1969.

That same year the Government appointed a committee under the chairmanship of Sir Lionel Russell to find 'the most effective and economical deployment of available resources to enable adult education to make its proper contribution to the national system of education'. The Committee discovered an 'accelerating rate of social and educational change' and evidence that 'adult education has proved remarkably adaptive to [these] changing conditions' (DES, 1973: iv, 1), although in the event, the recommended expansion did not take place for reasons which are explained in later chapters.

During the 1970s the deterioration of Britain's condition began to accelerate. The Government attempted to reduce the bargaining power of the trade unions which the commitment to full employment had given them, by introducing incomes policies (1965–70 and 1972–4) and legal regulation of the unions (1969–71). But this only stimulated increased militancy and widespread industrial strife, culminating in the three-day working week and the miners' strike in January 1974. Economic problems were further exacerbated by the 1973 oil crisis and continued to mount up during the later 1970s. These led to rising inflation (which reached 26 per cent in July 1975); the long-term decline of Britain's manufacturing industries (resulting in a fall in the number of people employed in manufacturing from 8.6 million in 1966 to 5.4 million by 1985); the resultant deskilling of the workforce; and rapidly rising unemployment (which reached over three million by 1983). The consequence of all this economic turmoil for adult education was that the Government increasingly used its influence to render it more directly vocational in the hope and expectation that this would contribute to economic recovery.

What made the growing unemployment particularly aggravating was that it disproportionately affected the working class, the ethnic minorities, the inner cities and almost all geographical areas beyond the south-east of England. The result was a dramatic rise in poverty, homelessness and crime, and an increase in dependence on state benefits which steadily declined in real value. For example, in 1971 unemployment benefit was 70 per cent of average earnings: a decade later it was 43 per cent (Moran, 1985: 195–6). A significant underclass of seriously deprived people was being created, within which the ethnic minorities were disproportionately represented. In 1981 this gave rise to large-scale race riots in London, Liverpool and many other cities, and further riots occurred from time to time in subsequent years. By the 1980s British society had become increasingly divided and beset with a variety of escalating social problems, ranging from structural unemployment to rising criminality, homelessness and racial discrimination. At the same time there had been a weakening of the socially protective forces, from the trade unions to the paternalistic left wing of the Tory Party (dismissively dubbed 'wets').

The Thatcher administrations of the 1980s made a radical attempt to tackle the growing social problems by rolling back the support of the welfare state and attempting to create an enterprise culture which would stimulate more adventurous and innovative action on the part of individuals. Initiative was encouraged by reducing regulations and direct taxation and by giving priority to tackling inflation. Dependency was discouraged by reducing social benefits and emphasising the 'old-fashioned Victorian values' of self-help and thrift. Unfortunately, by reducing regulation and state controls, the Thatcher Governments threw away the means of influencing economic and social policy. The consequent planning vacuum, together with the emphasis on an anti-inflation policy at all costs, considerably weakened Britain's industrial base. The resultant unemployment, which again reached over three million in 1993, after a temporary reduction in the late 1980s, placed enormous strains on the economy. Moreover, the patent unfairness of the unregulated enterprise culture which was the legacy of Thatcherism gave rise to despair and resentment and created a socially deprived underclass. In some parts of Britain, by the early 1990s, a culture of crime, violence and selfishness, and a relentless social deterioration towards anarchy, had very largely destroyed the liberal values which had predominated in Britain for much of the previous two hundred years.

At the same time, Thatcherism's ideological antipathy to professionals (including the teaching profession) and local government undermined the basis of both university and local authority adult education. The 1991 Education White Papers, *Higher Education: A new framework* and *Training for the 21st Century*, and the 1992 Higher and Further Education Act, reflect the ideological shift and the growing demand for vocationalism. The emphasis in the 1944 Act on a partnership of providers collectively securing an adequate and broadly-based provision of further and adult education for all who were able and willing to benefit by it was largely displaced by more individualist, self-help values; by a narrower functional approach; and by the encouragement of greater competitiveness between providers. The sense of collective effort and social worth, which raises societies above the selfish pursuit of individual gratification, although not completely lost, was much more muted by the early 1990s than it had been half a century earlier.

2

# The Nineteenth Century

## Roger Fieldhouse

In the previous chapter it was suggested that the experience of industrialisation and the gradual drift from a *laissez-faire*, self-help ethos towards collectivism formed the wider background to the development of adult education in the nineteenth century. At the end of the First World War the Adult Education Committee of the Ministry of Reconstruction concluded that the history of adult education reflected the religious developments, economic reconstruction, scientific discoveries and inventions, political agitation and social ferment of the nineteenth century. It had drawn inspiration from 'churches and chapels, from the achievements of physical science, from the development of cheap literature and of a popular press, from Co-operation and Trade Unionism, from Chartism and more recent political developments' (Ministry of Reconstruction, 1919: 9). The Committee also noted that the development of adult education in the nineteenth century was 'hampered by the absence of any universal system of elementary education as well as by the demoralizing industrial conditions'. The absence of adequate child education meant that 'experiments in adult education too often ... resembled an attempt to roof a house before the walls were completed' (*ibid.*: 10).

### State Involvement in Adult Education

Early nineteenth century *laissez-faire*, self-help ideology made its impact on one aspect of adult education with the repeal of the Statute of Artificers in 1813-14. Since 1563 this statute had provided legal protection to seven-year apprenticeships. With its repeal employers were no longer legally required to provide this training: it was left to the voluntary force of self-interest to ensure such provision. In many cases this proved inadequate. By the middle of the century employers generally were making very little provision for workers' education. But by this time there was a swing away from crude liberal *laissez-faire* thinking, towards a degree of collectivism (see Chapter 1). In the field of adult education, as elsewhere, the Government began to be persuaded that some intervention was necessary, although it was still felt that this should fall short of interference (Keane, 1982: 357; 1988: 13--21).

The Government established a Science and Arts Department in 1853 which became the agency for promoting and assisting workers' education by offering grants on a 'payments-by-results' basis for science teaching. In 1859 regular payments based on students' examination successes were introduced. By the 1860s it was widely accepted that voluntaryism was insufficient and that some government involvement and funding was necessary to stimulate an adequate provision of adult education, although this government assistance was still very *ad hoc* and inadequate for sustaining much of the 'rich diversity of voluntary contribution' that was available. At the Paris Exhibition of 1867 British industry achieved pre-eminence in scarcely a dozen of the 90 classes and this failure was attributed by the jurors to the lack of suitable educational facilities (Vincent, 1989: 114; Keane, 1982: 357, 1988: 19–28).

Government involvement in adult education during the nineteenth century very much reflected broader ideological developments, from a withdrawal from paternalistic protectionism at the beginning of the century, through a period of *laissez-faire* non-intervention, to a gradually increasing, if reluctant, state involvement and support from the middle of the century onwards. But first it will be necessary to look at some of the voluntary activities which owed very little, if anything, to government support.

## *Literary, Philosophical and Scientific Societies and the Royal Institutes*

From the end of the eighteenth century a variety of literary, philosophical and scientific societies sprang up in many provincial towns to meet the growing demand of the middle classes for scientific and philosophical knowledge, intellectual stimulation and a fuller cultural life. They reflected the general inadequacies of scientific education in the grammar and public schools and the universities and a widespread desire to understand the scientific or quasi-scientific developments of the industrial revolution. They 'hold an honourable position in the nineteenth century's history of self-help, and particularly for the middle-class self-improver' (Roderick and Stephens, 1973a: 28; Stephens and Roderick, 1983: 16, 45). The desire of the Plymouth Institution 'to encourage research, particularly in objects of local interest in science, literature and art' sums up the character of the societies, many of which established libraries, museums and art galleries and offered lecture programmes of variable quality. 'At each such meeting' during the first session in Plymouth in 1812, 'one of the party read and discussed an original essay on some subject of a scientific or literary nature, political or religious subjects being carefully avoided' (*ibid.*: 44; Freeborn, 1986: 62; Roderick and Stephens, 1973a: 29).

Some societies' upper-class founders and sponsors cherished a mission to give instruction to the working classes; to keep them within the established order of church and society; to 'stimulate the ingenuity of the young, to promote industrious habits among the working classes, and to elicit the inventive powers of the community at large'; to 'facilitate the general introduction of useful mechanical inventions and improvements'; and promote 'the application of science to the common purposes of life'. But more generally they were a reflection of middle-class tastes and actively excluded those from a more 'humble situation of life' for fear that 'the element of amusement would predominate over intellectual instruction and mental energy'. When the Maxwelltown Astronomical Society installed a camera obscura in the Windmill Tower in Dumfries in 1836 it was open to the general public with the exception of 'members of the working class' who were not admitted until the later 1840s. When the camera obscura in Edinburgh was opened in 1853 it also was only open to members of the upper classes (*ibid.*: 29, 33; Roderick and Stephens, 1973b: 39; Freeborn, 1986: 62–3, 159; Stephens and Roderick (nd): 3; information at the Edinburgh Camera Obscura). For similar reasons many of the societies were also reluctant to admit women to their proceedings. The Cornwall Philosophical Institution in Truro cautiously agreed in 1839 to allow ladies to attend every alternative monthly meeting (Roderick and Stephens, 1973b: 43).

A small number of literary and philosophical societies (London, Liverpool, Manchester, Cornwall, South Wales) evolved into Royal Institutions, acquiring the prefix 'royal' to enhance their prestige and finances by attracting influential members and royal subscription (Freeborn, 1986: 61; Stephens and Roderick, 1983: 21–2; Roderick and Stephens, 1973b: *passim*). In other respects they differed very little from the other literary and philosophical societies, many of which survived well into the nineteenth century and sometimes into the twentieth century. But their heyday was the earlier nineteenth century: later their functions were gradually taken over by state-aided institutions (Freeborn, 1986: 159; Roderick and Stephens, 1973b: 46).

## Growing Interest in and Concern for Working-Class Education

It has already been remarked how some of the founders and sponsors of literary and philosophical societies harboured a desire to educate the working classes either to teach them their allotted social position and respectful behaviour or to render them more efficient labourers. There remained a considerable body of old-fashioned Tory opposition to educating the lower orders in the belief that this would make them uppity and give them ideas beyond their station, but the early nineteenth century saw a growing belief that the new industrial society required a better educated population and that 'the ground to be cultivated' was the emerging working class (Harrison, 1961: 3–5). The middle classes became increasingly aware of the value of adult education as a means of moulding society to their image (*ibid.*: 218). The Benthamites, Utilitarians and philosophical radicals were among the first to advocate universal education: their cosmic view of a harmonious society required that the working classes should be educated to understand that their interests coincided with those of the industrial capitalists. The bourgeoisie needed to control and direct the thoughts and actions of the increasingly powerful working class (Simon, 1974: 126–7, 132). With the extension of the political franchise and the successful incorporation of working-class institutions within the bourgeois state during the second half of the nineteenth century, the opposition to educating the working class gave way almost completely to an awareness of the need for a better educated society and workforce.

Meanwhile the working classes developed their own educational processes, which did not always coincide with what their betters thought was good for them.

## The Autodidactic Tradition, Self-Help and the Mutual Improvement Societies

Self-help and individual learning were an important aspect of nineteenth century adult education, carried over from the end of the previous century, 'with the result that many working men were widely read not only in contemporary radical literature, but also in the political and social writings of the eighteenth century Enlightenment' (Harrison, 1961: 43; Simon, 1974: 186). Edward Thompson has described how this autodidactic tradition contributed to 'planting the liberty tree' in early nineteenth century England: how 'in every town and in many villages throughout England' there were working men 'with a kist or shelf full of Radical books, biding their time, putting in a word at the tavern, the chapel, the smithy, the shoemaker's shop ... And the movement for which they waited did not belong to gentlemen, manufacturers, or rate-payers; it was their own' (Thompson, 1968: 201).

One of the most remarkable examples of the autodidactic tradition was the Chartist Thomas Cooper, who, by the age of 24, planned to have mastered the elements of Latin, Greek, Hebrew and French, taught himself Euclid and algebra, committed *Paradise Lost* and seven Shakespeare plays to memory, and read extensively in history, religion and contemporary literature (Kelly, 1992: 142). During much of the nineteenth century this movement for intellectual self-development flourished among sections of the working class. Samuel Smiles's *Self Help* and many other books for 'young men of the lower orders' encouraged self-improvement (MacIntyre, 1980: 70; Harrison, 1961: 204–9). It often started from an interest in religion and bible reading but then broadened out in many directions including political radicalism, philosophy, cosmology, science and history. 'From the beginning, autodidactism had had affiliations with non-conformity, radicalism and secularism.' By the end of the century there were connections with socialism (MacIntyre, 1980: 71; Harrison, 1971: 4–5; Ree, 1984: 8–9, 15). Much of the effect was reformist rather than revolutionary, introducing working-class intellectuals to middle-class ideas, particularly liberal-bourgeois notions of individualism and self-improvement. But they were not all attempting to become members of the middle class: others 'sought to define themselves in terms of a working class culture' and to become leaders of working-class organisations (Ree, 1984: 9; Harrison, 1961: 44, 1971: 5, 9). But these socialist autodidactics had a problem: much of 'the learning which they revered was embodied in persons and institutions which they resented'. Moreover, they often displayed a disproportionate confidence in the authority of the text, and 'belief that the ultimate solutions to questions which perplexed these questioning minds were locked up in the printed pages'. This made them particularly susceptible to the influence of those authorities as they read book after book long into the night and attended evening classes in whatever spare time they could find. The sacrifice and devotion is unquestioned. As John Burns, the trade union leader, declared, 'I have deprived myself, as many of my class have done, of hundreds of meals on purpose to buy books and papers'. But within this autodidactic tradition there is more than a hint of 'university fetishism or bibliomania, rather than genuine intellectual curiosity' and 'a treacherous social ambition masquerading as devotion to truth' (Ree, 1984: 6–8, 15; MacIntyre, 1980: 95).

The collective form of this self-education was the mutual improvement society, which promoted 'friends educating each other' amongst the working class. They also date back to the eighteenth century, although then they were predominantly middle class and religious. In the nineteenth century they were more autonomously working class and motivated by political and educational aims. They had a significant influence on working-class education for much of the century, perhaps more so than formal, institutional provision, but they were especially popular in the 1840s and 50s (Keane, 1982: 355; Graham, 1983: 2; Harrison, 1961: 50). Almost from the beginning, these mutual improvement societies tended to admit women as well as men (Radcliffe, 1986: 2).

The fact that approximately half the population as a whole, and a much greater proportion of the working class, was illiterate at the beginning of the century and that this illiteracy improved very little before the middle of the century, is one of the main reasons for the spread of the mutual improvement societies. They concentrated on elementary subjects, particularly learning to read. 'The better informed and more literate imparted their hard-won knowledge and skills to the less experienced and less educated.' A combination of independent study in the societies' reading rooms and instruction by one's peers was the usual form of learning. Thus their main direct contribution to working-class adult education was the diffusion of literacy rather than tackling broader philosophical or political issues, but they did help to establish a working-class culture (*ibid.*: 1–2; Graham, 1983: *passim*; Harrison, 1961: 51–2).

The early societies were managed and run very largely by working-class people: they have been described as 'the most truly indigenous of all the early attempts at working class adult education' (Graham, 1983: 40–1; Harrison, 1961; 53). But they often ran into organisational and financial problems and therefore were prone to impermanence. They sometimes attempted to gain support and security by organising social events or by seeking partnerships with other institutions such as Mechanics' Institutes, the Chartist movement, the Nonconformist churches, or, later in the century, the Independent Labour Party. But this laid them open to being taken over by the middle class or absorbed into more formally constituted bodies. They lost much of their indigenous autonomy (Graham, 1983: 45; Radcliffe, 1986: 6–11; Harrison, 1961: 53–4). With the improvement in literacy rates in the second half of the century, the mutual improvement societies gradually disappeared (Graham, 1983: 30, 47), but they had made a very considerable contribution to working-class adult education. 'While providing a substantial minority of working people with remedial education ... they also gave a small politically conscious elite information and training in a democratic, co-operative environment' (Radcliffe, 1986: 11–12).

The revival of radicalism at the end of the eighteenth century, the impact of the French Revolution, and the experience of industrialisation brought into existence many other indigenous working-class organisations which exerted an influence on, and were influenced by, adult education.

## Radical Working-Class Movements and Adult Education

Innumerable radical working-class organisations used education to further their aims during the first half of the nineteenth century, without necessarily formulating any elaborate educational philosophy. They sought *really* useful knowledge which would enable them to take political action, gain political power and bring about a radical transformation of society, and therefore they needed forms of education which they controlled. They tended to ignore or oppose the bourgeois-tainted elementary schools, Mechanics' Institutes, or the Society for the Diffusion of Useful Knowledge; or to use them instrumentally (Harrison, 1961: 101; Simon, 1974: 218–22; Johnson, 1983: 23).

If technical education in England springs ultimately from the Mechanics' Institutes, social and civic education, though its history runs for long periods underground, can be traced to the educational idealism which was one side of most working-class movements up to 1850 – of Co-operation, of Chartism, and of early Trade Unionism (Ministry of Reconstruction, 1919: 16).

'*Really* useful knowledge' consisted of a combination of political knowledge, social science (the principles of social explanation), and labour economics or political economy (i.e. explanations of economic exploitation and why labourers remained poor in the midst of the production of so much wealth). Together, these elements of really useful knowledge provided the working class with an understanding of existing circumstances which they could use to change them. In this radical working-class world, education without politics or politics without education were both deemed inadequate (Johnson, 1983: 29–30, 33).

Education was not regarded as separated from other social or political activities, nor adult education from childhood education. It was informal, ephemeral, often non-institutional, lifelong. It embraced communal reading and discussion groups in pubs, clubs, coffee houses, workshops and private homes and the provision of reading rooms and other facilities for reading collectively-bought newspapers and radical literature (*ibid.*: 23–4; Yeo, 1981: 172). The radical James Watson described how he saw a notice in Leeds one evening in 1818 which stated that the Radical Reformers held their meetings in a room in Union Court. Curiosity prompted him to go and hear what was going on. He found them reading Wooler's *Black Dwarf*, Carlisle's *Republican*, and Cobbett's *Register* (Harrison, 1961: 96). The literature was often read aloud in declamatory style by those who could read for the benefit of those who could not (Johnson, 1983: 26.). One only has to look at some of the quite intricate, complex, sometimes biblical language of Chartist propaganda to realise that it was intended to be declaimed aloud like a sermon. In 1799 and again in 1819 the Government outlawed unauthorised lectures, debates and reading rooms open to the public – demonstrating how these activities were feared by the authorities (Kelly, 1992: 136).

Corresponding societies, Hampden clubs, secular Sunday Schools and numerous parliamentary reform societies emerged out of the mass of political agitation of the 1790s. They promoted discussion, lectures, correspondence and public reading of the radical press with every intention that such education would lead to political action. They sometimes adopted the Methodist plan of weekly class meetings and a small weekly subscription (Simon, 1974: 180, 186–9; Kelly, 1992: 135).

In 1835 Robert Owen founded the grandly titled 'Association of all Classes of all Nations to effect an entire change in the character and conditions of the human race', more modestly re-named three years later 'The Universal Community Society of Rational Religionists'. Owen possessed an infinite belief in the power of education to perfect the human character and improve the human condition. The Owenites saw education as the key to social reform. Therefore education was included in all their plans. In 1839 they began to build Halls of Science or Social Institutions where this educational activity could take place, and by 1840 halls had been erected or were being built in many of the major towns of England and Scotland. The Owenite movement appealed to middle-class reformers but also to working-class radicals disillusioned by the utilitarian character of many Mechanics' Institutes. 'Owenites were not concerned to produce capable machine minders, but fully developed men and women able to take their place in building a new society' (Simon, 1974: 235, 238–9; Harrison, 1961: 108–18; Kelly 1992: 138, 145; Bonner, 1970: 1–19).

Closely associated with the Owenite movement were the early Co-operative Societies of the 1820s, 30s and 40s which attempted to implement the Owenite ideals of co-operation and brotherhood. Education was seen as the means by which people could be persuaded to adopt these ideals and therefore many of the Co-operative Societies gave prominence to educational activities. They established schools, libraries, reading and lecture rooms, debating clubs, and various other means of education. In 1844 the Rochdale Equitable Pioneers Society introduced the dividend on purchases and decided to devote a percentage of their profits to educational purposes, thereby launching the co-operative movement's later nineteenth century educational initiative (*ibid.*: 25, 54–5; Ministry of Reconstruction, 1919: 20–1; Simon, 1974: 214; Kelly, 1992: 146).

When the British Association for the Promotion of Co-operative Knowledge collapsed two years after it was founded in London in 1829, many of its leading members, including William Lovett and Henry Hetherington, formed a new body known as the National Union of the Working Classes. This in turn transformed itself into the London Working Men's Association in 1836. Under Lovett's guidance, the Association gave high priority to educational activities. Its aims included the creation of 'a moral, reflecting, yet energetic public opinion; so as eventually to lead to a gradual improvement in the condition of the working classes, without violence or commotion'. It sought to achieve this by collecting relevant information and disseminating it through a reference library and class meetings which were generally held in members' homes. There, a subject for conversation or discussion was chosen, or selections from radical writers such as Paine, Godwin or Owen were read, or the radical periodicals of the day were studied. According to Lovett, 'in this manner hundreds of persons were made acquainted with books and principles of which they were previously ignorant'. The Association also proposed state-aided lifelong education, with 'finishing schools' or colleges to continue education for the over-12s who wanted to acquire higher branches of knowledge after they had left elementary school (Kelly, 1992: 138–40; Peers, 1958: 26).

Lovett was also a leading figure in the educational activities of the Chartists who also organised lectures, discussion meetings and classes; provided reading rooms; built public halls or 'schools for the people' where discussion and debate took place; and promoted Chartist churches which carried out a variety of educational work. These educational activities were not exclusive: they were available to a wide cross-section of the population. But like the other forms of radical working-class education, they were intended to prepare people for political action (Kelly, 1992: 140–2; Simon, 1974: 243–50; Yeo, 1981: 161–2; Murphy, 1985: 8–13).

There is little doubt that the free enquiry and socially purposive dimension of the Owenite and Chartist and other radical education attracted and influenced large numbers of working people (Simon, 1974: 254–5). It is not fanciful to claim that it greatly influenced the tradition and even the form of later voluntary, purposive liberal adult education (Peers, 1958: 29). But the financial commitment to the Owenite and Chartist halls was something of a contradiction to the non-institutionalised informality of radical adult education, drawing it closer to institutional provision (Yeo, 1981: 163).

The trade unions which began to gain strength and take on a national role in the 1830s and 40s also made attempts to provide educational facilities for their members, although it was less central to their activities than to those of the other working-class organisations described above. In 1850 the Flint Glassmakers' magazine urged its readers: 'get knowledge, and in getting knowledge you get power' (Ministry of Reconstruction, 1919: 20).

By the mid-century, with the defeat of Chartism, independent working-class education, like the political movements which harboured it, found itself increasingly isolated. It survived, but more emphasis was placed on the individual, autodidactic route, or on demands for state education. After 1848 the working-class movements increasingly turned away from political to economic solutions – how to obtain a share of the profits of capitalism rather than how to overthrow it. 'Each advance within the framework of capitalism simultaneously involved the working class far more deeply in the *status quo*.' This delivered working-class adult education more into 'the pragmatic if compromised' hands of the surviving Mechanics' Institutes. The notion of an alternative working-class education was replaced by demands for more equal access to facilities provided by and for the middle class and by the State. Opposition to state education was transformed into a more reformist agitation for a share of it. In the process, education was largely depoliticised and institutionalised, and the seamless robe of lifelong education was replaced by notions of separate child and adult education (Johnson, 1983: 31, 34; Thompson, 1965: 343–4; Keane, 1982: 356).

The significance of this radical independent working-class education is without doubt, but its achievements were not always obvious. It did not bring about the political changes the radicals advocated and it did not always meet the working-class educational needs it uncovered. These needs were often more basic and more prosaic than the interests of the activists. However, it did begin 'to create an alternative formation, deeply, incompatible with the structural subordination of industrial capitalism' and it helped to determine and change class relations by the middle of the century. But because of its potential threat to the social *status quo* it also called into being a middle-class cultural counter offensive from commercial and philanthropic providers (and the state), who felt it was time that they became more involved in providing the working class with safer forms of education (Yeo, 1981: 172, 180).

## Newspapers and Cheap Literature

The importance of newspapers and other literature to radical working-class education has already been indicated. They were 'saturated with educational content' and were 'read aloud in declamatory style in pub or public place' as well as being read privately by the more literate (Johnson, 1983: 26–7). But the authorities used the libel laws and taxation to try to minimise their effectiveness. At the beginning of the century the press was shackled by the constant threat of the law of seditious libel. Three decades of radical opposition eventually caused the libel laws to fall into disuse (although they were not repealed) in the 1830s. But the 'tax on knowledge' continued to maintain the price of newspapers beyond the means of working people, so that they could only have recourse to them in reading rooms, coffee houses and pubs. Cobbett and then Wooler had found a way of evading the newspaper tax in 1816 by publishing their *Political Register* and *Black Dwarf* with comment but no news, but this loophole was closed by one of the Six Acts in 1819. Henry Hetherington challenged the law in 1831 by publishing the *Poor Man's Guardian*, unstamped, as a penny weekly. This launched a new campaign which led to the taxes being reduced between 1833–6, but the new stamp duty law was rigorously enforced, causing the cheap unstamped press to virtually disappear. It was not until 1849 that a new campaign was started for the abolition of the remaining taxes, significantly opposed by the Prime Minister, Lord John Russell, on the grounds that he disliked all plans for a popular press or popular education. But slowly the battle was won in stages during the course of the 1850s. The effect of the abolition of the stamp duty was staggering: the number of newspapers in the United Kingdom rose from 563 in 1851 to 1,294 in 1867. In particular the provincial press in all the large cities and most towns flourished as a result (Kelly, 1992: 158–64).

A cheap literature movement existed at two levels from the 1820s onwards: at the higher level making 'quality' literature available at moderate prices and at a lower level producing 'useful knowledge' for the working masses. The Society for the Diffusion of Useful Knowledge was founded in 1826 to sustain the work of the Mechanics' Institutes. Until its demise in 1846 it produced a variety of cheap publications but they did not always satisfy demand. Like many Mechanics' Institutes, they tackled political and economic issues in a patronising or frankly *laissez-faire* way intended to stifle the demands of the working class for change, such as the 'Address to the Labourers on the Subject of Destroying Machinery' at the time of the Swing Riots in 1830. The Society also over-estimated the intellectual level of its working-class clientele, producing texts which were too scientific or difficult for many of its readers. There were many other publishers, such as the Chambers brothers in Edinburgh and John Cassell in London, whose 'labours ... went to swell the ever-growing flood of popular literature' (*ibid*.: 164–73; Simon, 1974: 159–63).

There were numerous libraries in existence in Britain during the first half of the nineteenth century, before the passing of the Public Libraries Act in 1850. Apart from the special London libraries and provincial city libraries in Manchester, Preston and Glasgow, there were libraries attached to cathedrals and many churches; village libraries promoted by the clergy, landowners and manufacturers; and numerous libraries attached to the literary, scientific and philosophical societies, the Mechanics' Institutes, the mutual improvement societies, the Co-operative Societies and many other institutions. There were working men's libraries often formed because the local Mechanics' Institute library would not stock 'controversial' religious or political publications. And it was estimated by Lovett in 1849 that of some 2,000 coffee houses in London, largely frequented by working people, about a quarter had libraries. There were also a variety of private circulating libraries. But although the list of libraries sounds impressive, the total book supply, particularly for poorer people, was very inadequate and frequently dull and inappropriate (Kelly, 1992: 173–6).

The first rate-aided public libraries were founded under the 1845 Museums Act, at Canterbury in 1847, Warrington in 1848 and Salford in 1849 (*ibid*.: 176–7). But for many people, this was all largely irrelevant because they could not read.

## Literacy and Basic Education in the Early Nineteenth Century

Much of the adult education offered by the various radical movements and by middle-class philanthropic and not-so-philanthropic providers was at too high a level for the many poor people who had had little or no schooling and were totally or virtually illiterate. Taking the ability to sign one's name as an indicator of basic literacy, marriage registers suggest that about half the population was basically literate in the 1750s, rising to 58 per cent by 1840. But this national average conceals considerable geographical variations and differences between types of community and in broad class and gender terms. From 1840 onwards, the literacy rate steadily improved: between 1841 and 1885 the illiteracy rate at marriage in England and Wales fell from 42 per cent to 12 per cent, although regional variations persisted, while Scotland boasted a superior level of literacy. There was also a remarkable improvement in the relative literacy of women from the 1850s, narrowing the gap between males and females that had existed earlier in the century (Stephens, 1987: 2–53).

One of the major functions of adult education (not always recognised at the time) was teaching the three 'R's to this large illiterate section of the population, particularly during the first half of the century. But this basic education was not only about the three 'R's: it represented part of the attempt by the middle classes 'to help the working classes to assimilate themselves more completely into the new society'. By the 1860s these middle classes 'had been wonderfully effective in suffusing their ideals and precepts throughout the 'lower orders'' (Harrison, 1961: 38–43). By the same process the informal, non-institutionalised, ephemeral working-class autonomous adult education and popular culture had been very extensively undermined by a more formal, 'provided' adult education in the adult schools, the Sunday Schools and night schools and, to some extent, the Mechanics' Institutes and Working Men's Colleges.

## The Churches, Sunday Schools, the Adult School Movement and the YMCA

The new evangelical religious fervour emanating from Methodism and spreading to all churches by the early nineteenth century had two contradictory although not mutually exclusive effects on middle-class attitudes. It stimulated a considerable amount of philanthropic activity which tried to mitigate the worst excesses of industrial capitalism without changing the basic social structures, but also pointed some people towards more radical social reforms. For the working class it acted both as a sedative and an inspiration for social justice. At the beginning of the century, Anglican clergy generally favoured education for the working classes, if at all, only to teach them their duties to society, but Nonconformist ministers were somewhat more inclined to see education as enabling working people to improve themselves and their position. By the middle of the century, Anglicans also had been increasingly converted to this view, and were likely to give their support to Sunday Schools, adult schools, Mechanics' Institutes and night schools (Harrison, 1961: 172–3, 177–9).

A small but important body within the Nonconformist tradition, particularly Unitarians and Quakers, even in the first half of the century, argued for full educational opportunities for girls and women in the then unusual belief that females' intellectual capacity was equal to males'. After 1850 this movement gathered momentum, despite considerable opposition, and made a significant contribution to the development of female education. It concentrated mainly on childhood schooling, higher education and teacher training, but had a spin-off effect on adult education, encouraging the consideration of women's needs as well as men's (Watts, 1980: 273–86).

Sunday Schools, which were common to all denominations, began to appear during the last two decades of the eighteenth century in England and Wales, but less so in Scotland, where they were regarded as an infringement on the preserve of the parish schools. They concentrated on teaching bible reading to children but in Wales and the north of England the practice of admitting adults as well became widespread. Before the end of the eighteenth century there were some Sunday Schools exclusively for adults, and there was a swing away from soley religious instruction, and beyond literacy, to more varied forms of adult education. In north Somerset in the 1790s the sisters Hannah and Martha More instructed the mining population in the scriptures, at the same time encouraging their students 'to see more clearly the advantages you derive from the government and constitution of this country, and to observe the benefits flowing from the distinction of rank and fortune' - largely as an antidote to the influence of Tom Paine's *Rights of Man* (Harrison, 1961: 194–5; Kelly, 1992; 75–9; Ministry of Reconstruction, 1919: 11).

In Wales and the north of England all-age Sunday Schools continued to serve the educational needs of their communities. Throughout the country, Sunday Schools spread rapidly in the nineteenth century, particularly during the 1830s and 40s. Although their general ethos was obviously religious and socially conformist, this culture merged, consciously or unconsciously, with wider social and moral ideas and even political considerations. They gave large numbers of people a basic training in literacy, enabling them to become 'readers, writers and speakers in the village meetings for parliamentary reform' and many other social and political activities (*ibid.*: 17; Harrison, 1961: 201–2; Kelly, 1992: 149–50, 206).

Meanwhile, an adult school movement emerged, closely allied to Sunday Schools but devoted exclusively to the education of adults rather than treating themas something of an afterthought to children's education.

In 1798 William Singleton and Samuel Fox, a Methodist and a Quaker, opened the first adult school in Nottingham, to teach bible reading, writing and arithmetic to young women employed in the lace and hosiery factories. A few years later, in 1811, the Rev. Thomas Charles opened a Sunday School exclusively for adults in North Wales. But it was really the founding of an Institution for instructing Adult Persons to read the Holy Scriptures in Bristol the following year that launched the adult school movement. From Bristol, adult schools spread rapidly through the south of England and the Midlands and South Wales and to a lesser extent into northern England (*ibid.*: 79–80, 149–50; Ministry of Reconstruction, 1919: 11).

The aim of the adult schools was not only to teach the poor to read the scriptures, but also to improve their morals and to inculcate habits of thrift, industriousness and social obedience. Dr Thomas Pole, a leading member of the movement in Bristol, expressed these aims in an address published in 1814. 'We are now called upon to become instrumental in opening windows to admit celestial light into the habitations of darkness and ignorance; that those who sit in the valley of the shadow of death may be brought to the saving knowledge of the Lord ...' he declared. He went on to recommend industry, frugality, economy, meekness, Christian fortitude, and resignation to the fortunate lower classes favoured by the benefactions of the adult schools. The practice of the adult schools following the Bristol model was to concentrate very largely on reading, and dismiss anyone once they could read the Bible distinctly; but in time the the adult schools came to include some basic education in other subjects such as chemistry, maths, grammar, geography, drawing and sewing, as well as reading and writing. Despite their very real limitations and their patronising approach, these early adult schools did help to promote the cause of adult education and demonstrate that adults were capable of learning (Ministry of Reconstruction, 1919: 12; Martin, 1924: 29, 31; Peers, 1958: 9, 11–12; Kelly, 1992: 151–2).

Many of the adult schools led a somewhat impermanent existence and there was a decline in the movement during the 1830s and 40s, partly because of a lack of competent teachers and partly because of financial difficulties. But there was a revival in the 1850s: largely under the influence of the Society of Friends, they dropped their patronising attitudes and became more democratic, adopting Quaker notions of brotherhood and fellowship. Under this influence they laid less emphasis on instruction, more on discussion. This tendency was encouraged by the 1870 Education Act which anticipated that the new School Boards would ensure that children were educated to a standard that would make adult basic education unnecessary in the future. The adult schools broadened both their educational curricula and their social functions. There was a steady growth during the last quarter of the century and the movement peaked in the early years of the twentieth century. But despite a willingness to embrace almost any literary, philosophical or scientific theme, the movement was still firmly rooted in nineteenth century Sunday School scriptural traditions and insisted on political neutrality. Moreover the academic level, especially in the schools for women, was generally low (Martin, 1924: *passim*; Simon, 1965: 74–5; Peers, 1958: 35; Charlton, 1985: iii).

The Young Men's Christian Association (YMCA), founded in London in 1844, was similar in intent to the adult school movement although it attracted a somewhat younger, lower middle-class rather than working-class, clientele. It was a non-denominational organisation founded to improve the spiritual and moral condition of young men in the drapery and other trades. Originally it had three specific aims: comradeship, united prayer and bible study. It soon came to combine religious instruction with a range of social and educational activities, including lectures and classes; and established libraries and reading rooms. By 1850 it had spread to the provinces and it expanded and developed steadily during the second half of the century. By its jubilee year in 1894 there were 651 branches in the UK with nearly 850,000 members and associate members. In 1855 a women's counterpart, the YWCA, was founded but this concentrated on social relief work rather than educational activities (Sadler, 1907: 50–1; Simon, 1965: 60; Kelly, 1992: 126–7, 205–6).

## Technical Education

For the greater part of the nineteenth century, from the abolition of statutory apprenticeships in 1814 to the passing of the Technical Instruction Act in 1889 there was a marked absence of government support for technical education. This was partly due to a general complacency about the importance of technical education – one of the legacies of an early successful industrial revolution which appeared to owe little to formal education. But more importantly, it was the inevitable consequence of the dominant liberal, *laissez-faire* philosophy which discouraged state intervention. Despite the repeal of the Statute of Artificers and its legal enforcement of apprenticeships, most teaching of occupational knowledge continued for much of the century to be 'undertaken by working men in the context of formal or informal apprenticeships. A century after the abolition of the Statute of Artificers, there were more than a third of a million apprenticeships in any one year.' Such training on the job was regarded as both cheap and adequate, although it often provided very little real instruction and very few opportunities for any grounding in scientific principles or even basic education. Indeed, there was a general deficiency in technical education before the 1880s, except for a combination of work manuals and evening classes provided by the Mechanics' Institutes and, after 1853, the Department of Science and Art (Vincent, 1989: 107, 117–8; Green, 1994: *passim*).

## The Mechanics' Institutes

The origins of the Mechanics' Institutes lay partly in the lectures which George Birkbeck gave to large assemblies of working men in Glasgow between 1799 and 1803 (which established the predominance of the lecture format in the institutes' provision for many years); and partly in the variety of working-class adult educational activities occurring at the beginning of the century, which have been described earlier. Thus from their very beginning, the Mechanics' Institutes were a mixture of autonomous working-class enterprise and paternalistic middle-class provision. They stem from a strong belief in some quarters of both the middle and working classes at that time that a better educated work force was desirable, together with a desire to spread to the working class the benefits accruing to the middle class from the literary, scientific and philosophical societies. After the first institutes were formed in Glasgow in 1823 and London in 1824 they spread rapidly to almost every sizable town and to many villages by mid-century. By 1851 there were some 700 Mechanics' Institutes in the UK. However, although some of the city institutes attracted very large numbers of members, these were not typical: three-quarters of the institutes in existence in 1841 had less than 200 members (Kelly, 1992: 117-25; Inkster, 1985: 3–5; Tylecote, 1957: 28–30; Watson, 1987: 12; Cowan 1968: 202; Ministry of Reconstruction, 1919: 13–14).

The impetus for founding and financing the institutes sometimes came from within the working class; sometimes from above. Evidence from the Midlands and north Lancashire suggests that they were not necessarily dominated by wealthy patrons, nor by middle-class radicals. The pattern varied from locality to locality and each institute reflected the characteristics of its own community. 'In any institute, there could be support from all political, religious and occupational classes.' There could be quite mixed representation on management committees and some institutes undoubtedly did belong to working men (Kelly, 1992: 125; Turner, 1968: 65–70; Watson, 1987: 16–17; Royle, 1971: 315). However, in a majority of cases control either rested from the beginning with middle-class patrons, who might be radicals, as in London, or conservatives; or it gradually passed out of the hands of the mechanics into those of the middle class who possessed more management skills and financial wherewithal. Indeed, management was often confined to those who subscribed quite substantial sums. Despite early working-class involvement in promoting and managing some institutes, they were essentially a middle-class venture. It was mainly wealthy representatives of the propertied and governing class who provided the patronage and the impetus to the movement, for a mixture of philanthropic and social reasons (Kelly, 1992: 120–21; Simon, 1974: 154–7; Stephens, 1958: 75, 267; Harrison, 1961: 57; Tylecote, 1957: 27, 282–4; Watson, 1987: 17).

The clientele of the institutes also differed from place to place, and over time. It is important to remember that Birkbeck's original aim had been to attract the *skilled* mechanics to his lectures in Glasgow, and the early

Mechanics' Institutes were likewise intended for the craftsmen - the labour aristocracy and natural working-class leaders in both a technical and political sense. But quite quickly there was a tendency for the institutes to be taken over by the lower middle class: artisans were displaced by clerks, shopmen and tradesmen, and many institutes completely abandoned all efforts to attract the working class. Nevertheless mechanics and artisans did continue to represent a sizable proportion, if a minority, of the clientele in many institutes. There was also a marked geographical difference in the social composition of the institutes' membership: in Yorkshire it remained significantly more working class. But in England and Wales as a whole, by 1849 only about one-fifth of the institutes were predominantly working class. Moreover, there was also a growing practice of including large numbers of non-adults in the membership. By the middle of the century the Mechanics' Institutes nearly everywhere had ceased to be agents of mass working-class adult education. They had become 'select rather than popular institutions'. They had certainly failed to attract the labouring poor, although they were not alone in this and, indeed, had not set out to do so. But even with their intended skilled working-class clientele, they had over-estimated the level of education required by all but a few; and by the time they realised that the real need was for basic education to make good the lack of even an elementary education, they had lost the bulk of the working class (Royle, 1971: 305, 310–12; Roderick and Stephens, 1985: 61–2; Thompson, 1968: 819; Harrison, 1961: 65, 71; Peers, 1958: 17; Laurent, 1984: 588–9; Tylecote, 1957: 258).

Just as the patronage and clientele of the Mechanics' Institutes was quite varied, so there were a number of motives for promoting, supporting and participating in the activities of the institutes. They do not all apply to all institutes: indeed some are mutually contradictory. But these various reasons for supporting or using the institutes do illustrate where they were placed on the nineteenth century adult education stage.

One reason for supporting the Mechanics' Institutes (either as patron or participant) was to provide or acquire intellectual and moral improvement, cultural enrichment, and personal fulfilment as an antidote to the alienating effects of industrialisation; together with a better understanding of the fundamental changes which the industrial revolution was imposing on people's lives. Birkbeck expressed this kind of motivation in 1800 when he spoke of the *pleasure* and the filling of a mental vacancy which would be brought about by the meditation of a few systematic philosophical ideas by mechanics at their leisure. Middle-class support for the Mechanics' Institutes was stimulated in part by this wish to compensate for some of the social ill-effects of industrialisation, and to enrich working-class life, although this was probably very much a minority motive (Harrison, 1961: 66; Kelly, 1957: 29, 1992: 123; Watson, 1987: 21; Ministry of Reconstruction, 1919: 15).

A second motive was to provide the skilled workforce for the rapidly growing industries by inculcating an industrious culture and improving the scientific and technical skills of the new mechanics of the industrial revolution. Certainly this was the rhetoric of many of the Mechanics' Institutes when they were first founded:

This society was formed for the purpose of enabling Mechanics and Artisans of whatever trade they may be, to become acquainted with such branches of science as are of practical application in the exercise of that trade, that they may possess a more thorough knowledge of their business, acquire a greater degree of skill in the practice of it, and be qualified to make improvements and even new inventions in the Arts which they respectively profess ... There is no Art which does not depend, more or less, on scientific principles, and to search what these are, and to point out their practical application, will form the chief object of this Institution (Manchester Mechanics' Institution, Preamble to the Constitution, 1824).

At Leeds the stated object of the Mechanics' Institute was:

... to supply at a cheap rate, to the various classes of the community, the advantages of instruction in the various branches of science which are of practical application to the various trades or occupations. Such instruction ... will greatly tend to improve the skill and practice of those classes of men who are so essentially conducive to the prosperity of this large manufacturing town (Statement of the aims of the Leeds Mechanics' Institute, 1824).

However, it has to be said that this rhetoric was to some extent window-dressing, to attract both patronage and participants. There is little evidence that the institutes made any serious attempt to instruct working people in their crafts, or succeeded in spreading scientific knowledge which led to new discoveries or technical inventions (Tylecote, 1957: 32–8; SCUTREA (nd): c3; Watson, 1987: 13–14; Harrison, 1961: 64).

For the participants, the motives were somewhat different from those of the patrons. For many, their interest in education was not predominantly altruistic nor cultural nor recreational: it arose from their wish to get better jobs or raise themselves from a state of poverty. This was recognised by the Stockport Institute in its first annual report in 1835 when it stated that 'at a small expense the workman may not only be better qualified to advance himself in the world, but he may also be better enabled to secure himself and his family the means of comfort and enjoyment.' For the labour aristocracy, one of the reasons for acquiring education was to distance themselves from the labouring poor and enable them to rise into the ranks of the middle class, and there is little doubt that some institutes were successful in this and in helping people to enter and rise within clerical grades of work (SCUTREA (nd): c4; Tylecote, 1957: 262).

It will be noticeable from the quotations from the institutes' statements that their language was very male-specific. This partly reflects the way language was used at that time, but it also reflects the predominantly male orientation of the institutes, especially when they were first founded. They saw their target clientele as mainly men. But membership of most institutes was not exclusively male, and women came to make up a higher proportion later in the century. The institutes did do something to draw attention to the neglect of education for girls and women, although their response was very largely traditional - i.e. to provide instruction to enable women to become good wives and mothers and to run a household, even though large numbers of working-class women were also wage-workers (Tylecote, 1957: 263, 266).

In some institutes there was a minority of working-class political activists who sought knowledge for power – to enable them to challenge the political and social system and to learn an alternative social and economic philosophy. It was precisely a fear of this revolutionary effect that caused many conservatives to oppose the Mechanics' Institutes, along with all forms of working-class education, although not always quite so crudely as the country gentleman who asked:

Suppose that some friend of humanity were to attempt to improve the condition of the beasts of the field – to teach the horse his power, and the cow her value – would he be that tractable and useful animal he is, would she be so profuse of her treasures to a helpless infant? Could anything be more impolitic?

At a meeting held in Swansea town hall in 1826 to form a Mechanics' Institute, it was objected that:

... educating servants would unfit them for the discharge of their duties. The working class would be taken out of their proper station in life, and there would be none left to perform the menial tasks of societ ... (They might) become wiser than their superiors. The spirit of subordination and combination would be generated, and the working classes (might) get a vain habit of reading novels and writing love letters.

In 1847 a Yorkshire vicar complained that 'our little Institute is a spark which if encouraged will burst into a prodigious conflagration, and destroy every desire for labour and order' while a year later the *Ashton Chronicle* solemnly declared, in language borrowed from John Ball and the fourteenth century peasants' revolt, that:

Teach the hungry poor to read, and they will read the long roll of their wrongs, in being robbed of their lawful hire, till they have them at their tongue-end; teach them to write and they will write their sufferings in words never to be blotted out, till the day of reckoning with their oppressor come; teach them to cast accounts, and they will one day show tyrants to what a fearful amount they can cast up the sum of their accumulated miseries.

There is little hard evidence of the Mechanics' Institutes contributing directly to radical or revolutionary ideas in this way, but there is no measuring the indirect effect of improved education. They have been described as 'essentially co-operative institutions, used to further both the social advancement and the social solidarity of the British working class'. Towards the end of the century, the Yorkshire Mechanics' Institutes were closely associated with the Labour movement and socialist education (SCUTREA (nd): i: 1–2; Ministry of Reconstruction, 1919: 14; Roderick and Stephens, 1985: 62; Laurent, 1984: 586, 598–608).

Many potential working-class recruits to the Mechanics' Institutes feared the exact opposite to the conservatives: that the institutes were a form of 'social policeman' inculcating attitudes of subservience, obedience, sobriety and social conformity; training people to accept bourgeois culture. 'Despite the altruism and sincerity of many promoters, the overall emphasis clearly implied some form of social control in that working-class energies were to be attracted to an area of education considered potentially supportive rather than disruptive of the status quo' (Keane, 1975: 256–7). The aim, conscious or unconscious, was in part to point the emerging working-class organisations in the 'right' direction and contribute to social stability by extending an appreciation of bourgeois values to the potential leaders of those organisations and to allay social agitation by rendering the artisans more intelligent and useful. It was also widely anticipated that this education would reduce two of the perceived major social problems amongst the working class: immorality and alcoholism. There were strong links between the Mechanics' Institutes and the teetotal movement (Simon, 1974: 153; Harrison, 1961: 75–9; Tylecote, 1957: 44-5; Watson, 1987: 12–25).

To avoid alienating one sector of supporters or the other, most institutes claimed to ban politics, political economy and religion as being too controversial. Indeed, a report in 1841 suggested that the institutes were only too willing to explain physical sciences or demonstrate atomic theory or the orbit of the planets, but would not discuss the political constitution – 'a question which every newspaper more or less raises' and which 'the Chartists in the next street handle ... quite freely'. But in practice it was only radical politics or agnostic religious discussion which was banned. Orthodox forms of liberal political economy were very prevalent, extolling the virtues of *laissez-faire* free enterprise capitalism and helping to correct 'popular errors' and to extend an understanding of 'immutable' economic laws to the working class. Thus at the Halifax Mechanics' Institute in Yorkshire it was considered 'especially important that the working classes should appreciate the real nature of political economy so that their inevitable hardship might be both understood and alleviated' (*ibid.*: 18; Kelly, 1992: 134; Harrison, 1961: 80–3; Tylecote, 1957: 47–8). In 1844 Frederick Engels noted:

Mechanics' Institutes also offer classes in that brand of political economy which takes free competition as its God. The teachers of this subject preach the doctrine that it does not lie within the power of the workers to change the existing economic order. The proletariat is told that they must resign themselves to starving without making a fuss. In the Mechanics' Institutes the teaching is uninspired and flabby. The students are taught to be subservient to the existing political and social order. All that the worker hears in these schools is one long sermon on respectful and passive obedience in the station in life to which he has been called (SCUTREA (nd): i: 3).

Even if Engels exaggerated a little there was much truth in his assessment. It is not altogether surprising that 20 years earlier a contributor to the *Mechanics Magazine* in October 1823 warned that 'men had better be without education ... than be educated by their rulers; for then education is but the mere breaking in of the steer to the yoke; the mere discipline of the hunting dog, which, by dint of severity, is made to forego the strongest impulse of his nature, and instead of devouring his prey, to hasten with it to the feet of his master' (*ibid.*: i: 1).

It is apparent that the purposes or functions of the Mechanics' Institutes were, or at least were perceived to be, varied and sometimes contradictory. They were expected to produce a more skilled workforce; enhance intellectual development and act as an antidote to the alienating effects of the industrial revolution; assist social and occupational upward-mobility for sections of the working class and lower middle class; improve the educational facilities for women; provide knowledge for power in order to enable the political activists in the working class to bring about social and political change; or contribute to social stability by encouraging an acceptance of the *status quo*. 'Denounced by the Tories as hot beds of Radicalism, and by the Radicals as strongholds of Toryism, the institutes ... had the worst of both worlds' (Kelly, 1957: 226). They also offered opportunities for social life, recreation and entertainment and as the century wore on, this became an increasingly significant part of their activities.

The curricula of the institutes reflected this diversity of purpose. They quite clearly intended to spread 'useful knowledge' in the form of scientific and technological instruction. At Leeds, for example, such instruction was 'to be given in the evenings ... (and) by Public lectures on Mechanics and Chemistry and other branches of science which are immediately applicable to, or connected with, the useful Arts.' But in attempting to improve the much neglected area of science education in England the institutes encountered resistance and doubts about the value of such education. Within a few years this scientific and technical education had very largely given way to more varied and less demanding topics, including light entertainment and basic elementary education, which was very largely what was needed; although in Scotland and the north of England there remained a greater commitment to technical education. Nevertheless, in 1850 only one quarter of the 11,183 members of the 59 Yorkshire institutes were attending classes, and four-fifths of these were in elementary classes. By this time, classes had very largely replaced the large lectures which had been the early practice, but which had not proved very successful. This was a more expensive form of teaching if good, qualified teachers had to be hired for the relatively small classes. Therefore another reason for recreational provision becoming more common was that it could attract larger numbers for little cost. In some institutes, little or no formal instruction was being given, whilst programmes of single, unrelated popular talks displaced systematic study in most places. However, this decline in standards was not solely the result of financial pressures or intellectual apathy: it reflected the general lack of adequate elementary education which made the original educational aims of the institutes somewhat unrealistic. Nor was the decline into basic education or recreational activities absolute: Science and Art Department classes began to take place in some institutes after 1853, and although they had little direct relevance to industrial technical requirements they did encourage speculative thought, particularly in the field of natural history and evolution, even though this was straying into that other taboo area – religious controversy (Harrison, 1961: 64–7, 74, 131; Ministry of Reconstruction, 1919: 16; Kelly, 1992: 128, 198; Roderick and Stephens, 1985: 24; Peers, 1958: 19; Tylecote, 1957: 50, 279; Royle, 1971: 308–9; Laurent, 1984: 590–7).

In terms of numbers and membership the Mechanics' Institutes peaked around 1860, although again there was regional variation. In some places, particularly in the north of England, new ones continued to be established well into the 1870s and 80s. The Yorkshire Union of Mechanics' Institutes was most active *after* 1850. But the substantial capital and recurrent costs of maintaining their buildings laid a considerable burden on many institutes. And after 1850 they became more and more vulnerable to competition from other forms of adult education, and grew increasingly indistinguishable from them. As previously mentioned, they became centres for Science and Art

Department classes and from 1859 were able to gain government grants for this work. This gave a new impetus to what remained of their technical and vocational curricula, and provided a home for many efficient night schools. But this was not universally popular because it was just another step towards the loss of any distinctive character. By the time that substantial state aid became available with the passing of the Technical Instruction Act in 1889, the Mechanics' Institutes and their amateur approach were doomed. They found their work being taken over by the new technical education committees (see below). Many of the institutes likewise were taken over, to become local authority technical schools or colleges or libraries (Kelly, 1992: 198–9; Harrison, 1961: 212–6; Laurent, 1984: 588–9; Yeo, 1981: 166; Tylecote, 1957: 285, 290; Peers, 1958: 19; Keane, 1988: 26–7; Roderick and Stephens, 1985: 31; Ministry of Reconstruction, 1919: 15).

What is the final judgement on the Mechanics' Institutes? It has been claimed that:

They failed to become all that they might have been, they failed to be what they were thought to have been, and they failed to live up to the expectations of their patrons. They did not attract the majority of working men, and they did not teach science (Royle, 1971: 320).

But Royle also reminds us that they varied greatly according to local circumstances (*ibid.*: 318). It is true that their attempts to stimulate scientific education were largely thwarted by apathy and a lack of adequate basic education on which to build. They did not succeed in attracting large numbers of unskilled workers, partly because of their early unrealistic educational goals but also because they did not really aim at that sector of the working class. They did attract numbers of the labour aristocracy and the lower middle class, although they alienated many others with their predominantly bourgeois ethos and refusal to tackle the controversial political issues which appealed to active members of the working class. However, they were not completely taken over by the middle class, especially in the north of England and Scotland. They appealed to the same social group to which other working-class movements appealed, and supplied them with one of their most necessary requirements - elementary education. 'Behind the appearance of institutes with a large middle-class membership, hearing middle-class lectures, lies solid achievement - an achievement which helped other, more ostensibly working-class, movements to improve the condition of working men'. They significantly extended the coverage of adult education in the nineteenth century (*ibid.*: 306–7, 320–1; Tylecote, 1957: 291; Kelly, 1992 127–8; Roderick and Stephens, 1985: 30).

But they also tended to concentrate the learning of many working-class activists on the 'right' political and economic theories and thereby helped to divert their minds from independent political activity. 'The net result was a powerful and sustained propagation of the ideology of the middle class' which may have inhibited the development of a true proletarian class consciousness (Simon, 1974: 158; Harrison, 1961: 89; Royle, 1971: 315).

## Working Men's and Women's Colleges and Institutes

A People's College was founded by the Nonconformist Rev. Robert Bayley in Sheffield in 1842 with the aim of making humane higher education accessible to working men and women in a spirit of comradeship. Within a year there were 50 classes per week in a range of subjects, including English grammar, Euclid, geography, history, literature, Latin, Greek and modern languages. The college journal insisted that the students needed to learn more than just how to read and write: they needed to learn to think. The college aimed to be free of sectarian religion or party politics, but it was dependent on the goodwill of the educated middle class to provide the teaching. After Bayley's departure from Sheffield in 1848 the emphasis became more vocational. A reorganisation of the college in 1853 established it as a self-supporting, self-governing institution which decided to make the classes more relevant to the occupations of the working population of Sheffield. Latin and Greek were replaced by 'the application of chemistry to the Sheffield trades'. The reorganisation met with initial success, with nearly 200 students recruited to the classes, but increasing competition from other educational providers in similar fields led to a decline by 1860 and the eventual closure of the college in 1879 (Moore Smith, 1912: *passim*; Kelly, 1992: 182–3).

The Sheffield People's College was the inspiration for a number of similar institutions established in other towns within the following quarter century, including the London Working Men's College founded by the Christian socialist F.D. Maurice in 1854. Like the Sheffield College, it aimed to be self-governing and free of patronage, and to provide university-style, liberal non-vocational education and culture for working men, not to enable them to 'get on', but for its own sake. It was quite consciously intended to replicate the education that Maurice and the other promoters of the working men's colleges had experienced at university. The education provided was not only intended to be humane rather than technical or vocational; but also tackle socially and politically controversial issues by systematic study rather than single, unrelated popular lectures (thus differentiating it from the Mechanics' Institutes' activities); and to promote human fellowship which was an essential ingredient of Maurice's Christian socialism. The college was intended to be a place not just for lectures but where 'rational enjoyment, mingled with hard work and education, was mixed up with, and to a great extent derived from, the formation of friendships.' The curricula covered politics, science, language and literature and art. Maurice succeeded in involving numerous men of letters and culture in the London college and it became a significant cultural centre. But, as we have seen elsewhere, this attempt to impose a middle-class, liberal culture did not meet the wishes of many working-class or lower-middle-class people. Despite the intentions of the founders, they came to advance themselves and they demanded more practical subjects. As the century progressed, the curricula turned to more professional and technical studies, including drawing, grammar, maths, languages and shorthand. Even so, the college attracted only a very small number of students. It remained very much an exclusive 'club' – infinitely cosy for the small number of members but failing to touch the vast majority of potential students. In the early years the clientele was similar to that of the Mechanics' Institutes, mainly clerks and lower professionals rather than working class, although to some extent this depends on definitions. In 1904 it was claimed that more than 50 per cent of the college students were working men. For all its renowned place in the history of British adult education, the comment that Maurice's 'contribution to the structural development of nineteenth century education was peripheral' is probably a fair judgment of the London Working Men's College (Davies, 1904: 236–40, 247, 251; Ministry of Reconstruction, 1919: 24–5; Peers, 1958: 43; Kelly, 1992: 183–6; Gibson, 1986: 298–312).

During the 1850s and 60s a number of working men's colleges were founded in English provincial towns, including Manchester, Wolverhampton, Cambridge, Oxford, Salford, Halifax, Liverpool, Leicester, Ely, Huntingdon, Ipswich and Southwark (south London), and two in Scotland, at Ayr and Prestwick. With the exception of the college in Leicester, few of these survived very long despite, or perhaps because of, their greater emphasis on vocational education. The growing competition from a variety of other forms of education, including state-aided elementary schools and night schools, rendered them largely superfluous (Kelly, 1992: 187–8; Ministry of Reconstruction, 1919: 23; Davies, 1904: 245; Cowan, 1968: 203–6; Purvis, 1981: 243).

The Working Men's College movement, as the name implies, was primarily aimed at men, and women had to struggle to gain admission to the colleges. The masculine ethos of fellowship and brotherhood tended to exclude women. Indeed, Maurice believed it would not be possible to create a sense of fellowship if women were present, so they were excluded from the London college in the early years. They were admitted to some colleges later, but did not enjoy equal status. They paid lower fees, which justified their marginality, and were offered a narrower range of classes, which included basic education and practical subjects, but not politics, history, geography or theology. The only co-educational classes were for singing. Moreover, many colleges were open only during the daytime, which was not suitable for many women, or indeed for working-class people generally. By 1860 classes for women had disappeared altogether. It was in this context that Elizabeth Malleson founded the London Working Women's College in 1864, more as a matter of expediency than through any belief in separate women's education. Over the next 10 years the college struggled to survive, gradually increasing the number of students from 157 at the outset to 250, but in 1874 it began to admit men. However, a separate women's-only college was formed at that time as a breakaway from the co-educational institution, supported by those who believed in single sex education for women. It represented a more conservative and orthodox view of women's education – emphasising their different, subservient role in society and fostering attitudes of self-sacrifice, prudence and forethought or consideration. It catered for shop assistants, domestic servants, milliners, nurses, teachers, etc. and taught domestic subjects such as dressmaking, cookery and hygiene, as well as more academic subjects. The original college struggled on in the shadow of the Working Men's College until it closed in 1901. The more successful breakaway college maintained its separate existence until it was amalgamated with the Working Men's College in 1966 (*ibid.: passim*; Kelly, 1992: 187).

The Working Men's and Women's Colleges did not play a large part in nineteenth century adult education, but their emphasis on liberal and humane studies and the enrichment of the personality as opposed to more practical skills helped to secure the liberal dimension in later British adult education. Indeed, it contributed to the later harmful dichotomy between vocational and non-vocational adult education and the preference given in influential circles to the latter.

A growing number of working men's clubs and institutes were founded in the second half of the century, particularly in London and the Midlands and north of England, but not in Scotland or Wales. After 1862 they were given some support by the Club and Institute Union, but many still enjoyed only a precarious and short life. Their interest in education was always secondary to their social functions, but some clubs did organise occasional lectures and classes and, after 1864, participated in a successful circulating library (*ibid.*: 189–92).

A People's Palace was opened in the East End of London in 1887 as a centre of organised recreation, orderly amusement and intellectual activity. It was soon taken over by the Drapers' Company and turned into a polytechnic, later becoming the East London Technical College and then Queen Mary College. Meanwhile, across the river in Lambeth, Morley College (named after its financial benefactor, Samuel Morley, a millionaire hosiery manufacturer) emerged in the 1880s from a coffee tavern and working men's club within the Old Vic Theatre. Open equally to working-class men and women, it offered classes and lectures 'not directly connected with or applied to any handicraft, trade or business'. By 1901 there were 55 classes in 32 different subjects which, despite the original intentions, included elementary, technical and commercial subjects and various practical classes (e.g. cookery, dressmaking, woodwork), as well as a wide range of liberal studies and a vigorous social life. Apart from the welcome given to women, Morley College had evolved into a very similar institution to the London Working Men's College. There was nothing particularly novel in its provision of liberal non-vocational courses, its elementary instruction or its conception as a college for working people rather than the leisured classes. But the combination of these characteristics in one stable institution was rare (*ibid.*: 192–4; Richards, 1958: 86–100).

## Evening Schools

From the 1830s onwards an increasing number of elementary day schools opened in the evenings for adult students as well as children and adolescents, particularly in the north of England and in Scotland. These were mostly small, private ventures run on the same lines as the elementary day schools, and very often by the same teachers, using the same premises. They charged a small fee, from one penny a week upwards, to teach a little reading and writing, with sometimes some number work and other subjects such as history, geography and grammar. Where they were associated with the Church they included religious knowledge. Many were of a very low standard, as were the common day schools; run by people with little or no qualification for the job who were eking out a meagre existence as school teachers. Very often these evening schools enjoyed a precarious, short-lived existence. But more than any other form of adult education, they met the needs of large numbers of adults for basic literacy and therefore played an important part in nineteenth century adult education. 'It was in these schools, perhaps more than anywhere else, that the illiterate or semi-literate adult acquired the elements of education' (Sadler, 1907: 53; Kelly, 1992: 155-7).

The 1851 census recorded 1,545 evening schools for adults in England and Wales with 39,783 students (mostly in England, very few in Wales where Sunday Schools continued to be the main form of adult education); and 438 schools, 15,071 students in Scotland. However, it is unclear from these census statistics how many of the students were really adults and how many were children or adolescents studying in the evenings (*ibid.*).

In 1851 the Committee of Council on Education introduced government funding for these evening schools, to assist elementary education. Two years later the Department of Science and Art was established to encourage science and technical education in all kinds of institutions. Some of its funding was directed to the evening schools for this purpose, enabling them to offer Department of Science and Art examination courses, although such evening classes encountered problems of inadequate funding and continuing doubts as to whether scientific education was really suitable for artisans (Sadler, 1907: 57-8; Ministry of Reconstruction, 1919: 22; Roderick and Stephens, 1985: 28-9, 66-7; Vincent, 1989: 14).

By 1858 there were reported to be over 2,000 evening schools in England and Wales, most of them attached to day schools and three-quarters of them connected with the Church of England, but it is clear that a majority of their 81,000 students (two-thirds male) were adolescents. Under the Committee of Council's 1862 revised code, evening schools qualified for government grant on the same basis as elementary day schools, except that their students were older. This introduced the payments-by-results system whereby schools received grant on the basis of numbers of attendances and examinations passed. It tended to narrow the curriculum to the 'three Rs' and religious instruction. In Wales, Sunday Schools continued to play a more important role while in some of the more remote parishes in Scotland there was a practice of some young farmworkers taking a break from their farm service and returning to day school (Sadler, 1907: 60; Kelly, 1992: 200-1).

After the passing of the new Education Act in 1870, which set up School Boards to found elementary schools wherever they did not already exist, the need and demand for elementary evening schools gradually declined, although some School Boards themselves promoted evening classes (*ibid.*: 202; Sadler, 1907: 61; Ministry of Reconstruction, 1919: 22-3; Cowan, 1968: 205-6; Bird, 1991: 190).

During the 1870s the London guilds concluded that there was a need for more technical education relevant to industry and established the City and Guilds of London Institute in 1878 to develop technical education and administer examinations. Many evening schools prepared adults for these examinations in the years to follow. The stimulus of the City and Guilds and the Department of Science and Art did gradually extend scientific education in the evening schools, although in a limited form. Their activities, together with increasing foreign industrial competition, did give rise to some improvements in technical education during the last two decades of the century, although it was still significantly inferior to that available in many European countries (City and Guilds, 1993: 12–45; Vincent, 1989: 118–9; Roderick and Stephens, 1985: 30; Green, 1994)).

Meanwhile, in 1885 a Recreational Evening Schools Association had been established to encourage the use of school buildings for a wider and more practical and recreational use than the grant-aided evening schools with their narrow, revised-code curricula. The emphasis of the Association was on provision for adolescents, but it did include adults. More importantly, it pointed the way for the development of local authority evening classes in the twentieth century (Sadler, 1907: 91–6; Kelly, 1992: 202).

The gradual shift from *ad hoc*, voluntary evening schools to more organised, grant-aided provision towards the end of the century did not eliminate the gender differential that was frequently to be found in the curricula. While both men and women were able to study basic literacy and numeracy, women were encouraged to do physical exercises whereas men were more likely to learn shorthand and book-keeping, reflecting the gender structure of occupations at that time (Bird, 1991: 191). Meanwhile, after the decline in the 1870s and 80s, the numbers in evening schools began to increase again in the last decade of the century. This was partly a result of a relaxation of the grant regulations but more a consequence of the passing of the Technical Instruction Act in 1889 which revolutionised evening schools and enabled them to provide a wider range of adult education built on the foundations of compulsory childhood schooling (see below) (Sadler, 1907: 62–7; Ministry of Reconstruction, 1919: 23).

## Libraries, Museums and Cultural Societies in the Later Nineteenth Century

The existence of numerous libraries before the passing of the Public Libraries Act in 1850 has already been mentioned, as has their generally poor quality and the fact that for the large proportion of the population that was barely literate, they had little significance. But with the extension of educational opportunities in the second half of the nineteenth century and the gradual reduction of illiteracy, the libraries became an increasingly important adjunct to adult education. The 1850 legislation permitted municipal authorities in England and Wales to provide library premises (but not books) from the rates if two-thirds of the ratepayers approved. In 1853 similar permissive powers were extended to Scotland and Ireland, and in 1854 and 1855 the legislation was amended to allow expenditure on books as well as premises. Relatively few local authorities took immediate advantage of this legislation: by 1869 only 35 had done so. However, over the next 30 years a further 266 public libraries were opened in England, Scotland and Wales. This reflected the increased demand; an easing of the cumbersome process for obtaining taxpayers' approval in 1893–4; and a flow of private benefactions for public libraries, notably from the Scottish-American Andrew Carnegie. His benefactions started with his native Dunfermline in 1881, extended to other Scottish towns, and then into England in 1897. But in rural areas, where ratable income was too low to establish a public library, the population had to rely on the scatter of Mechanics' Institute, literary society, Sunday School and circulating libraries. These were sometimes supported by such organisations as the Southern Counties Adult Education Society in order to 'improve the moral and spiritual character of the working-classes and to persuade them to accept their assigned role in society' and become better and more productive workers in rural Hampshire (Kelly, 1992: 177, 213–4; Field, 1980: 101, 104–5; and see Chadwick and Stannett, 1995: 11–22).

Public museums and art galleries were virtually non-existent outside London in the early nineteenth century but over forty museums of one kind or another came into existence between 1820 and the passing of the Museums Act in 1845. They were mostly attached to universities or literary and philosophical societies, natural history societies or antiquarian societies. Their collections of local antiquities and curiosities were of little educational significance. The 1845 Act empowered local authorities to use rates to support a museum, but as with the libraries few did so before the 1880s. Even then, there was a marked reluctance on the part of local authorities to burden their rate payers with the cost of a museum or art gallery. Although 1880–1920 was the richest period of museum development, nearly half the public museums created during those four decades originated as private collections. Many society or institutional museums were handed over to local authorities during this period, although numerous cultural societies (literary, musical, dramatic, historical, antiquarian, geological, natural history, mutual improvement, etc.) continued to prosper and contribute to the educational development of their members during the last decades of the century. Not least, they assisted the autodidactics in their heroic studies, described earlier (Kelly, 1992: 177–9, 210-11, 214–5).

## The Co-operative Movement in the Later Nineteenth Century

Reference was made earlier to the attempt of the Co-operative Societies in the 1830s and 40s to implement Owenite ideals, and the Rochdale Society's decision in 1844 to devote a percentage of its profits to educational purposes. After 1850 the Co-operative movement's commitment to adult education survived but it lost its radical, socialist dimension. Its educational work came to resemble that of the other later-nineteenth century organisations providing education for the working class. The Rochdale Society continued to be a major educational provider: in 1877 it had 14 libraries scattered throughout the area, with over 13,000 books, and subscriptions to numerous daily, weekly, monthly and quarterly periodicals. It ran a large programme of classes, mainly scientific in character, most of which were supported by the Science and Art Department. But few societies were as committed as Rochdale and outside the north-west only a minority made any significant contribution to adult education. Those that did operated like an evening school or Mechanics' Institute rather than in any distinctly co-operative way. In Yorkshire the attitude of the leaders of the Co-operative Societies was favourable to adult education but they did not consider it their duty to provide it. This was perhaps typified by the view expressed at a Co-operative Society meeting in Leeds in 1872 that 'we want no eddication, give us a bonus'. In 1880, only a quarter of the 912 societies made grants to education, and nearly half of these were in the north-west, which accounted for more than three-quarters of the total educational expenditure. And in most cases, the activity was limited to the provision of a library and newsroom with perhaps a few popular lectures and one or two classes. A report of 1884 listed 47 lending libraries, 69 circulating libraries and 194 newsrooms, together with 134 lectures and 2,253 students in classes (*ibid.*: 207–9; Ministry of Reconstruction, 1919: 29; Harrison, 1961: 105–6; Bonner, 1970: 59–86).

During the last 10 or 15 years of the century, the need for the Co-operative Societies to provide these forms of adult education was reduced by the spread of public libraries and local authority evening classes, particularly after the passing of the Technical Instruction Act in 1889. But a new form of education began to be provided, concerned with promoting the ideas and improving the practice of co-operation. With the founding of the Women's Educational Guild in 1883 there was also more emphasis on training women to fill leading roles in the Co-operative movement and also in other social and political organisations. This training included public speaking, committee work and policy formulation. In 1896 a special Committee on Co-operative Education found that 269 out of 402 Societies that responded to its enquiry had educational funds and that the total amount they spent on education in 1895 was £36,336. Four years later, almost £60,000 was spent on co-operative education. But only a small proportion was spent on classes: much more went on libraries, reading rooms and recreational lectures and concerts that were educational only in name. Nevertheless, serious educational work was being done by some of the Co-operative Societies towards the end of the century, which included education in co-operative values and also the training of men and women 'to take part in industrial and social reforms and municipal life generally'. They provided co-operative halls where political and social adult education could take place, and gave support to other forms of adult education, particularly in the north, including university extension and, after 1903, the Workers' Educational Association (Kelly, 209–10; Ministry of Reconstruction, 1919: 30; Simon, 1965: 41–6; Jepson, 1973: 169–77; Bonner, 1970: 118–21).

## University Extension

From the 1830s onwards there was increasing pressure to reform the obsolete ancient universities of Oxford and Cambridge, to make them more relevant to contemporary educational needs and to develop and extend their limited provision. This involved discussions about how university culture could be taken to a wider population, which led in 1850 to an unsuccessful proposal from William Sewell, a fellow of Exeter College, Oxford, that the University should appoint peripatetic teachers in some of the larger provincial cities and supply literary, scientific and Mechanics' Institutes with university lecturers. A few years later, in 1857, both Oxford and Cambridge did adopt schemes for examining secondary school pupils. Although this did not constitute a form of adult education, its significance for the future of university extension was that it involved the universities in a more direct role in the wider field of education, beyond the walls of the universities. It also helped to make them more aware of the educational needs in that wider world, and established an administrative system at central and local level which could later be adapted to the provision of extension lectures (Kunzel, 1975: 34–9; Harrison, 1961: 220–1; Marriott, 1984: 15–17; Jepson, 1973: 13–30).

In 1867 James Stuart, a fellow of Trinity College, Cambridge began a programme of lectures for ladies' educational associations in Liverpool, Manchester, Sheffield and Leeds. This led to the foundation of the North of England Council for promoting the Higher Education of Women, in order to organise lectures in literary, historical and scientific subjects and promote higher examinations for women. The following year lecture courses were organised in nine northern towns and were all given by lecturers from Oxford or Cambridge. In 1871 the Council, together with Crewe Mechanics' Institute, Rochdale Co-operative Society and the Mayor and inhabitants of Leeds, petitioned the University of Cambridge to open the University 'to those whose circumstances prevent them from being able to reside there'. Their proposal was accompanied by a letter of support from Stuart. The spirit of reform was stronger by then than it had been at the time of Sewell's proposal, 20 years earlier, and so in 1873 Cambridge agreed to organise courses of lectures in a limited number of centres. University extension had formally arrived. Three years later a London Society for the Extension of University Teaching was launched, and in 1878 Oxford agreed to make arrangements for university extension lectures on its own account, although the reform impetus was less strong there than at Cambridge at that time and very little happened at Oxford before 1885. Cambridge's and Oxford's involvement in university extension was induced at least in part by a wish to maintain their national influence during a period of rapid change, and to prevent their positions being weakened or usurped by newer institutions. A general lack of collaboration prevented a rational geographical organisation or distribution of extension work or sharing of responsibilities. University extension was not so much a united movement as a series of competing schemes in an adult education free market, with some quite cut-throat competition between the two ancient universities and London University (*ibid.*: 31–45, 80–91; Harrison, 1961: 221–3; Kunzel, 1975: 46; Marriott, 1984: 13–69; Goldman, 1995: 61–102).

By 1875–6 there were 112 extension lecture courses being run at 37 different centres. The next five years saw a reduction to 37 courses in 17 centres by 1880–1 but then there was steady expansion during the 1880s. Because of the increase in shorter courses, the statistics are not directly comparable, but by 1889–90 there were over 100 Oxford extension centres and 67 Cambridge centres. During the next few years, collaboration with the local authority Technical Education Committees set up under the 1889 Technical Instruction Act (see below) and the availability of 'whisky money' under the terms of the 1890 Local Tax Act led to considerable expansion. The peak was reached in 1891–2, with 279 Oxford centres and 295 run by Cambridge. After 1895 the local authority work dried up and the level of provision fell back to approximately that of 1889–90, becoming fairly stabilised at that level for the remainder of the century. By 1902 the two universities had established contact with well over 900 centres, although many of these had quite a short life (Jepson, 1973: 99-103; Marriott, 1983: 7-10).

Apart from meeting the universities' own agendas, university extension was part of wider educational changes that were taking place, and a response to a number of more general aims: to improve the general state of education, particularly by improving the potential supply of school teachers; to help satisfy the growing demand for better education for women; to improve on the limited success of other forms of adult education; to contribute to the democratisation of higher education and the more general democratisation of society; and to meet the demand from a section of the politically conscious working class for *really* useful knowledge, to help them in their struggles for social justice (Jepson, 1973: 92–5; Harrison, 1961: 226, 235–9; Goldman, *op. cit.*).

In 1891 university extension was described by one of the pioneers as being 'for the whole nation'. Unlike other forms of nineteenth century adult education, it was not aimed specifically at the poor or the working class. It was more inclined to adopt a *laissez-faire* approach, responding to demand rather than targeting a particular social group. Stuart believed that it should cater for all classes together. But Michael Sadler (the rather aggressive secretary of the Oxford Extension Committee from 1885), while confirming that university extension was not intended for workmen only, claimed in 1894 that it 'desired to meet the needs of three different classes – ladies, young men engaged as clerks and shop-assistants, and working people' (Jepson, 1973: 128, 215; Kunzel, 1975: 47; Rowbotham, 1981: 63).

In practice, university extension in the late nineteenth century was predominantly middle class, and was particularly popular with middle-class women. We have seen that this was where it really began, with Stuart's lectures to the ladies' associations in Lancashire and Yorkshire. This continued to be the major source of demand. It was the champions of women's education who had the clearest idea of how extension could help them achieve their aims. Although the statistics are unreliable, probably two-thirds of the participants were women and schoolgirls. Undoubtedly, university extension contributed to the higher education of women (and at the same time to the higher education of school teachers), although there was little attempt made to reach working-class women, who were still assumed to need little or no education (Jepson, 1973: 104–19; Harrison, 1961: 227; Kunzel, 1975: 47; Bird, 1991: 185–6; Rowbotham, 1981: 71).

But the promoters of university extension were troubled by their failure to recruit other constituents. They failed to attract young middle-class men in large numbers, and they generally failed to attract working-class students, despite considerable assistance from the Co-operative Societies in the north of England. No more than 20 or 25 per cent of students were working class, and they were concentrated mainly in Yorkshire and Lancashire (Jepson, 1973: 105, 119–40, 169–77; Harrison, 1961: 243). One of the reasons, common to almost all nineteenth century adult education, was that the universities over-estimated the demand for this kind of education amongst working-class people, the majority of whom still had had no more than a basic elementary education. However, that was not the only reason: many working-class people felt uncomfortable with the alien bourgeois culture of university extension and the academic approach of some of the lecturers, who had difficulties in crossing the cultural and class divides and making their lectures meaningful to a working-class audience. Equally, working-class expectations that adult education should be either social and entertaining or politically useful were at odds with the university lecturers' perceptions of education. This mutual lack of understanding between lecturers and working-class students was reinforced by the middle-class local committees, who unwittingly alienated working-class people by their condescension and patronising manner (Jepson, 1973: 143–78; Harrison, 1961: 240; Rowbotham, 1981: 63–6, 72; Kunzel, 1975: 40).

There was another, more pragmatic, reason for the lack of working-class participation: the costs involved. Extension lectures received no financial aid until the 1890 Local Tax Act made the 'whisky money' subsidies available for some extension work, which, as previously mentioned, did boost numbers considerably for a few years. But apart from this, the courses had to be financed from students' fees and local support. This meant that the fees were often beyond the means of even the keenest working-class potential students. 'How can you expect such as myself to keep a house over my head, support and keep things respectable, and be able to pay 6 (shillings) down on the nail for a course of lectures out of a little over a pound a week?', one such student complained. And that was without taking into account the other costs of books and travel on top of the course fee. As Professor Jepson has noted:

the cost of courses remained such as to compel the local centres either to charge comparatively high admission fees, or to rely upon local support ... The former was an obvious hindrance to working-class support. The latter, in that it often took the form of middle-class support, tended to create a social barrier which, in an age of comparatively acute class consciousness, was not easy to overcome.

This was demonstrated at Exeter, where the local committee attempted to overcome the problem by charging workmen a lower fee and then admitting them by a separate entrance and sitting them apart from those who paid a full fee. This was hardly conducive to making them feel welcome! (Jepson, 1973: 181–208; Harrison, 1961: 240; Peers, 1958: 56–7; Rowbotham, 1981: 67; Clapp, 1982: 14–20).

Despite all these difficulties, university extension did attract some 'rather special' and very determined, mainly upper working class students. They were very much the same breed as the working class autodidactics. They greatly admired the culture of the 'strange country' into which they were admitted and were intensely effected by it – almost in the nature of a religious conversion (Rowbotham, 1981: 67–70, 73–7).

This culture was very much a reflection of the universities from which it flowed: liberal, arts-dominated and extolling the virtues of social harmony, rather than technical, scientific, vocational or politically 'extreme'. This liberal (in all senses) culture was a little modified in the early 1890s when collaboration with the Technical Education Committees and acceptance of the 'whisky money' gave an impetus to the scientific and technical side of extension work (ibid.: passim; Jepson, 1973: 215–44).

The universities were very anxious that this extension of their activities into what was a 'strange country' for them should not undermine the quality of higher education. They tried to ensure this by insisting on the high quality and qualifications of the extension lecturers (although this was sometimes made difficult by the insecurity of the job), and by the structure of the courses. This almost invariably consisted of four parts: an hour's lecture, a class either preceding or following the lecture, the students' private study and an examination. The lectures were generally considered to be of a high standard, but the classes gave greater cause for concern. Although fewer students attended the classes than the lectures, there were still frequently far too many to be able to give them individual attention in the time available. Certainly they did not conform to the Oxbridge tutorial tradition that they were supposed to resemble. The other problem that lecturers encountered was apathy. Students were prepared to sit and listen, but not necessarily to do more than this. This also affected the quality of their reading and written work, which was very variable. It was also adversely affected by inadequate book supplies and insufficient time for lecturers to mark and comment on the students' work. It is therefore not surprising that the examinations, which were optional, were taken by a disappointingly small proportion of the students (*ibid.*: 245–87).

Summer meetings were introduced by Oxford in 1888 and by Cambridge a few years later in an attempt to supplement and enhance the educational value of the normal extension courses. Certainly some of the working-class students found these summer meetings in the rarefied atmosphere of an Oxbridge college the most intense aspect of the extension experience. Both Co-operative Societies and private individuals awarded scholarships to poor students to enable them to attend these meetings (*ibid.*: 320–3; Rowbotham, 1981: 83–7).

Perhaps the most problematic aspect of the courses, as far as standards were concerned, was the lack of opportunities for thorough and systematic study. The 12-lecture courses were intended to provide such opportunities, but in practice most students were left high and dry at the end of them. Many centres had a very temporary existence, and even where they were more permanent, there was little likelihood of continuity as far as subject matter was concerned. For the vast majority of students, study was at best disjointed, and frequently discontinued after 12 weeks. Even that level of thoroughness was undermined by Oxford's preference for less demanding six-week courses (Jepson, 1973: 288–322; Marriott, 1984: 38–42).

At the vast majority of centres ... the normal provision consisted of short and unconnected courses. As such it would appear that, whilst indeed these courses brought the public into closer contact with the Universities through the presence of University teachers, they fell far short of the standard envisaged by the founders of the movement, who regarded the provision of thorough and systematic courses as the ultimate and primary, though not the sole, aim of University Extension (Jepson, 1973: 327).

University extension made a notable contribution to the expansion of higher education in England by helping to found, or paving the way for, a number of local colleges which were used as premises for extension courses and later became university colleges. These included Bristol, Leeds, Nottingham and Sheffield and the three specifically extension colleges at Reading, Exeter and Colchester. Their motive was partly to liberalise or humanise these local colleges, which many Oxbridge academics such as Benjamin Jowett, the influential Master of Balliol, considered too technical and utilitarian. But there was also an element of empire-building in their approach: encouraging the local colleges to act as outposts of Oxford or Cambridge, and prising them away from London University's external degree provision. However, the local colleges did not always relish this role and, as at Reading, quickly forsook their extension origins and assumed the outlook of a conventional university (*ibid.*: 88–9, 224, 327; Harrison, 1961: 227; Peers, 1958: 58; Bird, 1991: 186–8; Marriott, 1984: 23, 64; Clapp, 1982: 14–20; Macrae, 1994: 3–18; Goldman, 1995: 26–7).

Any assessment of university extension during the last three decades of the nineteenth century must conclude that it failed to provide for the 'whole nation'; it failed to develop a social conscience; and it failed to maintain the high educational standards anticipated by its founders. Its lack of public funding (except the 'whisky money') meant that it was forced to chase popularity instead of quality, and price itself beyond the means of most working-class people. It promoted social harmony and aimed to persuade 'the working classes ... to take a broad view of things, and feel in sympathy with the richer and more cultured classes' as one of the advocates of extension argued in 1901. In this way it sought to integrate the working class within middle-class socio-economic structures and modify working-class consciousness and political opinions. Not all were 'nobbled' in this way, but it did alienate some of these working-class scholars from their roots and helped to foster their perception of the middle-class world as benevolent, liberal and philanthropic, thereby countering socialist political theory based on antagonistic class relationships (Kunzel, 1975: 47–8; *The Cambridge Graphic*, 16 November 1901; Rowbotham, 1981: 77–83, 91–2).

However, extension did help to take Oxford and Cambridge 'along the paths of democracy' and, by opening the doors of the universities a tiny crack, it made it a little easier for the Labour movement to bid for seats of power. It established the practice of the universities entering into partnership with local bodies and helped to liberalise some of the local colleges; but it also helped to establish the hegemony of the arts in liberal adult education and perpetuate the division between non-vocational liberal and vocational utilitarian adult education, with major consequences for the twentieth century. It contributed to the improvement of education for middle-class women (Peers, 1958: 60; Harrison, 1961: 244–5; Kunzel, 1975: 47–8).

Finally, although many of the large extension lectures did suffer from serious pedagogical defects, some of this early extension work can claim to have established the tutorial practice which later became the hallmark of the twentieth century tutorial class movement (see Chapters 7 and 8). 'The Cambridge 'Local Lectures' under James Stuart's leadership inaugurated extramural education and were the source of a non-vocational, humanising 'movement' which was to find imitators in other English-speaking lands, and until recent times was to dominate conceptions of adult education in this country' (Lowe, 1972: and Welch, 1976: *passim*; Dixon, 1965: 5; Marriott, 1984: 35).

## University Settlement

In 1883 Samuel Barnett, vicar of St Jude's, Whitechapel, presented a paper entitled *Settlements of University Men in Great Towns* to a small group of academics in St John's College, Oxford. From this meeting the university settlement movement emerged. It shared many of the motives of university extension, particularly the wish to democratise higher education and take it out into the wider world to people who could not come to the universities. It also shared the same liberal desire to extend social harmony and build bridges between the classes. It was very much a response of liberal, educated middle-class people to the growing sense of social crisis and instability. But it also had a stronger social conscience than was apparent in university extension: a missionary zeal to right the manifest wrongs of society. Barnett and his supporters felt that one of the problems was a lack of understanding between people of different social backgrounds. They believed that much educational work, such as university extension, suffered because the privileged providers could not appreciate the points of view of those they intended to educate. The idea of university settlement was to overcome these social barriers by organised intermingling of young men from the universities and working-class residents and to find a common ground for all classes. This is what was to distinguish a settlement from a proselytizing mission. As the socialist MP Keir Hardy explained in 1901: 'A University settlement in itself was a very simple affair, six, eight, ten or twelve men living together in some part of a great city ... The settlement was a training ground, into which the young of both sexes came, gained their experience, and passed on to make room for others.' While there, they would teach the local residents and at the same time learn to appreciate the values and aspirations of the working class. The aim was to plant the idea of a people's university based on a fellowship of teaching and learning (Simon, 1965: 77–9; Peers, 1958: 45; Meacham, 1987: 32–4; *The Cambridge Graphic*, 16 November 1901).

In 1884 Toynbee Hall, the first and best known of the university settlements, was established in the East End of London, with Barnett as warden. It promoted a variety of educational and social activities and followed the ideas laid down by Barnett in his earlier paper. But whatever his theories, in practice Barnett's liberalism, like so many other middle-class paternalists', hid a basic contempt for working-class culture. He was incapable of seeing beyond his liberal-bourgeois values or appreciating that the working class of the East End had their own distinct cultural traditions. Toynbee Hall, for all its supposedly democratic sentiments, was authoritarian and mission-like in expecting the fortunate poor to follow the example set by their betters. In this sense it was 'a continuation of the philanthropic campaign to educate the poor that had flourished throughout much of the nineteenth century'. By the end of the century, Toynbee Hall had gained a reputation as a training ground for bright, young, reform-minded middle-class men who were destined for the civil or colonial service. Between 1884 and 1900, 102 residents lived there. But it is questionable whether it had much impact on the working class of the East End of London (Briggs and Macartney, 1984: 1–60; Simon, 1965: 79; Peers, 1958: 45; Meacham, 1987: 35–85).

A second Oxford settlement was established in 1885, in Bethnal Green, and by the end of the century 20 or more settlements had been founded, not only in London, but in Bristol, Ipswich, Liverpool, Manchester, Edinburgh and Glasgow. About half of them were associated with the universities, and several, such as the Women's University Settlement established in Southwark in 1887, were organised by women (Kelly, 1992: 239–40). Despite its paternalism and authoritarianism, the university settlement movement did also have a strong Christian socialist basis inherited from Maurice, which contributed to the more radical, egalitarian strands of adult education in the twentieth century.

## Technical Education Committees and the 'Whisky Money'

Meanwhile, as already noted, the Government had gradually become involved in the provision of adult education, reflecting the gradual drift from *laissez-faire* to collectivist intervention as the century wore on. The availability of some government funding from 1851, and the establishment of the Science and Art Department in 1853 gave some encouragement to the development of scientific and technical education although it was really only in the last 20 years of the century that much progress was made in this respect. In 1879 the City and Guilds Institute founded what is sometimes regarded as the first technical college, at Finsbury, later to become a school of the University of London; and this was followed by the spread of polytechnics for 'the promotion of industrial skill, general knowledge, health and well-being of young men belonging to the poorer classes'. But the real stimulus to improved technical education came with the passing of the Technical Instruction Act in 1889, which empowered county councils and county boroughs to devote the proceeds from a penny rate to technical instruction committees; and the Local Taxation Act in 1890 which provided further resources for the new committees from a duty on beer and spirits (the so-called 'whisky money'). This replaced the previous payments-by-results funding with more substantial, if variable, funds which facilitated a considerable expansion of technical education in local authority evening classes during the 1890s. In 1891, nearly three-quarters of a million pounds was paid out in whisky money grants: by 1900 it was over one million (Kelly, 1992: 197–8; City and Guilds, 1993: 35–6, 46, 50; Sharp, 1971: 31).

The distribution of the whisky money was somewhat haphazard and based on a very unfair formula which did not take local authorities' size of population or educational needs into account. Some authorities received three or four times as much as others per 1,000 of population. Moreover, authorities were not obliged to use the whisky money for educational purposes, and whilst many did, some used it for the relief of rates. But 'despite minor losses to the relief of rates, the 'whisky money' grants were much larger that other public contributions to technical education in the 1890s' and did contribute to its expansion. Similarly, as previously noted, it re-directed university extension into scientific and technical education for a few years in the early 1890s, and enabled it to expand rapidly until the local authorities turned the tap off in the mid-1890s. At the same time it had the effect of putting university extension at the mercy of 'blinkered and bureaucratic local government' (*ibid.*: 32–6; Marriott, 1983: 7–15; Jepson, 1973: 231).

## The Nineteenth Century's Adult Education Legacy

Professor Peers once suggested that by the end of the nineteenth century 'the first coherent national movement for adult education' was emerging, 'in which all the preceding elements were finally merged', providing a setting for the modern movement (Peers, 1958: 48). This is perhaps a somewhat Whig interpretation of the history of adult education, seeing the nineteenth century leading inevitably towards the apotheosis of twentieth century achievement. We might be rather less optimistic, more cynical about progression now. Nevertheless, the nineteenth century did undoubtedly leave a legacy to the twentieth century.

With the exception of the literary, philosophical and scientific societies and university extension, most nineteenth century adult education was aimed primarily at the working class, for a variety of reasons: to educate them to conform happily to their allotted roles in society; to produce a more efficient workforce; to alleviate the alienating effects of industrialisation; or to assist them in their struggles for social justice. But whatever the motive, much of this adult education ended up being colonised by the middle class, either because it reflected their culture or because the educated middle-class was better equipped to take advantage of it. In many cases it was culturally and ideologically alien to the working class; or cast at too high a level for the many people who had had little or no education at even the most basic, elementary level. Much of it suffered from being patronising and bourgeois, even if well intentioned.

Much of it was also conceived of as mainly for men, reflecting the orientation of education generally, but there were notable exceptions, and increasingly women did find ways of adapting it to their needs.

There was a strong emphasis on voluntaryism and self-help and this gave a strength and a degree of independence to much nineteenth century adult education, but it also revealed the limitations of depending solely on voluntaryism. As the century advanced, so did the extent of government support. This rescued much adult education from oblivion, but also overshadowed autonomous or independent working-class adult education. However, it did not destroy it altogether: the autodidactics struggled on a little longer yet and independent working-class adult education gained a new impetus with the founding of Ruskin College in 1899 and the subsequent formation of the Plebs League and the Labour Colleges in the twentieth century (see Chapter 10).

The nineteenth century revealed the importance of informal adult education that takes place outside the bounds of formal provision. It also showed the crucial importance of providing a firm base of basic, elementary education on which more esoteric and ambitious forms of adult education can be built.

One of the major detrimental legacies was that, despite some correction late in the century, adult education carried into the twentieth century a tradition and a practice which greatly undervalued, if it did not despise, utilitarian, technical, vocational education. It reflected the liberal, humane, non-technical ethos of the ancient universities, which gloried in not being useful. The extent to which this anti-vocational prejudice was passed on to the twentieth century adult educators can be seen in the pages of the influential *1919 Report*. The spin-off of this was the separation of vocational from non-vocational adult education for much of the twentieth century, and the widely assumed superiority of the latter.

More positively, the twentieth century inherited a strong tradition of socially purposive adult education and the belief that adult education could and should contribute to political and social action.

How this legacy was used in the twentieth century will be considered in the following chapters.

*3*

# An Overview of British Adult Education in the Twentieth Century

## Roger Fieldhouse

This chapter, like the previous one, will be mainly concerned with the provision of formal adult education in various modes, by a variety of organisations. However, it is important to remember the continuing significance, at least in the early part of the twentieth century, of the autodidactic tradition, even if this tradition was being slowly eroded or undermined by the gradual opening-up of the universities to working-class seekers of intellectual enlightenment (Ree, 1984: 15). The emphasis on formal systems of adult education also leaves the extent of other non-formal adult learning and distance education somewhat neglected. These major aspects of adult education are easy to overlook and very difficult to quantify but Tough's estimate that about four-fifths of learning projects are initiated by the learners themselves or some other amateur planner, and only one-fifth by professionals (Tough, 1983: 143–4), has already been referred to in the Preface. This submerged part of the adult education 'iceberg' needs to be constantly borne in mind. The of nature some of this non-formal adult learning in Britain in the twentieth century is examined, if not quantified, later in Chapter 12.

### New Adult Education Structures

The century began with a flurry of educational activities, the first of which was the passing of the 1902 Education Act. This attempted to bring order to the imbroglio of public education that had emerged from the nineteenth century. By this legislation the Government created local education authorities (LEAs) to take over responsibility for the provision of elementary and some secondary education, funded by local rates. The LEAs also inherited the adult education responsibilities of the recently created technical education committees. How they exercised these responsibilities and gradually developed a comprehensive provision of nightschools and other adult education activities is described in the next two chapters.

A year later, in 1903, the Workers' Educational Association (WEA) was founded with the aim of making university education available to working-class adults who had had no opportunity to acquire such education through the normal, very restricted, routes that existed at the beginning of the century. At first utilising the University Extension Movement, the WEA fairly quickly developed its own network of tutorial classes and other provision, as detailed in Chapter 7.

In 1907 Albert Mansbridge, the founder of the WEA, convened a conference at Oxford of various working-class interests together with a group of reformist Oxford academics and some influential churchmen, politicians and civil servants, to debate the contribution that the University could make to working-class education. Mansbridge very astutely harnessed both the reform movement within the University of Oxford and the Liberal Government's eagerness to promote a programme of social reforms intended partly to divert the leadership of the emerging Labour movement from socialist or Marxist 'extremism'. The outcome of the conference was a report, published the following year, which advocated various reforms within the University intended to open it up to a wider cross-section of society, and the establishment of a tutorial class movement which would feed working-class students into the University and also provide the working class with access to university education in tutorial classes located throughout the length and breadth of the country. This adult education provision was promised financial support from central government grants. How the 1908 Report fundamentally influenced the subsequent development of both WEA and university adult education is shown in Chapters 7 and 8.

Meanwhile, an alternative 'independent' working-class movement, free from the political constraints or strings allegedly attached to the WEA's and the universities' government grants, grew out of the Ruskin College strike in 1908. The Plebs League and the National Council of Labour Colleges were founded to promote 'independent' working-class education. They did so often with bitter hostility to the WEA. This strand of British adult education, together with the involvement of the trade union movement, are depicted in Chapter 10.

## The 1919 'Final Report' and Board of Education Adult Education Committees

The Ministry of Reconstruction, set up during the First World War, established an Adult Education Committee under the chairmanship of A.L. Smith, Master of Balliol College and a longstanding and influential member of the adult education fraternity. The Committee's *Final Report*, published in 1919, has been variously described as 'probably the most important single contribution ever made to the literature of adult education'; the 'Bible of British adult education' and 'the most notable and useful monument in our adult education literature' (Tawney, 1956; Waller, 1967: 4; Taylor, 1976: 147). Within the context of the post-war euphoria, the Report provided a sense of a new beginning (Kelly, 1973: 113) although in some respects it was based on pre-war models and experience of adult education (Tawney, 1956). Its influence and importance lay in its emphasis on the social purpose of adult education in developing a notion of responsible citizenship. The rationale of adult education was presented as the creation of a 'well ordered welfare state or Great Society' organised in support of 'the common good'. It was 'a blue print not only for adult education but for a free and fully participatory democracy'. And it was from this vision that the foundations were laid for the democratic teaching methods and learning environment which became the hallmark of much British adult education (Small, 1975: 152; Waller, 1967:

45). The Report was successful in 'depicting adult education not as a side issue to be resigned to the fanatic or the crank but as an activity indispensable to the health of democratic societies and to be regarded therefore as a necessary and normal part of the country's educational system' (Tawney, 1956). This was stressed by A.L. Smith in his letter addressed to the Prime Minister in which he described adult education as 'not ... a luxury for a few exceptional persons here and there' but as 'a permanent national necessity, an inseparable aspect of citizenship' (Ministry of Reconstruction, 1919: 5).

However, although the Report was extremely effective in justifying a system of adult education with a social purpose, aimed at the broad mass of the population, it was not particularly successful in stimulating a mass popular demand (Small, 1975: 152). This was perhaps partly because its vision was not the same as the more prosaic, bread-and-butter interests of the mass of the population. The Committee's field of vision was very wide, but the heart of the report was liberal studies 'without thought of vocational advantage' (Waller, 1967: 5). It is not surprising, given the background, beliefs and experience of the majority of the Committee, that the Report 'strongly underlined the virtues of the university connection'. Indeed it perhaps idealised the tutorial class movement and enhanced the universities' contribution to adult education, encouraging the formation of extramural departments by most universities between the wars. But it underestimated the LEAs' contribution and undervalued the vocational aspects of adult education (Tawney, 1956; Kelly, 1973: 118; Taylor, 1976: 137). It was partially responsible for perpetuating, or indeed widening, the gulf between vocational courses and liberal studies which became such a dominant and harmful characteristic of British adult education for much of the century.

In 1921 the President of the Board of Education set up an Adult Education Committee to promote and develop liberal adult education; to bring together national organisations concerned with the provision of adult education; to secure mutual help and avoid waste of effort; to further the establishment of voluntary organisations and their co-operation with the LEAs; and to advise the Board. At first the Committee supported the Board's desire to aid adult education mainly through the LEAs rather than by direct grants to other bodies, but it came to favour the work of the voluntary bodies and emphasise the importance of voluntary, non-statutory bodies as equal partners. Between 1922 and 33, the Committee produced 11 papers which helped to influence the Board's adult education policy. In particular it influenced the drafting of the very important Board of Education (Adult Education) Regulations in 1924 which allowed the universities and WEA Districts (and other appropriate organisations) to obtain recognition as adult education 'Responsible Bodies' which were entitled under the new regulations to direct grant, not only for three-year tutorial classes but for a whole range of shorter and less demanding courses. This was a retreat from the Board's previous view that all, or most, further education below the standard of university tutorial classes should be the responsibility of the LEAs (Ministry of Education, 1954: 7–8).

The same WEA-universities-liberal studies-non-vocational-non-LEA axis was further strengthened with the foundation of the self-proclaimed 'World

Association of Adult Education' in 1919 and of the British Institute of Adult Education in 1921.

## The 'World Association' and the British Institute of Adult Education

In July and November 1918, two meetings were held in London, with Albert Mansbridge (founder of the WEA and member of the Ministry of Reconstruction's Adult Education Committee) in the chair. The purpose was to consider the formation of one association of all movements connected with adult education in the overseas dominions and elsewhere, and to promote adult education throughout the world. The inaugural meeting of this 'World Association' was held on 29 March 1919. In June a provisional committee adopted a constitution which stated that the Association's objects included assisting 'the establishment, or development, in all parts of the world, of movements and institutions for promoting adult education, and to promote co-operation between them'. It would do so by establishing a Central Bureau of Information in London, the publication of a journal and bulletins, and the establishment of branches, groups, commissions or research committees in various countries of the world. In its early years the Association received reports from overseas, organised conferences and gave advice about educational aspects of the developing media of cinema and broadcasting. It attempted to encourage an international outlook (NIACE Archive (n), (p)).

On 19 January 1921 another meeting was held, again with Mansbridge in the chair, at 20 Tavistock Square, London, to consider the formation of a British Institute of Adult Education as a branch of the World Association. The inaugural meeting of the British Institute was held at the University of London Club in Gower Street on 28 May 1921, with 60 to 70 members and friends present. The 'World Association' formulated its initial publicity and approved the nomination of its officers. By the fourth meeting in September, there were 267 members (NIACE Archive, (a), (b), (n)).

The Institute acted as a general national forum for adult education, holding public meetings and exerting parliamentary pressure. It provided support to the WEA, the 'World Association' and the Educational Settlements but apparently not to the LEAs. It gave consideration in its early days to adult education in rural areas, adult education for fishermen (a particular interest of Mansbridge's), adult education among women, and broadcasting and adult education. In April 1923 the 'World Association' asked the Institute to investigate the position of education in broadcasting in England and it subsequently arranged a conference of all voluntary adult education bodies likely to be interested in the use of broadcasting for educational purposes (*ibid.*).

A year previously the Executive Committee of the British Institute had decided that it was not the Institute's function to undertake any teaching work, and subsequent minutes show it to have acted mainly as a discussion forum and pressure group. At its first AGM, on 15 July 1922 (by which time the Institute's membership had risen to 397) the President, Lord Haldane, declared that 'the primary function of the Institute was to be a centre for common thought by persons of varied experience in the adult education movement'. It was to be a representative body and 'a 'thinking department' or general staff to help the movement over its various difficulties.' He also insisted that they must hold rigidly to university standards, thus revealing the Institute's bias towards university adult education (NIACE Archive (b), (c)).

Early in 1925 the Institute decided to separate itself from the 'World Association', become an autonomous body with its own membership and produce its own journal, although it remained 'in association' with the parent body. Each organisation agreed to nominate one representative to sit on the other's governing body. In 1926 it commenced the publication of a half-yearly *Journal of Adult Education* (which became a quarterly entitled *Adult Education* in 1934), and a handbook and directory of adult education, as well as starting an adult education library. In 1928, the Institute held its first Scottish conference and established a Scottish Committee (*ibid.* (c), (f), (n)).

By the mid-thirties the Institute could look back on its early activities as mainly devoted to 'the more formal work of adult education - for instance, its instigation of an inquiry into the methods and principles of adult class teaching'. At the same time it noted that it had more recently developed an interest in 'various auxiliary services' although 'the University Tutorial Class and the University Extension Class still represent(ed) the metropolis of adult education' as far as the Institute was concerned. But now, some 'remoter provinces' were being explored. These included collaboration with the BBC in evolving an educational use of the wireless; setting up a Commission on Educational and Cultural Films; assisting loan exhibitions of pictures in small towns and villages; and, in 1933, setting up an unemployment committee. It concluded that 'the work of the Institute is analogous to that of a research laboratory. It conducts the experiments; it prepares the blue-prints ... Since its establishment in 1921 ... it has set itself to discover where the defences of adult education were weakest; it has devised a strategy for the advance into new territory; it has brought together every kind of interest and expert opinion to consider the revision and development of educational policy' (*ibid.* (f)). Between 1921 and 1934 it set up commissions, undertook enquiries and produced reports on Educational Settlements and Adult Education Centres; the relation of library services to adult education; the possibilities of broadcasting in adult education; educational and cultural films; the educational uses of the gramophone; the supply and training of tutors in adult education (in collaboration with the Tutors' Association); mechanical aids to learning; and started a book scheme for the unemployed. It continued with similar activities over the next decade, including the initiation of an 'art for the people' scheme in 1935 and a hospital education scheme in 1937; the creation of the Trust for Educational Work among the Unemployed (also in 1937); supported a Council for Encouragement of Music and the Arts as well as Air Raid Shelter Libraries and Reading Rooms in 1940; initiated an Army Study Centres Scheme in 1941; and produced a report on *The Housing and Equipment of Adult Education* for the Ministry of Education in 1945; before being subsumed in the new National Foundation for Adult Education in 1946 (*ibid.* (m)).

## The YMCA and the Co-operative Movement

Meanwhile, two national bodies, the YMCA and the Co-operative Movement, both of which had contributed to the development of adult education in the nineteenth century, continued to play an important role. The YMCA always took its educational function seriously, aiming to stimulate and challenge its members to be responsible, moral and achieving members of society, and to help them understand the world in which they lived so that they could come to terms with it (rather than change it). At the beginning of the century there were some 650 YMCA branches and approaching one million members. They were offered a mixture of religious instruction and social and educational activity, with an emphasis on physical and recreational activity; but many branches also provided libraries and reading rooms and organised lectures, including university extension courses. During the First World War the YMCA carried out a great deal of educational work with members of HM Forces in many parts of the world and carried over a greater emphasis on education into the post-war period. This was recognised by the Board of Education in 1924 when it included the YMCA as one of the approved associations for grant aid for adult education. However, the momentum was not maintained during the 1920s and 30s, although the Association continued to promote a considerable amount of informal education through discussion groups, study circles, etc., as well as helping to promote university and WEA classes. During the second world war it again played a significant part in the civilian contribution to education for HM Forces (see below: 55–7). After the war. the YMCA continued to make educational provision through its local associations, at its three residential colleges (and in association with other residential colleges), and through its Youth and Industry Department which was set up in 1960 to organise regular educational activities for young employees during work time. The latter programme concentrated on the problems of growing up in contemporary society, and on current affairs (Lowe, 1970: 182–4; Legge, 1982: 137; Kelly, 1992: 205–6, 276–7, 286, 305–6).

The YWCA also began to develop educational programmes in the 1920s, concentrating on classes for young women ranging from Bible study and international affairs to physical education, singing and domestic crafts (ibid.: 277).

The Co-operative societies had played an important role in nineteenth century adult education and contributed to the foundation of university extension, the WEA and the long-term residential colleges, and after the First World War the Co-operative Union established its own residential college. (See Chapters 2, 7, 8, 9.) Immediately before the war there were some 1,500 adults attending co-operative classes in co-operation, citizenship, industrial history, economics and elocution in addition to a good deal of less formal education. Between the wars, summers schools, weekend schools and classes for members increased, as did the number of students from 21,000, including young people, in 1918–19 to nearly 70,000 in 1939. Educational provision embraced the supplying and maintenance of libraries and reading rooms; evening classes in literature, science and the arts; popular lectures and entertainment; introductions to the principles of co-operation; technical training for employees (e.g. accounting and book-keeping); and propagandist lectures and public meetings to spread the ideals of co-operation. But despite this apparent hive of activity, Sidney and Beatrice Webb in 1921 considered there was an uncertainty of aim and infirmity of purpose, little enthusiasm or energy, and even less activity. In their view, the Co-operative movement only occasionally took a lead in the new developments of adult education and it was failing to meet the needs of its widely scattered membership (*ibid.*: 259; Bonner, 1970: 183–7; Webb, 1921: 37–8, 85–6, 307).

Like other adult education bodies during the Second World War, the Co-operative movement sought to keep its educational commitments alive by developing correspondence courses and study circles. After the war, in 1948 it formed the National Co-operative Educational Council to supervise and co-ordinate all the educational work, including the Co-operative residential college, national scholarships, technical education, adult education and youth work. There was a marked increase in student participation in the years following this development. The overall aim was not merely to provide employee training, but to educate both staff and members in the ideals and principles of co-operation. Perhaps its most significant aspect was emphasising these principles within the post-war Labour movement. But it was less successful in forging links with other parts of the adult education 'movement' (Bonner, 1970: 219–20, 246, 297–9, 390–4; Lowe, 1970: 167–71; Rees, 1982: 98).

## *Other Adult Education 'Auxiliaries' and Early Community Education*

A number of other organisations and movements with significance to the development of adult education came into existence before, during and after the First World War. These included the Carnegie UK Trust – a very important source of finance for rural adult education – founded in 1913; the Women's Institute Movement in 1915; the rural department of the National Council of Social Service, established in 1918; and the British Broadcasting Company which began 'wireless' broadcasting in 1922 and became incorporated as a public body with a statutory monopoly four years later. The county libraries also significantly expanded their services at this time. (See Chapters 12 and 14.)

The appointment of Henry Morris as Assistant Secretary for Education in Cambridgeshire in 1921 and his promotion to become Secretary of Education for the county the following year also proved to be important for the education of adults when, in 1924, he produced his policy document, *The Village College*, which has been called the detonator of a revolution in British education (Ree, 1981). Morris saw the village college as the nucleus of a holistic lifelong educational system for the local community, housing all the vital activities of village life.

As the community centre of the neighbourhood it would provide for the whole man (sic), and abolish the duality of education and ordinary life ... The dismal dispute of vocational and non-vocational education would not arise within it ... There would be no leaving school – the child would enter the college at three years old and leave only in extreme old age. In all seriousness it might be said that the school leaving age would be lifted to 90' (Morris, 1924).

Morris's vision was, in one aspect, intensely conservative in that it disregarded the growing mobility of the population. Indeed one of the policy's aims was to prevent the migration from the countryside and reverse the decay of rural areas such as Cambridgeshire. But in other ways it was revolutionary and it became the corner stone of community education in Britain, with its emphasis on lifelong education, community of purpose and an 'organic whole' which was greater than the mere sum of the parts. It was intend as 'a true social synthesis' (ibid.) The first village college opened at Sawston in Cambridgeshire in 1930 and three others opened before the war. Similar imitations were developed in other counties before and after the war and the concept of community education gradually entered into the field of British adult education, with results which are described more fully in Chapter 5.

## Adult Education for the Unemployed

The high levels of unemployment between the wars demanded some new approaches to adult education. At first the targets were demobilised ex-service men and women, displaced women wartime workers, and unemployed juveniles. The training department of the Ministry of Labour and the semi-autonomous Central Committee on Women's Training and Employment (which in practice was a dependency of the Ministry of Labour) promoted an *ad hoc* programme of training courses and established both residential and non-residential training centres (Field, 1992: 30–43). 'It was a classic example of the way in which the politics of the British labour market developed through a process of disjointed incrementalism ... The frontiers of the state were pushed forward incrementally to deal with the practical problems of mass unemployment' (ibid.: 41–2). When this *ad hoc* training and other short term policies, such as encouraging resettlement of the unemployed in the colonies and the land settlement schemes, proved unsuccessful in significantly reducing unemployment, the Government turned to other remedies including 'transfer instructional camps' (where the unemployed were 'reconditioned' to equip them to transfer to areas with lower unemployment), and work camps. Britain was in fact amongst the first countries to open state-owned residential camps for the long-term unemployed in the mid-1920s, before they were established in Germany which is usually regarded as the main instigator of work camps. Their primary aim was 'education through labour and for labour'. During the 1930s there were widespread protests and resistance within the camps, occasionally organised by the National Unemployed Workers Committee Movement, but more frequently at a local level (ibid.: 44–99).

From 1920 the Central Committee on Women's Training and Employment undertook the organisation of training of women for industrial and domestic work. Starting as a special scheme for women affected by the war, this became a long-term project in training unemployed women in Home Training Centres. Their emphasis, like much LEA provision targeted at women, was very much on equipping women for their perceived 'natural' sphere in the home, either as wife or domestic servant, although most young women avoided the latter if at all possible (*ibid.*: 100–17).

Meanwhile another government department, the Board of Education, was encouraging the LEAs to develop new forms of adult education, other than liberal studies, which would help the unemployed in practical ways (Marks, 1982).

In 1933 the British Institute of Adult Education set up a National Advisory Committee in co-operation with the National Council of Social Services (NCSS), to develop educational work with the unemployed. This brought objections from the TUC, which was very sensitive about the political dimensions of educational work for the unemployed if it made unemployment more palatable. Using a grant from the NCSS, the Institute published details of the kinds of educational work which was feasible for unemployed groups and the agencies which were able to provide them. The Institute claimed that this publicity helped to stimulate both the supply and demand for adult education in occupational centres and unemployment clubs, although it is impossible to verify this. It also created a book scheme for the unemployed. Later, the Institute concentrated more on investigating the nature and organisation of educational work for the unemployed, keeping more of a distance from direct involvement (NIACE Archive (d)).

The WEA had rejected the overtures of the NCSS to undertake some joint educational work for the unemployed, possibly for fear of becoming involved in unacceptable political activities regarding unemployment, but Tawney and William Temple did negotiate financial support for the WEA from the Pilgrim Trust for much the same purpose. This led the WEA into involvement in occupational centres for the unemployed, such as the Settlement at Maes yr haf in the Rhondda Valley and the People's Service Club in Lincoln, which helped to relieve the tedium and degradation of unemployment. The WEA, together with the universities, in fact became heavily involved in providing large numbers of classes, weekend schools and summer schools for the unemployed in many parts of the country during the 1930s. In doing so they wittingly or unwittingly nudged adult education away from political concern towards containment of the problem of unemployment. The predominantly recreational activities and leisure pursuits operated as palliatives which diverted the attention of the unemployed from political action. When the WEA did offer more political fare, such as a course on economics at Southport, to teach the unemployed *why* they were unemployed, the proposal was rejected as altogether inappropriate. It was decided that it would be more suitable for the unemployed to do woodwork and other practical work. The WEA meekly agreed to provide courses in art, painting and music. Similar courses were offered in many other centres (Fieldhouse, 1984: 111–3).

A number of other bodies also made special provision for the unemployed, including the Education Settlements Association, the Society of Friends and several of the adult education residential colleges. The result was a greater variety of provision, 'much of it experimental and almost all of it aimed at a wider and less educationally motivated social group than had previously been touched' (Marks, 1982: 1), but essentially functioning as a political palliative.

Meanwhile the LEAs were developing as major providers of adult education, in some areas their programmes becoming very extensive. This was particularly true in London. Other LEAs could not emulate the London County Council, but they were providing a growing programme of mainly practical and recreational courses, as well as giving some support to the voluntary bodies' more academic programmes. (See Chapter 4.)

## Adult Education in HM Forces During and After the Second World War

Developments during the Second World War had some long-term effects on the nature of British adult education. When the Secretary of State for War refused to include statutory education in the terms of the Military Services Bill in 1939, attempts were made to introduce a voluntary scheme. This was dismissed by the War Office at the outbreak of war, but the universities, the WEA, the YMCA and several other bodies went ahead and formed a Central Advisory Council (CAC) in January 1940 to set up an educational scheme for services personnel. Within a short time, 23 regional committees had been formed, covering the whole country. Meanwhile, in April 1940 a small committee was set up under the chairmanship of the Vice-Chief of the Imperial General Staff to draw up a scheme for non-military training for the Army. But it was not really until the end of 1940 that the Services showed much enthusiasm for such frivolous matters as education (Fieldhouse, 1988: 99).

The first of the Services' own schemes was the Army Bureau of Current Affairs (ABCA), which was established in August 1941 to organise weekly current affairs talk-and-discussion sessions conducted in each unit by regimental officers who were assisted in their task by the publication of two ABCA pamphlets, *Current Affairs* and *War* issued in alternate weeks. The ABCA discussions are frequently credited with major educational achievements, and particularly with engendering a political awareness that contributed to the election of the Labour Government in 1945. ABCA did undoubtedly promote a great deal of excellent and challenging adult education and also some of the earliest professional training for adult educators. However, at the time it was set up, it was suspected in several quarters that ABCA was intended in part to undermine the growing civilian adult education schemes for Services personnel organised by the CAC regional committees, and to replace them by a politically safer programme under the control of regimental officers. Even the Board of Education was suspicious (*ibid.*: 100). Although it was frequently claimed that the ABCA publications were free of official censorship, they were in fact scrutinised by numerous authorities before publication – one estimate putting the number of 'vetters' at 16. The purpose of this multiple censorship was to ensure that the pamphlets on which the Army officers based their talks avoided controversial matters. Although the pamphlets contained excellent background material, in the hands of some educationally inexperienced officers who knew little about the subject and used them as their only source of information, they could give rise to a somewhat biased presentation, reflecting orthodox government thinking. The most famous case of censorship was the withdrawal in December 1942 of the *Current Affairs* bulletin summarising the contents of the recently published Beveridge Report on the future Welfare State, on Churchill's instructions. It was considered too difficult or controversial for ABCA groups in its original form. When a revised version appeared six months later, it warned against easy promises and laid much greater stress on the need to pay for social security (*ibid.*: 100–102).

In September 1942 the Army Council approved another scheme, known as the Winter Scheme. Initially it was intend to run for four months during the winter of 1942, but it was later extended until May 1944. It provided for three hours' compulsory education each week: one hour for military training, a second for personal interests and general subjects, and a third hour for education in citizenship. This third hour, which became known as the 'British Way and Purpose' (BWP) consisted of talks and discussions intended to clarify the Allies' war aims and 'to give a fuller understanding of the achievements and possibilities of the British way of life and of the responsibility of the individual for their present defence and future development'. BWP derived its name from the monthly booklets which were produced by the Directorate of Army Education for the guidance of instructors. They covered domestic, imperial and international affairs. These BWP sessions supplemented the ABCA talks and provided more systematic current affairs instruction than did ABCA. But as with ABCA, problems of bias and propaganda arose where relatively inexperienced instructors relied on the BWP booklets as their sole or primary source of information, for they presented a remarkably complacent and uncritical picture of British domestic, colonial and international politics and activities, laying 'too much stress on a rosy future without squarely facing real difficulties and controversial issues'. Indeed, in 1944 the Secretary of State for War openly boasted in the House of Commons of the propagandist value of BWP which was quite clearly intended to reinforce British liberal-imperialist ideology (*ibid.*: 102–3; Scarlyn Wilson, 1948: 59; Hawkins and Brimble, 1947: 304; *The Times*, 3 March 1944).

A third major Services educational scheme, the Release Scheme, was launched towards the end of 1944. It was not supposed to provide training for specific jobs but more general preparation for vocational training and civilian duties that military personnel would embark on after demobilisation. In practice the main interest was in vocational training that would lead to a job in 'Civvy Street'.

Meanwhile, from the end of 1940 the CAC and its 23 regional committees became increasingly involved in making provision for units of the three Services stationed in Britain (but not overseas) and also for the Women's Auxiliary Territorial Service (ATS) and Auxiliary Air Force (WAAF); the civilian defence forces including the Fire Service; and for workers in wartime munitions, industrial, agricultural and construction camps, factories and hostels all around the country. This provision consisted of single lectures, short courses (of three to six meetings), classes (of 10 to 12 meetings), and a variety of intensive schools, courses and conferences, many of which were residential. The regional programmes began to grow rapidly from late 1940 onwards, and more than quadrupled between the beginning of 1941 and September 1943. The peak was reached in 1943–4, when more than 110,000 lectures, courses and classes were arranged. Altogether, in the three and a half years between October 1940 and March 1944, the regional committees provided over one-quarter of a million single lectures; nearly 15,000 short courses and nearly 9,000 classes of 10 to 12 meetings. In addition, they made certain contributions to the three major Services schemes – ABCA, the Winter Scheme and the Release Scheme (Fieldhouse, 1985: 69–71, 1988: 99, 104).

The regional committees aimed to provide adult education for the Services in as similar a form as possible to the 'traditional' Responsible Body liberal adult education, based on the notions of education for social purpose or citizenship-training; voluntary participation; absolute freedom in the choice of teacher and topics to be studied; freedom from propaganda; and the maintenance of standards through regular, continuous and sustained study. The Services, on the other hand, were not much impressed by voluntaryism and were dubious about, if not hostile to, freedom of discussion, particularly of the controversial subjects so often beloved by adult educators. On the whole, the Services preferred to regard education as an extension of military training – to make better soldiers. It was seen primarily as an aid to military efficiency and anything that did not contribute to this was considered undesirable. There were thus quite fundamentally different, indeed conflicting, civilian and Service perspectives on the purposes of education, giving rise to inevitable friction. This led to the banning of lectures and lecturers by the Services, through an elaborate system of vetting, certification and surveillance. Tutors who were considered politically unreliable were not issued with certificates of employment while those who strayed into prohibited areas were liable to find their certificates withdrawn. The civilian adult education providers were forced to accept these restrictions, which prevented the discussion of many political and controversial topics which would normally be the very stuff of adult education (ibid.: 108–20)

After the war the Services dispensed with the work of the regional committees and the CAC was wound up in 1948, but the 1947 National Service Act required them to make appropriate educational provision for the young national servicemen who were really civilians temporarily in uniform. The Services turned to the university extramural departments to help them with this work. (See Chapter 8.)

## The 1944 Education Act and Post-War 'Further Education'

The general wartime trend in adult education, both within the armed forces and in civilian life, towards shorter, less academic, more recreational or vocational provision, convinced some educational policy-makers that the LEAs' type of courses were the most likely to be in demand in the future (Evans, 1983: 92–3). Quite early in the war a number of bodies, including the British Institute, the Council for Educational Advance, the NUT, the TUC and various women's organisations began campaigning for improved adult education after the war, although one of the main adult education bodies, the WEA, was strangely muted because it felt it was more important to maintain its own autonomy than 'become sullied by too close an association with the LEAs'. The wartime adult education lobby was thus 'a curious amalgam of idealism and self-interest' (*ibid.*: 95–100). More generally, the lobby was somewhat restricted by the focus of educational reform being very largely on secondary education and the belief that any new funds would be allocated mainly for improving secondary schools and for technical education. There was a widespread feeling that it was better to concentrate efforts where success was most likely. However, the 1943 White Paper on *Educational Reconstruction* did cite developments in army education as a catalyst for adult educational reforms and stressed the need to reduce ignorance and provide a proper training in democratic citizenship through adult education. The LEAs were promised a supervisory role for the future which the WEA was confident would prevent them from 'trespassing' on its patch (*ibid.: passim*).

The 1944 Education Act organised the statutory system of public education into three progressive stages: primary, secondary and further education, and laid a duty on the LEAs to secure efficient education throughout those stages for the population of their areas, as far as their powers extended. As far as further education was concerned, it became the duty of every LEA to secure the provision of adequate full- and part-time further education for persons over compulsory school age. When preparing their schemes of further education, LEAs were required to take into consideration any facilities for further education provided in their area by universities, educational associations and other bodies, and to consult with them (Education Act, 1944, clauses 7, 41, 42(4)).

In 1946, in accordance with clause 42(1) of the Act, the Minister of Education, Ellen Wilkinson, required the LEAs to draw up detailed further education schemes to be submitted by 31 March 1948; and in 1947 the Ministry published a 200-page pamphlet, *Further Education*, to provide guidance for the LEAs in drawing up their schemes (Ministry of Education, 1947). The most far-reaching (and ultimately doomed) proposal was the attempt to introduce compulsory part-time education for everyone up to the age of 18, first proposed in an Education Act in 1918 and reintroduced in the 1944 legislation. Financial difficulties prevented the Government from implementing this and other aspects of its further education policy, but 'learning for leisure', intended to extend individual happiness and promote a 'civilised community', did receive considerable impetus. Despite the WEA's somewhat sanguine belief that the new Act would not threaten its own rather privileged position in the world of adult education, it was the LEAs that particularly gained from this impetus. The number of evening institutes more than doubled between 1947 and 1950, from just over 5,000 to nearly 11,000 and the number of students increased from 825,000 to nearly 1,250,000 (Jepson, 1959: 106). (See Chapter 4.)

The university extramural departments also expanded after the war and adopted various new initiatives, but the WEA was squeezed between the expanding LEAs and the universities and found it increasingly difficult to maintain its privileged position or identify a new role for itself in the post-war world. (See Chapters 7 and 8.)

Another post-war development was a revival of interest in residential adult education which particularly stimulated the LEAs and various voluntary and private bodies, with a certain amount of encouragement from the Ministry of Education, to found a number of short-term residential colleges. (See Chapter 9.)

## Post-War National Adult Education Bodies

An initiative taken by the WEA's national officers during the latter part of the war led to the setting up of a National Foundation of Adult Education (NFAE) to act as a general advisory body for adult education and to promote understanding and co-operation between the bodies engaged in adult education. This initiative was felt necessary partly because the 'World Association for Adult Education' had recently been disbanded and because the British Institute of Adult Education was regarded as ill-equipped to respond to the changed emphasis of the new Education Act; but there was an obvious danger of overlap with the British Institute. Nevertheless the NFAE was constituted in June 1946 and by the following January, 68 LEAs, eight universities, three university colleges and 13 voluntary societies had responded to invitations to join. The National Council of Girls' and Mixed Clubs was refused admission on the grounds that, while recognising the links between youth work and adult education, it was not considered an appropriate body for membership of the NFAE. Thus the new organisation, whilst clearly more welcoming than the British Institute to the LEAs, was no more attuned to the wider notions of community education (NIACE Archive (f), (g); Public Record Office (PRO) ED 80/45, 46).

During 1947 the NFAE laid ambitious plans to establish a central library, hoping to use the library of the disbanded 'World Association'; to review the relationship between statutory and voluntary bodies in adult education; to undertake a survey of the voluntary sector; to influence the Ministry of Education's further education planning; to co-ordinate the publicity of all adult education providers; to influence the character of the BBC's programmes; to carry out a survey of adult education students in order to identify the best teaching methods and most suitable aids; to look into the possibility of establishing a training centre for studying techniques in adult education; and to examine the problem of book supplies. However, by 1948 it was becoming apparent that there was widespread confusion and misunderstanding about the separate functions of the NFAE and the British Institute. Some efforts were made to identify their different functions and characters (not least the fact that the British Institute admitted individual members whilst the NFAE admitted only corporate bodies) but, with the encouragement of the Ministry of Education, it was decided to merge the two organisations into one body which would combine the characteristic functions of both. This was agreed by an NFAE Executive Committee meeting in September 1948. The merged organisation, known as the National Institute of Adult Education (NIAE), came into being on 1 April 1949 (*ibid.*)

The new body adopted the broadly-based pattern of institutional representation of NFAE but also allowed representation of individual members on its Council. In all other respects its constitution, aims and objects were very similar to the NFAE. Its general terms of reference were to advise on the liberal education of adults but it came to interpret this very broadly. It fairly quickly embarked on a major survey of developments in adult education arising from the 1944 Act, in particular the notable increase in LEA student numbers. This survey and the subsequent report, *Social Aspects of Further Education: A survey of LEA action*, published in 1952, were the main preoccupations of NIAE in its early years. However, during its first decade the Institute also undertook a number of other activities, including the continued publication of *Adult Education* (also incorporating the *Tutors' Bulletin* from 1958) and publication of a half-yearly *Calendar of Residential Short Courses* from 1950; and initiated enquiries into technical institutions (1952), library development (1955), obstacles to the fuller use of museum resources in adult education (1956), education and retirement (jointly with the Nuffield Foundation, 1957), and residential and technical education (1959). Most of these enquiries resulted in reports published by the Institute, which also published a directory of adult education organisations (1950) and *A Select Bibliography of Adult Education* and the *First* and *Second Handlists of Studies in Adult Education* (with the Universities Council for Adult Education, 1953) (NIACE Archive (h), (j), (k), (l), (m)).

During its first two decades, under the direction of its first Secretary, Edward Hutchinson, NIAE became an authoritative source of major policy developments and successfully welded together the diverse interests of its disparate members, including the LEAs, the university extramural departments, the WEA, libraries, the BBC and ITV, the Women's Institutes, the Townswomen's Guilds and many other voluntary bodies (*Education*, 11 November 1994).

By the 1970s NIAE had become a prominent national focus and source of information and ideas about adult education. It encouraged by experiment and enquiry; maintained international links; and published the journal *Adult Education*, an annual yearbook, and valuable monographs. Its outstanding achievement had been 'to extend the terms of reference of adult education' beyond the WEA/universities preoccupation with liberal adult education (Lowe, 1970: 278–81; Small, 1975: 161–2). The Russell Committee in 1973 regarded NIAE as 'a major non-government force in the development of the adult education service' that helped to promote understanding both nationally and internationally; undertook important enquiries; served as a centre of information on all aspects of adult education; and represented a consensus of opinion about adult education to Government and to commissions and committees of enquiry (Department of Education, 1973: 141). In the 1980s it was seen as having a useful independent role in developing co-operative relations in the field of adult education, both nationally and internationally, although its achievements were limited by inadequate resources (Legge, 1982: 183–5). It spawned a number of important and influential units and agencies (see below: 66–8) and changed its name to the National Institute of Adult Continuing Education (NIACE) in 1983. It continued to be an influential promoter of formal and informal adult learning throughout England and Wales, seeking to take positive action to improve opportunities and wider access to learning opportunities. It did so by convening conferences, seminars and meetings; collecting and disseminating information; conducting enquiries, research and development work; publishing and distributing publications; undertaking special projects and administering special agencies; developing co-operative relations with adult education organisations in the UK and other countries; and representing the interests of adult learners and the organisations that serve them. It came to interpret its remit as covering the whole range of post-school learning, but especially emphasising the requirements of those groups who had not had equitable opportunities to pursue learning, including women, older people, adults who are low-skilled, low-waged or unemployed, people from black and other ethnic minority communities, and adults with learning difficulties and disabilities (NIACE, 1992–93: 4, 1994–95: 4).

In Scotland a separate Institute of Adult Education was established as a successor to the Scottish branch of the BIAE. It maintained close links with its English counterpart and with similar organisations in other countries, thereby helping to keep adult educators in Scotland in touch with developments elsewhere. It fostered inter-institutional collaboration in Scotland and experiments and new techniques in adult education, and acted as a general promoter of adult education interests. It was almost totally dependent, financially, on grants from the local authorities and the Scottish Education Department and when this support was withdrawn in 1991, the Institute closed (Scottish Education Department, 1975: 9).

## The Ashby Report and After

To return to the early 1950s, the adult education Responsible Bodies (the universities and the WEA) were faced in 1952 with a freeze on their grants (the first serious check to expansion for 20 years); and threatened with a 10 per cent reduction in 1953. This caused a storm of protest. However, the Minister's cost-cutting plans were undermined by the Prime Minister, Winston Churchill, when he responded to objections from the TUC by stating (in his usual flowery prose) that:

There is, perhaps, no branch of our vast educational system which should more attract within its particular sphere the aid and encouragement of the State than adult education ... I have no doubt myself that a man or woman earnestly seeking in grown-up life to be guided to wide and suggestive knowledge in its largest and most uplifted sphere will make the best of all the pupils in this age of clatter and buzz, of gape and gloat. The appetite of adults to be shown the foundations and processes of thought will never be denied by a British Administration cherishing the continuity of our Island life ... (Ministry of Education, 1954: 66–7).

Although Churchill went on to say that this was no reason 'for not looking through the accounts', the cause of economy was undermined and the threatened 10 per cent cut in grant aid in 1953–4 was not imposed, although the earlier freeze was not lifted. It was in these circumstances that the Minister, Florence Horsbrugh, set up a committee under the chairmanship of Eric Ashby, 'to review the present system by which the extra-mural departments of universities, the Workers' Educational Association and the other responsible bodies provide local facilities for adult education, with special reference to the conditions under which the facilities are organised, and are aided by grant from public funds ...' (*ibid.*: 1–2, 67).

The Committee recommended no fundamental changes, largely favouring the preservation of the existing partnership between Responsible Bodies, the LEAs and central government, and the continuation of voluntaryism. However, the Committee did recommend one potentially significant change – that the amount of grant aid to individual Responsible Bodies should be determined not historically but after consideration of the quality and standard of work being done, the needs of the region and the activities of other bodies in the region. A number of other recommended technical changes had the cumulative effect of reducing regulatory restrictions on the activities of the Responsible Bodies, but also further blurring the distinction between them and the LEAs (*ibid.*: 48–9). Following the Committee's general vote of confidence, 'the old system continued to muddle along without firm central direction' (Small, 1975: 157-8), although there was an increased responsibility laid upon the Ministry to determine policy and to supervise and guide the implementation of that policy, informed by inspectors who enjoyed increased powers and influence (Raybould, 1959: 222–4, 228, 231).

In the years following the *Ashby Report* there was some modest growth in Responsible Body provision, but the post-war euphoria and expectation of unlimited growth had evaporated. 'Progress was now slower and more hesitant, and plans for expansion were inhibited by a sharp sense of what the Ministry was likely to be able to approve' (Kelly, 1992: 342). In local authority evening institutes there was an overall decline in attendances of some 30 per cent during the 1950s. Although this was partly the result of young people staying on longer at school or attending further education courses, it was also the result of financial pressures forcing LEAs to raise their fees and become stricter about closing small classes (*ibid.*: 342–3).

The 1960s witnessed a reversal of this LEA decline, and a growing optimism and sense of purpose in university adult education and the WEA. To some extent this stemmed from the influence of the sixties culture on a new generation of adult educators who brought a more positive attitude and confidence of purpose into adult education. They believed that adult education could and should enable people to work for a better world, and this belief introduced greater determination and drive into the whole field of Responsible Body adult education (Fieldhouse, 1993a).

## The National Extension College, the Open University and the Polytechnics

The foundation of the National Extension College (NEC) in 1963 as a non-profit making organisation committed to improving access to higher education was part of the more optimistic, purposeful mood of the 60s. It sought to combine broadcasting (both television and radio), correspondence courses and residential schools to create a prototype 'University of the Air' (Jackson, 1964: 24). It started with residential schools for London external degree students, held at Cambridge, Keele and Leeds Universities during 1963–4, but quickly progressed to television teaching. The 'Dawn University' was a series of six first year Cambridge lectures transmitted on successive mornings in October 1963, and this was followed by an experiment linking research seminars by television from Cambridge, London and the University of East Anglia. At the same time the NEC launched nine correspondence courses. Its next step was to combine the various distance learning media. In May and June 1964 the NEC collaborated with Anglia TV to provide a 'College of the Air' a series of six Saturday morning programmes designed to support correspondence students studying O-level maths and English. A month later a correspondence course was launched to provide back-up to a television series on the history of technology, while in the autumn of 1964 the English O-level course was linked to a year's BBC radio series plus residential schools provided by Oxford and Keele extramural departments. Keele also agreed to allow the NEC to follow up its 'Dawn University' with a year-long television transmission of its Foundation Year course. Within an 18-month period the NEC had approached its target of combining correspondence courses, broadcasting and residential adult education from almost every angle (*ibid.*: 22–4).

The NEC's plans were somewhat upstaged in 1966 with the publication of the Labour Government's White Paper, *The University of the Air*, and the foundation, three years later, of the Open University (OU). The NEC was almost totally left out of these developments and denied any government funding for its planned 'University of the Air'. It had to cut its cloth accordingly and concentrate very largely on providing high quality correspondence courses. Its attempts to link these with face-to-face teaching met with only limited success (Kelly, 1992: xxxv–vi). Meanwhile, the OU registered approximately 25,000 students during its first teaching year (1971) and expanded rapidly. Twenty years later it awarded its 100,000th BA degree. By this time it was responsible for producing nine per cent of the country's graduates, as well as a growing number of higher degree and continuing education students. The OU not only offered a new opportunity for large numbers of adults to undertake systematic study by distant learning methods, and to obtain a degree without any required prior academic qualifications: it also had a profound impact on teaching methods and pedagogic thinking throughout further, higher and adult education. (See Chapter 11.)

Another important development of the 60s was the creation of a binary higher education system following Anthony Crosland's two major policy speeches at Woolwich and Lancaster in 1965 and the publication of the 1966 White Paper, *A Plan for Polytechnics and Other Colleges*. At Woolwich, Crosland declared that:

There are tens of thousands of part-time students who need advanced courses either to supplement other qualifications or because for one reason or another they missed the full-time route. There are immense fields of talent and aspiration here; common justice and social need combine to demand that they should be harvested.

This paved the way for many adults to study full-time or part-time on a wide range of degree and sub-degree level courses at the newly created polytechnics as well as further education colleges (Scott, 1984: 158–71), although it is somewhat ironic that just as the Labour Government was getting rid of selection in schools it was introducing a binary division into higher education. This made it possible for the university sector to ignore the demands from adult 'non-standard' students for many years. As late as 1978 the DES view was that there was no evidence of unsatisfied demand for part-time degrees in existing institutions (DES, 1978), although the OU was by then turning away several thousand applicants each year.

## The Russell and Alexander Reports

Meanwhile, in 1969 the Labour Government set up a committee under the chairmanship of Sir Lionel Russell to review non-vocational adult education in England and Wales and to recommend ways of obtaining the most effective and economical deployment of available resources for a national system of education 'continuing through life' (DES, 1973: v). Thus the Committee, which produced its Report in 1973, was restricted by its terms of reference to the deployment of available resources, and to a perpetuation of the traditional British separation of liberal/non-vocational and technical/vocational education. It was therefore somewhat shackled from the outset, and it is not altogether surprising that the Report was criticised for lacking the breadth and vision of a grand design (Baynes, 1975: 228). It tended to concentrate on recognised adult education agencies and miss new developments, and new forms of continuing education being pioneered by the polytechnics and the CNAA. Its perception of adult education was still as the 'poor cousin' (topping up existing knowledge, second chance and leisure-time learning) in relation to 'proper' education, which took place in schools, colleges and universities (ibid.: 229; Hughes, 1977: 283; Kelly, 1973: 121).

The Report contained a thorough review of existing provision but largely failed to provide the leadership or the vision to build a new beginning, perhaps because the Committee adopted a pragmatic strategy of proposing what seemed politically feasible, in the hope that its proposals would be implemented. In the event, even this modest expectation was unrealised because neither the Government nor local authorities showed any inclination to meet the 'very modest rise in total expenditure' from £17.4m to £40.65m over a five- to seven-year period (DES, 1973: x; Small, 1975: 163–4; Jones, 1974: 74; Hughes, 1977: 284–5, 1981: 58). There were two major reasons for the Government's failure to fund the Report's recommendations: the economic situation caused by the international oil crisis, which unfortunately coincided with the publication of the Report (see Chapter 1); and the Treasury's view that any extra funding for adult education had been more than swallowed up by the newly established Open University (see Chapter 11). Because of this, it is not altogether surprising that the Report is now 'sometimes regarded somewhat nostalgically as a promise of a new future for British adult education which, for various reasons (mainly political), never materialised' (Fieldhouse, 1993a: 41).

Nevertheless, despite the Report's limitations and the failure to support its recommendations with a modest increase in public expenditure, it did help to re-focus adult education, encouraging it to concentrate once more on socially committed, political work with disadvantaged groups, and to devote more resources and energy to the needs of the 'adult education untouchables' (*ibid.*: 43–5; Kelly, 1973: 122, 1992: xix).

In Scotland, a similar Committee was set up in 1970 under the chairmanship of Professor K.J.W. Alexander, with virtually the same terms of reference as the Russell Committee. It produced its report, *Adult Education: The challenge of change* (Scottish Education Department) in 1975. It proposed a doubling of the number of adult education students within 10 years and the structural merging of adult education with the youth and community services into a unified system of community education under a Scottish Council for Community Education. Like Russell, the Alexander Report encouraged adult education to concentrate on the disadvantaged and areas of multiple deprivation. The Report did have an important impact in promoting the idea of 'community education' and stimulating structural changes to implement that idea, as well as encouraging the provision of education for change. However, its implementation was hampered by a vagueness in its definition of the 'community education' it was proposing; a lack of leadership or any clear vision of what its strategic aims were; and the same severe constraint in public expenditure in the years following the Report's publication that afflicted the Russell Report. Ultimately the Report led to little more than a rationalisation of existing provision. Although a Scottish Council for Community Education was set up in 1979, and most local authorities implemented the recommendation to merge adult education with the youth and community services, the effect on adult education was not very dramatic. Indeed, far from doubling the number of students within 10 years, there was a marked decline in the number of local authority enrolments and non-vocational classes between 1975–85. This was partly counterbalanced by significant increases in the number of mature students entering further and higher education in Scotland and by the development of open learning opportunities. However, these and other developments, including basic education and an increased provision of adult training, were not outcomes of the Alexander Report (Scottish Education Department, 1975; Jones, 1975; Small, 1976: 262–5; Smith, 1980; Horobin, 1983; Gerver, 1985; Barr, 1987; Kelly, 1992: xix–xx).

## *The Advisory Council for Adult Continuing Education*

One of the Russell Committee's recommendations was that the Secretary of State should establish a Development Council for Adult Education for England and Wales (DES, 1973: 54–5). Four years later, the Government agreed to set up an Advisory Council for Adult and Continuing Education (ACACE) under the chairmanship of Richard Hoggart. Its 22 members were all nominated by the Secretary of State. Its brief was to advise generally on the provision of adult education in England and Wales, to promote co-operation and to develop policies for lifelong education. It received £50,000 per annum from the DES. Despite its modest resources it managed to make some significant contributions to the debate on the future direction of adult continuing education (and indeed helped to popularise the change in terminology from 'adult' to 'continuing'). It saw itself as an authoritive voice for the education of adults which could make itself heard at the highest levels of policy making (Legge, 1982: 188). But it was an altogether more modest affair than the Development Council envisaged by Russell (*ibid.;* Boaden, 1988: 173–4).

Nevertheless, it did make representations to the Secretary of State concerning the financial cuts being imposed on adult education, and attempted to develop a whole new paradigm of continuing education (Taylor, 1978: 211; Duke, 1986: 257). In its six years of existence, the Council produced 36 reports on such issues as educational guidance, basic education, education for the unemployed, education for the black communities, etc. They provided both information and much practical advice (Kelly, 1992: xx).

The Council's most significant report was *Continuing Education: From policies to practice* (1982). This was hailed as the most important adult education publication since the Russell Report: a 'milestone document' (*Education* Digest, 1982: i; Goodwin, 1983: 98; Duke, 1986: 256). It proposed a radical shift of emphasis for the whole post-school sector, abandoning the boundaries between education and training or between vocational and general adult education in a comprehensive, integrated system of continuing education. Its priorities were very similar to the Russell Report's emphasis on the disadvantaged, but it did look more broadly to the benefits of credit transfer systems; educational guidance; access to higher education; the application of new technology; open and distance learning; independent study; grants for part-time students and educational entitlements (*Education* Digest, 1982).

The underlying message of *Continuing Education: From policies to practice* worried many adult educators at the time because of its assumption that the new developments it was recommending could be funded through the reallocation of existing resources. This was seen as a very real threat to traditional non-vocational liberal adult education, which was already under attack from the Government (see below: 68). At best, ACACE appeared to be adopting a very naive approach; otherwise it was abetting the Government's efforts to divert adult education providers and resources away from 'liberal adult education' into new forms of continuing education, with a much grater emphasis on training and meeting manpower requirements (Goodwin, 1983).

## Development 'Units' in the 1980s

After two three-year terms, the ACACE was abolished, to be replaced in 1984 by a Unit for the Development of Adult Continuing Education, (UDACE) under the auspices of NIACE. Like its predecessor, UDACE was underfunded and temporary: a far cry from the Development Council envisaged by the Russell Committee. On the other hand, the setting up of an adult education unit with the word 'development' in its title could be regarded as an accomplishment (Evans, 1987: 192). Its agenda very much reflected the concerns of the DES – initially concentrating on guidance and counselling; education for older adults; and voluntary/statutory relationships. Access was added in 1986. By the end of the 1980s it was still concerned with educational guidance and access to education and training but less so with education for the elderly or the promotion of partnership.

Instead it was concentrating on strategic planning and management issues; open college networks; performance and quality; and learning outcomes and competence. Its changing remit very much reflected the latest preoccupations of the DES. UDACE's overall objective was to help improve the range, quality and accessibility of education and training opportunities for adults (ibid; NIACE, 1989–90: 13; McNair, 1992; O'Rourke, 1992). Its research and development work and its publications and other forms of dissemination (conferences, seminars and workshops, etc.) were widely valued by practitioners. It was successful in stimulating cross-sectoral collaboration and raising the profile of adult education as well as a wide range of issues. But UDACE was always constrained by its remit and its close relationship with government departments and policies. It is also questionable whether it was ever adequately resourced or sufficiently influential to fulfil this role effectively. It is therefore not surprising that a final evaluation of UDACE's eight year's work identified a large number of issues not addressed and opportunities missed (O'Rourke, 1992: 36–8).

In 1991 the DES decided to merge UDACE with the Further Education Unit (FEU) in preparation for the implementation of the Further and Higher Education Act (see below: 75–6). The merged unit, which came into being in 1992, was expected to promote more flexible, effective and relevant learning opportunities for both 16–19-year-olds and adults. It was particularly concerned with issues of progression and accrediting competence and achievements, thereby reflecting the Government's educational policies of the 1990s, especially its desire to distinguish qualification courses from 'leisure education' (NIACE, 1991; UDACE, 1991). However, after only three years the reformed FEU was itself merged with the Further Education Staff College to become a new Further Education Development Agency (FEDA).

A very important dimension of adult education which received surprisingly little attention for much of the century was literacy and basic education. But in response to the 'right to read' campaign in the early 1970s, the Government made a £1m grant for 1975–6 to establish an Adult Literacy Resource Agency (ALRA) under the aegis of the National Institute. Its purpose was to support and promote a rapid expansion of literacy teaching. The government grant was renewed for a further two years and then in 1978 ALRA was replaced by an Adult Literacy Unit. This unit in turn was reformed in 1980 to become the Adult Literacy and Basic Skills Unit (ALBSU), in realisation that the adult basic education needed was broader than just literacy. ALBSU existed under constant threat of impermanence and DES reviews and redirection until Tim Boswell, junior education minister, announced in 1995 that following yet another review the DES had decided that it should continue as an 'independent, centrally-funded basic skills unit'. Its new responsibilities included basic skills training in the workplace, for the unemployed, and for young people, as well as its traditional concern with the needs of adults. Despite these frequent changes and lack of adequate funding, ALBSU and its predecessors have been a major influence in promoting learning materials and methods and stimulating experimentation and innovation in England and Wales, although adult literacy was less successful in Scotland where the Educational Institute of Scotland complained in 1989 that adult basic education had been left to atrophy north of the border (Jones and Charnley, 1983: 115—20; Evans, 1987: 119—23; Kelly, 1992: xxii–iv; Boswell, 1995: 261). The development of this adult literacy and basic education is fully described in Chapter 6.

## Government Intervention and 'Quangos' for Education and Training

From the various reports and initiatives that have already been outlined in this chapter, it will be apparent that after relative government indifference for many years, adult continuing education became an important policy issue in the 1970s and 80s. It was increasingly shaped by government actions and policies and by a progressive decline in public expenditure on education. As a non-statutory provision, adult education was particularly vulnerable to this financial stringency, which was first heralded by the DES in an administrative memorandum in 1967. Reductions in expenditure were exacerbated by mounting inflation. Providing bodies were forced to reduce programmes and steadily increase fees (Jones, 1978; Kelly, 1992: xlviii).

At the same time, the Government became increasingly selective about the kinds of adult education that it wished to promote or encourage and used its control of funds to direct it, particularly after 1979 when the Thatcher Governments were determined to use adult education for ideological purposes – to contribute to the creation of a culture of enterprise, competitiveness and individualism. But the seeds were sown much earlier. A challenge in 1973 to the notion that adult education should aim for social transformation seemed an aberration at the time: a denial of the great tradition (Paterson, 1973). But it turned out to be a harbinger of the future. The gradual displacement of 'adult' by other adjectives – 'lifelong', 'recurrent', and above all, 'continuing' – proved to be more than a semantic act (Hostler, 1973). It signified the end of a tradition and the dismantling of an adult education *movement* which was to be gradually subsumed into a general education and training system. The defence of that tradition and that movement was 'left in tatters by the systematic re-alignment of popular education as a social and technical preparation for the market place' (Clissold, 1987: 238).

The Government increasingly wanted adult education to aim at specific targets. Some of these reflected old traditions and the Russell and Alexander priorities – the disadvantaged, community groups and the unemployed. With rising unemployment, this group became as much a priority as it had been in the 1930s.

But above all, there was an increasing emphasis on vocationalism. This led adult education in two complementary directions: into training and retraining (for the unemployed and for those in work) and into accreditation, qualifications and awards which would enable individuals to utilise their learning in practical ways, which would be beneficial to the economy. Economic revival and wealth generation rather than social improvement became the major driving force. An assessment of continuing education trends in 1986 concluded that the Government had 'made considerable strides in formulating and giving effect ... to an adult training campaign intended to galvanize industry (in the broadest sense) into putting more resources into retraining its workforce' (Duke, 1986: 268). A full analysis of the developments in vocational education and training will be found in Chapter 13.

In 1972, in the face of growing economic difficulties and widespread disquiet about the quality of British technical education in general and the effectiveness of the industrial training boards in particular, the Government announced the formation of a Manpower Services Commission (MSC) with a brief to co-ordinate employment and training services nationally. It was formally set up under the 1973 Employment and Training Act and came into being on 1 January 1974 (Evans, 1992: 1–18).

During the next seven years the MSC exercised a substantial influence over the national industrial training policy. It was powerful and very well funded compared with other adult education agencies. At first it operated on a tripartite basis, reflecting the views of the CBI and TUC as well as the Government, but it gradually fell more under government control (Evans, 1987: 131–3; Low, 1988: 215–6). The Government considered the MSC, through its two divisions, the Employment Services Agency (ESA) and the Training Services Agency (TSA), more capable than the education system of producing relevant training experiences. Indeed, the MSC was intended to force changes on the education system (Green, 1994).

In practice, the ESA and TSA were swamped by the introduction of a string of special programmes (e.g. the job creation programme, the work experience programme, the youth opportunities scheme (YOPS), etc.), each seeking quick solutions to the growing unemployment crisis brought about by the recession following the oil price rises. They were more of an attempt to reduce dole queues than meet long-term training needs, but they did introduce 'a new vocationalism' onto the agenda (Evans, 1992: 31). The MSC was intended to be a catalyst, to provide manpower information and improve manpower planning which would lead to the development of relevant training initiatives, but increasingly the Government pushed it into work experience activities with the unemployed and other short-term palliatives to deal with unemployment. After the urban riots of 1981, YOP was given yet more money. 'Once again a special programme concerned with crisis management had taken precedence over a proper national skills training initiative' (ibid.: 45). Indeed, during its first seven years, the MSC was largely overshadowed by the unemployment crisis and responded by developing a set of special programmes rather than establishing a training strategy. It frenetically moved from scheme to scheme without allowing the benefits of the previous one to emerge (Low, 1988: 219–20).

A new national training initiative was published as a White Paper in 1981 which committed the MSC to three new developments: the conversion of YOPS into a youth training scheme, the development of an adult training strategy (ATS), and the reform of the apprenticeship system to take effect in 1985.

The ATS was intended to provide leadership in the whole field of vocational education and training but it turned out to be more of a set of proposals than a coherent programme: another 'quick fix'. However, it was welcomed by many who felt that the DES had been neglecting adult education (ibid.: 223). Indeed, adult education's revived interest in the educationally under-privileged coincided with the MSC's developing interest in basic education and this led to some MSC funding for adult education projects. But there was still a wide gap between the educational perspective of most adult educators and the short-term project/quick-result expectations of the MSC. It was not only drawing adult education into the vocational world, but also into instant consumerism with its disposable projects and schemes.

The period between 1981 and 1987 was the most active phase of the MSC. It became a different kind of body with a different mission as it fell more directly under government control and was used 'in an ever more interventionist and authoritarian fashion to impose new forms of vocationalism on the education system' (Green, 1994). Unfortunately the policies of this period were largely misconceived and misdirected and the range of programmes was chopped and changed so frequently that it lacked any real coherence (ibid.; Evans, 1992: 83–9). The ATS was based on inadequate market intelligence and consequently lacked any real sense of direction. This caused confusion as to what was required of providers to the programmes.In 1987 the National Audit Office concluded that the MSC had no idea of the skill base of the adult population and very little information about the effectiveness of its training programmes and whether they were meeting the needs of industry (Low, 1988: 224).

In 1988 the MSC was converted into the Training Commission (TC) with a brief to concentrate on adult training but after only a few months it in turn was replaced by the Training Agency and then in 1990 by the Training, Education and Enterprise Directorate (TEED) of the Department of Employment.

A new White Paper, Employment in the 1990s, published in December 1988, proposed the creation of regional training and enterprise councils (TECs) in England and Wales and local enterprise companies (LECs) in Scotland which would examine local labour markets, assess needs and create opportunities. They were a return to a demand-led, employer-controlled training system: a shift of control in the provision of training from educationalists to employers who dominated the management of the new TECs and LECs, which were also expected to reflect the Government's wish to transfer more of the cost of training to employers. They represented both 'a retrogressive move towards a new form of the old, discredited voluntarism which had so little success in the past' (Green, 1994). and the Government's practice of decentalising through central control. (For a further discussion of TECs and LECs, see Chapter 13.)

Over two decades, numerous initiatives had been introduced and vocational education and training undoubtedly rose higher on the political agenda, yet 'the policies ... had limited success in reversing the historic backwardness of British vocational education and training' (ibid.)

Meanwhile, the DES felt upstaged by the Department of Employment's programmes for the unemployed promoted through the MSC, the Training Agency or TEED. It wanted to encourage its own protégés – the LEAs and the Responsible Bodies – to become more active in this field (Evans, 1987: 123–4). Therefore in 1984 it used some of the funds it had cut from LEA and Responsible Body adult education budgets to initiate a three-year programme to support innovative research and projects to develop educational opportunities for unemployed adults under the auspices of NIACE and the FEU. This REPLAN programme was blatantly a means of earmarking these resources to force the adult education providers to address the needs of the unemployed (Uden, 1987: 9).

REPLAN was not universally welcomed by those educational providers, partly because it was funded with what had previously been their money and partly because it was regarded as 'a bureaucratic creation consuming resources which could be put to more direct use' (Evans, 1987: 125). In fact only 13 per cent of the initial budget was earmarked for direct provision: the remainder was spent on curriculum development, staff training, co-ordination and administration. A team of national field officers managed by NIACE sought proposals and supported and supervised local projects. It was an inter-agency, collaborative scheme involving close liaison between the DES, NIACE, the FEU, the LEAs and other project fundholders. This collaboration was not without its tensions e.g. over DES expectations that sponsoring organisations would gradually meet part of the costs of the projects, which adult educators regarded as unrealistic; or conflict over the involvement of 'unemployed activists' and public sector trainers (Blaxter, 1992: 9–10).

Early REPLAN projects were heavily geared towards community action. They involved outreach work and collaboration with community work agencies (ibid.: 5). And according to the NIACE Associate Director in 1987, REPLAN aimed to promote the education of the whole person, not merely job-specific training. But by this time (when the scheme's renewal was under consideration) it was attracting criticisms that it was not sufficiently vocational or concerned with job training (Uden, 1987: 11, 14).

An evaluation of the first 21 FEU projects expressed concern about their lack of transferability or wider application, and also about a lack of liaison between the two arms of REPLAN – the FEU and NIACE. But it considered that one of the strengths of the scheme had been in its 'energising educational provision for unemployed adults and in producing policy, attitudinal and institutional change' (Percy, 1989: 41).

The scheme was continued into a second term in 1987 but it moved more specifically towards training for the workforce. In 1989 the NIACE REPLAN Committee endorsed involvement with the TECs. It was becoming increasingly difficult to distinguish it from the TEED/TEC strategies and in 1990 the DES announced the scheme would end in October 1991. It claimed that the objectives of REPLAN had been achieved and that it was up to adult education providers to work with the LEAs and TECs to make educational opportunities available for the unemployed.

One assessment of REPLAN's achievements concluded that it had 'raised awareness of issues and possibilities, created collaborative networks, stimulated new provision' and embedded these new initiatives in the mainstream activities of LEAs (Fordham, 1992: 225). While this may have been partly the case, it is difficult to see what REPLAN encouraged that the providers would not have done anyway, if they had the funds to promote their own projects for the unemployed – given the widespread commitment to this form of community education. More significant was the extent to which REPLAN served as a government agent: it was a means by which the DES exercised an influence over the LEAs and other educational providers. The various bodies involved became 'agents of DES policy rather than influential actors in the field' (Fordham, 1991: 154; Evans, 1987: 127).

Nevertheless, although REPLAN 'reeked of rank political opportunism' some of its effects were 'highly desirable in strictly educational terms', helping people to understand the options open to them and challenging the fatalism and apathy which overwhelms so many people in crisis situations such as unemployment (Field, 1986: 4–5).

The DES was also keen to establish a hold over the growing provision of training and retraining for those in work, as well as the unemployed. In the same year (1984) that it switched some of its previous grant-aid for adult education to REPLAN, it diverted a second tranche to PICKUP, another three year scheme. PICKUP was intended to encourage higher and further education institutes to undertake 'professional, industrial and commercial up-dating'. Like REPLAN, PICKUP continued for a second term, but then the DES decided it had outlived its usefulness, and wound the scheme up. (See Chapter 8.)

The Government always regarded PICKUP funding as a temporary measure: it was planned as a pump-priming exercise to stimulate the educational providers to respond to market demand for training, and to persuade employers to meet the full cost. This was always difficult in a political culture in which education was regarded as part of the social infrastructure, paid for by taxation. Small and medium sized enterprises (SMEs) were particularly reluctant to accept the whole financial burden, but some larger companies did respond more enthusiastically to the challenge. Their programmes were at times extensive and imaginative. For example, in 1987 the Ford Motor Company responded to increasing Japanese competition by establishing its Employee Development and Assistance Programme (EDAP). The aim of EDAP was to try to change the workplace culture by raising levels of literacy and numeracy, raising morale and motivation, developing an awareness of quality, and improving industrial relations. It offered all employees up to £200 per annum to spend on a wide range of personal and career development education and training in their own time. The only restriction was that the courses should not be directly related to the participants' own jobs (such training was provided separately by the Company), nor should they be wholly recreational. The scheme was particularly successful in attracting non-traditional learners into continuing education. By 1993, one-third of the workforce was taking part: equivalent to one per cent of all adult education in the country (Moore, 1994; UACE, 1993; Kelly, 1992: lii). Ford's EDAP and a number of other similar schemes began to demonstrate that significant numbers of non-traditional learners could be enticed into participating in continuing education if it were held at the workplace or was otherwise work-related, without its being remotely job-training (Corlett, Gibson, Mannion-Brunt and Moore, all 1994)). (For an interesting antecedent to these schemes, see Chapter 9).

## 'Access', Open Colleges and the University of the Third Age

Meanwhile, as British society was becoming 'increasingly divided by social, gender, regional and racial inequalities and beset with a variety of escalating social problems, ranging from structural unemployment to rising criminality, homelessness and racial discrimination' in the 1970s and 80s, the Government attempted to relieve some of the tension by widening access to post-school education, including higher education (Benn and Fieldhouse, 1991: 80–1). It was not a new strategy: the socialising or 'normalising' tendency and incorporating effect of education had influenced educational policy throughout the twentieth century. But the Access to Higher Education Scheme which was initiated by the Labour Government in 1978 and enthusiastically continued throughout the 1980s and into the 1990s by successive Conservative Governments, was intended to be a very specifically targeted affair.

Educationally, if not politically, Access owed much to the Fresh Horizons programme introduced into the London City Literary Institute in the mid-sixties by Enid Hutchinson. Although it was never intended exclusively as a route into higher education for non-qualified women, from the very beginning Fresh Horizons was used very largely for that purpose (Groombridge, 1995: 8–11, 15–19). The Access scheme began in 1978 when the DES invited seven local authorities, including the Inner London Education Authority (ILEA), to establish a pilot Access programme with a view to increasing the opportunities for members of ethnic minorities to enter higher education and the professions. This invitation was eagerly seized upon by tutors in LEA and university further and adult education, for whom 'Access' became a social movement which harnessed their vision of a more just society. It very quickly became a national movement. Six courses were started in 1979: in 1985 there were 130; in 1990 the number had risen to over 600 and by 1994 to over 1,000 courses with more than 30,000 students. The targets were gradually widened to include women, the unemployed and the working class as well as the ethnic minorities. On the whole this targeting worked well, although as 'Access' became a significant route into higher education it became increasingly attractive to all sections of the adult population as a second chance if they had missed out at 18 (Benn and Fieldhouse, 1991: 81–2; Lieven, 1989; Hansard, 23 February 1993: col. 210; Benn, 1994: 75; Benn and Burton, 1995; HEFCE, 1995: 11–12).

By the late 1980s the need for some form of regulation of Access courses became apparent and so in 1989 the CVCP and CNAA jointly established a national framework for their recognition. It operated at three levels: a national central body responsible for policy and review (originally the CNAA itself but subsequently this responsibility was transferred to the Higher Education Quality Council (HEQC) when the CNAA was abolished following the 1992 Further and Higher Education Act); regional Access Validating Agencies (AVAs) which validated individual courses; and individual providers of Access courses. Those providers wishing to operate within the national framework, and obtain a 'kitemark' of recognition, were required to provide mainly for mature students and specific groups in the community identified as under-represented in higher education; to cater for those without conventional qualifications who did not feel ready for direct entry to higher education; and to design and teach programmes to meet the needs of these target groups. The majority of Access providers did seek recognition by their local AVA. Although the AVAs were answerable to a national Standing Conference of Access Validating Agencies (SCAVA) which belonged to HEQC, the emphasis on responsiveness to local requirements gave them considerable freedom in shaping Access programmes in their area. Consequently, these varied considerably, according to how local needs were interpreted (Benn and Burton, 1995). However, in the 1990s many AVAs and Access programmes became closely linked to Open College Networks and to some extent constrained by their aims and processes.

Open Colleges first appeared in the 1970s, essentially to accredit courses and students' learning (Browning, 1991a: 72). The first was founded at Nelson and Colne College in Lancashire in 1976 and became a model for similar developments in many parts of the country. The early Open Colleges concentrated on developing alternative curricula to A-levels which were more appropriate for many adults, but in the early 1980s they began to tackle the issues of accreditation more widely, in order to facilitate progression. This led them into the closer collaboration with the Access movement. These early developments were essentially local or regional: a 'second generation' of Open Colleges later extended the early principles beyond course-based work, to more widespread learning activities, including voluntary activities and learning at work; and began to develop a national framework of Open College accreditation and a national network. This led to a credit accumulation and transfer agreement between 10 of the 11 Open Colleges in 1991. They were located in Merseyside, Greater Manchester and Cheshire, Inner London, West Yorkshire, South Yorkshire, the Midlands and South Wales. There were a further twenty embryonic Open Colleges covering most of the remainder of England and Wales by the early 1990s, but none in Scotland (Browning, 1991a: 78, 1991b).

SCAVA and the National Open College Network (NOCN) collaborated closely in the 1990s to establish a nationally recognised credit framework and an effective lobbying body. This facilitated national recognition of courses but it required an intensive process of moderation and review which some critics found excessively bureaucratic, centralised and complex. While this criticism may be somewhat harsh, nevertheless the guidelines and directives issued by the national Network did erode the early informality and diversity of both the Open College and Access movements, and reduced their freedom of response to individual and local needs. Such guidelines and directives inevitably implied a degree of conformity (Browning, 1991a; Davies and Parry, 1993).

Another 'movement' of the 1980s was the 'University of the Third Age' (U3A) – an idea imported from France. The first major British U3A branch was founded in Cambridge in 1982. Four years later, there were some 115 groups, 7,000 members and a national committee. Each group consisted of a body of older adults who undertook to learn and help others to learn on a self-help basis (Midwinter, 1984: 7–17; Kelly, 1992: xxx). Supposedly the U3A did not rely on public funding, but in practice many groups tapped into the publicly-funded educational system indirectly. The level of learning within the U3A varied enormously – not all of it could be equated with university education. But in an age when public funding for adult education for the elderly was increasingly under threat, U3A was an important development. (See Chapter 12.)

## Into the 1990s: Legislative changes and changing patterns of adult education

Major new educational legislation, the Education Reform Act (ERA), was passed in 1988. It made no direct reference to adult education: like its predecessor, the 1944 Act, it subsumed adult education within further education. Nevertheless, ERA had a significant influence on how LEAs were able to finance, plan and provide education for adults, which is described in Chapter 4.

A survey of participation in adult education carried out in 1990 found that approximately one quarter of all adults had engaged in some form of adult education within the previous three years, although the participation rate appeared to be somewhat lower in Scotland. The rate varied considerably with social class, from 42 per cent amongst the upper and upper-middle classes, 37 per cent lower-middle class, 29 per cent skilled working class, to 17 per cent of the unskilled working class. Overall there had been a 7 per cent increase in participation since a similar survey carried out by ACACE in 1982. During that time the proportion of men studying had increased more rapidly than women, particularly in qualification courses, but women continued to predominate in non-qualification courses (Sargant, 1991: 11–12, 92, 95–6). Vocational subjects had increased in popularity since the early 1980s, and dominated the list of subjects studied, while the arts and social sciences, academic and domestic subjects generally and some vocational topics traditionally favoured by women had all declined. Sports and physical activities had also apparently declined dramatically, but in reality this reflected a change of terminology, as they had transferred from educational to leisure activities (*ibid*.: 14).

A MORI survey of 4,000 adults in England, Wales and Scotland, carried out for NIACE in May 1994, confirmed a participation rate of about 10 per cent in any one year and 25 per cent over a three-year period. As in the 1990 survey, it found that social class, unemployment, income and previous education all affected the participation rate. It was still clearly the middle classes who were benefiting the most. Age was also a major factor, with only 3 per cent of people over 65 currently studying (NIACE, 1994: 1).

Meanwhile, the dust had hardly settled from ERA before the Government produced a flurry of educational White Papers in 1991 (DES, 1991a, 1991b; Scottish Office, 1991), followed by another major education Act, the Further and Higher Education Act, in 1992. This legislation did not follow the same pattern as 1944 and 1988: it created a newly defined further education sector which became responsible for securing adequate provision of certain categories of education, listed in Schedule 2 of the Act. These included vocational and qualification courses, Access to higher education, basic education, and skills acquisition for those with learning difficulties. The Act left LEAs with residual statutory duties to secure non-Schedule 2 adult education – i.e. recreational, social and leisure provision. They lost their strategic planning function, which the 1944 and 1988 Acts had recognised, and left them with a reduced and potentially financially non-viable range of provision. Not surprisingly, some LEAs began to contract out their residual responsibilities to private or voluntary agencies (see Chapter 4).

A survey of adult education in the early 1990s contrasted the 'romantic' 1930s, 50s and 60s, when a 'range of moral and social imperatives ... informed our work and our discourse' with the 'modernist' 1990s: 'frequently utilitarian, pragmatic, instrumental, targeted, and often brutish' (Stock, 1992: 27). Another overview concluded that the past 'pluralism of provision, of providers and participants is threatened by prescriptive norms and performance indicators' (McNay, 1993: 23). More generally, the 1980s and early 90s witnessed a serious erosion of adult education's fundamental commitment to serving a collectivist social purpose – to make the world better. It was being displaced by individualist ideology and the pursuit of essentially individual goals – sometimes theoretically justified (under the influence of North American andragogical theory) as self-actualisation. This seemed to presage the end of the adult education *movement* with its distinctive social purpose (Benn and Fieldhouse, 1994). But at the same time adult education was presented with a vast new challenge: to introduce its social values into the mainstream. 'As traditional adult education is marginalised, its best aspects may be entering mainstream provision' (McNay, 1993: 23).

# 4

# The Local Education Authorities and Adult Education

## Roger Fieldhouse

The 1902 Education Act swept away the structures created 32 years earlier by the previous major Education Act of 1870, including the school boards, and replaced them by local education authorities (LEAs). They inherited the uneven but significant educational activities of the technical education committees established under the terms of the 1889 Technical Education Act, whose importance during the 1890s has already been mentioned in Chapter 2. Much of the 1902 Act was concerned with elementary education, but under Section 2 the LEAs were given powers to use income from rates to supply, or aid the supply, of other than elementary education. This led to the provision of LEA secondary and further education in technical colleges or institutions or in LEA schools.

'By unifying secondary and further education under a single set of authorities' the 1902 Act achieved an administrative coherence and 'settled the pattern of technical and commercial education in the maintained system until the Second World War' (Pimlott, 1970: 52). Provided they met certain conditions laid down in new further education regulations, the LEAs received grant aid from the Board of Education on a *per capita* basis. The regulations disallowed any grant for under-12-year-olds and required at least 25 per cent of expenditure to come from non-government sources – i.e. rates, fees and subscriptions. They laid down certain categories or 'divisions' of grant-aided work: literary and commercial; art; manual instruction; science; home occupations and industries; and physical training. This amounted to predominantly low-level technical and craft education together with basic instruction in the 'three Rs' and practical, 'domestic' courses for women – mainly needlework, dressmaking and cookery. The technical-vocational bias of this adult education was carried over from the work of the technical education committees of the 1890s. There was also some purely recreational provision but very little attempt to offer 'academic' courses, although the Board of Education did try to encourage the LEAs to provide some full-time courses at more advanced levels and even some higher education of a liberal character in the Oxbridge tradition (*ibid.*; Sadler, 1907: 105–10). After 1902 the LEAs were in many ways the obvious location for an expanded adult education provision but, 'with the exception of crafts, the potentialities of the LEAs in liberal adult education remained greater than their achievements' (Harrison, 1961: 314).

As the *1919 Report* recognised, the LEAs were only interpreting 'the utilitarian spirit of the times' by concentrating very largely on technical studies. The authors of the Report felt that the distinction between vocational and non-vocational education is one which may usefully be made, more especially because the distinction is one which exists in the popular mind and has taken root in practice (Ministry of Reconstruction, 1919: 104–5, 149).

It was this attitude which perpetuated the division between vocational and non-vocational ('liberal') adult education for much of the twentieth century. This vocational bias in the LEA sector was one of the reasons why Robert Morant, the Permanent Secretary at the Board of Education, was favourably inclined to the foundation of the Workers' Educational Association (WEA) in 1903, and to providing public funding for the Association a few years later, to promote non-vocational liberal adult education (Pimlott, 1970: 52 and see Chapter 7).

Apart from its technical, vocational, practical bias, what was the character and nature of LEA adult education? One of its characteristics was that its quality and volume varied very considerably from authority to authority. LEA adult education in London was very different from what developed in Scotland or Suffolk. But it has been argued that most LEAs emerged only slowly 'from the atmosphere of the restrictive evening school codes of the later nineteenth century' and that the 'subsequent entanglement in the complexities of technical and commercial education still further hampered them. Local Authority adult education lacked intellectual glamour or status' (Harrison, 1961: 314). Even the LEAs themselves frequently regarded it as of lesser-importance, dealt with separately from schools by a sub-committee of the main Education Committee. It was very much the poor cousin within the local authority structure, and for many years was also conferred low status vis-a-vis the more prestigious voluntary bodies - the universities and the WEA.

Physically, LEA adult education took place in a mixture of evening classes in LEA schools (many of them junior schools equipped for small children!); single-purpose adult education centres equipped for adults and open in the daytime as well as the evening; and multi-purpose community centres such as the village colleges founded by Henry Morris in Cambridgeshire during the 1930s, or the special further education colleges when they began to appear (Legge, 1982: 100–7). It was most frequently taught by schoolteachers or specific 'experts' brought in from all walks of life. Until quite recently, very few had any training in adult education and many had no educational training at all.

On the other hand, LEA adult education was easily accessible, and despite the lack of structured pathways it offered many people for whom school had been an unsatisfactory experience, a way back into education at an appropriate level, and a way to progress to other things. Frequently, it altered people's views or challenged their ideas and prejudices, just by being in an educational environment. This could happen in the least likely setting, such as the class attended by the same group of women in south London year after year, ostensibly to learn the same dressmaking skills each year, but which was in reality a multicultural discussion group. (I owe this information to Alan Tuckett.)

One other general characteristic, or consequence, of LEA adult education in Britain was that, because of its relatively large quantity and accessibility, it may well have helped to prevent the involvement of social movements in adult education in this country to the extent that they became involved in other countries such as Germany and Scandinavia, although the involvement of the trade union movement is described in Chapter 10 and many other informal organisations in Chapter 12.

## Early Developments

By 1904 the LEAs were operating under the revised Board of Education regulations governing 'further' education (which encompassed adult education) and by the following year there were some three-quarters of a million part-time students in LEA evening classes inspected by the Board of Education, 60 per cent of whom were men. Although Michael Sadler claimed that the number of students attending classes under government inspection was increasing at the time he made his survey of continuation schools in 1907, and that 'in no other country is greater zeal shown in attendance at evening classes organised upon a purely voluntary basis', in reality the total disappointingly did not significantly increase over the next 35 years (Sadler, 1907: 111–2; Kelly, 1992: 289; Pimlott, 1970: 52).

In his survey, Sadler noted a considerable number of problems. He believed that not enough was being done to encourage pupils to pass from elementary education to either secondary school or evening class. A much closer link between the elementary day school and the continuation classes was needed. There was also the problem of poverty: not everyone could afford to pay the fees. Perhaps linked to this, he identified a general apathy to education in most country districts and more specifically noted that farmers disliked modern developments in education. More generally, employers failed 'to recognise their responsibility towards the further education of the young persons in their employment'. There was also the problem of the long working hours and poor working conditions of evening class teachers. 'The continuation school especially needs fresh ways of teaching and a departure from the routine of the day school' (Sadler, 1907: 115–26). But apart from the London County Council, few LEAs were able or willing to tackle these problems in what was regarded very much as a peripheral activity.

During the period between 1902 and the First World War, and indeed during the war, the contribution of most LEAs was 'largely confined to trying to remedy at an adult level the deficiencies of primary education, and to provision of vocational and technical training' (Jepson, 1959: 83). They left the non-vocational, liberal adult education very much to the universities and the WEA, although an increasing number of them provided valuable financial support for this work (Ministry of Reconstruction, 1919: 106, 109; Fieldhouse, 1984: 456).

In London, the LEA did make more of an effort to broaden the scope of its adult education provision. A report from the Education Officer in 1912 formed the basis of a major reorganisation in the capital the following year. Recognising the problems for adults studying with young people, adult education was taken out of schools and moved to special institutions for the over-eighteens. In September 1913 242 evening institutes were opened, including a number exclusively for women. The emphasis was still predominantly on technical and vocational subjects, or practical domestic subjects for women, but 12 of the institutes were non-vocational, although few of these survived beyond the outbreak of war in 1914 (Devereux, 1982: 61–76; Hughes, 1992: 44–5; Kelly, 1992: 289).

In 1917 the Board of Education issued draft revised regulations for further education which were intended to strengthen LEA adult education; encourage greater co-operation and joint planning between LEAs; and between LEAs and the voluntary bodies. The regulations heralded an end to direct grant by the Board to voluntary bodies, proposing instead that this responsibility (and the attendant control) be handed over to the LEAs. Only university tutorial classes were to be exempt from this arrangement (ibid.: 107, 162–4; Ministry of Education, 1954: 4–5). A year later the 1918 Education Act (the Fisher Act) created no new statutory adult education duties for LEAs, but echoed the proposals of the draft regulations and required the LEAs to provide for 'the progressive development and comprehensive organisation of education' in their areas – sometimes interpreted as an encouragement for lifelong learning (Ministry of Reconstruction, 1919: 107). The Act also brought LEAs under the closer control of the Board of Education and the Treasury (Thoms, 1974). The 1918 Education (Scotland) Act had less direct bearing on adult education.

However, the 1919 *Final Report* opposed those aspects of the 1917 draft regulations which would have increased LEA control over the voluntary sector and, possibly for this reason, the draft regulations were not confirmed. But the *Final Report* did argue very forcefully that the LEAs should play a greater part in the development of adult education, including non-vocational adult education (Ministry of Reconstruction, 1919: 106, 170; Ministry of Education, 1954: 5–6). This set the scene for the development of LEA adult education during the 1920s and 30s.

## Relations between the LEAs and the Voluntary Sector

The spirit of the 1917 draft regulations was not immediately discarded. One of the objectives of the Adult Education Committee established by the Board of Education in 1921 was to foster collaboration between the LEAs and other providing bodies and to make all adult education, except university tutorial classes, the responsibility of the LEAs (see Chapter 3). The Committee gradually retreated from this objective, coming to value the separate and independent activities of the 'Responsible Bodies', but it was not so readily abandoned by the Board of Education or the local authority associations. New adult education regulations introduced by the Board in 1924 were prefaced by a note stating its belief that the LEAs should assume 'the main financial responsibility for work of lower standard'. The Board was worried that as the volume of Responsible Body adult education grew, it would not be able to monitor it. However, in practice the regulations not only increased the range and types of grant-aided university courses, but also provided for the recognition of other 'approved associations' (for which the WEA was the model) which would receive direct grant for a wide variety of non-vocational liberal adult education as 'Responsible Bodies' (Ministry of Education, 1954: 6–8). The authors of the 1919 Report appeared to have won the battle.

But not yet the war! A year later, when the WEA fell foul of the Board of Education because of its flirtation with the TUC's educational scheme, Lord Eustace Percy, President of the Board, and the Association of Education Committees were very inclined to take the opportunity to impose greater local authority control over the WEA. Although direct control, 'financial or otherwise', was not conceded, the LEAs did gain greater powers of inspection and approval of 'responsible Body' adult education as a result of the incident (Fieldhouse, 1981: 56–60 and see Chapter 7).

It has been suggested that few LEAs gave any significant support to the voluntary sector during the inter-war period (Lowe, 1970: 43) but this assessment is 'a trifle harsh' (O'Hare, 1981: 55), if not downright wrong. The picture is really one of considerable and growing collaboration, with the LEAs looking very much to the 'Responsible Bodies' to supplement their own programmes. Most LEAs provided some financial assistance to these partners. The Board of Education's annual report for 1922-3 recorded this assistance for the first time. It showed that a considerable number of LEAs were contributing varying degrees of financial assistance for university tutorial classes and extension lectures and WEA classes. A rather smaller number were also assisting classes organised by Women's Institutes, Educational Settlements, literary and other societies and the St John Ambulance Association. Other investigations by the Association of Tutors in Adult Education in 1926 and the British Institute of Adult Education in 1926-7 revealed a similar picture, with LEAs providing direct and indirect grants and also bursaries and scholarships for students and assistance with publicity. In some cases, such as the West Riding of Yorkshire, the LEA assumed full financial responsibility for all courses of one year's duration or less. In many areas the LEA promoted some form of adult education joint planning committee. Normally such committees enjoyed merely advisory powers but sometimes they were more executive. For example, in Devon the Adult Education Committee allocated the Board of Education grants to the University College of the South West and the WEA District as well as for the county's own adult education activities, and attempted to co-ordinate the provision of the three partners. Many LEAs also enjoyed rights of representation on university adult education committees (Kelly, 1992: 287–8; Jepson, 1959: 84; Fieldhouse, 1984: 458–9, 461–3, 469; Public Record Office (PRO), 1931 and 1939, ED 73/38 and 59, Board of Education files re WEA SW District and the University College of the South West).

This support provided by the LEAs to their adult education partners continued and increased during the inter-war period. It was regarded as a significant part of their statutory duty to supply, or *aid the supply*, of further education in their areas. The last report of the Board of Education's Adult Education Committee, entitled *Adult Education and the LEAs*, in 1933, indicated that many forms of collaboration existed and that they generally included some kind of practical assistance provided by the LEA to the 'Responsible Bodies' and other organisations.

This financial support did provide the LEAs with some control over the activities of the voluntary bodies. This was evident even before the 1924 regulations and the controversy surrounding the 1925 TUC scheme, but became more explicit after that, ranging from consultation to inspection of classes and approval of syllabuses and tutors. A sample survey of 37 English, Welsh and Scottish LEAs carried out jointly by the British Institute and the Tutors' Association in 1928 revealed no overall pattern of LEA supervision and control, but it did indicate that at least a sizeable minority regarded the payment of grant aid as entitling them (or perhaps obliging them) to watch over the subject matter and the teachers of 'responsible Body' classes. In Scotland the LEAs made no grants to the universities, and therefore exercised no control over them, but they were directly responsible for appointing and paying WEA tutors.

For most of the time this LEA surveillance was cursory or desultory, or was more concerned with the enforcement of technical regulations such as minimum numbers; but it could, and occasionally did, allow officials or councillors to object to what they regarded as the politically subversive nature of certain classes or tutors. The occasional murmur of disapproval or polite enquiry about certain undesirable activities did constitute a constraint on the freedom of the 'Responsible Bodies' (Fieldhouse, 1984: 456–71, 474–5).

Nevertheless, the dual system continued, with the 'Responsible Bodies' providing most liberal adult education and the LEAs largely vocational and recreational adult education:

It was an odd situation. Not only was liberal adult education in large part separately administered, but classes met in different buildings, the teachers were more highly paid, and it came to enjoy a higher prestige than vocational education' (Pimlott, 1970: 53).

LEA adult education in the inter-war period remained very much the poor cousin.


## Expansion During the Inter-War Period

Despite its apparent marginality, there was a 'general quickening' of LEAs' own direct provision during the 1920s and 30s (Kelly, 1992: 294–5). This included a 'tremendous increase in the provision of social and recreational courses'; a considerable growth in technical education; and a smaller increase in academic or non-vocational adult education, although this last declined as a proportion of the total during the 1930s because most LEAs, apart from London, continued to leave this very much to the 'Responsible Bodies'. The great bulk of this expansion was in practical and recreational, as distinct from academic classes (Jepson, 1959: 85). The 1933 report on *Adult Education and the LEAs* identified the reason for this when it stated that in the past adult education had been designed very largely to 'make good in a limited field the deficiencies of the public system of education' but it was believed that by the 1930s these gaps had been filled and therefore practical and recreational pursuits were seen to have a value in their own right and also as preparation for more serious study (NIAE, 1951: 2). The report also noted that outside London, over one-third of all LEA provision was dedicated to 'domestic instruction' for women – reflecting the growing proportion of women in LEA classes (Pimlott, 1970: 53).

Expansion during the 1930s was due very largely to the continuing interest in recreational and handicraft subjects (Jepson, 1959: 85). Nevertheless, in 1936–7, two-thirds of LEA enrolments in England and Wales were still in vocational classes (professional, commercial, science, English, industrial and language courses). The remaining one-third covered women's subjects, physical culture, handicrafts, music, art, hygiene and first aid. Fifty-six per cent of the students were now women. Well over 90 per cent attended evening, as opposed to day-time classes (NIAE, 1951: 7, 9, 12). In Scotland evening school provision was on a smaller scale than in England and Wales, even allowing for the difference in population (Kelly, 1992: 300).

London County Council (LCC) remained outstanding amongst LEAs, developing a 'comprehensive adult education service of quite remarkable educational and social breadth'. The 1933 Report of the Adult Education Committee on *Adult Education and the LEAs* noted that London had much more scope and variety of adult education than other places (Devereux, 1982: 111, 126). The number of evening institutes in London had declined temporarily during the First World War, to 193 by 1916–17, but there was an expansion again after the war. This included the creation of a number of men's institutes which frankly recognised the need for the non-intellectual, practical-craft activity, hobbies and recreation so often ignored or belittled by well-meaning adult educators. By 1925 the LCC had established six men's institutes and five junior men's institutes alongside the 37 women's institutes offering mainly domestic instruction and recreational classes (Hughes, 1992: 47; Kelly, 1992: 290–2). The LCC also established a number of literary institutes to provide cultural and academic courses, such as languages, literature and the natural sciences. In 1929 the Board of Education saw these as a valuable and expanding provision for the growing number of people who had experience of secondary education and desired 'further education for its own sake'. There was some danger of these institutes duplicating the work of the 'Responsible Bodies' but their ethos was less politically, socially or religiously committed. By 1939 there were 12 of these literary institutes in London (Kelly: 292–4). All of London's institutes also laid great stress on social activities.

Much of London's success in promoting non-vocational adult education during the inter-war period was a result of its targeting the unemployed, particularly through its men's and junior men's institutes. The Board of Education encouraged other LEAs to make specific provision for the unemployed but with only limited success. Much of this work was undertaken by central government departments and voluntary agencies (Devereux, 1982: 111; Marks, 1982; and see Chapter 3).

During the 1930s some LEAs moved towards a community education approach, following the example of Henry Morris and Cambridgeshire. They aimed to integrate all aspects of education in a holistic approach to lifelong learning based on village colleges (see Chapter 5). Several LEAs, including Leicestershire, Nottinghamshire, Derbyshire, Cumberland and Coventry imitated the Cambridgshire example, at least in part, during the 1930s.

## The Second World War and the 1944 Education Act

As in the First World War, after 1939 the experience of war gave an impetus to wide social reforms, including educational reforms. R.A. Butler's predecessor at the Board of Education, Herwald Ramsbotham, issued a consultative Green Paper in 1941 and this was followed by a vigorous campaign to include compulsory part-time continuing education for everyone up to the age of 18 and improvements in technical education and training in any future legislation (Evans, 1982: 46–50). The Green Paper was followed by a White Paper, *Educational Reconstruction*, in 1943 which envisaged the LEAs playing a much larger part in further education in the future, involving them not only in an expansion of technical, commercial and art education and compulsory part-time education between the ages of 15 and 18, but also in 'a more extensive and flexible system of cultural and recreative provision for adolescents and adults'. Further education was to be the third stage (after primary and secondary stages) of an educational system intended 'to bring up a healthy and happy population, to train a balanced team of workers able to develop a prosperous economy, and to rear a people eager to advance its civilization and culture' (Jepson, 1959: 86; Peters, 1967: 275).

The 1944 Education Act which emerged from this wartime campaigning and the White Paper imposed upon the LEAs 'a statutory duty, as distinct from an enabling power, for which no provision had been made in the Education Acts of 1902 and 1918' (Ministry of Education, 1954: 9). This duty was laid out in section 41 of the Act:

... it shall be the duty of every local education authority to secure the provision for their area of adequate facilities for further education that is to say:
(a) full-time and part-time education for persons over compulsory school age; and
(b) leisure-time occupation, in such organized cultural training and recreative activities as are suited to their requirements, for any persons over compulsory school age who are able and willing to profit by the facilities provided for that purpose ...

Section 53 of the Act required the LEAs to secure adequate facilities for recreation and social and physical training and Section 42(4) to have regard to any facilities for further education provided for their area by universities, educational associations and other bodies. The LEAs were required to carry out these duties only in so far as they were in accordance with schemes for further education which they would prepare and submit to the Minister. This was intended to force LEAs 'to examine, in its entirety, the provision of further education, which had previously grown up so haphazardly' (Jepson, 1959: 86–8; Dent, 1952: 45–6).

Despite this intention to bring order to the system, the LEAs all interpreted their duties rather differently, so that 'instead of one system there (were) over a hundred' which grew out of the 1944 Act. (There were, in fact, 146 LEAs in England and Wales of widely different sizes, ranging from Rutland serving a population of 17,370, to the LCC with a population of over two-and-a-half million.) There were, for example, very wide variations in the level of fees charged. Some LEAs continued to interpret further education very largely as technical and vocational education provided on a day-release basis in addition to part-time attendance at continuing education classes at the proposed new county colleges. Others saw further education more broadly, but they all interpreted 'adequacy' in convenient ways, and tended to reassess what it meant every time there was a financial crisis. Indeed, as will be seen, the failure of the 1944 Act to define 'adequate' in either quantitative or qualitative terms proved to be a crucial weakness as time went on (Legge, 1982: 23–5; Owens, 1969: 30; Cantor and Roberts, 1983: 277).

Nevertheless 'a system' did emerge from the 1944 Act which remained very largely intact for the next 40 years. In this system, the LEAs had a responsibility for securing 'adequate' adult education facilities in their area, whatever that meant, and this statutory responsibility made them the key players, supported by the 'Responsible Bodies'. Central government set a certain minimum standard and a maximum overall expenditure limit. Both of these were overseen by His/Her Majesty's Inspectors. Within each LEA area, individual adult education institutions enjoyed a fair degree of autonomy and flexibility. Professional control of institutions rested to a considerable extent with the professional staff, but they were governed by Education Committees of elected councillors and very often by governing bodies representing the voluntary members and students. The system was flexible, varied and, at its best, allowed innovation and development to emerge 'from below', reflecting grass roots needs and experience. There was the capacity to 'grow innovation organically from the bottom up', although this decentralised system also resulted in wide variations in quality and quantity, and in very varied administrative practices (Elsdon, 1994: 321–3).

The partnership between the LEAs and the 'Responsible Bodies' remained a very important part of this system. As already shown, this was not a new phenomenon, but the duty laid upon the LEAs in the 1944 Act to have regard to any further education provision made by other bodies, and to consult with any such bodies, created a firm basis for genuine partnership. Section 42 recognised 'the leading part which voluntary bodies have always played in the provision of adult education', and in effect invited them 'to co-operate on a basis of equal partnership with the statutory authorities' (Dent, 1952: 46). The centrality of this partnership approach was recognised by the Ministry of Education in its *Further Education* pamphlet issued in 1947 to assist the LEAs in drawing up their further education schemes:

The first need is co-operative action by authorities, universities, and voluntary organizations of every kind. We need generosity and trust between the teaching bodies themselves, so that we may use our teaching resources to the best advantage. We need a close and confident relationship between those teaching bodies ... There is an opportunity to advance, if we march together (Ministry of Education, 1947: 32).

However, that was some way into the future. Immediately after the Act was passed, the Government announced that, at that juncture, it was not requiring the LEAs to submit new schemes of further education (Evans, 1982: 54). This meant that the further or adult education sections of the Act did not become operative until after the 1945 general election which swept the Labour Party into power.

## Great Expectations, 1945–51

The new Labour Government was certainly committed to planned social and economic reconstruction, but did not regard education as a major component of those plans. Many members of the Government, including 'red' Ellen Wilkinson, who became Minister of Education in 1945, and George Tomlinson who succeeded her after her death in 1947, were quite traditionalist in their education policy, aiming to make the existing system fairer rather than introducing a more radical system of comprehensive education. It was assumed that 'all would be well if only the advantages of the old heaven and the old earth were spread more evenly' (Barker, 1972: 138). The Government confined its educational objectives very largely to implementing the 1944 Act which many of its members had been involved in shaping. And within that policy, top priority was given to raising the school leaving age by 1 April 1947. The only reference to education in the King's speech after the 1945 general election was to raising the school leaving age (*ibid.*: 81–97, 137; Pelling, 1984: 113–14, 117; Rubenstein, 1979: 161–2; Morgan, 1985: 174–8; Vernon, 1982: 202, 206; Blackburn, 1954: 169–70, 175–7; Tawney, 1943: 13; Pritt, 1963: 93; Hughes, 1979: 157; Gordon, Aldrich and Dean, 1991: 62; Simon, 1980: 31–43; Dean, 1986: 157; Fieldhouse, 1994: 287–90).

If the Labour Government was somewhat lukewarm about education (apart from raising the school leaving age), the new Ministry of Education was more enthusiastic. A Further Education Schemes Committee was established in April 1946 and at its first meeting it decided to issue a directive to LEAs, asking them to prepare their further education schemes. The circular, which eventually went out in March 1947, directing them to submit their schemes by the following March, requested a considerable amount of general information, together with details of their current further education activities and a costed five-year programme. However, it was already evident that the anticipated costs were causing the Government to back-track on some aspects of the 1944 Act, despite Ellen Wilkinson's determined attempts to protect those plans. Indeed, it was concern about the cost which delayed the circular for nearly six months (*ibid.*: 291).

The circular was accompanied by 'an official publication designed to survey the whole field of further education as an entity'. This was the Ministry's pamphlet, *Further Education*, which the FE Branch adopted as its 'bible' (Ministry of Education, 1947a and b; Fieldhouse, 1994: 292). While the LEAs' schemes did produce something of a 'patchwork-quilt' of local or regional FE plans (Cantor and Roberts, 1983: 3; Jepson, 1959: *passim*), the 200-page 'bible' must be regarded as a reasonably comprehensive and coherent national plan or blue-print. The further education that local authorities were expected to offer was 'a synthesis between the utilitarian and the cultural – so that a wide choice of educational opportunities may be brought within the range of the imagination of all' (Ministry of Education, 1947b: 76).

According to this blue-print there was to be a college of further education (which might have originated as a technical, commercial or art college, an institute of adult education, or a village or county college) in every centre of population. They were to 'serve as power houses ... (and) provide the framework of further education as a whole'. Within this framework a pattern of smaller centres was to be fitted: 'community centres, youth clubs, village halls and the like' (*ibid*.: 8–9). Different patterns of organisation were laid down in detail for large urban areas, smaller towns and scattered rural communities (*ibid*.: 78–80).

The Ministry felt that 'the replacement of a great deal of evening class work by part-time study during the day (was) long overdue, especially for young people' (ibid.: 16). This was to account for the bulk of vocational and technical training. 'Preparation for work' was the primary purpose of this further education: 'to produce both skills and social leadership' (*ibid*.: 12-13). The core of this vocational FE was intended to be the re-introduction of the proposals first contained in the 1918 Fisher Act, for compulsory part-time education for all school-leavers up to the age of 18. This was to be provided mainly in the proposed new county colleges, although there were to be some more specialised regional and national colleges. It was envisaged that this vocational further education would not only afford opportunities for the development of technical skills but also provide 'a variety of courses including handicrafts and the domestic arts' which would keep the students' minds alert and provide 'resources of satisfaction and self-development', together with 'some education in the broad meaning of citizenship' (Jepson, 1959: 98).

Unfortunately, the worsening economic crisis from 1947 onwards, together with a lack of real political determination, undermined this grand plan for compulsory part-time vocational further education. It was constantly postponed and eventually abandoned in 1950. Reliance continued to be placed largely on *voluntary* part-time vocational education and training for young people, to the very real detriment of the country's needs for a better trained workforce. Although the number of part-time vocational students did increase very considerably, they were mainly on relatively low-level courses. There was very little improvement in higher technical education, apart from the establishment of six specialist national technical colleges (Fieldhouse, 1993b: 98–103; 1994: 292–6).

Although the policy of compulsory part-time further education in county colleges for all up to the age of 18 was never implemented, it nevertheless had the effect of concentrating vocational education in further education (FE) colleges and major institutions. This came to be identified as '*further*' (as opposed to '*adult*') education, separate and set apart from the rest of the education system, although legally 'further' education embraced all post-compulsory education apart from higher education. Meanwhile, part-time, predominantly evening adult education, located mainly in evening institutes, became increasingly non-vocational. Thus the old vocational/non-vocational divide was perpetuated but the dividing line moved after 1944. It no longer lay between the LEAs and other providers, as it had done before the war, but between LEA 'further education' and 'adult education'. Thus the 1944 Act and the subsequent FE plan contributed to a uniquely British separation of vocational FE from non-vocational, recreational and leisure adult education.

As already noted, the 1944 Act required local authorities to secure adequate facilities for organised cultural training and recreational activities for anyone over compulsory school age who was able and willing to profit by them. The Ministry's 1947 further education 'bible' describes this as 'learning for leisure'. Local authorities were expected to greatly extend educational and social resources which would enable people 'to deal competently and democratically with the complex political questions of our time, or to develop those interests and activities which go to the making of a full and satisfying life', thereby 'making for individual happiness and ... a civilised community'. This very ambitious intention was built on the belief 'that, given understanding, the human spirit can rise to the challenge of events' (Ministry of Education, 1947b: 32). Therefore 'the aim of any programme of adult education must be to provide men and women with opportunities for developing a maturity of outlook and judgement, for increasing their sense of responsibility and awareness, for helping them to evolve a philosophy of life, and to develop interests which will enrich their leisure' (ibid.: 44). After 1944, LEA adult education became identified much more with this recreational, leisure and 'general', as opposed to vocational and technical, education.

The evening institutes were the focal point of much of this LEA 'learning for leisure'. As a result of the gradual development of technical and commercial FE colleges, and the government policy to transfer most or all vocational work from the evening institutes to these colleges, the institutes became 'less junior vocational institutes and much more adult non-vocational centres', concentrating on leisure, recreational and general cultural adult education (Jepson, 1959: 106–8; Lowe, 1970: 54; O'Hare, 1981: 56)

Local community centres also increased considerably after the war, encouraged by a pamphlet published by the Ministry of Education in 1945. They could be provided by LEAs themselves, by other local authorities, or by voluntary organisations assisted by the LEA, the National Council of Social Services or directly by the Ministry of Education (Jepson, 1959: 102; Ministry of Education 1947b: 53–4). Village or Community Colleges, based on the ideas and practice of Henry Morris in Cambridgeshire, also made some progress although Morris's advocacy of village colleges was considered rather doctrinaire and superficial within the Ministry of Education. In 1948 the Central Advisory Council suggested to the Ministry that it should investigate one of the cornerstones of Morris's Community College idea – what extraneous community duties a school should adopt, and what village schools could contribute to village life.   Perhaps as a result of this investigation, in 1950 new primary schools were allowed to exceed the maximum permissible capital cost if they were making provision of facilities for evening work beyond the ordinary requirements of the day school (Fieldhouse, 1994: 297–8).

It was also felt that there was 'scope for considerable experiment in the organisation of short residential courses' and that it was 'reasonable to expect that every authority will require ... a (residential) centre, either for its own area or in partnership with other authorities' (Ministry of Education, 1947b: 61–2). (See Chapter 9).

The very considerably increased responsibility placed on the LEAs by the 1944 Act meant that their relationship with other providing bodies became of great significance. Circular 133 reminded them that the Act required them to have regard to the provision by the universities, educational associations and other bodies, and to consult with them when preparing their schemes for further education (Ministry of Education, 1947a, para. 5). The 'bible' stated that 'further education is a community effort in which the authority must play a leading part', but that co-operative action between the various partners was essential (Ministry of Education, 1947b: 32–3). It was envisaged that LEAs would continue to subsidise the 'Responsible Bodies' and other organisations such as Women's Institutes, the YMCA, Young Farmers' Clubs, youth organisations, drama and music societies, etc., to make provision which the LEAs were unable or unwilling to make themselves (*ibid.*: 41; Jepson, 1959: 104–5).

This post-war LEA adult education was expected to cover three broad categories - theoretical studies, foreign languages and practical activities. The theoretical studies would develop an appreciation and understanding of cultural traditions and achievements. Although the number of people interested in this category would be small compared with those engaged in the practical activities (which were 'far the most popular form of adult education'), nevertheless the importance of the group interested in theoretical studies far outweighed its size 'for from its ranks come many of the leaders of those groups and associations which are such an important part of democratic society' (Ministry of Education, 1947b: 44–7).

'Women's specialized interests' which would enable 'young women contemplating marriage, as well as those already married, to increase their skill in housecraft' were also to be encouraged, as were the use of exhibitions, films, public libraries and broadcasting. To encourage the serious use of the last it was suggested that establishments of further education might equip a small room with a wireless set to be 'at the disposal of those who wish to listen to the third programme' which had just been launched by the BBC (*ibid.*: 47–52). The 'bible' also recommended, as a matter of some urgency, the acquisition of convenient sites for playing fields, together with the provision of village halls. If necessary, they were to be funded by grants or loans from the Carnegie Trust or the Development Commissioners (*ibid.*: 56–8).

Interestingly, in this broad, if somewhat traditional, recommended programme of formal and informal adult education, there was no mention of literacy or what would now be called adult basic education, which is surprising considering the Services' extensive experience of illiteracy during the war.

The expansion of LEA adult education between 1945 and 1950 was real but patchy. The number of evening institutes more than doubled between 1947 and 1950, from just over 5,000 to almost 11,000 and the number of students increased from about 825,000 to nearly one-and-a-quarter million (Jepson, 1959: 106). But this did not amount to the grand plan envisaged in the Ministry of Education's 1947 pamphlet. And it depended less on the drive from central government than on the inclinations of individual LEAs. Nevertheless, a survey carried out by the National Institute of Adult Education into the relations between adult education and other forms of further education in England and Wales, but excluding Scotland, in 1951 concluded that 'one of the striking features of the post-war development is the increase in the number of people of full adult age who have responded to the increased opportunities stimulated by the 1944 Act' (NIAE, 1951: 8). The statistical survey (*ibid.*: 5–11), despite the need for cautious interpretation of the figures, nevertheless showed a remarkable growth in adult demand for evening classes, especially from women. The number of enrolments in evening classes in evening institutes and major establishments (but excluding art establishments) had increased from 568,000 in 1936–7 to 1,295,000 by 1949–50. Sixty per cent of these students were women, and 17 per cent were aged between 18 and 20. Despite quite desperate accommodation problems and overcrowding (*ibid.*: 13–14), the authors of the survey found that:

the total volume of activity in further education is now more than twice as large as it was pre-war. Despite a notable growth of full-time and part-time day attendances the demand for evening classes from both sexes has increased. The increase extends to all age groups, and is most marked amongst women over 21 years of age. Side by side with the absolute growth in numbers of evening students there appears to have been a transfer of certain types of work from evening institutes to evening classes in major establishments. Evening institute classes are increasingly catering for a body of adult students who turn to them for the satisfaction of personal and social needs, rather than for the continuation of basic education or the development of occupational skills (*ibid.*: 10).

But the LEAs' plans for expansion and development were constantly thwarted by lack of resources, which prevented them from building the planned new adult or community centres or improving existing accommodation. The growing economic crisis in the late 1940s made such improvements ever more unlikely. Then in 1949 the LEAs were advised to increase fees for evening class students and in 1951 were asked to consider making recreational classes self-supporting (*ibid.*: 13–14; Kelly, 1992: 338).

## Stagnation and Recovery During the 1950s and 60s

As part of the partnership with the 'Responsible Bodies' and other providers, there was an increase in the number of consultative and advisory committees, but also 'a certain conflict of views as to their usefulness'. More positively, there was considered to be no lack of administrative co-operation and in many areas these formal arrangements were 'supported by the friendly daily contact of officers round practical details – availability of rooms and equipment, provision and approval of teachers, interpretation of regulations, the "borrowing" of chairmen and speakers for meetings and conferences' (*NIAE*, 1951: 39–40). Most LEAs collaborated quite happily with the universities, and there was less political antagonism towards the WEA; but there was a steadily growing belief that the LEAs could take full responsibility for all non-vocational adult education below the level of university tutorial classes, thereby dispensing with the need for the WEA altogether (Fieldhouse, 1984: 471).

This stemmed very largely from the ever-growing overlap between the increasingly non-vocational LEA adult education and much of the work of the 'Responsible Bodies'. In 1954 the Ashby Committee, set up to review the organisation and finance of 'Responsible Body' adult education, noted that many local authorities had developed a lively interest in the field of liberal adult education which had once been very largely the preserve of the 'Responsible Bodies'. At the same time it found a degree of resentment in LEA quarters against the perceived privileged position of the 'RBs', which were able to charge lower student fees and pay higher rates to their tutors. While identifying a generally amicable relationship, the Committee uncovered a considerable amount of mutual distrust. In particular, the Association of Education Committees advocated that the LEAs should take over total financial responsibility for all adult education below university level, but the weight of evidence and opinion was against them (Fieldhouse, 1977: 36–7; Ministry of Education, 1954: 28–31, 39–40). The Report came down in favour of the *status quo*:

We do not agree that local authorities should take over the functions of the voluntary responsible bodies. We believe they should take every opportunity of liberalising their own provision of further education and we think they can, as many of them do at present, give voluntary bodies substantial help in their work (*ibid.*: 40).

In particular the Committee encouraged LEAs to offer accommodation free of charge for classes provided by their partners, and contribute towards their administrative expenses, but said nothing about the problem of differential fees. In practice, collaboration was hampered by distrust and overlap for many years. In 1959, at the North of England Education Conference, it was again suggested that LEAs were quite capable of becoming the main providers of adult education and the domination of the universities was questioned. A few years later, Professor Harold Wiltshire, the influential Director of Adult Education at Nottingham University, advocated closer collaboration and a coming together of the two parallel but separate systems of adult education. He suggested that there should be a shared purpose and common philosophy, but he saw this very much in terms of the LEAs adopting the values of the 'Responsible Bodies' by concentrating on 'liberal' adult education to the exclusion of vocational and mere recreational subjects. He also acknowledged that the disparity in fees and payments to tutors, and the different status of adult education in the 'parallel systems', remained a problem. The following year, 1964, the Somerset County FE organiser argued that the LEAs now had the resources and the machinery to take the dominant role and provide a comprehensive programme rather than merely concentrate on lower-level work, as they had done over the previous 20 years.(*ibid.*: 40, 48–9; Jepson, 1959: 116–9; De Bear Nichol, 1959: 60; Wiltshire, *passim*; Mitchell, 1964: 6–12).

LEA adult education went into apparent decline during the 1950s after its initial post-war expansion: the number of evening institute students in England and Wales fell from over one-and-a-quarter million to 877,000 by 1961, and the number of evening institutes reduced from over 9,000 in 1956 to about 7,500 by 1963. There was a similar pattern of decline in Scotland, although the recovery began earlier north of the border, in 1957–8, compared with England and Wales, where it was delayed until 1961–2 (Kelly, 1992: 343, 358–9; Jepson, 1959: 106–7; Cantor and Roberts, 1983: 8). There were a number of factors which contributed to decline or stagnation during the 1950s. Government pressures to economise led to increased fees and stricter attendance requirements. At the same time, many LEAs still gave adult education very low priority, and in the face of any financial stringency it carried more than its share of cuts. The increase in the number of women working may also have contributed to the fall in student numbers, which was particularly acute amongst females (Kelly, 1992: 343; Jepson, 1959: 107).

However, the decline was more apparent than real: a matter of different terminology rather than absolute decline, highlighting the constant difficulties in interpreting adult education statistics. At least some of the apparent decline reflected the increasing number of younger vocational students who transferred from evening institutes to the FE colleges. There was both a relative and absolute increase in leisure-time activities and in LEA provision of certain liberal adult education subjects (*ibid.*: 107–8, 115).

Moreover, despite the failure to implement the compulsory part-time day-release provision of the 1944 Act, the number of mainly young people (but also some adults) participating in voluntary day-release vocational schemes also steadily increased, but they were located increasingly in FE colleges rather than evening institutes. In 1939, attendance on such courses provided by LEAs or employers numbered only some 42,000. By 1950 this had risen to nearly 250,000 and by 1956 to over 380,000, although this still included only about one in eight of the 15 to 17 age group eligible to attend. There had also been an increase in the number of full-time students attending major establishments from under 30,000 in 1947 to some 53,000 in 1956, and during the same period there was a 30 per cent increase in the number of people attending FE evening classes in subjects related to commerce and industry (*ibid.*: 91, 98; Venables, 1955: 5).

During the 1960s the expansion in LEA adult education accelerated, although it remained somewhat sporadic and uneven. In 1963 Professor Wiltshire identified a greater LEA interest in adult education and a willingness to commit more resources. By the end of the 1960s the LEAs were quite clearly the major providers in terms of the volume of provision and the resources they commanded. During 1968–9 there were reported to be 1,701,070 students aged 18 and over on LEA non-vocational courses in England and Wales, of whom 69 per cent were women and 87 per cent were evening students. The claim that this represented about one in 20 of the adult population was probably an exaggeration because the returns represented enrolments rather than individuals (some of whom almost certainly enrolled on two or more courses). Nevertheless, it did represent 'about six times the number in university extra-mural and WEA classes' and formed 'the largest number of individual students served by any type of post-school education'. And although the amount of money spent by the LEAs on adult education had declined as a proportion of the total local authority education budget (to 1.1 per cent by 1968–9), it had nevertheless increased substantially in absolute terms, to over £16m in net expenditure. This had made it possible to greatly increase the number of adult education staff. In the early 1950s there were very few full-time staff: by 1968–9 there were 1,205 full-time staff (inspectors, organisers, advisers, principals, centre wardens and teachers) in

England and Wales, as well as 1,713 part-time principals and 76,093 part-time teachers. This was the vital factor which had changed the face of LEA adult education (Kelly, 1992: 358–9; Lowe, 1970: 44–5, 51; Wiltshire, 1963: 184; Legge, 1977: 13; O'Hare, 1981: 57; DES, 1973: 28, 204, 207, 209).

## The Russell and Alexander Reports

The Russell Report in 1973 described LEA adult education in England and Wales as very diverse in atmosphere and activity, ranging from little change since before the Second World War, when evening institutes provided continued education for elementary school-leavers, to situations where adult education institutions were major centres of community education and cultural life. Organisational form was similarly varied. In many areas, adult education took place in 'evening institutes', 'FE centres', 'adult education centres' or 'adult institutes' located in day schools and run by full- or part-time adult education principals. Sometimes it was provided by a 'community college' on the Cambridgeshire model. Elsewhere, FE colleges had been given the responsibility for providing adult education in their catchment areas. Most LEA adult education took place on the premises of day schools or FE colleges. The growing use of FE colleges for adult education was leading to a gradual convergence of the non-vocational adult education and vocational further education streams which had become separated after 1944, although this convergence was not altogether apparent in 1973 (ibid.: 29–32; Lowe, 1970: 59–60; Cantor and Roberts, 1983: 276–7).

Despite the diversity, much LEA adult education shared a number of common characteristics: it was primarily concerned with interests and skills relevant to personal as compared to vocational life; the subjects were those with a mainly practical or creative content rather than academic studies; the great majority of classes were not designed to prepare students for examinations leading to recognised qualifications; and most classes took place once a week between September and April. Seven out of eight classes took place in the evening. Although there were local variations, 'in most authorities domestic subjects, physical activities, arts and crafts, music and drama, foreign languages, and practical activities such as woodwork and car maintenance' accounted for about 80–90 per cent of the programme. During the previous 20 years there had been a substantial increase in the number of foreign language courses; a steady development of shorter courses on a specific aspect of a subject; a great increase in the range and complexity of programmes, particularly concerned with outdoor pursuits; and a growth in the provision of academic subjects such as astronomy, psychology, sociology and local studies (thereby increasing the overlap with the 'Responsible Body' programmes). There had also been an important development of induction and in-service training courses for the large number of LEA part-time tutors on which this provision depended (DES, 1973: 28–9, 32).

The Report found continued variation in both the form and effectiveness of LEAs' collaboration with their 'responsible Body' partners. Such collaboration could, but did not necessarily, include consultation and joint planning; the free use of local authority premises; joint publicity; and financial grants, although such grants constituted only 3.3 per cent of LEA adult education expenditure (*ibid.*: 32–3, 209).

The Report did identify some serious weaknesses in the LEAs' activities. Teaching techniques too often lacked 'the skills that enable adults to learn effectively', while teaching was 'sometimes insensitive to the particular needs of adults'. There was an unevenness of standards of achievement; students were not sufficiently challenged; and there was 'inadequacy of provision, particularly of equipment in certain subject areas like modern languages'. As the Report gives no source of evidence for these generalisations it is not possible to evaluate them critically. However, they almost certainly stemmed from HMI reports and reflected some real weaknesses resulting from 'the shortage of professional staff (despite the increase in recent years), the limited provision of training and a failure to develop curriculum studies in this area of education' (*ibid.*: 33). The Report also noted that although LEA classes attracted the whole social and educational range, 'the lower middle class (C1) group' was the most highly represented proportionally, while 'less privileged social groups and those who had a more restricted previous education' were under-represented (*ibid.*: 28), But of course this only reflects a failure that has haunted British adult education for 200 years.

In Scotland, the Alexander Report, published two years after Russell, noted that the 35 County and City education authorities had sole statutory responsibility for securing adequate and efficient provision for voluntary adult education classes and courses, either directly or in co-operation with other agencies such as the extramural departments or the WEA, which might be assisted with grants, or by making accommodation, lecturers or other services available to them at no or reduced cost. It was not anticipated that the transfer of these responsibilities to nine regional and three islands authorities in 1975, under the 1973 Local Government (Scotland) Act, would make any significant difference (Scottish Education Department, 1975: 12).

LEAs directly provided the majority of the Scottish adult education classes, accounting for 87 per cent of the enrolments in 1972–3. Slightly more than half the enrolments in these classes were in physical education, country dancing, handicrafts and hobbies, and 28 per cent, almost entirely women, were in cookery and needlework classes. The remainder were in a broad range of subjects, often overlapping with the provision of the WEA and extramural departments. Overall, including the provision secured from other providers, this adult education was reaching no more than 4 per cent of the adult population in Scotland and, as in England and Wales, they tended to be 'the older, the better-educated and the more affluent. Those to whom adult education should be of most value are least involved' (*ibid.*: 12, 14–15, 104–5).

Most local authority adult education in Scotland took place in evening institutes, adult centres or further education centres, normally housed in schools. The total number of staff solely responsible for adult education was very small. The evening institutes, even the larger ones, were run by part-time heads who were usually day-school teachers. There was also a substantial number of classes run by the youth and community service, and the Alexander Committee could find very little difference between this provision and that of the LEAs. The separation led to a certain amount of duplication and the creation of artificial barriers (*ibid.*: 13).

In England and Wales, the Russell Report encouraged the LEAs to further develop their major role as direct providers, including all the categories of work they had previously covered and also an enlarged range of liberal adult education. They were also recommended to make opportunities for adults to complete their formal general education, and to make more efforts to attract a wider cross-section of the population, including 'those hitherto untouched by adult education'. Although this was encouragement to the LEAs to extend their provision, it did not constitute a major switch of objectives, nor a *carte blanche* for the provision of a 'comprehensive service' as has been suggested (DES, 1973: 58–63; Hughes, 1977: 284). Indeed the LEAs were specifically advised to ensure co-operation and enhance their partnerships with other providing bodies by setting up broadly representative local development councils to facilitate discussion and consultation (DES, 1973: 57-8).

Organisationally, Russell envisaged things continuing very much as before, with LEA adult education based in evening institutes (variously named), community colleges or FE colleges; but the Report did recommend that the LEAs should give greater encouragement to the FE colleges and other educational institutions to contribute to adult education programmes. It also made a number of recommendations concerned with improving accommodation, equipment, facilities, staffing and staff training (*ibid.*: 63–7, 104–38). Its comments on training were quite radical but suffered from 'an indifference to developments at that very time occurring in the whole field of teacher training', including further education, and particularly failed to relate to the 1972 James Report on *Teacher Education and Training* (Foden, 1992: 189).

The Alexander Report's major recommendations for Scotland were that responsibility for adult education should continue to be vested solely with the LEAs, but that it should be regarded as part of a wider youth and community service, overseen by a national Council for Community Education which would advise the Secretary of State and the providing bodies. High priority was to be given to a community approach to adult education; to making it more accessible and relevant; and to meeting the needs of disadvantaged groups (e.g. young mothers, the elderly, those with literacy problems, immigrants, inmates of prisons, the physically and mentally handicapped and those working unsocial hours). Areas of multiple deprivation, minority interests, and Scottish cultural subjects were to receive special attention. The Report also encouraged the development of more correspondence courses and distance learning. Like the Russell Report, Alexander encouraged the use of adult and community centres and further education colleges, rather than children's classrooms, for adult education. Overall, the service was expected to double the number of students within 10 years. In practice, although many of the LEAs responded positively to the recommendations, the Report had relatively little impact. Indeed, the result was a loss of focus on adult education, which was swamped by the youth service, and a decline in participation. Instead of doubling the number of participants, the decade after the publication of the Report saw a marked decline in LEA non-vocational courses in Scotland (Scottish Education Department, 1975: 34–93; Gerver, 1985; and see the more detailed analysis of the Alexander Report in Chapter 5).

## Difficult Times, 1973–88

Although it was not apparent at the time, the picture of LEA adult education in the early 1970s painted by the Russell and Alexander Reports proved to be its twentieth century apogee. The recommendations of both reports were crucially based on assumptions of increased public expenditure on adult education, whereas in practice the opposite happened. In England and Wales, LEAs' net expenditure on adult education as a proportion of their total expenditure continued to fall from the 1.1 per cent noted by Russell for 1968–9 to 0.66 per cent in 1975–6 and 0.4 per cent in 1980–1. By 1980 the national picture was bleak. This of course reflected the deteriorating economic climate following the international oil crisis which coincided with the publication of the Russell Report (see Chapter 1), and the diversion of any available extra funding for adult education to the Open University (see Chapter 11). Nevertheless, few other sectors of public service experienced reductions on this scale (DES, 1973: 209; ACAE, 1981: 16; Small, 1982: 88; O'Hare, 1981: 57). Scottish LEAs appeared somewhat more generous: although they averaged only about two-thirds the *per capita* income, they spent just as much per student on adult education as their English and Welsh counterparts (*ibid.:* 58). But in the context of the decline in numbers in the decade after the Alexander Report, this still represented a fall in overall expenditure.

Despite the unencouraging economic situation, some of the developments recommended or inspired by the reports did occur. In particular, many LEAs laid greater emphasis on special provision for disadvantaged students, however they defined this term. The Inner London Education Authority (ILEA) was outstanding in this respect, although not necessarily because of the Russell Report: its positive promotion of 'second chance' opportunities and courses for the disadvantaged pre-dates the publication of the Russell Report. For example, the Fresh Horizons Course, a forerunner of later Access courses, began at the City Literary Institute in 1966. ILEA adopted a policy of positive discrimination in favour of disadvantaged groups and concentrated on outreach provision for those groups. It also promoted an active campaign against illiteracy and made special provision for people with disabilities (as far as possible integrated into normal classes). By the mid-80s nearly half of ILEA's students had no formal qualifications, and 45 per cent were from black or other ethnic minorities (Groombridge, 1995: 8–11, 16–19; Kelly, 1992: xxvii–xxxii; HMI, 1991: 12).

Many other LEAs increased their commitment to 'the disadvantaged'. For example, Nottinghamshire produced a booklet, *Access for the Unemployed*, which explained what educational provision was available, from basic adult education to higher education. Many of the courses were free (Stephens, 1990: 87). ILEA's Fresh Horizons course was imitated in many parts of the country from the later 1960s onwards in the guise of 'return to study' courses, 'new opportunities for adults' or 'new opportunities for women'. This trend pre-dates the publication of the Russell Report: indeed, the report reflected rather than started the trend, but it did give it impetus. This was given a further boost in 1978, when the DES invited ILEA and a number of other LEAs to provide 'Access to Higher Education' programmes aimed initially at ethnic minorities. These courses very quickly widened their target to include other 'disadvantaged' groups, including women and the unemployed, and rapidly increased in number (see Chapter 3).

Following specific recommendations in the Russell Report, a national Advisory Council for Adult Continuing Education was set up in 1977, (although it was only 'advisory' rather than a 'development' council as recommended by Russell – see Chapter 3); and a number of LEAs established local development councils or modified their existing consultative machinery. But they were still not very effective (Taylor and Warburton, 1981: 43).

Another development in the 1970s, stemming partly from the Russell Report's criticism of the level of tutor training by the LEAs, was an improvement in opportunities for adult education training. An increasing number of universities also began to offer advanced courses in adult education. However, much of this was less a result of Russell or Alexander than a response to the James and Haycocks Reports. The James Report, *Teacher Education and Training* (1972) made a number of important recommendations aimed at improving the in-service training of full-time further education staff, but had little to say about part-time staff. The Government accepted that a higher proportion of full-time staff should receive initial training, and that they should have opportunities for further in-service training. It saw a clear need to encourage polytechnics and some further education colleges to undertake this training, in addition to the four existing colleges of education (technical) (O'Hare, 1981: 62; Foden, 1992: 119–22). A further education sub-committee of the Advisory Committee on the Supply of Training for Teachers (ACSTT) was set up under the chairmanship of Professor Norman Haycocks. In 1975 it produced a report on training full-time teachers in further education. The Haycocks Report (published by the DES in 1977) made 26 recommendations for improving full-time staff training which were greeted less than enthusiastically by the Government and regional advisory councils. Nevertheless, by the 1980s an in-service training system 'actually got into motion and began to make inroads in the backlog of teachers without training' (Foden, 1992: 123–6).

A second, unpublished Haycocks Report (1978) addressed more specifically the training needs of full-time staff in non-vocational adult education. LEAs were encouraged to ensure their continued professional development 'through supervision in the provision of structured opportunities for consultation and exchange of experience'. However, despite some progress, most of the problems remained unresolved. This was because most adult education was taught by very part-time, transient adult educators. In many areas in the late 1980s, the ratio of full-time to part-time staff was as low as 1:300. Most teaching in adult education centres was still undertaken by part-time staff who typically were contracted for two hours per week. It was very difficult to bring them into any satisfactory training scheme. The second Haycocks Report suggested an 'ingenious and simple' system of training for these part-time staff that progressed from induction, through basic pedagogical skills to a third stage comparable with the level of training for full-time staff. But the report singularly failed to address the practical issue of how to persuade part-time staff to take up such training (*ibid.*: 127–30, 175–8; HMI, 1991: 13–4).

This problem was partly tackled by the introduction of LEA training grants which stimulated many LEAs to provide a comprehensive in-service training scheme for full-time staff and some training for part-time staff by the late 1980s, although funding was very varied and often inadequate. The City and Guilds 730 course was the main vehicle for the lower level training. It was not very satisfactory and rarely reflected real needs, although it was substantially restructured and improved during the 1980s (*ibid.*: 14; Foden, 1992: 134, 140-54, 180–1, 192–8).

Towards the end of the 1980s, the HMI concluded that part-time adult educators were still receiving very little academic or curriculum leadership from their full-time colleagues, and a significant minority lacked expertise in teaching adults. Too often they were not encouraged to undertake appropriate training. However, by this time most LEAs had improved the training opportunities for part-time staff, and the participation rate was also improving. At the same time, it was reported that full-time adult education staff were generally well qualified and an increasing number were obtaining diplomas or higher degrees in the education of adults. Nevertheless, most initial and in-service training was still of very variable quality and many of the in-service schemes lacked coherence (HMI, 1991: 13, 15; Stephens, 1990: 88).

What really rendered the general expectation of development which was at the heart of both the Russell and Alexander Reports inoperative was the rapid deterioration in the national economy following the 1973 oil crisis. Instead of the anticipated increase in funding there was a steady decline. As the *Times Higher Education Supplement* reported in June 1977: 'In 1952, adult education faced 10 per cent cuts in government grants. In 1977 there are fears of 100 per cent' (Legge, 1977). This was the first time in the memory of many people that educational expenditure faced an actual cut-back. Their fears were compounded by a DES circular recommending fee increases. A few months later, the *THES* was suggesting that adult education was a threatened service. It reported shorter courses; a reduction in teaching hours; and the adoption by some LEAs of a role of provider of accommodation and some administrative support for an essentially self-financing activity. It all contributed to an 11 per cent decrease in student numbers in a single year. Research at the University of Nottingham similarly identified a real decline in LEA adult education and wondered whether it was doomed. LEA cut-backs to meet government economies were partly to blame, but there was also evidence that some LEAs were wantonly attacking adult education because it was seen as a soft target with little political support. It was less protected than schools education and was regarded as an optional extra: it could be attacked with impunity. Although the 1944 Act required LEAs to secure adequate facilities, there was no satisfactory interpretation of what that meant. This ambiguity enabled LEAs to reduce the service without being challenged in court. In 1979 the Director of NIACE stated that education, particularly adult education, was facing the worst climate in years. Many LEAs were severely cutting back and some were ceasing to provide courses altogether, as in Derbyshire and Humberside. The pattern varied considerably from one LEA to another. Some attempted to keep fees down by reducing the length of courses or by charging different rates for courses considered 'educationally less worthwhile'. Elsewhere it became an acceptable argument that adult students should cover the costs of their education from their own pockets. In some areas, although not everywhere, the result was 'profligate fee increases'. The predictable result was that it was the less well-off students who suffered. While there had been a growing emphasis on work with the disadvantaged, these were the very students who were in danger of being excluded. Thus economic forces, ideology, and perhaps some indifference, were leading adult education in exactly the opposite direction to that recommended by Russell and Alexander: not so much for the disadvantaged or the poor as for those who could afford the ever-increasing fees (*THES*, 17 February 1978; Mee and Wiltshire, 1978, *passim*; Stephens and Lawson, 1979; Mee, 1980: 1–2; O'Hare, 1981: 59; Legge, 1982: 110–11; Evans, 1987: 154-8, 161–2).

The situation was summed up by Stephens and Lawson in an article in *Education* in November 1979:

There appears to be little commitment to adult education by many education committees and they often seem to be pleased at the prospect of shedding their obligations. At best they want a financially self-supporting service and this inevitably means that only the popular and profitable classes will survive. We are in danger of a service which is accessible only to the well-to-do (Stephens and Lawson, 1979).

The ACACE 1979 discussion paper, *Towards Continuing Education*, gave rise to demands that LEAs should be more explicitly obliged to plan a broad range of post-compulsory education, but the new decade did not bring any immediate improvements. In February 1980, *Education* reported that many LEAs were introducing further very steep fee increases and that it was becoming clear that 'the poorer people were falling off and pensioners were cutting down on classes'. The Minister of State, Lady Young, had told the House of Lords that there was no evidence of any deterioration of adult education services. A survey of student enrolments in November 1979 had shown 'only an eight per cent drop overall'. This in itself is strangely incompatible with the claim that there had been 'no deterioration' but, as the article pointed out, these figures concealed 'the very large fall-off in several hard-hit areas and the changes in clientele that have occurred as well as reductions in the range of courses' (*Education*, 15 February 1980).

The national picture in the early 1980s remained gloomy and confused. The ACACE in 1981 considered that the diminished resources and financial cuts experienced by LEA adult education over the past few years seriously threatened the essential fabric of the service. Other commentators felt that the service had 'changed out of recognition in little over half a decade' and by 1981 was the weakest it had been for several years. In some areas the cuts were seen to be fatal, while elsewhere they had created two-tier adult education, consisting of a leisure service for the well-off and a compensation service for the 'conspicuously disadvantaged' (ACACE, 1981: 6, 14–17; Small, 1982: 86–8; Evans, 1987: 154). Yet despite these difficulties, the LEAs still had much to offer: indeed they still catered for two million adult students in more than 100,000 courses in England and Wales each year, providing over 85 per cent of all courses available for adults. But they needed to be both efficient and flexible and to avoid the narrow, functional role being wished on them by the Government (Small, 1982: 91–3; Legge, 1982: 23, 99; McGivney, 1990: 122).

Unfortunately, this functional view was becoming more pervasive, encouraging LEAs to make value judgements about the relative importance of certain forms of adult education, such as vocational updating, basic education and courses for the unemployed and other disadvantaged groups, at the expense of the much broader, liberal curriculum which had emerged during the first three decades after the Second World War. It was at least in part a consequence of central Government policies and priorities. 'The sad effect of current government policies' was that many of the most popular adult education courses were 'being given low priority and (were) being almost priced out of existence in an attempt to make them self-financing'. This was very much the order of the day at the DES: in 1982 Sir Keith Joseph, Secretary of State for Education, argued that adult education should be self-financing or run by commercial organisations. Certainly the DES no longer regarded the LEAs as the most appropriate deliverers of vocational training, which it preferred to see in the hands of the MSC or the private sector. LEA adult education was suffering from a general lack of central Government confidence (Evans, 1987: 155–6; O'Hare, 1981: 60; Small, 1982: 90–1; Elsdon, 1994: 324).

Many of the difficulties did emanate from central Government but, as in the 1970s, some LEAs over-reacted and made disproportionate cuts because there was a lack of political commitment to adult education. When money was scarce they took the easy option and cut this unprotected service. Or they failed to give it their full support - for example over the question of mandatory awards for predominantly adult part-time students in higher education which the LEAs continued to oppose. Or they diverted funds intended for adult education and training to ease their general financial difficulties. This encouraged the Government to transfer 25 per cent of further education funding from the LEAs to the Department of Employment, thereby further weakening the LEAs' already tenuous control of adult education and causing a rapid decline in the quality of courses for the unemployed (Evans, 1987: 159; O'Hare, 1981: 64–5; Elsdon, 1994: 324).

In 1981 the ACACE concluded that there was no single national picture or strategy, largely because of the failure of the 1944 Act to impose specific statutory requirements. There was not one policy but more than 100 separate local policies in England and Wales, and access to adult general education depended increasingly on where people lived and on what they could afford or were willing to pay (ACACE, 1981: 19, 51). A few years later, in 1987–8, the Inspectorate found that the amount spent on general and basic adult education varied widely, from over £10 per head to just a few pence. In the low spending LEAs, fees were expected to cover the main costs. In many areas, the level of funding permitted only a very limited range of activities.

The resultant participation rate varied enormously: while nearly five per cent of the English and Welsh LEAs achieved 110 or more enrolments per 1,000 adult population, 6.7 per cent achieved less than 30 enrolments per 1,000 adults (HMI, 1991: 2–3, 5).

In her survey of non-participation in the late 1980s, Veronica McGivney also identified great variation from one LEA to another, particularly in their policies and practices for attracting social groups who were under-represented in adult education. These ranged from the positive targeting of such groups by ILEA to the complacent recruitment of a narrow, self-perpetuating clientele in some of the shire counties. In many LEAs, provision had largely retained its traditional image and ethos, with limited experimentation and few attempts to widen participation. In some areas efforts were being made to facilitate wider access and provide programmes for special groups, but in general the same students tended to return year after year. The usual mix offered by the majority of LEAs was 'a combination of general education, interest, leisure and qualification-based courses, with some initiatives for specific groups – the unemployed, women, older adults'. Some authorities had gone further, introducing special 'innovation' budgets, new learning units and mobile services (McGivney: 122–3).

Although there was this great variation across the country, the 1980s saw a general strengthening of the market model introduced in the 1970s whereby the individual beneficiaries were expected to pay the bulk if not the full market price for their adult education. At the end of the decade Professor Michael Stephens concluded that:

Efforts to challenge such views have met with varying degrees of success, but overall there has been a notable decline in the State's and local government's subsidy for non-vocational adult education since 1979 ... Underfunded local education authorities have been forced to give priority to their clearly defined mandatory obligations. Adult education classes still mainly use other people's buildings, rely on part-time teaching staff, and face ever-increasing fee levels. There are some more favoured areas of provision, such as classes in literacy and numeracy or those for ethnic minorities, but this is often a matter of modest differences ... (Stephens, 1990: 85, 88).

The deterioration in the LEAs' funding position put an increasing strain on their always fragile partnership with the 'Responsible Bodies' and other voluntary organisations. The climate of growing uncertainty led to greater competition rather than collaboration between providers. Financial support dwindled and there was a growing reluctance to make accommodation and equipment available for classes provided by the LEAs' partners. It appeared that the LEAs did not want them to fill the gaps left by their own decline (ACACE, 1981: 24–7; Evans, 1987: 162–3; Mackenzie, 1989: 3).

At the end of the 1980s, some 70 per cent of students enrolled in LEA adult education centres attended in the evenings, and nearly four-fifths of LEA adult students were women. In general, participation rates tended to be higher where LEAs concentrated their provision in adult education centres rather than through further education colleges, but by this time many colleges were becoming increasingly involved in general adult education as opposed to further education predominantly for young people (HMI, 1991: 3–5, 12; Sargant, 1991: 43).

In the quarter century between the mid-fifties and the early eighties, further education had outgrown its narrow technical and vocational confines. Britain was the only country in Europe which made the distinction between this 'further education' and predominantly non-vocational 'adult education' voluntarily undertaken by people over the age of 18. By the 1980s this distinction was very largely obsolete. Local government reorganisation in 1973 had encouraged local authorities to adopt a less compartmentalised approach generally, while developments in both further and adult education were tending to blur the distinction. LEA adult education had become increasingly 'an integral part of the business of living', and found 'vocational continuing education falling very much within its ambit' once more. Meanwhile, 'further education', reflecting general structural changes in society and particular requirements of government departments and agencies, was likewise becoming 'increasingly concerned with education in the broadest sense. Its remit might more fairly be described as continuing education of all kinds.' This was recognised by the DES in its 'Review of the Legal Basis of Further Education' in 1981, which stressed the need to re-define further education in statute, to include the full spectrum of adult and continuing education. This was the embryo of a policy which was to come to fruition in the Government's White Papers 10 years later (Williams, D., 1973: 348–51; 1977: 165–7; Cantor and Roberts, 1983: 285–6; O'Hare, 1981: 66–7; Shrimpton, 1985: 3–5; Mackenzie, 1989: 6–8).

This awakening of interest in adult education in further education colleges did not mean that it fared any better there than in LEA centres: it also 'suffered severe financial cutbacks in the 1970s and 1980s' (Shrimpton, 1985: 6). There also continued to be considerable barriers to an effective partnership between the further education colleges and LEA adult education services. Apart from the lack of any tradition of working together, the climate of cuts and commercialism tended to breed competitive rather than co-operative attitudes. Indeed, as their missions and practice moved ever closer, there was a greater sense of fear and mistrust. There was also a lack of adequate consultative machinery; no common set of criteria guiding their work; and various staffing problems, such as different pay scales (Mackenzie, 1989: 12). Nevertheless, by the late 1980s the clear distinction that had emerged after 1944 between the LEAs' mainly non-vocational adult education, the 'Responsible Bodies'' concentration on liberal adult education, and the further education institutions' commitment to meeting the vocational needs of adults, was disappearing. The Inspectorate noted these structural changes that had taken place amongst adult education providers, as well as changes in provision reflecting the very different political climate in the 1980s (HMI, 1991: 2, 18). Likewise, in her survey of adult learners in 1990, Naomi Sargant found one of the main differences since the ACACE had undertaken a similar survey in 1982 was the increased awareness of the local further education colleges as providers of adult education – reflecting both the shift to vocational courses and the extending of further education from its traditional 16–19 clientele to the whole adult age-range (Sargant, 1991: 18, 80–2).

## Statutory Changes 1988–92, and Beyond

The Education Reform Act (ERA) which was passed in 1988 echoed its predecessor of 1944 in laying upon LEAs in England and Wales the duty to secure adequate facilities for further education including vocational, social, physical and recreational education for adults. As in 1944, the new Act did not insist that LEAs *provide*, only that they *secure*, adequate provision; it repeated the requirement that the LEAs consult with other bodies and have regard to their provision; but, as in 1944, it failed to define 'adequate'. In all these respects, ERA was very similar to its predecessor and frequently repeated its wording verbatim.

Some LEAs regarded ERA as an opportunity to expand the scope of their adult programmes but others feared it would reduce them, particularly the more highly subsidised provision for disadvantaged groups, because of increased pressures on the education budget as a result of other aspects of the Act. The DES attempted to allay these fears by issuing a circular emphasising the need for LEAs to take account of the need to secure an appropriate range of opportunities for adults who may have disadvantages, but this exhortation was not backed by any resources or protection for adult education budgets. Moreover, ERA had introduced crude numerical performance indicators which militated against experimentation and innovation (Field, 1988: 18; McGivney, 1990: 134–5; Stephens, 1990: 82–3). And in one very important respect – the abolition of ILEA, which had maintained its radical policies until the end – ERA fatally undermined what was undoubtedly the most successful model of adult education for disadvantaged groups in the country (Payne, nd, *passim*; *THES*, 30 March 1990: 10).

As previously mentioned, the DES had for some years wanted to break down the non-statutory but traditional boundary between adult and further education. This was done by defining further education in ERA as including part-time and non-vocational education and the education of adults, thus returning to the *de jure* position of 1944 rather than the *de facto* situation which had arisen in the years after the Second World War. This strengthened the position of further education colleges as providers of adult education, in competition with their LEA. The powers of the LEAs to plan and control, or even secure, adequate adult education were further reduced by the right of schools to opt out of LEA control, and the provision in the Act for school governing bodies to control school premises outside normal school hours. As a result of ERA, both colleges and schools were in a position to compete with their LEA as provider, and inhibit its use of premises for adult education. The Act thus significantly contributed to the fragmentation of local planning and delivery of adult education and encouraged competition rather than collaboration. At the same time, it had a centralising aspect, giving the Secretary of State control over a number of key features of the new infrastructure, including all delegation schemes and governing bodies (Field, 1988: 17; McGivney, 1990: 135).

The changes introduced by ERA were given little opportunity to have any significant effect before the Government heralded more radical changes in two White Papers published in 1991, *Education and Training for the 21st Century* by the DES, covering England and Wales, and *Access and*

*Opportunity: A strategy for education and training* by the Scottish Office. The English and Welsh paper laid out the Government's intention to create new Further Education Funding Councils which would fund further education colleges directly, thus freeing them from LEA control. The LEAs were to be left with much reduced residual powers and responsibilities. The Scottish White Paper focused on improved vocational training for 16–18-year-olds, but it similarly promised independent legal status for the 46 Scottish further education colleges.

The 1992 Further and Higher Education Act duly established the two Further Education Funding Councils for England and Wales with a statutory responsibility for securing sufficient full-time further education for the 16–19 age group and adequate facilities for certain specified part- and full-time further education for those over 18. This adult education, which was unequivocally removed from the LEAs to the new further education sector, was laid out in Schedule 2 of the Act:

- (a) a course which prepares students to obtain a vocational qualification ...;

- (b) a course which prepares students to qualify for (i) the General Certificate of Secondary Education, or (ii) the General Certificate of Education at Advanced Level ...;

- (c) a course ... which prepares students for entry to a course of higher education;

- (d) a course which prepares students for entry to another course falling within paragraphs (a) to (c) above;

- (e) a course for basic literacy in English;

- (f) a course to improve the knowledge of English for those for whom English is not the language spoken at home;

- (g) a course to teach the basic principles of mathematics;

- (h) in relation to Wales, a course for proficiency or literacy in Welsh;

- (j) a course to teach independent living and communication skills to persons having learning difficulties which prepares them for entry to another course falling within paragraphs (d) to (h) above.

All but the last had appeared, in slightly different form, in the White Paper. The last category was added to the Bill at Committee stage as a result of lobbying.

For the first time in legislation, the 1992 Act attempted to define 'adequacy'. The new Funding Councils were expected to 'secure that facilities are provided at such places, are of such character and are so equipped as to meet ... reasonable need for education ...,' and 'take account of the different abilities and aptitudes of persons among (the) population'. The definition still contained the ubiquitous term 'reasonable' but government ministers did stress that they expected the Funding Councils and colleges to ensure that provision was accessible to all local communities.

'My vision is ... of colleges making "accessible" provision in a variety of convenient locations – on campus and off campus – and making full use of provision under contract from other providers serving local communities' (Powell, 1992a: 14). However, other parts of the Act, which redoubled the financial responsibilities of the colleges, militated against this 'vision' of adequacy by rendering it imprudent for colleges to engage in too much high-risk provision in sparsely-populated communities away from the campus.

Not surprisingly, this new corpus of adult education subsequently became known as 'Schedule 2 work'. Its rationale was explained at the time by a series of government ministers and spokespersons: it would provide a 'tree of progression' for adults that would take them from basic skills to higher level qualifications; it would be secured at national level, not at the whim of local authorities, so that it would be accessible to all adults, wherever they lived; and it encapsulated the courses which the Government considered to be of national economic and educational priority (Powell, 1992b: 26). The significant factors were that this 'Schedule 2 work' was unambiguously oriented towards the acquisition of skills and qualifications; it was clearly aimed at meeting certain national priorities; and the LEAs were considered unfitted to secure this provision. The responsibility was removed from them to a newly defined, separately funded further education sector.

The LEAs were left with the statutory duty to meet other priorities which were not national, but 'best decided and delivered at a local level.' These consisted of the residue of public sector adult education – the recreational, social and leisure provision. The LEAs continued to receive central Government funding for this work under the 'standard spending assessment', but these funds were not earmarked for adult education. The Government took the view that it was up to LEAs to decide how best to use their assessment. For this reason, and also because the LEAs had lost much of their vocational work which had previously offered an opportunity to cross-subsidise other adult education, this residual provision was even more vulnerable than before (Powell, 1992a: 21–2; 1992b: 26–7).

Under the 1992 Act the LEAs lost the strategic planning function they had had since 1944. The Funding Councils inherited this role for 'Schedule 2 work' but the overall planning and co-ordination of all adult education, including the partnership with voluntary and other bodies, was seriously undermined. It became much more liable to fragmentation. Indeed, the Act was designed to promote competition rather than collaboration. The further education colleges were encouraged to take on non-Schedule 2 adult education if they could make it pay, while the LEAs were empowered, but not funded, to undertake 'Schedule 2 work'. They were now set in open competition with each other, with the assumption that this competition would eliminate waste and inefficiency (those twin vices which Conservative Governments had long ascribed to local government). But the dice were very firmly loaded in favour of the further education sector. LEA adult education faced an uphill struggle for survival.

The other consequence of the 1992 Act was that it resurrected in a new form the old division between vocational and non-vocational – now dubbed 'Schedule 2' and 'non-Schedule 2'. This was despite a loud public outcry against this anachronism between the publication of the White Papers and the passing of the Act.

There were widespread fears expressed in a debate in the House of Lords in February 1993 that the LEAs' 'non-Schedule 2' provision was at risk because of inadequate government funding and the failure to ring-fence the adult education funds which were allegedly being diverted to schools and social services. The LEA services were said to be significantly declining, and there were indications of increased fees, shorter terms and redundancies of adult education teachers throughout the country. In reply, the Minister of State, Baroness Blatch, clearly reaffirmed the priority being given to the further education sector and 'Schedule 2', but claimed that the LEAs retained 'their duty to secure the provision of all kinds of further education for adults which do not come within the funding councils' duties'. She also confirmed that the Government did not regard it as its duty to 'tell local authorities what they must spend on their remaining responsibilities for adults. That is for them to decide in the light of local circumstances' (*Hansard*, 23 February 1993, 179, 181–2, 190–2, 203–8).

A national survey carried out a month or so later by the National Association of Teachers in Further and Higher Education and answered by 78 per cent of the LEAs in England and Wales, reinforced the fears expressed in the House of Lords that the effect of the 1992 Act, plus the *laissez-faire* attitude of the Government to LEA use (or misuse) of their standard spending assessments, was endangering the future of LEA adult education. Most LEAs continued to maintain a distinct adult education service but adult education budgets were being cut in real terms in the majority of LEAs. Over a fifth of the LEAs responding to the survey had cut their 1992–3 adult education budget by 50 per cent or more. There was a clear trend towards consolidating adult education onto fewer sites; higher priority was being given to providing progression routes into 'Schedule 2 work' and there was a growing trend towards accrediting adult education courses (to qualify for Schedule 2 funding); fees were increasing faster than the rate of inflation; concessionary fees were becoming less widespread and less generous; full-time adult education posts were being reduced and the adult education services were becoming more dependent on part-time teaching staff (NATFHE, 1993: 1–2, 24–42; *THES*, 25 June 1993). At the same time, the funding methodology in the new further education sector was militating against part-time provision in the further education colleges (*THES*, 11 June 1993).

Another survey carried out for NIACE in 1994 highlighted the continuing decline in LEA adult education services, which it found 'had been hit by dramatic cuts in many parts of the country because of pressures on local government finance and an increasing national emphasis on courses leading to qualifications' (NIACE, 1994: 1). Even tighter expenditure settlements for local authorities at the end of 1994 meant further depressing news for adult educators. While resourcing for FEFC-funded Schedule 2 work carried out by the LEAs and other non-FE college institutions had increased by 20 per cent between 1993–4 and 1994–5, the funds available for

LEA non-vocational adult education and other non-statutory expenditure, such as discretionary awards, continued to decline. Many LEAs made further swingeing cuts in their funding for adult education in 1995–6, and 1996–7 promised to be worse. The prospect of becoming little more than a franchising agent for the FEFC in their adult work was facing an increasing number of LEAs (*THES*, 10 March and 14 April 1995; *Adults Learning*, March 1995: 198).

*Commentary* in the NIACE journal made the situation all too clear:

Year in, year out, over the last decade local authorities have been squeezed into ever tighter expenditure limits, and year in, year out, this has led to LEAs cutting back on the small number of areas of expenditure over which they have discretion. As a result, there are each year horror stories about the collapse of youth or adult services. A similar pattern was evident in the 1970s and early 1980s, but then a bad year tended to be followed by a number of years in which the services to learners gradually improved. The difference now is that a bad year tends to be followed by a worse one (*Adults Learning*, January 1995: 138).

What was happening was that changes in the balance of provision and funding mechanisms had actually increased opportunities for some categories of student who wanted FEFC-funded Schedule 2-type courses, while excluding other groups who did not want certification and progression – particularly older learners and many women (*Adults Learning*, March 1995: 198).

The Conservative Government's poll tax fiasco of the 1980s and their rate-capping policy, combined with the 1988 and 1992 Education Acts, had led to an apparently permanent leeching of resources for LEA adult education. At the same time, as part of the same process, the system of democratic control and capacity to reach out to the whole community and respond to its needs, which the LEAs had built up, however imperfectly, over the previous 90 years, had been ruthlessly undermined. The result was a crude emphasis on narrowly conceived vocational training and a diminution of some of the best aspects of British adult education, such as its flexibility and variety; aspects of second-chance education and role education (including political education and citizenship); and adult education for personal fulfilment. The last, which contributed fundamentally to the 'spiritual and moral, the aesthetic and psychological health of a nation' used to be one of the major strengths of British adult education, but it had become 'fiercely curtailed'. It was accessible only to the well-off or the 'conspicuously deprived' who were eligible for concessionary rates. 'The majority of the population falls between these groups and has disappeared from adult education' (Elsdon, 1994: 325–7).

It is true that some of the abandoned LEA activities were taken up by other agencies including further education colleges, schools, other educational institutions and voluntary bodies (see Chapter 12); and it has been suggested that the LEAs should concentrate on becoming 'local support for lifelong learning services', providing neutral information, advice and guidance to these other providers (Foster, 1992: 10). This may happen, but there is no sign of it yet, and little likelihood of such a development without adequate resourcing.

5

# Community Education: The Dialectics of Development

## Ian Martin

The literature of community education tends to be both ahistorical and partial. Community education is treated as a free-floating and timeless concept and is often related to a single institutional form, e.g. community schooling. The argument presented in this chapter is that the history of community education describes no simple or linear chronology. In its relation to education, 'community' should be viewed as an ideological construct which is both historically and contextually specific. 'Community education' therefore only makes sense if it is located historically and situated in relation to state policy in a systematic and discriminating way. Analysis is therefore directed towards the dynamics of the tensions and contradictions that are generated both between and within policy and practice. It is here that the dialectics of development in community education are to be found and that the deeply ambivalent nature of the idea of community, with its radical and reactionary connotations, can best be exposed and explored. Particular attention is paid to the role of the state, both national and local, as it has sought to adapt education policy and practice to changing material and ideological conditions. As Baron (1989) rightly emphasises, what needs to be examined to make sense of the history of community education interventions is 'the use of community at times, and in places, of structural change and at times of change within the state itself' (pp 97–8).

The force of this chapter is therefore to draw attention to the continuous struggle for control over the meaning of community education in relation to adult education as it has evolved through distinctive phases of formal education policy, on the one hand, and through the informal politics of practice, on the other. As Brian Simon (1985) argues, education policy and practice are always the site of contention and struggle, and the unintended outcomes of policy may be as significant as its intended outcomes:

The historical record clearly shows that there is nothing inevitable about educational advance. Far from progress being linear, advances are more often met by setbacks, by new crises, by ideological and political struggles of all kinds (p 52).

This argument is elaborated by focusing on key stages in the development of community education and the dialectics of policy and practice characteristic of each of these.

It should be emphasised at the outset that the focus of this account is restricted to the adult education dimension of community education. Other aspects, such as the compulsory schooling stage or youth work, are only considered in so far as they impinge on this.

## The Community School and College Movement

Our greatest need is for the elaboration of a communal system of education (Henry Morris, quoted Ree, 1973: 87).

The origins of the British community school and college movement are usually attributed to Henry Morris and the development of the first 'village colleges' in Cambridgeshire in the 1920s and 1930s. The claims of this orthodoxy represent not only an over-estimation of the significance of Morris in relation to subsequent developments but also an under-estimation of his distinctive achievement. In the post-war period the spread of community schools and community colleges was primarily a response to a new policy context, although it is certainly true that some of Morris's ideas influenced the pattern of development. Orthodox accounts of this movement (e.g. Ree, 1973, 1984; Poster, 1971, 1982), on the other hand, simply do not do justice to Morris's calculated and creative reading of and response to the specific and concrete conditions in Cambridgeshire in the inter-war period. The village college was, above all, the product of a 'situated rationale' (Baron, 1989: 91).

Henry Morris was the Chief Education Officer of Cambridgeshire from 1922 to 1954. Throughout this period he consistently used the idea of the 'village college' to sponsor a particular, if idiosyncratic, vision of what a rural community should be and how education might relate to it. This proved to be a long struggle: the first village college was opened at Sawston in 1930 and a fifth had been established by the time of Morris's retirement (Poster, 1982).

To understand Morris's achievement, as well as its inherent limitations, it is necessary to clarify the socio-economic and political context of his early work in Cambridgeshire in the 1920s and 1930s and to locate schooling within this. Morris confronted a situation in which he believed the rural way of life to be dying and the traditional culture of communities disintegrating. The rural economy had become impoverished and offered few opportunities for employment. Local people, especially the young and ablest, were drifting to the urban areas in search of work and entertainment, leaving the countryside depopulated and in danger of becoming, in Morris's view, degenerate.

Moreover, there was an acute crisis of local leadership. Both the squire and the parson had become the vestigial and anachronistic authority figures of another era, incapable of grasping the challenges of change. This left a critical vacuum of leadership in the countryside which Morris feared would be filled by the commercial interests of urban-based capital, sounding the death knell of rural culture as a distinctive way of life. In this respect, it is worth noting that Morris always considered the 'passive amusements' of commercialised leisure to be decadent and dehumanising. This connects with a strong and consistent strain of anti-urbanism in his thinking and his conviction that state policy was preoccupied with urban issues: 'The immense development of the State system of education in England during the nineteenth and present centuries has been almost wholly an urban development' (Ree, 1973: 144). At the same time, he was convinced that rural problems called for rural solutions.

The education provided for the vast majority of local children took place in very basic, all-age elementary schools, most of which still remained under church control, offering an extremely limited curriculum. The development of a better resourced and more coherent system of primary and secondary education, however, was frustrated by continuing rivalry between the main providers, the church and the state. His commitment to the extension of public sector education meant that Morris had to fight a long battle with the local church authorities to gain overall control.

Morris's distinctive vision and prescription were spelt out in his famous 1924 memorandum *The Village College: Being a memorandum on the provision of educational and social facilities for the countryside, with special reference to Cambridgeshire* (see Ree, 1973: 143–57). Despite its ponderous title, this was a bold and detailed statement which called for an extension of public sector education in Cambridgeshire to form a unified system of junior and secondary schools and for the establishment of a radically new institution for the countryside in the form of the 'village college'.

It should be emphasised that Morris's idealism was rooted in a hard-headed pragmatism. The village college was to be a practical way of exploiting the economies of scale in order to provide a range of co-ordinated and accessible public services to a poor and widely dispersed rural population. Unlike the Danish Folk High Schools, the village colleges were intended to be essentially local institutions. This pragmatism also included a clear reading of the wider context: the emerging demand for a general extension of secondary education, evidenced by the publication of Tawney's *Secondary Education for All* in 1924 and the 1926 Hadow Report on *The Education of the Adolescent*, as well as the 1919 Report of the Adult Education Committee which had made a forceful case for the expansion of liberal adult education.

The village college, he proposed, should become the focal point for communal regeneration: an holistic institution, integrating educational, social, cultural and recreational activity in 'a new institution, single but many-sided, for the countryside' (Ree, 1973: 147). This would provide an alternative set of interlocking structures and relationships to sustain, invigorate and enrich learning and living in the rural areas.

Morris believed that education should be open, inclusive and integrative. Not only did he never tire of criticising the 'insulated school', he was also an early advocate of both lifelong education and deschooling:

The first need is that we should reconstruct our conception of education and the system by which it is to be realized so that it will be coterminous with life. Education should be the impulse and method by which the community in all directions realizes the best life for itself. At the present moment our state system is concerned almost wholly with children and the teachers of children. We ought to see our way to the organic provision of education for the whole adult community. ... We must institutionalize our places of education so that they become centres of corporate life and not congeries of classrooms for discourse and instruction (Ree, 1984: 38–9)

The village college was therefore conceived as a new kind of educational, cultural and social institution for the countryside that would provide a catalyst for communal regeneration. What was envisaged was an all-age, multi-purpose centre designed to serve the educational, social and cultural needs of all age groups. The village college would therefore form the hub of

all the various vital but isolated activities in village life – the School, the Village Hall and Reading Room, the Evening Classes, the Agricultural Education Courses, the Women's Institute, the British Legion, Boy Scouts and Girl Guides, the recreation ground, the branch of the County Rural Library, the Athletics and Recreation Clubs (Ree, 1973: 154).

Fundamentally, the ideal of the village college was an expression of Morris's own idiosyncratic vision of community and his prescription for filling the vacuum of leadership left in 'our squireless villages'. The village college would, in effect, sponsor a particular vision of communal life:

A building that will express the spirit of the English countryside which it is intended to grace, something of its humaneness and modesty, something of the age-long and permanent dignity of husbandry; a building that will give the countryside a centre of reference arousing affection and loyalty of the country child and country people, and conferring significance on their way of life (Ree 1973: 153).

As already noted, it was a long and hard-fought struggle to convert this vision into reality, all but two of Cambridgeshire's village colleges being completed after the 1944 Education Act introduced compulsory secondary schooling. Without this legislation, it remains doubtful whether Morris's ideas would subsequently have been pursued in Cambridgeshire, let alone taken up and extensively developed in the community colleges of Leicestershire, Devon and Cumberland in the post-war period. Indeed, Jeffs (1992) suggests that, but for the Butler Act in particular and the post-war welfare settlement in general, Morris's village colleges 'might have remained no more than fondly recalled educational Brabazons' (p 22).

Morris's strategy, therefore, was to use the growing demand for universal secondary schooling as an opportunity to propose a radical and ambitious redefinition of the meaning of education and its social purpose in a particular economic and cultural context. He was in many ways a radical and imaginative thinker who succeeded in extending the role of the local state as the main provider not only of schooling but also of adult education at a crucial stage in the evolution of a national system of public education. Moreover, he incorporated into this struggle a unique attempt to reconnect education with his own reading of the current of community life. In this sense, he was a popular educator: his interest was in the well-being of communities and his proposals firmly located in a systematic, if eccentric, analysis of their needs.

On the other hand, Morris was also a paternalist. He knew what was good for local people – as, no doubt, the significantly named 'Wardens' of his village colleges were expected to. This paternalism was at the heart of the ultimately rather blinkered notion of community he sought to sponsor. The emphasis on 'nostalgic organicism' and his celebration of 'folk ways' (Baron,

1988: 94) were essentially backward rather than forward looking. Fundamentally, Morris attempted to use education to sponsor a vision of community in which the value placed upon organic relations and social consensus belied the underlying differences in power and conflicts of interest within rural society.

This blurring of issues of power, interest and difference was carried over into the subsequent development of community colleges and community schools influenced by the village college model:

The concept of community, consensual in nature and, therefore, capable of being promoted by a single institution, is reflected in the vocabulary of many of the early writers who saw schools, particularly the village colleges, as replacing the churches as centres of community cohesion, enshrining the shared values of, and exercising a benevolent influence over, an assumedly homogeneous community (Wallis and Mee, 1983: 13).

This may help to explain Morris's antipathy to the WEA and the more radical of its allies in the university adult education movement. These perceived advocates of class struggle, based in urban areas, represented in his view the very antithesis of the supposedly organic and consensual social relations of the countryside.

In the post-war period the spread of the community school and community college movement is largely explained by both the opportunities and constraints presented by the developing policy context. In this respect, it is worth emphasising how Morris sought to fill the vacuum created by the absence of state policy in the inter-war period. The post-war years, in contrast, were increasingly characterised by 'top-down', policy-led initiatives. State policy was driven by both social and educational purposes as well as, increasingly, the pressure to combine development and expansion with economy. The transposition of the community school and community college idea from rural to suburban, urban and, eventually, inner city areas was therefore the product of both political commitment and pragmatic considerations. It is important to qualify the 'great men' tradition in the literature of the community school and community college movement by emphasising that it was in this context that several forceful and dynamic Directors of Education and headteachers were able to pursue their own versions of the educational sponsorship of community.

The 1944 Education Act's proposal to establish 'county colleges' to provide part-time education and develop leisure and recreation provision for young people not in full-time education (see Chapter 4) created an opportunity to extend some elements of Morris's thinking to the post-war context. Although the county college idea was not subsequently pursued by central government, it did encourage LEAs like Leicestershire, Devon and Cumberland to plan the first phase of post-war community college development. As far as adult education in particular was concerned, this was a chance for LEAs to catch up with the 'responsible bodies' as providers of non-vocational adult education, an area in which they had remained weak, as was pointed out in the 1954 Ashby Report on *The Organisation and Finance of Adult Education in England and Wales*. It is worth noting that London was slow to develop this holistic model of community education – largely because London County Council had been unique among local authorities in the inter-war period in developing an extensive range of specialist services in both adult education and youth work, perhaps recognising the limitations of consensual approaches in cosmopolitan areas with shifting populations (*ibid.*).

The need to combine a rapid expansion of secondary school provision with economy created a strong practical case for the extended use of school buildings to provide additional services and facilities for the wider public. In 1955, for example, the Department of Education responded to increasing public demand for adult education by providing a small but significant financial incentive for schools to be used as adult education evening institutes. Similarly, in response to the recommendations of the 1960 Albermarle Report to expand youth service provision, central government funding was made available for the building of youth wings on school sites to accommodate statutory and voluntary sector youth work. At the same time, joint use of school premises and the development of dual purpose facilities were further encouraged.

Some LEAs, Leicestershire in particular, took advantage of the post-war policy context to plan systematically to combine a commitment to comprehensive education with the development of school-based provision of adult education and youth work. Generally, however, this pattern of development was slower and more incremental elsewhere until the wider, national trend towards comprehensivisation gathered pace in the 1960s and 1970s. At a practical level, comprehensivisation required the development of bigger schools at a time of increasing economic stringency. This, in effect, created a strong case for rationalisation and co-ordinated planning in order to make the most of the economies of scale. Thus, for example, the government responded to the 1960 Wolfenden Report's recommendation for the general expansion of public sports and leisure provision by encouraging LEAs and District Councils to develop shared facilities on secondary school sites.

As they implemented comprehensive reform in the 1960s amd 1970s and were themselves reorganised in 1974, many local authorities came to regard the development of 'community provision' on school sites as a practical and cost-effective measure. Joint funding and shared use were explicitly advocated in the Department of Education Circular 2/70 *A Chance to Share: Co-operation in the provision of facilities for educational establishments and the community*. This encouraged LEAs to respond to the growing demand for adult education, youth work and recreational provision by collaborating with District Councils and the voluntary sector to ensure 'a *variety* of community facilities when building new schools or making additions to existing ones' (Jones, 1978: 9). The circular went on to suggest how such potential economies of scale could lead to multiple service provision on school sites.

It is important, therefore, to recognise the economic, and essentially pragmatic, element in the rationale for post-war community school and community college development. In some cases, this model of community education was as much the product of the need to combine expansion with economy as any kind of progressive educational vision or socially redistributive intent. On the other hand, the significance of the latter should not be under-estimated, especially in those authorities most committed to comprehensivisation, where integrated provision for the 'whole community' came to be seen as the logical expression of the comprehensive principle. For example, Henry Swain, the Nottingham County Council Architect responsible for the design of the Sutton Centre (see Fletcher, 1984), suggested in his address to the Royal Institute of British Architects in 1968 that the logic of comprehensive education was expressed in a universalistic notion of community education:

There are signs that a radical new concept for the comprehensive school is emerging generally which demands a building designed deliberately for use by the community (Poster, 1971: 106).

Coventry, under the leadership of Robert Aitken, represented perhaps the clearest example of the commitment to comprehensive education being interpreted in terms of an integrated, all-age community education service which would 'bring together individuals, families, statutory and voluntary organisations in its area ... to think and act for the common good' (Poster, 1982: 62).

In the post-war period, then, the community school and college movement progressively spread from rural and suburban areas to urban areas, the New Towns and eventually the inner cities. The most systematic and comprehensive development of the community college idea took place in Leicestershire. In this respect, it is significant that Leicestershire was the first authority to commit itself to comprehensive reform and to pioneer the delegation of financial control to College Councils (see Fairbairn, 1979). The 1949 Leicestershire Scheme for Further Education and Plan for County Colleges was the pre-eminent example of the integrated community college becoming the basis for LEA policy development. It represented a self-conscious attempt to apply Morris's ideas to urban and suburban areas and, in the process, sought to develop 'a model to show how the front-line institutions of a mass, comprehensive local education service might come into being' (Flude and Parrot, 1979: 134). The main thrust under the leadership of both Stewart Mason and his successor Andrew Fairbairn was for the development of community colleges around comprehensive secondary schools, but similar forms of integrated provision were subsequently encouraged in both further education colleges and primary schools. Development took the form of both ambitious *carte blanche* schemes as well as more modest, incremental change.

Similar, if somewhat less ambitious, developments took place in Devon and Cumbria, which represent the most striking early examples of secondary school-based community education in predominantly rural areas. Devon committed itself strongly to an integrated model in which generic 'community tutors' were employed as members of the school staff with combined responsibilities for youth work, adult education and classroom teaching. Cumbria, a relatively poor and sparsely populated county, on the other hand, moved more slowly from dual use of school buildings to planned integration based on co-operation between County and District councils.

New Towns such as Peterborough, Telford and Milton Keynes, the sites of ambitious social engineering projects, boasted their own distinctive versions of the integrated community education campus or complex built around the school as the intended focal point for the educational sponsorship of a consensual vision of community. In this respect, it is significant that Henry Morris was appointed as a part-time consultant to the New Towns Commission in 1946, his opinionated and autocratic style doing nothing to endear him to his fellow commissioners (Poster, 1982: 39).

Eventually, the community school and college movement spread to some inner city areas, where it represented the most ambitious evidence of reformist state intervention, a theme taken up in the next section of this chapter. In some inner city areas, community college complexes on a grand scale played a part in the local and national state's attempts to address the effects of economic decline and 'multiple deprivation'. As such, these grandiose, if futile, initiatives in social engineering aimed in a more or less self-conscious way to echo Henry Morris's concern to regenerate social coherence and a shared sense of identity in areas where they were notable for their absence.

Any attempt to assess the efficacy of the community school and college movement from an adult education perspective immediately comes up against the problem that there is little disinterested research or systematic evaluation to call upon. Characteristically, the mainstream literature is descriptive, rhetorical and anecdotal, often presented in the form of case material which makes little distinction between aims, claims and performance. As Jeffs (1983) notes, the case tends to be made 'by the careful, often skilful, use of case study, guided tour and anecdote' (p 12).

Stock describes 'community education' as 'a useful integrating principle' (Jennings, 1980: 9), and goes on to quote, apparently with approval, from a memo by Stewart Mason, Director of Education in Leicestershire, presented to his Education Committee in April 1949: 'Here the approach was essentially one of *integrating* facilities and resources, of decompartmentalizing much of the public offer of educational, social and cultural provision'. However, Jennings notes that there is no reliable research evidence for the kind of claims that are typically made by these institutions, i.e. that they offer a wider range of provision to a greater variety of people and a 'balanced neighbourhood programme' that is relevant to the locality, or that they promote participation by 'the whole community' (p 46).

The point is that the principles of integration and continuity that inform this pattern of institutional development make any assessment of its costs and benefits, in relation to adult education in particular, difficult precisely because, as Mee and Wiltshire (1978) put it:

Their claim is that education is a continuous and lifelong process, and that it should not be artificially divided into separate sectors or stages. Instead, it should be conceived as a totality and administered through institutions which provide for the whole range of educational needs from childhood through adolescence to adulthood and old age. Adult education therefore ceases to exist as a separate entity with separate institutions; it is replaced by community education which is addressed to all age groups and all sectors in the population (pp 14–5).

Such consensual and universalistic rhetoric all too easily leads to hyperbole – for example, the suggestion of Flude and Parrot (1979) that these institutions represent the seedbed for a fully fledged 'recurrent education system' in Britain.

One of the difficulties, therefore, in reaching a realistic assessment is the ambitiousness and vagueness of the claims sometimes made for the community college approach. In view of this, it is worth noting that in straightforwardly organisational terms the provision of adult education within a school context is intrinsically problematic. Again, as Mee and Wiltshire (1978) point out,

As a host institution for adult education the school seems to have certain inbuilt disadvantages:
(a) There is a wide gap between school and adult students.
(b) School education is compulsory and full-time, adult education is voluntary and part-time; there are wide organisational and attitudinal differences between the two services.
(c) The school tradition tends to be one of central control rather than departmental independence.
(d) The school-youth-adult integration excludes Further and Higher Education, the very sectors of education with which adult education is likely to have most in common (p 109).

There is also the problem of whether like is being compared with like. Baron (1988), for example, distinguishes between 'organic' and 'implanted' patterns of institutional development and argues that huge inner city community complexes like the Abraham Moss Centre in Manchester, for instance, have no more than a superficial resemblance to the original idea of Morris's village colleges. Economies of scale can mean very large institutions indeed. Fletcher (1984) warns that 'the greatest hidden pressure ... [is] to become a hypermarket of corporate life' (p 315). The danger is that sheer size impedes the articulation of the institution with any identifiable community. In other words, economics impedes social purpose.

In attempting to assess the efficacy of the community school and college model of community education in terms of its implications for adult education, therefore, a general caveat should be entered that its effectiveness is likely to vary in proportion to the size of the institution and scope of the claims it makes. In this respect, the limited and predominantly school-focused claims of the more modest community school approach tend to be easier to sustain (although less relevant to adult education) than the characteristically holistic aims and grandiose claims of the more ambitious community colleges.

McCloy reviewed the provision of adult education in village colleges (Jones, 1978: 16–17). His research indicated 'minimal' provision of adult day-time further education, lack of local (i.e. catchment area) use of college facilities, and reactive rather than proactive forms of provision with very little sustained attempt at local 'needs assessment', outreach or networking. In addition, there was a uniformly low rate of adult user involvement in decison-making, allied to a tendency for school governing bodies to see the school's interest as both separate and dominant. These rather negative conclusions are generally confirmed in other accounts (e.g. Jennings, 1980; Titmuss, 1981; Wallis and Mee, 1983). In particular, there is evidence that the adult education role and responsibilities of the generic 'community tutor' are constantly diverted and diluted by competing institutional demands. The community tutor's role is weakest in precisely those aspects which are least reinforcing of the mainstream school concerns.

The general implication of Wallis and Mee's research, therefore, is that the rationale of school-based community education is primarily pragmatic, reflecting the 'ubiquity' of the school as a public institution rather than its suitability for the extended role conferred upon it by the community college concept. Their overall assessment is blunt: 'adult education on the cheap' (p 8). Indeed, several studies suggest that the economies of scale intended in large-scale, multi-purpose complexes of this kind encourage a process of retrospective rationalisation by means of which social and educational objectives are identified after economic objectives have been achieved.

Moreover, the sheer size of the larger community colleges and the logic of the economies of scale built into them can encourage a socially regressive definition of community in terms of a community of consumption, i.e. those who can afford to use their facilities and are sufficiently motivated and confident to do so. Even Andrew Fairbairn (1979), one of the most ardent advocates of the community college, quotes research on the Leicestershire colleges which showed that adult participants 'come from educationally and occupationally favoured groups', and he therefore goes on to argue for a supplementary 'network of more local provision' (pp 63–4).

The complexities of managing such large institutions, sometimes funded by several departments, seem to lead to persistent and intractable problems in terms of efficiency, accountability and equity. Consequently, as already noted, the literature on community colleges tends to be preoccupied with the debate about different models of management. In short, unitary management under the headteacher skews power decisively towards the school interest; joint management structures, on the other hand, can become extremely complicated. Responsibility for the Abraham Moss Centre in Manchester, for instance, was originally shared between the local departments of Education, Recreation and Social and Cultural Services (Poster, 1982: 61).

Given the lack of systematic evidence, it is difficult to offer firm conclusions about the efficacy of this model of community education as an agent of adult education. In general, however, research suggests that at best the case remains not proven. Titmuss (1981) goes further, stating that there is 'cause for doubt'. Perhaps the most consistent and striking feature of the case that is made for this approach is that its benefits are mainly judged in terms of what the internal school community has to gain from closer association with the wider external community. Given the characteristically hierarchical nature of British schooling and the power of the headteacher, the partnership is never equal and the statutory priorities of the school inevitably tend to become dominant, especially when the priorities are judged primarily in terms of cost-efficiency.

In institutional terms, the school is an intrinsically problematic base for adult education because its power relations are inevitably so unequal. In ideological terms, the democratic ethos of adult education does not fit well with the authoritarian culture and hierarchical structure of British schooling. The outcome for adult education can be very precarious. Not surprisingly, therefore, one of the few research-based accounts of community colleges which focuses specifically on their work in adult education concludes:

The present difficulties of sharing and of attitudes to adult education in multi-purpose institutions must raise serious doubts about their stated advantages both in terms of the resources available and of their effective use. ... adult education is still too often the unwelcome borrower of other people's premises or alternatively the unequal partner in a sharing situation (Mee and Wiltshire 1978: 77–9).

Moreover, as the pressure for economy mounts, the logic of cost recovery is towards a regressive rather than progressive distribution of educational opportunities. It must also be emphasised that the scale and cost of the most ambitious developments of the 1960s and 1970s simply did not represent replicable models in the stringent economic climate of the decades to follow.

The evidence, therefore, suggests that many of the post-war community colleges bear no more than a superficial resemblance to the original village colleges established by Henry Morris in Cambridgeshire. Morris was certainly a patrician and a paternalist, but his vision was fundamentally radical, prefiguring developments in state policy by 20 years, and his strategy was firmly grounded in the social and economic realities of the local community context. In contrast, the subsequent development of the community school and college movement was primarily driven by an imposed rather than a popular politics of education. In this sense, the dialectics of its development were essentially regressive, and the mantle of radicalism in community education was left to others to assume.

## Reformist Intervention and the Problematic of 'Community'

The potential control of the state increases the more closely the working population is knit to the state system (Cockburn, 1977: 101).

A basic distinction can be drawn between the notion of *sponsorship* through the 'ideological construction of homogeneous communities' (Westwood, 1992: 234), characteristic of the mainstream community school and college movement, and that of the *co-option* of deficient or disadvantaged communities which was implicit in the 'community' approaches that developed from the initiatives in compensatory education in the late 1960s. While the former started in rural areas and gradually spread to urban areas, the latter were primarily focused on inner urban areas and made a significant impact on both schooling, especially primary schooling, and adult education.

The process of co-option, as well as the dialectics that emerged within it, can be located in the purposes of state intervention in areas of 'multiple deprivation' in the late 1960s and early 1970s in general and in the Educational Priority Area (EPA) and Community Development Project (CDP) programmes in particular. Nevertheless, these action-research initiatives have to be related to the wider policy context of the time: in particular, the British Urban Programme, which was initially heavily influenced by essentially colonial thinking about community development; in more general terms, the characteristic concerns with 'educational disadvantage' (the 1963 Newsom and 1967 Plowden reports on schooling, and, subsequently, the 1973 Russell and 1975 Alexander reports on adult education), public participation (Skeffington Report 1969) and generic welfarism and corporate management (Seebohm Report 1968).

Several general points should be made about the EPA and CDP interventions. The programmes were partly a response to the so-called 'rediscovery of poverty' in a society that had only recently been told it had never had it so good. More significantly, however, they were prompted by fears of racial conflict following Enoch Powell's notorious 'Rivers of Blood' speech and the spectre of the race riots in American cities in 1967–8. In this respect, it is no coincidence that social and educational initiatives in areas of multi-racial settlement were complemented by the introduction of new controls on immigration. It is also significant that the problem of poverty was defined in terms of its symptoms and supposed effects rather than its causes. This 'culturalist' analysis (Cowburn, 1986: 138) focused attention on supposed patterns of individual, family and subcultural pathology in pockets of 'multiple deprivation' rather than material conditions and structural position of the poor. Finally, it is important to emphasise that selective interventions of this kind could be accommodated within the consensus politics of the time because they apparently raised no fundamental questions about the nature of inequality or the distribution of power – and when they did, they were rapidly terminated (see e.g. Loney, 1983). They were also small-scale and cheap enough to be acceptable to the Treasury.

It is not surprising, therefore, that policy in the areas specially selected for these experiments in social engineering was highly flavoured with assumptions about 'needs meeting', compensation and social pathology (i.e. attributing perceived problems to the apparent characteristics of local communities and 'subcultures'), and about the validity of the so-called 'deficient agency' hypothesis, by which it was inferred that technical solutions could be found for what were taken to be essentially 'service delivery' problems. In both cases, education was seen to be the principal instrument and locus of intervention as well as the best guarantor of success.

Baron (1989) identifies three underlying processes at work in this co-opted construction of community which help to explain the dialectics that emerged within it. First, the projects facilitated the surveillance of deprived communities. This was achieved partly by encouraging various kinds of local participation:

It is by integrating the local population into predictable 'families' and 'community groups' and by setting up 'joint committees' between itself and them that the state can develop the level of information flow that amounts to 'governance' (Cockburn, 1977: 100–1).

Second, women and family life, the key agents of social reproduction, became the primary focus of reformist intervention. Much attention, for example, was paid to child rearing, 'parenting skills' and pre-school 'enrichment'. Third, and most significantly perhaps in terms of the process of co-option, 'community education' was used to re-present the community to itself as a problem, deviating from the healthy norm and in need of rescue and re-integration.

In terms of the subsequent dialectics of practice, therefore, two linked but distinctive themes became especially significant: the first attached to the notion of the adult constructed as parent in the community school-based work of the EPAs; the second was the range of responses to the idea of working-class community in the community development oriented work of the CDPs. In both respects, developments in the EPA and CDP projects in Liverpool were of particular importance. For instance, Tom Lovett's experimentation with 'community development approaches' in adult education in the Liverpool EPA subsequently influenced the thinking of the Russell Report (DES, 1973) on the problems of 'educational disadvantage' and 'non-participation'. They also made a significant impact on the recommendation of the Alexander Report (Scottish Education Department, 1975) for the establishment of a Community Education Service in Scotland.

The EPA project started in 1968, jointly funded by the Department of Education and Science and the Social Science Research Council over a three-year experimental period in five selected areas. According to the Plowden Report (Central Advisory Council for Education, 1967), which originally recommended EPA intervention as an experimental action-research programme, the general aim – far from modest for a relatively modestly funded and staffed project – was to ensure 'equal opportunities for all'. More specifically, it should seek 'to raise educational standards, to lift teacher morale, to solder home and school links, and to assist in giving communities a sense of responsibility'.

As Director of the Liverpool EPA Project, Eric Midwinter's name is particularly associated with the development of the community primary school. Midwinter was an energetic, innovative and controversial educationalist whose work has come to be associated with a 'reformist', school-based model of community education (see e.g. the extensive publications of the Coventry-based Community Education Development Centre). For Midwinter community education was essentially a means of 'oiling the wheels' of community development, which he understood as the process of reviving grassroots democratic processes in communities that had become alienated and disaffected by the scale of mass society and the impersonality of the state apparatus (see Midwinter, 1972, 1973, 1975). The basic task of education in such areas was to enable local people to gain more control over their immediate circumstances and develop a sense of their own citizenship.

Midwinter's central concern, therefore, was to reconnect education, and schooling in particular, with the realities of life in the locality and thereby to promote communal identity and social purpose. The emphasis in his work was on translating the rhetoric of community development about participation, partnership and self-help into educational practice. The primary school was, in his view, the obvious starting point for such a strategy because of its local character and its potential links with parents and the home and neighbourhood life of children. Two themes of particular relevance to adult education emerged from Midwinter's work: the concern to develop home–school relations, including parental education, and the interest in the socially relevant or 'community' curriculum.

In Midwinter's view, parental involvement in their children's schooling was necessary both to ensure active educational support within the home and family and to harmonise what was learnt in the school with what was learnt outside it. At the same time, such educational partnership with parents could draw members of the adult population into the community development process. Moreover, the community curriculum, whereby learning was related to the immediate local environment, would support both aims. It would enable parents to contribute with authority and enthusiasm to the education of their children, as well as help them to gain the motivation and confidence to become involved in the wider community development process. This new kind of educational partnership and engagement was to be strengthened by adult education initiatives focused on practical, local issues, e.g. decisions about the environment, planning, transport and housing, as well as education. Adult educators, like school teachers, should be prepared to adopt much more imaginative and flexible ways of working in order to interest and involve local people. Adult education in this sense would function as an integral part of a generic, localised 'community service'.

For Midwinter this kind of educational intervention was an urgent necessity if a 'double crisis of injustice and nonidentity' (1973: 42) was to be addressed. 'Community education is not phrased in terms of a docile exercise in educational reform but as a possible alternative to social dislocation' (p 57).

He was careful, however, to eschew what he regarded as an unrealistic radicalism. He identified himself as an 'actualist', distinguishing between

the 'actualist', who attains workable results within the organic social frame, and the pseudo-idealist who achieves nothing and risks much. If achievements were a criterion, the 'revisionist' should often carry the 'revolutionary' mantle (Midwinter, 1975: 93).

The emphasis on developing a partnership between child, parent and teacher, which was at the heart of Midwinter's thinking, was premised upon the key assumption of gender roles, located within a traditional model of the nuclear family. This, in effect, constructed the adult as parent, and the parent primarily as mother. Much well-intentioned home–school work has proceeded uncritically – and, in its own terms, effectively – on these lines. Jane Thompson was the first adult educator to identify the contradictions inherent in a view of women's education predicated on an ideology of unproblematic domesticity and familism. Thompson's critique of this and her development of a feminist counter-practice (see Thompson, 1983) subsequently became influential in forging an alternative model of women's education. At the same time, Midwinter's interest in curriculum and, in particular, his interpretation of social relevance provoked an important debate among adult educators, the repercussions of which have continued to reverberate through community-based adult education.

It is certainly important to recognise the significance of the EPA action-research projects in stimulating more progressive and child-centred practice in British primary education in the post-Plowden period. Nevertheless, they also showed how reformist intervention of this kind could serve to co-opt potentially dissident communities back into the very structure which, ultimately, oppressed them – in effect papering over the cracks of the real inequalities arising from class, gender and race divisions in the wider society. In this respect, what Harold Entwistle (1978) derided as the 'retreat into localism', which was characteristic of this particular construction of community, could be both disingenuous and disabling.

It is significant that A.H. Halsey, Director of the national EPA Project, called the introductory chapter of the final evaluation report on it 'Political ends and educational means'. The school's potential as a primary agent of community co-option as well as the marginality of its impact on poverty and structural inequality were both implicit in what he went on to identify as the tendency to use

education as the waste paper basket of social policy – a repository for dealing with social problems where solutions are uncertain or where there is a disinclination to wrestle with them seriously. Such problems are prone to be dubbed 'educational' and turned over to the schools to solve (Halsey, 1972: 8).

Underlying the critiques and counter-practice which emerged from EPA and CDP work was the view that the idea of 'disadvantage' implicit in such approaches facilitated key evasions. As Thompson (1980) put it:

... the notion of disadvantage was uncritically related to a wide range of physical and personal defects and social conditions in which diverse groups were linked together, and by which complex social, economic and political manifestations of inequality went unchallenged (p 87).

It was precisely this idea, however, that got firmly embedded in both official thinking and professional practice. For example, it informed Peter Clyne's influential study The Disadvantaged Adult (1972), commissioned for the Russell Committee, and was carried over into subsequent work in the field (e.g. Fordham et al., 1979).

As has been noted, the characteristic focus of intervention on women served to exacerbate rather than resolve their basic problem because 'it is as appendages of homes, husbands and children that they are usually assessed and catered for' (Thompson, 1983: 85). The Second Chance to Learn for Women project in Southhampton, which developed from a critique and rejection of this approach, was an attempt systematically to address the interests of women students as a particular community of interest who shared a common experience of male oppression and professional paternalism at home, in the community and at work (see Thompson, 1983; Taking Liberties Collective, 1989). It should be emphasised that the project's commitment stemmed as much from a rejection of the patriarchal power structure and value base within agencies of traditional liberal adult education as the somewhat muddled thinking of officially sanctioned versions of community education and community development.

What is particularly striking about Thompson's account of this important project is the clarity of analysis which informed the initiative and the consistency with which this was addressed in the curriculum. It was from the start conceived as a serious and challenging educational process. No concessions were made in this respect. The relevance of the curriculum was defined in terms of its engagement with the demonstrable realities of sexual inequality, discrimination and oppression, as evidenced as much in the personal experience of students as in academic study. In direct contradiction of much mainstream community education work with women, the task was precisely to render as problematic their traditional roles and to examine gender as a social construction rather than a 'natural' phenomenon.

Educational purpose and process were 'practical' in the original radical sense of the 'really useful knowledge' tradition (Johnson, 1979), i.e. rooted in the concrete circumstances of people and committed to analysing, challenging and changing them. This was reflected in Thompson's summary of the aims of the project:

to redistribute the kind of educational opportunities which well-satisfied adult students in the most favourable kind of learning environments are entitled to expect, to those who, for a variety of social, political and economic reasons, had received least from the education system in the past. This meant positive discrimination in favour of women and working class women in particular (Thompson, 1983: 151).

Given the nature of the critique of conventional community education provision and its influence on the subsequent development of feminist practice, it is important to emphasise three particular features of this kind of work. First, it proceeded from a recognition that curriculum reflects the relationship between knowledge and power. Social relevance was therefore interpreted in terms of developing a rigorous and challenging analysis which would enable women to make sense of their lives and, if necessary, to change them. Second, the project was quite specifically and unapologetically aimed at working-class women without formal educational qualifications. This redistributive purpose was subsequently vindicated, consistent over-subscription and the sustained level of participation and commitment giving the lie to the conventional wisdom of 'apathy' and 'fecklessness' implicit within the dominant discourse of educational 'disadvangtage' and 'cultural deprivation'. Third, it was increasingly recognised that such work was difficult to sustain within mainstream, male-dominated educational institutions in which there was the constant danger of its incorporation and neutralisation. The logic of this was to secure automony, as the project succeeded in doing when it moved out of university premises into a community-based Women's Education Centre (see Taking Liberties Collective, 1989) – although it was always recognised that ultimately the challenge was to change mainstream provision and practice rather than escape it.

This type of work, targeting precisely the kind of working-class women officially defined as being in need of compensatory intervention and 'parenting' skills, has become an important and subversive – if always precarious and under-funded – strand in community-based adult education (see, for example, Taking Liberties Collective, 1989; Highet, 1991; Rogers, 1994). Essentially, what is important about it is that it treats women as subjects in their own learning rather than the objects of professional intervention, and values their gendered experience as an educational resource to be used rather than a deficiency to be rectified.

The action-research brief of the British Poverty Programme initiatives of the late 1960s and early 1970s presented adult education workers employed in the EPA and CDP projects with the opportunity to experiment with a variety of new methods and approaches aimed at addressing problems initially defined in terms of 'educational disadvantage' and 'non-participation' in working-class communities. This stimulated a range of innovatory practice, particularly in Liverpool, where Keith Jackson and Bob Ashcroft worked in the CDP project and Tom Lovett was seconded by the WEA to the EPA project. Their attempts to test locally-based, 'community development approaches' to adult education, and in the process to challenge its pervasive 'ideology of individualism' (Keddie, 1980), led to a lively debate about the nature of the problem and appropriate adult education responses to it. Both this debate and the emergent practice of community-based adult education had a formative influence on subsequent developments.

Before examining the practice that emerged, it is important to identify the dialectic generated within this work between the neighbourhood-based community development orientation of Lovett's work and the increasingly structuralist critique that developed in the work of Jackson, in particular. The latter was neatly summed up in the title of an influential paper Jackson wrote at the time: 'The marginality of community development: implications for adult education' (see Fryer, 1989). This reflected the rejection by the more radical CDP workers of what they had come to regard as the social pathological premises of the original CDP brief and the redefinition of the key issues in structural terms. As the *CDP Inter-Project Report* (1974) put it:

Problems of multi-deprivation have to be redefined and reinterpreted in terms of structural constraint rather than psychological motivations, external rather than internal factors. The project teams were increasingly clear that the symptoms of disadvantage ... cannot be explained adequately by any abnormal preponderance of individuals or families whose behaviour could be defined as 'pathological'. Even where social 'malaise' is apparent it does not seem best explained principally in terms of personal deficiencies so much as the product of external pressures in the wider environment.

Jackson's writing and the development of his own work, therefore, demonstrated increasing scepticism about what another CDP worker characterised as the use of 'community' as 'a kind of aerosol word to be sprayed on to deteriorating institutions to deodorise and humanise them' (Benington, 1974: 260). In particular, he became critical of the tendency of officially sanctioned 'community' approaches to obfuscate both the structural determinants of local problems and the bogus ideology of consensus they embodied. Their logic was a disabling parochialism, remedial education based on an impoverished curriculum, and social control rather than social action. Given, therefore, that 'The idea of community obscures the most important social and economic relations' (Jackson, 1980: 42), he withdrew quite deliberately to the firmer ground of class. It is important to emphasise, however, that Keith Jackson has never rejected locally-based approaches to adult education in working-class areas out of hand. Rather, he has insisted that these should be systematically grounded in a wider analysis, and located historically within the tradition of autonomous working-class education with its characteristic emphasis on the relationship between knowledge, power and action.

At about the same time, another but related debate took place in the pages of the journal *Adult Education*. Kenneth Lawson (1977) attacked community education for what he dismissively described as its 'practical instrumentalism', which he compared unfavourably with the established liberal values of 'cultural diffusion and personal development'. In Lawson's view, the current interest in community education was dangerous because it disguised its political and partisan nature in a disingenuous coyness about its aims and purposes. Lawson's critique provoked a sharp rejoinder from Colin Kirkwood (1978) to the effect that there was nothing neutral or unproblematic about the liberal tradition, which, he suggested, was more like the problem than the solution in trying to develop relevant adult education practice in working-class communities.

In the midst of all this debate, the practice of community-based adult education had begun to take shape. As already noted, it influenced the thinking of both the Russell and Alexander reports on appropriate responses to what continued to be defined as the problems of 'disadvantage' and 'non-participation'. Subsequently, in the 1980s, state intervention in the management of structural unemployment, increasingly under the aegis of the Manpower Services Commission, stimulated further developments. Many adult educators, however, became ambivalent about participating in this (see e.g. Johnston, 1992) Although MSC-funded initiatives were often narrowly vocational, DES funds did provide small but significant opportunities for developmental work and innovation. In this respect, the DES-supported Pioneer Work conducted by the Department of Adult and Continuing Education at Leeds University was particularly important (see Ward and Taylor, 1986; Fraser and Ward, 1988).

What is now known as *community-based adult education*, therefore, originated from attempts to harness adult education to the professed aims of community development: in brief, stimulating grassroots participation and processes of self-help, developing relevant responses to local needs, and enabling people to see the practical value of education as a problem-solving activity (see e.g. Calouste Gulbenkian Foundation, 1968). It is significant in this respect that the Open Univeristy identifies the rationale of its Community Education programme in terms of its learner-centredness as distinct from subject-centredness, i.e. focusing on the interests, needs and problems of people in their various adult roles and at different stages of the life cycle, and its experiential as distinct from academic frame of reference, i.e. the concern to enable adult learners to understand and address the practical problems and challenges of everyday life (see e.g. Calder, 1983; Farnes, 1988, 1993). In community-based adult education, therefore, curriculum is derived as far as possible from the circumstances and concerns of participants and it aims to be both problem-posing and problem-solving in Freirean terms.

As a form of practice, it certainly reflects a critique of the 'enrolment economy' of much traditional liberal adult education. The latter is criticised for its organisational ritual and intellectual rigidity, as well as its failure to connect with the concrete realities of people's lives, concentrating on 'satisfying intellectual need alone' without any attempt to address 'collective economic and social needs' (Thompson, 1980: 14). Before his disillusionment with community development, Keith Jackson identified the 'most substantial challenge' for adult education in working-class areas as that of 'helping community groups whose members have received little formal education and have restricted opportunities to develop social, organisational and intellectual skills in their working lives' (Jackson, 1970: 167).

This implies new ways of thinking and new ways of working:

Pedagogically, there must be a ... change towards an outreach and needs-oriented educational delivery system. Whilst this requires considerable political and structural change to achieve full success, potentially important beginnings can be made through educational programming that is *based* in the community, that *recognises* community needs, and is attractive and relevant to adults in the community (Taylor and Ward, 1988: 260).

'Community', therefore, is reappropriated from being the site of co-option to become not simply the locus of educational activity but also an educational resource that informs curriculum development and the object of critical engagement.

The logic of this it that it may turn out to be more radical methodologically than ideologically. Indeed, despite the liberal anxieties of Paterson (1973) and Lawson (1977), the real danger is that adult education becomes merely handmaiden to a community development process which, true to its colonial origins, is cheap, co-optive and profoundly conservative (see Mayo, 1974). It is essential, therefore, to avoid the pitfalls of localism and culturalism. On the other hand, community-based adult education at its best also challenges the crudely reductionist nature of traditional class analysis. Pioneer Work, for example, aimed quite clearly to confront structural inequalities in ways which recognised how class position is mediated by geographical location, gender, race and age (Ward and Taylor, 1986). Its work was therefore informed by the notion of 'double disadvantage' whereby the inequalities of class and unemployment are compounded by other identities and positions.

Since the early work in the 1960s and 1970s there has been considerable interest in using community-based approaches to adult education as a way of seeking to redistribute educational opportunities and to reconnect issues of community, culture and class in the curriculum (see e.g. Lovett *et al.*, 1983). However, it is in the nature of such work that generalisation is difficult because its focus is local, its funding precarious and its status marginal. The remainder of this section, therefore, focuses on three key concerns which arise out of developmental work in community-based adult education: curriculum, the role of the worker and strategies for inter-agency collaboration. These are illustrated by reference to three examples of practice which have had a formative influence on subsequent work: the original Second Chance to Learn project in Liverpool, Tom Lovett's early work, and the Leeds University Pioneer Work initiative.

The original Second Chance to Learn project was established in Liverpool in 1976 as a direct result of the CDP/EPA experience. In particular, it reflected Keith Jackson's critique of the parochialism and lack of rigour characteristic of some 'community development approaches' to adult education and his experience of working with local people in opposing the 1972 Housing Finance Act. Second Chance was essentially an attempt to salvage the positive features of this experience and avoid its pitfalls. In particular, it sought to work specifically with local working-class activists and to relate locality to structure by developing within the curriculum an analysis that reconnected not only community and class but also contemporary struggles with the historical tradition of autonomous working-class self-education and the precepts of 'really useful knowledge'. What this implied was not a rejection but a redefinition of 'relevance' in terms of an education that would promote critical understanding and lead to action, i.e. *praxis* (Edwards, 1986: 2). The principle of positive discrimination was to be effected through targeted recruitment, systematic provision for learning support and relatively generous staffing and resourcing.

The concern to combine local relevance with social and educational purpose led to considerable debate about the nature of curriculum. The original intention of Second Chance to Learn was quite specifically to build curriculum on a common political position and purpose and to develop it in an historically informed and intellectually demanding way. Lovett's work, on the other hand, was more modest and pragmatic, although the central concern to relate adult education in working-class communities to local social, cultural and economic conditions was sustained. Pioneer Work was explicitly rooted in the intention of maintaining a dual commitment to the aims and values of liberal and social purpose education across a wide curricular range. In the process, it consistently demonstrated how local definitions of 'relevance' can become effective starting points for critical and contextual analysis as well as local social and cultural action (Ward and Taylor, 1986).

Subsequently, Second Chance-type initiatives proliferated and became an important influence on the development of Access courses to further and higher education. There is now a wide variety of both community and college-based courses which use the term 'Second Chance'. However, their aims and methods have become more conventional. This is almost inevitable, given the fact that the original work derived from a very clear and specific political commitment forged in a concrete situation (see Yarnit, 1980). In addition, the changing policy context, continuous cutbacks in funding and the hegemony of individualism have all made it difficult to sustain the original aims and purposes of such work.

The logic of the Second Chance programme was, in fact, more evident in the work which Keith Jackson subsequently developed at Northern College. There, despite constant financial pressures and an increasingly hostile political climate, something of the original vision and commitment were sustained, reflecting the conclusion Jackson drew from his Liverpool experience that adult education needed 'internal institutional and professional reform; the establishment of new types of relations with working activists; the development of means by which social consciousness and awareness can become an explicit feature of an education programme' (Fryer, 1989: 27). In its continuing work with trade unionists and community activists, for example, Northern College sought to sustain the radical tradition and to develop its students as 'organic intellectuals' (Cowburn, 1986: 169) who were committed to social and political action in their own communities. It should also be noted that Northern College responded to the critique of the original Second Chance work for its emphasis on white, male, working-class culture. Although the class analysis was maintained, there was a much more explicit recognition, both in recruitment and curriculum, of the salience of issues of gender and race in the lives of its students (Jackson, 1989) (see Chapter 9).

Second Chance practice made few concessions to 'progressive methods' – largely because its own agenda was so clearly defined. As Keith Jackson put it, 'Solidarity with working class activists sits unhappily with non-directive help offered to autonomous community groups' (Lovett, 1988: 154). Pioneer Work was more flexible methodologically, but it insisted on the importance of clear educational purposes. Thus, although much of the work was conducted in relatively informal and non-didactic ways, both tutors and students were expected to be systematic and rigorous.

Tom Lovett, on the other hand, was ready to be more experimental and flexible. Midwinter (1972), emphasising that Lovett had to start from scratch, working with groups who had no overt interest in adult education or explicit commitment to political action, described how 'His technique – the searching-out of non-formal groupings and the gradual extrapolation of problems for educational action – turned the usual practice of adult education on its head. The course came last' (p 155). It should, however, be emphasised that in all of his work, from the early years in Liverpool to his current work in Northern Ireland, Lovett has been concerned to link adult education with social or cultural action, this being understood in the Freirean sense of 'an examination and exploration of communities in all their complexity in order to encourage the embracing of options which improve people's sense of identity, integrity, security and dignity' (Lovett, 1994: 157).

Three key features of community-based adult education emerge from Lovett's account of his early work in the Liverpool EPA project (Lovett, 1975), all of which have practical implications for the role of the adult educator. First, he found it necessary to do a great deal of time-consuming and labour-intensive groundwork, familiarising himself with the local environment and developing personal relationships. These demanded the skills of the community worker more than those of the adult educator. Second, he came to see that the basic task of the worker was to reverse the conventional 'centre-periphery' model of provided classes and courses – and to challenge the power relations embedded in it. In Lovett's view, 'The problem lay with the providers, not the community' (1983: 32–3). The local worker therefore had first to assess interests and needs in the community and then deploy educational resources in order to respond to them on the terms set by local people rather than those of the traditional providers. The primary role of the worker was understood in terms of managing a network of relationships and resources in such a way as to ensure that educational work developed from the experience and concerns of local people rather than the preconceptions and convenience of outsiders. Third, Lovett argued that the 'community adult educator' had to become much less precious about 'education', to be ready to blur the distinctions between cognitive and affective processes and, indeed, to build the former on the latter. He argued that community-based adult education should be essentially person- rather than subject-centred. As Fordham et al. (1979) put it, reflecting on their own subsequent experience of developing adult education 'learning networks':

'The tutor must become skilled as the organiser of learning processes rather than more and more expert in a particular academic discipline' (p 219).

Tom Lovett's work has always been primarily about connecting adult education with the latent educational interests and resources within existing informal community networks. In contrast, the Leeds Pioneer Work proceeded from the view that more formal inter-agency collaboration should be understood as a 'central operating principle' (Ward and Taylor (eds), 1986). It demonstrated how community-based approaches to stimulating local demand for adult education could catalyse the educational work of a range of local agencies. This project also showed that such collaboration and co-ordination are a practical precondition for effective practice where, as is invariably the case, funding is meagre and personnel are over-stretched, because such arrangements encourage joint funding as well as student progression and the hand-over of successfully piloted work to other agencies.

It was also clear from this work that both targeting and progression were heavily dependent on coherent inter-agency working. Thus, for example, courses offered in local community-based settings were particulary effective in making opportunities available to unwaged working-class women with minimal educational qualifications, whereas very few of them were attracted to officially designated unemployment centres – not least because most were not formally registered as unemployed (Ward and Taylor (eds), 1986: 69). Similarly, working with educational institutions like LEAs and the WEA helped to prevent wasteful duplication, ensure continuity and identify opportunites for project staff to undertake appropriate professional development and consultancy work.

Community-based adult education remains an important but highly marginal and vulnerable area of work. It is plagued by problems of short-term funding, part-time staffing and rapid staff turnover. Its precarious nature leads to the danger of such work becoming no more than temporary, one-off and tokenistic. Projects come and go, often disappearing almost without trace. The labour-intensive nature of the work leaves little time for systematic monitoring, evaluation and dissemination. As traditional providers have been forced by national policy to develop more narrowly vocational and market-oriented provision, so this kind of work has become progressively squeezed. Alternatively, it has had to adapt to the new climate, becoming institutionally-based, increasingly individualistic and meritocratic. As already noted, there has been a proliferation of 'Second Chance' courses which bear little resemblance to the original Liverpool initiative. Neverthess, in a generally hostile environment, community-based adult education at its best remains one of the few spaces on the current map of adult education where there is still the possibility of sustaining a commitment to the progressive redistribution of educational opportunities in community settings. It is important precisely because it stubbornly continues to address the real if unpalatable facts for any social purpose adult education of structural inequalities as they are manifested at the local level.

## Developments in Scotland: Adult education within the Community Education Service

Those to whom adult education should be of most value are least involved (Alexander Report, 1975: 15).

Community education in Scotland has developed in a distinctive way. It takes the form of a single local authority Community Education Service which aims to combine the provision of non-vocational adult education with youth work and community work. The Scottish Community Education Service is the major structural outcome of the Alexander Report *Adult Education: The challenge of change* (Scottish Education Department, 1975), the Scottish equivalent of the 1973 Russell Report.

The report's conception of an integrated service was influenced by several factors. It sought to address the comparatively weak position of non-vocational adult education in Scotland. Local authority adult education provision had been slow to develop, despite the historical evidence of distinctive Scottish liberal and radical traditions (Bryant, 1984; Alexander and Martin, 1995). This weakness can be partly explained by the fact that the long-established pattern of relatively open and democratic access to higher education in Scotland diverted attention from the development of non-vocational liberal adult education. In this respect, it is worth noting that in Scotland the university extramural departments and the WEA were never granted Responsible Body status, thus becoming almost entirely dependent on local government funding and reducing the resources available for the development of a separate local authority adult education service. In addition, there was no developed community school or college tradition in Scotland at that time.

The Alexander recommendations were strongly influenced by the belief that adult education should help to counter 'disadvantage'. This key concern was reinforced by the evidence of research commissioned for the report which indicated highly regressive rates of participation in adult education, compounded by a widespread problem of non-participation. This provided both a conveniently cost-effective administrative and a potentially socially redistributive rationale for exploiting the relatively extensive local infrastructure of the Youth and Community Service as a basis for developing more localised and responsive forms of provision. In this respect, the report reflected the general interest at the time, stimulated in part by the influential 1968 Gulbenkian Report on community work, in inter-agency strategies for local service delivery as well as the 'community development approach' to adult education which had been introduced in the CDP and EPA projects. It did not, however, take into consideration the very different ideological roots and cultural practices of liberal adult education, youth work and community development.

There seemed to be a compelling case in pragmatic terms for some kind of integration of adult and youth services. This would not only make fuller use of the resources already committed to youth and community work, which had been significantly expanded in response to the recommendations of the 1964 Kilbrandon Report *Children and Young Persons in Scotland* (the Scottish equivalent of the 1960 Albermarle Report). It would also enrich the work of adult educators with the supposedly responsive, neighbourhood-based knowledge and skills of existing local authority personnel, as well as strengthen links with the voluntary sector. At the same time, there seemed to be a strong case for infusing youth and community work with a clearer educational purpose.

It is significant that the combination of pragmatic and redistributive rationales, characteristic of reformist social democratic intervention, had already been demonstrated in the concern of the Standing Consultative Council on Youth and Community Services' 1968 report *Community of Interests* to 'promote, within the sphere of informal further education, further development of the youth and community services and to foster cooperation among the statutory authorities and voluntary organisations concerned' (SCCYCS, 1968).

Finally, it should be noted that the publication of the Alexander Report in 1975 was timed to coincide with local government reform and the advent of the nine new double-tier regional and three single-tier island authorities in Scotland. These unprecedentedly large-scale units would, it was assumed, provide an adequate resource base for the development of the new service. At the same time, the Alexander recommendations reflected the dualism inherent in state policy between centralisation, conferring the economies of scale and the advantages of strategic planning, with the concern characteristic of the time to foster local democracy by encouraging devolution, accountability and participation at the local level. This dualism was at the heart of the proposals of the 1969 Wheatley Commission, which formed the basis of subsequent local government reorganisation in 1974. The locally-based Community Education Service would, in Alexander's view, have an important part to play in nurturing 'pluralist democracy' by helping to manage the tension between the representative politics of the state and the participatory politics of communities. In short, the time seemed ripe for adult education to meet the 'challenge of change'.

In terms of the subsequent development of the Scottish Community Education Service and, in particular, the future of adult education within it, it should be emphasised that the Alexander Committee's brief was very narrow. Its terms of reference were specifically restricted to the provision by local authorities of non-vocational adult education, or what the 1945 Education (Scotland) Act had termed, rather curiously, 'informal further education'. As such, the implementation of a report specifically intended to strengthen adult education in Scotland had the unintended effect of isolating this particular, and traditionally weak, aspect of provision from the wider field of adult and continuing education. In subsequent years this significantly impeded the development of a national policy framework for adult and continuing education in Scotland. In this respect, it is also worth noting that the definition of informal further education in the 1969 Education (Scotland) Act as 'the provision of adequate facilities for social, cultural and recreative activities and for physical education and training' did nothing to clarify the specifically educational rationale of the new service.

It is important to stress that the fundamental aim of the report was to raise the profile of adult education in Scotland and make recommendations that would enable it to help people face up to the demands of the rapid pace of economic, technological and cultural change. Underlying this was the view that adult education had a key role to play in strengthening 'pluralist democracy', reflecting both the anxieties and imperatives of the state's reformist interventions of the time. The central concern to address issues of social and educational 'disadvantage' meant that the 'challenge of change' was conceived primarily in terms of adult education's capacity to respond to the interests and needs of those groups it identified as being most likely to suffer the negative consequences of change and, potentially, to become alienated and disaffected from the political process. This helps to explain the report's central interest in developing approaches to adult education which such people would perceive as relevant, attractive and accessible. It also suggests why the committee recommended closer links between the adult education and youth and community work services, to be catalysed by the chemistry of community development. Not only did youth and community work have a much more developed local infrastructure, but it was also perceived as being closer to people, more accessible and 'user friendly' than traditonal subject-centred and institution-based adult education provision. The intention, in this sense, was both to democratise and popularise adult education. As Tett (1995) puts it, the Alexander Report

sought to create the conditions through which adult education could move from being a leisure pursuit of a more affluent minority who had the confidence to return to educational institutions, to becoming a more relevant and locally based enterprise which involved the mass of people who had traditionally not participated in its provision (p 59).

Sir Kenneth Alexander (1993), reflecting back on the committee's recommendations, confirmed that the basic intention was that adult education's use of the youth work base in communities, spanning both statutory and voluntary sector provision, should create 'a wider network within which more people could become aware of educational opportunities' (p 36). Incidentally, he also admitted that some of the difficulties that were to arise from this proposal had been under-estimated.

The main recommendation of the Alexander Report was, therefore, that 'adult education should be regarded as an aspect of community education and should with the youth and community service be incorporated into a community education service' (Scottish Education Department, 1975: 35). The major structural outcome was the establishment, with some local variation, of an integrated Community Education Service in most of the new Scottish regional and island authorities. It is worth re-emphasising that the work of the service was to be characterised by locally-based, community-oriented approaches with a pronounced emphasis on positive discrimination in favour of 'disadvantaged' and traditionally non-participant groups.

In view of subsequent developments, it is essential to underline two points about the Alexander Report's original conception of the status of adult education within the new service. First, it was recommended that adult education should be a function of a new integrated service within which adult educators and youth workers would work together as 'committed allies' with a 'common purpose'. It is important to stress that there is nothing in the original report to justify the subsequent transubstantiation of committed allies into multi-purpose generic workers. Second, the conditions stipulated by Alexander as a basis for the development of the new service, which were specifically designed to strengthen its adult education arm, were never fulfilled. The report called for substantial investment in new appointments, training and research in adult education in order to equalise the partnership with youth work from the start. This reflected the fact that at the time its recommendations were published, it has been calculated that youth workers outnumbered adult educators by a 7:1 ratio (Kirkwood, 1990: 297). In effect, the implementation of the major structural recommendation of the Alexander Report without any attempt to meet the requirements identified as necessary preconditions for its success ensured that the new partnership was from the outset a very unbalanced and unequal one.

The problems consequent upon adult education's position of relative weakness from the inception of the new service were compounded by a pronounced trend in the years following the implementation of the report towards the development of community education as a generic entity in its own right. As has been noted, the Alexander Report recognised the potential benefits of an integrated model of community education for both adult education and youth work. The closer working relationship envisaged would involve identifying a 'common core of knowledge and expertise', developing patterns of functional collaboration, and infusing practice with community work skills. Subsequent attempts to apply this idea of a new partnership to the training of community education workers, however, progressively replaced Alexander's essentially practical proposal for greater integration with the overarching concept of genericism. Thus, for example, the Carnegie Report *Professional Education and Training for Community Education* (Scottish Education Department, 1977) introduced the idea of a common and transferable core of generic knowledge and skills required of all community education workers. The loss of focus and dilution of function implicit in this were exacerbated by the Scottish Community Education Council's subsequent report *Training for Change* (Scottish Community Education Council, 1984) This proposed a pattern of training based on a dominant core of generic 'process skills', largely derived from community work practice, and downgraded the constituent specialisms in adult education and youth work to the status of mere 'options' appropriate to particular 'settings'. The implications of this for adult education are epitomised in the fact that many members of the service now describe themselves simply as 'community workers', making no explicit reference to their educational role. The general point therefore requires restatement: the Scottish Community Education Service has developed in a way that is very different from the relationship originally envisaged in which 'committed allies' would use their distinctive specialisms to develop co-ordinated local strategies.

The professional identity problem of the service created by the generic principle was heightened by the increasingly hostile climate in which the new service had to develop (see Chapter 1). Kirkwood (1990) suggests that from the start there was also a more fundamental problem: the very conception of community education as a generic, inter-disciplinary service had already become an outmoded hangover of the corporate welfarism of an earlier and more expansive era.

It is very difficult to assess the efficacy of the service because little systematic research has been conducted. One of the few detailed studies that exists (Alexander et al., 1984) suggested that the development of generic approaches had had systematically negative effects on the adult education elements of the work. Genericism had led to a disabling confusion of purpose and a loss of any clearly identifiable educational rationale. It found that the dominance of youth work traditions of non-direction and facilitative group work impeded systematic learning and cognitive development (see Kirkwood, 1991). It also confirmed earlier evidence of an actual decline in formal enrolments in non-vocational adult education in the period immediately following the implementation of the Alexander Report and a general failure to raise participation rates among traditionally non-participant groups. Subsequent research confirmed that the problem of socially regressive participation rates remained (see Munn and MacDonald, 1988; Gerver, 1992) and that men were notable by their absence from most types of adult provision (Tett, 1994).

It is, nevertheless, clear from observation – in the absence of more systematic evidence – that most community education workers do concentrate their efforts on 'disadvantaged' areas and 'non-participant' groups, as Alexander intended. The problem for the adult education component of their work seems to be that it either takes the form of a fairly standard menu of conventional class programmes or, alternatively, it dissolves into a wide range of generic activities which, whatever their merits, are not primarily educational. This creates a real dilemma for adult education within a Community Education Service of which, it must be emphasised, it was intended to be the main beneficiary. Thus, Barr (1987) argues that 'One of the less discussed problems of adult education in Scotland at the moment is that it is hard to see' (p 329).

Part of the difficulty is summed up in Bryant's (1984) phrase 'education by stealth'. This suggests that the educational elements of the service's work tend to be presented in covert , or at least very oblique, terms. The idea that learning is an incidental accretion rather than substantive objective is, for instance, implicit in the Principal Community Education Officers' vague statement that, 'The Service supports a wide range of groups and activities and its role is to enhance the learning element which is intrinsic to these groups and activities' (PCEO/SCEC, 1991).

This is certainly not the kind of community-based adult education discussed in the previous section of this chapter. Nor is it what the Alexander Committee intended. It is also interesting to compare with the argument presented in an earlier report, significant in terms of both its title *Adult Education: Now ... and then* and the fact that it was never officially published, that,

... education is not seen as an accidental process happening by stealth when the participants believe themselves to be taking part in something else ... but rather a service responding to adults' own requirements which will change at different stages of their lives (Scottish Community Education Council, 1988: 14).

In view of this, it is important to note that the Adult Basic Education element within the service, which has on the whole retained a distinctive identity, has sustained a much clearer educational rationale and continued to develop effective and significantly redistributive practice (Scottish Office Education Department, 1992). On the other hand, there is no doubt that the national profile of adult education in Scotland has suffered severely from the closure of the Scottish Institute of Adult Education (under the auspices of which ABE provision developed) in 1991 and the consequent absorption of the Scottish Adult Basic Education Unit into the Scottish Community Education Council. In addition, the continuing struggle for survival of Newbattle Abbey, Scotland's only public sector adult residential college, seems to be a depressingly significant sign of the times (Gerver, 1990) (see Chapter 9).

Nevertheless, it can be argued that in recent years the very existence of community education as a distinct local authority service may have helped to preserve some kind of administrative and professional framework in which a public sector commitment to adult education, youth work and community development has been maintained in increasingly hard times. This, in turn, has also helped to ensure that some of the genuinely innovative work developed in local projects, often funded initially through Urban Aid, has eventually been absorbed into mainstream local authority provision (see e.g. Thomson, 1991).

The most obvious example of developmental practice in community-based adult education is the Gorgie-Dalry Adult Learning Project (ALP), which is located in an inner city district of Edinburgh (see Kirkwood and Kirkwood, 1989). The work of this project has become widely known both nationally and internationally. It is highly regarded as one of the few systematic and fully documented attempts to develop community-based adult education according to the philosophy and methodology of Paulo Freire in a British urban context. It is significant, however, that from its inception this project was quite clear about its educational purpose and adult constituency – and, indeed, that the original initiative came from a group of local women.

More recently, ALP's work has concentrated on the development of a community-based adult education curriculum focusing on issues of Scottish identity and culture. This connects with a genuinely popular social movement in contemporary Scotland, which has been significantly strengthened by the growing disillusionment of the Scots with a political system that simply does not reflect or represent their interests. Indeed, Galloway (1993) argues that any authentically popular form of community education in Scotland is well placed to tap into and articulate the rich vein of cultural politics which has evolved from the rejection of what is commonly perceived to be the alien and alienating culture of representative politics. In this respect, it is also important to recognise that some workers in the Community Education Service played a significant part in the successful community-based campaigns in Scotland against, for example, the poll tax and water privatisation. There is some evidence, therefore, of a dynamic emerging within the work of more radical and innovative workers which articulates some of the real and concrete concerns of people in Scottish communities.

There were also signs in the early 1990s of these currents of social and cultural action beginning to make an impact on the training curriculum. In this sense, the cultural politics of Scotland might eventually help to transform the professional culture of its Community Education Service. This dynamic was strengthened by the appointment of new staff in some of the training institutions who had a much clearer sense not only of what popular education in Scottish communities might be but also what this implied for curriculum development (see e.g. Shaw and Crowther, 1995). Finally, the growing interest in developing a more coherent theoretical base for the practice of community-based education and social action in Scotland has been demonstrated by the success of the journal *Concept*, which was established in 1990.

The changing policy context also created new opportunities for community education workers in Scotland to develop a more explicit educational role. In particular, as education became increasingly marketised, there was a growing recognition of the critical need for accessible, locally-based forms of educational guidance (Steward and Alexander, 1988) which the Community Education Service should be well placed to provide. This, however, would have significant implications for the training of workers. In addition, it became clear that some further education colleges saw their future within the educational marketplace as all-age, multi-purpose institutions along the lines of the North American community college model (see Scottish Community Education Council, 1994). There was also evidence that secondary schools, particularly in Strathclyde Region, were very successfully marketing 'in-fill' places to local adults in order to compensate for falling rolls (HMI, 1992). It should be emphasised, nevertheless, that this was hardly the kind of community-oriented adult education envisaged in the Alexander Report.

At the same time there appeared to be a growing contradiction between the drive towards the professionalisation of community education in Scotland and the demands of practice. On the one hand, for example, Strathclyde Regional Council acted to confront the dilution of function and purpose inherent in genericism. It sought to rationalise and co-ordinate responsibility for community development by locating it entirely within the Social Work Department and to encourage community education workers to adopt more specialised roles in either adult education or youth work, albeit utlilising appropriate community development approaches in their work – much as Alexander had originally intended (Strathclyde Regional Council, 1978). On the other hand, the introduction of a system of competency-based endorsement of professional training courses by the Scottish Community Education Council in 1990 had the effect of instantiating genericism as the hallmark of professionalism – a development which confirmed the logic of Hamilton's research on the dynamics of professionalisation within the Community Education Service (Hamilton, 1991). An ironic, if unintended, consequence of this was the closure of Edinburgh University's postgraduate course in community education (see Alexander and Martin, 1995). This effectively removed from the scene the only institution involved in initial training for community education in Scotland with a distinctive, and distinguished, tradition of postgraduate teaching and research in both adult education and community development.

Finally, the prospect of local government reform in 1996 posed many uncertainties about the future of the Community Education Service (see e.g. Mathers, 1995). Moves towards professionalisation and performance assessment may have helped to give the service a higher profile and a clearer sense of its own identity. It remained to be seen, however, whether all of the new and much smaller unitary Scottish local authorities would have an adequate resource base to sustain the the full range of non-statutory provision such as that made available by the Community Education Service.

## Conclusion: Education and communities in 'New Times'

... a new politics is marked by local narratives, a point of special interest to those in community education (Westwood, 1992: 243).

The increasing conflict between local government and the central state became the dynamic of a new but short-lived construction of community education in the 1980s (Martin, 1986, 1992). In this case, the term was widely used by LEAs, mostly but not exclusively Labour controlled, as an organising concept for the development of a more coherent, comprehensive and equitable local education service (see e.g. AMA/CEDC, 1991). Essentially, this was an attempt to mobilise popular support for a defensive local politics of education articulated around the notion of 'community', defined in terms of common residence, shared interests and social purpose. Adult education was therefore presented as an integral part of a coherent range of local education services that should be publicly accountable and democratically controlled.

This construction of community education held out a vision for the development of education as a locally delivered public service that was the antithesis of the fragmentation and competition of a marketised system. It also sought to engage policy development with the local context in a systematic way, recalling Henry Morris's concern to ground education in the community. This manifesto was perhaps best expressed in Newham's policy statement:

Community education will not in itself produce a just society, nor will it guarantee to solve the social, educational and economic problems of Newham. What is important about community education, though, is that it offers a coherent approach to this range of issues. Fundamentally, it is about recognising people's right to education ... [and] encouraging and empowering people to take charge of their own institutions, their own education, and their own lives (London Borough of Newham, 1985: 17).

Five principles were identified as fundamental to this construction of community education as a rationale informing the development of the local education service as a whole:

- access and equal opportunities

- lifelong education (including developing the capacity for learning throughout life)

- inter-agency co-ordination and collaboration in order to ensure coherent service delivery

- curricular relevance to local people's interests, problems and aspirations

- representative partnership in institutional governance.

The reality, of course, is that the potential for this kind of policy development at the level of the local state was already being systematically undermined by the central government drive towards the marketisation, commodification and privatisation of public goods and services. The general effect of educational legislation throughout the 1980s, and in particular the 1988 Education Reform Act, was to centralise power while at the same time deregulating control, emasculating local government and eventually challenging its very legitimacy (Bogdanor, 1994; Allen and Martin, 1992; and see Chapter 4). 'Community education' could do little about this.

The idea of 'New Times', on the other hand, pointed to both the possibilities and the problems presented by the conjunction of political intervention with changing social conditions (see Hall and Jacques, 1989). The argument was that the convergence of economic, cultural and political forces in Britain and other advanced capitalist societies in the 1980s, as well as their globalised effects, called for new ways of understanding and engaging with the lived experience of people in communities. Some commentators saw in the complex and unpredictable chemistry of this conjuncture the possibility for the construction of a new dialectic out of which a more genuinely popular and radical politics of education could emerge.

For Westwood (1991, 1992), for example, 'New Times' represented an opportunity for the radical tradition in adult education to abandon once and for all the crude forms of class analysis that had, in her view, impoverished its theory and practice in the past. She contended that radical adult education had been both the perpetrator and the victim of the crass distortions and exclusions of modernist grand narratives. Consequently, it had became locked into

a reductionist account of socialism – an account that emphasised a unitary view of the working class which was itself homogenised through the emphasis on white, male workers whose politics were tied to production (Westwood, 1992: 223).

In the context of 'New Times', new constructions of community education seemed to offer the possibility of reappropriating community as a site of struggle, working with progressive social movements in order to develop a radical educational agenda that sought both to recognise and respect difference and to reconcile it with solidarity. Gilroy (1987), for instance, argued forcefully that the black experience in contemporary British society could only be adequately understood in terms of the mediation of class position through the struggles and celebrations of community life. Moreover, he suggested that the dominant interests and concerns of most black people, excluded from the labour market, focused more around the politics of consumption in the community than the politics of production in the workplace.

Part of the 'New Times' argument was, of course, levelled against paternalistic and oppressive forms of statism. In this respect, it should be noted that the unintended outcomes of state policy began to open up opportunities for new forms of community-based education. On the one hand, marketisation and 'parentocracy' encouraged the development of certain perverse mutations of community education as a commodity or simply a public relations exercise. On the other hand, they also presented novel possibilities for community educators to exploit the 'new forms of representation ... [and] to move from dependence upon local state patronage towards the acceptance of popular power' (Field, 1989: 26). Similarly, increasing fragmentation and differentiation within the education system embodied the potential for more 'genuinely alternative and democratic agendas' to emerge at the local level (Jeffs and Smith, 1991: 70). Certainly, there was evidence of new communities of resistance developing as, for example, schools opted out of local authority control in order to maintain their commitment to comprehensive education, institutions struggled to co-operate rather than compete, and parents and governors marched on Westminster to demand more realistic levels of funding for state education.

The conflation of democracy with the marketplace combined with a widespread disillusionment with representative politics to generate an equally widespread sense of a 'democratic deficit'. One consequence of this was the ideological recycling of community in the form of the debate about 'communitarianism'. It also helped, however, to stimulate a renewal of interest in the cultural politics of progressive social movements.

The 'New Times' argument was always, of course, contentious and its implications deeply ambivalent (Martin, 1993). Capitalism was being re-formed, not transformed, and any approach that seemed to be naive or complacent about issues of power and distributive justice had to be regarded as suspect. In addition, the relativism and particularism celebrated in some forms of postmodernist thinking could all too easily be appropriated for reactionary purposes. On the other hand, 'New Times' potentially gave a voice to groups who had been marginalised, even silenced, in some traditional forms of class analysis and the dominant discourse of radical adult education - thus the attraction of the argument to many women and black people.

What 'New Times' did seem to suggest was that in a rapidly changing and uncertain world, community educators were well placed to engage with the increasingly fragmented and dislocated realities of people's individual and collective experience. The real challenge of 'New Times' for community education was, therefore, to forge out of this engagement more genuinely popular and democratic forms of education and, in the process, to reconnect the cultural politics of communities with the vision of a common political culture that simultaneously respected diversity and promoted solidarity.

6

# Literacy and Adult Basic Education

## *Mary Hamilton*

While the development of universal literacy has been an urgent international theme for the whole of this century, Adult Basic Education (ABE) has only recently been identified as a field of adult continuing education in industrialised countries. It first emerged in the USA in the 1960s, and developed in the UK after what was initially seen as a temporary literacy campaign in the early 1970s. Other European countries followed. With the introduction of the Further and Higher Education Act of 1992, ABE became a statutory form of provision in the UK for the first time.

However, teaching literacy and other basic skills to adults has gone on throughout the nineteenth and twentieth centuries under different guises and circumstances. It has been affected enormously by the development of free universal primary schooling, which has always been centrally concerned with the teaching of reading, writing and mathematics. The history of ABE, therefore, must be understood not only in the context of adult education and attitudes to lifelong learning. It is intimately tied up with the history of compulsory state schooling, the hopes that we have had for it, and the realities of what it has achieved.

A critical history of ABE that looks back to this earlier period has to be a history of the different (often conflicting) strands of work and understandings of literacy and basic education that have fed into the field of ABE as it has now emerged, and of how these have contributed to the discourses that have shaped it, the insitutional frameworks within which it is carried out and the resources it has been able to draw on. When we approach ABE in this way, we can see many historical continuities with long-standing struggles over the purposes and control of education and basic literacy. As Withnall (1994) says in her detailed study of the origins of the adult literacy campaign: 'an essential preliminary to understanding the sequence of events in a particular country is to reconstruct the process by which the idea of adult illiteracy as a social problem requiring public recognition and government intervention is interpreted and developed' (p 67).

This chapter begins such a reconstruction by identifying the major historical periods that adult basic education has passed through in the nineteenth and twentieth centuries; and the main ideological strands that have fed into adult basic education, from literacy education itself and from parallel fields, such as special education. An understanding of this larger socio-political context is especially important for ABE (and adult education more generally), for while basic literacy through schooling has always been a major policy issue, formal literacy opportunities for *adults* have developed in the margins of social policy.

The main primary sources for this historical account are policy documents, public records, some accounts from teachers and others involved in education (inspectors, politicians, civil servants) and, particularly in the twentieth century, an increasing number of research reports and surveys. There is very little firsthand material on the experience and attitudes of those adults who were the students: different voices are unequally heard in the construction of the historical account. However, because of the student publishing that has always been a special part of the UK literacy scene, there are some firsthand records of adult students' motivations and experiences (e.g. Gatehouse, 1985).

It is also important to have a sense of the lived experience of literacy in the community at different times, its uses, values, the imperatives surrounding the practice of reading and writing in everyday life and the ways in which it was learned and supported outside of formal educational settings (see e.g. Howard, 1991; Barton, 1988). This is especially important, since in the nineteenth century, as Johnson (1983) points out, knowledge was not so institutionalised, and there was less formal division between education and the rest of life: adults and children learned alongside one another and collaborative use was made of informal resources and venues.

## Historical Roots

The history of the struggle for universal access to a basic education has been tied up with the struggle for political enfranchisement, and in both of these adult education played a significant role. The context of these struggles through the first half of the nineteenth century, to 1870, has been described in broad terms in Chapter 2. A range of opportunities for adults to learn to read and write were organised during this time, and while access was by no means guaranteed, especially for women (see Purvis, 1989; Taylor, 1983) many thousands of working-class adults learned the basics of reading and writing during this period before the advent of universal primary schooling.

The period 1870–1900 saw the development of universal, compulsory primary schooling for children. Whilst this undoubtedly had effects on the development of literacy, exactly what these were is the subject of considerable dispute. The dispute centres on the extent to which state education was motivated by the desire to control and tame the already fast developing working-class literacies, and how far it was a response to popular demand for increased access to literacy and other learning (Webb, 1971; Lawson and Silver, 1973; Mitch, 1992). Perhaps the most far-reaching effect of compulsory schooling was to change expectations about literacy norms: where there is no universal access to schooling, there is less stigma attached to illiteracy. When it is assumed that everyone has learned to read and write in childhood, an adult who is not literate is treated as a 'special' case (Rose, 1993; Barton, 1988).

The centrality of literacy to Christian religious traditions is described in detail by Kapitzke (1995). Strategies for teaching literacy in the nineteenth century were deeply saturated by the religious ideologies and practices which were dominant at the time. This religious heritage pervaded both state schooling and adult education of all political hues. Strong traces of it remain

today in our beliefs about the moral and character-building powers of
literacy and in traditional teaching methods which emphasise rote learning
and ritual question and answer routines derived from the use of the
catechism as a teaching aid.

It survives also in the otherwise inexplicable privileging in schools of
reading over writing and numeracy. Religious learning emphasised the
reading, memorisation and interpretation of biblical texts, and the only role
for writing was in copying or responding to these. In the nineteenth century,
therefore, reading was taught in school before writing and many children
with limited schooling would have left without having learned to write
(Stevens, 1990). Writing was seen to be potentially subversive of the status
quo and particularly unsuitable for the working classes to practise.
Consequently it was tightly controlled both in terms of educational and
publishing opportunities.

Whilst basic education for adults was a lively feature of the nineteenth
century, it was eclipsed by the development of compulsory state-supported
primary education. The twentieth century has therefore, in contrast, been
pre-occupied with initial schooling for children and its success or failure in
creating mass literacy. Throughout this period there have been surveys of
young people's reading performance and periodic worries about declining
literacy standards. Rogers (1984) collected quotations from Board of
Education reports from 1921, 1925 and 1939 which indicate concern from
employers and educators alike that standards of basic literacy and numeracy
were falling short of some notional but desirable level. Lewis, writing in
1953, talked about a 'universal anxiety about illiteracy'. These sources make
fascinating reading because they are so similar to contemporary claims, and,
as Rogers argued 'one thing these pronouncements have in common is the
omission of any objective supporting evidence'.

By way of contrast, as observed in Chapter 3, literacy was conspicuous
by its absence in the concerns of the adult education establishment (e.g. the
British Institute of Adult Education between the wars and the National
Institute in the 1950s and 60s). During the first half of the century, up to 1944,
there was a huge development in collective working-class activity and
organisation, including new developments in independent adult education
(see Chapter 12). LEAs became heavily involved in providing evening
classes, and in some areas, notably London, began to develop strong
innovatory traditions in adult education. However, as a result of universal
primary schooling the important role that the adult schools had played in
developing literacy in the nineteenth century was much reduced (Hall, 1985).
New organisations such as the WEA and the more radical Labour Colleges
focused on a wider social science, philosophical and literary curriculum
which generally assumed a level of basic literacy and operated methods of
learning through discussion which allowed those with limited reading and
writing to take part. There is some evidence, as Frank and Hamilton (1993)
report, that these colleges addressed the reality of limited literacy among
students through courses such as English grammar, but this was not given
high priority. Frow and Frow (1992) give the example of a Lancashire
woman, Alice Smith, who 'did not find her education easy'. She continued
playing a part in trade union work as well as in independent working class

education, but admitted in the early 1920s to having nearly wept over Joseph Dietzgen's *The Positive Outcome of Philosophy* and she made an impassioned plea for a simplified textbook on the subject – 'something the average man can lap up with his Quaker oats – something he can read (and understand) as he runs.' Frow and Frow comment that 'her difficulties probably reflected a weakness in the work of the Labour College classes which may have contributed to a narrowing of the circle of students in later years.' Marks (1982), in describing the response of adult education to unemployment in the 1930s, revealed that attempts to cater for 'unbookish' students involved offering practical subjects, rather than help in developing literacy.

As soon as universal state primary schooling was in place, the business of classifying and grouping children according to individual differences in ability and various kinds of 'defects' began. The discourse of backwardness and remedial education grew as universal access to education was assumed and a new problem was identified: the differential response of learners to these opportunities. At the end of the nineteenth century the fields of medicine and psychology were developing rapidly and psychometric methods and approaches to assessing ability and educability became dominant, based on models of 'fixed intelligence' and other individual characteristics. As Tomlinson (1982) argued, during this whole period, a great deal of attention was paid to elaborating various categories of defect and developing 'suitable' educational responses to those labelled as in need of special treatment.

In practice, literacy was heavily implicated in measures of intelligence and school performance. The backward child (and later, the adult) was also the child with reading and writing difficulties. This led to an over-identification with remedial education which ABE inherited and has always found problematic.

One important outcome of compulsory schooling, then, was that it allowed closer scrutiny and definition of individual performance in literacy. Definitions of literacy were shaped by the ideology of an elite culture and education system. The psychologist Cyril Burt personified this approach and was an influential figure in promoting it for most of the first half of the century, beginning with his appointment with the London County Council in 1913, where he developed tests for sorting and selecting children for different kinds of educational experience.

The period from 1944 to 1970 began with an Education Act that extended compulsory schooling to secondary level, and continued with reforms to this system and extension of state support into further and higher education. The system that developed enshrined the notion of different needs and fixed abilities among different social classes and elite aims for education. It produced a divided education system which relegated most children to secondary modern schooling with little concern or expectation for their achievements. This led to a majority of children reaching adulthood without formal educational qualifications or high literacy levels and with a low estimation of their capabilities, but this was regarded as inevitable given their limited potential for learning.

During this time UNESCO was developing its mission as promoter of world literacy (Jones, 1990). Its focus then, however, was entirely on developing countries without universal primary schooling and on the issues of providing access to literacy for both children and adults under these circumstances. It was not until much later (the end of the 1980s) that its attention shifted to industrialised countries.

Basic literacy continued to be ignored by adult educators and was not part of the policy agenda of the National Institute of Adult Education. The extension and rationalisation of a national compulsory schooling system into the secondary years was still the major pre-occupation of policy-makers.

Experience in the army during the wartime years of 1939–45 gave the lie to this complacency, however, when it was found that many recruits had missed out on schooling or had very limited experience of it. Basic skills needs among wartime recruits were widespread, and in 1943 for the first time the army responded by setting up Basic Education Centres to address these needs. *Ad hoc* tuition had been available in the army since 1846, when a Royal Warrant established the Corps of Army Schoolmasters, engaged during the day in teaching the children in army schools and during the evening in teaching writing and reading to the soldiers themselves (White, 1963). The Basic Education Centres, however, represented a much more serious and systematic attempt to address literacy needs. Attendance on the full-time courses was compulsory and needs were identified through personnel selection tests and sometimes psychiatric screening (Stevenson, 1985). Whilst an element of remedial therapy was involved in these courses, the over-riding motivation was vocational training and efficiency, making these forerunners of the functional vocational basic skills programmes that are now a familiar part of ABE. However, experience was not generalised from within these spheres to civilian life or adult education policy.

The need for basic education courses in the army continued after the war. Many of those recruited in the 1950s had had their education interrupted by the war. Later, almost all recruits had been through initial schooling but a proportion still had not learned to read and write. This suggested that compulsory schooling had not produced universal literacy and also that literacy is a matter of degree – the demands of literacy move on, and what had once been sufficient writing and reading was no longer functional. This more subtle and shifting definition of literacy in its changing social context is a discovery made by the army that has still not fully reached the public consciousness

The urgency that had propelled the development of literacy provision in the army during and after the war later disappeared. The School of Preliminary Education that was established in 1956 as a residential centre offering full-time courses was struggling for funding by the mid-sixties and eventually closed in 1981 as more limited and selective recruitment led to fewer people with needs for basic literacy training entering the army (Stevenson, 1985).

The institutional separation of military education and civilian adult education is probably one reason why the experience of basic education in the army did not generalise into other contexts (see Hawkins, 1947). The fact that army education was compulsory and closely identified with official wartime propaganda activities, and that literacy was seen as military-related vocational training increased the distance between the expertise developed in the army and the liberal adult education establishment which might have made use of that experience (see Chapter 3).

The other context in which adult literacy education became established was in prison. Prison education began early in the nineteenth century through the concern of social reformers such as Sarah Martin and Elizabeth Fry. In practice, the education on offer was often basic literacy and had strong moral and religious overtones. The supposed link between crime and lack of education and literacy has been a strong theme from the social reformers of the nineteenth century onwards and recurs in contemporary moral panics about literacy (see Cameron, 1995: 92). It is part of the view of prisoners as pathological 'others', and the adult education service that developed in prisons has had strong reformative and therapeutic motives (Banks, 1958). Funded and organised by the Home Office, it was outside the general adult education service and slow to develop links with it (see Hannam, 1982). For example, the 1973 Russell Report hardly mentioned prison education. Neither did the 1979 ACACE report on ABE, which relegated prison education to an appendix, alongside initiatives for other special (i.e. 'deviant') groups. Even now, the relationship between prison education and educational opportunities for ex-offenders is still problematic.

In both of these cases the fact that concern for ABE did not spread into mainstream adult education has much to do with the separation of the populations in prisons and the military from general public and civilian life and the different definition and goals of literacy work within these settings from the way that liberal adult education has defined it.

Adult literacy therefore remained a hidden issue during the 1950s and 60s. It did not figure in the LEAs' post-war plans for further education (see Chapter 4) and was addressed in a marginal way by voluntary welfare groups, individual LEAs, or where adults were subject to particular disciplinary regimes, as in the army or in prison. It was hidden by dominant assumptions about schooling and fixed abilities, expectations of differential achievement of children from different class backgrounds, and a lack of belief in the efficacy or necessity of learning in later life. There were many unskilled jobs and few worries about the low educational attainments of those who filled them. Concerns about skills and training did not arise until later decades, when alarming levels of unemployment brought a whole new group of adults under state scrutiny.

## Competing Ideologies of Literacy

From this brief historical sketch we can begin to identify some of the strands that have contributed to the development ABE. Whilst literacy is an emotive word that evokes almost universal agreement about its desirability, beneath the rhetoric are widely differing views about the definition and purposes of literacy. These reflect competing interest groups and their ideologies, which make appeals to both the moral and the utilitarian bases for literacy. Jones (1990) describes the way in which literacy thus became a central focus for UNESCO policy, since it was an issue that governments of very different ideologies could (at least superficially) unite around.

In the history of adult basic education the different ideologies can be traced through the choice of institutions offering literacy tuition; through the characteristics of those who became teachers – who they were, how they were recruited, their motivation and interpretation of what they were doing; through policy and curriculum discourses; and through the developing public understandings of the reasons for illiteracy and their relationship to school practices and perceptions of schooling.

Some of the strands that can be identified are the same ones that have characterised adult education more generally throughout the nineteenth and twentieth centuries, described in the earlier chapters, but there are others that are particular to literacy and ABE. In common with the rest of adult education are the competing discourses of literacy for emancipation or social control.

**Literacy for emancipation** implies a radical critique of elite culture, selective schooling, state or religiously controlled curricula and existing unequal power relations among different social groups. This is a continuation of the oppositional traditions of independent working-class education described in Chapters 8–10, where adult education is linked to political organisation and action and serves the interests and purposes of working people (Simon, 1992). It is also part of the tradition of community education, where education is linked with efforts to change power structures in order to increase the resources available to communities (see Chapter 5).

Within this discourse, ABE addresses issues of power and representation by emphasising the need for social and political change to redress language-based inequalities. Issues of access to reading and writing are seen as issues of power, not just technical issues of language. Whilst this strand resonates strongly with the Freirian approach to literacy (Freire, 1972) it would be a mistake to think that Freire's ideas were a widespread inspiration for ABE work in this country. Those who were aware of his ideas *did* try to make the connection with their own work, and also with the other mass literacy campaigns that have taken place as part of revolutionary social change this century (Brown, 1973; Arnove and Graff, 1987). The challenge for the new ABE was to adapt Freire's analysis to a society where in principle everyone has access to basic education through primary schooling (Kirkwood and Kirkwood, 1989). A critique of the existing system of schooling was therefore needed.

In the competing discourse of **literacy for social control** by dominant groups, literacy is seen as a way of maintaining the status quo, functionally shaping responsible, moral and economically productive citizens. It may be seen in its purest forms in relation to employer-led workplace training or in prison education, but elements of the social control discourse also occur in the most prominent ideological strand in British ABE whereby literacy education is seen as a welfare activity promoted by the middle classes for disadvantaged 'others' as a way of offering enlightenment – opening access to literacy, classical or religious culture – a kind of **cultural missionary activity**. Whilst this discourse is almost entirely secular in its expression in contemporary society, we have already noted the very overt social and moral control of literacy that sprang from religious motives in earlier days, and which has left a powerful legacy (Graff, 1987).

Discourses of social control within ABE make frequent appeals to liberal and democratic arguments, but in practice the definition of culture on which they are based has generally been extremely narrow – ridden with class-based hierarchical notions of 'good' and 'bad' language, high and low culture. It has also been shaped by imperial notions of the superiority of the English language as a symbol of nationhood, leading to racist, deficit notions of bilingual speakers and a total neglect of serious policy to address the needs of linguistic and cultural minorities. Such attitudes, of course, pervade language policy and practice across the whole educational system and ABE has had to work within the constraints posed by these (Carby, 1982; Brumfit, 1985). An important issue in evaluating the contribution of ABE is, then, how far it has managed to resist and critique this discourse.

Another legacy from the general educational discourse as described above has been the **deficit model of literacy** carried over to ABE from remedial or special needs education and, more broadly, from the selective educational tradition. How could ABE and ABE students define themselves in ways other than this remedial discourse and develop positive views of those adults who do have learning difficulties?

One way is to move away from an individual, skills-based approach to ABE towards a view of literacy and numeracy as community resources to which ABE can improve access for individuals and groups.

These four strands (emancipatory, social control, cultural missionary work and remedial views of ABE) have been tightly interwoven in the fabric of ABE in the UK. Most programmes show evidence of a mixture of them and any analysis must focus on the shifting balance of power between these different ideologies at different points in time, or in different institutional and policy settings.

Nevertheless, they are useful pointers for evaluating the changing shape of ABE as it moved from the early days of the literacy campaign and for identifying the areas in which a truly effective ABE would have to develop a critical stance. These are: (1) a critical analysis of the social and economic relationships framing literacy in the UK, especially in respect of the world of work; (2) a cultural critique exposing and contesting the elitest assumptions in discourses about language and literacy; and (3) a critique of the formal educational system, especially the ways in which it creates deficit models of literacy learners.

The next section will look at how ABE has developed over the last two decades and assess how far such critiques have emerged from the field.

## Naming the Moment: The Adult Literacy Campaign

ABE as a part of adult continuing education in the UK emerged when central government support for adult literacy began in the 1970s. The motivation for the original literacy campaign among those who promoted it was a liberal, welfarist approach that emphasised wider access to cultural and educational opportunities. During the course of the 1980s, this original motivation was overtaken by the rise of vocationalism in education, as ABE was caught up in political agendas that led to a widespread reform of education and training more generally and a heightening of social and political control.

*Ad hoc* provision of literacy in both voluntary groups and LEAs had been rising unremarked during the late 1960s. A survey carried out by Haviland in 1972 showed that there were more than 230 literacy schemes in England and Wales on the eve of the literacy campaign, catering for around 5,000 adults. Around half of all LEAs were involved in such provision (Clyne,1972) and the rest were organised by voluntary schemes or prisons. The later pattern of voluntary tutors, part-time courses (typically two hours per week) and small groups or individual tuition was already established by these schemes (Haviland, 1973).

The literacy campaign was spearheaded by the British Association of Settlements (BAS, 1974) which had its roots in the nineteenth century cultural missionary activities of university extension. These activities had become overlaid with a more distinctively twentieth century idea of welfare for disadvantaged groups. The rhetoric was of rights, access to a literary heritage, arts and the quality of life – the classic 'enlightenment' approach to working-class education that had increasingly come to dominate liberal, individualistic adult education (Keddie, 1980).

The background and history of the adult literacy campaign and its aftermath has been reasonably well documented. (Those interested in more details can consult Jones and Charnley, 1978; Mace, 1979; Hargreaves, 1980; Charnley and Jones, 1981; Limage, 1986; Fowler, 1988; Charnley and Withnall, 1989; Hamilton, 1989, 1992; Street, 1994; Withnall, 1994.)

Briefly, in 1973 a national campaign was launched as the result of pressure from community workers and adult educators. In 1974, one million pounds of central government money was released from the DES for the campaign, and this, combined with an enormous amount of volunteer effort and the involvement of public television and radio, quickly established adult literacy provision in England and Wales. It became part of adult eduction in every LEA, supported by a central agency (now known as the Basic Skills Agency). This unit, originally the Adult Literacy Resource Agency (ALRA), was set up to fund special development projects, to publish resource material and develop staff training. It developed and promoted accreditation for staff and students, developed quality control measures and funded a considerable body of research. Its remit was later broadened to include basic reading and writing, numeracy, oral communication and, from 1985, English for speakers of other languages (ALBSU, 1987 and see Chapter 3).

Provision in Scotland initially followed a similar pattern, but the Scottish Adult Basic Eduction Unit was integrated into the Scottish Community Education Council in 1991, and ABE has always been treated as part of the strong community education service (European Bureau of Adult Education, 1983). In this way it has had a less distinct presence than in England and Wales but has retained a firmer committment to collective social and political change (see Chapter 5).

It is clear from Withnall (1994) that there were really two linked campaigns in which the BBC and the British Association of Settlements (BAS) joined forces. The BAS led the political campaign, whilst the BBC organised a public awareness campaign and referral service. It is also clear that the initial money was given by central government as the result of persuasion by committed individual politicians. Most visibly, these included

Christopher Price, Labour MP for Lewisham West who introduced a private bill which gathered all-party sponsorship (Withnall 1994: 77). Fowler (1988) also cites the positive support of the Minister for Higher Education in finally authorising the release of central government funding.

But there was far from a wholehearted policy commitment: the money that was released was a relatively small amount, slipped through in the margins of educational policy and seen as a temporary measure. By the time ABE was made a permanent part of adult continuing education in England and Wales a very different policy rationale was in ascendance: that of economic efficiency, rather than the right to read.

It is revealing to juxtapose the advent of the adult literacy campaign with other aspects of contemporary social, educational and training policy, including developments in the mass media. Thus the campaign occurred in the context of the arrival of comprehensive schools during the mid 1960s, and the expansion of higher education through new universities later in the same decade, along with the creation of the polytechnics and later, in 1971, the Open University.

After the expansionist period of the 1960s, the 1970s saw a growing realisation that compulsory schooling as developed since the war had not achieved a basic education for everyone as hoped. The National Foundation for Educational Research had carried out research which suggested that after a steady upward trend, improvements in standards of literacy and numeracy had slowed down during the 1960s (Start and Wells, 1972). The notion of compensatory education was at its height: this was the moment of the Halsey Report into Educational Priority Areas (1972) and the era of Community Development Projects as a radical intervention intended to solve well-recognised but intractable problems of social inequality (see Chapter 5). There was concern for access for working-class and other disadvantaged groups to higher education generally, of which the establishment of the Open University in 1971 was a part (see Chapter 11). This concern was strongly expressed in the Russell Report, which specifically recommended that 'LEAs should make available and widely known opportunities for men and women to complete formal general education' (DES, 1973: xx, in reference to para. 183), though this was still couched in terms of 'remedial' education rather as than part of lifelong learning.

The publication of the first of the Black Papers in 1969 was the first sign of the right-wing 'back to basics' movement which blamed supposed falling standards of literacy and numeracy on the failure of progressive teaching methods and comprehensive schools. As we saw earlier, such attacks on education have surfaced periodically and reveal more about the political climate of the time than about real trends in literacy. At this time, it was, as Deem (1981) says, 'only part of a more general move to cut welfare expenditure and restructure social relations'.

The Manpower Services Commission, responsible for the massive expansion of vocational education and training during the 1980s, was also established at this time through the Department of Employment. It was the first national training agency in the UK and it reflected an already growing government concern about the changing structure of employment and the perceived need for new training strategies (see Chapter 3). Manufacturing industry was beginning to decline and the traditional apprenticeship system had collapsed. This posed a major problem for the further education colleges, which had built their provision around the day-release system. Callaghan's watershed speech at Ruskin College, which made a firm link between education and economic investment, followed in 1976. Despite these signs of a change of direction in government policy, the people attracted into the field of ABE as teachers were more influenced by a 1960s ideology and had motivations and ideals similar to other liberal adult educators (Fieldhouse, 1993).

Beyond the small world of adult education, there was also a new belief in the possibilities of lifelong learning – that adults *could* learn later in life. The ideals of lifelong learning and recurrent education were embodied in reports by the OECD and UNESCO at the beginning of the 1970s (OECD, 1971; OECD/CERI, 1973; UNESCO, 1972). These signalled a change in the debates around education at international level which filtered through into national policy, though unevenly in different countries. Ironically, these ideas were not much visible in the Russell Report, but gained momentum in the UK during the 1980s and 1990s in relation to vocational education and training and in the movement to widen access to higher education.

Other international influences included the US federal 'Right to Read' programme which was put in place in 1971 (see Limage, 1990) and almost certainly provided some stimulus to the campaign in the UK, although this is not widely acknowledged. The most tangible link is through the Ford Foundation which provided some financial support to the BBC campaign (Hargreaves, 1980: 7).

The name was the same, although the motivation in the US was already linked with economic efficiency and had the explicit aim of improving the quality of schooling as well. There had also been a literacy campaign in Southern Italy, but like the literacy work of UNESCO this was aimed at adults who had not had an initial schooling. The UNESCO rhetoric of 'eradicating' illiteracy and contemporary definitions of functional literacy coined by UNESCO were cited. The campaign style of mobilising public interest and volunteers typical of mass campaigns in countries such as Cuba and the Soviet Union were also clearly visible in the original BAS campaigning documents (British Association of Settlements, 1974).

## *The Role of Central and Local Government*

The initial grant was given to the Adult Literacy Resource Agency (ALRA) in 1975–6 on the basis of temporary need, but by 1979, the Advisory Council for Adult and Continuing Education's Report *A Strategy for the Basic Education of Adults* was recommending that ABE be consolidated as a permanent feature of continuing education – though the funding would still be subject to regular review.

The central resource agency went through several incarnations (formerly ALRA, ALU, ALBSU, and, from 1995, BSA – the Basic Skills Agency (see Chapter 3). Over time the agency came to fulfil all the criteria of a national 'quango' – carrying out government policy whilst retaining a quasi-independent facade. It began as a resource agency, but became more of a monitoring and quality control body. This involved a political balancing act as it continued to fund special development projects; promote major initiatives such as open learning, workplace and family literacy; document the need for ABE; research good practice and produce publications, while maintaining relationships with LEAs and colleges as the main providers of ABE. The latest name change, which dropped the 'adult literacy' label and extended the BSA's remit to 14–16-year-olds, had important implications for an adult-focused service.

Funded by central government, ALBSU played only a supporting role in the field. The vast expansion in provision was funded by LEAs. Further funding came from voluntary bodies, whilst prison education and ESOL obtained money through the Home Office. European Union money became increasingly available and important in helping support innovatory programmes. The Department of Employment was another major funder of basic skills courses, largely for unemployed school leavers and adults.

Local government was very influential on ABE and some (particularly the large metropolitan authorities) developed extensive programmes of learning opportunities. In London the ILEA set up its own Language and Literacy Unit as a focus for advisory and development work in ABE. Disputes which flared in the 1980s and 1990s between local and central government, particularly the radical metropolitan LEAs, were a legacy from earlier periods. The 1992 Further and Higher Education Act gave LEAs a much reduced role. FE colleges became the main conduit for funding for all vocationally relevant courses, giving them a great deal of local influence. Whether ABE becomes a central part of college provision and retains its community base or whether it is subsumed under other college activities (becoming transformed into learning support for mainstream college students, for example) depends on the management, philosophy and history of individual colleges.

The demise of the Inner London Education Authority (ILEA) seriously affected the comprehensive and innovative ABE that had been developed in London as part of its extensive adult education service (Lobley and Moss, 1990; Herrington and Moss, 1991). The former ILEA Language and Literacy Unit, which pioneered much important work, still exists but in a much weaker form, without the resources or the networks to be effective.

After 1992, when the funding for ABE became channelled through the FE colleges directly rather than through the LEAs, very little money was available for non-vocational, community initiatives, and there is an increasing reliance on other non-statutory sources for these types of literacy programmes.

## The Influence of Broadcasting

Public broadcasting already had a well-established educational mission, with a philosophy of broadening access to culture (Robinson, 1983 and see Chapter 14). It enthusiastically embraced the new educational technologies explored in the development of the Open University (see Chapter 11).

Following the publication of the Pilkington Report in 1962, the BBC appointed a team of further education officers, who conducted a survey of adult interests and needs. The ITA also carried out a questionnaire survey. Both revealed the extent of practical and functional interests among the adult community, as opposed to 'academic' and 'subject' interests, and this research gave new direction to the planning of programmes. Programmes on basic literacy and numeracy were regarded as ideal candidates for addressing the needs identified through this research and television and radio were thought to have particular potential for reaching adults who could not read or write.

In developing programmes for recruiting and teaching adult literacy learners, the BBC created a powerful public image of literacy: this has always been a problematic aspect of media publicity, in the press as well as the broadcasting media. The literacy campaign programmes made great efforts to present potential literacy learners as 'just like us', rather than as isolated, maladjusted, remedial figures – almost to the extent of obliterating any patterns of social class or other differences. The message was that the person in need of literacy help was as likely to be a bank manager as to be an unemployed labourer. This was not true, of course, as findings from national cohort studies revealed (Hamilton, 1987; Eckinsmyth and Bynner, 1994). This research clearly showed that although people across the socio-economic spectrum report difficulties with literacy and numeracy, the incidence of such difficulties is strongly related to social class background and current occupation. Nevertheless, the media campaign was an attempt to overcome the stereotype of the illiterate as a stigmatised 'other' and to present literacy as an issue which affects all our lives.

## The Institutional Setting of ABE

From the start ABE was located in the LEA adult education sector under the control of the DES, rather than with the Employment Department or social services. The exception to this was ESOL, which, as we discuss later, has been funded through the Home Office.

The fact that ABE was put under the control of the DES signalled a great deal about the vision behind the provision and how it was intended to develop. Comparisons with other countries, such as France and Canada, show that this was a policy choice to which there are a number of possible solutions (Hamilton, 1989). According to whether ABE is linked to employment, social services or citizenship and immigration, the provision develops under a different set of priorities.

The fact that ABE was defined and located as adult education, meant that it took on the ethos and characteristics of that provision: that is, a concern with the educational rather than the social aspects of ABE, a liberal curriculum, a philosophy of informal, student-centred teaching and assessment, part-time staff, classes without dedicated space or facilities, often housed in school premises and timetabled in two-hour slots, mainly in the evenings.

Where ABE did take place in other institutional settings, such as FE, voluntary sector and employment programmes, prisons and the forces, it took a correspondingly different shape. For example, the early preparatory Training Opportunity Programme courses, funded by the Department of

Employment, were the first and only full-time basic skills courses set up (apart from those in the army). The effect of institutional setting was well recognised in the early years of the literacy campaign in the UK, and ALBSU encouraged developments in a wide variety of settings within the community: voluntary agencies, schools, family centres, prison and probation service, libraries, as well as adult centres and FE. There was concern to foster links with the voluntary organisations which had pioneered literacy work, and an assumption that a diversity of settings for ABE was important to cater for the range of needs of potential students. Adult education was well-placed for this, since in its 'community education' role it was used to the notion of outreach.

It has always been important that ABE link with other educational and training opportunities, and again the institutional base can make for more or less access and flexibility. Seeing literacy and numeracy as more than just isolated skills problematises the whole naming of ABE as a separate subject – always a contentious issue for practitioners. Should we call ABE Communication Skills? Essential Adult Learning? Second Chance to Learn? Brush Up Your English and Maths?

## Staffing Conditions and Professional Development

The great majority of tutors and organisers in ABE have from the start been women, a gender bias which reflects the fact that related fields such as primary school teaching and special education are feminised. This explains the poor conditions of service and part-time nature of many of the posts in ABE. The use of volunteers, which was very extensive during the initial literacy campaign, was later much reduced. ALBSU argued that properly trained and paid professional teachers were preferable, and volunteers could only supplement, not replace, the work of such staff. The idea of one-to-one pairings of volunteers and students in their own homes came to be seen as suitable only in particular cases as a transitional stage towards participation in a group. The argument against volunteers as providing an 'ABE on the cheap' are persuasive, and there were undoubtedly problems in adequately selecting, supporting and training volunteers. However, there are benefits to the volunteer model which have perhaps been overlooked in the reaction against it. There is the potential to recruit volunteers from a wider range of backgrounds than current professional ABE teachers have. Much greater support and understanding of students' personal circumstances are possible through the more individual relationships that are developed by volunteers, especially where these are not limited to the college setting.

Initial training and accreditation for tutors in ABE became tightly controlled by ALBSU, which developed special qualifications through the City and Guilds validating body. There were few opportunities for higher level, in-service training, however, and this, together with the lack of real career structures in ABE, meant that experienced workers tended to move sideways out of ABE if they wanted to develop their work. Although local and regional networks did emerge (such as those that evolved through training activities, for example) ABE staff were slow to develop a strong professional voice. Consequently they had little systematic input into the policy changes that have taken place.

## Teaching and Learning Methods

Teaching and learning methods evolved since the literacy campaign, with a move away from the one-to-one tutoring pairs that were originally common, towards small groups and, increasingly, drop-in workshops or open learning centres offering supported self-study. Whilst each of these methods has its good and bad points, ideally a choice is needed to suit different students' needs. For example, the flexibility in timing offered by open learning was welcomed by many adults, but not all ABE students were able to benefit from such self-organised study methods, which offered less opportunity for the discussion and mutual support that proved to be an important part of developing confidence to tackle basic skills (see Bergin and Hamilton, 1994). The move toward open learning fitted in with more general moves in this direction in further education, where it was seen as a cost-effective method, reducing the need for tutor contact and making use of new technologies.

The materials and curriculum commonly in use in ABE were heavily influenced by ALBSU, which consistently published high quality resource packs. These materials are aimed at tutors, for them to adapt with their students. ALBSU never produced primers or a fixed syllabus for use in ABE but kept to the principles of student-centred teaching. However, in the late 1980s and early 1990s it developed national accreditation for ABE in the shape of two competency-based schemes: WordPower (for literacy) and NumberPower (for numeracy). These were developed in response to pressures to fit in with a framework of National Vocational Qualifications (NVQs) and linked to strong concerns with cost-effectiveness, measurement, accountability and control of programme outcomes. While WordPower and NumberPower are not in themselves a curriculum, in practice they strongly affected the content and format of learning.

Alternative accreditation was developed in conjunction with the burgeoning Open College Networks, which enabled pathways to be built from ABE into higher education. The student writing and publishing movement also developed its own set of methods, including the use of residential writing weekends and reading evenings (Gardener, 1986). These methods were well-developed through community bookshops and publishing projects such as Gatehouse Books, Centerprise and Write First Time (a collectively produced newspaper that closed after 10 years amidst political controversy; see Mace, 1979). Student writing not only creatively solves the problem of what adult learners can be offered as reading matter, it also fits in with the idea of participation and validating the experience of learners. A recent survey of student writing and publishing showed that such activities still existed in many ABE programmes (O'Rourke and Mace, 1992). However, there was a lack of staff training to support it and few opportunities for residential weekends or for national circulation of the work. Training is particularly important if staff are to develop creative ways of integrating this kind of activity within the WordPower framework.

As standardised accreditation and outcomes were increasingly demanded by funders, the tension between these and the original student-centred approaches to teaching and measuring progress became stronger. Perhaps more than anything else, this changed the face and the feel of ABE.

## Research and Reflection on Practice

The British ABE movement was rooted in a strong practical tradition that was slow to theorise or make links with other fields. Whilst this was in some ways a strength, it also made ABE particularly vulnerable to outside pressures to change practice. The academic work that flourished in the 1980s and 1990s in the new field of literacy studies made little impact on ABE work in the UK because links with higher education had never really developed (see Barton, 1992 and 1994 for reviews of this research).

International links were weakened by the UK's withdrawal from UNESCO during the 1980s. This was particularly obvious during 1990, UNESCO's International year of Literacy, which had considerable impact worldwide, but received only marginal official publicity or support in the UK.

ALBSU itself sponsored a range of policy-oriented research, which included a comparison of styles of provision and a study of drop-out and progression in ABE (Abell, 1992; Kambouri and Francis, 1994). ALBSU was particularly active in sponsoring research that tried to establish the extent of the need for adult basic education (ALBSU, 1989, 1993; Eckinsmyth and Bynner, 1994). Whilst this research was important in raising the profile of basic skills work, it took for granted many questionable assumptions about the definition and goals that underlie the field and did not therefore encouraged an atmosphere of debate. Other bodies which sponsored evaluation and development work, such as the ILEA, disappeared, leaving very few opportunities for local and regional co-ordination and information exchange. One organisation that spanned this period of change since 1986 to the present is the Research and Practice in Adult Literacy (RaPAL) group, which aimed to improve communication between researchers and practitioners. It has supported and promoted new models of research, which emphasise co-operation between all those involved in the research and treat the learners experience as central to any enquiry (Hamilton and Barton, 1989; Hamilton et al., 1992; Hamilton, 1994), and publishes a regular bulletin. It has acted as a network to keep people in touch with changes and debates in the field, with the aim of promoting a sense of professional community.

## English for Speakers of Other Languages (ESOL)

Concern with the language needs of linguistic minority groups, whether in-comers or indigenous groups, had very weak support at policy level. Controlling the relationship between English and other language groups has always been a feature of nation-building in the UK and of immense concern in the maintenance of 'empire'. This has led to struggles over the survival of the Welsh and Gaelic languages, promotion of English as the standard language of the empire and belief in its superiority over other languages. Cameron (1995) has called the consequent obsession with purity of standards (in which literacy has been implicated) 'verbal hygiene'.

This legacy from the empire, and the wider mentality, attitudes and prejudices of which it is a part, pervaded the development of ABE and literacy work generally. Specifically, it shaped, and in the main restricted and deformed any provision that developed for ESOL. This is one of the areas where international comparisons are sobering. In Canada and Australia (societies not devoid of racism themselves), literacy and ABE policy developed with a genuine recognition of the relationship between literacy and language variety, the underlying social relationships of power and subordination which determine which language is adopted as the dominant standard, and the need to address these relationships in a co-ordinated fashion.

In the UK, whilst there were some shifts in public attitudes and policy between the 1970s and the 1990s, the response was muted and halting, to say the least. The only concession was to recognise the equality of the Welsh language in Wales as part of ABE policy, and the BSA pursued this assiduously.

Nicholls (1985) described the development of adult ESL provision since the mid-1960's:

Although Britain has always had non-indigenous second language speakers, it was not until the forced migration of large numbers of East African Asians started to arrive in the 1960s that the need for language provision for adults was officially recognised and ESL schemes came into existence (p 101).

Official recognition came in the shape of funding from the Home Office to LEAs (the infamous Section 11 funding of the 1966 Local Authority Act) and this was used to set up ESOL courses in areas where the demand was greatest. The fact that funding was entirely separate from ABE and was never offered in terms of a 'campaign' in the same way meant that what should have been overlapping provision developed quite separately, and it was only gradually that connections were made. (ALBSU took ESOL into its remit only in 1985.)

Funding until the early 90s was restricted to immigrant groups from the new commonwealth and so did not cover many ESOL groups who arguably had equal or greater language needs (such as those from Eastern Europe or Vietnamese refugees). LEAs were not encouraged to make provision through their mainstream education budgets for bilingual learners (ALBSU, 1992; Hartley, 1992). Speakers of minority dialects, such as Afro-Caribbean adults, were also casualties of this irrational provision. Their literacy needs were addressed neither by national ESOL funding nor by mainstream literacy programmes. The most notable work was done in some outstanding local projects developed with Afro-Caribbean speakers in London and Manchester (Craven and Jackson, 1986; Schwab and Stone, 1987; Morris and Nwenmele, 1994).

The fact that funding for ESOL came from the Home Office rather than the DES meant that it was treated as a 'social' problem resulting from immigration rather than as an educational issue. Bilingual adults and their children were pathologised and treated as deficient rather than a resource, and mother tongue and bilingual literacy programmes were never officially sanctioned and funded. There were some examples of bilingual literacy work funded outside of Section 11 funding, such as the Black literacy campaign (Gurnah, 1992); the Kweyol project (Morris and Nwenmely, 1994, and see *RaPAL Bulletin*, issue 25, Autumn 1994).

Within mainstream provision, however, the aim was only for adults to learn the English language. As Robinson (1985) says:

compensatory education programmes are provided to try to assimilate the immigrant communities into what is perceived as the traditional, monocultural, monolinguistic heritage. This has been a very powerful trend in the British Education System and it is only comparatively recently that it has begun to be questioned (p 32).

In the late 60s there was an ideological shift from 'assimilation' to cultural pluralism, and then to anti-racism which acknowledged the way in which different cultures were produced and existed in social relations of power, of dominance and subordination (Carby, 1982). However, these ideological shifts have been far from straightforward. They were contested at every step, most recently in terms of threats to the continuation of Section 11 funding without any replacement (Wardle, 1994).

The MSC-funded Industrial Language Training (ILT) programme was the only other centrally-funded initiative during this period. Though it did some ground-breaking work, it never connected with ABE and did not survive the 1980s. It was set up to address the needs of ESOL in the workplace (Munns and Strutt, 1981; Roberts *et al.*, 1992). ILT began in 1974, the same year as the adult literacy campaign, but had a management and support structure entirely separate from it, with its own National Centre for Industrial Language Training (NCILT). The original aim had been to contribute to racial equality by addressing the English language needs of ethnic minority workers but issues that at first were defined as communication or langage deficiency issues began to be seen more as aspects of racism and disadvantage in the work context. The attention of the programme shifted towards those providing services for ethnic minority groups and to the skills and attitudes of their colleagues and managers. By the time its funding was withdrawn in 1989, the agenda of ILT work had become, therefore, much more radical and controversial (Brooks and Roberts, 1985).

## Changing Discourses of ABE: From compensatory education to economic efficiency

The fact that the political climate was already changing from the expansive welfarism that had inspired it when the literacy campaign started meant that the original impulse behind the campaign was already becoming out-dated by the mid-1970s when it took shape, and the project of developing a permanent ABE service went on under changed policy assumptions about educational goals and priorities. The 1979 ACACE Report still justified the need for ABE in terms of equality of opportunity, but it was out of step with the increasingly influential MSC and acknowledged that no coherent policy commitment had yet materialised.

Through the 1980s public discussions about literacy increasingly invoked the vocational discourse of human resource investment. Talk was of literacy skills, rather than wider knowledge or practices; training rather than education; and literacy and numeracy were linked into wider discourses about national training and economic needs and the development of functional competences. In areas such as prison and army education, the functional/instrumental aspects of literacy had always been stressed, but during the 1980s and 90s the social control aspects became more overtly political in mainstream ABE, linked with unemployment through Youth and Adult Training Schemes, workplace and family literacy programmes. Programmes which started from community definitions of literacy and numeracy and which focused on the process of negotiation of purpose and curriculum became derided and discredited.

These developments were of course part of the attempt to redefine education more generally (Ball, 1990). Another manifestation of this was the bitter war waged in the late 1980s and early 90s over content and methods of English teaching in schools through the development of a National Curriculum. In the course of this another 'literacy crisis' was fomented and the moral basis of literacy in our culture was once again revealed. Cameron (1995) summarises the hysteria in this way:

Newspaper columns and editorials were haunted by the spectre of a language and culture under threat: a nation disinherited, illiterate, populated by school leavers unable to fill in a simple job application form or make themselves understood at an interview – not because they were intrinsically stupid but because no one cared enough to teach them proper English. The malign and destructive ideologies that gripped these young people's teachers would have their full flowering in the later careers of the young people themselves: ignorant, inarticulate and unemployable, they would turn to anti-social and criminal behaviour. These images were powerful, and they resonated across the social and political spectrum (p 92).

## Failure/Deficit Models

We have seen how ABE inherited from schooling a view of literacy difficulties which was rooted in psychological deficit models, learning difficulties and special educational needs. At the beginning of the literacy campaign there were few available materials other than those used to teach initial literacy to children. In the secular 1970s, the catechism no longer seemed appropriate and in any case, the biggest demand was for help with writing and spelling rather than with reading (Hamilton and Stasinopoulos, 1987). There were attempts to import the expertise that had been developed through remedial work with children, and ABE had to remove itself from this stigmatising 'special education' label. There was a conflict of perspectives between teachers coming from primary schooling and traditions of special education who felt expert by virtue of their experience with children's initial literacy and those from an adult education background and philosophy who felt that a different kind of teacher–student relationship was appropriate and that new materials and methods needed to be developed for adults.

The issue of how to work with adults who have general and specific learning difficulties is nevertheless a real one, and, over time, ABE developed its own body of expertise. It remained a sensitive and controversial area. One model that gained considerable ground despite surrounding controversy was the medical disability model of dyslexia. Dyslexia was first identified at the end of the nineteenth century but has never been fully accepted by the educational establishment (Miles and Gilroy, 1986; Pumfrey and Reason, 1991). Interest in it has been perpetuated by a strong voluntary lobby of parents and individual teachers and there are many adult students who are enthusiastic about finding a physical rationale for persistent difficulties with reading and writing, especially as diagnosis now brings LEA recognition and resources as an official 'special need' (Herrington, 1995).

## Emancipatory Literacy Education

The notion of an independent, emancipatory adult education serving a collective movement for social and political change was never a mainstream part of ABE, but flourished in selected, influential pockets, especially in the voluntary sector and the metropolitan LEAs. Some voluntary adult education providers and the WEA had retained a commitment to community development and to democratic self-management in their programmes in a way that had never been part of the tradition of LEA adult education. This was a strand that got taken up in some ABE programmes (see Mace, 1979 and the Lee Centre Problems of Representation series; National Federation of Voluntary Literacy Schemes/ALBSU, 1983; Edwards, 1986). From the notion of participatory literacy grew notions of a radical research agenda, controlled by student and staff concerns (Baynham, 1986; Hamilton *et al.*, 1992; Hamilton 1994) This agenda was taken up and developed by the Research and Practice in Adult Literacy group (RaPAL), as we saw above.

The emancipatory strand did emerge in a different way in ABE, through the development of a student publishing movement which never received a great deal of official state support but survived to produce innovatory materials and methods of working on literacy (Gatehouse, 1992; O'Rourke, 1992; Mace, 1995). This way of working was born partly out of expediency (since there were few materials available for new adult readers and writers) and partly from the inspiration of innovative work on writing going on in London schools at the time, by people such as Chris Searle and Harold Rosen.

The approach was pioneered by voluntary sector schemes and had its roots in the 'history from the bottom up' approach, evident as far back as the Mass Observation archive established in the 1930s (Sheridan and Calder, 1985) and the impulse to working-class autobiography, as in the Ruskin College History Workshop. Those involved in ABE made links with community/working-class publishing (Morley and Worpole, 1982; Gatehouse, 1985; Gregory, 1991) and those working to develop oral history (Thompson, 1978) to develop a political critique of the welfarist discourse in literacy work (Shrapnell, 1974). The Federation of Worker Writers and Community Publishers, which links self-organised writers' groups across the country, was formed in 1976. The *Oral History Journal* also began at this time.

In terms of other emancipatory forces, feminist ideas developing through a strong women's movement in the 1970s were influential in adult education more broadly (see Thompson, 1983), but less obviously in ABE. Mace (1993) and Mace *et al.* (1993) argue that much of the process and oral culture aspects of ABE were shaped by women's consciousness as the main workers in the field. However, this did not happen so explicitly as in Canada, for example, where literacy workers developed a critique of the role of women as literacy tutors as well as the values of literacy and literacy education in women's lives (Rockhill, 1987; Horsman, 1990; Lloyd, 1991).

The trade unions always had a presence in ABE from the initial literacy campaign, but never took the major initiative on literacy as a public issue for their members. In this sense, there was never a feeling that ABE was a grass-roots, collective movement for change. NUPE developed WORKBASE, a pioneering and influential collaborative approach to workplace basic skills programmes (Bonnerjea, 1987) and there were other scattered initiatives, such as the Trade Union Basic Education (TUBE) project in Manchester. In the 1990s, UNISON and other trade unions sponsored programmes of general education for their members (see Chapter 10). However, during the 1980s government attacks on the trade union movement kept it fully occupied with more urgent struggles for their survival as collective organisations themselves. This elbowed out more peripheral concerns such as education and training, and this was especially unfortunate given the subsequent government interest in workplace basic skills which appears to have been largely inspired by management interests (Frank and Hamilton, 1993). The trade union influenced lobby for paid educational leave (Mace and Yarnit, 1983) went strangely quiet.

## Conclusion

At the beginning of the literacy campaign, there was a great deal of potential to develop an ABE which would elaborate the ideals behind 'lifelong learning" and develop a robust critical stance in relation to the forces identified above: these were the social, political and economic structures within which ABE was developing; notions of culture and language variety embodied within ABE programmes; and thirdly, the formal education system. How far did it fulfil this potential and manage to sustain a radical critique of these areas?

In the 1970s, the UK offered a role model for other adult literacy campaigns in countries such as Canada, Australia and France and was seen as an innovatory force within adult education. The literacy campaign pushed forward the development of a comprehensive local authority provision, albeit of uneven quality, and attracted a new constituency of working-class adults (especially men) into adult education. It challenged the boundaries of adult education by insisting on outreach and a diversity of settings. It drew on the practices and resources of voluntary organisations and developed a variety of new partnerships.

It was influential in getting mainstream further and adult education to take issues of literacy and numeracy seriously in subject-based courses. More recently it achieved statutory status within the FE sector.

The literacy campaign marked a major new development in educational broadcasting and co-operation with the adult education service. The BBC support services grew from the referral service set up during the campaign. The campaign and subsequent follow-ups put adult literacy on the public agenda. ABE has been successful in distancing itself from the remedial image by production of high quality resources and materials but has not yet won this battle with the media, who still speak in terms of deficit models and 'illiteracy', making any publicity double-edged. This is partly because ABE has not managed to make use of the discourse of the new literacy studies now current in higher education research or to link in with it. Too often the media reflect limited or outdated views of the 'need' for adult basic eduction fed to them by particular interest groups.

Despite the successes of ABE in the UK, over the last 10 years the innovatory cutting edge of ABE has moved to other countries. Perhaps this was to be expected, as a new field of state-funded education matured into the mainstream and reached compromises around issues of professionalisation, accreditation and so on. With the advent of national accreditation through WordPower and NumberPower, ABE was forced to work in partnership with the demands of FE and training and this left little room to develop any effective critique of vocationalism. The downside of achieving statutory status was the narrowing of the definition of literacy and numeracy and the assimilation of ABE into formal education, away from the more radical potential of informal community education. No legislative guarantee of the right of individual adults to a basic education has been forthcoming from government, not even in terms of the workplace. There has been much rhetoric, but the substantial funding that would indicate real political will has not materialised and ABE has only ever reached a small proportion of adults who report basic skills difficulties (in Hamilton and Stasinopoulos, 1987, the figures were one in 10).

Given the marginal power of ABE in the policy spectrum, to survive at all in the current climate could be seen as a major achievement. If it *has* failed, this is due in part to a failure in the wider vision of adult continuing education in the UK that it has had to live within. Kallen (1979) pointed out how a failure to take on board the full implications of the lifelong learning approach and strategy leads to new initiatives being incorporated into the existing patterns of provision at the risk of losing their innovative characteristics. Finch (1984) in looking at education and social policy since the 1940s noted the tension that has existed between the individual good and the benefit of policies to society as a whole. She claims that policy proposals that address individual needs and benefits are less likely to get implemented than those appealing to the social good, or, if they *are* implemented, are very likely to get co-opted for other purposes.

This analysis is highly relevant to the development of adult literacy policy in the UK over the last 20 years. Its force can be seen in the care with which literacy workers and students themselves have constantly to present arguments to the media and to funders in justification of adult basic education. Two hundred years ago Martha More had to convince farmers to allow their employees to take part in reading classes by claiming:

we ... said that we had a little plan which we hoped would secure their orchards from being robbed, their rabbits from being shot, their game from being stolen and which might lower the poor-rates' (Kelly, 1992: 77).

Such appeals to employers' and tax-payers' interests have been commonplace in the 1990s in order to secure policy support for work which is also motivated by the pursuit of other, less marketable benefits. The danger of such appeals is that they deform and narrow the discourse of adult basic education even while trying to raise awareness and funds.

ABE has been further deformed by the wider political and educational agendas that have dominated the UK since the end of the 1970s. ABE has been squeezed between two versions of the "social control" approach, neither of which is adequate to define it: these are the discourse of disadvantage and compensatory education, and the discourse of economic efficiency. The emancipatory, collective discourse has always been weak and had no power in official policy circles so it has remained a fairly ineffectual counter-discourse. Those working within this tradition have shown convincingly what can be done practically in individual programmes, but this work has been sparsely documented and has not been able to develop any strategy or professional base from which to affect policy and practice more widely.

The central dominance and astute publicity strategy of ALBSU in the field has meant that there has been one official version of the scope, goals and practice of ABE since 1974. ABE has therefore become incorporated into mainstream educational practice, limiting its potential to act radically on literacy issues and to influence the rest of adult education. It could be argued that this outcome is better than the ghettoisation of ABE within the low-status non-vocational adult education sector, but it does mean that ABE has not so far fulfilled its potential as a leading innovator in lifelong learning.

This *potential* remains, however, to force a change of perspective that would bring ABE closer to community concerns and definitions of literacy and numeracy. Such a change of perspective would move the public and media image of literacy and numeracy away from a 'skills-based' approach to a 'social practice' view. The social practice view of literacy and numeracy starts from people's everyday, vernacular uses, meanings and purposes for reading, writing and maths and the resources available in communities to support these practices. Finding pathways between these vernacular cultures and the learning opportunities developed for adults remains a major challenge for ABE policy in the UK.

That ABE has not realised its potential is due to a failure to reflect and a failure to connect. The failure to *reflect* has been a lack of processes and mechanisms whereby this can be done, such as through professional development and stronger links with theory and analysis through higher education. There has been a failure to *connect* and situate ABE in its larger national and international context of struggles for basic education and the forces which act against this happening. These failures have meant missed opportunities to link with collective resources and movements both at home and internationally.

# 7

# The Workers' Educational Association

## Roger Fieldhouse

### The Beginning: Foundation principles

At the Oxford University Extension summer meeting in 1899, Albert Mansbridge, an employee of the Co-operative Wholesale Society, proposed that there should be a closer alliance between the University Extension Movement and workers' organisations such as the Co-operative Society and the trade unions. He returned to this theme in three short articles contributed to the *University Extension Journal* in 1903. By May of that year the idea had crystallised into a firm resolve to form a new organisation to make the benefits of university education more readily available to the working class (Mansbridge, 1920: 9–11, 1944: 1–9; Jennings, 1973: 9–12; *University Extension Journal*, May 1903).

The Association to Promote the Higher Education of Working Men (renamed the Workers' Educational Association two years later) was founded, with Mansbridge and his wife as the first two members. By July 1903 a provisional committee had been formed and within a few months, district committees had been established in the southwest and northwest of England. The first branch was founded at Reading in October 1904, followed by others at Derby, Rochdale and Ilford in the early months of 1905 (Jennings, 1973: 12; Mansbridge, 1920: 11–17).

As described earlier in Chapter 2, the nineteenth century had seen numerous attempts to provide adult education for the working class, while the Extension Movement was already offering university learning to the general, non-university public. The unique contribution of the new Association – the WEA – was to combine these two objectives, so that the provision of a *university* education for *working-class* people became the overriding justification for the Association's existence, the standard by which its success or failure should be judged. Mansbridge himself emphasised the absolute necessity for the Association to become 'in distinct and immediate relationship equally with the Universities as with Working Class Movements' (Mansbridge, 1920: 13).

There was no doubt among the founders and early pioneers that the purpose of the WEA was to stimulate the demand for education 'in the interests of those who are largely occupied by manual labour'. Mansbridge claimed that 'all the public utterances of the time make it clear that the first condition of the power and life of the Association was that at least three-quarters of its members should be actual labouring men and women', or, as G.D.H. Cole more forthrightly stated, 'the WEA is nothing, or worse than nothing, unless it is based firmly in the support of the working class movement' (Mansbridge, 1913: 4, 1920: 19; Cole, 1925: 6). There was predictably less agreement about what the terms 'worker' or 'working man' or 'working class' actually meant, or what proportion of the student body should fall within these categories. Mansbridge warned that in time the tutorial classes would be likely to attract the already-educated general public and that the presence of too many teachers could be a danger, but he was prepared to tolerate 25 per cent non-working class students, and defined 'workers' more broadly than most trade unionists would then accept. Indeed, on occasions Mansbridge appears to have approved of the WEA as 'a replica in miniature of English life', which is rather different from an exclusively working-class organisation. The problem of defining who were workers and whether the WEA was catering for them became a perennial preoccupation of the Association (Mansbridge, 1913: 54–5, 1920: 12; Raybould, 1949: 38–9; Harrison, 1959: 14–17, 1961: 265).

If working-class involvement was one leg on which the WEA claimed to stand, 'university standards' was the other. An unassailable belief prevailed that there were many workers who, having been denied the opportunity in their youth, were both capable and desirous of a university education. The WEA 'started with the idea ... that ordinary men and women working in the day in manual occupations can do work of high intellectual quality, and of persuading them to undertake it. It did so, not by minimising the exacting character of the demands which it made on them, but by emphasising it,' claimed R.H. Tawney, the tutor of the first tutorial classes at Rochdale and Longton and later President of the WEA (Tawney, 1948). At first the WEA hoped and attempted to achieve this goal by supporting and promoting University Extension courses, but it experienced the same financial difficulties as had the Extension Movement, which tended to make the courses too expensive for working-class people and too short for the work to be of 'high intellectual quality'. By 1905 Mansbridge was fearing that the WEA would fail 'unless intensive class teaching up to university standard was developed' (Mansbridge, 1944: 1–9; Jennings, 1975: 53; Jepson, 1973: 181–208; University Review, Aug. 1905).

During the next couple of years the WEA waged a well-organised campaign to democratise Oxford University so that its resources should become available to poor scholars and working men as well as the wealthy. This campaign culminated in the 1907 Oxford Conference and subsequent report on Oxford and Working Class Education, which recommended the establishment of a network of tutorial classes in industrial towns 'specifically adapted to the needs of workpeople' together with machinery to ensure that a proportion of these working-class students passed on into the University (Joint Committee, 1909: 55–81, 87–8; Harrop: 149–175, 181–2). In the event, the tutorial classes spread rapidly but the attempt to open the doors of Oxford itself to working-class students proved to be a much more elusive objective, partly because of inadequate funds but also because the WEA itself, particularly at the grassroots, began to doubt the desirability of expending so high a proportion of its resources on sending relatively few students to Oxford. The responsibility of achieving 'university standards' therefore fell squarely on the tutorial classes themselves, which are examined in more detail in Chapter 8.

Mansbridge and the early WEA emphasised objectivity and study for its own sake, uncontaminated by the pursuit of material goals. Indeed, Mansbridge suggested in 1903 that education would raise the workers above such aspirations, whether material, political or social: 'the deep draughts of knowledge drunk by those within the currents of correct thought will provide that power and strength which, in spite of stressful and baneful days, will divert the strong movements of the people from the narrow paths of immediate interests ...' (Jennings, 1973: 5, 11; Mansbridge, 1944: 6). He regarded education as a way of life rather than a means of livelihood: a spiritual pursuit of knowledge for its own sake (Mansbridge, 1913: vii, 1, 36). When recording the early story of the WEA in 1920, Mansbridge emphasised that 'education has never been confused (by the WEA) ... with the acquisition of the means of getting on in life' (Mansbridge, 1920: xv, xvii). Students supposedly did not join WEA classes to improve their material or social position or for any *specific* purpose, but out of a 'yearning after spiritual perfection' – 'to develop the mind and body in the power of the spirit' (*Boston Evening Transcript*, 5 April 1922); *The Highway*, 16, 3, 1924: 135), although in reality the motivation of many students was a mixture of this 'ideal' and their more material interests. The emphasis on a spiritual, non-materialistic, apolitical form of education, which he equated with university scholarship, caused Mansbridge to find great encouragement in the WEA's repudiation of the 'ephemeral power' of diplomas and certificates, whose existence he believed threatened the belief 'that true study is its own sufficient reward' (Jennings, 1973: 30; Mansbridge, 1913: 57, 128).

The third fundamental principle claimed by the WEA (in addition to its affinity to the working class and its commitment to university academic standards) was its voluntary and democratic nature. It was always the pioneers' intention to 'allow each part of the country to develop on its own lines, and in its own way, within the natural limits of the work of the whole Association'. Gradually it became more of a federation of districts, each represented (with other affiliated bodies) on the national committee. Individual branches, which were represented on their District Councils, enjoyed considerable autonomy and often undertook very independent activity. This democratic principle was also manifested in the organisation and running of the WEA's classes. According to Mansbridge, WEA students discovered their own needs, organised in their own way and studied as they wished to study. When he addressed the Congress of the Universities of the British Empire in 1912 he claimed 'the students control the class ... It is *the* class of the students – each student is a teacher, and each teacher is a student; the humblest is not afraid to teach, and the most advanced is willing to learn'. This concept of democracy within the Association and within its classes, which was reiterated in numerous later policy statements, must be regarded as the third founding principle of the Association (Mansbridge, 1920: 29, 34, 69–72, 1944: 24; Joint Committee, 1909: 57–8; Legge, 1982: 126).

## Establishment and Expansion

The Mansbridgean WEA was welcomed with open arms by the reformers of the Oxford Catiline Club, who harboured a sense of guilt about the social exclusiveness of the universities. Edwardian liberalism decreed that 'it has become incumbent upon Universities to watch carefully every sign that a new class is ready to receive their guidance, in order that the seed of University culture may be deposited wherever it has suitable material on which to work' (Joint Committee, 1909: 53). The Oxford reformers were seeking a clement working-class seedbed for this university culture. The new Association promised to be just such a safe beneficiary of their liberalism, an ideal opportunity for acquiring a veneer of working-class participation and support without risking any fundamental social upheavals (although its opponents believed that it would foment the very social discord they feared). Many of the Oxford supporters of the WEA were strongly influenced by the Christian socialist ideas inherited from F.D. Maurice, including his belief that education could bring about 'God's order' in the world in the form of a Christian-inspired social democratic society. This idea in turn was a major influence in shaping the development of the WEA (Jepson, 1973: 51; Harrison, 1961: 266, 299).

The WEA was equally welcome to the new Liberal Government after 1906 as a moderate political influence on the emerging working class and Labour movement. It was felt that it was likely to educate the leaders of the Labour Movement to exercise their influence moderately and in the interests of social harmony, thus helping to keep class conflict and full-blooded socialism at bay (Fieldhouse, 1987b: 30–47). The famous offer of a share of the 'golden stream' (i.e. government grants) for the WEA, made at the Oxford Conference in 1907, which enabled the WEA to break out of the financial confines restricting the university extension movement and to establish the tutorial class programme, did not come out of the blue. Mansbridge had long been in close contact with Sir Robert Morant, Permanent Secretary to the Board of Education, and had so impressed him with the WEA's moderation that it had become 'irresistible'. Support for the WEA was seen as a sound political investment against extremism (Jennings, 1973: 25–6, 1975: 58). It was also (as explained in Chapter 4) regarded by the Board of Education as a useful means of developing more academic, non-vocational adult education in contrast to the predominantly technical and vocational early LEA provision.

The 1908 Report of the Oxford Conference duly recommended that half the cost of running tutorial classes should be met by the providing university and the other half by the WEA, which would receive grant aid from both the Board of Education and the local education authorities. The universities, the central government and the local authorities thus became the main support for the infant WEA, supplemented by certain charities such as the Cassel, Carnegie and the Gilchrest Trusts, and by WEA membership and affiliation fees. Securing this direct grant aid was probably Mansbridge's greatest achievement, because without it the tutorial class movement would almost certainly have failed at an early stage (Jennings, 1973: 17, 25, 1975: 61; Mansbridge, 1913: 114–5; Central Joint Advisory Committee, 1910–27, *passim*). But as we shall see, it had implications for the Association's independence and its voluntary status.

The history of the WEA between 1903 and the end of the Second World War is indisputably a story of growth. As previously mentioned, the first branch was formed at Reading in October 1904. Two years later there were 13 branches and 110 by 1912, increasing to over 200 by 1919. Branches continued to be founded, rising in number to 635 just before the Second World War and 932 by 1946–7. WEA membership increased in much the same way, from Mr and Mrs Mansbridge in 1903 to over 7,000 in 1912; climbing steadily to around 17,000 in 1919; 28,652 in 1938–9 and 45,320 by 1946–7. A large number of organisations (including trade unions, co-operative societies, universities, local education authorities, working men's clubs, adult schools, and many others) affiliated to the WEA. They totalled nearly 2,500 by 1919 (Mansbridge, 1920: 67–8; WEA, *Annual Reports, passim*).

Branches were grouped into districts, of which there were 16 by 1924. Subsequently, another five were formed. Members could join either individual branches or the districts. The districts were governed by a council representative of the branches, the affiliated societies and the district members, and were virtually autonomous organisations. When the WEA was granted the right in 1924 to provide classes itself (in addition to the university tutorial classes) with government funds, each of the districts was recognised as a separate 'Responsible Body'. They were only loosely federated by a national central council. Although national policy was promulgated by an annual conference, the power and independence of the districts (particularly after they became separate Responsible Bodies) was such that they could interpret and execute the Association's policies in very different ways. The WEA cannot, therefore, be described as a uniform organisation throughout the country, and it was often seriously handicapped in attempting to carry out any nationally agreed policy (Ministry of Education, 1954: 13, 36).

The Board of Education's 'golden stream' of grant aid was originally intended only for university tutorial classes, but the WEA was also able to use some central and local government money for less advanced classes. This funding was threatened in 1917 when the Board proposed to divert all such resources to local education authorities, making them solely responsible for all forms of adult liberal education with the exception of the university tutorial classes. However, the Adult Education Committee of the Ministry of Reconstruction concluded that voluntary organisations such as the WEA had an important part to play and recommended in its *Final Report* in 1919 that in certain circumstances these organisations should receive direct grants for the provision of one-year classes. The 1917 draft regulations were not confirmed and no substantial changes were made for a further five years (Ministry of Education, 1954: 4–6; Ministry of Reconstruction, 1919: 112–19, 162–7). Nevertheless, in these early years the financial resourcing for those less advanced courses was haphazard and the hard evidence for their quantity or quality is somewhat obscure. As Mansbridge remarked in 1920:

Many people regard the WEA and the University Tutorial Class Movement as one and the same thing. They treat the terms as interchangeable, probably because the system of University Tutorial Classes has been the most prominent constructive work of the Association ... The rest of its work, even though it may have been more important, has been intangible, and elusive ... Such work cannot be estimated, statisticised, visited, seen (Mansbridge, 1920: 36).

This statement suggests that non-advanced courses were numerous, even if the evidence is elusive. In fact, it was not always possible to know whether a particular educational activity was a WEA one or not, as the Association inspired or supported many activities which were financed by some other body, or were completely self-financing. Some of these activities consisted of serious and prolonged classes, either for organisations such as the adult schools, trade unions and co-operative societies, or for specially established groups. Sometimes they were 'reserve classes' formed alongside a tutorial class, to train men and women to fill vacancies in the tutorial class as they occurred. These and many other classes and lecture courses were taught by unpaid tutorial class students who were encouraged to undertake such missionary work. WEA branches also sponsored many less formal activities, including single lectures, study or reading circles, discussion groups, art exhibitions, plays and concerts; even rambles through the countryside. Indeed, as Mansbridge observed, 'almost every kind of educational method was adopted' (Mansbridge, 1920: 24–8, 69–72; Fieldhouse, 1977: 21). With such a variety of informal as well as formal educational activity, it is indeed impossible to quantify the work, although WEA branch records tend to support Mansbridge's statement that these may have been more important in numerical terms than the tutorial classes from very early on in the life of the Association (Jennings, 1976).

## *New Regulations, 'Responsible Body' Status, and 'Soft Options'*

In 1924 important new grant regulations were introduced. They formally regularised the payment of grants to other 'approved associations' to provide one-year and shorter courses in liberal adult education. Each of the WEA districts in England and Wales (but not Scotland) became recognised 'Responsible Bodies' in receipt of grant aid and a providing body in its own right. The grant-aided shorter courses gradually replaced the previous confused pattern and 'voluntary' tutors were gradually displaced by paid tutors. In Scotland they remained dependent on local government funding. Gradually more of the WEA's energy and limited human resources became diverted from its original objective of organising and stimulating a demand for tutorial classes into that of offering shorter courses not required to be so demanding of the students and serving increasingly as soft options or easier alternatives to the rigours of the tutorial classes. In these shorter courses students were not necessarily obliged to do any written work at all (Ministry of Education, 1954: 7–10; Raybould, 1951: 94–114, 1964: 26–30).

The number of WEA one-year classes had in fact exceeded tutorials as early as 1919-20 (328 to 229), and the gap thereafter grew wider year by year. But the WEA also promoted an increasing number of even shorter courses. In 1928 its programme of 1,826 courses consisted of approximately one-third tutorials, one-third sessional and terminal classes (lasting one or two terms) and one-third other. During the Second World War the WEA was a partner in the Central Advisory Council (CAC), which became heavily involved in making educational provision for units of HM Forces and the Auxiliary Services stationed in Britain, as well as the civilian defence forces and many other wartime workers, which consisted very largely of single lectures and short courses (see Chapter 3). By 1946–7, tutorials represented only 14 per cent of the total programme of 5,276 classes, whereas over half the classes were shorter than 10 weeks. The proportion of tutorial class students relative to all WEA students had fallen to 20 per cent by 1931–2. It remained approximately at that level throughout the 1930s, but dropped as low as 8 per cent during the Second World War. By 1946–7 the figure had risen slightly, to 11 per cent (Raybould, 1949: 3–5, 102–6, 1951: 118–20, 1959: 248–51; Fieldhouse, 1988: 104; WEA, 1943, appendix 1; Central Joint Advisory Committee, 1930; Ministry of Education, 1947: 157–8).

The overall picture that emerges from the rather unreliable statistical evidence is one of very considerable growth in the WEA class programme during its first 40 years. In the beginning the greatest commitment and fastest growth were in tutorial classes, but later expansion was more rapid in courses which were shorter and did not involve regular study or written work on the part of the students. The amendment to the grant regulations in 1924 in particular resulted in an easing of the demands made upon the students with regard to the length of time they were expected to study and the amount of reading and written work they were expected to do. This, together with the general switch to shorter courses, could only mean a lowering of academic standards. Not all the courses suffered in this way but the trend was away from an emphasis on high academic standards, towards the provision of a greater quantity of more popular courses (Ministry of Reconstruction, 1919: 61–72; Raybould, 1949: 54–74). By the third and fourth decades of the Association's history, there were far more students than in the early years, but most of them were receiving a much more elementary form of adult education than the university level education originally regarded as an essential justification for the Association's existence. This was recognised by R.H. Tawney in 1948, when he wrote to the head of the new Leeds University Extramural Department:

The main effort of the Association down to 1914, and indeed after the First World War, down to about 1925, was devoted to organising tutorial classes, and such classes, with the exacting standards that they implied, were regarded as the Association's distinctive contribution ... In recent years the WEA has been criticised ... on the ground that it demands from the unsophisticated worker intellectual standards of an inhuman rigour. The valid - and very serious - criticism is precisely the opposite. It is that, in its eagerness to increase the number of classes and students, it has steadily relaxed the demands which it makes upon them ... There is too much running of classes for all and sundry, and of begging people to join them whether they mean business or not ... As things have worked out in many areas, short classes have not been a preparation for, or supplement to, tutorial classes, but a substitute for them, a substitute attended by students of whom many would have been in a tutorial class if the softer option had not been offered. And this change has taken place, not by any deliberate act of policy on the part of the WEA but through, in most cases, a mere following of the line of least resistance (Tawney, 1948).

## Working-Class Participation and Links with the Labour Movement

How attractive was the WEA to the 'worker intellectuals' or indeed to the working class in general? When the Association was set up, it was blithely assumed that the workers would be attracted to its network of tutorial classes in industrial towns 'specifically adapted to the needs of workpeople' (Joint Committee, 1909: 55). But as early as 1913 Mansbridge feared that some tutorial classes attracted large numbers of middle-class students, including more prosperous clerical workers and a sprinkling of teachers (Mansbridge, 1913: 54–5, 160). However, the question of 'how many workers?' has always been dogged by the difficulties in defining social class or identifying it from the available statistics. When the WEA was first formed, there was little doubt that the working classes could be clearly identified by their association with the trade unions and co-operative societies, the Labour Party, manual work, public elementary education, chapel and cheap housing, and by their speech, their dress and even the food they ate. But gradually the twentieth century has blurred if not eradicated many of these social differentiations, while the statistical records, which are generally based on students' occupations, are very crude indicators of students' social class – especially female students, who are frequently classified merely as women or housewives or by their husbands' occupations. These statistics therefore do not provide a very accurate picture of the social class of the WEA student body: nevertheless they do show a significant decline in the proportion of manual workers among WEA students. In 1931–2 33 per cent of the students were recorded as manual workers; 23 per cent as clerical, shop and postal workers; 23 per cent engaged in domestic and home duties; 14 per cent as teachers, social and professional workers; and 7 per cent 'miscellaneous'. Fifteen years later the proportion of all the categories had risen except the manual workers, who had declined from 33 to 23 per cent. Even accepting the unsatisfactory nature of the statistics, they do confirm Mansbridge's fear that the WEA would prove 'congenial to the general adult mind' and become increasingly colonised by the middle class (Raybould, 1947: xii, 5–10, 38–53, 102–3).

Apart from seeking trade union affiliations, little attempt was made by the WEA in the early years to attract organised labour although some districts such as Yorkshire under the leadership of its first District Secretary, George Thompson, did attempt to secure trade union support and cultivate the working-class leadership (Steele, 1987: 110–12). But after J.M. Mactavish, a Portsmouth dock worker and trade unionist, took over as WEA General Secretary from Mansbridge in 1916, greater effort was made to forge closer links with the trade unions. G.D.H. Cole, the guild socialist, was also an important influence at this time. In 1916 he said he looked forward to the day when the WEA would be funded by the labour movement, thus freeing it of dependence on state funding, which could be inhibiting (Millar, 1979: 79). In 1925 the WEA journal described Cole as having been 'for some years ... the most powerful influence in our movement' in four spheres, the first of which was in bringing the WEA 'up to date in its machinery and closer to the trade union movement in its policy' (*The Highway*, 1925–6, 18: 3).

Cole and Mactavish helped the WEA jointly with the Iron and Steel Trade Confederation and the Union of Post Office Workers to establish the Workers' Educational Trade Union Committee (WETUC) in 1919 in order to attract more trade unionists to WEA classes. Trade unions that joined the WETUC contributed funds directly to the WEA and their members were then permitted to attend WEA courses and weekend schools free of charge. Although trade union support for the WETUC declined somewhat in the years immediately after the general strike, by the mid-1930s interest and support began to pick up again. By 1946 the number of unions affiliated to the WETUC had risen to 34. However, it was not always easy to convert this official blessing into rank-and-file participation. In fact the number of local trade union and other working-class affiliations to the WEA at branch level had declined since the 1920s (WETUC, 1944: 5–9; Fieldhouse and Forrester, 1984: 5–6).

Under the WETUC arrangements, the unions could make use of existing WEA and tutorial class provision or ask for special trade union courses, and the emphasis became increasingly on separate provision of informal activities, discussion groups, study circles and day and weekend schools, although lip service continued to be paid to the tutorial class as the WEA's major contribution to working-class education. Thus, quite contrary to the intentions of the early founders of the WEA and the WETUC (who had envisaged WEA and tutorial classes as being essentially for the workers and recruited partially through the trade unions), there grew an ever-widening gap between the WEA's general provision organised through its branches and its trade union provision, organised separately through direct trade union contact and recruitment (Fieldhouse and Forrester, 1984: 6).

While people like Cole and Mactavish regarded the WEA's contribution to the trade union movement and the working class as essentially empowering, others saw it more as education for responsible citizenship. The growing power of the trade unions and the emergence of working-class political associations at the beginning of the twentieth century, together with the success of the new Labour Party in winning 29 seats in the 1906 general election, were causing many people to advocate education of the working class for responsible democratic citizenship. This had been recognised by Mansbridge in his blue-print for the new Association in 1903, when he declared that 'if it be admitted, reasonably enough, that working men ... should be represented on governing bodies, it must also be admitted that lack of thinking power in the rank and file tends to nullify the good effect of such representation'.(Mansbridge, 1944: 2). This need for responsible thinking to inform political action was forcefully expressed by the authors of the 1908 Report on *Oxford and Working Class Education*, who regarded it as imperative that the working class 'should obtain the knowledge necessary to enable them to show foresight in their choice of political means ... The Trade Union secretary and the 'Labour member' need an Oxford education as much, and will use it to as good ends, as the civil servant or the barrister. It seems to us that it would involve a grave loss both to Oxford and to English political life were the close association which has existed between the University and the world of affairs to be broken or impaired on the accession of new classes to power' (Joint Committee, 1909: 47–8). The WEA was the chosen agent for ensuring that the close association between the liberal values of the University and 'the new classes of power' was not broken. It was envisaged that the working-class beneficiaries of this largess would either return to their former occupations, suitably enlightened, or 'become the future teachers and leaders, the philosophers and economists of the working class', thus uplifting their peers to the level and way of thinking previously considered the preserve of the middle class (*ibid*.: 50, 86).

There is little doubt that some working-class potential students were alienated by this close link between the WEA and the universities, its academic image and its refusal to offer or espouse the more political education for social change that they were seeking. They believed that it was impossible for the WEA to combine this neutral position with a genuine offer of education for social, economic and political emancipation which would equip them for the class struggle. This was certainly what the Plebs League and the National Council of Labour Colleges believed (see Chapter 10). Therefore there was a distrust of the university connection and an undercurrent of demand within the Association for a more radical social purpose. There were many in the WEA, such as Mactavish, Tawney and Cole, who argued passionately that the Association should promote socially purposive education – education which would contribute directly to reforming and improving society. In 1918 Mactavish advocated education which would equip the students 'for the great task of ... moulding their social and industrial environment' (Mactavish, 1918: 329). Seven years later Cole argued that:

We have seen too many branches wrecked by the well meaning educationalist, who is so keen on fostering what he calls the 'student mind', that he has no desire, or no power, to attract the militant Trade Unionist who wants to turn his education to definite and practical purpose ... I want to serve the live-wired practical worker, who wants guidance in facing the practical problems of living.

Cole went on to tell WEA students to act as proselytes in the working-class bodies and not to leave the WEA to be run by those who believed in education 'as an opiate for social discontent' – a fairly open rejection of Albert Mansbridge's later, somewhat romanticised view of the Association (Cole, 1925: 8).

## Dynamic, Constraints and Controls

There were many others within the WEA who were unhappy with Mansbridge's vision of its role being to 'divert the strong movements of the people from the narrow paths of immediate interest' (Mansbridge, 1944: 6). George Thompson, who was appointed WEA District Secretary for Yorkshire when that District was formed in 1914 and remained in office (except for a six-year interval in New Zealand) until his retirement in 1945, scorned Mansbridge's hopes for class reconciliation and the concept of education as a bridge from one class to another. He believed that workers' education was intended to deepen the students' understanding of class solidarity, to equip them to serve their class, and to achieve social justice and industrial emancipation. Subjects such as economics, economic history and social theory, which enabled the workers to defend themselves against an exploitive capitalist system, were the most important ones in Thompson's opinion. He was representative of 'a whole generation of working men who devoted their time and energy to the WEA ... Socialism was the new evangelical movement from which they derived their peculiar strength and inner direction' (Harrison, 1961: 290–9; Thompson, 1938: 3, 11–19; Steele, 1987, passim). It was from this source that the WEA derived its main dynamic over many years.

But it was this dynamic, this commitment to education for social purpose and social change that brought the WEA into conflict with its central and local government paymasters from time to time. In 1917 the War Cabinet solemnly discussed the danger of the WEA spreading revolutionary ideas to the working class and dispatched Mactavish to Buckingham Palace to reassure the King that the Association was not fomenting social revolution (Cole, M., 1952: 96–7). In fact, as soon as the WEA became a recipient of government grants, from 1907 onwards, it was subject to Board (later Ministry or Department) of Education regulation and scrutiny by HM Inspectors. While this was partly to ensure that the grants were correctly used, it also provided an opportunity for a degree of political control.

This was recognised very clearly by the Conservative President of the Board of Education, Lord Eustace Percy, when he defended the adult education grants to the WEA (and the universities) against Treasury scepticism in 1925, because in his view '£100,000 spent annually on this kind of work, properly controlled, would be about the best police expenditure we could indulge in' as a protection against socialist ideas being spread abroad by such bodies as the National Council for Labour Colleges (NCLC) (PRO, T.161/186/S. 17166, Lord Eustace Percy to Walter Guinness, 7 Oct. 1925). There is no doubt that on occasions the power to grant or withhold essential financial aid gave both central government and local authorities a means of influencing the WEA.

In 1922 a Treasury official inserted the word 'bolshevism' in the margin against a reference to political science and economics tutorial classes, and two years later Board of Education officials expressed their concern about the political tendency of the WEA (PRO, ibid., B.P. Moore to Secretary of HM Treasury, 8 August 1922 and ED 73/7 and 19, Board of Education memoranda, 1924). This immediately preceded one of the major conflicts between the WEA and the Board of Education, sparked off by the WEA's plans to participate in a TUC education scheme in 1925, which would have brought the WEA and the NCLC together, under the control of the TUC General Council, to jointly provide an educational service for the trade union movement. At the instigation of the NCLC, which distrusted the WEA's ideological commitment to working-class education, the TUC advisory committee persuaded the WEA to agree that the purpose of the scheme should be 'equipping the workers ... in the work of securing social and industrial emancipation' – a distinctly anti-capitalist, subversive objective which immediately rang alarm bells in Whitehall. During the following summer and autumn the WEA was under intense pressure from both central and local government to withdraw from the scheme or lose its grant aid. The WEA leaders tried to defend the Association by minimising the political significance of the scheme, fudging its intentions or arguing that it was a lesser evil to allowing trade union education to fall completely into the hands of the Marxist NCLC. In protracted negotiations between Lord Eustace and A.D. Lindsay, Master of Balliol, representing the WEA, a series of compromises was reached. Assurances were sought from the WEA about its future behaviour, and certain conditions for grant aid were imposed, including a very restrictive interpretation of the TUC scheme, the abandonment of the Association's traditional identification with the working class (i.e. there should be no specific working-class targeting in the recruitment of students), and a stricter interpretation of the WEA's non-party political status. The authorities also insisted that WEA classes should in future be open to inspection by the local education authorities, and subject to their approval. Investigations were made as to whether the LEAs could keep the Association under careful scrutiny or indeed replace it altogether 'where the work of the WEA becomes unsatisfactory' (Fieldhouse, 1981, *passim*, 1985a: 124, 1990: 154–7). Although the TUC scheme was never implemented, the affair demonstrated how grant aid was used to impose more effective machinery for supervision and control where the authorities believed the WEA was straying too far into the realms of political extremism.

During the subsequent two decades there was little evidence of heavy censorship or control, but there were a number of controversial incidents which were investigated by HMIs or local government inspectors or raised by MPs in Parliament or privately with the Board or Ministry of Education. These investigations established a code of practice - always with the explicit or implicit threat that failure to comply with the code would result in withdrawal of grant aid. This was clearly recognised by Tawney and others in the WEA when he warned the annual conference in 1944 that seeking a much larger measure of public funding as advocated by the General Secretary, Ernest Green, in order to solve the Association's financial difficulties, would threaten its political freedom and independence. He was successful in persuading Conference to reject this risky strategy in 1944 but the following year it was carried, with the rather naive proviso that such grants should not endanger 'the degree of independence now enjoyed by the Association'. In practice, the WEA was influenced over the years by its dependence on government subsidies to loosen its close ties with the working class and the labour movement and to pay less attention to specifically working-class interests. It was encouraged to see itself as a general adult education provider for all sectors of society. It was warned against 'intemperate' left-wing bias or over-concern with mere social or working conditions instead of larger (more worthy) national issues (Fieldhouse, 1984: 435, 1985a: 124–5, 1990: 158–65).

The outbreak of war not unnaturally increased the political pressures and brought the conflict between the WEA's notion of adult education and what the Establishment paymasters might consider to be in the national interest much closer to the surface. In the early months of 1940, HMIs Jack and Dann submitted reports to the Board of Education on the problem of controversial topics in adult education. They were anxious for the Board to realise the inflammable nature of many of the topics dealt with in adult education classes. A Board official warned that if indiscreetly handled they might give rise to storms of protest and questions raised in the House of

Commons which the Board would find extremely embarrassing. A circular stressing the need to treat such topics objectively and impartially and avoiding giving any grounds for complaint about encouraging an anti-national point of view was planned although in the end it was dropped for fear of appearing over-censorious. Nevertheless, wartime nervousness and the expansion of informal provision referred to earlier did give rise to a number of incidents and official warnings. In particular, it was the provision made for HM Forces that caused most difficulties because of the military fears about security and the differences in concepts of education. Many Services personnel were dubious about, or even hostile to, the free discussion of controversial subjects which seemed normal to WEA tutors. Moreover, the Services' security vetting caused a number of tutors to be banned from this work. Although the number of such bannings was relatively small, it was sufficient to induce a wariness and caution amongst the approved tutors when dealing with political and controversial subjects. This was exactly what was intended. It created a pressure to conform (Fieldhouse, 1985a: 125–7, 1988: 104–20, 1990: 166–70).

After the war, the spread of Cold War attitudes soon affected adult education, including the WEA, imposing upon it a much narrower definition of acceptability and a much restricted consensus. This caused a number of controversies and constraints, especially in the growing field of trade union education. The WEA became very sensitive to accusations of subversion, and over-anxious to prove itself innocent of McCarthyite charges. Complaints about the WEA's alleged left-wing bias led to action being taken on a number of occasions against those who, in the Cold War climate, were deemed to have shown too much affinity with communism or left-wing politics. A number of tutors were subject to rigorous scrutiny, criticised, or even encouraged to seek another job (Fieldhouse, 1985a: 125–7, 1985b: 22–8).

In 1942 R.A. Butler, President of the Board of Education, was able to dismiss a complaint against the alleged partisanship and contentious political pronouncements of the acting President of the WEA, Henry Clay, by stating in the House of Commons that 'the acceptance by a body of grant from the Board in respect of its educational work should not be taken as placing a limitation on the right of free speech enjoyed by its officers and members' (The Highway, 1943, 35: 58). But even when refuted, such questions act as warnings for the future. There was not constant conflict between the Association and the authorities. For most of the time the boundary between the legitimate and the unacceptable was appreciated by all concerned. The incidents that did occur were often petty and of little consequence. But they were just serious enough, and just frequent enough, to ensure that temperance, responsibility and judiciousness (to use the terms favoured by the HMIs) and an acceptable orthodoxy did prevail. The result was that the WEA became very largely confined within the broad centre of the British political spectrum, avoiding political extremes. In fact it is arguable that the WEA's chief influence on the working class was not that it seduced many of its leaders and activists from loyalty to their class (as sometimes claimed), but that it encouraged them to think in terms of non-Marxist politics.

## Prevailing Orthodoxy: Political activism

A detailed examination of economics teaching in WEA and university classes from the 1920s to the 1940s revealed it to be broadly liberal, sometimes radical, sometimes pluralist, but overall consisting very largely of predominately orthodox empirical studies of the capitalist system in operation (Fieldhouse, 1983, *passim*). It is not surprising that an HMI report on WEA economics classes in the West Midlands in 1934 found they had 'developed a sobriety of outlook, a detachment of mind and a recognition of the complexity of the subject' in the students (PRO, ED 73/1, HMI Report on WEA and university classes in the West Midlands, 1934).

This detachment of mind was exactly what Cole had earlier scornfully described as the 'student mind', the effect of which could be to so confuse the students by the complexities of the subject or daunt them by the enormity of social problems and the difficulties of alleviating them that they lost their previous certainties and any confidence in action. One economics tutor described how adult students 'approaching the subject in the hope of discovering cures for society's economic ills ... find their tutors willing to describe theoretically the workings of the economic system but unwilling to diagnose its diseases and unable to prescribe any cures' (Michaels, 1938: 115–16). It is therefore not surprising that a 'consumer's view of adult education' written in the 1930s quotes a description of a class as 'not inspired or inspiring'. It went on:

In the discussions, the tutor never had any definite points of view, and seemed to restrain those who wanted to go to the left or the right. The student rapidly gained the idea that no problem was capable of solution, that there was so much to be said on all sides of a problem that one should take no action at all. It was only fools who gave adherence to a party, or had plans of action for changing the status quo (Williams and Heath, 1936: 206).

As the Ashby Committee approvingly noted in 1954, 'WEA classes have equipped thousands of workers of all kinds to approach contemporary social and economic problems with the critical objectivity of the student rather than the impassioned prejudice of the agitator' (Ministry of Education, 1954: 36). Here again was the ubiquitous 'student mind', but there were inevitably some contradictions and tendencies which ran counter to this general trend. As George Orwell pointed out in 1943, 'the bigger the machine of government becomes, the more loose ends and forgotten corners there are in it' (Orwell, 1943). The WEA did find quite a number of forgotten corners where it could escape from scrutiny. In practice neither the state nor the WEA itself had adequate machinery to monitor all that was being taught under the Association's auspices. Tutors enjoyed a very considerable *de facto* independence in offering a great variety of courses in a variety of ways. Many did heighten the social and political consciousness of their students and encouraged them to take a more active part in social and political affairs. There seems little reason to doubt the claim made in 1949 that the WEA over the years had permanently altered the tastes, the standards of judgement, and the capacity to think independently and responsibly of many of its students (Raybould, 1949: 77).

A survey of 410 tutorial class students and 128 Ruskin College students carried out in 1936 revealed that many WEA students had been prepared or stimulated by their courses to become 'active citizens' (Williams and Heath, 1936, *passim*). Another survey in the autumn of 1938 claimed widespread public activity amongst past and present WEA students. It covered only 16 WEA districts, and took no account of work with the trade unions, political parties or cultural and social organisations. Nevertheless it uncovered 15 WEA Members of Parliament, almost 1,800 students active in various levels of local government, 250 magistrates, 165 managers or governors of schools, and more than 100 in other forms of public service (WEA, 1938). During the war the WEA produced a report on its 'service to democracy since 1918', which it presented 'as evidence that the real value of workers' education is determined by the extent to which it leads to social activity outside the classroom' (WEA, 1943: 3). This was perhaps borne out by the general election in 1945, which produced a Labour Government with 14 ministers, including the Chancellor of the Exchequer, and a large proportion of MPs, who had close ties with the Association either as former tutors or students or as members of the WEA Executive (Stocks, 1953: 143; King, 1955: 265; Jennings, 1979: 50).

A more recent survey relating to 92 WEA classes held before 1951 confirmed that the Association had generated a considerable amount of social activism. But it is clear from this survey that it was the more active people who were the most strongly influenced by their WEA experience. In other words, the WEA reinforced activism as much as it caused it (Fieldhouse, 1983: 29).

## Difficult Times after the Second World War

Like the universities (see Chapter 8), the WEA entered the post-Second World War era in a mood of optimism. Just as the early pioneers had conceived it as their job to educate the leaders of the growing Labour movement, so now the WEA believed it could play an important role in preparing people for the greater democratic participation in the affairs of the nation expected under the new Labour Government. In 1945 the Association's branch officers were told that 'a new social order is arising before our eyes, which working people must play their part in shaping, and the conditions of a changing world have enormously enlarged the opportunities of service by an educational organisation such as ours to the working-class movement' (WEA, 1945: 3, 1947: 3–4). But despite the failure of the schools to meet the growing educational needs of the post-war society, the WEA did not expand as rapidly as had been anticipated. In the decade after the war the Association did achieve a 15 per cent expansion in terms of the number of classes it provided, which rose from 5,400 in 1945–6 to 6,239 in 1954–5. But the number of students only crept up from 98,700 to 102,100. The tutorial classes and tutorial class students increased from 651 classes, 10,730 students to 845 and 11,480 respectively during that time. As a proportion of the WEA's total class programme and student body they remained fairly constant at around one-eighth of the classes and one-tenth of the students. But the number of one-year sessional and one-term classes, and the number of students attending them, declined in both absolute numbers and as a proportion of the whole. The real growth at this time was in short courses of less than 20 hours' duration, together with day and weekend schools and single lectures. They increased from less than 22 to 34 per cent of the WEA's activities, and from 20 to over 43 per cent of the student body. If the WEA's progress in the decade after the end of the war were measured in terms of student hours or the academic rigour of its programme, then it was slipping backwards. The next two decades did see a revival of the sessional and one-term classes, although the tutorial classes went into terminal decline. By 1973–4 the total number of classes had risen to 9,300 and the students to 167,000. But over 40 per cent continued to attend classes or activities of less than 20 hours' duration (Fieldhouse, 1977: 19, 40).

This lack of real growth and decline in academic rigour was part of the 'severe crisis about its effectiveness, its purpose and its identity' which the WEA faced by the early 1950s (Jennings, 1978: 6). One of the reasons for the crisis was the merging of the British working-class movement with its culture of 'club, co-op and chapel ... and interlocking network of grassroots working-class organisations' into the apparently classless post-war welfare society. The Government had already done its best to separate the WEA from its working-class roots: now the task was being completed by social trends (ibid.). Another related cause of the crisis was the WEA's loss of its political dynamic. It was no longer in the van of various political campaigns. Nor was it actively involved in the local self-help pressure groups or visibly engaged in the community action which was developing during the 1950s. This was partly because the welfare reforms introduced by the Labour Governments between 1945–51 had taken some of the wind out of the sails of old political crusades, and partly because in many cases 'the WEA members who had carried the banners outside the Town Hall in the 1930s were now inside the Town Hall running the Education Committee' (ibid.: 6–7; Rees, 1982: 3). One way or the other the 'undermining of the ideal of social emancipation by welfare economics slowed down the main dynamic of the WEA' (Harrison, 1961: 350). A few years later a critical study of adult education described the WEA as having 'a national executive and headquarters apparently exercising less drive and authority than in the past; a few energetic and markedly successful districts; some districts holding their own; other districts showing signs of decay; and striking disparities in achievement from branch to branch within the same district'. Many branches were too cautious and reluctant to try new ventures (Lowe, 1970: 117). This reflected the decline of voluntaryism and of the WEA's social purpose dynamic described below.

At the time it was felt that the main reason for the WEA's difficulties was the increasing competition it was facing from the universities and the local authorities. As they expanded from their narrower specialised bases into more general provision while the Association also adopted the role of a more universal provider, the demarcation between the various bodies was becoming blurred. The WEA felt itself increasingly squeezed into a tight corner (WEA, 1953a: 11–18; Harrison, 1959: 1-29).

As described in Chapter 8, the special relationship between the Association and the universities grew weaker as non-WEA university extramural provision began to expand after the war. In 1946 approximately 90 per cent of university adult education was still organised through the WEA but a decade later the proportion had fallen to below 50 per cent. Moreover, an increasing amount of university provision consisted of one-year and shorter courses indistinguishable from the WEA's own classes. In 1954 the Association complained to the Ashby Committee which was reviewing adult education organisation and finance that its position was being undermined by some extramural departments. By this time some universities favoured a partial dissolution of the partnership between the Association and the universities and the Committee did seriously consider recommending the dissolution of the WEA as an independent provider, possibly only being prevented from doing so by the forceful advocacy of one of its members (WEA, 1947: 4, 1953a: 13, 1966a: 49; Raybould, 1959: 230–4, 1964, *passim*; Ministry of Education, 1954: 22, 26–7, 37; Shaw, 1971: 7–13; Fieldhouse, 1989–90: 16–17; information given by Professor Raybould to the author).

The WEA also felt threatened by the expansion and diversification of local authority adult education (see Chapter 4). In 1954 the Association of Education Committees recommended to the Ashby Committee that direct grant to the WEA should be abolished, and that it become merely a recruiting agency for courses provided by the LEAs. To the WEA's relief this advice was rejected by the Ashby Committee, but there was an implied threat in the Report that grant arrangements should remain unchanged only so long as the 'voluntary bodies prove themselves equal to their responsibilities' (Jepson, 1959: 101–17; Ministry of Education, 1954: 28–31, 40–1; *Times Educational Supplement*, 29 October 1954: 1016).

## Trade Union Work

A third post-war development which significantly affected the WEA was the changing attitude of the trade union movement to adult education (see Chapter 10). The WEA still considered trade union education as 'one of the most important aspects' of its work at that time because it was really the only means by which it could fulfil its oft-stated commitment to *workers'* education. The Trades Union Congress (TUC) still preferred to rely on the WEA and the National Council of Labour Colleges (NCLC) to provide this education rather than do it itself. Trade union affiliations to the WEA increased during the post-war years and so did the courses organised by the Workers' Educational Trade Union Committee (WETUC). In 1949 the WEA established Trade Union Advisory Committees in each district to promote more trade union education and began to appoint organisers specifically for this task. Fourteen such appointments had been made by 1951, financially supported by the WETUC (WETUC, 1944, *passim*; WEA, 1947: 3, 1953a: 19–23; Ministry of Education, 1954: 14; Gregory, 1958: 310–15).

In 1953 a working party on trade union education concluded that 'the basic aims and purposes of the WEA require that it should give a clear priority to the educational needs of the Trade Union Movement' (WEA, 1953b: 79) and favoured closer liaison with the trade unions. Following the working party's report, three pilot schemes were set up in industrial areas to investigate ways in which these aims could be achieved. Six years later, the pilot schemes demonstrated that a considerable expansion in certain types of trade union education was possible with the assistance of increased resources, although there were unresolved problems about linking this work with the WEA's other activities and branch structure. The Association continued to show a special concern for trade union education and was especially successful in pioneering day-release courses for trade unionists during the 1950s and 60s (*ibid., passim*; Raybould, 1959: 39–41; Clegg and Adams, 1959: 11–38, 86–9; WEA, 1958: 7; DES, 1973: 39). Meanwhile certain developments in trade union education were beginning to challenge the WEA's special relationship with the trade unions through the WETUC. One was the tendency for some unions to make their own educational provision independently of any other agency, or to approach the universities without using the WEA as intermediary. In 1947 the TUC began to make facilities available for training officials and active trade unionists, deciding in 1956 to establish its own training college. At the same time, the TUC encouraged individual unions to provide such facilities for their own members, and many unions appointed full-time education officers. Others approached extramural departments directly, with the result that the number of university day-release courses began to expand after 1953 (Raybould, 1959: 33–51; Clegg and Adams, 1959: 56–70).

The other major development was a shift in interest on the part of the trade unions from general social and political education to a more utilitarian concern with union organisation, negotiating procedures, communication, and the specific tasks of training trade unionists to be effective officials. As the unions began to involve themselves under a Labour Government more in the running of a complex modern society and economic system, they became more concerned with methods of operating the socio-economic machine than understanding its nature. The demand was increasingly for skills in the techniques of trade unionism rather than for wide-ranging social-purpose liberal education. The TUC and individual unions' entry into the field of direct educational provision was very much geared towards this technical training, which offered them certain advantages over the old liberal approach, but this put the WEA in a quandary. It wanted to maintain its close relationship with the unions and increase its trade union work, but did not wish to abandon its liberal approach to education. The solution conceived was to relate the courses initially to the practical training being demanded and gradually to broaden them to cover a much wider range of liberal subjects. This approach generally proved feasible, at least until the mid-sixties (WEA, 1953a: 29–32, 1958: 7; Raybould, 1959: 33–5; Clegg and Adams, 1959, *passim*).

When the WETUC was wound up in 1964, at the same time that the TUC took over the NCLC, the WEA's influence on the curricula of the courses financially supported by trade union funds was severely curtailed. The TUC now set up an Education Committee to supervise all education for which it gave financial assistance. Syllabuses were required to be submitted to the Committee for approval, even if the WEA was paying the teaching costs. Regional education officers were appointed to administer the provision. At first the WEA was a major provider under the new arrangements. In 1969 it provided some 200 courses and 350 weekend schools, about half the total TUC educational programme, but subsequently the WEA's share steadily declined in most parts of the country (WEA, 1966a: 45, 1969: 9, 1970: 8, 1975: 10–11; DES, 1973: 38–9; TUC, 1975: 203, 1976: 178–9).

There was an ever-widening gap opening up between the WEA's concept of workers' education as concerned with 'great issues of purpose, truth, justice and beauty' and the TUC Education Committee's belief that 'training those responsible for conducting trade union affairs in the knowledge and skills essential to conducting those affairs efficiently' was the primary object of workers' education (Sedgwick and Winnard, 1971: 4–5). This made it increasingly difficult for the WEA to promote trade union education, at least in its traditional way. There was a steady retreat from liberal education in an attempt to satisfy the wishes of the TUC Education Committee and maintain the volume of trade union work. In 1973 a WEA working party on trade union education rendered the obligatory lip-service to the need for liberal education but put much greater emphasis on recognising the trade unions' needs to enable their representatives and officials to improve their skills in the performance of their trade union functions. It sought to involve the WEA more in this narrower field of training. This set the pattern for the WEA's continuing participation in the TUC education scheme 'in its first priority of providing training for work place representatives' (WEA, 1975: 9–10). Not for the first time, nor the last, the WEA adopted a pragmatic approach in the interests of survival but in reality it lost all credibility as a promoter of liberal education for trade unionists by accommodating too readily the TUC's demands for training.

It is true that some individual unions continued to support a more liberal approach and that the WEA was also able to persuade some students and ex-students of TUC day-release courses 'to continue and extend their education ... into wider fields' (ibid.). A few WEA industrial branches were formed. It was argued that it was sometimes possible to introduce a more liberal element into the narrowest of training syllabuses, or at least to awaken an interest in broader issues. But this was very much against the general trend. Ultimately the justification for continuing to participate in the TUC scheme was that it was the only way in which the Association could maintain any real links with the unions, and that realistically was the only way it could still claim to be serving the working class.

## The Drift to Universal Provision

Certainly, while trade union and WETUC courses were an important part of the WEA's activity it could still make a real claim to be maintaining its special commitment to working-class education. Nevertheless, the proportion of WEA students who fell within the category of manual workers steadily declined from about one-third in the early 1930s to less than one-quarter by 1946, to one-sixth 10 years later. By the 1950s manual workers were being replaced by a category of 'non-manual, technical and supervisory' workers and by an increasing number of 'housewives' (Harrison, 1959: 4; WEA, 1960: 8–9; Malone, 1960: 116). Of course, to some extent this reflected the more general changes in British society. 'Many of the working class had become middle class and some thought it necessary and inevitable that the WEA become more national and less sectarian in its appeal' (Rees, 1982: 101). Within a very approximate social classification, the working-class proportion of the WEA student body (excluding 'housewives' and a small miscellaneous category) was estimated to have declined from 47 per cent in 1931–2 to 33.5 per cent in 1946–7 and to 28 per cent by 1958–9 (Malone, 1960: 117). Moreover in 1960 a WEA working party exploded the cosy myth which the Association had clung to for many years, that the many housewives in its classes would turn out to be mainly working class if only their social class could be ascertained. A sample survey revealed that 'in general married women (in WEA classes) tend to come from the "higher social categories"' (WEA, 1960: 59).

In 1948 the WEA Annual Conference agreed that the Association should make its main concern in the future not the working class, but the educationally underprivileged. However, there was never any firm agreement about what was meant by the term 'educationally underprivileged'. While some interpreted it very specifically, others used it to include almost everyone (Malone, 1960: 118–20). This hastened the WEA's transformation into a universal adult education provider, 'serving a representative cross section of the adult population' (WEA, 1954: 4). A year before the 1948 Annual Conference decision about a change in orientation, Tawney claimed that the WEA served 'all those, whether in factory, mine, office or home, who render useful service to their fellows', and in the same pamphlet it was stated that the WEA 'must continue to recruit students and members widely, limiting its appeal only to the expectation that those who join in its activities share the desire of the WEA for an educated democracy' (WEA, 1947: 4–5, 11–12). The Association continued to stress its concern for the 'whole community', for 'all men and women' and for 'people of all kinds' (WEA, 1958: 7, 1960: 18; Harrison, 1959: 20). In 1966 it amended its constitution to refer to stimulating and satisfying the demand of 'adults' for education instead of 'workers', although it did add the phrase 'in particular, members of workers' movements' to mollify the opponents to the change (WEA, 1966a, appendices 5, 6, 1966b: 9). Despite this sop, it was clear that the WEA had drifted a long way from its original commitment to the working class. It was attempting to be all things to all men, a general providing body within the field of adult education.

There were people in the WEA who were very unhappy with this drift. Most influential of this faction was G.D.H. Cole, who argued in the early 1950s that unless the WEA maintained its distinctive character and purpose it might just as well hand its responsibilities over to the local authorities and other agencies. He believed the WEA was forced to make a choice: it 'cannot have it both ways. It cannot be a general adult education provider and at the same time the educational representative of the working-class movement' (Cole, G.D.H., 1952: 6–9). In fact, the WEA's choice was to become a general provider and by the late 1960s, if not before, the social composition of WEA classes differed little from those of other providing bodies (Wilderspin, 1968: 7; DES, 1973: 38).

## Retreat from Academic Standards

The Association's claim to be serving the educationally or socially underprivileged was also undermined by its shift away from the three-year tutorial classes to short courses. Unless it abandoned all pretence to academic standards, it was bound to cater for a reasonably educated clientele because the short courses gave no real opportunity for educationally underprivileged students to 'start where they were' (at a fairly elementary level) and progress to university level work in the time available, which had been the hallmark of the early tutorial classes. The short course programme was more often a top-up for the already well-educated. In the later 1950s and early sixties, only some 45 per cent of the national school population was staying on at school beyond the then minimum age of 15, but in 1960 nearly 60 per cent of WEA students had remained at school beyond the minimum leaving age (Central Advisory Council for Education, 1959: 6; WEA, 1960: 60). To counter this trend, those within the WEA who advocated a continuing commitment to the working class or the educationally underprivileged were forced to advocate more elementary work and a retreat from academic standards. In 1969 the WEA published a policy statement entitled *Unfinished Business*, which probably more clearly than ever before recognised the Association's dilemma that its concentration on short courses combined with its insistence on disciplined study, scholarship and academic standards alienated the very people it wished to serve (WEA, 1969: 8–9).

## Decline in Voluntaryism and Democratic Participation

Another founding principle of the WEA which began to look less secure by the 1950s was its voluntaryism and dedication to a democratic structure. Branches had become somewhat moribund or incapable of organising and stimulating classes and membership was declining. Particularly in large towns, the job of organising adult education was felt to be beyond the capacity of the voluntary movement, and a paternalistic professionalism was gradually taking over, either through a growing body of WEA tutor organisers or, in some areas, through university resident tutors who organised classes in the name of the WEA, but with little reference to it. Indeed, some (although not all) extramural departments began to feel they were carrying the WEA: doing the work of the voluntary movement (Ministry of Education, 1954: 36; WEA, 1954: 6–7, 1958: 9–12; Harrison, 1959: 6, 9; Shaw, 1959: 209–11, 1971: 7–13; *Times Educational Supplement*, 1954, 2061: 1016). Over-dependence on public funds was also believed to be weakening the Association's voluntary character, reducing it to just another public body.

Certainly, after a post-war boom in 1946 and 1947, membership began to decline. Branch membership fell from 39,092 to 30,095 between 1947 and 1953. Numerically, it remained steady during the later 1950s, but as a proportion of WEA students it continued to fall. By 1956–7 less than 40 per cent of WEA students belonged to the Association (WEA, 1954: 6; Harrison, 1959: 8; Raybould, 1954: 248). When a WEA working party investigated the Association's structure and organisation in 1966, it found that the existing branch structure was not capable of coping with the demands made upon it.

More professional assistance and regular and systematic training of voluntary officers were considered necessary. At the same time, the WEA changed its constitution to admit almost all students in WEA classes, as well as individual subscribers, into automatic membership of the Association. This was an attempt to counter the decline in voluntary membership by giving all students the democratic right to participate in its affairs (WEA, 1966a: 11–20, 1967: 5–7). However, it failed to stimulate more active involvement and may well have weakened the very concept of voluntaryism still further.

The 1966 working party also recommended a devolution of power (particularly in financial matters) from the districts to more participatory local representative committees (WEA, 1966a: 29–33) but this was never effectively implemented. Three years later the WEA's policy statement *Unfinished Business* recognised the continued weakness of the branch structure and the necessity of strengthening the Association's voluntaryism. Despite the extension of membership, there was still a real need to find a way of involving the many students who were not active in the branches (WEA, 1969: 13–15). One of the problems of the voluntary branch structure was that it tended to perpetuate existing attitudes and provision. Branch committees became self-perpetuating, inward-looking elites, reluctant to break new ground and unable or unwilling to attract new types of member. 'An effective WEA branch is plugged into a network of people in the community ... (which) covers a limited spectrum of the community in which the branch operates. (The larger the community, the smaller the spectrum.) The real task of development is to plug into other networks', concluded the WEA National Committee in 1973 (WEA, 1960: 61, 1969: 6, 1973: 32). In a survey of nine WEA district secretaries carried out a year or two later (by the author), the majority considered that branches were only moderately effective in assessing the adult education needs of their local communities. Despite this, the evidence submitted to the Russell Committee was sufficiently positive to persuade it to give qualified approval of the WEA's voluntaryism. It concluded in 1973 that 'although branch organisation may have lost some of the vitality that marked the pre-war years, the amount of voluntary effort is still substantial' and that classroom democracy was still better than in most local education authority establishments or university extramural departments (DES, 1973: 38). This was probably a somewhat optimistic view.

In 1976, when the WEA undertook a national survey of 908 branches, it came to the conclusion that 'there is no need for alarm and despondency about the vitality of our branches but neither is there room for complacency' (*WEA News*, ns. 11, 1976: 1). Individual subscribing membership had become an insignificant part of the voluntary movement, while an average of only 14 per cent of branch members attended their branch AGM. Moreover, there was clearly no rapid renewal of committee membership. Indeed, some branches specifically expressed the need for infusion of new blood and complained about the difficulty of involving student members in WEA affairs. The small branches tended to involve more of their members than the large ones, but overall it was not a picture of very active member participation. Rather it was a picture of small, dedicated and hard-working oligarchies running WEA branches and providing a semblance of voluntaryism amidst general apathy. The branches' involvement in the wider movement presented the same picture. Although regarded by the WEA as a basic criterion for recognition as a branch, less than two-thirds of the branches attended even one of their quarterly District Committee meetings. Only one branch in five managed to send a representative to all four District Council meetings in 1975. And a clear majority of branches also failed to send representatives to any of the previous four biennial conferences of the Association (WEA, 1976a, *passim*).

## Growing Professionalisation

It had long been argued that more professional assistance was necessary to foster the voluntary movement: more organisers and organising tutors in the field and more administrative staff in district offices were regarded as essential support for the voluntary workers in an ever-more-complex field of adult education. The WEA and national and local government, which jointly contributed towards the salaries of the professional staff, yielded to this pressure over the years. In 1954 the Association was operating with 36 full-time tutors and 82 administrative and clerical workers in the whole of England and Wales. By 1966 the number of organising tutors had risen to 68 (plus four in Scotland) and there were also 17 organisers. By 1975 the total number of organising tutors had increased further, to 123: three-and-a-half times the number employed 20 years earlier. Much of the new 'work with the disadvantaged' which had been recommended by the Russell Report (see below) was planned and organised by the professional tutor organisers, with very little involvement by the branch voluntary workers. Perhaps the complexities and challenge of such adult education made this inevitable, and in any case the size of the professional staff was still small in relation to the overall size of the WEA's programme. Nevertheless, by the mid-seventies the National Committee felt that the Association needed to 'review carefully the role it expects its professional workers to fulfil and the position it expects them to assume in the movement' (WEA, 1954: 6–8, 1966a: 16, 20–7, 73, 1969: 13–14, 1975: 13; Legge, 1982: 128–9). The growing administrative burden of running an educational organisation in close conjunction with the state system was one undoubted cause of the dwindling strength of the voluntary movement.

## Decline of the Social Purpose Dynamic

The post-war decades also witnessed a gradual evaporation of the social purpose dynamic of the WEA. Despite some weakening during the 1930s, the belief that the Association should aim to be the educational arm of the Labour movement and equip workers to take up the struggle for political, social and economic emancipation was still strong after the Second World War. 'Students are not to be regarded as individuals, self enclosed in routine academic studies' declared the WEA in 1953: rather they sought 'to clarify their views of social good, and to strive to realise their ideal, through political action' (WEA, 1953a: 35). The WEA continued to declare unequivocally that it was concerned to encourage and equip students to take an active role in modern democratic society (WEA, 1954: 4, 1960: 3–7; Cole, G.D.H., 1952: 2–11).

But after the Second World War this 'knowledge for power' motive became gradually less strong, partly because the need for it in the post-war welfare state was less apparent than in the social and political turmoil of the earlier twentieth century which had been experienced by many of the WEA pioneers. The desire to change society was no longer the main motivating force of WEA students (Harrison, 1959: 11–13, 25–27; WEA, 1960: 8).

With the decline of the traditional dynamic, the quest for personal fulfilment or knowledge for its own sake came gradually to predominate, especially as the WEA grew more middle class and adult education came to be regarded primarily as a leisure activity. 'Cultural emancipation' was accepted by many as a valid alternative to economic emancipation. Very few students expressed any desire to equip themselves for social or political purposes. Although, of course, students often had mixed motives for joining a class, it was clear that very few did so out of a desire to change the world (Ministry of Education, 1954: 26; Harrison, 1959: 5; WEA, 1960: 57–8; Shaw, 1959: 213).

From time to time the WEA attempted to infuse a new sense of social purpose alongside this 'cultural individualism', but at best it was a rather feeble alternative 'community purpose' (WEA, 1958: 5–9, 1960: 13–14; Legge, 1982: 128). Its objectives were one stage removed from social or political *emancipation*. They amounted to a more neutral, objective, undynamic interpretation of social purpose, educationally valid but lacking the inspiration of the earlier commitment. In 1966 the WEA's policy statement still hankered after social relevance and claimed that it was a false antithesis to set the aim of individual fulfilment in opposition to social or political emancipation. As the educated individual could contribute to society more effectively, both were valid and complementary objectives. The following year, in its evidence to the Russell Committee, the WEA again claimed that its purpose was to help people to attain a richer personal development *and* to undertake responsible social action (WEA, 1969: 4–6, 11–12, 1970: 3).

Although they made a valiant effort to marry the cultural individualism to the old dynamic, such statements lacked something of the old fire or commitment to changing society for the benefit of the working class. In particular, it is significant that the term 'social and political *responsibility*' was preferred to 'emancipation' (*ibid.*). The result was a rather vague social message. Most people regarded the WEA merely as a providing body rather than a living organisation with social aspirations and dynamic. A lack of positive identity or uniqueness of purpose rendered it increasingly vulnerable to the encroachments of the local authorities and the universities. The WEA still needed, perhaps more than ever, to tackle the tasks it had set itself in 1958: to give its members 'the feeling that they are really joining a movement when they join the WEA, a socially relevant movement' (Harrison, 1959: 25–7; Fieldhouse, 1967, *passim*; WEA, 1958: 11).

## Re-Emergence of Social Purpose and Response to the Adult Education Reports

Periodically the WEA was urged to recover its radicalism. In 1955 the *Times Educational Supplement* advised it not to try to imitate the universities but to be 'an agent of democracy, bold, positive, engaged in the conflict of ideas' (*Times Educational Supplement*, 2053, 11 April 1955: 262). By the late 1960s there were indications that the Association (or a part of it) was responding to the pressure to rediscover its social purpose. A flurry of discussion papers and policy statements, culminating in *Unfinished Business* in 1969, advocated a more positive approach to changing social demands (Lowe, 1970: 121). The WEA evidence submitted to the Russell Committee that year emphasised the priority it felt should be given to work with the educationally deprived and socially disadvantaged (WEA, 1970: 24–30). There was nothing particularly new about this except the urgency and high priority now being given to such activity within the Association.

Even before the Russell Report was published, many of the WEA districts were promoting some kind of community adult education which aimed to contribute to social change in areas 'of social, economic and educational deprivation' as well as a variety of courses concerned with specific social problems, such as civil liberties, welfare rights, drug addiction, etc. (Jackson and Lovett, 1971: 102; Lovett, 1975, *passim*; WEA, 1973: 31–8). Then in 1973 the Russell Report, closely following the evidence that the WEA and others had submitted to it, nudged the Association quite definitely towards 'a shift of emphasis from a wide range of general provision to more specific priorities', leaving some of its previous functions to other providing bodies. The 'specific priorities' consisted of four areas which the WEA itself had identified as of special interest, and which became known as the WEA's 'Russell-type work'. They were:

education for the socially and culturally deprived living in urban areas – of an experiential and informal character;
work in an industrial context (predominantly trade union education);
developing greater social and political awareness (which the Report considered to be of 'special value'); and
liberal and academic study below the level of university work.

In the last category, it was envisaged that the WEA would move gradually to a more promotional role for other bodies rather than making direct provision itself, and that there would inevitably be a weakening of the links with the universities in providing joint courses. All-in-all, the Report argued that this shift in emphasis would 'once again cast the WEA largely in the role of educational pioneer' (DES, 1973: 77–81; Fieldhouse, 1993a: 42).

Two years later the Alexander Report recommended that the WEA in Scotland should make a major contribution to meeting the educational needs of those adults 'who by virtue of social, economic or educational deprivation are less able to articulate their needs'. This would enable the WEA to place practical emphasis on its social commitment. The Report also attached much importance to the special relationship with the trade unions and urged continued collaboration with them (Scottish Education Department, 1975: 64–5).

There was an immediate increase in WEA manpower and other resources devoted to 'Russell-type work'. In England and Wales, 13 new tutor organisers were appointed during 1974–5 and 1975–6, all of them to work in the priority areas and similar developments took place in Scotland following the publication of the Alexander Report. Much of this work, particularly in social and political awareness, was much the same as the WEA's traditional provision. It was the programmes for the deprived or disadvantaged which led the Association furthest into new ventures, including more community adult education, provision for the mentally ill and handicapped and the physically disabled (both in and outside institutions), prisoners, the unemployed, immigrants, the elderly, women, single parents and alcoholics. Courses were given in welfare and citizens' rights, and training for voluntary community workers. Over half the districts also became involved in the rapidly developing adult literacy schemes (see Chapter 6). The WEA National Committee concluded that a 'different kind of educational provision' was necessary, with a greater emphasis on relevance than on academic standards (WEA, 1973: 31–2, 1975: 8–12, 1976b, *passim*).

Until 1976 it was generally assumed within the WEA that it would be able to maintain previous levels of traditional/cultural classes as well as pursuing its new priorities, but then the Minister of Education warned that the Government's over-riding intention to reduce public expenditure meant that desirable expansion in the priority areas could not necessarily be achieved by growth, but rather by abandoning some existing activities. Prolonged negotiations eventually led to a 'new deal' whereby the WEA was awarded an extra £100,000, but this was coupled with a requirement that it produce 'a coherent plan to shift the emphasis away from liberal and academic studies and towards the Russell priorities of work' and meet specific targets set by the Minister for expansion in the priority areas (Circular from WEA General Secretary to District Secretaries, 16 July 1976; *WEA News*, ns 14, 1978: 1; Doyle, 1980: 130). This really marked the final abandonment by the WEA of its commitment to providing or promoting specifically *university* level adult education.

By the end of the decade the WEA claimed remarkable progress, with work with the disadvantaged and social and political education each increasing by 12 per cent from the 1975–6 baseline, and trade union education and industrial studies by as much as 31 per cent, although in reality it was impossible to quantify the growth accurately because of the imprecision of the Russell categories (*WEA News*, ns 14, 1978: 1, 6–7; Jennings' 1978: 7; Doyle, 1980: 129–39; Hopkins, 1978: 21; Stephens, 1990: 101–3). By 1980 the trade union work represented approximately one-quarter of all the WEA's provision and the number of specifically industrial branches, which had first appeared in 1972, had increased to over 25 (McIlroy and Brown, 1980: 91–5). But there was a price to pay for these developments. Within the WEA, and particularly within the voluntary movement, it was felt that there was too little contact between the expanding industrial studies field and the rest of the programme, and that the expansion of the Russell-type work generally was responsible for a decline in the Association's traditional liberal studies programme (although the expansion in the local authority and university sectors, and the establishment of the Open University were almost certainly contributory factors). 'The 'traditional' work acquired a slightly musty odour' (Jennings, 1978: 7). Moreover, there was more than a hint of opportunism in the WEA's pursuance of its goals. There was little sense that principles, values or belief should be determining its purpose. In 1986 the Association's national Assistant Secretary complained that 'discussion of the WEA's concern for education for social purpose demonstrates at best a lack of clarity and at worst utter confusion, whereas in the period up to 1939 social purpose constituted the very core of policy review' (Doyle, 1986: 141).

## Mounting Tensions and Lost Opportunities

There was increasing concern about the shift in the balance between the professional employees (particularly those tutor organisers appointed specifically to develop the Russell-type work, or who had moved into that area) and the voluntary movement, 'to the detriment, and the obvious concern, of the latter' (*ibid.*). This was vigorously challenged by those closely involved in the Russell-type work, who saw it as an opportunity to re-establish the WEA's radical purpose and commitment to the working class (Caldwell *et al.*, 1975: 5). Although many tutor organisers considered the Russell Report as having little long-term influence, this was not so much the view of the more politically committed, who saw it as an opportunity to bring about a change of direction or at least a change of emphasis. It provided 'a platform from which to change the very conservative nature of the WEA – particularly to concentrate on disadvantaged groups and to bring a more politically social purpose dimension to the work' (Fieldhouse, 1993a: 43–5). But a large proportion of the voluntary movement was 'terrified of things like social and political (purpose) and the unemployed' (*ibid*). The result was a dangerous polarisation within the Association between the professional/working-class axis and the largely middle-class voluntary movement. In a number of districts this caused a great deal of turmoil and dissension and lost opportunities during the early 1980s.

The decline in trade union work after 1980, due partly to the change in TUC educational policy (see above and Chapter 10) and partly to the increase in unemployment and the government attacks on the trade unions, did not immediately reduce the tension within the Association. Rather it led to a greater diversification into other Russell-type work. Between 1981–2 and 1988–9, industrial studies and trade union work declined from over 20 per cent of the WEA's activity to 10 per cent but work with the disadvantaged, including the unemployed, increased from 24 to 34 per cent (Kelly, 1992: li). When the national biennial conference resolved to 'examine afresh the nature of the WEA' with the intention of establishing clear goals for the Association in 1989, it confirmed that it had become increasingly difficult for the WEA to sustain the level of its trade union provision because of financial pressures, but that there had been new initiatives in other areas of provision. These included personal development, access to higher education and return to learning courses, work with ethnic minorities, women's education, work with the disadvantaged including the unemployed, the handicapped and people confined to institutions, and role education for such groups as parents and school governors (WEA, 1991a, paras. 1.1, 1.5, 2.2, 2.11).

## Funding and Financial Problems

The internal conflict and tension within the WEA was further exacerbated by increasing financial difficulties brought about very largely by changes in Government policy following the election of the Thatcher Conservative Government in 1979. In 1983 the DES announced its intention to claw back some £45,000 from WEA district surpluses (i.e. working capital) and then imposed a phased reduction of 8.3 per cent in its grant to the WEA over the next three years. In line with government ideology, it was expected that the shortfall would be recovered from increased student fees. (Of course, this was in almost total contradiction with the previous policy of encouraging the WEA to concentrate its provision on 'the disadvantaged'.) At the same time, cuts in the government grants to the universities and in local authority resources meant that the WEA's partners became less supportive. In many districts there was a reduction in subsidies to the WEA or in the proportion of fees from jointly-provided courses that the WEA was permitted to retain (Evans, 1987: 163–5).

Meanwhile the Government introduced a crude measure of cost-effectiveness, based on attendance rates, which forced the WEA to concentrate on safe, popular subjects and abandon much of the more exciting, innovative work which had been developed since the publication of the Russell Report. This payments-by-results system threw the Association into a state of permanent uncertainty, making it impossible to plan ahead. The DES did offer the WEA an opportunity to recover some of its lost grant by bidding for contracts for work with the unemployed under the REPLAN programme (see Chapter 3) but this did not provide any financial security. As districts encountered increasing financial difficulties they were forced to shed staff, or not renew posts when they fell vacant. Eventually two districts (North Staffs and the Southern District) had to be wound up and their responsibilities transferred to neighbouring districts (WEA, 1991b: 3).

However this reduction in the professional staff did not lead to a revival of the WEA's voluntaryism. Instead of being driven by its own professionals, it found itself increasingly answerable to government departments. Indeed, in the mid-eighties the DES defined the WEA 'as a mainly statutory body' – as opposed to a voluntary organisation – because its work was supervised by the government inspectorate and because of the volume of grant it received which, by this time, accounted for over two-thirds of the Association's total income (Evans, 1987: 163; Fieldhouse, 1989: 89). Although these were not new factors, and the WEA vigorously rejected the allegation, it is true that the degree of professionalisation, together with the gradual eclipse of the voluntary element in the Association, and the size of its grant from central government, made it very difficult to catagorise the WEA any longer as a voluntary body. It is true the WEA national executive committee and some district councils were still heavily influenced by voluntary 'representatives', but there was often only a tenuous link between these representatives and the majority of the student body. In 1991 the WEA itself acknowledged that 'available evidence suggests that the level of voluntary activity as measured by the number of Branches is in decline' (WEA, 1991a, para. 9.1).

After the promise of revival in the 1970s, following Russell, the eighties were not a happy decade for the WEA. A vast amount of time was spent by both professional staff and voluntary members in the task of survival. It was 'a deflection from the real educational purposes of the WEA and, in terms of potential students and student groups, a wasted opportunity' (Boaden, 1988: 176).

## Incorporation into the Further Education Sector

The WEA was thrown into further confusion and struggle for survival in 1989 when the Government announced that part of the central government grant to the English WEA districts was to be routed through the local authorities in future. This was a matter of major concern in view of the increasing financial difficulties faced by the poll tax-capped local authorities, which were causing them to reduce their discretionary grants to the WEA. The Association did manage to negotiate a compromise agreement with the DES, whereby the WEA national executive committee became responsible for all central government grant aid to the English districts (WEA, 1991b: 1-2). However, the Government announced a totally new plan for the WEA in its 1991 White Paper *Education and Training for the 21st Century*, whereby the Association in England and Wales was to be funded via the new Further Education Funding Councils while the Scottish Office would fund the WEA in Scotland directly (*ibid.*: 2; DES and Welsh Office, 1991, para. 2.8). This apparently locked the WEA into providing certain prescribed forms of what became known as 'Schedule 2' adult education (see Chapter 3). There seemed little opportunity for the WEA to continue to receive funding for its traditional liberal adult education, or what was somewhat dismissively described in the White Paper as 'the leisure interests of adults' (*ibid.*, paras 3.2, 3.5, 3.6).

The WEA became involved in campaigning against some of the proposals contained in the white paper (WEA, 1991b: 2, 1991c, *passim*). When the Further and Higher Education Bill was published, the WEA took some comfort from the changes that had been made to the original proposals, but was still very concerned that its funding via local authorities was at risk (Emergency motion passed by WEA National Conference, December 1991; Hansard, 1993, cols. 189, 191, 207–8). In fact, the Government's emasculation of the local education authorities, together with the proposed changes in the funding of university continuing education and the total withdrawal of government grant to the TUC for trade union education, meant that the WEA could expect less support from, or collaboration with, its erstwhile adult education partners in the future. By 1991 a significant number of local authorities had announced plans to cut back or abolish their grants to the WEA (WEA, 1991d: 4, 1993a: 4–5).

The Further and Higher Education Act placed the WEA as a 'designated institution' under the Further Education Funding Councils for England and Wales. The WEA recognised that 'this status places us more firmly within a statutory framework and within mainstream education than ever before'. It did represent survival of sorts. In 1993–4 the WEA received £3.28 million recurrent grant from the English FEFC for 100,282 enrolments (Wales having become constitutionally separate, see below). The following year this grant increased by 23 per cent to over £4 million. But there was 'a considerable price to pay' in terms of greater accountability to a quango funding body. Within the WEA this caused 'a widespread feeling that the Association (was) becoming finance led'. But more significant was the question of whether it had lost all control over its ethos and purpose. The eight categories of fundable courses listed in Schedule 2 of the Act had very little relevance to the WEA's traditional roles. In fact, 89 per cent of the 1993–4 enrolments fell outside Schedule 2, and the WEA also had a further 30,000 enrolments in courses funded from other sources, including joint courses with the universities. It was questionable whether the WEA had a long-term future in the new further education sector into which it had been manoeuvred. The Association itself feared that it had become 'simply ... ring-fenced as a 'protected species' whose survival is only sought out of sympathy for a past tradition' (WEA, 1993a: 3–4, 1994: 6; FEFC, 1995: 3).

The WEA's new statutory position certainly meant that it would 'have to compete for contracts and "service level agreements" ' within the further education sector and 'speak the language of measurable outcomes, accreditation, quality assurance and output-related funding.' It faced 'the fundamental problem of reconciling quite different philosophies of education within a common framework of funding and accreditation' (WEA, 1992b: 7). The WEA President warned in a lecture to the South West District in Plymouth in June 1993 on 'The Next Ten Years' that it was not possible for the Association to swim against the tide of recent legislation. More funding would be directed towards the Schedule 2 work and the WEA would have to accept this because of the Association's dependence on government funding. However, he predicted that the range of provision would continue to be a mixture of traditional and specially targeted work; that the Association would remain a large national provider of adult education; and that it would probably continue to expand.

Other assessments of the WEA's role in the adult education context of the 1990s were equally positive. In London it was claimed that

The opportunities are there for the WEA to develop further its role as a small but important provider of adult education in Inner London building upon its aims to provide adult education for all and especially for working-class people ... (particularly) where cuts in funding have led to often greatly reduced adult education programmes and significant gaps in provision (Lewis, ?1992: 110).

In 1995 the WEA General Secretary stated that the Association had radically reorganised itself over the previous few years, to fit into the new further education sector. His assessment was that it had become an integrated national organisation, full of innovation and diversity; infused with a 'culture of change'; and developing many new kinds of programme (Lochrie, R., address to the Eric Bellchamber memorial meeting, Rochester, 8 July 1995). The WEA's 1995 *Annual Report* listed some of these changing roles, including outreach work, working with unemployed people, returning to learning, pre-Access and Access, working with ethnic minority communities, courses for people with special needs, and women's education.

Its national strategic plan identified certain target groups within the community for whom courses were specifically designed: unemployed people, low paid people, ethnic minority communities, refugees, community groups, women, retired people, and people with physical disabilities and learning difficulties (WEA, 1995: 4–15). In fact many of these roles were not so new: they were very similar to the 'Russell priorities' and reflected what the WEA had been attempting to do for sometime. FEFC funding and Schedule 2 gave this work a new impetus.

What was much less secure after 1992 was the 'liberal adult education in the branches' – still some 70 per cent of the WEA's work in 1995, and the bulk of the branch-delivered programmes – which was less generously funded than the programmes which qualified for funding under Schedule 2. The FEFC Inspectorate reported that the provision targeted at specific groups and geared to more specific outcomes was increasing, and assumed without question that this was desirable. There was a growing division between these targeted programmes and the branch-based liberal adult education, reminiscent of the division between the branch programmes and the TUC work in the 70s (Lochrie, 1995, *loc. cit.*; WEA, 1994: 6, 1995: 2; FEFC, 1995: 4–5).

There was also a conflict between the need 'to meet the requirements of the FEFC' and the traditional democratic, voluntary and decentralised character of the WEA. By the mid-90s pressure was being applied by the FEFC on the WEA to develop management systems which enabled the FEFC to monitor and measure output. In 1995 the Inspectorate reported that there was still 'considerable work to be done to ensure (the WEA) can effectively demonstrate to itself and to outside bodies that it is achieving all the targets it has set in its mission and strategic plan' (*ibid.*: 7–9).

## Constitutional Changes

Meanwhile, the changing nature of the Association, together with an industrial tribunal decision which cast doubts on the legal independence of the districts, necessitated a constitutional revision in 1991. Two new constitutional models were considered: the creation of a unitary or 'integrated' body, with delegated powers but less independence for the districts and branches; or a confederation to which a number of independent WEAs were affiliated (WEA, 1991e). A third model – an 'Association of Four Nations' with independent status for Scotland, Wales and Northern Ireland – was mooted because there had been general unhappiness for sometime in the six Celtic districts about the way in which the affairs of the English districts had tended to dominate the agenda of the national organisation. However, the executive committee decided not to put this alternative to the national conference at Manchester in December 1991. Therefore the constitutional conference did not resolve the fundamental issue of whether the WEA could survive as a genuinely national body or would become a federation of four independent national associations. This was shelved until after the conference when it was referred to a small working party (WEA, 1992a, 1992?).

The 'integrated' constitution was adopted by the Manchester conference, as a consequence of which all the English districts were dissolved and incorporated into a single Association with effect from 1 April 1993. The three Scottish districts formed themselves into a single Scottish Association which was also incorporated into the new 'integrated' WEA, but the Northern Ireland and Welsh districts opted out because of fears about the erosion of the WEA's democratic principles and structures (WEA, 1993a: 2–3).

Under the new constitution the English districts and the Scottish Association became subject 'at all times ... to the ordinance of the National Executive Committee' (Clause 8). The districts lost their charitable as well as their Responsible Body status and in effect became subject to the control of the national executive. District councils were reduced to a largely advisory role, although District Committees were left with some delegated powers. All professional staff became employees of the national Association rather than the districts. Similarly, branches became subject to the ordinances of the districts (Clause 7). More than ever before, it was a top-down rather than bottom-up relationship. It made a nonsense of Mansbridge's vision of an Association run by the students! As the WEA's own magazine recognised, it was 'a period of coming to terms with things not clearly of democratic choosing' (WEA, 1993b: 5).

The WEA also reviewed the automatic membership that had been introduced in 1966. It was felt that there had been a confusion between 'the idea of 'democracy' as government by an active membership' with the Association's 'ethos of 'democracy' in the class where the direction of learning is determined by the students'. As a result, the WEA 'must be one of the few organisations where someone can be a member without his or her knowledge and where membership brings no obligations whatsoever' (WEA, 1991e). Nevertheless, the new constitution retained automatic membership, although it did introduce a mechanism for excluding anyone from membership 'for conduct inimical to the welfare of the Association' (Clauses 6.2 and 6.5).

Incorporation into the further education sector meant that the WEA's traditional close linkage between membership and provision (essential to a voluntary body) was in danger of disappearing. This was clearly demonstrated by the 1995 FEFC report, which, although recognising the key role of voluntary members, was critical of the branches; identified the districts (rather than the branches) as the 'key organisational units'; and stressed the importance of greater central monitoring and control at national level. The Association had become 'subject to inspection and targets which are without reference to the notion that it might be seen as primarily accountable to its members' (FEFC, 1995: 2, 5–7; Bown, 1995: 7). This had created an identity crisis for the WEA:

Its core activities are for and by its members, but the discourse of 'provision' and the funding conditions mean that more and more of its work is done for others, who are not members and whom existing members do not see as sharers in the inherited WEA project. It will not be long before an open decision will have to be made: will it continue to organise learning activities mainly for members and assume that learners in all its classes are seriously offered the choice of becoming members? or will it transform itself openly into an organisation of members contributing subscriptions to help others gain access to learning, that is operate more like the Educational Centres Association in this country or Oxfam when it runs educational programmes in poor countries? Either position is tenable and respect-worthy, but at present the Association has not openly faced up to the choice (*ibid.*: 14).

It is an assessment which was echoed in the FEFC Inspectorate report: 'The challenge for the organisation is to sustain the participation of the voluntary membership whilst achieving its mission' (FEFC, 1995: 5).

Thus the last decade of the twentieth century saw the WEA as a very different organisation from the one founded in 1903, with very different objectives, membership and working methods, and with a rather uncertain future.

# 8

# University Adult Education

## *Roger Fieldhouse*

### *University Extension Struggles into the Twentieth Century*

It has already been noted in Chapter 2 how university extension began at Cambridge in 1873, followed by Oxford a few years later; and how the fortunes of this 'movement' fluctuated over the last quarter of the nineteenth century. The peak was reached in the early 1890s, with the support of the 'whisky money' but there was a falling away in the later 1890s. Nevertheless by 1902 the two universities had established well over 900 centres, although many of these were quite short-lived. A very conservative estimate of the numbers attending extension lectures in England in 1901–2 would put the figure at between 20 and 25 thousand. This university extension had been particularly important in contributing to the improvement of women's education at the end of the century but had been less successful in attracting poorer or working-class students, or in providing opportunities for systematic and sustained study. Its lack of public funding meant that it had been forced to chase popularity rather than promote quality, and had never been really secure financially. (See Chapter 2.) Despite these shortcomings and difficulties, university extension continued to enjoy some success in England during the first decade of the twentieth century, although less so in Wales and Scotland. Some extension lecturers and organisers did make valiant attempts to provide opportunities for more sustained and systematic study, such as the classes promoted by Canon Barnett at Toynbee Hall or A.W. Bateman-Brown, first secretary for the Extension of Higher Education in North Staffordshire, which can be viewed as genuine forerunners of the later university tutorial classes (Kelly, 1992: 246–7; Jepson, 1973: 102; Marriott, 1983: 286–8; Lowe, 1972).

However, more generally, university extension was exhibiting severe strains by the beginning of the century. The 1908 Report on *Oxford and Working Class Education* identified several reasons why it was not offering satisfactory university adult education to working-class people. The report confirmed that it was providing very little continuous and systematic teaching of a university standard. This was very largely because the cost of such education, without public subsidy, was prohibitive. Therefore efforts had been made to make cheaper provision by offering popular lectures to large audiences. Although numbers varied enormously, an audience of 200 was quite normal, and in the larger centres, 800 or 1000 might be found. Even at the supposedly more intensive classes that followed the lectures, where the 'real students' were to be found and which offered more of an opportunity for proper educational work, attendances could still be 50 or 60, or more. In these circumstances, it was impossible to provide the necessary individual guidance and supervision, although some of the local associations organised follow-up discussions 'under the advice of the lecturer'. Lack of secure fee income also meant that it was not possible to guarantee continuity of study in one subject or discipline for any length of time. All this was the consequence very largely of inadequate funding. By the time university extension obtained a modest amount of public financial support it had already fallen into fatal decline (Joint Committee of University and Working-class Representatives, 1909: 36–8; Ministry of Reconstruction, 1919: 184–5, 188–9; Dixon, 1965: 5; Jepson, 1973: 177; Marriott, 1981b: 43).

The 1908 Report also considered extension work flawed because it failed to employ only university lecturers, or teachers with 'recognised status as members of the teaching body of the University ...'. Extension continued to suffer from a lack of suitable lecturers, mainly because of the absence of any career structure or steady employment. By the end of the First World War, the supply had almost completely dried up (Joint Committee, 1909: 39–40; Ministry of Reconstruction, 1919: 188).

Some years before the publication of the 1908 Report, the Oxbridge domination of extension had begun to be threatened, firstly by the replacement of the London Society for the Extension of University Teaching (which had worked with Oxford and Cambridge) by a University of London Board to Promote the Extension of University Teaching in London in 1902; and then by the promise of similar developments by the University of Durham, the newly independent Universities of Birmingham, Liverpool, Manchester and Leeds, and the rumoured new federal university for the south west. Their tendency to claim regional 'territories' undermined the Oxbridge notion of a universal extension movement which allowed Oxford and Cambridge to respond to the 'free choice' of voluntary extension committees anywhere in the country (Marriott, 1984: 70–4; Burrows, 1976: 24, 28).

The fate of the University Extension College that had been established at Reading in 1892 illustrates some of the difficulties faced by the movement. In its early days the College did reflect the social ideology of the extension movement, but even before the end of the century it was claiming not to be a typical extension college, but rather a broader institution where 'extension work is done ... as part of a College scheme'. In reality, extension work was becoming a less integral part of the College's activities, so that in 1902 it changed its name to the University College, Reading. 'In the pursuance of funds and status, the middle-class, liberal-minded men who governed the college moved, usually unconsciously, away from the social ideology that had spawned the college, towards a more conventional idea of university education.' The foundation of the first WEA branch at Reading in 1904 was a direct consequence of the College retreating from its original commitment to extension provision. In 1907 W.M. Childs, who had become Principal in 1903, published a 17-page 'vision' of the University College which made no mention of evening classes or public lectures. It was a vision of full university status: a national rather than a local institution. The College's emphasis on full-time degree study eclipsed the extension style courses and by 1907–8 the College stopped employing university extension lecturers. Four years later the College Council formally announced its intention to pursue full university status, which was eventually obtained by royal charter in 1926 (Macrae, 1994).

In many respects the experience at Reading can be seen as representative of the failure of the whole university extension movement. Exeter University Extension College underwent a similar development, although at a slower pace ... Colchester, the only other Extension College to be founded, followed a divergent course ... dropping all extension work and becoming a Technical College in 1919. Other University Colleges which owed their origins to university extension work include Firth College, which became the University of Sheffield in 1905 and Nottingham University College, which became Nottingham University in 1948 (*ibid.*: 15).

The decline of extension in the early years of the twentieth century reflected the failure of the movement to become the means whereby 'the great mass of people' could gain access to university education; the greater emphasis on, and public funding for, technical and vocational education; and the emergence of the WEA and its redirection of the original social aims of extension into the tutorial class movement, which soon attracted the support of such bodies as the London University extension board. It was, in fact, the rapid rise of the WEA and the new method of extramural organisation which it promoted that was the fatal blow to the old extension movement. Although it set out to promote extension lectures and classes, by 1906–7 the WEA was convinced that it had to find an alternative to extension for the working class, and this led to the plan for tutorial classes. 'From 1907 the Extension system became increasingly troubled by the actual and anticipated effects' of the new tutorial class movement (*ibid.*: 15–17; Burrows, 1976: 35–8; Marriott, 1984: 76–9).

Meanwhile, the universities had begun to look for financial support for extension from both the Board of Education and the new LEAs. While this was not a very successful financial strategy, it tended to further weaken the Oxbridge stranglehold on the movement because the local authorities were more inclined to favour their local universities. These made a small but valuable contribution, but this caused some internal tensions within the movement, with increasing competition from the provincial universities leading to price-cutting and the establishment of territorial spheres of influence. Nevertheless, extension continued to be dominated by Oxford, Cambridge and London, which respectively had 114, 72 and 74 active centres just before the First World War. Liverpool secured some extension work in the north west, but other would-be participants found it difficult to support the work (Ministry of Reconstruction, 1919: 186–9; Marriott, 1984: 74–6).

During the years immediately preceding the First World War extension was still the predominant form of university adult education statistically, but the writing was on the wall:

... enrolments began to fall, there was less and less evidence of really serious commitment, and its continued vitality came into question. Extension's voluntarist foundations were showing signs of age, and in a changing social and educational world there were doubts about the viability of an expensive mass-lecture system which depended ultimately on a capacity to deliver polite recreation ... Any marked zeal on the extramural front associated itself with the new working-class adult education, and was fully absorbed in the effort to establish the tutorial-class system ... By 1914 university adult education was a house divided against itself ... supporters of the tutorial classes were prepared to denigrate other forms of extramural activity in order to establish the WEA's claim to define the essential character of adult education and to have the pick of university resources ... University Extension ... had not solved the problem of how to reconcile the interests of Oxford and Cambridge with those of the provincial universities, and the impending war was simply to delay the time at which a new dispensation must be agreed (*ibid.*: 79–87).

Although university extension did not come to an end in 1914, terminal decline had set in. After the war, the anticipated revival did not take place, the large lecture audiences dropped off and its voluntary base crumbled. The old extension movement 'declined to its nadir in the early 1930s' as local centres wound themselves up, leaving the WEA and the tutorial class movement in possession of the field (Ministry of Reconstruction, 1919: 186; Marriott, 1985: 86; 1981a: 93).

## *Partnership with the WEA: The tutorial class movement*

The WEA was, to some extent, an 'outgrowth of university extension' and perhaps even owed its existence in part to Albert Mansbridge's ability to hi-jack the more viable remnants of the extension movement (Marriott, 1983). Its foundation in 1903 and subsequent campaign to promote university adult education accessible to working-class people, culminating in the 1907 Oxford Conference, and the establishment of a network of tutorial classes in industrial towns 'specifically adopted to the needs of workpeople' have been described in Chapter 7.

Following Oxford's lead, most of the universities in England and Wales set up joint committees for tutorial classes. The WEA played an active role in most of these joint committees and assumed virtual command of some of them. Thus the new form of university adult education – the tutorial classes – was to a very considerable extent controlled by a friendly but external body – the WEA. It was aided-and-abetted in this by the Central Joint Advisory Committee (CJAC), set up in 1909 to co-ordinate and promote the tutorial classes. It consisted of representatives from 10 English universities, the University of Wales, six university colleges, and the WEA; but three of its four officers (D.J. Shackleton, vice-chair; W. Temple, treasurer; and Mansbridge, secretary) were WEA men. The CJAC was, in practice, closely associated with the national WEA (Marriott, 1984: 86; CJAC, 1910; Ministry of Reconstruction, 1919: 198–200).

This new university tutorial class movement inherited a broad liberal ideological perspective from its predecessors, which has already been referred to in Chapter 7. It also exuded the Balliol philosophy of Benjamin Jowett and T.H. Green, which provided it with a range of values or an 'ideological agenda' for much of the twentieth century. This agenda encompassed notions of individual self-fulfilment, social purpose, public service, social justice and class emancipation 'provided they were pursued through a dialectical process rather than by propagandising'. That was what university adult education existed for (Taylor *et al.*, 1985: 15–23; Fieldhouse, 1984: 37–45).

This ideological perspective corresponded to 'the reformist current and the social democratic centre of the political spectrum'. It is epitomised by the philosophies of four of the most influential early leaders of the tutorial class movement – William Temple, R.H. Tawney, A.D. Lindsay and G.D.H. Cole. It represented a libertarian socialism which nevertheless, most of the time, displayed comfortable affinities with the mainstream British liberal tradition and the emerging Labour movement. Although sometimes accused of being dangerously left-wing, a tutorial class movement informed by this ideology was regarded by more politically sophisticated observers as an invaluable alternative to the revolutionary socialism which was perceived as such a threat to the British State both before the First World War and in the aftermath of the Russian Revolution. It was a means of educating the leaders of the emerging working class and labour movements in the virtues of liberalism, and 'protecting' them from the enticements of Marxist socialism. As such, the state considered it a worthy recipient of public funds (*ibid.*: 38, 45–80, 102–8; Fieldhouse, 1987b). One of the main aims of the 1907 conference on Oxford and Working Class Education, and the Report that was published the following year, was to secure university control of the education of the leading members of the working class in order 'to guide their general outlook ... towards social harmony' and class reconciliation: an aim the tutorial class movement shared with its predecessor, university extension (*ibid.*: 41; Rowbotham, 1969). For all its occasional lapses, this adult education movement was welcomed by the Establishment as a bulwark against revolutionism, a moderating influence and a form of social control. It helped to channel and reduce pressures and conflict, neutralise class antagonism and integrate the working class into British society (Fieldhouse, 1985a).

It was partly for this reason that the Board of Education and the local authorities were prepared to fund tutorial classes after 1908. Between then and 1913 the Board provided £12,000, the LEAs £6,100, and various other bodies such as the Gilchrist Education Trust another £2,000. Together, these sums amounted to over 50 per cent of the total funding for tutorial classes during the six years before the First World War, the remainder being found by the universities (Ministry of Reconstruction, 1919: 197).

As with the WEA (see Chapter 7), once the universities accepted government funds to support tutorial classes, they became subject to inspection by HMI, who were then in a position to watch out for any ideological lapses. Long before they gained the right to inspect university teacher training, HMI exercised considerable influence over university adult education, partly through the gradually acquired right to approve (or withhold approval from) the appointment of full-time staff in extramural departments and the syllabuses of university adult education courses, and partly through their inspection of, and reporting on, the classes provided by the universities. In this way HMI exercised a discreet but very real surveillance which might have been regarded in other parts of the universities as an infringement of academic freedom. There were times when the controlling influence was quite heavy – for example during the Second World War and the Cold War. But for most of the century it was a very British, benevolent and consensual relationship. For all its shortcomings, public funding allowed much valuable adult education to develop and flourish, which otherwise would not have done so. It provided a space that would not have existed without grant aid. This pervading liberal ideology produced a form of adult education that was essentially democratic – valuing students' wishes about what and how to study. It was dialectical rather than propagandist or didactic, encouraging students to be critical of everything, question all existing assumptions and discuss everything freely, although this was very largely within the framework of the liberal, white, male-dominated canon of western culture. It aimed to enable them to formulate, or at least understand, alternative interpretations; challenge their conceptions of their own environment; widen their experience and understanding; and increase their awareness of alternative views. And it was non-utilitarian in that it was more concerned to enable students to fulfil themselves intellectually or to become better educated citizens, rather than be turned into better trained workers (Taylor et al.: 15–19; Fieldhouse, 1985b: 2).

During the first decades after the 1907 Oxford Conference, a spectacular rise took place in the number of tutorial classes and students, although some caution has to be used when addressing the rather unreliable statistics. In 1908, immediately following the publication of the Conference report, eight tutorial classes were arranged in conjunction with Oxford University. In the following year seven English universities were co-operating with the WEA in the provision of 38 classes and within five years there were approximately 150 tutorial classes with over 3,200 students. By 1914 all the universities in England and Wales were involved, and classes had also been started in Scotland, although the Scottish universities generally showed less interest in adult education because of the long tradition of reasonably effective schools education and the relatively easy access to Scottish higher education. The Scottish universities were also hampered because, unlike their English and Welsh counterparts, they had no direct access to public funds for adult education. Grant aid could only be made to the Scottish School Boards, which retained financial responsibility and therefore ultimate control. Nevertheless, university joint committees with the WEA were established in Scotland (Fieldhouse, 1977: 19; Shearer, 1976: 10–13; Ministry of Reconstruction, 1919: 191–3, 197–9).

The First World War caused a temporary decline, but by 1918–19 there were 145 tutorial classes in England and Wales and six in Scotland, catering for an estimated 3,300 students. Before the war, men outnumbered women by four or five to one, but during the war the proportion of women had rapidly increased. The next two decades saw a further increase of more than 500 per cent in the number of tutorial classes in England and Wales, reaching 810 in 1938–9. The Second World War then caused another temporary decline (Ministry of Reconstruction, 1919: 191; Fieldhouse, 1977: 19).

The aim and intention was that the work undertaken in these tutorial classes should be of university honours degree standard. Some doubts were expressed (for example in the Report of the Board of Education on the universities and university colleges in 1908–9) as to whether this could really be considered to be university education. However, the early class reports claimed that the work being done was of exceptionally high quality and a crucial special report by HMI Mr Headlam and Professor L.T. Hobhouse for 1909–10 judged them to be up to the required standard. This they defined as courses which were scientific, detached and impartial in character and which taught the students to be critical of authorities and sources of information, thorough in their investigation and empirical in their method, valuing of truth, able to distinguish fact from opinion and to argue all points of view (Jennings, 1973: 20–21; 1975: 63; Mansbridge, 1913: 5, 137–8, 145, 166; CJAC, 1910: 13–14). This was to be achieved by ensuring that tutors had sound academic qualifications and were brought regularly into contact with the critical atmosphere of the university in order to maintain their scholarship; by limiting the size of classes to a maximum of 30 students; by imposing a two-year minimum length for classes (soon increased to three years); and through the commitment of the students to attend every class as far as was possible, engage in reading at home, and write 12 essays each year, although the last was widely recognised as more of an aspiration than a requirement. Many of the Joint Committees followed Oxford's example in supplementing the tutorial classes with opportunities for some students to experience more intensive study in a university atmosphere at residential summer schools – a practice borrowed from the extension movement (Joint Committee, 1909: 60–67; Mansbridge, 1913: 38; Ministry of Reconstruction, 1919: 189–90, 200–2).

The most popular subjects during the early years of the tutorial class movement were social studies, industrial and political history and economics. This was considered natural because these were the fields in which 'the immediate interests of working people' lay (ibid.: 194–5).

Something of a mythology grew up about the standards achieved in the early tutorial classes, fostered to some extent by Mansbridge. In reality the standards were very variable. Students came to the classes with very different levels of prior education, and equally different levels of commitment. Some students failed to maintain regular attendance and dropped out, although generally attendance was surprisingly regular considering the difficulties of shift work and overtime. The quality of the written work varied enormously and the goal of 12 essays per year was never widely achieved. Indeed, after three years the CJAC significantly stopped recording the number of essays completed by each student. But in any case, whatever the quantity, the quality was affected by the students' prior educational experience, by lack of convenient access to good academic libraries and, above all, by lack of time. There was also inevitably an unevenness in the quality of teaching: it could not be universally excellent. And there was a real and continuing barrier to effective learning caused by the lack of time and opportunities for adequate individual tuition (ibid.: 62–8, 190–1, 196; Fieldhouse, 1977: 23–6).

For all these reasons, it is not surprising that actual achievement in terms of written work fell somewhat short, even in the earliest days, of the idealised picture of every student toiling away by the midnight oil while the family slept, and handing in scintillating essays regularly once a fortnight. To say such things in no way belittles the real efforts and achievements of the students during the first two decades of tutorial classes (ibid.: 26).

This early tutorial class movement did not aim to serve the whole community, because it quite clearly saw its role as redressing the social imbalance in the educational system by making university scholarship accessible to the have-nots – the working class who quite clearly had not enjoyed much chance of progressing from school to university. The extent to which it can be considered successful in this depends on the vexed question of social class definition, as explained in Chapter 7. By any definition it is clear that the early tutorial classes did attract a predominantly working-class clientele but even before the First World War some of them contained large numbers of non-manual workers, such as clerical workers and teachers. During the first two decades, the link between the trade unions and the tutorial class movement ensured a degree of working-class involvement but between the wars the trade unions became increasingly attracted to informal educational activities and short courses rather than the three-year tutorial classes. The number of manual worker students steadily declined (Fieldhouse, 1977: 28–9).

## The 1919 Report and 1924 Adult Education Regulations

The influential *Final Report* of the Ministry of Reconstruction's Adult Education Committee was generally enthusiastic about the state of university adult education immediately after the First World War and suggested that it remained to reap the fruits of what had already been accomplished. But it also concluded that the number and remuneration of tutors and administrators was inadequate and therefore universities should employ more and ensure that they were paid more. It recommended that there should be more systematic public funding and that the universities should also provide increased financial resources and recognise adult education as one of the most important of their services (Ministry of Reconstruction, 1919: 92–8, 160, 167).

Organisationally, the Committee felt that tutorial classes should no longer be regarded as an off-shoot of extension work, but rather that the two areas of work should be brought together with any other forms of university adult education in equal partnership and equally funded, within newly established extramural departments in every university. The new departments should have an academic head but continue to be subject to the governing authority of joint committees made up of university and outside members, representing the students or their organisations – a model which ensured that university adult education remained outside the mainstream of the universities for most of the century. The Committee also argued that despite the different educational traditions in Scotland, Scottish universities should enjoy similar public funding and extramural organisation, with a Scottish standing joint committee (*ibid.*: 97–9; 103–4, 159).

The Committee laid great stress on the role of the extramural department as a link between the university and the non-academic world. 'The bridge which it would help to build between the Universities and the world of industry would not be the least of the advantages offered by the establishment at each university of such a Department.' Moreover, this was not the only way the Report sounded remarkably like a late twentieth century document: its vision of a diffusion of high education into every community, so that it became 'as universal as citizenship'; and of wider access to mass, lifelong higher education and continuing professional development (although it did not use those terms) sounds remarkably modern and forward thinking for 1919 (*ibid.*: 99–103).

The three-year tutorial classes and more advanced one-year classes were grant aided between 1908–13 under the Board of Education's regulations for technical schools, schools of art and other forms of provision of further education in England and Wales, but from 1913 onwards they came under special adult education regulations which changed the basis of the grant from a *per capita* to a *per* class payment. There were also regulations for shorter courses, but these were not intended for the universities, although advantage was occasionally taken of them by the Tutorial Class Committees to obtain funding for one-year courses which were preparatory to tutorial class work. In 1924 important new regulations were introduced which gave full recognition to university preparatory classes for grant purposes and also made provision for the payment of grants to other 'approved associations' – particularly the WEA Districts – which became recognised as 'Responsible Bodies' in their own right, providing a multitude of grant-aided short courses as well as university tutorial classes. The new regulations were supposed to establish a clear demarcation between university adult education and other, non-university, adult education, but almost immediately the Board of Education allowed Birmingham University and Nottingham University College to fudge the difference. It became increasingly tolerant of (if not enthusiastic about) this lower-level 'pioneer work', as it became known. The consequence of these reforms was to encourage both the universities and the WEA to put more effort into promoting the easier short courses at the expense of the three-year tutorial classes, and so began the slow decline of the latter. Further revisions of the regulations in 1931 and 1938 allowed the universities to undertake more short courses and less demanding elementary work (*ibid.*: 154–5; Fieldhouse, 1977: 19; Raybould, 1951: 92–110; Marriott, 1984: 93–5).

The regulations had a number of effects on university adult education. By encouraging universities after 1924 to abandon tutorial classes in favour of the shorter courses, they tended to make extramural work indistinguishable from other forms of adult education while at the same time widening the gap between extramural and intramural work and therefore hampering those departments which were aiming for parity with the rest of their university. By prescribing conditions for grant aid, they also allowed the Ministry, or its officials, including HMI, to proscribe what might or might not be taught (Raybould, 1951: 60–1; Kelly, 1992: 272; Fieldhouse, 1984: 435).

Scotland was not covered by the revised regulations of 1924, and the position there remained largely unchanged. The University of Glasgow established an extramural committee in 1924 and Edinburgh did likewise five years later, but there were no major attempts to change or improve the funding position until 1934 when Scottish adult education regulations were introduced. These empowered LEAs to co-operate with voluntary bodies including the universities more on the English and Welsh model. However, responsibility for, and control of, adult education remained firmly with the LEAs (Shearer, 1976: 12; Scottish Education Department, 1975: 4).

## University Extramural Departments

Meanwhile, in England, Nottingham University College was the first university institution to follow the 1919 Report's recommendation to establish extramural departments. Robert Peers was appointed as its head for the start of the 1920-1 session. Five years later the staff had increased to five, and by 1928 to eight staff tutors. The number of classes and students likewise rapidly increased, but from the very beginning the programme contained a high proportion of one-year and preparatory classes and even more elementary forms of 'pioneer' adult education. This was partly the result of the new regulations after 1924, but also stemmed from the University College's unusual right, acquired before the First World War, to mount short courses in the East Midlands which would have been the responsibility of the WEA in other parts of the country. Peers regarded this as an advantage and an opportunity for the College, but it had serious consequences in undermining the claim of university adult education to be of genuinely university standard (Brown, 1981: 5-9; Nottingham University College, 1926: 43).

Most English universities and university colleges followed Nottingham's example in establishing extramural departments or at least appointing a Director of Adult Education, so that by 1939 the only institutions not to have done so were Leeds, Sheffield and Reading. The whole country by then was covered by a network of 23 extramural areas (three of them belonging to Oxford). There was a steady expansion of full-time staff during this period, so that by the outbreak of the Second World War there were 84 in England and Wales (Kelly, 1992: 269).

These new extramural departments collaborated with the WEA in organising tutorial classes, but they did not necessarily share the WEA's social and political belief in adult education as a means of creating a more egalitarian society. This led to a modest resurgence of university extension, as some of the universities, with Nottingham very much to the fore, sought ways of promoting adult education by other means than directly through the WEA (Marriott, 1984: 93-7; Brown, 1981: 10-11).

Given the lack of universal enthusiasm for tutorial classes and egalitarian social purpose, it is not altogether surprising that the inter-war expansion of extramural departments was marked by a decline in the proportion of working-class students and in the commitment of the students to sustained study at genuinely university level (Fieldhouse, 1977: 26-30; Kelly, 1992: 270). There was also increasing conflict between the fledgling departments and the WEA; a growing assertiveness at the expense of the WEA; and a considerable amount of territorial empire building which caused some bitterness between universities (Brown, 1981: 6-7; Marriott, 1984: 88-9; Mayfield, 1965: 29).

There were probably several reasons for this bullish behaviour, the most straightforward being that having established extramural departments and appointed directors, they saw it as their mission to expand. But particularly for the smaller universities and university colleges, which were amongst the most assertive, there was a strong desire to make themselves better known in their regions. This was partly a matter of simple public relations: to increase their importance and extend their influence. But being seen to be making a significant contribution to adult education was also regarded as helpful in supporting the universities' appeals for financial endowments and LEA grants (Marriott, 1984: 97–110).

## Political Orthodoxy

The dominant liberal ideology of this university adult education and the discreet political surveillance exercised by HMI as well as local and central government elected representatives, to try to ensure that it kept within accepted political bounds, have already been mentioned. But as with the WEA (see Chapter 7), there were occasional 'bouts of suspicion' that the universities were overstepping these boundaries of political correctness (Bruce, 1974: 12). At various times, university courses were adjudged to be giving too much attention to working-class interests and too little to national interests. It was felt that occasionally there was too much intemperate, pejorative and injudicious bias being permitted if not encouraged by tutors. HMI were asked to make visits; reports were compiled; discussions took place. The university authorities were reminded of the necessity to ensure that their adult education staff acted 'responsibly' (Blyth, 1983: 77, 84; Fieldhouse, 1990: 158–65).

Of course there were some cases of political extremism in university adult education classes. Given that an important aim, at least in the early days, was to educate the leaders of the labour movement, it would have been surprising if there had not been some political activists amongst the student body, who wished to use the classes to propagate or reinforce their political views. However, the investigations by HMI revealed very little hard evidence, and the accusations were not infrequently based on erroneous information (*ibid.*). A detailed examination of economics teaching in WEA and university classes from the 1920s to the 1940s, referred to in Chapter 7, revealed them to be overwhelmingly orthodox in their capitalist orientation (Fieldhouse, 1983: 18–28). Similarly, an investigation of some 300 Cambridge University extramural syllabuses covering the period 1925–39, and 61 Oxford syllabuses of the early 1930s, indicates a widespread absence of political interest (particularly in the Cambridge syllabuses) and a predominantly liberal-orthodox ideological approach in the majority of the more political classes. A left-wing slant or any suggestion of a Marxist perspective was quite rare. This picture is reinforced by the recurrence of certain predominantly liberal recommended books and authors, which were clearly enormously popular and influential, in the class reading lists (*ibid.*: 14–18). Rather than promoting political protest, the effect of many of the classes could be the exact opposite: the creation of a feeling of detachment and academic neutralism leading to political non-commitment or sitting uncomfortably on the fence, although there is some evidence to suggest that attendance at classes did reinforce the activism of some students who were already politically active (*ibid.*: 28–30; MacIntyre, 1980: 89–90; See also Chapter 7).

## Staffing Issues

One of the reasons for the mainstream political orthodoxy of university adult education (and the WEA's) was the insecurity of most of the tutors, which made them very vulnerable to pressure, and liable to the exercise of self-restraint. Just after the First World War there were 150 tutorial classes taught by 76 tutors. These were a mixture of permanent university staff teaching adult classes as an extra activity; some full-time adult education tutors who might also do a bit of intramural work; and a number of non-university occasional tutors. The method of payment for all categories was almost universally a fixed fee per class, per session. Thus the income of the full-time or occasional tutors was highly precarious, depending on the efficiency of the universities in mounting their programmes. If they failed, or if the tutor was ill, there would be no payment. Moreover, except at Nottingham, there were no pensions rights for these tutors (Ministry of Reconstruction, 1919: 123–4).

With the establishment of extramural departments, there was an increase in the number of full-time adult education staff. Some were paid a regular salary and enjoyed security of tenure, but there was a growing army of 'intellectual casuals' in university adult education. The total number of full-time tutors had risen to about 100 by 1928. Some of these enjoyed the same status and security as other university teachers, but most did not. Many lacked any guarantee of employment from year to year, while others worked under short-term contracts and were excluded from superannuation schemes. A Tutors Association was formed in the 1920s, and tried to tackle these problems, but a request for 'full status as teachers on the staff of the University, including pension rights and reasonable security of employment' in 1925 was rejected by the Central Joint Advisory Committee for Tutorial Classes because the Board of Education's grant aid was paid on the number of successful classes run each year. Despite this, there was some advance during the later 1920s and 1930s towards establishing some permanent posts with fixed salaries, or at least three-year contracts. But most university adult education continued to be taught by part-time tutors who lacked security. These increasingly came to include what became known as full-time part-time tutors who had no security, but depended almost wholly on teaching four, five or six classes for their livelihood. Indeed, during the 1930s such employment, together with short-contract posts, increased at the expense of more secure employment (Fieldhouse, 1987a: 36–9).

The consequence of this insecurity was that tutors felt very vulnerable to pressures from their employers, and frequently were obliged to fall into line with their wishes or risk the loss of their livelihood through dismissal or, more often, non-re-engagement. This was particularly true when tutors were dealing with controversial matters or attempting to introduce innovative or unorthodox methods or subjects. They were liable to be asked to exercise 'common sense' or to be reasonable, or to adopt a more orthodox approach to their subject and to avoid any challenge to the *status quo*. The authorities did not often have to use the big stick of dismissal: it was sufficient that everyone knew it was in the cupboard. Most tutors exercised self-restraint (*ibid.*: 39–43).

## The Second World War and After

Soon after the outbreak of the Second World War, the universities together with the WEA, the YMCA and several other interested organisations formed a Central Advisory Council (CAC) to promote adult education for HM Forces during the war. Within a short time, 23 regional committees had been formed, each covering a university extramural area. During the course of the war they provided many thousands of single lectures, short courses, longer classes and intensive residential courses not only for home-based units of the three Services, but also for the Women's Auxiliary Territorial Service (ATS) and Auxiliary Air Force (WAAF), the civilian defence forces including the fire service, and for workers in wartime munitions, industrial, agricultural and construction camps, factories and hostels. In addition, they made certain contributions to the three major educational schemes organised directly by the Services themselves – ABCA, the Winter Scheme and the Release Scheme. (See Chapter 3.)

One effect of this wartime activity was to draw the universities into much greater involvement in the provision of short elementary courses and 'popular' single lectures, thus accelerating the drift away from the sustained tutorial classes at recognised university level. It also, as with the WEA, increased the political pressures and difficulties over the treatment of what were considered to be controversial or 'inflammable' topics. (These difficulties have been described in Chapters 3 and 7.)

The 1944 Education Act did nothing to change the nature or context of university adult education in England and Wales, except in its requirement that the LEAs should have regard to the university programmes in their area when preparing their schemes for further education. But the new regulations brought in in 1946 did have a significant effect, by dropping many of the previously highly detailed requirements regarding class work and written work and minimum and maximum numbers of students. This reduced the distinction between the work of the universities and that of other responsible bodies to next to nothing. While this gave the universities greater freedom in the construction of their programmes, 'inevitably this entailed a somewhat greater danger of overlapping between universities and other responsible bodies in the provision of shorter courses. Nor was the three-year tutorial class protected to anything like the former extent.' The regulations thus further undermined the commitment to sustained university-level adult education: a process which had begun well before the Second World War, and accelerated during the war (Ministry of Education, 1954: 9–10; Raybould, 1954: 110–16).

In Scotland the 1945 Education Act did offer opportunities for new financial and administrative arrangements between the universities and the LEAs which resulted in more co-operation and financial support for university adult education. Seven years later the 'Report on Further Education' by the Advisory Council on Education in Scotland gave a further stimulus by drawing attention to the LEAs' duty to ensure the provision of adequate facilities, and arguing that it was therefore 'the merest common sense that any work in this field by the universities should be undertaken in co-operation with the education authorities and be regarded as part of the public system of further education'. As a consequence of the Report, Scottish Education Department grant aid was extended to voluntary organisations, and new regulations (1952) were introduced which permitted 'approved associations' to be assisted in respect of their administrative costs. This enabled the university extramural committees as well as the WEA to apply for financial assistance (Shearer, 1976: 13–4; Scottish Education Department, 1975: 5–6).

After the war there was very rapid expansion in university adult education in England, Wales and Scotland. The last remaining English universities (apart from Reading) established extramural departments. In Scotland the University of Glasgow did likewise in 1946, and Edinburgh three years later. Many of these extramural departments created a number of new full-time, established posts and appointed young men and women, often with wartime experience, who regarded adult education as an opportunity to help create a better post-war society, and set about their task with energy and enthusiasm (ibid.: 6; Shearer, 1976: 15–16; Mayfield, 1965: 33). This post-war generation of university adult educators included a number of exceptionally talented individuals such as E.P. Thompson, Raymond Williams and Richard Hoggart, who went on to make a major academic and cultural impact. It was a characteristic of their work which sprang from their experience as adult education tutors that it transcended traditional academic boundaries and was frequently both inter-disciplinary and intellectually innovative, challenging traditional conceptions of historical, literary and sociological disciplines.

Many of the universities participated in the post-war expansion, taking advantage of the lack of any apparent restriction on central government funding, so that the number of full-time staff trebled from 83 in 1945–6 to 244 by 1951–2. Oxford was the most expansionist, appointing seven new full-time tutors in 1946 without any prior consultation with the Ministry of Education. This somewhat precipitate action did heighten the concern that was already beginning to be felt in the Ministry and elsewhere about the tendency throughout the country for the universities to alter the pre-war balance between full- and part-time tutors, and between voluntaryism and professionalism, not least because of the increased cost. Between 1946–7 and 1949–50 the Ministry grant aid for university adult education rose from £147,000 to £243,000. Oxford was warned that their proportion of full-time staff in the North Staffs area would require special justification as a long-term policy, and that in future they should inform the Ministry before making appointments (Rees, 1982: 171; Fieldhouse, 1985b: 29; Kelly, 1992: 361–2; UCAE, 1961: 28).

## The Universities' Council for Adult Education and Changes in Direction

In 1947 the universities founded a Universities Council for Adult Education (UCAE), and the following year issued *A Statement of Principles* which reiterated their commitment to educational work 'at the University level' (primarily ensured by the scholarship of the teacher); and stated that although liberal studies had always been the principle concern of the extramural departments, they would not ignore technological subjects. 'The primary duty of the University in adult education is to contribute to the general welfare of society by training capable minds to know and understand the nature of the society in which they live', but it was also necessary 'to offer opportunities for technologists, administrators and other professional persons, to keep abreast of the developments affecting their work'. In order to carry out their adult education mission the Council believed the universities would require a much greater number of full-time staff who should be treated in respect of salary and status in exactly the same way as the staff of other departments (UCAE, 1948). This statement reflected the way university adult education was developing in the post-war world.

The Council's statement also declared that although the universities still attached special importance to the tutorial classes and to the relationship with the WEA they could no longer 'regard their services as available exclusively to any one organisation or section of the community'. Together with the new Ministry regulations, this put the universities on a collision course with the WEA, which felt that the universities used their much increased funding and their prestigious position to alter the balance of their joint relationship. The rapid expansion of post-war university adult education was very largely in the field which the WEA had previously regarded as its own – one-year and shorter courses. Between 1945–6 and 1961–2, the number of university three-year courses in England rose by a mere 17 per cent; the number of university one-year courses by 156 per cent and shorter courses by 254 per cent. An increasing number of university programmes lacked any specific requirement that students should undertake any written work. Moreover, in most parts of the country the decline of the tutorial class was even greater because its survival was concentrated very largely in two areas: London and the Yorkshire North WEA District served by Leeds and Hull Universities. The growing competition with, and independence of, the WEA is also illustrated by the decline in the proportion of extramural work carried out in collaboration with the WEA, from at least 90 per cent immediately after the war to some 40 per cent by 1956 (*ibid.*; Fieldhouse, 1977: 34–6, 41; Kelly, 1992: 363–4).

As the 1948 UCAE *Statement of Principle* indicated, there was also a shift away from the concentration on liberal studies. Many of the new shorter courses were more vocational in orientation and a growing number were highly technical and specialist. They were aimed largely at a professional clientele, including particularly the professionals of the new welfare state, rather than the traditional WEA student body. These more vocational courses were therefore to be found mainly in the expanding new extension programmes promoted independently of the WEA. There was also a growing demand for the certification of these courses, which could more easily be satisfied in extension programmes, as the WEA was still opposed to the idea that learning should be for individual credit rather than social purpose. By the early 1950s Cambridge, Leicester and Leeds were all offering extension certificates, while London trebled the number of its longstanding extension diploma courses from 41 to 126 between 1946–7 and 1951–2 (*ibid.*: 367; Marriott, 1981a: 95–6; Ministry of Education, 1954: 16; Burrows, 1976: 92).

## The Cold War

Meanwhile, the regional committees established in 1940 to promote adult education in HM Forces continued in existence until 1948, thereby continuing the universities' involvement in this work. But as early as January 1946 the War Office set up an Army Education Advisory Board which came to the conclusion that there was no insuperable reason why the War Office and Home Commands should not take over the function of the regional committees. In the end it was decided that whilst the Services should take full responsibility for compulsory general education in working hours, the universities should be invited to contribute to programmes of higher level voluntary education, particularly for the young national servicemen, many of whom were (like the wartime conscripts) really civilians temporarily in uniform. Fourteen university committees for forces education, together with a sub-committee in London, were set up, the most important being at Bristol, Leeds and Southampton. Most of them appointed full-time staff for this purpose. They took over this work from the regional committees in 1948. Their contribution continued to be a mixture of single lectures, short courses, tutorial classes and various intensive residential and non-residential courses and conferences. There was still a conflict between the universities' educational objectives, based on their traditional values of open discussion of all topics with an emphasis on social purpose or citizenship-training, and the Services, which tended to regard education as an extension of military training – to make better soldiers. This led to a continuation of the wartime restrictions, particularly after the outbreak of the Cold War in 1947–8. Security vetting procedures were tightened up and were more rigorously and arbitrarily enforced, in order to ban any suspected 'communist' tutors and prevent the discussion of any ideas which even remotely challenged conservative military prejudices (Raybould, 1951: 81–6; Fieldhouse, 1985b: 71–75, 78–91; Kelly, 1992: 372–4).

However, it was not only in Services' education that the universities felt the effect of the Cold War. Irrational fears and prejudices against communism surfaced in many extramural departments, and there was greater pressure to conform to an ideological consensus which embodied those fears and prejudices. The greater security of tenure enjoyed by many of the full-time staff appointed after the war protected some of them, but they were still subject to many pressures, both overt and covert. Other full-time and part-time tutors who did not enjoy such security or, as at Oxford, had only limited-term contracts (for three or five years) found their services no longer required, or their teaching subject to surveillance. While many departments were affected, some were more affected than others, particularly the Oxford Delegacy, which had appointed a large number of left-wing tutors after the war. This had posed little difficulty during the immediate post-war 'popular-front' period, but the situation changed rapidly with the polarisation into ideological camps from 1947 onwards. The high hopes for a new socialist society built on liberal foundations, which had attracted so many of the tutors to adult education, came to be regarded as unacceptable support for an alien ideology. University trade union education and the Oxford Delegacy's exported extramural programmes in West Africa became especially prone to both internal and external politically-motivated pressures and interference (Fieldhouse, 1985b: *passim*; Titmus and Steele, 1995: 25–102).

## The Ashby Report

In 1953 the Government set up a committee under Eric Ashby, Vice-Chancellor of Queen's University, Belfast, to investigate the organisation and finance of responsible body adult education, following the row that arose from the proposal to cut the level of government grant by 10 per cent (see Chapter 3). The Committee found that 'the main initiative' for the provision of liberal adult education lay with the extramural departments. Aided by their access to Treasury money, via the Universities Grants Committee (UGC), as well as to Ministry of Education grant aid, the universities had seized the dominant position. The Committee recognised that while some of the universities still valued the partnership with the WEA, others felt that it was obsolete. Indeed, it identified a real hostility to the WEA from a minority of universities which found the constraints of the traditional partnership irksome. Likewise, it found that some departments resented the financial ties to the Ministry of Education. They wanted to escape from both the traditional partnership and the government regulations – to be free to develop in more varied and flexible ways (Ministry of Education, 1954: 25–8, 37).

Nevertheless, the Committee concluded that the partnership between the universities, the WEA, the LEAs and the Ministry of Education as joint providers of the whole spectrum of adult education should be maintained. For this reason, it opposed the suggestions that the responsibility for funding university adult education should be transferred from the Ministry of Education to the UGC, although it did suggest that sooner or later this transfer would be desirable, and that university adult education would then have to fight for a full recognition within the higher education sector. The question of whether it was beneficial or damaging for university adult education to remain linked to the other sectors of adult education but separated from the rest of higher education by its different funding stream via the Ministry of Education or its successor, the Department of Education and Science (DES), continued to exercise and divide extramural directors long after the Ashby Report was published. In 1970 a minority of universities was still advocating that all funding should derive from the UGC on the grounds that it would make extramural departments the equal of other university departments whereas DES funding and regulations inhibited academic freedom (*ibid.*: 35; Raybould, 1959; Allaway, 1959; UCAE, 1961: 27, 1970: 51–2).

The Ashby Committee was reluctant to take sides in the controversy about whether universities should confine themselves to a particular 'sphere of influence', or be free to make whatever provision they wished. But it did not support the argument that they should be restricted to providing three-year tutorial or sessional classes. Indeed, the Committee recommended exactly the opposite – that the regulations should be amended to give less prominence to length of course compared with 'other equally important criteria' when calculating grant aid. It rather weakly suggested that universities should satisfy themselves that their provision was appropriate for a university and that they should impose a self-denying ordinance on themselves to avoid too much overlap with other bodies – particularly the WEA (Ministry of Education, 1954: 37–9, 43). As this had patently failed in the past, there was no reason to expect it to be more successful in the future, which it was not.

Having lent support to the more flexible school as far as length of course was concerned, the Ashby Committee also recommended that vocational courses and classes promoted for special groups of students should be eligible for grant aid in future, thus encouraging the universities in other forms of diversity which they had already been moving towards (*ibid.*: 43). It also gave its support to the argument for parity regarding salaries and status for full-time staff vis-a-vis other university lecturers, and better remuneration for part-time staff (*ibid.*: 25, 43, 45).

## The Demise of the 'Great Tradition'?

In the two decades between the Ashby Report and the Russell Report (1973), the universities pursued the diversity recommended by the Ashby Committee. They did not feel themselves tied to the special relationship with the WEA (although they frequently paid lip-service to it); nor to provision for any one section of society. Indeed, they prided themselves on serving the whole community indiscriminately, and saw nothing wrong if this very often meant that they were providing more for those who already knew education was a 'good thing' and were only too happy to seize the opportunity to monopolise more of this state-subsidised service! Increasingly reflecting the social make-up of their parent universities, the extramural departments became very skewed towards satisfying the intellectual hunger of the educated middle-class for greater self-fulfilment. While the joint programmes with the WEA, lacking a coherent *raison d'etre* and suffering from the deteriorating relationship with the Association, tended to stagnate, extension programmes re-established themselves and grew rapidly in all kinds of ways – for example, more technical and vocationally-oriented courses, role education for select groups, certificated courses, etc. Whereas the total number of university courses rose from 2,635 in 1947–8 to 7,957 in 1968–9, and the extension courses from 1,065 to 5,788 during the same period, the joint programmes with the WEA grew very little, from 1,570 to 2,169 courses. During the 1960s the number of joint courses remained almost constant at around the 2,000 mark. In 1970 the UCAE noted that 'since the war, the number of courses arranged jointly between the universities and the WEA has remained relatively static, while the courses provided by universities independently have increased nearly six-fold' (Raybould, 1957: 250; UCAE, 1970: 25, 70).

In 1956 Harold Wiltshire, head of the Nottingham Department, suggested that the 'Great Tradition' of university adult education had lost its old dynamic, principles, purpose and relevance. This dying tradition, he argued, had consisted of small tutorial groups which learnt through discussion and were open to all; committed to humane, non-vocational liberal studies 'as a means of understanding the great issues of life'; and which therefore deplored examinations and awards. It had been replaced by a new tradition, more technical, professional and vocational; more examination and qualification oriented; aimed at the educated elite. Wiltshire suggested that this new tradition lacked conviction (Wiltshire, 1956).

Wiltshire's thesis was roundly criticised by a number of people, who felt he had failed to see the new purpose of university adult education. Collins (1956) argued that it was a good thing that it should shed the social aims of the old movement and become more of a service to the modern welfare state. The primary aim of universities was 'to enquire into and to teach certain areas of knowledge at the highest possible intellectual level': any social, moral or spiritual aims, however good in themselves, should be secondary. Universities did not have the resources to seek out those who failed to attend grammar school. They should not despise or refuse to accommodate those who wanted qualifications or had vocational motives. Kelly (1956) and Raybould (1957) both regarded the 'new clientele' produced by an improved secondary school system and higher education as appropriate for university adult education. Echoing Collins, Raybould argued that the previous desire to create a welfare state, or a more egalitarian society, had been transformed into 'the desire to administer it well' and that was giving rise to the new type of courses. Hogan (1957) also welcomed the increased opportunities for vocational training and quoted Eric Ashby's 1956 address to the Scottish Institute of Adult Education: 'education for leisure and for personal satisfaction is now our purpose'. He dismissed Wiltshire's 'Great Tradition' as nostalgia.

The debate trundled on for years (e.g. Bowl, 1992). In 1961 and again in 1970 the UCAE tried to marry some of the traditional values of university adult education (liberal studies to promote co-operation, tolerance and a better understanding of society and to create an alert, critical and informed public opinion) with the newer notions of recurrent education (up-dating and renewing education obtained early in life and rendered obsolete in an age of rapid change). The Council did make some concessions to 'traditional' social purpose. In 1961 it still claimed that university adult education should make good the deficiencies of initial education for the 'educationally under-privileged' and in 1970 it rejected the idea that it should merely be a topping-up process for graduates because this would 'perpetuate the inadequacies and inequalities ... in selection for higher education' (UCAE, 1961: 5, 18–19, 1970: 11–12). But these statements lacked any *particular* commitment to the working class or the disadvantaged through a policy of positive discrimination in programme targeting. As Wiltshire (1957) remarked in reply to his critics: with limited resources the universities could not do everything. They needed clear priorities. In the 1950s and 60s, university adult education lacked any real sense of priority of purpose: it was too anxious to respond to all demands from the 'whole community', and willing to bow to any new pressures.

In 1963 two memorial lectures highlighted the loss of social purpose within university adult education. David Thomson, the Master of Sydney Sussex College, Cambridge, articulated a widely held view in the William F. Harvey memorial lecture, that university adult education should forsake its earlier special concern for the educationally underprivileged and concentrate instead on lifelong education for all – renewing obsolete knowledge rather than making good the inequalities of the initial educational system (Thomson, 1964: 237–40). That same year Charles Morris, Vice-Chancellor at Leeds University, regretted in the first Mansbridge memorial lecture that 'the discussions and studies which so satisfied and delighted Mansbridge and the early WEA students are now thought to have been no more than a snare and a delusion ... The whole belief in the immense value of "education" was woolly-minded mysticism ... In Mansbridge's sense of the word, the contemporary world has no belief in, and no use for, education at all' (Morris, 1963: 5–6). The 'sense' that Morris was referring to was the sense of adult education for social purpose and as a door to a better world. This was what had very largely disappeared from university adult education in the 50s and 60s.

The 'new clientele' was increasingly made up of those seeking technical and vocational training and those who already had grammar, further and frequently higher education and wanted to continue their learning beyond formal education (Rees, 1982: 172–6; Shearer, 1976: 17). Morris, in his 1963 lecture, suggested that the original idea of the tutorial class – to allow working class students to make up for their lack of formal education and bring them by a different route to the same level of attainment and understanding as more conventional higher education – had been largely displaced by the belief that everyone who was able and willing to do so could take the meritocratic route right through the educational system. There was therefore no longer any perceived need for tutorial classes, which were everywhere in serious decline (UCAE, 1961: 19; Shearer, 1976: 17; Fieldhouse, 1977: 40–2). Their replacement by shorter courses could only mean a retreat from provision for the educationally disadvantaged or a decline in standards. These shorter courses could 'only lay claim to a reasonable academic standard by assuming all the students have some previous knowledge of the subject and educational know-how, and therefore starting way above the level of the educationally under-privileged. These short courses must either do this or start *and finish* at a very low academic level,' although of course this was less true of the expanding extension programme catering for the better-educated 'new clientele' (*ibid.*: 42–3; UCAE, 1961: 17).

In 1961 the Universities Council quite unambiguously stated that 'university adult education does not normally imply on the part of the students any fixed standard of attainment ... (only) that the teacher is either a member of a university staff or person of comparable academic standard' (*ibid.*: 8). Thus standards had come to be measured exclusively in terms of teaching (and that rather oddly), but not at all in terms of student learning. By 1970 the Council approached the question rather more sophisticatedly, claiming that the essential character of university adult education was contained in its scholastic approach, intimately connected both with research and the experience of adult students (UCAE, 1970: 15–18). This at least was a return to the recognition of the particular contribution of adult students' experience to the level of learning that took place, but it still did not really explain how educationally disadvantaged students, even with their life experiences, could achieve genuine levels of higher education during the limited period of a short course.

What the Council did believe was that universities should make their provision more popular and 'glamorous' by experimenting boldly with new approaches; collaborating more closely with other bodies or media, including television, libraries, art galleries, and various voluntary bodies; and above all, forging closer links with the LEAs in jointly securing programmes of adult education. This last objective they shared with LEA chief education officers (UCAE, 1961: 20–6; 1970: 26; Chief Education Officers and the UCAE, 1964).

## Ad Hoc Expansion

Above all, there was a belief in the benefits of expansion and professionalisation. By the early 1960s there were 23 extramural departments with full-time heads and a collective total of 265 full-time tutors. Despite the government threat to cut grant aid at the beginning of the decade, it in fact increased during the 1950s from £243,000 to £496,000 *per annum* for university adult education by 1959–60. But the Universities Council was still pressing for more resources and 50 per cent more full-time staff. They argued that every extramural department should have a core of full-time staff, professionally committed to their work and enjoying the same status and conditions as 'intramural' staff, in order to ensure proper professional competence. The Council argued in 1962 that the proportion of teaching undertaken by full-time staff (estimated at between one quarter and one third) was too low. Eight years later, the Council was still arguing a similar case for greater professionalisation and an increase of at least 25 per cent in the number of full-time staff, but it recognised that in reality the extramural departments were bound to rely heavily on part-time tutors employed from outside the universities, and therefore recommended an immediate increase of 25 per cent in the fees paid to part-time tutors, to attract properly qualified people (UCAE, 1961: 27–30; 1962: 1–3; 1970: 37–42).

Behind this sometimes strident advocacy of expansion and professionalisation was a sense of insecurity, of not quite belonging to academia, and of the constant danger of being disowned by the parent universities. This was the reason why some directors continued to press for 'mainstream' funding through the UGC rather than the separate funding system via the Ministry of Education (or Department of Education and Science as it became in 1964). This feeling of weakness and insecurity was heightened in the 1960s with the emergence of new universities whose desire to offer a service to their regions was seen as a further threat to the fragile extramural departments. Any fragmentation of their territories would place them in an even more vulnerable position. The Universities Council therefore advocated complementary collaboration rather than cut-throat competition (Beet, 1960; UCAE, 1961: 31; 1962: 3–8). This was a reasonably successful strategy in the 1960s, but the problem did not go away. It led, for example, to the later cession of parts of Oxford's extramural empire to the Universities of Kent and Sussex, and Birmingham's to Warwick. And later still, with the conversion of polytechnics into universities in 1992, to a further redistribution of responsibilities.

Meanwhile, the 1950s and 60s did witness an expansion of university adult education, despite its sense of insecurity. However, as remarked earlier, this expansion was not in the traditional programmes run jointly with the WEA, but very largely in new extension programmes promoted independently by the universities. One such area was training and up-dating courses for the growing number of welfare state professionals. For example, a survey carried out in 1969 found that one third of all university social work courses were located in extramural departments (UCAE, 1961: 18; Cunliffe, 1969).

Another area was the continuing Services education, even after the abolition of national service in 1960. The emphasis then switched more towards vocational education. However, the relationship between the Services and the universities continued to be somewhat strained at times. The system of annual estimates and the uncertainties and frequent changes of policy affecting defence affairs often created insecurity, particularly for the full-time staff involved. For example, in 1966 the Ministry of Defence set up a scheme for Higher Defence Studies which was independent of the existing collaborative arrangements with extramural departments. Nevertheless, in 1970 the Universities Council still anticipated a continuation of 'the natural link between the Services and universities', not least because the likely future recruitment of a highly qualified officer corps would make the university facilities for post-experience training of even greater importance (UCAE, 1970: 82–3).

Another area of growth in the 1960s was in certificated courses and the beginnings of a movement towards university adult education becoming part of a wider structure of accredited further and higher education leading ultimately to part-time degrees. By 1970 a sharp increase in demand for 'courses in adult life leading to degrees, diplomas or certificates' was expected. The Universities Council was aware of the danger of assessment undermining one of the highly valued characteristics of adult education – its freedom from examination tyranny. Nevertheless, it advocated that the universities should respond to this shift in demand (Jennings, 1983; UCAE, 1970: 32–6).

A growing area of university adult education that crossed the division between extension and the joint programmes with the WEA was the day-release courses for shop stewards and trade union officials (UCAE, 1970: 24). Some departments, such as the Oxford Delegacy, offered very practical courses which stressed 'immediate relevance' and 'practical application'. But others attempted to fuse practical with theoretical issues, to generate a consideration of techniques for action from a critical understanding of society. From the early 1950s the Universities of Nottingham, Sheffield and Leeds offered two- and three-year day-release courses for members of the National Union of Mineworkers which, at their best, perceived skills training as flowing organically from this understanding of society. A number of other universities followed suit with courses for a wide range of workers. (See Chapter 10.)

Another area which was common to both extension and joint programmes was the increasing number of courses which put a greater emphasis on 'learning by doing'. This had long been precluded by the Ministry regulations which, for example, differentiated art or music appreciation which was considered appropriate for the universities, from practical art or playing music, which were not. Languages had also been excluded from university liberal adult education. But these arbitrary boundaries were gradually being broken down, and other subjects, such as archaeology, local history and field biology, with their peculiar opportunities for student involvement in primary research, were increasing in response to demand (UACE, 1970: 21–2; Jepson, 1972: 297–8).

During the 1950s and 60s the universities also considerably increased their provision of training for the growing number of full- and part-time staff in both the Responsible Bodies and the LEAs, and the significant number of other people, such as clergy, whose job involved an adult education role. They also developed a slowly growing interest in adult education research. A number of universities appointed staff with special responsibility for this adult education training and research and a growing number of departments changed their names from 'Extramural Studies' to 'Extramural Studies and Adult Education' to signify their new role. Manchester went further, and established a separate academic Department of Adult Education. In 1961 and again in 1970 the UCAE advocated further development of the adult education and research functions of the universities. By the latter date seven universities (Edinburgh, Glasgow, Hull, Leicester, Liverpool, Manchester and Nottingham) were offering certificates, diplomas and/or master's degrees in adult education. The combined enrolments on the courses at the five English universities in 1969–70 totalled 241 students (some full-time, some part-time).(UCAE, 1961: 31; 1970: 43–5, 84–6; Jepson, 1972: 293; Dees, 1981: 9).

By the time that the Labour Government set up a committee 'to assess the need for and to review the provision of non-vocational adult education in England and Wales ...' in 1969 and a similar committee to consider the aims and achievements of adult education in Scotland in 1970, university adult education was beginning to rediscover some of its social purpose. This was a reflection of the more radical, challenging culture of Britain in the 1960s, and the fact that the growing number of full-time tutors appointed to extramural departments at that time brought this culture with them into the world of adult education. A survey of this generation of adult educators (Fieldhouse, 1993a) showed that they tended to be left of centre, politically active, and somewhat anti-Establishment. They believed the world could and should be changed for the better.

What they expected to achieve in adult education varied very considerably, but a belief that it would (and did) help individuals to achieve their personal potential and live more fulfilled lives was certainly the predominant motive. However, this was not seen as being at variance with the social purpose which many also shared. A sense of social guilt or social conscience made many want to promote a social purpose through adult education. By providing knowledge and informing people, by extending understanding and rationality, by building confidence and by raising consciousness, it was felt that the students would be empowered to challenge authority, take on the Establishment, and work for a better world. Adult education would provide the intellectual tools (or weapons) for this process, although for some this was regarded not so much as the central purpose as a by-product of adult education (*ibid.*: 48–9)

In 1972 the new Professor of Adult Education at Leeds, Norman Jepson, concluded his inaugural lecture by suggesting that one of the challenges facing university adult education in the 1970s and 80s was how to revive its social relevance so that it might contribute to the active and committed community education which was then emerging (Jepson, 1972: 303–4; and see Chapter 5). A year later the long-awaited Report of the Russell Committee on the future of non-vocational adult education in England and Wales was seen by some as the necessary stimulus to the universities to take up this challenge although, as already noted in Chapter 3, lack of funding for the recommended developments rendered the Russell Report something of a damp squib.

## *The Russell and Alexander Reports*

Russell recommended that the universities should concentrate specifically on work of university quality, or 'intellectual education'. It recognised that this would always be a minority concern, but one which it expected to 'enlarge rapidly' over the following decade. The implication was that the universities should pull back from too great an involvement in low-level adult education, but in practice the Report's recommendations for the universities involved little change from the practice of the previous decades. It proposed that the universities should concentrate on:

1. liberal studies of the traditional kind, characterised by intellectual effort by the student;
2. 'balancing' (or conversion) continuing education;
3. role education for groups whose common element was their role in society;
4. industrial education at all levels, from management to the shop floor;
5. project research work; and
6. training for those engaged in the education of adults and research in adult education as an academic discipline (DES, 1973: 72–4).

None of this would necessarily have involved the universities in changing their activities very much. More radical was the recommendation that they could also undertake more elementary pioneer work 'to open up the cultivation of new fields which, once cultivated, could be handed over to other agencies', although even this was a variant of the short-course 'pioneer' work which many universities had engaged in since the 1930s. However, it was envisaged that this work would include courses in new fields for professional and vocational groups; work for disadvantaged groups; and provision for adult access to higher education and other qualifications at an advanced level. The Report saw the last as a 'mounting need', and expressed the hope that the universities would 'explore this field energetically' (ibid.: 72–3).

Organisationally, the Report gave support to existing specialist extramural or adult education departments, but also to those universities which wished to integrate their adult education more closely with their day-to-day teaching and research (ibid.: 74–6). Although the Committee recognised that the universities did, or at least should, make a unique contribution, it very definitely saw this as part of the comprehensive service of adult education. It urged that 'in their adult education work the universities must be brought visibly and directly into participation in the public system of education' and therefore advocated the continuation of the direct grant 'as the most sure and economical means of achieving this' (ibid.: 71). Russell thus shared the Ashby Committee's view that university adult education should be regarded, and funded, as part of a comprehensive adult education service rather than as an integral part of higher education.

In Scotland, the Committee set up under the chairmanship of Professor Alexander to consider the 'not specifically vocational' adult education north of the border, produced its Report in 1975. Like the Russell Report, the Alexander Report recommended relatively little change for the universities, except that they should improve their provision of refresher or up-dating courses for professional groups and consider offering certificates or diplomas to mark the successful completion of such courses; and promote more courses, conferences and seminars to examine social issues and controversial matters which the education authorities might feel unable to tackle. The Committee felt that the impact of university adult education on large sections of the Scottish population had been slight, particularly in urban areas, and therefore recommended that the universities adopt a community development approach. It recognised that this would require a substantial injection of resources. It recommended that the education authorities and the regional advisory councils which it proposed should be established in each education authority area should support additional university appointments, to improve the promotion and organisation of university adult education. It also recommended that all universities should become involved (St Andrews had appointed a Director of Extramural Studies in 1967, thus joining Glasgow, Edinburgh, Aberdeen and Dundee in promoting adult education, but unlike the others it received no government grant aid). The Report did not suggest any fundamental change in the system whereby the universities received grant aid from the Scottish Education Department only towards administrative and organising costs, not for teaching. But it did recommend that the Department should make grants towards teaching costs in respect of certain approved developments such as special needs, community development and industrial studies (Scottish Education Department, 1975: 11, 61–3, 75). In practice, in Scotland as in England and Wales, few of these proposed new resources became available.

Despite the lack of extra funding to finance the developments recommended by Russell and Alexander, the years following the publication of their Reports did see some shifts in direction in university adult education. Although these were brought about more by economic factors following the 1973 oil crisis, nevertheless the Reports helped to create a favourable climate for certain changes, and even led to the creation of new centres or departments of continuing education at Strathclyde in 1976 and Stirling in 1977. Meanwhile a joint working party established by the UCAE and the CVCP endorsed the Russell categories (Gerver, 1985: 24–6; McIlroy and Spencer, 1988: 32).

## From Adult Education to Continuing Education

A number of universities in England as well as Scotland took up the challenge to adopt a more informal community approach in programmes aimed specifically at the unemployed or other target groups, including women and ethnic minorities. There continued to be an expansion in courses which offered opportunities for 'learning by doing' (local history, archaeology, natural history, etc.), and in the study of adult education; but a decline in some 'traditional' areas, particularly the social sciences and trade union studies (the latter largely because the TUC and individual unions took over much of this work – see Chapter 10), although conversely some provision around unemployment with trade unions and the TUC was developed. Overall the traditional liberal adult education declined as a proportion of the totality of university adult education in the 1970s (*ibid.*: 43; Ward, 1983; Ward and Taylor, 1986; Dyson, 1978: 11–15; Dees, 1981: 5–6, 9; Gerver, 1985: 19–26).

Stemming more from the 1972 Government White Paper, *Education: A framework for expansion*, and the economic crises of the mid-70s, than directly from the Russell or Alexander Reports, there was a growing expectation that university adult education should contribute to economic reconstruction and that this should take precedence over other aims. This led to a steadily growing emphasis on vocational training, post-experience courses and continuing professional education. The same utilitarian and instrumentalist forces encouraged a hastening of the trend towards certification and part-time degrees – to give credit for learning which could then be recognised and utilised in the job market. The universities also began to offer opportunities of access to higher education for 'non-standard' mature students for the same reason – to improve their employability (*ibid.*: 19–21, 26; McIlroy and Spencer, 1988: 32, 37, 40–1, 43, 46; Dyson, 1978: 19–21; Dees, 1981: 10). Growing competition from an increasing number of vocational education organisations offering education and training for specific occupational groups, and the shift towards a more utilitarian rationale within both further and higher education, put the extramural departments under pressure to change their ways. It was 'within this context that developments of a more directly professional and post-experience kind within university extra-mural work should be seen' (Taylor and Ward, 1981: 13). Within a few years, and stimulated by the funding changes described below, the universities were competing with each other to promote vocational continuing education which would attract the new PICKUP funding from the DES.

The 1978 DES discussion document, *Higher Education into the 1990s*, seemed to offer university adult education an expanded, indeed a crucial role, filling the hole in undergraduate recruitment which it erroneously predicted for the coming decade because of the decline in the number of potential 18-year-old entrants. This, and the contribution which adult education (or continuing education as it was now increasingly being called) was expected to make to economic regeneration, made it too important to be left to extramural departments in some people's view. The idea began to gain ground that the whole university should take on a continuing education role, now that it had become something of value; something more than a tolerated peripheral activity. The central administrations and the big academic departments began to eye the spoils. They were no longer willing to leave the responsibility for the public face of the university to adult education. Integration of university adult education into the mainstream of higher education, which Ashby, Russell and Alexander had all rejected on the grounds that it belonged in a comprehensive *adult education* movement, now emerged as a credible idea. The need for separate, identifiable adult or continuing education departments was critically examined and several universities commenced the process of incorporating continuing education into their mainstream institutional structures by dispersing continuing education staff and responsibilities across all departments (McIlroy and Spencer, 1988: 32–3, 41–3, 46–7; Stewart, 1974: 2, 9).

By the end of the 1970s university adult and continuing education found itself in an ambiguous situation, apparently courted by Government and by the parent universities, but at the same time facing a threat to its traditional structures. It often reacted idiosyncratically to external pressures. It lacked a coherent strategy or collective sense of purpose. It was haphazardly expanding here, declining there, blown in the wind rather than changing according to plan. 'Despite rhetoric about "disadvantage" many (universities) were obviously chary about involvement in this difficult area. There was overall a refusal to adopt strategies of positive discrimination in favour of educationally deprived groups ...' (McIlroy and Spencer, 1988: 48–9; Forster, 1990: 107). The then Honorary Secretary of what had become the Universities Council of Adult *and Continuing* Education (UCACE) later recalled of that time that 'an element of drift had come into the system; a mixture of imagination, ingenuity and idealistic traditionalism, along with a sense of being all things to all men (*sic*), whilst producing some very fine programmes, had diffused our sense of specific purpose, priorities and motives' (Forster, 1989: 14).

## Financial Difficulties, Funding Changes and Government Intervention

By this time many adult education departments were also facing a deteriorating financial position, particularly in their LEA funding, which was compounded in 1981 by a reduction and reallocation of UGC grants to the parent universities. Within university adult education there was a widespread feeling of defensiveness – of being questioned and threatened – and increasing anxiety (Gerver, 1985: 20–2; Forster, 1989: 7, 1990: 107–8).

Then in December 1983 the Government announced a 14.7 per cent cut in the global Responsible Body grant for the English universities, although some universities were later able to recover a proportion of the lost funds by applying for the short-term PICKUP grants for continuing vocational education (see below). A few months later the DES announced complex proposals designed to change radically the method of allocating the remaining grant. The objectives of the new formula were stated to be to improve the exploitation of the universities' teaching and research resources for continuing education; to increase value for money and enhance the quality of provision; to obtain optimum volume of work and programmes of subjects; to better target defined priority groups ('disadvantaged', unemployed, older age groups, ethnic minorities, handicapped); and to promote innovation and co-operation. The proposed mechanisms for achieving these objectives included reserving five per cent of the grant for innovative projects and allocating the bulk of the remaining grant according to a crude measure of student attendance (Forster, 1989: 5–6).

Over the next two or three years the UCACE attempted to influence the DES to avoid what it considered would be damaging changes in the funding arrangements, although it was somewhat handicapped by being internally divided and constitutionally not in a position to negotiate on behalf of its members, which were all autonomous institutions. Nevertheless it was quick to note that there was a contradiction between the objective articulated by the DES of wanting to encourage outreach work with the 'disadvantaged' and the imposition of an output-driven formula which would encourage universities to concentrate on easier programmes and clientele to produce maximum numbers. The emphasis on volume was also potentially incompatible with quality assurance. There was also a likelihood that the competitive ethos would drive some departments into a spiral of decline and ultimate extinction because any above average growth in the output of one department would reduce the grant to another (ibid.: 4–8).

Nevertheless only a slightly modified version of the original proposals was announced in November 1984, and brought in for the 1985–6 session (but determining only 10 per cent of the grant) as a trial. By May 1986 it had become clear that the effects of the formula were very uneven and unpredictable. They were potentially damaging for some universities, particularly those that had in the past, with DES encouragement, undertaken major commitments to promote work with the 'disadvantaged'. As predicted by UCACE, there were indications that the formula mitigated against 'disadvantaged' work and minority subjects. Rather like the payments-by-results scheme for elementary education introduced by Robert Lowe in 1862, it encouraged concentration on safe and mainstream subjects at the expense of experimentation or the satisfying of minority interests (ibid.: 9–11).

The new formula evoked considerable hostility within university adult education, where it was widely regarded as very damaging to quality and innovation and to the work targeted at the 'disadvantaged'; and likely to reduce extramural departments to non-academic administrative agencies (Stephens, 1985: 50–1; Durucan, 1986: 116; Spencer, 1987: 44–6; and see many objections quoted in McIlroy and Spencer, 1988: 69).

A meeting in May 1986 between representatives of the DES, HMI and UCACE arrived at an unusually frank understanding of their respective positions in relation to the formula. The UCACE was anxious to maintain the professionalism of full-time adult education staff and departments whereas the DES expressed grave doubts about the nature of extramural departments and the need to fund expensive full-time staff when a cohort of part-time teachers could maintain a series of courses much more cheaply, and was sceptical about the universities' long-term commitment to 'disadvantaged' work and minority interest subjects (Forster, 1989: 11).

By the end of the year it was recognised by the DES that the formula was unwieldy if not unworkable. It had already begun to make a number of 'exceptional' special case awards outside the formula. The following February, UCACE produced a rationale for maintaining a body of professional full-time academic staff. In May a simplified formula was agreed, to be applied to only just over half the grant (the rest being in recognition of the need for infra-structural support), and subject to a safety net which prevented any university's grant from varying by more than five per cent in any one year, to provide a degree of stability (*ibid.*: 12).

## *The Abolition of 'Responsible Body' Status*

Meanwhile, the UGC had published the Report of its Continuing Education Working Party in January 1984 which questioned whether the 'anomalous' Responsible Body system was worth preserving, and recommended that the DES should review it. In December 1987 the Government announced that it would indeed scrap it and transfer funding responsibility from the DES to the new Universities Funding Council (UFC) as from April 1989. This aroused fears that once the specifically earmarked DES grant was consolidated in universities' block grants, it would soon be diverted to other areas of higher education. There was also concern that universities other than the designated 'responsible body' ones would become entitled to a share of the limited funds and that resources would then be spread too thinly to maintain specialist adult education departments or units; and also that there would be nothing to prevent the diversion of the funds from their traditional support for liberal adult education into subsidisation of vocational courses. A joint DES/UGC/CVCP working party (with the Honorary Secretary of UCACE as one of the CVCP representatives) was set up to implement the transfer of funding responsibility to the UFC. It produced a report towards the end of 1988 which recognised that 'liberal adult education has always required subsidy' whereas post-experience vocational education (PEVE) 'on the whole ... should be self-supporting in the medium term, with pump-priming to enable development and expansion to take place'; and recommended that:

(a) funding should be based in future on output, reflecting the number of full-time-equivalent (FTE) students taught;
(b) in addition to PEVE, four categories of activity would need to be distinguished for funding purposes – i.e. liberal adult education; credit-bearing courses leading to a degree or other award; access courses to higher education; and courses for disadvantaged groups entailing a high level of central support;

(c) the grant per FTE should reflect the cost and income potential of each category;

(d) the cost of developmental work and research in adult education should be recognised for funding purposes;

(e) each university should maintain a core of full-time academic staff (not administrators) to ensure that academic quality, educational effectiveness and innovation were maintained;

(f) there should be a five year transitional period, during which geographical areas should be rationalised;

(g) collaboration with the WEA and the LEAs should continue; and

(h) the grant to individual universities for 1989–90 should not vary by more than five per cent from that for 1988–9.

Through the UGC, the nascent UFC agreed to follow the recommendations of the working party and specifically that 'the extra-mural grants paid under these arrangements will constitute special additions and will be paid subject to their being used only for the purpose of providing courses of liberal adult education'. University adult education had thus obtained most of the paper safeguards it had sought but the UGC also made it clear that the UFC would be considering its future policy not only in the light of the working party report but also 'as part of its general review of arrangements for the funding of extramural and continuing education' (Forster, 1989: 3–4 and 1990: 108–9; 'Report of the Official DES/UGC/CVCP Working Party', 1988; UGC circular letter 54/88).

This transfer of responsibility to the UFC ended the 65-year-old relationship between the 23 designated universities, the DES and the Inspectorate, and finally abolished the conditions of the adult education regulations. It changed the status of university adult education from poor relation or marginal activity to a more equal and integrated part of higher education, which a minority of interested parties had advocated for decades. Its future had become 'inextricably bound up with the wider battle for the soul of the university', bringing it face-to-face with what Professor Raybould in 1964 had predicted would be its 'acid test' (Raybould, 1964; McIlroy, 1989). It also rendered the recently agreed DES formula for funding university adult education obsolete almost before it had been put into operation.

The protracted struggle between university adult education trying to protect itself and its liberal values (however woolly they had become) and the emerging new right ideology in the DES had been incredibly time consuming and energy sapping. But it did force the universities to review their commitment to adult education so that by the end of it they were possibly a little clearer about their mission (Forster, 1989: 14). However, the price was a heavy one. University adult education may have freed itself from DES controls but it became subject to close scrutiny and direction by a government quango – the UFC, and later the Higher Education Funding Councils (HEFCs) – and by the parent universities. Funding became more short-term, insecure and subject to Government-determined priorities and criteria which were much more to do with financial viability than academic quality or appropriateness. There was an almost imperceptible shift from concern about content and academic disciplines to managerial preoccupation with process, accountability and systems of delivery (Forster, 1990: 108–11).

Most significant of all, the abolition of the 'Responsible Body' system destroyed the comprehensive adult education movement which had existed for much of the century.

## Growing Predominance of Vocational Continuing Education

Meanwhile, the shift in emphasis towards more vocational adult education continued apace. The tendency for the universities ever since the 1950s to circumvent the adult education regulation requirement that grant-aided provision should be exclusively liberal, non-vocational, has already been mentioned. Vocationally-oriented short courses began to thrive and multiply. The Ashby, Russell and Alexander reports all encouraged greater diversity, including a shift towards more vocational courses and professional up-dating. In the 1970s and 80s, the requirement that the universities 'subordinate themselves further to the exigencies of manpower planning intensified' (McIlroy, 1987: 32–3). In May 1982 the DES launched a new pump-priming initiative intended to induce colleges, polytechnics and universities to undertake more professional, industrial and commercial up-dating, which became known as the PICKUP scheme. In 1984 a proportion of the 'Responsible Body' liberal adult education funds in England and Wales was diverted to the PICKUP initiative while the cost of extending the scheme to Scotland was met from the government grant to Scottish extramural departments (Duracan, 1986: 43; McIlroy and Spencer, 1988: 64, 71). A letter from the under-secretary for higher and further education at the DES to the University of Exeter's working party reviewing adult education in 1985 made it clear that the DES wanted 'to see major new growth of PICKUP activity in the universities' and that this would require 'a flexible and entrepreneurial charging policy, professional marketing technique, a hard-nosed managerial approach to cost effectiveness and a readiness to take advantage of all possible sources of income.' The PICKUP contracts issued to universities were short-term and extremely interventionist, giving the Secretary of State absolute means of controlling the projects and any outcomes.

This vocational work, variously described as PICKUP, PEVE (post-experience vocational education), human capital development, or more generically 'continuing education' (as opposed to liberal 'adult education'), became much more the centre of attention, not only for specialist departments but throughout the universities during the 1980s. In 1983 Harold Wiltshire doubted whether it really had a 'vigorous and assured future' in the universities but a snapshot of university continuing education at the beginning of the 1990s showed that more than half of university adult education was PEVE and that nearly half of all courses were located elsewhere than in continuing education departments. The general climate of opinion put pressure on the universities to concentrate much more on this form of continuing education. Forging a new servicing relationship with industry became the 'received wisdom'. Extramural departments began to restyle themselves as 'departments of adult and continuing education' to reflect the changed emphasis, reflected also by UCAE's change of name in 1983 to the Universities Council for Adult *and Continuing* Education

(UCACE) for the same reason (Taylor *et al.*, 1985: 70–2, 76–7; Spencer, 1987: 46; McIlroy, 1987: 39–40, 46; Wiltshire, 1983: 5–6; Tight and Sidhu, 1992; Duracan, 1986: 52; Forster, 1989: 4).

This transformation was not wholly unwelcome within the universities as a whole (as opposed to the adult and continuing education departments): the new continuing vocational education fitted rather more comfortably into their missions than any commitment to the working class or disadvantaged sections of the population, or to any semblance of egalitarian social purpose had ever done (McIlroy and Spencer, 1988: 82).

This greater concentration on vocational education was very much a reflection of Government policy expressed directly in the 1985 Green Paper, *The Development of Higher Education into the 1990s*; through the PICKUP contracts, as already mentioned; or indirectly through the UGC. The 1984 UGC Continuing Education Working Party clearly advocated a greater emphasis on PEVE which was seen as 'a necessity if the national economy is to avoid being handicapped by critical skill shortages' (p 2); although later in the year (as a result of pressure from the UCACE) its *Strategy for Higher Education in the 1990s* did stress the importance of 'personal development and social progress' in addition to continuing education's 'essential role in promoting economic prosperity' (p 1).

## Changes in University Liberal Adult Education

Despite this sop from the UGC it was feared that the 'rightful development of vocational adult education' would cause the demise of rich traditions of liberal adult education. There was concern that resources and effort were being diverted from the disadvantaged sections of society to business-oriented courses and to an already highly educated clientele. This subsuming of liberal adult education represented a further marginalisation: a retreat from liberalism (Stephens, 1985: 52; Taylor *et al.*, 1985: 77; Spencer, 1987: 51; McIlroy, 1987: 43, 52, 1988: 11). On 23 February 1993 Lord Judd warned the House of Lords that adult education was becoming too vocationally orientated at the expense of other forms of education (*Hansard*, col. 201).

These fears and warnings were not unjustified. There was a major switch of resources and effort into continuing vocational education. But the despondency about liberal adult education proved to be somewhat misplaced. In fact UCAE/UCACE was more successful than many critics allowed in persuading government Ministers and DES officials to continue funding this area of work. As a consequence, the 1980s saw a number of innovations and developments in university liberal adult education, although there was a tendency for them to be a piecemeal reaction to pressures and demand rather than development based on any theoretical or strategic concept (Duracan, 1986: 122).

Innovations included an involvement in the Access movement (see Chapter 3); various 'new opportunity' courses specifically designed to give certain target groups a 'second chance to learn'; issue-based courses; an extension of the community-oriented work previously mentioned; and further developments in certificated and other credit-bearing courses leading to awards, including further progress towards the establishment of part-time degrees for mature students (e.g. at Hull and Kent). These last were particularly favoured by those who disliked the political agenda of the more traditional liberal adult education with its commitment to egalitarian social purpose, or who believed it was a thing of the past (Ashmore, 1990; Crombie and Harries-Jenkins, 1983).

On the whole, the universities were content to be receivers of successful Access students rather than providers of Access courses, although a number did become providers, either directly or in collaboration with further education colleges. What the courses certainly did was open up a new route into higher education for mature students without standard entry qualifications. There was some scepticism about the quality of these courses as an alternative mode of entry, but as the number of Access students who not only entered higher education but were successful there began to increase rapidly, this prejudice diminished.

In Scotland the universities of Aberdeen, Dundee. Edinburgh, Glasgow, St Andrews, Stirling and Strathclyde continued to received funding from the UFC for the provision of non-vocational courses (£2.5 million in 1991–2), plus variable amounts of financial assistance from the local authorities. In 1991–2 the seven universities collectively enrolled over 40,000 students in non-vocational adult education courses, of whom about 1,200 were on university part-time Access courses. Other courses included both award-bearing and uncertificated work, but with the emphasis firmly on the latter. They were predominantly in the arts and social sciences but also in science, engineering, law, medicine, music and divinity (UCACE (Scotland), 1993).

## Continuing Education Research

The increasing interest in adult education as a subject of research and of specialist certificate, diploma and master's courses has been mentioned previously. In 1983 Harold Wiltshire advocated greater concentration on these areas in order to create a more 'strategically defensible position' for adult education departments in the 'no doubt increasingly difficult times ahead' (Wiltshire, 1983: 8). This trend was given a considerable boost by the creation of a special fund for continuing education research by the new UFC when it took over responsibility for funding university adult education. For a four-year period from 1990–1 to 1993–4 the UFC and its successors, the Higher Education Funding Councils (HEFCs) (see below), made earmarked grants totalling approximately £1.7 million *per annum* for specific research projects in the field of adult continuing education. Most of the projects were for one or two years' duration. The bidding process was highly competitive and resulted in the concentration of these research resources in some 26 universities. The funds proved to be an effective change agent – enabling a number of continuing education departments to establish a research identity and adapt to the new world of research assessment. A considerable number of publications derived directly from this pump-priming and in several universities the opportunity was taken to establish a continuing education research centre. However, there was an overall lack of coherence about this project-driven research, much of it carried out by assistants on short-term contracts with no security (Duke, 1995; Field and Taylor, 1995: 247–8, 253, 256).

Universities were less successful in obtaining funding for adult education research from other sources, such as the Economic and Social Research Council (ESRC), although in 1993 the University of Edinburgh and the Scottish Council for Research in Education did obtain ESRC funding for a seminar series in adult education. A number of government departments, most notably the various sections of the Employment Department, also funded research projects, particularly focused on vocational education and training and aspects of policy and institutional change (*ibid.*: 250–2).

Graduate students working towards higher degrees also undertook a growing amount of research. In 1990 it was estimated that there were over 300 people registered for research degrees in university adult continuing education departments and a number of MEd students also made a significant contribution to research in their dissertations. Most of these graduate students were highly experienced professionals in the field, carrying out research work on a part-time basis (*ibid.*: 256).

Overall, the nature of this adult education research was somewhat disparate. Most studies were small-scale and somewhat eclectic in nature, drawing on various disciplines including sociology, history, political science and, to a lesser extent, psychology and philosophy. However:

This general picture should not obscure the smaller number of enquiries whose importance is widely recognized by the adult continuing education research community. Empirically, there have been highly influential studies of the educational exclusion of disadvantaged groups, and of attempts to overcome this exclusion process; of relations between training and the labour market; of trade union education; of the history of adult education and training, particularly in the 20th century; of the ideological role(s) of adult continuing education, usually in the context of radical historical and cultural studies; of change in the organizational settings of adult continuing education; of the application of new technologies to teaching and learning; of adult learning as a process; and of patterns of participation in different kinds of adult continuing education provision. There have also been important contributions to philosophical debate, as well as a number of methodological interventions (*ibid.*: 254).

## *Towards the Mainstreaming of University Adult Education*

The end of the 1980s and the early 1990s saw a spate of educational White Papers and legislation, some of which had important consequences for university adult education. The 1988 Education Reform Act had very little direct effect except that in undermining the role of the LEAs it reduced the opportunities for local collaboration between them and the universities, thereby further contributing to the destruction of the former comprehensive system of adult education.

The 1991 White Paper *Higher Education: A new framework* did not mention adult continuing education as such but it did envisage more adults and more part-time study in higher education, and more extensive use of credit accumulation and transfer, all of which was important for setting the context for the future development of university adult education. So also were the main proposals: the abolition of the binary line and the creation of separate higher education funding councils (HEFCs) for England, Wales and Scotland. The HEFCs were clearly not intended to be independent bodies: their allocations of funds were to be 'informed by the Government's general policy on higher education' (p 22). They were intended to render universities more directly accountable for their public funds which (despite concessions about academic freedom wrung from the Government in the House of Lords during the passage of the Act) meant greater central Government control. This was later confirmed by Tim Boswell, the minister for further and higher education, when he declared that 'the day of the unaccountable professional is over' (THES, 16 December 1994).

The binary line was abolished and the funding councils were established to replace the UFC by the 1992 Further and Higher Education Act for England and Wales and a similar but separate Act for Scotland. The abolition of the binary line and the conversion of the polytechnics into universities was a further step towards bringing university adult education into the mainstream of higher education. There was no such thing as extramural or adult education as a separate entity in the polytechnics. They did not regard their part-time provision for adult students or their service to their region as being separate activities from their mainstream undergraduate and postgraduate teaching. It was all part of their institutional mission. Therefore adult continuing education permeated the whole institution. This was a culture which the polytechnics brought across the binary line into the university sector after 1992.

Another important consequence of the 1992 legislation was the setting of precedents in the further education sector which subsequently influenced higher education. The separation of vocational, award-bearing and instrumental 'Schedule 2' further education from LEA non-Schedule 2 residual adult education (see Chapter 4) presaged a similar reform of university adult education by the HEFCs whereby continuing education would be brought into the mainstream higher education funding methodology. This implied treating continuing education students as 'normal' part-time students in the fashion of the former polytechnics, rather than exceptional extramural students. But this would mean confining funding to students qualifying for a university award (comparable to the further education 'Schedule 2' category) whilst excluding those on non-award-bearing liberal or, (as was sometimes said), leisure courses which were regarded as belonging to the same category as the non-Schedule 2 LEA adult education.

The English funding council (HEFCE) wasted no time is setting up an advisory group to review the continuing education policies it had inherited from the UFC, while the Scottish funding council (SHEFC) set up a very similar group a little later in 1993. The Welsh funding council joined forces with its English counterpart in issuing a consultative paper in December 1992 (HEFCE/HEFCW, 1992). SHEFC produced its consultative document exactly a year later (SHEFC, 1993), and subsequently followed an implementation timetable one year behind England and Wales. One of the objectives of these exercises was to align the conflicting concepts of continuing education derived from the very different sides of the old binary line (HEFCE, 1992)

The English/Welsh consultative paper proposed three options for the funding of non-vocational provision: to fund only award-bearing courses or courses leading to an award throughout the higher education sector as mainstreamed part-time provision with credit accumulation and transfer potential; or to continue specially designated funding for non-award bearing, non-vocational provision outside the mainstream; or to combine both approaches by having earmarked special funding within the mainstream system. Of the three options, it was made clear that the second was not acceptable to the funding councils.

For vocational provision, the two options proposed were the continuation of earmarked pump-priming funding for development work or an increase in universities' core funding which would be expected to be devoted to the development of continuing vocational education. Similarly, there were two proposed options for funding continuing education research: either to continue the existing special project funding, but extended to the whole higher education sector, or merge continuing education research into the mainstream research funding methodology.

Fifty-nine per cent of the English respondents favoured the mixed-mode third option for the funding of non-vocational provision; 71 per cent opted for the continuation of pump-priming funding for the development of vocational education; and 56 per cent were in favour of a continuation of project-based funding for continuing education research (HEFCE, 1993a).

The SHEFC Working Group consulted about very similar proposals for Scotland, except that they were expressed in terms of non-vocational 'continuing personal education' (CPE); vocational 'continuing professional development' (CPD); and continuing education research (SHEFC, 1993a).

UCACE (which was reconstituted in order to accommodate the 'new' ex-polytechnic universities, and became the Universities Association for Continuing Education (UACE) in 1993), was very active in responding to the consultative papers, assisted by the CVCP. Initially inclined to take a purely defensive position, it quickly turned its attention to the issues related to implementing the anticipated new funding methodology:

- What was appropriate for accreditation?
- What were appropriate credit units?
- What were the most appropriate performance indicators for accredited continuing education?
- How could the records be accurately kept and statistics returned?
- What effects would accreditation have on curriculum and pedagogy?
- What forms of assessment would meet universities' requirements and adult students' interests?
- What should be left out of the accreditation process and how could such work be continued?

In May 1993 the HEFCE announced its decisions. It would continue the allocation of specific funds for the development of continuing vocational education. These would be determined by a bidding process. For non-vocational continuing education, the Council expressed a wish to encourage universities to convert as much as possible to award-bearing courses, or courses carrying credits towards an award. This was the fundamental and anticipated mainstreaming decision, but it was modified by a recognition that 'non-vocational non award-bearing higher education (was also) both justified and worthwhile'. Therefore the Council announced its intention to maintain support for an unspecified amount of non award-bearing provision. The £1.7 million previously earmarked for research projects was to be added to the general research funding for education, despite a majority of institutions being against this change. The new arrangements were scheduled for introduction from 1995–6 onwards except for the change in research funding which was scheduled for 1994–5 (HEFCE, 1993b).

The following January the HEFCE issued a further circular with details of the plans for implementing the new funding methodology. There were no real surprises concerning the funding of continuing vocational education development or research or the mainstreaming of the non-vocational adult education. From 1995–6 and beyond, continuing education which resulted 'in a recognised higher education award, and also that continuing education which (was) accredited and (could) contribute to a higher education award (or was credit-bearing within a credit-bearing framework)' was deemed eligible for funding. On the basis of actual student numbers in 1994–5 falling within this definition, and anticipated numbers for 1995–6, all those universities which had previously received 'Responsible Body' funding had a proportion (up to 100 per cent) of their previous grant transferred to their core funding to support award-bearing non-vocational adult education (with the prospect of a claw-back if they failed to reach their targets). What was less expected was that the circular also announced that if resources allowed, supplementary funds would be made available to provide for access and work targeted at disadvantaged groups through a bidding process open to all higher education institutions and determined by clearly stated criteria. Wales followed virtually the same pattern as England and Scotland progressed on very similar lines, a year behind (HEFCE, 1994a, HEFCW, 1993, 1994; SHEFC, 1993b, 1994).

The main concern which preoccupied UACE and individual universities was how they could effectively accredit their adult education programmes to meet the tight timetable set by the funding councils, and what performance indicators would be used to judge which students qualified under the new formula and whether they had achieved their targets. A research survey carried out to examine the impact of the move towards accreditation at some 26 institutions found that the speed with which the changes were taking place was giving rise to feelings of uncertainty and fear, and provoking a resistance to change (Ambrose, Holloway and Mayhew, nd). Accreditation was also regarded as restrictive because courses might become limited to skills and asserted facts rather than open to ideas and critical discourse; and unpalatable because an externally controlled curriculum would not be so responsive to the wide variety of motives and purposes of adult learners. 'Credentials are not necessarily appropriate and may, in fact, be inhibiting to profundity of ideas.' (Bown, 1995: 5–6). Nevertheless, the need to protect their baseline funding persuaded most universities to overcome their misgivings and accredit significant proportions of their liberal adult education programmes.

It quickly became apparent that there might be two very important and positive effects of accreditation. One was that it forced universities to examine the quality of their continuing education programmes and decide whether or not they all merited credits leading to a university award. As has been indicated earlier, the displacement of the tutorial classes by programmes of relatively short courses had resulted in universities making much sub-standard provision. If the process of accreditation helped to eliminate this, that was a valuable by-product. The second consequence which immediately began to show itself was that accredited courses attracted a younger and less well-educated clientele. Some years previously, Owen Ashmore had argued that university liberal adult education had long denied the majority of the working class 'the very thing which might give them greater mobility and truly transform their lives and ... what the universities, uniquely among the providers, had to offer – degrees'. Not long afterwards, a survey of Birmingham's pre-accreditation liberal adult education programmes had shown that they attracted few working class, ethnic minority or younger adult students, and found that such students welcomed the notion of educational progression and recognition associated with accreditation and certification (Ashmore, 1990: 75; Bowl, 1992: 203–7, 214). But there had always been very good reasons for not accrediting liberal adult education: the absence of imposed assessment had allowed curricula to be flexible and adaptable to students' wishes. Some of this flexibility was now threatened. There was also a considerable number of students – particularly the elderly – who were not particularly interested in further qualifications and progression routes.

In November 1994 the HEFCE invited all universities to bid for continuing vocational education development funding and announced the outcome the following April. £15.1 million was made available for 1995–6 with the promise that similar amounts would be allocated for a further three years, until 1998–9. One hundred and fifteen bids were made for these funds: 29 were placed in an 'A' category which entitled them to a maximum of £300,000 *per annum*; another 29 in a 'B' category (maximum £145,000); 37 in category 'C' (maximum £100,000); and 20 were awarded no allocation. Two-thirds of the 'A' category were in the former polytechnics and altogether the exercise resulted in a considerable redistribution of the old PICKUP funds (HEFCE, 1994b; 1995b).

The last piece of the jigsaw was put into place in February 1995 when the HEFCE announced that it was making £1.6 million available *per annum* for non-accredited liberal adult education and £3 million for non-vocational continuing education provision specifically aimed at widening access to higher education (although ironically the very successful Access to higher education courses were excluded from both the funded accredited work and this new category on the grounds that they were covered by Schedule 2 of the 1992 Further and Higher Education Act and should therefore be funded by the FEFCs as further education). Both funds were open to bids from all higher education institutions and, as with the continuing vocational education, they were placed into one of four categories, with 42 out of 64 institutions being successful in obtaining some funding for non-accredited liberal adult education and 73 out of 91 for widened provision (HEFCE, 1995a and notification of funding allocations, 26 May 1995).

## The Beginning of the End or a New Beginning?

By 1995 the universities had experienced 15 years of constant change in the rules, regulations and funding methodologies for adult education, and in the underlying ideology. The outcome was a considerable change in the balance between vocational and non-vocational provision (in so far as those terms were mutually exclusive); the abolition of the 'Responsible Body' system for adult education and the binary line in higher education; a greater emphasis on continuing education research; and the mainstreaming of university adult continuing education. It is arguable that the 'new realism' had simultaneously rendered university adult education academically 'respectable' by integrating it into the mainstream of higher education, and brought about the end of adult education as a social movement (Benn and Fieldhouse, 1994: 8–9). In practical terms it meant that:

most continuing education students will be formally registered students of the universities and as such indistinguishable from most other students. The courses they attend will carry the same currency structure as that of the rest of the university's provision, the quality assurance mechanism will be the same and academics will have the same conditions of service as their non-continuing education colleagues (*ibid.*: 9).

The question which had emerged as the crucial one by the mid-90s was whether adult continuing education any longer existed as a separate entity. As the *Times Higher Education Supplement* noted as early as 1991, 'traditionally adult education has defined itself in opposition to the university mainstream, as an "open" tradition within an otherwise "closed" system. That will become more difficult as the old dichotomies between regular and extra-mural courses dissolve' (*THES*, 961, 5 April 1991). Even earlier, it had been predicted that many extramural departments would not survive integration into the mainstream (McIlroy and Spencer, 1988: 69–85). When UCACE held a conference on 'the organisation of continuing education within universities' in 1991, there was no consensus as to whether specialist continuing education departments or units would be appropriate for the future (Fieldhouse, 1991). Once-prestigious departments such as Liverpool had already been dispersed 'into the mainstream' of their universities, and within a short time others, including Durham, Hull, Keele and Manchester, followed suit whilst the London Extramural Department was subsumed into Birkbeck College (which was responsible for London University's part-time degree provision). It was increasingly felt that it was 'time to stop talking about ... adult education, and to see the universities as providers of part-time as well as full-time education across the range of faculties for whoever can benefit from their services' (Costello, 1990: 80). With accredited continuing education fitting snugly into the credit accumulation and transfer systems advocated by the HEQC Report *Choosing to Change* compiled by Professor David Robertson, and with the rapid move towards a mass higher education system in Britain, university adult continuing education was fast becoming just a modular, part-time mode of lifelong education within the higher education mainstream which, 'like a stick of rock ... has Continuing Education running all the way through it' (Wagner, 1995: 7). To complete the process, it was necessary for the funding councils to move to a credit-based funding system for all students, whatever their age and whether full-time or part-time:

The overall goal must be to normalise Continuing Education, to make it mainstream. Making it special implies it is deprived. Making it normal will be a recognition that it is integrated. The first step is a conceptual one, to stop thinking of Continuing Education courses and to think only of Continuing Education students. The next step is to find the operational levers to integrate Continuing Education students with all other categories of student. The best way of achieving that is the credit-based and funded system of Higher Education advocated by Robertson (*ibid.*: 10).

The HEFCE began to give consideration to converting to a credit-based funding system in 1994 (HEFCE, 1994c) but at the time of writing, no decision had been announced. When it is, it could round-off 120 years history of university adult education.

*9*

# Residential Colleges and Non-Residential Settlements and Centres

## *Walter Drews and Roger Fieldhouse*

In 1973 the Russell Report noted that 'two groups of (residential) colleges may be distinguished, the long term and the short term. The differences between them amount to much more than the duration of their courses; they have different objectives, attract different types of student, and are staffed and equipped in different ways' (DES, 1973: 44). This chapter will look at the two groups of residential colleges separately, and then briefly at how the non-residential settlements and centres evolved during the twentieth century.

### *Long-Term Residential Colleges*

The origins of residential adult education in Britain were very mixed. It derived partly from the university extension summer schools at the end of the nineteenth century, but was also influenced by the Adult School Movement, the Society of Friends and the Danish folk high schools (Legge, 1982: 69; Lieven, 1991: 31; Kelly, 1992: 393.) To some extent these colleges had very similar aims to the early WEA and tutorial class movement – to provide opportunities of higher education and sustained study for serious-minded working-class men and women whose full-time education had been cut short at an early age. And they shared a belief that this could most effectively be achieved under residential and collegiate conditions: that the best circumstances for learning occurred when students were removed as far as possible from their normal living conditions and experienced 'that intensity and at times frenzy in studying which can be achieved and encouraged in a residential setting'. But beyond that, they had no real common philosophy or culture. Some reflected their regional or national cultures, others a class culture. Some of the older colleges were influenced by liberal, idealistic and paternalistic philosophies of 'cultural uplift' for the working class (which caused conflict when they came into collision with less conformist socialist ideas). Others had a definite religious or ethical basis. However, most colleges shared a desire to prepare students for something other than just the 'disinterested pursuit of humane studies'. This 'something else' involved learning to put 'really useful knowledge' about social, political and economic ideas to practical use within the community: enabling students to participate effectively in a democratic society: developing 'active citizenship' (DES, 1973:

44; Lieven, 1988: 81–2, 1991: 31, 34; Lowe, 1970: 78; Houlton, 1978: 52, 60–2; Peers, 1958: 130–1).

The location of the long term residential colleges was very much a matter of chance circumstances and the action of committed individuals (Legge, 1982: 69). The first was Ruskin Hall (later Ruskin College) founded by three American philanthropists in Oxford in 1899. Woodbrooke (1903) and Fircroft (1909) were both Quaker settlements founded by the Cadbury family in Selly Oak, Birmingham. A small Co-operative College was established at Holyoake House, Manchester in 1919, and the first Residential College for Working Women (which became known as Hillcroft) was founded at Beckenham, Kent in 1920. A year later the Catholic Social Guild founded a Catholic Workers' College (Plater College) for men and women at Oxford; and in 1925 the Cadburys established another college, Avoncroft, at Offenham, Worcestershire, as an agricultural counterpart to Fircroft. The first non-English residential college was Coleg Harlech in north Wales (1927), and the last of the pre-Second World War foundations was Newbattle Abbey near Dalkeith in Scotland in 1937 (Ministry of Reconstruction, 1919: 31; Kelly, 1992: 259, 261–3, 280–2). Most of the colleges received grant aid from the Board of Education; Avoncroft from the Ministry of Agriculture and Newbattle from the Scottish Education Department (ibid.: 282). The only ones that did not, because they wished to retain their religious or political objectives, were Woodbrooke and the Co-operative College.

During the Second World War most of the colleges either closed down completely or greatly reduced the scale of their activities but after the war, although no new long term colleges were opened, there was a renewed interest in residential adult education. It was felt that it provided a good mix of intellectual work and socialising not easily achieved by other forms of adult education, and opportunities for pedagogic experimentation and curricular diversity, as well as having an intrinsic value located in its sense of community and friendship. All the colleges recommenced their work although Avoncroft had to close in 1952 because its form of agricultural education was increasingly being undertaken by farm institutes. Funding from the Ministry of Education (later the DES) and from LEAs improved during the 50s and 60s, putting the colleges in a reasonably sound financial position (ibid.: 390; Hunter, 1959: 121, 132).

This coincided with a change in the underlying purpose of many of the colleges. There was a shift from the idea of education to develop 'active citizenship' to an increasing focus 'on enabling working class students who lacked traditional entry qualifications to enter higher education, until by the 1970s this was widely perceived as the central purpose of the colleges' (Lieven, 1991: 34; DES, 1973: 85). They were very much in the vanguard of the Access and 'Second Chance' movements (which was to cause a crisis of purpose for the colleges in the 1980s by which time many other providers were catering for this demand). In the meantime, the emphasis on mature student entry to higher education was reflected in the founding of Lucy Cavendish College at Cambridge in 1965 as the first college in a residential university whose main function was to enable mature women to obtain university qualifications. None of the students came directly from school (THES, 218, 26 December 1975).

The colleges carried out an investigation into the demand for residential places in 1969 which claimed to reveal a pool of some 170,000 potential students (Houlton, 1978: 5). They presented this evidence to the Russell Committee which was sufficiently impressed by it to come to a positive answer to its own question 'whether, in a field so much in need of development as adult education is, the diversion of funds into this particular sector is justified'. The Report concluded, perhaps a little exaggeratedly, that:

Full-time study makes sustained intellectual demands and, when combined with individual tuition and the full life of the college, produces much more rapid intellectual growth than is possible under conditions of part-time study. None of this would be within reach of, for example, students from deprived backgrounds without the change of environment and the temporary release from voluntary activities and family responsibilities that a residential course offers (DES, 1973: 84).

It recommended that DES direct grant should continue for the colleges, and that there should be one further college established in the north of England (ibid.: 85). Very much as an outcome of the Russell Report, the 1975 Education Act introduced mandatory awards for adult college students on the same basis as those for degree course entrants, and Northern College was opened at Wentworth Castle, near Barnsley in 1978.

Under the 1992 Further and Higher Education Act the long term residential colleges were placed within the further education sector and became dependent on the Further Education Funding Councils for future public funding. This meant that their work had to conform to Schedule 2 of the Act (see Chapter 4).

## Ruskin College

Three Americans, Walter and Anne Vrooman and Charles Beard, who were interested in social reform and the labour movement, and admirers of John Ruskin, founded Ruskin Hall at Oxford in 1899 while they were temporarily in England. It changed its name to Ruskin College in 1903. The object was to provide residential education, not for individual personal satisfaction or qualification (there were no examinations in the early years), but to train working class men and women to undertake responsible leadership within their communities and organisations. (The Articles of Association stated that men *and women* would be admitted but in fact no women were admitted until 1919.) It was very much 'education for citizenship' in the fashion of the WEA, founded four years later, with which Ruskin quickly forged close ties (Yorke, 1977: 6–7; Jennings, 1977: 3–5; Pollins, 1984: 9–10, 15–16).

From the very beginning, Ruskin was not intended to be just an Oxford-based residential college: provincial Ruskin halls were established in Birmingham (2), Manchester, Birkenhead and Stockport to provide residential education for students who could not leave their jobs; and a correspondence and extension department was founded which promoted mixed-mode residential and correspondence courses and some classes, particularly in Yorkshire and Lancashire. The provincial halls proved to be financially non-viable, but the correspondence department was remarkably successful, enrolling some 8,000 students between 1899 and 1909. The

College began to abandon its outside activities after 1903 except the correspondence courses which continued until 1964 (Yorke, 1977: 12–15, Jennings, 1977: 1–2; Pollins: 14–16).

Finance was a major problem from the start, despite the Vroomans' initial generosity. The lack of any financial assistance for students influenced the length of residence (anything from one month to two years), and the kind of students able to come to Oxford (initially male, mostly unmarried and a high proportion from abroad who came to learn English). The need to seek support from private benefactors and patrons exercised a subtle influence on the nature of the courses: they did not want them to be too radical, socialist or atheist (Yorke, 1977: 6–7; Jennings, 1977: 4; Pollins, 1984: 16–17). Given the founders' interest in the labour movement, it was fitting that the College should increasingly look to the trade unions for support. It came initially from the Amalgamated Society of Engineers, in 1902, and a number of other unions were quick to follow suit. By 1907 they supplied £1,249 – five times more than in 1904. This trade union financial support brought more trade union activists to the College, some of whom were sponsored by their unions. Many of them were influenced by the industrial unrest of that period, and held strong socialist beliefs of one kind or another (Yorke, 1977: 18–26; Jennings, 1977: 4, 6; Pollins, 1984: 17).

This industrial militancy on the part of the student body brought it into conflict with the liberal, somewhat patronising ethos of the College, and also with the way in which the College was being drawn into a closer relationship with Oxford University, which was regarded as an agent of the class enemy by the militants. Rumours in 1908 that the Report on *Oxford and Working Class Education* would recommend closer links between the College and the University, transforming it from 'a Labour college into a college preparatory to university studies', contributed to the growing conflict although, as Bernard Jennings has pointed out, the 1908 Report and recommendations were not published until November, by which time the conflict was well advanced (Jennings, 1977: 5, 12; Simon, 1965: 312, 318).

For some time previously there had been student disquiet about the ideological nature of some of the teaching, particularly the free market economics teaching of H.B. Lees Smith, the Vice-Principal; and the perceived anti-socialist and anti-working class bias of other staff, reflecting their lack of knowledge or experience of working class culture or the Labour movement. Some of the teaching was felt to be condescending if not downright wrong! It was also very didactic, with some of the tutors seeing it as their task to correct the ignorant prejudices of the students or 'sandpaper' their rough edges. When Lees Smith, as Chair of the College Executive Committee, attempted to introduce a number of academic reforms intended to improve the standard of work in 1907, but which also involved abandoning the Marxist/Darwinian sociology course taught by the Principal, Dennis Hird, tension mounted. The students began to organise resistance to the new curriculum and hold their own discussion classes and eventually, in 1908, founded the Plebs League 'to bring about a definite and more satisfactory connection between Ruskin and the Labour Movement' by providing an alternative educational programme, less didactic and more sympathetic to socialist ideas. Hird was eventually sacked early in 1909 for supporting, or not sufficiently resisting, the students' demands. The students went on strike, demanding his reinstatement and a change in the character of the College, to make it a truly Labour College. But they did not have the financial independence or power to resist the authorities, and soon there was a split between the Plebs League and more moderate 'loyalist' students. The latter signed an undertaking to observe the rules of the College, while the former broke away to found the independent Central Labour College (see Chapter 10) (Jennings, 1977: 6–11; Simon, 1965: 319–23; Pollins, 1984: 17–23; Phillips and Putnam, 1980: 21–3).

Meanwhile a new constitution and a new Principal (and the departure of some of the previous staff) allowed the College to make a fresh start in closer collaboration with the trade unions, the Co-operative movement and other working class organisations, in a new building in Walton Street, opened in 1913. In line with the 1908 Report, the College forged closer links with the University, including altering its curriculum to enable the students to meet the requirements of the University diplomas in economics and political science, although only about one-third of the students actually sat the diploma examinations (Jennings, 1977: 13–14; Pollins, 1984: 23–7).

During the inter-war period, the educational work of the College continued to be largely determined by the requirements of the University diploma. Teaching was very orthodox, with little reference to Marxist or other alternative perspectives. The first decade after the war was marked by financial insecurity and deficits, which is possibly why women were admitted from 1919 onwards. But the Board of Education began to provide grant-aid, and financial support was also obtained from LEA awards, trust funds, TUC scholarships, and grants from individual trade unions, co-operative societies, working men's clubs and individual donors. The links with the WEA also became very close: of 174 British students admitted to the College between 1926-32, 111 were former WEA students (Pollins, 1984: 28–43; Kelly, 1992: 281; Legge, 1982: 70; Houlton, 1978: 13–15). The period was characterised by its lack of student unrest (except for a three-day strike in demand of eggs for breakfast!); an apparent disinclination to become involved in the political struggles around unemployment and international affairs; and an overall sense of gratitude for the privilege of being at Ruskin (Pollins, 1984: 42–3). Perhaps as an escape from the very real alternative of unemployment, this was not surprising.

The College closed between 1940-5 except for the correspondence department, which greatly increased its activities, catering especially for men and women in the Services. After the war, an increasing proportion of the College income came from public funds – from the Ministry of Education (later the DES) and discretionary awards from LEAs, although scholarships and grants from the labour movement were still important. Obtaining the University diploma remained the major student goal, but by the 1960s this was less for its intrinsic value: more as a means of gaining entry to higher education and the acquisition of a degree. This goal became more explicit in the late 1960s and early 70s, with the introduction of new college-examined diplomas which largely displaced the University qualification, and served more directly the purpose of access to higher education (*ibid.*: 43–8, 53–6; Hughes, 1961: 204).

In 1961 there were over 2,000 enquiries and over 400 applications for the 75 places at the College. Six of the successful applicants were women. The average age of the students was slightly over 28: half were from manual and half from clerical occupations. Nearly all had some former adult education experience (about half with the WEA or university extramural classes). All but a couple were members of a trade union and well over a third held lay office. Over half were active Labour Party supporters (ibid.: 201–3).

The general student and political unrest of the later 1960s and early '70s had its effect on Ruskin: there were some bitter controversies and demands for a more politically radical approach and greater student participation in running the College. But these were less extreme than in other areas of higher education, perhaps because of the trade union background of the students, many of whom 'were accustomed in industry to using agreed grievance procedures constitutionally' and who 'well understood the nature of institutionalised conflict' (Pollins, 1984: 56–7). The 1909 strikers would have felt totally vindicated in their predictions of how the College was becoming incorporated into bourgeois society! This would have been even more the case when the DES made mandatory grants available to students in place of the uncertain LEA discretionary awards in the 1970s. This improved the financial security of the College, but put it much more under the control of central Government. This became very apparent in 1987 when the Minister of State with responsibility for higher education used the threat of withdrawal of funding to try to force the College to protect what he termed the 'academic freedom' of one of its tutors who had publicly expressed violently anti-Labour views, thereby provoking a student boycott of his classes.(ibid.: 58; Lieven, 1991: 37–8).

It had always been the aim that students would come to Ruskin, not for personal advancement, but to acquire 'really useful knowledge' which they would then take back to their previous work places and communities and into the labour movement, or would disseminate through teaching adult classes. A survey in 1913 indicated that most of the students who left the College between 1909–13 had fulfilled this objective in one way or another. A review of the activities of 111 former Ruskin students in 1936 revealed that 17 were MPs or former MPs, 21 were in education (mainly adult education), 19 were trade union officials, 13 were officials in co-operative societies, and 20 were in social work. But it gradually became less common for students to return to their former occupations, and posts in the labour movement were limited. After the Second World War an increasing number went on to higher education or sought to use their education to escape from their previous ways of life, reflecting the more meritocratic nature of post-war society. Nevertheless, many continued to find work in the labour movement or education and in 1961 the Principal of Ruskin was able to claim that 'the proportion returning to their former occupations, and seeking full-time or part-time posts in the Labour Movement, has not significantly changed in recent years'. However, this practice became less and less prevalent, as upward social mobility became increasingly the goal (Pollins, 1984: 27, 53, 60–1; Yorke, 1977: 37; Hughes, 1961: 204; Legge, 1982: 70).

Two fundamental changes occurred in the College in the late 1980s and early 90s. Firstly, the Thatcher Government's attacks on the trade union movement made it more difficult to recruit students predominantly from there. Recruitment was widened and new courses introduced to attract a broader cross-section of society. Stephen Yeo, the Principal, claimed that 'Ruskin will become more female, more black, more international'. It was also becoming more middle class. This was partly the result of the second change, brought about by legislation. Under the 1992 Further and Higher Education Act, the College received a block grant from the Further Education Funding Council (FEFCE), but only by complying with Schedule 2 of the Act. It did so by emphasising the opportunities provided for access to higher education, but the FEFCE would only fund one year courses for this purpose, so the diplomas were shortened to one year. This allowed twice as many students to gain entry to Ruskin but it raised serious questions about whether it could adequately provide for the same kind of students as before. Either standards had to be lowered, or it was the most educationally deprived students who had gained most from the two year courses, who were least likely to cope in one year (*THES*, 22 July 1994).

These one-year courses led either to an Oxford University 'Special Diploma' in social studies or social administration, or a College diploma in social studies, labour studies, community studies, English studies, women's studies and history. There was also an Open College validated one year course in French communication and a social work professional qualification course, as well as various specialised short courses for trade unionists and a range of pre-diploma 'return to learn' and 'changing directions' courses (NIACE, 1994: 79–80).

Thus, after nearly 100 years, Ruskin had become a very different kind of college from the one founded in 1899. It was much more closely incorporated into the state, with far weaker links with the (admittedly far weaker) labour movement; and with the original aim of 'education for citizenship' largely displaced by the goal of 'education for personal advancement'.

## Woodbrooke and Fircroft

Woodbrooke, established in the former home of George Cadbury at Selly Oak in 1903, 'owed its origin to discussions at Quaker summer schools, in the closing years of the nineteenth century, on ways and means of bringing the traditional faith into line with modern discoveries in science and Biblical studies'. It was originally intended as a 'permanent summer school for the study and discussion of these problems' rather than as a long-term residential college, but gradually evolved into one, providing systematic courses for missionaries, teachers, Sunday School teachers and social workers. Although shorter periods of study were not abandoned, a term's residence became the norm. Like Ruskin, Woodbrooke also had an extension department: it arranged lectures, conferences, weekend schools and summer schools for adults interested in religious and social questions. Before the First World War and between the wars, the College drew its students mainly from Quaker and adult school circles. Because of its predominantly religious purpose, it did not accept government funding even when this was more readily available after the Second World War, and therefore experienced some financial difficulties. Nevertheless, it continued to prepare men and women 'of all faiths and none' for religious and social service and 'for responsible living', mainly in one-term courses although shorter courses were available by arrangement (Kelly, 1992: 261–2, 280–1, 390–1; NIACE, 1994: 80).

Fircroft was founded by George Cadbury junior in 1909, also at Selly Oak, very much as a sister college to Woodbrooke, but without the overtly religious objectives. It aimed to provide serious residential study opportunities from one week to a year, to enable working men to equip themselves better 'as citizens, adult scholars and teachers' and to enable them 'to develop their personal capacities so they could play a more responsible part in their communities both at work and at home.' The emphasis on *responsible* active citizenship was very similar to Ruskin's mission. From the start the College was sensitive to the comparative needs of women, but at that time it was not possible to consider a mixed sex residential college. In 1911 it offered six one-week summer courses for women which were heavily over-subscribed, and soon afterwards introduced a one-term course for women. However, this arrangement was not ideal and after the first world war the Trustees resolved the problem by founding Hillcroft as a sister college for women (see below) (Kelly, 1992: 262; Legge, 1982: 71; information from M. Lieven).

Like Woodbrooke, Fircroft soon became a predominantly long-term residential college, with some 90 long-term students attending either a two-term course for men or the one-term course for women. Also like Woodbrooke and Ruskin, it developed a range of extension activities including, in the early years, correspondence courses. Through its first warden, Tom Bryan, Fircroft developed close links with the Danish folk high schools and a strong emphasis on community living. Through its connection with the Danish movement, Fircroft attracted substantial numbers of foreign students (Kelly, 1992: 263, 281).

In practice, despite its original aims, many Fircroft students used the College for vocational purposes, and after the Second World War it increasingly served as a means of progressing to other further and higher education (*ibid.*: 391; Legge, 1982: 71).

In the early 1970s the College was torn apart by a dispute between the students and the College authorities over the nature of its provision. The students boycotted the classes and were supported by the staff. Eventually the Principal and the tutors were dismissed and the College closed in 1975 for five years. When it re-opened in 1980, women were admitted for the first time. A varied and more student-centred programme of short courses and workshops as well as longer residential courses, which aimed specifically at the disadvantaged, were introduced. The College sought to offer 'a new balance between liberal adult education and social purposes', based on a conscious commitment to the notion of education for equality and positive action to prevent the provision being colonised by the dominant groups in society. By the early 1990s new kinds of educational programmes in 'active citizenship' were being designed in partnership with other adult education agencies, which combined non-residential and residential elements, tailor-made to the needs of community groups and organisations. The student body and college activities also began to reflect more accurately the multicultural diversity of Birmingham and its region (*ibid.*; Kelly, 1992: liii;

Houlton, 1978: 6; Lieven, 1987; NIACE, 1994: 78; information from K. Jackson).

## The Co-operative College

Like Woodbrooke, the Co-operative College established at Holyoake House, Manchester in 1919 grew out of residential summer schools: in this case, the co-operative summer schools which had begun at Castleton in 1913. There was little difficulty in recruiting students supported by bursaries from co-operative societies, but there were insufficient capital resources, so in the early days students had to reside in lodgings. After 1924, a hostel did provide accommodation but at a considerable distance from the College. It grew slowly during the inter-war period, providing courses in co-operative subjects which ensured a supply of teachers for the co-operative movement with a reliable knowledge of co-operative principles (Bonner, 1970: 123–4, 180–3; Kelly, 1992: 281).

In 1945 the College was transferred to Stanford Hall, Loughborough, which at last provided adequate residential accommodation, but the move did cause some financial difficulties. The College continued to offer mainly courses in co-operative subjects and was dependent on financial support from the Co-operative Societies and Co-operative Union, although it accepted DES grant aid for one of its courses in 1969. By that time there were approximately 120 students in residence. Later the College also accepted some funds from the Overseas Development Agency for some overseas students to study co-operative development and management for a Loughborough University diploma (ibid.: 390–1; Bonner, 1970: 301; DES, 1973: 224–5; Hennessy, 1973; NIACE, 1994: 78).

In 1973 an article about the College in the THES described it as 'looking up after the lean years'. It reported that the main object of the College was to develop 'the democracy of co-operative organisations', still primarily through courses about co-operation. A variety of one-year, three-month and shorter courses covered a wide range of co-operative subjects. In addition, a small number of students took a more general Nottingham University diploma course in politics, economics and social studies. In 1984 this was replaced by a diploma course in policy studies aimed at voluntary community workers which, after 1992, became FEFCE-supported (ibid.; Hennessey, 1973; Kelly, 1992: 391; information from R. Wildgust).

## Hillcroft

Hillcroft was founded as a residential college for working women at Beckenham in 1920 by a group of people very representative of the 'liberal tradition' of early twentieth century adult education, actively encouraged but not financially supported by the YWCA, and financially endowed by Thomas Wall (the 'sausage philanthropist'). In 1926 it moved to larger premises in Surbiton. The aim of the College was to provide working-class women, who had made such a major contribution to the war effort, an 'opportunity for full time study and a spring board for a new life' through one-year, residential, non-vocational courses in general education with a Christian basis. Reflecting the liberal views of its founders, it was not intended to help the 'lower classes' rise in life or obtain social or industrial improvement, but rather to develop a 'fuller life' (Powell, 1964: 3–4; Cockerill, nd.: 1–18, 33–4).

Eleven students enrolled in February 1920 and the College grew very slowly, for many years experiencing financial problems resolved only by private donations, particularly from Thomas Wall. Some temporary improvement occurred with recognition by the Board of Education in 1929 which resulted in a *per capita* grant for each full-time student, but the early 1930s was a period of financial difficulty. Prospects began to improve again by the mid-30s with increased numbers of LEAs making discretionary awards, and with grants from several trusts. By 1939 the number of students had risen to 34 (Powell, 1964: 14–18; Cockerill, nd.: 19–27, 34–5, 43).

Within the educational resources available, every student followed a self-selected programme which was not so much academic, but intended to develop reading, writing, thinking and speaking skills which she could use to continue her studies later. In 1933, a new Principal introduced short, four-week courses for unemployed women, or the wives of unemployed men, to give them 'refreshment, stimulation and a taste of corporate residential life in pleasant and healthful surroundings'. In the relatively stable period before the Second World War, other short courses were added on the co-operative movement and new opportunities for women. Despite the intentions of the founders, a significant number of students used the College to equip themselves for a new occupation, not least because many saw their old jobs disappear into the well of unemployment during the 20s and 30s. A majority came from factory or retail jobs; a smaller proportion from offices. A survey in 1937 of the 400 students who had passed through the College in the previous 17 years showed that one-third had returned to their former work. Apart from those that got married, the others mainly entered nursing, or social, educational or church work. A tiny number of more academically inclined students went on to diploma or degree courses (Powell, 1964: 29; Cockerill, nd.: 28–43).

In 1940 the College migrated temporarily to Birmingham, but closed down in 1943, although the Principal developed and expanded a series of correspondence courses during the remainder of the war. The College re-opened at Surbiton in September 1945 with 35 students. It secured a block grant from the Ministry of Education and increased funding from the LEAs, although it remained never far from financial crisis and was dogged by recruitment problems because few women were free to go off to college or could easily obtain a local authority discretionary award for a non-qualifying course. The contradiction between the non-vocational ethos of the College foundation and the increasingly vocational intentions of the students became more marked in the 1950s and 60s. Most students were clearly interested in professional training. Out of 785 women who entered Hillcroft between 1945–60, nearly half afterwards took up teaching, social work or some kind of management. This interest led the College to introduce a two-year social studies course leading to an external University of London diploma in 1964. The diploma course, constituting a basic qualification which could lead on to professional social work training, caused two fundamental changes to the College's practices. It required candidates to have entry qualifications for the first time, and it introduced a fixed university syllabus in place of the individually constructed curriculum (Powell, 1964: 39–49; Cockerill, nd.: 44–65; Kelly, 1992: 391).

In 1974 London University withdrew the diploma as part of its contraction of its External Department, leaving the College with a vacuum which was filled by the CNAA agreeing to validate a new two-year course with three options in arts, social science and social studies, recognised as at least equivalent to higher education entrance and where appropriate, to exemption from the first year of a degree course. A small number of students continued to choose a one year course, but the majority opted for the two-year certificate. This drew the College even more firmly in the direction it had been following for some time, as a provider primarily of preparatory courses for higher education. However, by the mid-80s a two-year residential course was looking a decidedly expensive alternative to the new Access to higher education courses in further education colleges. The need to diversify and extend the recruitment net led to the admission of an increasing number of non-residential day students (rising to 45–50 per cent of the 70–80 full-time students by the early 1990s), and to other innovations intended to broaden the provision and the College's appeal. These included involvement in a prior experiential learning project and the introduction of new courses in computing and interdisciplinary arts, as well as more short courses. In 1991 the two-year course was converted into a one year Certificate of Higher Education in Combined Studies and Social Studies (with a two-year part-time option). With the demise of the CNAA, validation of the certificate was taken over by the Open University (Cockerill, nd.: 65–78; Hillcroft *Annual Reports* 1984–5, 1991–2 and 1993–4). However, one innovation the College surprisingly did not make was the introduction of a creche, which would have considerably improved its accessibility.

Over a period of 75 years Hillcroft experienced considerable change. In the mid-1990s it still offered a 'second chance' to women, but this was no longer to obtain education for a 'full life' (at least, not in the sense originally intended): rather it was for professional or vocational reasons, or to gain entry into higher education. The Principal, Eileen Aird, firmly believed that there was 'no dichotomy between self-development/personal development and access to other educational and training opportunities', but this does not adequately explain the drift from the College's original liberal principles to its recent mission statement: 'To enable adult women disadvantaged by educational or social factors to progress into Higher Education, vocational training and employment'. As the 75th Anniversary prospectus explained, 'the courses have changed a great deal over the intervening years as a result of evolving interests and needs'. It is true that the College's commitment was still 'to providing education for women' but the form, content and purpose were all very different. Nor was it any longer unambiguously working class but rather welcomed any women who were 'looking for opportunities to reflect, to acquire new skills or develop existing ones'. And it could no longer claim to be either exclusively long-term or residential. After 1992, not without 'major fears', the College became funded by the FEFCE and provided a programme of Schedule 2 work (Hillcroft *Annual Reports*, 1984–5:

3, 1991–2: 4-5, 1993–4: 2; 1995 *Prospectus*: 3–4; correspondence from E. Aird to the author, 17 October 1995).

## Coleg Harlech and Newbattle Abbey

Coleg Harlech, which opened in 1927, reflected the educational ideas of the man who inspired it, Tom Jones. Despite serving four prime ministers as Deputy Secretary to the Cabinet, he retained close links with adult educators in Wales and was a firm believer in the value of residential education to 'round off' the tutorial class experience. In its early days the College was heavily influenced by the traditions of Welsh nonconformity and the liberal adult education emphasis on 'study for its own sake' rather than for qualification or vocational purpose (Stead, 1977: 19–20, 27, 44; Ellis, 1992: 307). At the same time Jones's conciliatory view of industrial relations made him see Coleg Harlech as an opportunity 'to work with moderates, to build new bridges and to train new leaders'. There was more than a little paternalism in the enterprise. It was not surprising, therefore, that in the industrial climate of the 1920s the College was not fully accepted by the labour movement in South Wales, although the early students were nearly all Welsh industrial workers – miners, steelworkers, railway clerks and quarrymen. Its location in north Wales was also a distancing factor. There was a problematic contradiction and tension between 'the richness of life at Harlech and ... the real industrial and political world'. There was also a tension, as in the other colleges, between the founders' expectations that the students would return to their old life and jobs, and the students' intentions, even in the early days, to use the College as a means of entry to further education (Stead, 1977: 36, 47, 65, 77; Houlton, 1978: 61).

Although the University and Colleges of Wales, together with the WEA and LEAs, were represented on the controlling College council, the University declined any financial responsibility and the LEAs gave only patchy support for this non-qualification education. Like most of the long-term residential colleges, Coleg Harlech remained in a precarious financial position at least until the improvement in central government funding in the 1950s and 60s (Kelly, 1992: 282; Stead, 1977: 27–8, 91–3, 99).

From the beginning the College offered summer schools and acted as a conference centre and in the 1930s, like other residential colleges, provided short courses for unemployed men, in addition to its longer courses. There were only six long-term students in the first year but numbers gradually built up to between 30 and 40 for the one-year course. In 1939 the Transport and General Workers' Union instituted a scholarship to the College and various other unions subsequently followed this lead. On the eve of the Second World War the College remained largely dependent on such voluntary contributions but had nevertheless 'won for itself the position of a national institution'. However, 'it had not become part of a University nor was it like Ruskin a 'labour college'.' (*ibid.*: 52–4, 65, 80; Ellis, 1992: 346).

During the war Coleg Harlech was occupied by Liverpool University and then by ABCA as a training centre for army education officers. When it re-opened after the war, it began to admit women but the next decade was a difficult period until student numbers began to increase in the late 1950s. In 1969 a two year University of Wales diploma course in general studies was introduced and the range of subjects expanded as did the number of staff and students. By 1971 all but eight of the 139 students were taking the diploma course. It did mean major changes: not only the introduction of examinations – which went against Tom Jones's original intentions - but the recruitment of students from all parts of the United Kingdom as well as from overseas. By the 1990s, over 90 per cent of these students went on to higher education (Stead, 1977: 82, 90–118; Kelly, 1992: 391).

The policy review of the long-term residential colleges in 1991, prior to their incorporation into the FE sector, resulted in the two-year diploma course at Harlech, as in the other colleges, being reduced to one year. This required the College to double its annual recruitment to maintain student numbers. This was achieved by the mid-1990s when 140 students were enrolled on the one-year modularised diploma course. Nevertheless, the College felt insecure within the new FE sector. 'It has to compete in that jungle against animals much larger than and very different from itself' explained Lord Morris of Castle Morris to the House of Lords in February 1993 (*Hansard*, 23 February 1993, col. 196). The insecurity was well justified. Harlech's grant from the Welsh Further Education Funding Council (FEFCW) suffered large annual reductions despite its good educational record, confirmed by an FEFCW inspection in 1995 which found that 'the quality of teaching and the standards attained by students are outstanding' (Stead, 1977: 78, 90; FEFCW *Report*, March 1995).

Some six years after the opening of Coleg Harlech, the Marquess of Lothian offered his home, Newbattle Abbey, as a Scottish college of adult education. With help from the Carnegie Trust, and with considerable advice from Tom Jones, it was adapted and opened as a residential college in 1937. Unlike some of the other colleges, Newbattle Abbey was not burdened with too many founders' aims, other than that it should be used for adult education. The early students, who were both male and female, from the north of England as well as Scotland, and with quite mixed educational and social backgrounds, demonstrated a variety of aspirations and purposes. 'Some students are impelled by the disinterested love of knowledge; others by the consciousness of social purpose; others by a feeling of dissatisfaction with the life they are living and the desire to take stock of themselves. The methods of work adopted tend to encourage independent thinking and observation' claimed the sub-warden in 1938. The method of selection favoured students who had previous adult education experience (BIAE, 1934–5: 27; Ellis, 1992: 347–9; Mack, 1938, *passim*; Scottish Education Department, 1975: 5).

The College quickly attracted support from a number of trade unions, professional associations, co-operative societies, the independent Edinburgh branch of the WEA, and LEAs, and grant aid from the Scottish Education Department, but it had to face considerable hostility from the NCLC (which regarded it as a step towards the bourgeoisification of the working class), indifference from the Scottish TUC, and lack of enthusiasm amongst academics at the Scottish universities (*ibid.*: 5, 12; Mack, 1938: 16–18; Hughes, 1995).

The College was requisitioned during the Second World War, re-opening again in 1950. Over the next two decades the courses remained full-time and were analogous to certain further education courses. The College struggled to recruit viable numbers and to attract financial support. The LEAs frequently refused bursaries to accepted students and Edinburgh University found it 'too difficult' to support the College financially, although Glasgow University did so modestly on a regular basis. In 1973 the College introduced a two-year diploma course intended as Access to higher education. Within a short time, most students were taking the diploma, but the College was also used for short-term residential courses when the main courses were not in session (Scottish Education Department, 1975: 5, 11–12; Legge, 1982: 72; Hughes, 1995).

In December 1987 the Scottish Office announced, without consultation, that Newbattle would lose its core funding as from the end of the 1988–9 session. The College, threatened with closure, developed a wide range of short courses, and leased its premises to a number of education and training bodies, but in October 1989 it ceased to operate as a long-term residential college. However, it recruited Bill Conboy, the vice-principal at Ruskin, to help re-establish itself as a long-term residential college. This was achieved six years later, partly by selling a portion of the Newbattle estate to raise investment capital. In September 1995 it commenced new one-year, full-time, modularised diploma courses in European Studies and Scottish Studies for which students could qualify for grants, although the Scottish Office refused to restore the College's recurrent grant. 'Individual self-development' was the primary aim of the courses, but they also enabled students to proceed to higher education (Lieven, 1991: 38; THES, 3 February 1995; Hughes, 1995).

## Northern College

Northern College owes its origins to discussions between members of the Sheffield Extramural Department and the Derbyshire Area of the National Union of Mineworkers in 1964, and subsequent planning which also involved the four metropolitan authorities of South Yorkshire and the WEA. This culminated in evidence to the Russell Committee which resulted in its recommendation in 1973 that a new residential college should be established in the north of England. Northern College opened five years later at Wentworth Castle, near Barnsley, a recently-closed teacher training college, with an initial intake of 32 students on long courses and ten attending a short course. It shared some of the aims of the other long-term colleges, but also had a distinct philosophy of its own (Mitchell and Field, 1980; Northern College, 1983; Field, 1984; Fryer, 1989).

Its stated purpose was to provide a second chance for learning for both men and women (in equal numbers) who had left school at the minimum age but who 'had begun to be active in their communities and trade unions and felt the need for education'. It was not simply to benefit them as individuals, but also to enable them to be more effective and active in their organisations and communities, thus harking back to the aims of long term residential adult education of the earlier twentieth century. It was recognised that students would use the education gained for personal advancement, including entry into higher education, but this was not the main purpose. What was attempted was 'a genuinely new approach to Adult Education ... a major shift to bring the students' life and the educational process into a creative relationship'. This involved 'understanding the location of workers and of women in history, recognising the validity of class and gender experience including all the negative perceptions of formal education (and) bringing to that location and that experience the perspective of academic disciplines and the conflict of different ideologies.' This was done by devising curricula based on students' experience and adopting learning and assessment methods designed to be helpful to students with extremely limited previous education. Given the political and major financial support of the South Yorkshire metropolitan authorities, the College felt more able than some of its counterparts 'to resist absorption into the university dominated hierarchy of higher education, and to avoid the harsh labour market imperatives of the government's vocational training strategy'; although DES recognition and financial support did render the College subject to HMI inspection and some critical reports about the student-centred curricula. It felt threatened by government policies and local Conservative prejudices from time to time (*ibid.*).

There were no entry qualifications, not even an essay (which was felt might be too off-putting for some applicants), but they were required to have made a start in obtaining some further education through day release or evening classes, or in other ways. Particular emphasis was placed on trying to attract an equal number of women students, partly to counterbalance the male predominance in other residential colleges, by exercising positive discrimination in the selection process and by making creche and child care facilities available (with the help of the Rowntree Trust), and by being flexible about residence requirements. However, despite this action it was not possible to fill more than one-third of the long-term places by women. Particular encouragement was also given to ethnic minority students by devising appropriate curricula and building close links with Liverpool's black community and the Sheffield Caribbean community (*ibid.*; NIACE, 1994: 79).

One of the unusual features of Northern College was that it gave equal emphasis to short courses of up to five weeks as a matter of principle. They were particularly intended for men and women involved in voluntary and community work: some were planned and organised around the specific needs of a community organisation or group: others were open to individuals. But they all built on previous educational experience and were intended to lead on to continuing educational involvement. They fell within one of the three broad categories of long courses (see below). The short courses created enormous organisational problems but the presence of the short course students was seen as a valuable influence on the long-term students, preventing their being sucked too far into an ivory tower academia. The success of the short courses depended on their relevance to and links with the students' community experience, and the extent to which they were assimilated into the college and accepted by the long term students (Fryer, 1989; Northern College, 1990–1).

The longer one-year certificate and two-year diploma courses were offered in three areas, trade union and industrial studies; social and community studies; and liberal and gateway studies. They all built on the experience of the students, but also aimed to introduce them to recognised disciplines and scholarly discourse in political economy, history and sociology. They offered College qualifications and were assessed on course work, to avoid the rigidities of external syllabuses and examinations, but they were increasingly recognised as appropriate qualifications for entry to higher education. The liberal and gateways studies course was particularly planned to meet the needs of those wishing to enter higher education. A new one-year course in Women's studies was introduced in 1990 (Northern College, 1983, *passim*; 1990–1: 7–12; Field, 1984: 14).

By 1983 student numbers had been built up to 65 on the long courses and some 700 on short courses – 35–40 at any one time. By the 1990s the residential capacity of the College had been extended to 140 places, at least half of which were allocated to students on the short courses. There were by then over 2,000 short course registrations *per annum* and a small number of non-resident students. The students were drawn almost exclusively from working class occupations and backgrounds. 'Northern was seen as a College of the South Yorkshire Labour Movement recruiting mainly from lay workers in a wide range of Trade Union, Co-operative, Community and other voluntary associations in the region' (Northern College, 1983: 3, 5; 1990–1: 1, 4, 14; Field, 1984: 14; NIACE, 1994: 79).

## One Hundred Years of Long-Term Residential Adult Education

The long-term residential colleges have mostly shared a commitment to providing education that will in some way enhance active citizenship and democratic participation for working class people whose formal education had been minimal. In the earlier part of the century this aim was predominant, although how successful it was was questioned a long time ago (Blumler, 1962). Gradually, with an ever increasing premium being placed on certification, the emphasis shifted from social objectives to personal advancement, firstly vocational and then to entry into higher education, although there was (and is) no clear-cut distinction between these social and individual dimensions. However, this function was to some extent outflanked by the rise of the Access movement in the 1970s and 80s, with much cheaper and more accessible means of achieving the same goal increasingly available at local further education colleges. This caused a crisis of purpose and risk of redundancy for the colleges in the 1980s, although surprisingly the Government still regarded this as their primary purpose in 1993 (Lieven, 1991: 34; *Hansard*, 23 February 1993, col. 206).

The reason why it is surprising is that this form of provision has always been expensive and has catered for very small numbers. In 1969–70 there were 483 long-term students, and a decade later, before the addition of Northern College, the total had risen to about 700 (DES, 1973: 224; Houlton, 1978: 4; Legge, 1982: 73). The colleges frequently experienced recruitment problems and almost always lived on a financial knife edge, at least until the State (both central and local) undertook more of the funding. By the 1970s, central government funding was meeting 40 to 50 per cent of total expenditure, and local government was also contributing significantly (Lowe, 1970: 78). This led to closer incorporation into the State; closer control; more direction of the form and content of courses; and threats of funding withdrawal if the college failed to meet government expectations (Lieven, 1991).

Most of the colleges did experience external interference either from the Government or from other bodies that felt they had a claim on them, and also internal disputes and conflicts at some time. The latter were made more likely by the greenhouse intensity of long-term residential institutions. Sometimes these conflicts involved educational or political principles but often they were over domestic matters.

None of the colleges had been exclusively long-term, even from the beginning. They took on various external functions and increasingly added short courses to their provision, and even began to take in day students. It has been argued more recently (Lieven, 1991: 35) that this was a way for the colleges to 'reaffirm their historical and underlying purpose' by focusing on priority groups, for example at Fircroft and Northern. Much of the history of the colleges suggests that in fact they have been more successful than most forms of adult education in attracting working class and educationally disadvantaged students and giving them a genuine second chance (*ibid.*: 37; Boyden, 1970). This was less true for women who, apart from Hillcroft and Northern College, received a raw deal from long-term residential adult education. In 1969–70 about three-quarters of the long-term students were men (DES, 1973: 224). Some of the evidence suggests that women were only admitted when there was a recruitment problem (Ruskin, 1919) or when a college wanted to attract a less militant student body (Fircroft, 1980).

The fulsome claims for long-term residential colleges made by the Russell Report (quoted above) were certainly true for some students, but, as already mentioned, the number was very small. Inevitably they constituted a privileged elite amongst adult students, which became less justifiable the more they pursued individual advancement rather than a collective social purpose, or the same objectives could be achieved much more cheaply in non-residential further education.

## Short-Term Residential Colleges[1]

The mushrooming of short-term residential colleges after the Second World War (with some 25 founded between 1944–50) owes something to the same renewed enthusiasm for residential adult education that affected the long-term colleges, as described by Hunter (1959), and referred to above. But their origins lie in a variety of antecedents, some as far back as the nineteenth century, such as the University and Quaker summer schools and the related Chautauqua development in North America (Harris-Worthington, 1987: 10–17). These led to the establishment of a number of Adult School guest houses both before the First World War and during the inter-war years, but which closed with the outbreak of the Second World War. Other forerunners were the Co-operative Holiday Association, established in 1891 (and reformed as

1. Unless otherwise stated, this section on the short-term residential colleges is based on the research and doctoral thesis of Walter Drews, former principal of Wansfell College, Essex.

the Holiday Fellowship in 1913), which offered education, culture and physical recreation as well as social and international friendship in a residential setting. There is no real evidence of a direct line from the Holiday Fellowship to the post-war short-term residential colleges, but there were many similarities. Nor is there evidence of direct links between the residential provision for the unemployed between the wars and the later short-term colleges but again there are similarities of purpose as well as common personal associations (e.g. A.D. Lindsay) which suggest connections, not so much with the large work camps, but the small residential settlements such as Maes-yr-haf in the Rhondda Valley and others which sprang up in the Midlands and north of England (see Chapter 3). During the war the residential courses provided by the Services for HM Forces, and the Formation Colleges after the war (also outlined in Chapter 3) were important role models and many of those involved in setting up the short-term residential colleges after the war had had direct experience of army education.

There is evidence that a number of those involved were also familiar with the Danish folk high schools which had been founded almost a century earlier by N.F.S. Grundtvig and Christen Kold. Several of them visited Denmark, but they found the folk high schools rather Spartan and predominantly catering for young people, so the direct influence was not very great. Yet indirectly, through the vision and teaching of Sir Richard Livingstone, there was a connection between the Danish colleges and the English short-term colleges.

Two individuals, Ross Waller and Richard Livingstone, were particularly influential. Waller was appointed Director of Extramural Studies at Manchester University in 1936 and immediately looked to establish a residential centre for his department. This led to the founding of the Lamb Guildhouse at Bowdon, ten miles from Manchester, in 1938, to provide for weekend study groups; some opportunities for longer periods of study and recreation; and occasional conferences and branch rallies for the WEA. The first brochure, an expression of Waller's aims, stated that the Lamb Guildhouse (which had fairly primitive accommodation for 30 people) was 'a place where friendly people from far and near may meet on the common ground of respect and admiration for true, good and beautiful things, where they may find interest, good fellowship and peace. A place of refreshment, light and peace.' Unfortunately, the original Guildhouse only lasted a year because it was requisitioned to serve as a nursing home at the beginning of the war, but another, smaller house at Bowden was found which provided residential seminars for HM Forces during the war, in association with ABCA (see Chapter 3). Eventually it proved too small for this purpose, and the work was transferred to Holly Royde which was given to Manchester University in 1944. For the remainder of the war it served as a Forces College, but with regular monthly weekends reserved for the Lamb Guildhouse Association. In 1949 Holly Royde formally became a part of the Manchester Extramural Department.

Richard Livingstone, classics scholar, lecturer, broadcaster, Vice-Chancellor of the Queen's University, Belfast, President of Corpus Christi College, was an enthusiastic advocate of residential adult education which he believed was a much more suitable setting for cultural and intellectual studies and 'lighting the lamp' of adult learning than were the drab premises where many evening classes were held. He was also opposed to the policy of extending compulsory education to 15 or 16 years of age, believing that much more learning could be achieved in adulthood. In 1936 he used the opportunity of his presidential address to the British Association for the Advancement of Science to extol the virtues of the Danish folk high schools and urge that adult education in England follow their example both in their residential nature and their broad social curriculum. His book, *The Future in Education*, published in 1941 had a considerable impact on adult education. Livingstone's views influenced the nature of many of the short-term colleges founded after the war, such as Pendley Manor at Tring, Hertfordshire; Burton Manor, Cheshire; the Wedgwood Memorial College in North Staffs; and the Women's Institutes' Denman College at Marcham Park, Berkshire.

Livingstone and Waller used very similar vocabulary in arguing the virtues of residential adult education: 'graceful living', 'beautiful things', 'enjoyment', 'refreshment and light', 'fellowship', 'peace and inspiration', etc. – all in good and beautiful surroundings. But they did not have any sense of the social purpose, or belief in positive discrimination for the disadvantaged, that had inspired many of the long-term residential colleges. Their vision was of opportunities for cultural improvement available to everyone, regardless of their social or educational background.

In 1943 the British Institute of Adult Education produced an interim report on *Adult Education After the War* (finally published in 1945) in which it suggested there was 'a special need for residential institutes catering for shorter courses of a few weeks duration, for holidays and weekend schools and conferences' (BIAE, 1945: 58). This recommendation apparently influenced the writers of the 1943 White Paper, *Educational Reconstruction*, which reiterated the need to develop 'appropriate centres, including a number of residential centres' for adult education: the only time such a need has been acknowledged either by a white paper or in legislation. The 1944 Education Act made no reference to any such need, but the Ministry of Education's important pamphlet on further education three years later (see Chapter 4) did refer specifically to the value of short residential courses and stated that the Ministry considered it 'reasonable to expect every authority will require such a centre, either for its own area or in partnership with other authorities' (Ministry of Education, 1947b: 35, 61–2). However, the Government did nothing to make this financially possible. Nevertheless, by 1950–1 there were 24 short-term residential colleges (all in England) catering for 20,777 students, and by the end of the 1950s there were some 29 colleges with over 50,000 students. The vast majority of the students attended short courses of less than seven days, but there were a small number of longer courses.

Popular cultural courses embracing the arts, literature, languages, music, dance and handicrafts, and other recreational work 'for serious pleasure', rather than academic courses, constituted the predominant fare in a majority of the colleges. At one college, Belstead House (Suffolk) the main purpose was in-service training from the start: later, courses for teachers, probation officers, social workers, policemen and other branches of the service sector became common. At the Wedgwood Memorial College (jointly run by

Staffordshire LEA, the WEA and the Oxford University Extramural Delegacy), trade union courses were a major activity for some years. At some colleges such as Burton Manor (Liverpool) and Urchfont Manor (Wiltshire) attempts were made to offer non-vocational courses for industry in an attempt to find a source of recruitment where the cost was not the major concern (Peers, 1958: 132; Hunter, 1959: 124; Harris-Worthington, 1987: 19). This was more successfully achieved at Pendley Manor in Hertfordshire, a privately run college founded by Dorian Williams in 1945 as a means of making his ancestral home pay its way. Non-vocational residential courses were run for the employees of Vauxhall Motors (and later of other companies) at Pendley during the late 1940s and early 50s. Over 100 companies sent their industrial workers on week-long courses on full pay and with their fees paid. Although the employers' enthusiasm for this provision only lasted a few years, similar (but non-residential) schemes re-emerged as an important form of adult education in the 1990s (see the Ford EDAP scheme described in Chapter 3). Perhaps one of the main achievements of the short-term colleges generally was to bridge the gap between vocational and non-vocational adult education (Hunter, 1953: 35–48 and 1959: 135; Harrison, 1961: 317; Lowe, 1970: 90).

In 1952, D.M. Hopkinson, the warden of Grantley Hall in Yorkshire summarised the main purpose of the colleges as being

... to provide general courses for all-comers without qualification or restraint, to arrange special courses for particular groups such as teachers or supervisors in industry, and to give hospitality to other bodies seeking to hold courses or conferences of their own (Hopkinson, 1952)

although the last function was frowned upon by some of the first generation of wardens, most notably Guy Hunter of Urchfont Manor, who tried unsuccessfully to dispense with lettings to outside bodies. Most colleges found it economically essential to fill their places by letting the facilities to outsiders, or for in-service training, during the week, and to concentrate the general adult education courses between Friday evenings and Sunday afternoons, with some longer summer and winter schools. Another very practical reason for letting the premises to outside bodies was that it relieved the very limited staff in most of these colleges.

LEAs were the main sponsors or founders of the short-term colleges after the war, but they were not solely responsible. Several universities and WEA Districts, the National Federation of Women's Institutes, the YMCA, other voluntary organisations and trusts, and private individuals were also involved in founding colleges.

The growth in short-term residential adult education reached its peak around the time (1969) that the Association of Wardens and Principals of Short-Term Colleges submitted evidence to the Russell Committee. They listed 32 colleges, although the Russell Report identified 'something over thirty five' colleges (DES, 1973: 45). This constitutes the largest number ever recorded. They were catering for at least 100,000 people every year. Apart from one Welsh college (The Hill at Abergavenny), they were all in England. There were no comparable colleges in Scotland, although Newbattle Abbey did provide some short-term residential courses and two residential centres were opened in the 1960s in Midlothian and at Scottish Church House,

Dunblane, but they were not intended for general liberal adult education. A number of Scottish local authorities opened purely in-service residential centres, and the Scottish universities became increasingly willing to offer their student residences for short-term courses during the vacation (Scottish Education Department, 1975: 12).

The Russell Report recognised the short-term residential colleges' value as experimenters and pioneers in a wide variety of forms of adult education, and the advantages of the concentration of effort and the opportunities for informal group discussion that they provided; but also noted the tendency for colleges to lack a central purpose and for their programmes to 'approach the ephemeral' at times. Legge (1982: 80) similarly noted (amongst a number of positive educational values associated with these colleges) the tendency for the courses to be 'shallow and too short to allow for systematic study' and lacking coherence. But despite these weaknesses the Russell report recommended continued LEA support for the short-term colleges and the examination of the need for new colleges on a regional basis. It also recommended appropriate salary scales be established for the principals and wardens of the colleges (DES, 1973: xiii, xx, 45). But it failed to endorse the other points made in the submission of the Wardens, including the need for better staff and student accommodation, for an improvement in teaching facilities and equipment, and for adequate finance to publicise the work of the colleges nationally.

Even the two recommendations that did find their way into the Russell Report fell foul of the general economic crisis after 1973. Indeed, by then the growth in short-term residential adult education had more or less come to an end. Following local government reorganisation in 1974, the new authorities did examine the need for short-term colleges, but generally only in financial, not educational terms. The majority of colleges were administered by LEAs and over the years their support had risen to between 40 and 60 per cent of the total running costs. Wardens were now told to increase their income and aim for financial self-sufficiency. This led to fee increases (at variable rates, depending on local circumstances) and the adoption of a more market-oriented approach to managing the colleges. In some colleges, high educational standards were sacrificed at times for fiscal gain. With the retirement of wardens or principals, some were replaced by managers at a much reduced salary and with job specifications that reflected fiscal rather than educational objectives.

At the same time a number of universities, also under financial pressure (see Chapter 8), terminated their close links with the colleges.

A comparison of the general adult education curricula offered by the colleges in the period 1945–50 with the 1990s reveals great similarities. They remained rooted in the ideas of Richard Livingstone and Ross Waller. But the deteriorating economic climate brought about other changes. Reduced training budgets in the service sector led to a decline in residential in-service training. Some colleges promoted their own training sessions for industry or commerce, or increasingly offered their facilities to outside organisations to run their own conferences and seminars. This became the norm during the 1980s. But this move into the commercial conference market necessitated an improvement in the standard of accommodation which in turn led to higher charges, not only for the commercial customers, but also for the general public. This, of course, made them even less accessible to the less-well-off (Harris-Worthington, 1987: 24–5).

Most of the colleges survived by diversifying, but not always in the best interests of general liberal adult education. No new colleges opened after 1975, but some 17 have closed since 1955. The great majority of these closures occurred after the mid-1970s. Financial problems were the major reason for closure, but there were other contributory causes in some instances: the lack of an academic warden or principal; failure to establish good relations with the local community which could lead to hostility and complaints to local councillors which translated into opposition votes when the question of continuation came up; poor standing with county officers and elected members, which had the same effect; internal conflict of ideology (which led to an impasse and consequent closure of Kingsgate, the YMCA college); local government reform in 1974 which led to the closure of two colleges which found themselves the weaker of two in an enlarged authority; and the inability of some wardens, appointed for their educational expertise, to develop sufficient entrepreneurial skills. In some cases a warden, after many years of service and tired and worn out, was ready to accept early retirement rather than adopt new managerial skills, and this accelerated the closure of a college.

Nevertheless, despite all the problems and financial cuts faced by these colleges in the 1980s and 90s, the principals established an Adult Residential Colleges Association to promote their own training sessions, monitor standards, share the results of experiments with new ideas, and plan for the future. In the mid-1990s some 100,000 students *per annum* attended courses at these colleges, paying almost the full economic cost for them, thus testifying to the continuing demand for short-term residential adult education.

## Non-Residential Settlements and Centres

The university settlements which were founded during the last two decades of the nineteenth century were forerunners of the twentieth century non-residential centres. They were founded on the belief that settling educated middle-class residents amongst the working class of the big cities would be beneficial to both, bringing them closer together through better understanding, although in practice they tended to be dominated by bourgeois liberal values, with little appreciation of the distinctive working class cultural traditions. (See Chapter 2.) During the early twentieth century these university settlements continued their mixture of education and social enquiry, and several new ones were established. By 1926 there were 56 such settlements, 41 of them in London. They increasingly became centres for LEA, WEA and university classes, but also housed a great deal of informal educational activity, particularly music and drama, as well as being active in voluntary social work (Meacham, 1987: 111–29; Kelly, 1992: 261, 279). Indeed, the settlements posed an interesting dichotomy of voluntaryism versus state aid, illustrated by the case of Toynbee Hall which inherited the self-help, voluntary ethos of the nineteenth century Charity Organisation Society, but gradually forged closer links with the State at both local and central level. However, the underlying philosophy of voluntaryism and mutual aid was never forsaken, and in the 1950s became more dominant again, reflecting the growing disillusionment with Toynbee's close association with the welfare state. Briggs and Macartney (1984: 176) suggest that every kind of official support enjoyed by Toynbee Hall had made it 'increasingly difficult, as the year went by, to reach grassroots opinion' and therefore voluntary action was being canvassed once more.

Closely related to the university settlements, but also springing from the alliance between the Adult School Movement and the Quakers which had given rise to Woodbrooke and Fircroft residential colleges, was the foundation of eight non-residential settlements in the north of England during the first two decades of the twentieth century. They were intended as friendly centres for adult education in an atmosphere of fellowship. They shared many common features with the university settlements, but they were less overtly concerned with social work and reform: they were more properly educational. But they also had a strong spiritual basis. Their aim was 'to help men and women to enter fully into life, to be of service to the world ... to have wide interests and large views ... In other words it is to lead men (sic) out of the insular, the secular and the personal into the wider expansiveness of the Kingdom of God'. The essence of the educational settlement movement was classless fellowship: to lead people 'from their bondage to sect, party or class, and become members of a family' (Kelly, 1992: 261–5). It therefore had no room for the kind of adult education that aimed to provide the working class with the intellectual tools to wage war against their bourgeois oppressors.

In 1920 an Educational Settlements Association was founded and four years later the British Institute of Adult Education published a report entitled *The Guild House*, which proposed that each town and cluster of villages should have a centre for adult education. Although this goal was never achieved, several new non-residential settlements or centres were established during the 1920s and '30s. By 1939 there were 27 settlements and seven colleges affiliated to the Association. Their joint programme for 1938/9 consisted of 767 classes with nearly 15,000 students. About two-fifths of this programme was organised by the settlements themselves: the remainder consisted of 279 LEA classes, 76 WEA classes, 51 university classes and 44 YMCA short courses. Rather like religious houses in the middle ages, not all the settlements were able to maintain their original aims, but were driven by practical necessities to become all-purpose adult education centres, and providers of accommodation for a wide range of activities including, in some instances, paliatives for the unemployed (*ibid.*: 277–9; Stewart, Reynolds and Elsdon, 1992: 6).

Although there was no such thing as a typical non-residential centre, the Percival Guildhouse in Rugby, opened in 1925, is a good example. On a typically modest budget it soon became a lively centre for educational, cultural and social activities. Its educational programme included classes provided by the Adult School, the WEA, Birmingham University, the Educational Settlements Association and the LEA. In its early days it made a distinctive contribution to the cultural life of Rugby, but it later became heavily dependent on LEA funding, and dominated by its local authority programme, at least until the LEA grant aid was withdrawn in 1977. This caused the centre to make its warden redundant and threatened it with closure, but it continued to be run by voluntary effort (ibid.: 5–33).

In 1946 the Educational Settlements Association was transformed into the Educational Centres Association. Like the residential colleges, the post-war development of non-residential centres was heavily influenced by Richard Livingstone's advocacy of suitable and attractive centres for adult learning. For some years after the war there was little money to fund such centres, but a number of universities did use their resources to establish centres either independently or in conjunction with the LEAs. Leicester University's Vaughan College was a particularly successful development, but it was the Nottingham University Extramural Department, under the influence of Harold Wiltshire, which was the most prolific in establishing centres in Boston, Matlock, Loughborough, Lincoln, Stamford and Derby, as well as Nottingham. Wiltshire believed that centres should be devoted exclusively to adults in contrast to the all-age, all-purpose community colleges advocated by Henry Morris (see Chapter 5) (Champion, 1976).

Some LEAs, such as Kent, were also successful in establishing adult education centres in the years after the Second World War. They were located in converted houses, redundant schools, one-time Mechanics' Institutes, empty chapels, pubs, warehouses, factories, or anywhere where premises could be obtained cheaply. Other authorities established adult education centres within their community schools or colleges. By 1967–8 the Educational Centres Association encompassed more than 40 non-residential centres accommodating over 5,000 classes, the great majority of which were provided by LEAs. There was also a large number of community centres and village halls which provided facilities for adult education, mostly of a more informal, social and recreational nature (Kelly, 1992: 287–90). By 1984 the number of centres affiliated to the Association had increased to 150, catering for some 400,000 students (THES, 9 September 1984); and five years later it was claimed that the Association's centres accommodated one-fifth of all non-vocational adult students (Stephens, 1990: 86–7).

But with financial pressures mounting during the 1970s and 80s, the providers of classes at the centres (the LEAs, the universities and the WEA) became increasingly unable or unwilling to pay the extra costs or subscriptions involved in accommodating their classes in these centres. They began to rely more on their own premises or look for alternative accommodation which did not involve a subscription. This trend was exacerbated by the 1992 Further and Higher Education Act, which left LEAs even less well placed to fund the centres. Many had their grants drastically reduced, such as the Bristol Folk House, one of the earliest centres, which saw its £60,000 grant from Avon LEA reduced to virtually nothing. Like many centres, it was left to the vagaries of appeals, donations and having to charge full-cost fees in order to survive (*THES*, 10 March 1995).

*10*

# Independent Working Class Education and Trade Union Education and Training

## *John McIlroy*

In numbers of students and sustained provision Independent working Class Education (IWCE) never matched the work of the university-WEA alliance. It was for more than a decade tremendously influential and for more than half a century a familiar feature of the landscape, with strong roots in the Labour movement. Commonly associated with the Socialist agitators of the early years of the century, the movement provided through the 1920s an arena for the autodidactic tradition and anchorage for the pre-Popular Front tradition of intellectual Marxism. In the 1930s A.J.P. Taylor, V. Gordon Childe and Harold Laski taught for the National Council of Labour Colleges (NCLC). Proletarian novelists Lewis Jones and Harold Heslop studied at the Central Labour College (CLC). The thinning thread spanned the century. The key union leaders of the 1970s, Jack Jones and Hugh Scanlon, were graduates of NCLC classes. In the 1980s Neil Kinnock recalled attending NCLC classes with men who studied with Aneurin Bevan (Harris, 1984: 32).

IWCE is important as a creative movement from below, a sustained attempt by workers to control their own education in opposition to what they perceived as an externally imposed and hostile state curriculum. If it was always a minority movement struggling against the current, its real significance as a suppressed, alternative adult education should be recognised and critically addressed. The IWCE tradition requires reclaiming, to echo Edward Thompson, from the condescension of adult educators, and the romantic inflation of left intellectuals.

## *IWCE: Its development and decline*

The roots of IWCE lay in the classes developed by the Social Democratic Federation (later British Socialist Party (BSP)) and the Socialist Labour Party (SLP). Both emphasised the centrality of education in making socialists. Classes centred on Marxist economics and history. The SLP paid particular attention to pedagogy, organising study circles, correspondence courses and even examinations (Bell, 1941; Simon, 1965: 318–42; Challinor, 1977: 113–118). IWCE's early lineage ran from the Marxist study classes James Connolly organised in Scotland in 1903 through their tutors, such as William Paul, who was prominent in the Plebs League, the SLP, the Communist Party and the NCLC until the 1930s. IWCE's early historians acknowledged IWCE's organic relationship to the anti-capitalist militancy of 1900–21, symbolised by

Noah Ablett's role as midwife of IWCE *and* author of *The Miners' Next Step* –
the first major union manifesto supporting the replacement of capitalism by
workers' control of industry. And so have their successors (Paul and Paul,
1921: 53–4; Horrabin and Horrabin, 1924: 60; Kendall, 1969).

The inception of a distinct non-party but explicitly political IWCE as a
response to the increased state intervention heralded by the 1908 *Oxford
Report* was the product of events at Ruskin College 1908–9 (see Chapter 9).
The consequent dismissal of the socialist Principal Dennis Hird produced a
boycott of lectures and the creation in August 1909 of the CLC as an
alternative to Ruskin (Jennings, 1977; Yorke, 1977; Lewis, 1993: 48–90). The
CLC foregrounded independence and the need to equip students for class
struggle. Students were funded by scholarships from the unions, notably the
National Union of Railwaymen (NUR) and the South Wales Miners
Federation (SWMF) and the management committee was comprised of union
representatives. By 1914 the residential college was established, if in a fragile
way, and it was stating explicitly that its curriculum was 'grounded on a
Marxist basis':

[It] teaches the workmen to look for the causes of social evils and the problems
arising therefrom in the material foundations of society; that these causes are in
the last resort economic; that their elimination involves in the first place
economic changes of such a character as to lead to the eradication of capitalist
economy (W.W. Craik quoted in Ministry of Reconstruction, 1919: 222–3).

Broadening out from a grouping of ex-Ruskin students, the Plebs League
established local evening classes to complement the work of the CLC. Plebs
League and CLC extension classes co-existed with those of the BSP and SLP.
Students covered the spectrum of the labour movement and whilst
economics and history were central there were also classes in philosophy,
literature and English. Labour movement bodies often financed the classes
and the term 'labour college' with its antagonistic emulation of orthodox
education began to denote the nuclei of local activists involved in their
organisation. *The Plebs Magazine* ceaselessly argued the case for IWCE and
remorselessly criticised the WEA and the role of the state. Progress was
strengthened by the increase in union membership and intensification of
militancy from 1910 and the growth of support for industrial unionism and
rank and file control of unions and industry, rounding out in some cases to
syndicalism, but generally to a growth in class consciousness (Holton, 1976).
Reflecting on *The Miners' Next Step* and the creation of the NUR, Craik noted:
'A new kind of trade unionism became identified with a new kind of trade
union education' (Craik, 1964: 94).

By 1914 bridgeheads had been established in South Wales, Lancashire
and the North East. Scotland was dominated by BSP and SLP classes. But
progress was slower than is sometimes imagined. There were only 300
students in Plebs League classes in 1910 and the circulation of the magazine
remained at under 1,000. There was 'a heavy financial cloud hanging over
the League' and the immediate pre-war period was 'the most critical in the
[Central] College's existence, time after time it appeared as though we must
close down' (*Plebs*, 1914: 170).

In 1917 the college was forced to close 'for the duration'. By then
protracted negotiations had ensured its takeover by the NUR and SWMF

and when it reopened in 1919 its future seemed secure. Moreover the wartime militancy and the impact of the Russian Revolution was reflected in a qualitative expansion of the local classes. In 1917 1200 students were attending classes in South Wales and in Scotland there were 36 classes with 2,500 students (Ministry of Reconstruction, 1919: 291). By the end of hostilities IWCE had outstripped the WEA in these areas and was exercising a real influence in the labour movement nationally (Roberts, 1970; Duncan, 1992; Lewis, 1993: 111–41).

Its élan was reinforced by government reports identifying its work with the industrial unrest. The key leaders of the war-time shop stewards movement Tom Bell, Arthur McManus and J.T. Murphy were active in the Plebs League. In 1920 King George himself expressed concern about the Labour Colleges to the President of the Board of Education (Dean, 1971: 157–8). The WEA's attempts to benefit from the situation can be seen in the establishment of WETUC and communications to the Cabinet Office suggesting the important role it could play in curbing the study of Marxism (Commission of Enquiry into Industrial Unrest, 1916: 23–4; Public Record Office (PRO), 1917 CAB24/57, GT6792). The Directorate of Intelligence reports in 1919–20 described the CLC as 'the fountainhead of Marxian teaching in this country ... responsible for the training of more dangerous revolutionaries than all the Communist parties put together'. They deplored the weakness of the WEA: 'Unfortunately almost the only agency in the field is the Labour Colleges which is imparting instruction in false economics' (PRO, 1920, CAB24/96, CP462, CAB24/96, CP491).

This concurred with the estimation of the revolutionary pedagogues themselves. John McLean observed in 1917:

The greatest 'crime' I have committed in the eyes of the British government and the Scottish capitalist class has been the teaching of Marxian economics to the Scottish workers (McLean, 1917: 124).

In some ways this was the climacteric of IWCE. Although formal advance continued until 1927 it reflected the dissipation of the revolutionary mood of 1919–21, defensive militancy and a labour movement increasingly at odds with IWCE's radical dynamic. *Plebs* was selling 6,000 copies monthly. The publications department of the League established in 1917 sold more than 25,000 copies of pamphlets such as *What Does Education Mean to the Workers?* and its first short book, Mark Starr's *A Worker Looks at History* (1917), an accessible and considerable contribution to 'history from below'. Noah Ablett's *Easy Outline of Economics* (1919) also enjoyed a wide circulation. There was an attempt to adapt curriculum and method to meet the needs of a burgeoning audience. Classes moved from 24 evenings to 12 evenings and there were more trade union lectures and day schools. The League increased its membership to 800 in 30 branches attracting a layer of political intellectuals. With the classes still increasing the question of their co-ordination was raised.

The CLC was the natural body to take on this task. It demonstrated a lack of interest which together with concern about its curriculum and efficiency produced motions of censure and a Commission of Enquiry. Many already saw the leftism of the Plebs League as a liability in winning wider support. In consequence in 1922 a new organisation the NCLC was created with representation from the local colleges, the CLC, the League and affiliated unions.

The formation of the NCLC heralded a new phase. In the early years the labour movement was relatively plastic, the propagandistic cast of labour politics enabled IWCE to work across the spectrum. From 1921 recession and defeat took radical change off the agenda (Hinton and Hyman, 1975). The growing hegemony of Labourism produced bureaucratising tendencies and the marginalising of Marxism. The 'syndicalist challenge' was transmuted into Labourism or a sectarian Communism soon to be Stalinised (see, for example, Price, 1986: 135–74; Foote, 1986: 85–101). IWCE was squeezed between these tendencies. Many of its cadres joined the Communist Party (CP) in 1920–1, although they soon found it uncongenial and left. Their continued involvement in politics from the Minority Movement through to the Socialist League, as well as the continued presence in IWCE of CP members, sustained conflict with those hostile to a Leninist Party asserting a monopoly on Marxism. The latter group drew increasingly closer to the Labour Party and viewed left activism as a barrier to permeation of the unions (McIntyre, 1980: 78–85; Miles, 1984; Rée, 1984). Yet the failure to create a unified scheme under TUC aegis ensured the NCLC survived as a separate entity (Fieldhouse, 1981; Millar, 1979: 61–76).

The NCLC's drive towards the unions led by J.P.M. Millar was increasingly on the basis of adapting to them rather than transforming them (McIlroy, 1990a,b; McIlroy and Simon, 1991). On the model of WETUC, schemes were provided for unions across the political spectrum. They enabled members in return for an affiliation fee to attend classes with special courses being offered for branches or districts. The rationale for the NCLC had been co-ordination of the work of autonomous colleges. But the growth of national schemes with unions with affiliations paid to head office strengthened the leadership and the development of centralised organisation. So did the appointment of full-time organisers and the development of correspondence courses. The Amalgamated Union of Building Workers was the NCLC's first affiliation. By 1926, 32 unions with almost two million members had affiliated and the conflicts leading up to the decisive defeat in the 1926 General Strike propelled the classes forward.

The Plebs League asserted its continued mission to ensure the principles of IWCE were not diluted and to act as a think-tank and debating forum for the left. In the aftermath of 1926 it was in serious financial difficulties. Millar and Hamilton who viewed it as a political embarrassment and possible opening for the CP sought assimilation of this 'clique of intellectuals' and control over its press (National Library of Scotland, Acc 5120, Box 1, NCLC Correspondence; Millar, 1979: 86–7). Some in the League, its secretary accepted,

were taking the questions under discussion rather further than was good for the NCLC. The NCLC must keep the support of the Trade Unions and to have groups criticising the working class political parties does make life difficult (Horrabin, 1926: 322).

In 1927 the publications were taken over by the NCLC and the League transformed into the 'Plebs and NCLC Students Association'. This was stillborn and the last rites were read on 1 October 1930. Still suspicious of the

IWCE left, Millar transferred the head office from Edinburgh to London and increasingly exercised greater influence over *Plebs* than his co-editor Frank Horrabin – assuming full responsibility in 1932. The end of the League and the subordination of the left eroded much that was creative in IWCE, its radical inspiration and its conscience.

The NCLC's dominance was assured with the closure in 1929 of the CLC, its demise speeded by the decline in union membership and the problems facing the NUR and SWMF. The NUR's support had never been wholehearted and the inability of many blacklisted CLC graduates to return to their jobs raised the question of why residential education should be prioritised when evening classes could be provided for more people and more cheaply. In exploiting this Millar and his supporters were aided by disillusion with the CLC. Its staff were viewed by critics as inadequate, its curriculum academic: 'the college was not therefore a source of strength to the movement at the present time' (Woolf, 1922: 278; Starr, 1924: 77). Problems were exacerbated by unresponsiveness to student protests and the activities of Communist students. The lack of application of the principal and secretary Craik and George Sims culminated in misappropriation of funds, embarrassing IWCE in the labour movement (McIntyre, 1980: 83–5; McIlroy, 1980; Lewis, 1984: 156ff).

The NCLC's course was now set towards the established leadership although the closure of the CLC constituted a continuing problem in terms of renewal of tutors. By the mid 1930s 36 unions had schemes although the number of classes and students declined from the high point, in 1927, to 728 classes with 13,000 students in 1936. Whilst some of the more ambitious schemes, such as establishment of a research department, never got off the ground the correspondence courses grew from under 10 per cent of students in 1930 to 30 per cent in 1939. This was accompanied by a move to more practical training, with more courses in English, writing skills, public speaking and branch administration and emphasis on current affairs. Nonetheless classes in Marxism continued and history and economics continued to inform the programme. Particular attention was paid to Fascism and German refugee socialists found a home in the NCLC. The sympathetic hearing initially accorded Trotskyism and opposition to Popular Frontism ensured no rapprochement took place with the CP which as it grew in the 1930s felt little need for the NCLC. IWCE, at the heart of Marxism in Britain in earlier decades, was peripheral to its blossoming amongst intellectuals in the 1930s. The CP established its own alternative at Marx House and marked the divide by its designation of the Labour Colleges as 'a Trotskyist organisation' and finally 'an agent of Fascism' (Branson, 1985: 245).

Warfare with the WEA continued unabated while the NCLC was scarred by bitter, protracted internal conflicts. Grassroots autonomy was undermined and internal democracy limited. Millar's control was consolidated by links with Labour Party and union leaders and constitutional changes (rejected in principle in earlier years) which disqualified staff from the executive and institutionalised union dominance over the colleges by a block vote based on fees (Cohen, 1990: 109ff; Ellis, 1937). The NCLC still represented the tradition of IWCE (Cohen, 1990: 118) but with its radical activist edge blunted. Yet its identification with Marxism meant it had many enemies. The NUR leadership fought unsuccessfully against affiliation in 1930. In the TGWU Bevin had no time for the NCLC but was willing to give it token support 'to keep everyone happy' (Topham, 1992: 53). This was the attitude of many leaders. Certainly the active support IWCE received from George Hicks of the Building Workers or John Jagger of the Shop Workers Union was not replenished. The wartime move of the Head Office back to Scotland underlined the NCLC's move away from the centre of affairs and the ascendancy of the correspondence courses.

The post-war years saw terminal decline. Marxism was marginalised by Cold War, boom and consensus. Separate attempts in the 1940s to secure a takeover of the NCLC by the Labour Party and the TUC came to nothing. Educational expansion was undermining the NCLC's remedial role, the unions were turning to their own provision. Failure to gain affiliation from the two largest unions, the TGWU and GMWU, was accompanied by key disaffiliations in 1955–6 from the South Wales Miners and USDAW on the respective grounds that the NCLC was no longer providing Marxist education and that it failed to provide value for money. Sizeable unions wanted their own schemes. The purpose of the NCLC was increasingly to provide a small scale service on the unions' terms with a curriculum centred on organisational techniques and current affairs (Clegg and Adams, 1959: 43–5; Craik, 1964: 156–7). A remnant of 'the socialist forum' role provided an occasional base for left-wing activists (Martindall, 1964: 464–5). The NCLC's own Marxism was emblematic, support for the Labour Party and union leadership axiomatic and uncritical (McIlroy, 1990c). An ageing leadership was not renewed and the struggle to generate resources and compete with the universities and WEA was unremitting and unequal. By 1957, when an NCLC initiative again committed the TUC to a co-ordinated scheme, the NCLC was still running 782 classes with 11,625 students but much of its provision was slight and its statistics questioned. The formal takeover by the TUC in 1964 represented the extinction of an exhausted vein of socialist pedagogy.

## Ideology and the State

IWCE was based on the belief that the state was simply an instrument of the capitalist class. It adhered to a functional Marxism without contradictions in which the education system necessarily served only the interests of capital, unproblematically propagating bourgeois ideology and the reproduction of the division of labour. IWCE-ers did not need to wait for the publication of Lenin's *The State and Revolution* in Britain in 1919 or even William Paul's *The State: Its origin and function* (1917) to grasp this. Already in the first issues of *Plebs* Noah Ablett had pronounced permeation of state education by labour as 'ridiculous' (Ablett, 1909: 7). It was necessary for education to be controlled by the workers themselves for 'those who control education practically control our actions' (CLC, 1913). State support for the WEA was correctly viewed as part of wider social policy but its impact were overestimated, its contradictions and concessions ignored.

Dialectical conceptions of state education, with the degree to which capitalist values were received or rejected determined by struggle, were eschewed. Little attention was paid to the concessions the state had already made to Labour. IWCE was pessimistic about the degree to which educators could shape change through conscious organisation. It was unduly optimistic about the alienation of the working class, its receptivity to Marxism, its willingness to incorporate the new education into its dense associative culture. The majority of union leaders and cadres and the infant Labour Party did not share IWCE's analysis of the inherent bias of the state: they wanted more education, were not convinced of its class nature and saw the state as its natural provider.

We must not be ahistorical: more sophisticated analysis was not available. Moreover abstentionist views were not all pervasive. As early as 1917 Mark Starr argued that the movement should exploit local authority support (Starr, 1917a). For the leadership, IWCE's success, state surveillance, the support given to the WEA, as well as their awareness of the controls attached to state funds, justified their continued rejection. In 1923 the NCLC stated its willingness to accept grant aid on condition that there was no interference with its policy (*Plebs*, 1923: 194). There is little doubt that this would have been unacceptable to the state (Fieldhouse, 1981). When the NCLC *did* mount classes with local authority support in the 1920s the HMIs sought to have them taken over by the WEA or closed down (Simon, 1990: 55).

For most of its history there was little chance the state would have been prepared to fund much of its work. The siege mentality was reinforced by the refusal to allow it the place accorded the WEA on the Central Council for Broadcasting Adult Education and the ruling that civil service unions could finance the WEA but not the NCLC. All this strengthened IWCE's sense of exclusion, 'of how every part of the state machine is used against the Labour movement' (Millar, 1929: 66). Attempts in the 1930s to use local authority facilities again resulted in closure of classes (Brown, 1980: 115). When the issue came up for review under the 1945 Labour government, it was not pushed, for to start paying tutors to attract grant would involve more expenditure than would be saved in subsidy (McIlroy, 1990c: 190).

By this time theory was in internal disarray. Millar was arguing that the state was no longer capitalist, 'the capitalists in Britain haven't the power of the state at their disposal. That is in the hands of the Labour movement' (Millar, 1948: 97). But apparently the nature of the state no longer determined the nature of state education. For he also continued to argue that education 'whether it is provided by the school, the university, or the workers' organisation that collaborates with the university is part and parcel of the defensive mechanism of the capitalist system' (Millar, 1951: 3). The politics of the leadership were now conducted on the basis that the state was neutral. They remained imprisoned in an ideology dysfunctional to those politics.

IWCE asserted itself as a holistic educational philosophy. In 1918 IWCE intellectuals Eden and Cedar Paul pointed to the ideological role of elementary education and its impact on adult education:

Why should Labour not interpret Independent Working Class Education as meaning infant education and elementary school education as well as the teaching of socialist history and socialist economics to those who have outgrown the school age? (Paul and Paul, 1918: 6; Paul and Paul, 1921).

The Pauls were in a minority. IWCE-ers were constrained by limited resources and a confused estimation of schooling as at once too powerful to combat and as bearing minimal ideological impact in comparison with adult education (cf. Kean, 1990: 34ff). Thus despite occasional interventions in the Labour Party, Independent Labour Party and TUC (see, for example, Millar, 1979: 85) only the narrow ground of workers' adult education was contested. The content of schooling was periodically scrutinised (Starr, 1929; Millar and Woodburn, 1936). There were links with the Teachers Labour League. But IWCE never developed any programme for change (but see, for example, ILP, 1931). Meanwhile the movement IWCE sought to transform sought greater access to state education. And the early views that school teachers were 'helpless' to escape their role as purveyors of bourgeois ideology and that 'no working class student can undergo a university education and come through untainted' (Plebs, 1909a: 44) were revised piecemeal (Millar, 1943).

IWCE-ers who were involved in wider educational reform seemed conventionally more concerned with access than content. Meredith Titterington, one of the Ruskin strikers moved the 'Bradford Charter' at the 1917 Labour Party conference, novel in its advocacy of comprehensive secondary education, traditional in its neglect of curriculum (Simon, 1965: 347–50). Ellen Wilkinson, still a staunch supporter when she became Minister of Education in 1945, saw little connection between IWCE theory and practical politics (Simon, 1991: 96–115; Vernon, 1982: 204). Outside the domain of workers' education ideology was rarely a guide to action.

Other components of IWCE ideology, 'independence from the state' and 'working class control' were also problematic. For Ablett the emphasis on union control of IWCE was shorthand for *rank and file control* located in the strategy for transforming the labour movement outlined in *The Miners' Next Step*: IWCE was an essential weapon in the struggle to reconstruct the unions: education was organic to action. The practical problem of gaining sponsorship from leaders who were far from radical led to emphasis on the structural independence of IWCE rather than its transformative Marxist epistemology and its immediate, practical utility rather than its revolutionary objectives. The tensions between IWCE as the custodian of Marxism and opponent of conservative union leaders and IWCE as the educational arm of the *existing* labour movement, and between IWCE as a think tank for the left and IWCE as a school for equipping activists across a movement often antagonistic to the left, became more pronounced. Broad, vague statements of philosophy accompanied the growing ascendancy of Millar. In 1923 NCLC defined its objectives as:

The education of the workers from the working class point of view. In other words the provision of Independent Working Class Education, not merely controlled by the workers but of a working class character.

This flabby workerism was designed to possess a broad appeal as demonstrated when some sought to formally identify its content and character with Marxism. This was forcefully opposed by the executive and defeated (*Plebs*, 1925: 264–5). This symbolised the subordinate role Marxism was to subsequently play as a guide to action.

As early as 1915 Ablett had warned against the danger of union leaders 'who take a severely practical view of things' interfering with the Marxist basis of the curriculum (Ablett, 1915: 78). By the 1920s, defeat consolidated the control of these 'severely practical men', in Labour Party and unions. IWCE increasingly centred its ideology on freedom from the state and consequent contamination, rather than on a Marxism hostile to the labour bureaucracy. By escaping the state it did not solve the dilemmas of educational autonomy. Its primitive conception of internal conflict in the Labour movement based on a fault line between leadership and rank and file, with IWCE as the tool of an insurgent rank and file, faded. It was never replaced by a more mature address of the conflicts that did exist.

## Curriculum and Pedagogy

IWCE struggled to create a curriculum that went beyond absorption of the sacred texts. By the early 1920s the Horrabins classified its content as:

1. Elementary education for the rank and file of the workers' movement aiming at giving a sound grasp of broad essential facts and principles.
2. More advanced education for the minority who desire and are able to carry their studies further.
3. The training of tutors.
4. The training in the technical detail of their work of trade union organisers and officials, labour propagandists etc (Horrabin and Horrabin, 1924: 75).

The basis of elementary education was working class history and the development of modern capitalism. This should be followed by work in economic geography, psychology and the science of reasoning. Technical training included Branch Administration, Public Speaking, Electioneering and Trade Union Law (NCLC, 1923). English, Statistics and Esperanto also figured in a curriculum which strove to integrate theoretical understanding and technical expertise.

It still embodied a limited view of the knowledge required for emancipation. The strenuous attempts by Lyster Jameson and the Pauls to develop psychology were faltering by the mid 1920s. The study of literature was recommended by intellectuals and autodidacts and at times classes were in demand (*Plebs*, 1929: 120). It was generally seen as an adjunct to social studies and a means of attracting new students (Dana, 1925). A debate at the 1925 Plebs Meet demonstrated the depth of opposition. Workers took exception to 'purely cultural subjects as a waste of time' and argued '... they did not attract workers but brought in middle class dilettantes' (*Plebs*, 1925: 402–3). The study of literature never took root. Those like the Pauls who sought to push IWCE in the direction of an alternative cultural formation were marginalised after 1926.

IWCE's Marxism was cast in a propagandistic and determinist vein; accusations that its teaching was catechetical and abstract dogged IWCE from its inception (see, for example, Williams, 1915). Even sympathisers felt its classes produced 'a curiously academic view of life ... The secret of education surely lies in the power to relate what is learnt in the classroom to what happens in the streets' (Mellor, 1920: 135). IWCE leaders faced with catering for raw students often agreed. Academicism had to be confronted by addressing the three fundamental questions together: 'What the present position of the workers as a class is? *How* and *Why* it came to be so? *How* the workers can alter it?' (Horrabin, 1921: 3; Horrabin and Horrabin, 1924: 76). The difficulties were immense. Fred Casey has left us a vivid portrait of the realities of devising an effective method of teaching where the majority found it hard to follow detailed argument and often dropped out of the class (Casey, 1920).

There was however a continuing attempt to address current issues. The examination papers of the CLC, an institution often justly accused of academicism, contained questions on immediate strategy and union policy (Phillips and Putnam, 1980: 26). Postgate, Dobb, Jackson, Walton Newbold, Philips Price, sought to develop IWCE's understanding of changing capitalism. The Pauls attempted to raise wider questions of counter culture and draw on experience in the USSR and Germany. Whatever their inadequacies, the debates on philosophy demonstrated a desire to develop 'the science of thinking' (Rée, 1984). Nonetheless some still complained of 'pedants who saw education as a matter of memorising pages of Marx' (*Plebs*, 24, 8). For many still believed with William Paul that the aim was: 'whenever a working class head shows itself to strike with the club of independent working class education'. As Postgate remarked the result was: 'glassy-eyed paralytic silence of the students as if they had indeed been struck by a club' (Postgate, 1931: 5).

Such approaches were unlikely to develop students who could think and exercise leadership and some lamented 'we have not yet evolved a scientific system of socialist pedagogy' (Marcy, 1922: 295–6). Yet we must be careful of too black and white a contrast between a lecture-based IWCE and a discussion-based WEA (Brown, 1980: 119–20) Postgate's own classes stirred 'fierce debate' (Wicks, 1992: 33). From the early days IWCE leaflets urged that 'question and discussion time should be ample' and recommended study circles (Starr, 1917b). Fred Casey emphasised that tutors should stimulate questions by limiting explanations (Casey, 1920). Frank Phippen argued lecturing should be related to current issues and tutors should discuss learning methods with students (Phippen, 1921). There was argument as to whether lectures were outdated and discussion groups preferable. The need to draw on experience in the USSR and labour colleges in the USA was emphasised. Tutors were told to make the student a direct participant: 'never draw a conclusion the class can draw ... The teacher who answers the questions for the class without giving them a chance commits a crime' (Millar, 1922: 44). In consequence it was claimed in the early 1920s that classes

tend to an increasing extent to depart from the old idea of set courses of lectures conducted by throned or pulpitted 'experts' ... They are discussion classes' (Paul and Paul, 1921: 124).

This overestimates the demise of the lecturer. One experienced IWCE-er who visited a number of classes in 1924–5 found that, despite the advice in *Plebs* that revolutionary pedagogues should not treat workers, as the capitalists did, as 'empty vessels into which we pour our preconceived ideas' (Marcy, 1922: 295), 'the pulpitted expert' was still alive and kicking. Some classes involved 'not lectures at all but a series of denunciatory tirades' which stimulated phrasemongering not thinking (Williams, 1924).

There was diversity across classes and between IWCE and the WEA. Students in Lancashire in the 1930s who attended Labour College and WEA classes found discussion more vigorous and informal in the former (Cohen, 1990: 114). The Plebs League held conferences in the 1920s on teaching methods and textbooks and there was insistence on reading and writing in classes (Horrabin, 1929; Millar, 1930). The Pauls wrote in *Plebs* on the use of public libraries, Postgate on researching history. Classes were encouraged to research their employers (Paul and Paul, 1927; Postgate, 1926; Glyn Evans, 1927). The fact that the majority of tutors were unpaid and lacked training constituted a problem, particularly after the closure of the CLC. To combat this a series of annual 'training centres' were mounted enduring from the 1920s through the 1950s. The first in 1925 was an impressive event, three weeks at the CLC with courses taught by Dobb, Postgate, Jackson and Starr, a mix of conventional and worker intellectuals, lectures by union leaders, such as Alonzo Swales and George Hicks and intensive demonstration and criticism classes where aspirant tutors were put through their paces. Within the constraining framework of the belief that transmission of 'the pure and undefiled gospel of Marxism would of itself solve all problems' (Mellor, 1920: 134–5) there was a serious attempt to develop an active precursive pedagogy of workers' control of the classroom.

## Gender and Ethnicity

IWCE was strongly based on the working class: a large majority of students were manual workers and its staff were largely from that background (Millar, 1979: 195). Female shop assistants were told by fellow students they were not 'real workers': in a world of patriarchy the internal divisions of labourism were replicated in IWCE (Whittam, 1929: 117). The attempts by Mrs Bridge Adams between 1909–12 to establish a Women's Labour College were stamped with some of the assertion of the pre-1914 movement. She emphasised the need to develop women activists in the unions, inquiring '... where are the sisters of the young men who are doing such good work for their class in South Wales?' (Bridge Adams, 1912: 163). Her efforts were unsuccessful and gave way to the Women's League of the CLC which embraced socialists such as Dora Montefiore of the BSP and Rebecca West of *The Clarion*, as well as women trade unionists such as Grace Neal, General Secretary of the Domestic Workers Union. It was urged that 'the education of our working class women is just as important as that of the working class men'. But the role of the League was seen as subordinate and ancillary: to raise funds, establish a women's hostel and enrol more women students. Women were involved in cooking, cleaning and organising social events at the college (*Plebs*, 1909b: 188; Atkins, 1981: 78–9).

Members of the League believed education would help women out of the home and into industry and the unions. It would open their eyes to the way capitalism used them as cheap labour, strike breakers and a brake on working class progress. Little attention was paid to feminist arguments and women's specific oppression. There was no sex war only class war; men were as much its victims as women. Women's subordinate role within the working class was essentially taken as given (Brown, 1915: 44–5; Horrabin, 1915). The experiment was largely a failure. Apparently only three women, Alice Smith of the Lancashire Textile Operatives, Mary Howarth, another graduate of Plebs League classes in Lancashire, and Jean Dott studied at the CLC (Smith, 1915).

The League faded from the scene after World War I but a number of women continued to play important roles in IWCE. Winifred Horrabin, a committed Marxist who regarded feminism as 'futile', was the anchor of the Plebs League after 1915. Her sister-in-law Kath Starr was for many years the mainstay of the office. Ellen Wilkinson was a member of the League executive in her many incarnations as ILP-er, Fabian, Guild Socialist, Communist Party member and Labour MP. As a NUDAW official she played a key role in securing her union's affiliation to the NCLC. Christine Millar, a former teacher, was the force behind the expansion of correspondence courses. All of them, Horrabin and Starr perhaps unwillingly, seem to have accepted the prevailing imperatives of IWCE.

Other women who attempted to encourage a broader emphasis were viewed with suspicion and sometimes resentment. Myfanwy Westrope's unavailing attempts to encourage a study of literature that was more than reductionist evoked philistine hostility. Cedar Paul found her absorption with psychology, progressive education, coining a new terminology for socialism and organising recitals of Hebridean songs was not always appreciated. This represented an element of fear of the intellectual woman. But it is clear that, intellectuals and organisers alike, men dominated IWCE. From 1922 to its demise not one paid divisional organiser of the NCLC was a woman and few women were tutors. The ethos was overwhelmingly masculine. Colleges moved resolutions condemning the employment of the wives of full-time staff on the basis they were taking mens' jobs (*Plebs*, 1928: 182). Women students complained:

I've washed up for socialism, I've washed up for Disarmament but I'm not going to wash up for education because I want to be in class and not at the sink (Wilkinson, 1928: 13; Yow, 1993: 187).

IWCE never established a socialist feminist cadre although attempts to involve women continued. A women's committee was established in London in 1927 to mount classes aimed at women and there were similar shortlived experiments in Scotland and Wales. Ellen Wilkinson urged each college to establish at least one women's class (Wilkinson, 1928: 14). By the 1930s the majority of women students were in classes organised for Co-operative Women's Guilds and Labour Party women's sections and few classes dealt specifically with 'women's issues' (cf. Cohen, 1990: 128–9). Women gained in skills, knowledge and confidence: 'I feel I could talk for a week and I have learned more than I ever thought possible' (quoted in Yow, 1993: 195). But they only made up at most 20 per cent of students (Millar, 1979: 123).

Less attention was paid to racism. The Plebs *Outline of Imperialism* enjoyed wide circulation, Dobb wrote on colonialism (e.g. Dobb, 1921) and in the 1930s the NCLC provided a platform for black activists George Padmore and C.L.R. James. But when the American Communist Scott Nearing's *Black America* was discussed it was noted:

We have been too pre-occupied with immediate struggles at home to take overmuch interest in the wrongs and suffering of subject races (*Internationalist*, 1929: 75).

## Influence and Impact

IWCE provides a case study in admirable if flawed socialist endeavour, in oppositional history and the eventual incorporation of opposition. In its first period of *insurgency*, characterised by attempts to create *education for revolution* which ran from 1909 to 1921, IWCE exercised a strong influence – more specifically from 1916. This influence continued during the second period *of institutionalisation* which ran from 1922–40, faltering after the defeat of the General Strike, years which produced *education for reform*. The third period from 1940–64 was a period of *decline* characterised by growing loss of influence and *education for responsibility*, increasingly defined in technical rather than social terms.

IWCE cannot be examined within a limited educational discourse or autonomously: it developed and declined in response to changes in state policy and related changes in the labour movement (McIlroy, 1992). The reasons for its failure must be sought in wider explanations as to why Labourism conquered and why Marxism never became a powerful force in Britain (McKibbin, 1990: 1–41). But its own responses were important. It saw clearly that whatever the openings in state supported provision 'adult education is not an ideologically neutral activity whose political character simply reflects the dispositions of teacher and student' (McIntyre, 1980: 89). There *were* clear limits on what was permissible under state funding. Understanding the dangers of incorporation IWCE overestimated the radical autonomy 'independence' based on the labour movement would grant. In so doing it isolated itself from a strong potential constituency. G.D.H. Cole's position – the labour movement needed both the Labour Colleges and the WEA – is well known (Cole, 1916). But there must have been thousands like Agnes Reynolds, the daughter of an active ILP member brought up on vigorous socialist discussion, a reader of Marx and Engels, a woman who approached her Cambridge education critically and who brooked no external interference in the WEA classes she taught. She admired the NCLC but felt the more open method of WEA classes also made socialists. She could accept neither the NCLC's exclusiveness nor its hostility to what she saw as a complementary path. And of course she needed the money that the WEA, unlike the NCLC, paid its tutors (Millar, 1931a,b; Reynolds, 1931).

Even in its strongholds the IWCE's influence was limited and contradictory. In South Wales IWCE's initial impact was to reinforce the move from Liberal Labourism to independent Labourism with the revolutionary mentality of its leaders exercising limited purchase (Lewis, 1993: 88ff). The NCLC was fond of listing MPs and union leaders who attended its classes to demonstrate its influence. But the precise impact of classes on students remains elusive. John Campbell remarked wryly of James Griffith, Harold Wilson's Deputy Prime Minister and author at the CLC of an essay on Marx's *Eighteenth Brumaire*, that it was doubtful whether he ever gave another thought to Marx or Louis Napoleon (Campbell, 1987: 16). The leaders of the NCLC became dedicated supporters of the right-wing of Labourism practising politics the pioneers fought. If IWCE's impact was direct it worked in diverse and mysterious ways. From the miners' union alone it educated opportunists like Frank Hodges, Secretary of the Federation and later a coal owner; Sir William Lawther who emerged as an anarchist from the Little Moscow of Chopwell to become, with Arthur Deakin, a synonym for right wing trade unionism; the left wing General Secretary Arthur Cook, and his Communist successor Arthur Horner. Both Morgan Phillips, General Secretary of the Labour Party 1944–62 and his successor Sir Len Williams, later Governor of Mauritius, had long involvement but so did scores of lay activists in the unions, the Labour Party, the Communist Party and the Trotskyist groups.

It is impossible to simply relate experience of study to the development of a life, a philosophy and a practice. Many of those involved in IWCE did not bear its exclusive imprint because they failed to give it the exclusive philosophical commitment its leadership expected: they found IWCE *and* other educational routes useful. Jack Jones has spoken warmly of the influence on him of the Liverpool Labour College (Jones, 1984). But his further education also included a Ruskin correspondence course and at the time he was involved with IWCE he organised a WEA class for dockers. When he wanted courses for shop stewards in the 1950s he had no hesitation in going to Birmingham University's Extra-Mural Department (Jones, 1986: 24, 31, 35, 48). IWCE's contribution to Labour movement leadership at all levels is undeniable. But it was always a small scale movement based on a limited attachment by a minority of the minority: even at its zenith not more than 40,000 students were involved annually.

## The Trade Unions

In the early years of the century education had been left largely to IWCE and the WEA. By 1930 unions were bigger and more bureaucratic, their links with the Labour Party formalised. The growth of a full-time officer apparatus was linked to the consolidation of national negotiating machinery and the weakness of shop steward organisation. Leaders such as Bevin and Walter Citrine, General Secretary of the TUC, sought to centralise power, and marginalise the left. They worked in partnership with the state and employers in the interests of a new regulated capitalism (Middlemas, 1979: 174–213). This produced a distinctive but rudimentary trade union education resourced and controlled internally. It was explicitly distinguished by its architects from the 'workers' education for emancipation' of both IWCE and WEA in its emphasis on organisation and technique, rather than social understanding. Its direct objective was not the transformation of capitalism but the extension of the union apparatus through professionalising and integrating the work of lay activists, identifying them with union leaders and securing legitimacy for union policy (McIlroy, 1985a).

Education as the creation of skilled, committed functionaries could be clearly observed in the TGWU. Bevin took a personal interest in the establishment of an education department in 1938 and the creation of a curriculum based on the history and organisation of the union, the rights and duties of members, negotiating machinery and industrial legislation. The growth of union education was marked by opposition to leftism and rank and file movements (Topham, 1992: 53). Bevin's successors continued this approach (Allen, 1957: 243). But the scale of the project remained small: in the second biggest union the General and Municipal Workers lack of resources stymied emulation (Clegg, 1964: 145). Citrine saw internal education as an aid to centralisation and enhancement of TUC authority. A key purpose was weaning activists away from ideas of workers' control (Citrine, 1967: 42,330). Specifically the summer courses and weekend schools developed from 1929 were part of an attempt to establish the Trades Councils (the local TUCs) bastions of the left, as 'transmission belts of orders from leaders to the rank and file' (Clinton, 1977: 143). Courses dealt largely with union organisation and policy and 'propounded the views of trade union leaders on political questions' (Clinton, 1977: 139; McIlroy, 1985a: 35–6).

Increased access to the state convinced Citrine of the need to develop a compliant lay cadre 'trained in the concrete application of the policy and principles of our movement' (TUC, 1946: 449). In 1946 the TUC appointed a director of studies and began residential courses the following year. The curriculum was 'essentially practical in character' and union officials still needed the broader education the voluntary bodies provided (TUC, 1951: 170). The TUC's failure to act on the 1946 Congress resolution calling for a unified scheme involving the voluntary bodies affirmed a preference for what they termed 'trade union technical training' over 'social studies'. Courses dealt with organisation and collective bargaining. Criticised from the left, there was a struggle to fill places and secure funding. When the TUC training college opened in 1957 the TUC had established a specific role for itself as the sponsor of 'technical training'. It was a marginal, forced growth with around 600 students out of an affiliated membership of 8 million annually attending two week and one week courses (McIlroy, 1985a).

Some unions preferred to develop their own provision or to use the facilities of the WEA and the universities (see Chapters 7 and 8). The TGWU worked closely with the WEA, its summer schools attended annually by some 500 students. From 1949 the General and Municipal Workers financed one month courses at technical colleges and universities, switching, after the appointment of an education officer in 1954, to its own courses. The Electrical Trade Union opened a training college in 1953 and USDAW appointed an education officer in 1958 (McIlroy, 1990c: 183–6). This shifted activity from the voluntary organisations to the unions themselves. The emphasis again was on the mechanics of organisation and bargaining.

Problems with what was now sometimes perceived as the abstract tutorial class in economics or politics led the WEA to appraise its work less by seeking innovatory approaches to economics or politics than by emphasising work on industrial relations institutions and skills. The Association, it was argued, had to 'take seriously the unions' own assessment which gives priority to elementary training in a variety of practical skills' and develop 'intermediate education' which would analyse union organisation and industrial relations institutions and procedures (WEA, 1953; Clegg and Adams, 1959: 75ff). This approach was influential, through the TGWU-WEA Summer Schools and the work of the Oxford University Delegacy which stressed 'relevance', 'the need for practical application' and 'programmed discussion'. But other universities mounted courses for union activists which attempted to fuse the study of politics and economics with organisational concerns. The scale and scope of the university day release courses in the 1960s and 1970s should not be underestimated (McIlroy, 1990d: 218ff).

Trade union education was thus composed of contradictory currents. One stream attempted to reproduce internal authority relations, 'to benefit the unions directly by improving the performance by branch officials and shop stewards of their jobs for the union and by increasing their loyalty to the union' (Clegg and Adams, 1959: 71). The second stream based on university day release represented a refurbishment of liberal, often radical liberal, workers' education. These streams mingled in a diverse number of tributaries and many courses were mounted by employers or jointly by employers and union.

## Industrial Relations Training

By the 1970s this phase had given way to an extension of technical training bearing to a greater extent the imprint of the state. From the late 1950s growing awareness of relative economic decline focused on the unions, their bargaining power enhanced by full employment, as agents of inflation. Governments sought to involve unions in a partnership whose objective was wage restraint. Strong workplace organisation and aggressive bargaining in key industries was seen as the motor of disorder in industrial relations, and because of its relative autonomy from control by union leaders, a barrier to its solution via national tripartite accommodation. The growth of shop steward power, perceived as based on unofficial strikes and wage drift, threatened the 'ideal type' dominance of professional trade unionism in which the role of lay activists was subordinate to that of 'responsible' full-time officers. And it disrupted tendencies towards centralisation, focused on the TUC, necessary for successful bargaining with the state. Management viewed shop stewards as a threat to control of the workplace. The state viewed them as a stumbling block to political exchange. All three parties possessed an interest in strategies to reform workplace industrial relations and remould the shop steward (McIlroy, 1995a: 102-8). Industrial relations training was a pedagogy of control aimed at regulating lay activists, eliciting their commitment to political exchange and disciplining their militancy. When, in the years 1968-74, state strategies stoked the most aggressive militancy since the 1920s, training played an expanded role.

The left, in contrast, often welcomed the autonomy of shop stewards as a driving force of democracy and class struggle. Unlike the TUC they wanted to strengthen and unify shop floor militancy and give it a radical socialist content. The Communist Party and Labour Left were therefore suspicious of steward training (Palme Dutt, 1963; Park, 1969: 96–100). It was seen as undermining independence and militancy by encouraging stewards to accept the managerial conventions and compromise of negotiation and inculcating a debilitating commitment to procedures which constrained optimal deployment of bargaining power (Cliff, 1970: 218; Hyman, 1979: 57–8). But no clear cut ideological or organisational alternative was stimulated by the militancy of the 1960s and 1970s. The Centres for Socialist Education, putative successors to the NCLC, never took off and the main alternative was the network of conferences organised by the Institute of Workers Control. Here union activists worked with academics imbricated with the university day release courses such as Ken Coates, Tony Topham and Michael Barratt Brown (see, for example, Coates and Topham, 1974). Also, despite the narrow formal parameters of training courses, the inalienable core of classroom autonomy provided opportunities for those committed to broader education.

This goes some way to explaining why the TUC was prepared to establish a new scheme in 1964 based on an expansion of its own training tradition and elimination of the tradition of IWCE. Educationalists were excluded from any formal role and there was limited democracy with no decision-making body below Congress House. Day release courses, usually of 10 or 12 days duration, were sponsored with the universities, the WEA and technical colleges. Progress was slow: in 1966 there were only 21 courses involving 269 students. The essential context was the TUC's analysis of 'the shop steward problem' and its appreciation of training as an antidote to this (TUC, 1960; TUC/BEC, 1963; TUC/CBI, 1967). The centre of gravity shifted towards the state and TUC General Secretary George Woodcock was a member of the Royal Commission on Industrial Relations which recommended that all parties should support courses

with a view to using training of shop stewards as part of a planned move to more orderly industrial relations ... This is where shop steward training will be able to make its biggest contribution (Royal Commission Report, 1968: para: 712).

The judgement that the need for training was 'immense' was echoed by the TUC's own 1968 report which consecrated organisational and bargaining technique as 'really useful knowledge', insisting on weeding out economics and wider issues from the curriculum. Training was a legitimate control technique for unions and the 'common interest' of all parties lay in the management of the conflicts between them which would be facilitated by well trained stewards who would abide by union policy and procedures (TUC, 1968: 9, 11ff, 21).

With the advent of the 1970 Heath government a report by the Commission for Industrial Relations (CIR) recommended that management should be given greater influence over training and drew attention to tensions within the pluralist partnership (CIR, 1972). For the unions, training was a control mechanism required to improve efficiency and deliver bargains with government. Should too great a measure of control over training pass to employers or state the TUC would have less to deliver. They wanted integration of stewards into unions which would reach accommodation with management, not an unmediated integration between stewards and management. Management, in turn, wanted courses to explain their problems more sympathetically to commit stewards more strongly to their employer's position in the market (McCarthy, 1966: 11; Warren, 1971: 49).

The CIR report was never implemented. The TUC took advantage of the incoming Labour administration to assert its objectives. As a deeper response to militancy the 1974 Labour government offered an extension of training as part of the Social Contract. It was at once a concession, a lubricant for incomes policy and an instrument of industrial relations reform. Under the 1975 Employment Protection Act stewards were entitled to paid time off for training relevant to their workplace industrial relations functions subject to 'reasonableness' and 'the operational requirements of the employer'. Paid release would *not* be available for courses which dealt with stewards' wider trade union responsibilities: the curriculum was now firmly focused on workplace and employer. While courses required approval by the TUC or individual unions, disputes over relevance and release would be finally determined by the courts. A Memorandum of Agreement laid down categories of training for which state support – by 1979 more than £1 million a year – was available. Benefits were real if shortlived. For example, TUC basic 10-day courses increased from 684 with 10,640 students in 1975–6 to 1,208 with 15,701 students in 1979–80. There were in addition 383 'follow on' courses with 4,542 students and 1,441 Health and Safety courses with 18,700 student places. However, there were more than 12 million members and around 500,000 representatives, subject to high turnover: 40,000 places a year was far from a mass system.

The efforts of individual unions have to be added in. ASTMS, the NUR, the GMWU and the National Union of Teachers opened residential colleges. The National Graphical Association built up a residential scheme of week long courses. The Post Office Engineering Union operated a four-tier system of courses which emphasised social and economic education. USDAW's regional training officers specialised in in-plant courses. NALGO, NUPE and the TGWU qualitatively expanded provision which often went beyond the narrow confines of TUC courses. Perhaps most important was the appointment in unions like NALGO and the TGWU of regional officers able to give a majority of their time to education rooted in local membership activities. And, of course, the longer day release courses continued to flourish.

Until 1979 the state operated with the carrot of rights. After 1979 the carrot was maintenance, the stick the threat of withdrawal of support. Thatcherism had no time for corporatist strategies, but change was gradual. Public attention focused on state funding in 1982 when Employment Secretary Norman Tebbit argued it was illogical for the unions to take funds for training whilst refusing them for ballots as part of their opposition to the government's employment legislation. The government adopted a 'step by step' approach. Some Ministers wanted to terminate state funding; others believed TUC courses merely required correcting for pro-union bias (Lloyd, 1983). In 1983 grant was cut, with a proportion of funds available only for courses approved by employers. Congress House remained silent in the face of press reports headlined 'Unions accept employers right to ratify courses'. The lack of opposition suggested step by step manipulation of funding would encounter little future opposition (Gravell, 1983). And it was noted that acceptance of the new restrictions represented 'a departure from the TUC's solid defence of its right to make the sole decision on the courses' content' (Lloyd, 1983; Tribune, 1983).

Tebbit believed training within parameters accepted by the TUC did little harm. Properly supervised it could do some good in producing 'more intelligent, better informed trade union officials'. Until 1986 the grant provided a means for manipulating the unions: 'there was considerable advantage in funding union training activities to emphasise that it could not be a principled refusal which precluded unions accepting money for ballots' (Tebbit, 1989). Joseph, the Minister of Education, wished to use the courses 'to increase awareness of the links between jobs, prosperity and competitiveness and of government economic policies' (Joseph, 1989). Material on economics was introduced but Joseph's removal precluded its development. By and large Ministers were convinced these courses represented little challenge to government interests and policies. HMIs found classroom work in close accordance with the statutory rubric (DES, 1980). Against right-wing critics the government pointed out that the curriculum was limited and the TUC was 'required to seek departmental approval of any proposals for addition or amendments to the content of courses' (*Hansard*, 1987-8: 123, cols 10, 11). In a climate supportive of training, civil servants wished to maintain empires whilst maintenance of grant provided government with direct surveillance.

Government policy remained incremental. The TUC protested that the government was attempting to place 'unacceptable conditions' on the grant and questioned 'the educational validity' of course materials on privatisation (TUC, 1986a, 1991b). Under s.14 of the 1989 Employment Act training was formally tied to the steward's role as defined by the employer. The Department of Employment (DE) became the sole supervising agency. Grant was reduced annually and by 1991 was 75 per cent of its 1986 level.

The real limits became transparent when, in 1991, DE officials expressed concern about *Working Women*, a book used on courses, published by the TUC with no public funds involved. The DE view that the book was 'too political' was supported by the Secretary of State, who threatened withdrawal of grant unless it was banned from courses. Without consultation with TUC committees or affiliated unions, the TUC education department acted as agents for censorship. They instructed officers and tutors that the book should not be used (TUC, 1991a; McIlroy, 1993). The TUC argued that 'trade unionists had to live in the real world recognising that the whole of the trade union education grant was at stake' (TUC, 1991c). Moreover 'the lesson learned from this incident was that more care than ever needed to be taken in writing about government actions in education materials' (TUC, 1991b,c). The extent to which the TUC Education Department accepted such interference, recommending self censorship to avoid further intervention, demonstrated the degree to which it had become dependent on the state.

The TUC's contingent role was further underlined by its reaction to the White Paper *Education and Training for the 21st Century*. The TUC decided to adjust courses to the requirements of NVQ assessment to continue to qualify for funding (McIlroy, 1993: 54-8). However, in December 1992, the

Government announced funding would be phased out by 1996. The decision was related to desire to root out the last vestiges of corporatism and to the decline in collective bargaining and strikes. The purpose of the subsidy, Employment Secretary Gillian Shephard stated, had been to 'improve industrial relations'. That objective was now achieved.

TUC education was in serious decline. By 1992 there were only 512 ten day release courses with around 6,000 students although there were still 521 Health and Safety Courses with 6,500 students as well as a plethora of short course provision. It was clear that the termination of state aid would return TUC education to pre 1975 dimensions. Grant and the provision of training places was now split on a 50-50 basis between the TUC and affiliated unions. In 1991 the TUC retained £955,331 of the £1.78 million grant, the remaining £830,000 was passed onto affiliates who overall spent £3 million on education and training (TUC, 1990: 70). General trends made larger unions look to their own provision which stood up surprisingly well (Brown, 1992; Cosgrove, 1992). Fryer provides a picture of the range of innovatory work outside the mainstream, sometimes based on the residential colleges, universities and the WEA (see Chapters 7, 8 and 9), often self-organised work with the wageless, women's groups, black workers and local research groups (Fryer, 1990).

## Ideology and the State

The ideology that informed trade union education and industrial relations training was based upon Labourism's split between industrial and political. It emphasised a unitary, hierarchical, 'commonsense' conception of trade unionism with unproblematic goals, blurring differences of objective or interest between leadership and members and asserting politics as outside the realm of 'workplace industrial relations'. Education was a means of strengthening cohesion as defined by the leadership, the subject of top down delivery rather than democratic control. Critical thinking about society might liberate and empower activists and stimulate conflict. Even a *controlled*, issue-based education which might have been conceived as 'helpful' by developing understanding and acceptance of the economic logic of capitalism was refused. It was sometimes formally accepted that representatives needed both skills *and* critical understanding of the economic and social order. Scarcity of resources and 'relevance', it was claimed, dictated the primacy of the former.

The presentation of workplace skills training as neutral failed to acknowledge that exclusion of a critical examination of politics and power in unions, industry and society, taking the wider context as given, was liable to legitimise existing authority relations and the politics of the *status quo*. Or that industrial relations training carried a view of trade unionism as centred on workplace collective bargaining at the expense of a view of trade unionism as a social movement with a political mission. And a conception of lay activists as a subaltern stratum was at the expense of conceiving lay activists as a critical, empowered, cadre. The economistic ideology of skills training reduced real divisions of purpose and policy to a simplistic, conservative technicism.

IWCE's account of the interrelations of capital and labour was replaced by a pluralistic model: conflict was real but manageable by joint institutions maximising joint interests. The instrumental view of the state gave way to pragmatism. The TUC initially maintained an abstentionist stance. They feared direct state funding would pass control over training to the state and employers. Increased funding should flow through the educational bodies (TUC, 1966; 1970: 8). The *volte-face* in 1974 was part of a general change of attitude to state support at a time when the post-war consensus appeared guaranteed. The TUC believed that the 1975 settlement ensured them the right 'to determine the training of trade union representatives ... this is a principle from which we will not deviate' (TUC, 1975: 443). This glossed over the extent to which annual review of grant, vetting of materials, inspection of courses by HMIs, embodied state control. This – and the limits to the neutrality of the state – was demonstrated after 1979.

The acceptance by the state of the 1975 arrangements was scarcely a major achievement for corporatist approaches. Whether it constituted the right policy is open to serious doubt. At the zenith of union power, it beggars belief that the unions could not have secured release for courses in which economic and industrial policy and a wide political agenda were treated in a broad and balanced way. But industrial relations training was all the TUC leaders wanted and its limited nature scarcely made it a priority for execution. The TUC, moreover, used the threat of removal of grant to reinforce the existing limits. The view of some was that the nature of Thatcherism required a more radical approach and that, 'a reappraisal of the content of workers' education is needed' (Topham, 1981: 49; and see McIlroy, 1982a; Whitston, 1982). The argument that new challenges rendered a renewal of social and economic education urgent made few inroads. Whilst it was claimed that students exhibited a 'great thirst for making explicit the political and macro-economic dimensions of union activity' wherever it was possible 'to loosen the reins on narrower instrumental teaching', there was little active support for change by tutors (Moore, 1981: 53). For the majority it was probably not even a matter of self censorship: they were happy with training which discarded social knowledge for empowerment. The TUC refused genuine debate of the issues; instead those who took seriously arguments for a broader curriculum were excluded from teaching (McIlroy, 1995b).

Formal interventions were few; they emphasised the reality of state surveillance. By the 1990s continuing decline habituated the TUC to dependence. Any forceful assertion of the legitimacy of state funding of union education was eschewed in favour of bureaucratic manoeuvring. The fact that the increasingly debilitated system endured owed more to the modalities of government strategy than TUC resistance. The experience suggests the need to discard neutral and instrumentalist conceptions of the state in favour of emphasis on its real, if relative, autonomy (Poulantzas, 1978). Unions have little alternative to engagement with the state and the fact that the British experiment produced ephemeral quantitative, and little qualitative, advance has more to do with its specific nature than any iron law. Had the unions emphatically asserted the right to funding on their own terms arguing the state's role should be to ensure only quality (Ministry of

Reconstruction, 1919: 18–19) and fought energetically for this, then the story might have been different.

## Curriculum and Pedagogy

The belief that trade unionists should be 'equipped by education with the social, economic and political understanding needed for effective action' (TUC, 1922: 27) continued to inform the curriculum of many university courses into the 1980s. Length – with courses of up to 72 and 120 days – facilitated a curriculum which dealt in depth with economics, politics and industrial relations as well as skills (McIlroy, 1990d: 220ff). The training model, dealing with shop stewards' rights and responsibilities, procedures, negotiation techniques, industrial legislation and health and safety was strengthened by the decline in the 1980s of university day release associated, particularly after 1985, with the decline of the NUM (Bayliss, 1991) but there were some wider initiatives. The TGWU began to develop courses dealing with economics and politics on a distance learning model (Camfield and Fisher, 1987; Spencer, 1989). NUPE put special efforts into political education and NALGO into equal opportunities (Sutherland, 1985; Broome and Brown, 1987). There were new courses for local authority employees in Hull, London, Sheffield and Nottingham (Burke, 1987). In the TGWU there were programmes in Labour history, political education and equal opportunities in partnership with the Universities of Surrey, Liverpool and Manchester (Owens, 1989). There were courses dealing with legislation, privatisation, public expenditure. The TUC mounted from its own funds a range of campaign workshops on aspects of policy, short and explicitly propagandistic. Overall, provision addressing the social and economic context has been *ad hoc*, brief and subordinate. The view of the TGWU is generally true for the period since 1979:

subject matter has tended to be limited to what can be called the non-political or non-controversial aspects of trade unionism. By far the greatest amount of TUC and individual union courses concern themselves with what is essentially training in an established role of shop steward or safety representative (Cosgrove, 1983: 63).

From the late 1940s there had been an attempt to develop pedagogy with a greater emphasis on critical conversation and activism in the voluntary bodies and the universities (Murie, 1946; Lloyd, 1950; Styler, 1951). The wartime work of ABCA, the Ministry of Labour's courses and union education in the USA were all influential. J.E. Williams provides a memorable sketch of attempts to develop group work, negotiating exercises, student research and public expression on the Sheffield courses in the 1950s (Williams, 1954). On the whole changes in method were related to changes in curriculum towards skills: attempts to transform the teaching of politics or economics were limited. The work of Arthur Marsh who perhaps more than anybody laid the foundations for a programmed approach was related to skills and industrial relations institutions and procedures. This work linked with the efforts of Tony Corfield, the force behind the TGWU summer schools, and was disseminated through the annual conferences organised by the Oxford Delegacy and, after 1969, through the publications and conferences of the Society of Industrial Tutors (McIlroy, 1985b; Marsh, 1966; Coker and Stuttard, 1975).

By the early 1970s the ingredients of a pedagogic alternative to the lecture-discussion format which still dominated much traditional adult education had been assembled. Group work and discussion using pre-prepared materials was at its core with the tutor as democratic leader (Stuttard, 1975; Topham, 1979). Struck by the success of documentary methods in its campaign against the Industrial Relations Act, the TUC extended this approach. But the expansion of work brought in tutors more used to lecture based methods. Fundamentally, pedagogy was the instrument of politics: there was a desire to introduce a standardised, curriculum. Detailed timed packages were intended to control the classroom to ensure TUC requirements were met (McIlroy, 1985a,b). In the early 1980s planning of instruction continued but was replenished by an emphasis on self-direction, or rather externally controlled 'self-direction', for activities and documentation were again prescribed by the TUC and centred on workplace industrial relations (Gowan, 1982).

There was increasing emphasis on method at the expense of content. There were attempts to suggest that students' experience was sufficient and to limit the intervention and intellectual leadership of the teacher. This meshed happily with the desire to avoid issue based disputation and the attention detailed materials could (and did) attract from HMIs and Government (McIlroy, 1985a,b). It failed to impress many involved in union education. By the end of the decade it was replaced by a return to more traditional participative methods (SIT/TGWU, 1988; Grant, 1990).

## Gender and Ethnicity

Women played a marginal role until the 1960s and there was little address of gender issues (Lewenhak, 1977: 203–4). As the 1970s began, sessions on equal pay and sex discrimination began to appear on courses but 'women-only' courses remained a novelty (Beale, 1980: 24). As attention focused on the under-representation of women in union positions, attempts to increase participation were reflected in training courses. The TUC began to develop 'women-only bridging' courses and around 85 such courses of between three and five days were being mounted annually by 1986 (Elliott, 1982: 2–3). There was also an attempt to involve more women students in mainstream courses and ensure these courses dealt with the role of women and the role of sexism in the unions (Aldred, 1981; McIlroy, 1982b). 1988 saw the first TUC women's summer school.

These changes spread across individual unions and in several cases, notably NALGO and the National Union of Journalists, the organisation of women's courses and liaison over the wider programmes became part of women's self-organisation within the union (Williams and Nicola, 1982; Kibel, 1984). Progress in this area reflected progress in the unions generally: it was real but limited (McIlroy, 1995: 176–83). On TUC courses for example the number of women students increased from less than 10 per cent in 1976 to 25 per cent a decade later and 30 per cent by 1990 (TUC, 1990: 52). However estimates put the number of full-time women tutors at under 20 per cent. Particularly encouraging was the way many courses examined the historical and contemporary role of women in society as well as issues such as equal pay, sexual harassment and child care.

Progress on racism was arrested by the unions' position, sustained until the late 1960s, that no significant problem existed and there was therefore no need for positive action (McIlroy, 1981). The General and Municipal Workers Union played an important role in developing one week 'race relations' courses and the TUC began to mount short courses dealing with racism and courses specifically aimed at black workers from the late 1970s (Ball and Watterson, 1981; Murray, 1981). By 1987 there were around 75 such courses involving 600 students running each year. There was also an attempt to ensure that the issue of racism was introduced into mainstream provision and this sometimes involved a broad critical approach to the issue as distinct from a focus on legislation and bargaining (McIlroy, 1983). Several sets of imaginative materials were produced for work with trade unionists (Open University, 1983; TUC, 1983, 1986b). But there remained some tendency to moralise, denounce and assume that trade union consciousness was of itself anti-racist. This crude approach denied the particularistic and sectional in trade unionism, and minimised the need to *construct* anti-racism within a trade unionism that expresses its society (Rex, 1981; McIlroy, 1981: 17–22). In some unions, Unison, MSF and the NUJ, extensive educational provision was mounted by black members themselves whilst the TGWU ran regional black workers' workshops. It is difficult to estimate progress in this area. The TUC, for example, began ethnic monitoring in the mid 1980s but does not publish figures in its annual reports. Nonetheless the issue had a visibility and attention it had lacked during earlier decades.

## Influence and Impact

From the 1960s the number of courses and the resources they commanded developed on a scale unenvisaged by the pioneers. But it was still on a small scale. By 1986 only between ten and fifteen per cent of representatives received any training and this might mean only a day's course (Government Social Survey, 1968: 15; Daniel and Millward, 1983: 31; TUC, 1987). Membership education never got off the ground. In the context of tight resources – union subscription rates remained low in comparison with comparable countries – training remained a minority concern (McIlroy, 1995: 44–5).

For any critical history major interest lies in character and quality. There is no dearth of opinion on the value of this provision. Statements from providers registering satisfaction are abundant on the lines, 'the overwhelming majority of students attending TUC Stage I courses had found them most useful and reported they had given them confidence' (TUC, 1993: 91). Small scale studies register large majorities finding courses 'useful', helping skills development and increasing confidence – and so do TUC surveys (Smith, 1984; Kelly and Grooms, 1986; TUC, 1987). There are however intriguing hints as to the limits of skills training. In one TUC survey only 2.2 per cent of respondents mentioned 'development of skills' as a 'keyword' in the usefulness of courses 'disconcertingly low, given the emphasis on skills throughout the course' (Mahon and Stirling, 1988: 55). But successive Workplace Industrial Relations Surveys show both steward and management approval of training (Millward *et al.*, 1992: 118–20).

From the left the limitations have been emphasised. 'Managements were hardly likely to pay stewards to attend courses if they were going to be taught how to beat the "system" ' (Lane, 1974: 209).

Ideologically courses have never been independent of employers ... The aim of steward training, whoever does it, has always been to 'professionalise industrial relations' not to create a 'network of militants' (Lyddon, 1984: 95; see also Hyman, 1979: 57–8; Carter, 1983: 20; Beecham, 1984: 104–5; Freeman, 1984: 262).

We cannot assume the success of training in reproducing ideology and structure: resistance is always a reality. But the radical critique is backed by in-depth survey evidence:

The field work reported above would suggest that on balance shop steward training could be more accurately seen as encouraging a pro-management shop steward ideology and thus operating as a managerial control agent (Keithley, 1982: 245).

Adult educators refused the impossible task of disentangling cause and effect and evaluating the alchemy of education and life. Their *faith* was that education would stimulate and strengthen social action. The trainers, despite their belief in the measurement of competency, have failed to produce hard facts on the relationship between training and action. There is limited evidence of enhanced success in collective bargaining. Smith (1984: 84) reports that in the aftermath of a course stewards had some success but found it more difficult to achieve purchase at the level of strategic decisions. There is some evidence skill based courses have stimulated union activity and political involvement (Mahon and Stirling, 1988: 58; Spencer, 1989). Trainers who talk of a significant breakthrough (Holford, 1994) have not produced the evidence their philosophy demands. There remains 'a singular absence of systematic assessment of the concrete effect of courses on the quality of representation – let alone of wider activities' (Schuller and Robertson, 1984: 74).

It is difficult to see how matters could be otherwise. The 'role of the workplace representative' is fluid and contested even if this is evaded by trainers. However we define it it is contingent. And we possess only highly subjective measures of success and failure. The efficacy of the training paradigm is open to fundamental question. A moment's thought about the shop steward's situation

could be said to cast doubt on any very substantial claims being made for shop steward training. Moreover if it is also accepted that the steward performs his functions against a complex of largely impersonal factors beyond his control ... then it is arguable how far any course of training, in itself, could hope to affect his behaviour (McCarthy, 1966: para. 111).

We can draw no rigorous relationship between the dominance of workplace skills training and the crisis of trade unionism. What is clear is that crisis was created by the political mobilisation of economic and ideological forces beyond the scope of training, forces to which workplace organisation and training had no answer. To consign understanding of these forces which directly influence workplace industrial relations to 'educational needs' and demarcate training in organisational technique as 'trade union needs' is to make a false distinction. For trade unionists, as well as educators, skills are a secondary component in a complex power equation and cannot be developed in isolation from the economy and society. The 'need' to prioritize skills training was ideologically constructed by policy makers, union professionals and academics (cf. Armstrong, 1982). If one had to fragment an essential unity and prioritise either skills training *or* the development of a critical consciousness of the economic and political forces that create and constrain trade unionism, it is strongly arguable that the latter, not the former, is more 'relevant' and requires 'priority'. It is the second that has been lacking. Indeed, to some extent, it was the impulse to arrest the *success* of the bargaining skills of shop stewards that produced the need for training. Even within the discourse of priorities the case for an educational forum in which union representatives can examine the issues confronting the Labour movement as well as develop skills, remains a compelling one.

*11*

# The Open University

## *Naomi Sargant*

### *Origins and Environment*

The Open University (OU) has been widely described as one of the most significant innovations in education in this century. Analogues to it have been set up in over 30 countries. It operates on a very large scale. In 1994 it had 133,000 undergraduate students, 10,000 postgraduate students and together with its community and continuing education provision will reach over 200,000 learners in any one year. It is impossible in this chapter to do justice to the history of the OU as a whole, a task which still remains. What it attempts is to place the OU in the context of the history of adult education, and in the broader framework of the 'education of adults'.

Of course, the Open University was not the first educational institution to teach adults at a distance: it was preceded by many correspondence colleges including the Co-operative College and the National Council of Labour Colleges. But it was the first to extend the notion of openness to people as well as to methods and to systematically harness all available media, including broadcasting, to its purposes. It was set up as a University, but the designation of University was less important than the level of the new educational opportunities it was planned to provide. Its initial task was to provide higher education for adults and to use broadcasting and other media to assist it. Although it was set up for adults, it was not set up for 'adult education' in the conventional sense, a distinction which was to lead to some misunderstanding since, starting as it did, it incorporated many of the ideals and aspirations of the British tradition of adult education and many of its staff. The tension between access, equality and excellence this led to was noted early on and has proved a continuing dilemma.

Set up in 1969, it began teaching its first 25,000 students in 1971. It did not set out initially to rewrite the curriculum of higher education, but to make it more widely and explicitly available. It aimed, in the words of its first Chancellor, Lord Crowther, on the occasion of the Charter Ceremony, to be '...open as to people .... open as to places ... open as to methods ... and open, finally, as to ideas' (Crowther, 1969). How far it has succeeded in these aims can be judged by its graduates and their acceptability; the quality of its learning experience, widely utilised in other institutions in the UK and abroad; and by the interest of other countries in its system.

The roots of the Open University are to be found in diverse places: J.C. Stobart, working for the BBC, advocated a Broadcasting University as early as 1926 (see Chapter 14). Michael Young appears to be the first to use the actual term 'open university' in an article in *Where* magazine entitled 'Is your child in the unlucky generation?' (Young, 1962) in which he proposed an 'open university' to prepare people for external degrees of London University, many of whom were receiving poor teaching from private correspondence colleges. In referring to such overseas experience as the Soviet Correspondence Colleges and educational television in the US, he proposed the need for a National Extension College to act as the nucleus of an 'open university' with three main functions: to organise new and better correspondence courses for the external degree, to promote lectures and residential schools (working through the extramural departments of London and other universities), and to teach by means of television.

The BBC and the Ministry of Education were already discussing plans for a 'College of the Air'. Then in March 1963, a Labour Party study group under the chairmanship of Lord Taylor presented a report about the continuing exclusion from higher education of the lower income groups. It proposed an experiment on radio and television: a 'University of the Air' for serious planned adult education. Meanwhile Harold Wilson was impressed by Chicago's TV College and also by the experience of correspondence education in Russia. This variety of ideas was put together by Harold Wilson in an evocative speech in Glasgow, 8 September 1963, but did not reach the 1964 Labour manifesto. Wilson's ideas were not, however, for an independent, autonomous university, but rather for 'a new educational trust' bringing together many institutions and organisations to produce television and other educational materials.

The next move proved to be key: after Harold Wilson became Prime Minister in 1964 he asked Jennie Lee, then Minister for the Arts, to take on the project. Within days of her being moved into the DES, she scrapped the Department's detailed plans – described as ready to go to the Cabinet – for an experimental College of the Air, upsetting both civil servants and the BBC, and imposed two major changes of principle. First, it was to be a proper university: independent, autonomous, awarding its own degrees of comparable standard to any others. Second, it was to be open to all without any entrance qualifications. An Advisory Committee chaired by Jennie Lee herself had a rapid series of six meetings in mid-1965 and agreed the White Paper *A University of the Air*, which was published in February, 1966. A commitment to setting it up was included in the Labour Manifesto for the 1966 general election.

The White Paper was not well received and antagonism continued from the press, the Opposition and other members of the Cabinet, against a worsening economic climate. The Cabinet decision to set up a planning committee 'to work out a comprehensive plan for an Open University' (note the name change) was not made until September 1967. Jennie Lee determined to 'outsnob the snobs' and included five Vice-Chancellors on the committee, which was chaired by Sir Peter Venables, Vice-Chancellor of Aston University. The Planning Committee met over a two-year period and reported in January, 1969, the report being accepted by the Government on the day it was published, with the Privy Council granting the OU its Charter on April 23, 1969.

It is worth noting the political irony, which passed largely unnoticed, that the Labour Government was already setting up the polytechnics – a necessary step towards a mass higher education system – at the same time that it was setting up the Open University, but doing it quite separately, through separate Ministers and giving the Open University the elite status with its Charter from the Privy Council that the new polytechnics were to be denied.

The separation of the policies explains to some extent how it was possible for the sectors to develop in parallel but with so little contact for so long. Access for adults was not in the early 70s a matter of concern to most conventional institutions of higher education. Neither was there any particular incentive to make more use of the media for degree-level or vocational work. Qualification and participation rates for school-leavers, and hence demand for places, remained low. As late as 1978, the DES noted as its view that there was no evidence of unsatisfied demand for part-time degrees in existing institutions (DES, 1978) and yet the OU was already turning away several thousand applicants per year.

## Early Years

The Planning Committee Report (1969) laid down the academic aims of the OU in one sentence:

In summary, therefore, the objects of the Open University are to provide opportunities, at both undergraduate and post-graduate level, of higher education to all those who, for any reason have been or are being precluded from achieving their aims through an existing institution of higher education.

It proposed that the degree would be a 'general degree' in the sense that it would embrace studies over a wide range of subjects, that students would be allowed a great deal of choice from the courses offered, that the degree would be obtained by the accumulation of credits, that four 'foundation courses' would be offered initially in Mathematics, Understanding Science, Literature and Culture and Understanding Society and that these subjects would then represent 'lines of study'. The initial offer to applicants was a simple one: the chance to study for a degree, with an initial choice of four familiar subjects at an initial cost of £25. The numbers applying were within the guesstimates and the OU was in business.

Though the main aim of the OU was not seen to be to provide vocational opportunities for adults, the Planning Committee noted the pressing need for degree courses for practising certificated teachers and an early addition to the academic structure was a Faculty of Educational Studies, as well as a Faculty of Technology.

Teachers were to prove an important component of the undergraduate student population for the first few years, though their numbers later dropped dramatically. What had been underestimated by some in the planning was the very large numbers of teachers who held only certificates rather than degrees. Typically they had taught in primary schools and in secondary modern schools, not in grammar or private schools. Two factors coincided to put pressure on certificated teachers to up-grade their qualifications to degrees: the move from a binary to a comprehensive school system and the policy decision that teaching was to become a graduate profession. The system of 'credit exemptions' for previous qualifications benefited teachers as they only had to take one foundation course and could graduate more quickly. They were welcome as students, since they were expected to be both competent and motivated, but they gave the OU an initial middle-class image, which caused concern. In a real sense this was misleading as for many bright working-class children, particularly girls, getting into teacher-training college and primary school teaching was the first step to social mobility.

At the same time, although the OU was clearly reaching many people who had not had 'enough educational opportunities', many of whom had emerged from working-class backgrounds, they were not what would have been conventionally termed 'working-class' let alone 'manual workers', and the OU was therefore under fire from adult educators and other idealists for this failure (Pratt, 1971, 1973). However, early research into the social backgrounds of OU students confirmed that they were significantly more working-class in family background than conventional students (McIntosh and Woodley, 1974). OU students were asked to give the occupation of their father 'during the later years of schooling'. The fathers of 52 per cent of Open University students (both male and female) were in the 'manual worker' category, a further 28 per cent were in lower grade 'white collar' jobs and only 20 per cent had fathers in the 'middle class' categories. Later analysis showed differences between men and women, with more men suffering educational disadvantage at school and more women being prevented from continuing their education post-school. They recorded a high degree of intra-generational mobility as well as inter-generational mobility. Most interesting was evidence that women who were currently housewives, and therefore who would as adults conventionally be ascribed the social class of their husbands, were more middle-class in origin according to their fathers and more working-class according to their husbands. Note that all social mobility studies to that point limited themselves to the male parent (McIntosh et al., 1976)!

Apart from providing for teachers, the OU did not expect to offer vocational opportunities for adults. This has meant that other important vocational areas where the emergent polytechnics were already strong, e.g. social work, town planning, business studies and engineering, developed in the polytechnic sector rather than in the OU, though not always with adequate part-time provision for adults. In the postgraduate area, the Planning Committee felt that the critical need was for post-experience, up-dating or refresher courses rather than postgraduate courses, which it considered might be developed later.

Much of the history of the subsequent years is internal to the development of a large institution and does not impinge on the external world to a great extent. It tends to divide easily into three phases which coincide with the tenure of the OU's three Vice-Chancellors. The first phase is one of innovation and establishment, the second is of maintaining growth and quality against hard times and the third and current one is characterised by convergence and competition with the conventional system.

## Innovation and Establishment

The first phase was not without excitement. The political honeymoon was to be short-lived. The Conservative Government elected in June 1970 was committed to 'examine every aspect of Government expenditure'. William Van Straubenzee, in a lecture to the Open University Students' Association (Van Straubenzee, 1976), was clear about the threat this posed to the infant OU and the role that was played by Margaret Thatcher in saving it at the time.

Many Conservatives were known to be hostile to the infant Open University, not that they were hostile to the concept *per se*, but because of the continuing and growing public expenditure it would demand. It was generally known that Iain MacLeod, the new Chancellor of the Exchequer, wanted to look very closely at this expenditure. A study was prepared in the Department of Education examining the costs of closing the Open University down. I believe it to be true to say at that point in time, the very existence of the OU itself was in doubt. But Margaret Thatcher, the newly appointed Secretary of State for Education and Science, was also looking closely, not only at the figures, but at the whole concept, and she came to be convinced that the University was a project, admittedly in its infancy and yet to be proved, which should be given a chance to prove itself. I suspect that when history comes to be written and we can read all the Cabinet and other Minutes, we shall find that it was her advocacy, sometimes almost single-handed, which saved the University at that time.

Walter Perry (OU, 1979) describes a difficult dinner persuading Margaret Thatcher of the validity of the concept when she was opposition spokesman for education, and noted that part of the price of survival was to investigate the extension of Open University teaching to 18-year-olds. After the Conservative victory, what she had to do, as indeed Jennie Lee had to do before her, 'was to get money from the money going from your Ministry or Department' i.e. out of the overall Education budget, not extra money from the Treasury. In this, Van Straubenzee records, she was much helped by the friendship between a previous Secretary of State, Sir David Eccles, and Edward Heath, then Prime Minister.

What emerges strongly is the implicit competition for funds between the sectors of education. It is now clear that while the OU was certainly providing new opportunities for adults to learn at higher education level, these were not without their price and indeed were to be at the expense of the hoped for expansion of general adult education opportunities argued for by Russell. It was this possibility that Van Straubenzee describes as:

(making) liberally minded academics and other figures anxious at the amount of money that was going to be taken up by the OU. Put briefly, it was, and it remains the question as to whether it was right to commit so high a proportion of our available resources into this one type of adult education.

The point is made forcibly by the contrast in 1972–3, between the total revenue budget for the OU of £7.9 million and the budget for all the other DES-funded Responsible Bodies for Adult Education put together of £4.5 million. It is not surprising that many in adult education were aggrieved by the cuckoo in the nest, though many OU staff, including those who shared the traditional AE commitment to adults, were certainly not sensitive enough to this. The situation was not improved by the Government's lack of response to the Russell Report. Van Straubenzee's rather tough view, as an involved Minister, was that '... the tragedy of the Russell Report (was) that it missed the boat. ... It laboured conscientiously and with great industry for nearly four years.'

It is important to remember that the Russell Committee had been set up in February 1969, before the OU had even been given its Charter, but did not report until December 1972, as the initial cohort of OU students had produced its first graduates. Meanwhile the Government had published a major White Paper *Education: A framework for expansion* (DES, 1971) which paid little attention to adult education, presumably since it was waiting for Russell to report. Van Straubenzee records having 'tried to get the Committee to hurry up its deliberations and so the delivery of its report', but by the time it reported, 'the Government had already settled its main line of approach and its priorities in education'. His concluding words confirm this negative view.

...far from looking for increased expenditure in any field, we shall for some years, be searching for economies. This is particularly true when the Treasury can resist claims for increased expenditure on Adult Education with some justice on the grounds that such Adult Education is already receiving substantial and increasing sums through the Open University.

There was a more fundamental tension between adult education and the Open University which has rarely been articulated publicly . It stems from the very proposition that adults can be successfully taught at a distance. This was clearly threatening to many people who had themselves been taught, trained to teach and were now teaching others face-to-face in conventional institutions. It is not difficult to see why links between the OU and adult education were not particularly strong over those years, despite the numbers of OU staff, particularly in its regional offices, who had come from adult education backgrounds. University extramural departments were even more stand-offish, wishing to hold their own face-to-face traditions intact.

The White Paper was not to herald expansion but contraction in some areas and change in others. The birth-rate, which had continued to rise for many years until 1964, took everyone by surprise and started to drop. Harold Wilson had identified the problem the bulge would cause in his speech at the Charter Ceremony (July 23 1969):

The problem of providing enough places for all those qualified will be with us for some time to come, and there will certainly be a massive increase in the demand for higher education over the next ten years. It is not going to be easy to achieve the increase in places in our existing centres of higher education which this calls for and the Open University will have a vital role to play in complementing the efforts of other Universities in meeting this demand (Wilson, 1969).

It was this belief which ultimately led to the strongly-attacked proposal by the incoming Conservative Government that a group of 18-year-olds should be admitted to the OU on an experimental basis, a scheme which was implemented for three cohorts of 'younger' students entering from 1974 to 1976. In the event, younger students, whom the Vice-Chancellor had suggested 'would fall by the wayside like flies' did drop out at substantially higher rates than older students. However, a long-term evaluation of the programme (Woodley and McIntosh, 1980) indicated that there were some types of younger students whose circumstances were such that the OU could offer them a suitable opportunity for higher education and its regulations have since been amended to allow them to apply along with all other applicants.

## Access and Drop-Out

Previous research data on correspondence courses had shown that this was one of the most difficult modes of study, with high early drop-out similar to that experienced with part-time adult evening classes (Glatter and Wedell, 1971). The OU undergraduate programme was therefore designed to take account of this and allow new students to 'provisionally' register paying only a small proportion of the first year tuition fee enabling them to try out studying for two to three months before deciding whether to 'finally' register for the full course.

The advantage for the student was the chance to test out the system and to see if study would fit into their patterns of life and work, and their academic expectations. The advantage for the University was the economy in not providing course materials, tutors and summer school provision for that proportion of early drop-outs. It also allowed the University to use the more favourable calculation of student progress rates from the confirmation of final registration.

What this strategy masks is the variable early drop-out rate between students from different educational and social class backgrounds and between different subject areas. For example, Woodley (1989) records that while the overall early drop-out rate in 1989 was 28 per cent, it rose to 42 per cent for those who were unemployed and for those with no educational qualifications. Younger students and those in the London Region were also more vulnerable, at 35 per cent and 34 per cent respectively. Separating those with 'low' (below A-level) from those with 'high' (some HE) qualifications showed a gap between the two groups of around 15 per cent, with science and maths showing early drop-out rates of 43 and 41 per cent respectively for those with 'low' qualifications.

The majority of reasons for early drop-out are stated as relating to personal, work and domestic circumstances, with approximately only one in four referring to study problems, the form and content of courses or the OU system. While debate continues as to whether people give truthful answers about their reasons for dropping out, the stability of the size of the 'early drop-out' groups across part-time face-to-face and correspondence study is consistent with the explanation that early reasons have more to do with whether or not learners can, in practice, fit the extra demands of studies in with their life patterns than the more academic reasons: job changes, illness, pregnancy are all examples.

The issue of whether an 'open door' becomes a merely a 'revolving door' continues to be a live one for the OU and Woodley (1987) tracked the progress of students with low or no qualifications on entry. He noted that the proportion of applicants with low or no qualifications on entry has remained remarkably constant over the years at about the 10 per cent level and that the figure for those with O-levels or less had not risen since 1974. The proportion of applicants with teaching certificates had dropped from 29 per cent in 1971 to 7 per cent in 1987 and the increase in applicants has come from the 'medium' group with some A-levels or less.

Those with low or no qualifications had done best in arts and worst in maths. Their performance was around 20 per cent lower than that of the highly qualified in arts, social science, science and technology, but 35 per cent lower in Maths. Related to this is the question as to whether or not the performance of those with low or no qualifications is getting better or worse over the years. A proper challenge for the OU would be for it to become better and not worse at supporting students with low or no qualifications as it becomes more knowledgeable about the nature of their needs and experienced in its ability to support them. Remakes of courses should be more, not less, accessible than their predecessors.

Figures show (Woodley, 1987) that the performance of those with 'low' or no qualifications was remarkably constant over the years 1980 to 1986 with four out of 10 gaining a credit in each year. Similarly seven out of 10 of the highly qualified gained a credit in each of these seven years. Students with low qualifications do not have the advantage of any credit exemptions and need to gain the full six credits for a degree, which can, however, be accumulated over an indefinite period. Graduation rates, therefore, have to be looked at over a long time period. Woodley shows the cumulative graduation rates of the 1972 intake over a 15-year period broken down by specific educational qualifications and notes that the overall graduation rates for successive OU intakes appears to be decreasing. While each of the first seven intakes of teachers graduated at virtually identical rates over a 10-year period, the graduation rates of those with low or no qualifications, he noted, have tended to decline from intake to intake.

These issues were pursued by the OU's founding Dean of Science in the second Ritchie Calder Memorial Lecture (Pentz, 1991) using the same criterion of highest educational qualification on entry. Science pass-rates, he recorded, were better than maths and technology at the foundation level, better than technology at second level and better than all except arts at third level. Between 1971 and 1987 the proportion of students entering to study science with 'high' educational qualifications had decreased from 53 per cent to 30 per cent, and those with 'low' qualifications had increased from 26 per cent to 34 per cent, a 'step in the right direction in terms of the OU's basic aims as the University of the second chance', he noted, but 'only if those with low entry qualifications did not also show much lower pass-rates'. He used student progress statistics to measure the gap between the pass-rates of the well-qualified on entry compared with the low-qualified on entry, calling it an 'educational discrimination factor' and showed that for S101, the second science Foundation course, the 'low' group's pass rate was 64.6 per cent and the 'high' group was 85.0 per cent, giving a ratio of 1.32.

His proposition was that as students went on to second and third level courses, their progress should be less affected by their educational origin and the size of the factor should reduce. In fact the ratios did improve:

aggregating all the science second level courses gave a factor of 1.28 and all the third level courses gave 1.17. What these encouraging overall figures concealed were differences between the science subjects with biology and earth sciences improving, chemistry stable and physics getting worse. Thus, he suggested, the odds for a highly qualified entrant achieving a degree could vary even between science subjects from 6–7 to 1 for biology, earth sciences and chemistry to 15 to 1 for physics. These odds and the differences between them were not, he suggested, reasonable and the challenge was to work out how to apply what the faculty had learned in order to better support the less well qualified.

It is also arguable that the less well-qualified are not well served by a credit structure with at least six separate hurdles to overcome. The conventional exercise of norm-referenced assessment implicitly assumes that there will be a proportion who fail each course, whereas it is equally possible that everyone who has made it to third level will already have displayed the ability to pass.

Conventional higher education institutions have historically selected those that they believe are likely to succeed. Once in the institution, students both young and mature, are in the main well supported both academically and financially, with fewer internal hurdles to pass. The same is not true for OU students: though the quality of their courses are high, most of them have to continue to work while studying and to fund their own studies. Open admission brings in significant numbers of entrants with low or no qualifications. Woodley described this OU group as containing more women, somewhat more arts and social science students, more who were under 25, more who were 40–64, and more who were in blue-collar or routine white-collar jobs.

It also included more people from institutions, particularly prisons, and disabled students. While disabled students often have low or no qualifications, they have typically made good progress, since their lack of qualifications is more likely to be due to disruptions or inadequacies in their previous education. The OU now provides for some 4,500 adults with physical or sensory disabilities, a major extension of opportunity.

Access for minority ethnic groups is an increasing concern. The OU now takes in the same proportion of minority ethnic groups as are represented in the national population, but this is a far lower proportion than many of the new universities, for whom access and drop-out is also becoming an important issue. Since the majority of these are adult students, it will be increasingly important for the sectors to learn from each other in an endeavour to ensure that the 'open door' does not become a 'revolving door' (McIntosh, 1975).

## Transferability of Credit and Convergence between the Systems

The main task of the OU's first decade was to build up its profile of courses to provide a credible degree programme, and this pre-occupied its internal planning processes for several years. Meanwhile the very success of its own students put pressure on conventional institutions to review their admissions and recognition procedures. The Open University had, from its inception, a particular commitment to the notion of transferability. The Vice-Chancellor was on record as saying that the University was 'determined to act as a catalyst for credit transfer in Great Britain' (Perry, 1976). The credit structure adopted by the OU was at that time unusual in the UK, though such structures now, after nearly 20 years, have become commonplace.

OU students became interested in and interesting to conventional institutions in three ways:

- they wished to use their foundation course credits in lieu of A-levels for entry to degree programmes
- they wished to use a group of credits to gain advanced entry to degree courses
- they wished to use their OU credits to assist in gaining professional recognition ,e.g. in social work, psychology, engineering or town planning.

Given the autonomy of universities, it was necessary to negotiate with each one individually both on recognition for entry and for advanced standing. This was not an easy task as many conventional universities were obdurate in their insistence on their historic admissions requirements: the requirement of Birmingham University for matriculation was just one example. During 1975, ground-rules for equivalence were agreed with a small number of more open-minded universities, Lancaster, Kent, Salford and Sussex, and in 1976 a more ambitious agreement involving mutual availability of courses and a joint transcript was made with Bulmershe College of Higher Education. At the same time some individual polytechnics, notably Liverpool, started to accept individual students with advanced standing, thus building up valuable case-law.

These moves were given added weight by the James Committee's proposals that there should be a new general qualification called the Diploma of Higher Education, which could be terminal in nature or could lead on to a degree which could either be obtained through the same institution or though transfer to another institution. A serendipitous award of an Honorary Degree by the OU to Edwin Kerr, then Chief Executive of the CNAA, was the occasion for an informal understanding that the time was ripe for a comprehensive agreement between the OU and the CNAA covering all the students in both systems, a key move in widening opportunities for adults in higher education since it was to cover over 100,000 students on CNAA validated courses and over 60,000 OU students. The formal agreement – a reciprocal transfer of credit – arrangement was made in July 1977 and was designed to enable 'students to transfer between them with credit for past studies'. Its particular value was to allow more interchange between full and part-time study, improving real access within the system, particularly for adult students. An OU survey at that time showed 12 per cent of OU students not dropping out, but using their credits to 'drop-in' to other studies.

It was not an accident that this agreement was followed soon after by an initiative from Gordon Oakes, then Minister of State at the DES, who held a consultative meeting in 1977 and followed it up by setting up a steering committee to look at educational credit transfer. The committee was chaired by Clifford Butler, then Vice-Chancellor of Loughborough, and included all the major players: the OU, the CNAA, the Committee of Directors of Polytechnics (CDP) and the Business Education Council (BEC). It appointed Peter Toyne as Project Director of a feasibility study of 'educational credit transfer' the report on which gave undoubted impetus to the credit transferability movement (Toyne, 1979).

## The Development of Continuing Education

Meanwhile, the OU had not limited itself entirely to courses at higher education level, but had introduced a limited number of 'post-experience' courses outside the undergraduate degree programme. It set up a working group early in 1974 to look at the post-experience area in general and at the University's possible contribution to non-undergraduate work in terms of the objects stated in the University's Charter:

The objects of the University shall be the advancement and dissemination of learning and knowledge by teaching and research, by a diversity of means such as broadcasting and technological devices appropriate to higher education, by correspondence tuition, residential courses and seminars and in other relevant ways and shall be to provide education of University and professional standards for its students, and to promote the educational well-being of the community generally.

The second object opened the way for the University to take the broad view of 'continuing education' that many involved were working for and the University in January, 1975 set up a Committee on Continuing Education, under the chairmanship of Sir Peter Venables and with a majority of outside experts, to advise on the way ahead. In its report, it was argued that:

Far from threatening the undergraduate programme, we maintain that it is more likely that proposals for the various kinds of continuing education made in this report will improve access and performance both in the Open University and in other educational institutions (Venables, 1976: 18).

What was critical, of course, was that DES funding was only provided for the undergraduate programme, for which numbers and fee-levels were precisely laid down: to extend to non-undergraduate continuing education courses for adults would require additional funding to be sought from elsewhere.

Arguments were already raging internationally about the most appropriate name for a proper strategy for post-secondary or indeed for post-initial learning. While America favoured lifelong learning, the French were using education permanente and the OECD and the Scandinavians preferred recurrent education. The OU favoured 'continuing education' and the Venables Committee 'felt it to be sufficiently inclusive in character to allow adequate scope for consideration of the OU's role'.

Continuing education is thus understood by the Committee to include all learning opportunities which are taken up after full-time compulsory schooling has ceased. They can be full- or part-time and will include both vocational and non-vocational study. ... We have therefore chosen to focus attention on education for adults which is normally resumed after a break or interruption, often involving a period in employment (*ibid.*: 6).

The Committee accepted, it records, that the OU would only be able to meet its second Charter responsibility if substantial additional resources were made available for the non-degree programme. While it recognised that its undergraduate programme had broadened access to *higher education* the Committee was convinced that the OU was 'especially well placed to make an indispensable contribution, particularly in cooperation with many other interests to the future of continuing education' (*ibid.*: 83) and that it should seek further funds earmarked for this end.

The Committee's recommendations covered content and structure and suggested a number of ways in which the OU should collaborate with other providers: among others, in the development of an educational advisory service for adults; by offering experimental packages of learning materials which could be used by other institutions; in the development of 'adult concern' courses for which accreditation at O- and A-level could be offered; in collaboration with appropriate bodies to produce further post-experience courses; and in pilot experiments with polytechnics and colleges whereby part-time independent learning students might spend a day a week using their labs or other specialist work-space.

The emphasis on collaboration was significant and related to the Committee's concern that while reaction to its interim report had been generally supportive, some of the comments had 'charged us with planning to become some kind of "national comprehensive university" which building on its successful experience to date, would pose a threat by its (assumed) imperialist ambitions for the future' (*ibid.*: 14) In general, with some notable exceptions, there has been nothing like enough collaboration between the sectors though whose fault this is remains a difficult question to answer. Certainly OU materials are used in other settings, but often without acknowledgment. Heavily pre-structured materials designed for use in one setting are not always flexible enough for transfer elsewhere. The 'not invented here' syndrome tends to dominate, and has affected subsequent open learning developments such as the Open Tech, the Open College and the Open Learning Foundation (ex-Open Polytechnic). Moves to independence for and competition between higher education institutions makes collaboration more, not less difficult.

The Committee ended its introduction by emphasising the need to achieve cost-effectiveness.

To this end it will need to utilise to the full the savings which accrue when learning resources have standard elements which can be widely used, and which encourage independent learning (ibid.: 15).

It is not possible to map the development of the OU's continuing education provision in detail. Brian Groombridge (1979) noted:

The Russell Committee did not anticipate the extent to which the OU would itself wish to enter these other fields, but the Venables Report accepts that the OU would not seek any kind of monopoly ...

He continued acerbically, but with foresight:

If you approve the OU's move into other non-degree forms of continuing education, you will call it dynamic. If it worries you, you will brand it as imperialistic. Those of us who call it dynamic, must recognise however, that there are bound to be problems of adjustment, especially at a time when the world of higher education seems to lack self-confidence and the sector formally designated 'adult education' has been badly mauled in the spurious name of economy cuts. Complementarity must be the watch word (ibid.: 24).

A modest start was made with short community courses for parents; the 'Pre-School Child' with the Pre-School Play-groups Association was the first. Another significant decision was to permit people to study individual courses from the undergraduate programme as associate students, but paying a fee which was nearer full-cost, thus circumventing the control on overall undergraduate student numbers, but storing up trouble in relation to a future rational and equitable fees policy. The 1995 list available for non-undergraduate study comprised 263 packs or courses, but most of them were professional or vocational and adult and community education packs or courses formed only a small proportion.

By the end of its first decade, the OU was safely established, but was equally not the universal panacea for educational disadvantage. It was clearly a very hard way to learn, put a heavy premium on literacy, the use of the written word and the ability to be tough minded and study independently. In a 'good' world, it was argued, the educationally disadvantaged would go to Oxbridge and the elite to the OU.

## Maintaining Growth against Hard Times

Perhaps it was inevitable that an institution that grew so fast would face hard financial times. The 1980s saw a Government not sympathetic to public expenditure and increasingly hostile to the Open University, partly for political reasons. The OU was not seen as politically neutral by the Government. There were attacks on alleged Marxist bias, and the Government set up a new Visiting Committee to review the institution. Annual Reports repeatedly noted major reductions in funding: cuts of £3.5 million in 1980, a further cut of £1.5 million in 1981, the capital grant halved in real terms in 1982 and cuts amounting to £13.5 million over the three years 1984-6 (20 per cent in real terms) described as 'crippling reductions, requiring not just efficiency savings or marginal cuts but major and long-term reductions in levels of activity and in the quality of student services'. Between 1976 and 1982, the Government required the OU to increase the undergraduate student fee from £25 to £120 for a full-credit course (excluding summer school fees). This fee level was to put the OU's fees higher than those for part-time students studying part-time at Birkbeck College or at their local polytechnic. By 1995, the course fee had increased to £279.

The OU fought back strongly under the quiet but effective leadership of its second Vice-Chancellor, John Horlock, mobilising the support of the now large numbers of students, graduates, full- and part-time staff and resulting in the presentation of a 165,000 name petition at 10 Downing Street calling for restored funding. This political effort resulted in much media coverage and produced the highest number of applications to the OU in 1986 in any year of its history to date. On the occasion of the OU's twenty-fifth anniversary, Horlock described his effort as Vice-Chancellor as 'diversification': into management education, health and social welfare and, very significant, moving into Europe. Research was a major priority, enabling the OU to obtain a credible rating of 3.27 in the 1992 research selectivity exercise. He noted, however, that it had taken nine years to succeed in moving into foreign languages and only recently had Senate accepted a BSc as well as a BA degree. With his emphasis on research and the Business School with its successful launch of its MBA, the OU's focus was clearly on higher education or on professional up-dating.

In a speech on the same occasion, Walter Perry is on record as saying that he always believed that the most important role for the OU would be to update and refresh people's skills, i.e. to provide continuing education, but it would have been quite impossible for the University to start with that. It had first to gain credibility through its undergraduate degree programme. Its second stage was to come with the development of continuing education, and its third stage would be a technological explosion, a network of communications superhighways.

Its third Vice-Chancellor, John Daniel, recorded that on his arrival morale in the University was not high. While other countries admired its achievements, the external environment in the UK was at best indifferent, at worst hostile. The setting up by the DFE of a formal review confirmed these fears. The major explanation of these attitudes links back to the fears noted by Van Straubenzee 20 years earlier. The OU was one of only three institutions directly funded by the DES/DFE and its budget was larger than any other. The cuckoo had grown far too large for the nest, and whereas it had been possible at its inception to treat its funding as a one-off, separate from the rest of post-school education, with the overall increase in participation in higher education it became increasingly necessary to relate OU funding decisions to the decisions of the funding councils, the UFC and PCFC, that financed the rest of higher education. The University realised, Daniel noted in the same speech, that the Review was designed to help the Government decide how to fit the OU into the new structure of higher education that was about to be proposed, and indeed the White Paper *Higher Education: A new framework* (DES, 1991) called for the integration of the OU into the proposed new unified funding structure. The outcome of the Review was highly favourable and Ministers decided that funding some extra students at the OU was a good investment, and therefore permitted new growth in enrolment numbers.

Fortunately, Graeme Davies, the chief executive of the new Higher Education Funding Council, relished the task of finding a way to work out equivalences between conventional full-time institutions where part-time numbers were small with the massive part-time numbers of the OU. These calculations were to the OU's benefit, as was their decision to allow continued expansion of part-time student numbers with the result that in 1994 the OU received both the largest grant and the largest percentage increase of any UK university. The new funding methodologies emphasised cost-effectiveness and evidence that the OU operated at half the average cost of the HE system per equivalent full-time student put it in this favourable position.

By this means, the OU has become integrated into the higher education system of the UK, whether everyone approved of this or not. The integration was made even firmer when the CNAA was wound up under the 1992 Further and Higher Education Act and the OU was accepted by the DES as an appropriate body to take over some of the CNAA's residual functions, notably its Validation Services, now the Open University Validation Services (OUVS) and Quality Support Centre.

Many higher education institutions, predominantly polytechnics, had already followed the OU in moving towards modular structures and in providing credit accumulation and transfer schemes (CATS) within their institutions. However, unlike the original OU/CNAA transferability agreement which had been designed to facilitate transfer between institutions, the new schemes have been predominantly operated within institutions. OUVS plays a full part in the HEQC Credit and Access project and the development of a national framework for credit has become an important goal. Tracking of transferring students is not yet sophisticated enough for people to know how many and what sorts of people transfer between institutions, though the new Higher Education Statistics Agency (HESA) has undertaken to investigate this. It will be increasingly necessary if a comprehensive post-school modularisation of credit framework is developed.

The CNAA inheritance has also strengthened the reach of the OU into the conventional system, with its accreditation of awards in 59 institutions. By 1994, 15 per cent of the degrees awarded by the OU were in non-OU programmes, and most of them were earned not through distance but conventional education. The addition of the CNAA's Doctoral Programme doubled the number of OU research students to around 1,000.

Another significant move enabled by the acquisition of the skills of the Validation Services is that the OU became the first university to be granted awarding body status by the National Council for Vocational Qualifications. This is seen by the OU as an area of expansion under its five-year Plan for Vocational Qualifications, agreed in 1993 and more than 55 courses and study packs, involving nearly 3,000 students, now attract NVQ tax relief.

## Convergence and Divergence

The experience of the OU in providing a flexible part-time degree structure for adults, many without conventional qualifications, has clearly encouraged the increasing adoption of modular credit structures and increased acceptance of mature students. In this sense the sector as a whole has moved towards the practices of the OU, and the OU, by its example, has opened up even more opportunities for adults. Financial convergence has worked to the advantage of the OU and to part-time students, though these remain in a minority, except in further education and in post-graduate education. The new institutional funding arrangements, favouring part-time provision, at the same time encourage more competition from conventional institutions, increasing available opportunities for adult students. Part-time students in all sectors are, however, still disadvantaged compared with full-time students since they all have to pay their own tuition fees, from adult education classes through to MBAs.

Access and open learning have been placed firmly on the agenda of the whole of higher education. However, while funding and structures were converging, practices of teaching and learning and educational development were not. John Daniel claimed that the OU 'has broken, once and for all, the link between quality and exclusivity that was once taken for granted in higher education' (OU, 1995). It did this by using a wide variety of media-based approaches to teaching and learning which were still novel to many universities.

The OU is in the business of the provision of mass higher education, and uses both the mass media and other media to help it in its task. The reason for this is the obvious one, that though the media are not cheap, they become cheap when used for large numbers. This necessarily involves at some levels standardised content and a mass product. The OU has been criticised for reducing the educational experience received by its students through the combined use of independent learning and highly structured materials, with complaints about standardised tutor-marking procedures failing to allow for individual differences. It is true that content cannot be individualised for each learner. What can be individualised by the students themselves is their pattern of study; how they choose to use the pattern of learning resources, how long they spend over their studies, over what time period, their place of study and the pattern of subjects they choose. The tutors responsible for marking assignments must mark within an agreed framework set by the course designers if quality and standards are to be maintained and be equitable. It is the flexibility offered to students to choose how, what, when and where they study which is a major factor influencing large numbers of learners to continue to choose the OU rather than conventional part-time provision.

Otto Peters, founding Vice-Chancellor of the Fernuniversität in Germany, argues that distance education is the most industrialised mode of teaching and learning, but that this is 'in harmony with historical tendencies to become more egalitarian, more profane (sic), more determined by the students, more mechanised, more accessible by larger groups of students, and less tied to special persons, places and times' (Keegan, 1994). It is marked by the division of labour and Otto Peters suggests that 'judged in terms of (this historical interpretation) distance education is more advanced in the categories given and traditional instruction is lagging behind.'

The argument for face-to-face teaching is the importance of the (labour-intensive) interaction between teacher and learner. Most discussion focuses on the interactivity, conventionally provided through face-to-face teaching, usually without distinguishing whether the desired interactivity is between the tutor and the learner, the content and the learner or between learners themselves. Not enough is known yet about the depth of interactivity required, for what sorts of learners, for what sorts of content and at what sorts of cost-levels. Distance learning needs to have a high degree of interactivity built into the text and other materials *ab initio*. The challenge is to use the new technologies to individualise or personalise the mass-produced materials as effectively as possible.

Convergence in the structures of higher education, and maybe of all post-school education is being parallelled by convergence between television and communications technologies. At its inception the OU was concerned not to use media which were out of reach of many learners in order to maintain access and equity. For example, facilities were provided for viewing and listening in study centres. Increasingly, both for practical and economic reasons the OU has shifted more of the expenditure for such equipment from the University to students, with the result that such developments have been dictated by the advance of the domestic market. The OU is anxious to maintain its technological lead and remains in the forefront of experimentation with electronic teleconferencing, advanced computer courses and the use of the Internet and has agreed a Technology Strategy for Academic Advantage.

Its vision statement is revealing: it argues that priorities should now change, that developments should ensure that all students who have access to such technology can gain maximum benefit and that 'current access figures and trends show that the priority for the University's information technology policy can now be to concentrate on providing services for those students who do have access.' The down-side of this is that access to elements of the electronic superhighway is not cheap and is likely to deter a number of less advantaged applicants. It will be ironic if the information superhighway is only open to learners who already have or can afford the appropriate technology.

Where does this then leave the broader field of continuing education and more particularly the provision of general education for adults? It is quite clear that the latter is not now a primary concern of the University, though continuing education and more particularly continuing professional development is. As noted earlier, all courses and materials which are not part of the undergraduate programme have had to cover their costs, though of course cross subsidy is possible inside and between other programme areas. New developments are increasingly in vocational areas, where accreditation is possible or desirable. The move into NVQ accreditation is particularly significant: it also raises the issue of direct FEFC funding to the OU as a provider.

While there remains much general provision for adults, this is not a main goal, and the very way in which it is referred to in terms of 'packs sold' rather than 'learners reached' is indicative. Though packs may be used by many learners, and estimates of numbers reached are over 50,000, there is no hard learner-based research about the sorts of learners they are reaching. However, with the decline in provision of adult education by local authorities and the greater interest for good or bad reasons in open learning, such provision may become increasingly important as other traditional adult provision is cut back.

Brian Groombridge described the OU as having 'conferred social and political status on being an adult student' (1979: 23). Evidently, the OU has provided a very large number of adult learners with new learning opportunities. By its example and their success it has made the case for a substantial change in attitude and structure in conventional institutions and among decision-makers which has substantially increased adult opportunities particularly for higher and continuing education. What is less clear is how high a price has been paid in the historic diversion of funds and attention from general adult provision and whether this has been due to direct actions of the OU or is simply a by-product of its mere existence, almost as a monument. The charge still to be answered is its provision of support for and degree of openness to less well qualified entrants which, it can be argued, is still more apparent than real. The new danger is that, in its commitment to be in the forefront of technological innovation, it introduces new financial and technological barriers to access and forgets its historic commitment to be '... open as to people'.

*12*

# Adult Education Auxiliaries and Informal Learning

## *Peter Baynes and Harold Marks*

The importance in adult liberal education provision of a miscellany of agencies has been recognised since a British Institute of Adult Education pamphlet drew attention to what it dubbed adult education 'auxiliaries' (Williams, 1934). This chapter attempts an account of some of the changes in this growing but increasingly disparate provision.

It considers organisations with primary purposes outside adult education. Many have a largely social intention, sometimes restricted to particular groups. The expectation that these might become bases for increased, and particularly less formal, adult education work has generally been disappointed. Williams maintained that voluntary organisations often offered more accessible, flexible and appropriate educational opportunities for adults than the 'traditional' providers, and Thompson (1992: 156) argues that 'history suggests that voluntary associations may well survive to remain a cutting edge of adult education – provided that the new government funding body and the revamped Further Education sector co-operate'. To the older established voluntary bodies must now be added other providers for those seeking lifelong learning opportunities, whether at the radical end of a continuum (Thomas, 1982; Lovatt, 1988), or seeking enlightenment on more conventional lines.

Growing popular interest in specialised subjects and issues has led to a great development of voluntary organisations, with particular concerns and purposes often involving an adult education function. They too must be recognised as auxiliaries. So must commercial enterprises meeting the potential of demand for published material of adult educational importance, as well as for more course provision. The performing base essential to spreading aesthetic education, stressed in 1934 as so pressing a need, has grown enormously, and with it organisations concerned with the practice of the arts. Galleries and museums have also developed their adult education role, as have the public libraries, which have extended their provision to aid the development of individual study.

While broadcasting is the subject of Chapter 14, space does not allow an assessment of the significant contribution of film and the associated institutional developments, nor the contribution made to adult education by religious organisations and the youth service.

## The Bureau of Current Affairs

The Bureau of Current Affairs was established in 1946 in the hope that wartime interest in current affairs and related discussion as a staple of informal adult education, which had spread beyond ABCA (see Chapter 3) to the RAF and civilian war-work agencies, could be continued post-war.

Its director was W. E. Williams and its initiation, as with other adult education experiments of the time, depended on trust finance. The £150,000, in this case provided from the Carnegie United Kingdom Trust, turned out to be rather less than half of the total expenditure, the remainder coming from sales. Partly because of a fear that existing adult education organisations would not tolerate a subsidised competitor, the BCA did no organising or development but was only a servicing agency for other organisations. It provided briefs for group use, well illustrated, informative and provocative, written by experts and well designed to promote discussion. It also published informative and stimulating posters for wall display in educational institutions, and other public places willing to give them space.

The material covered later extended beyond political and social issues to include the arts. A handbook, *Discussion Method*, (BCA, 1950) usefully sets out the possibilities and the value and techniques of discussion in different settings. The Bureau also ran training courses which probably had more influence on the development of industrial training than on adult education.

The BCA put out 142 pamphlets and 141 Map Reviews, with a total circulation of 4.7 and 1.9 million respectively. It also produced a series of 17 more detailed background handbooks on various topics.

Sales to adult education bodies, libraries, and industrial concerns, never made publication economic. The Bureau received a serious blow when the armed services cancelled their mass orders and it then turned increasingly to satisfy a demand from secondary schools. It also gave much help to the growing West African Adult Education movement.

A victim of the decline in post-war idealism and also possibly of an over-extravagant approach to its role and certainly of the slowed immediate post-war growth of adult education, the Bureau closed in 1951. As its historian comments, the 'Bureau symbolised ... a widely felt disgust with propaganda and indoctrination. It stood for an independent service neither ineffectual or escapist. It represented standards of honesty and clarity that are not always much in evidence though they are probably quite widely appreciated' (Ford, 1951). It was not because of any lack of high standards that the BCA failed. The gap it left remains unfilled.

## The National Council of Social Service (later National Council of Voluntary Organisations)

Among the auxiliaries of adult education singled out in the phraseology of the 1934 BIAE pamphlet as important as 'societies for the development of civic values', were those which were established to improve life in specific neighbourhoods. Their development was a major purpose of the National Council of Social Service (NCSS), founded in 1919.

## The NCSS and Village Halls

Rural depopulation and measures to stem it by improving the quality of village life led to much NCSS help in the development of Rural Community Councils which had been established in most counties by 1954. Their purpose, the 'encouragement of social, economic and community life', included Village Hall provision. Grant aid towards this was secured from central government through the Development Commission. In 1924 the Carnegie Trust inaugurated an ingenious revolving loan system. By borrowing from it, Village Hall provision escaped from previous general dependence upon local landowners' charity, and had been extended to 775 villages by 1945 (Brasnett, 1969).

In 1985, 8,500 village halls existed in England, still an important facility for educational as well as social activity in spite of growing problems of maintenance and updating to modern standards. For this latter purpose they still had the use of the revolving loan fund.

Throughout its life the NCSS was a leading force also in encouraging and improving the quality of much other auxiliary educational activity, particularly in music making, amateur drama and the crafts for which it employed staff in the 1930s and 40s. It supported the voluntary organisations concerned, particularly through the organisation of 'standing conferences'. These brought them together often also with individual activists, and provided a valuable stimulus in a variety of areas of adult education. From the early 1980s a policy of 'hiving off' from the NCVO led to the establishment of independent organisations. Following this pattern, Rural Community Councils and village hall concerns were moved in 1990 to a new organisation 'Action for the Community in Rural England' as the successor 'champions of the rural disadvantaged' (ACRE, 1993). Rural education including adult education remained one among the growing number of its social, economic and environmental concerns.

## Community Centres and Associations

In urban, and more particularly sub-urban, neighbourhoods the NCSS encouraged provision to meet local needs which was more comprehensive, and was organised on the basis of a more sophisticated ideology, derived in part from the social settlement pattern. The first community associations, bringing together in groups with varying purposes the residents of the new municipal estates, came into existence in 1927. The needs of estate residents raised the concern of sympathisers who, through the NCSS, were able to enlist the support of trusts. Their social sympathy was strengthened by philosophical thinking about the nature of effective democracy, most notably by Follett (1929). The establishment of a movement, already spreading beyond council estates, was greatly helped after 1937 by growing government concern about the physical condition of a nation likely shortly to be at war. The resulting Physical Training and Recreation Act of 1938 increased the very modest government funding available by providing central grants towards buildings.

By 1940, and in spite of the difficulties caused by the outbreak of war, 220 Associations were active in many urban areas. All had as one of their objectives the acquisition of their own community centre buildings. With the coming of serious hostilities in 1940, the expansion of the movement ended, though some kindred war workers' and service clubs were established.

In 1944 the Board of Education committed itself to widespread development of community centres as an essential part of government policy for post-war social and adult educational provision (Board of Education, 1944). Though material shortages and financial difficulties restricted building, many neighbourhood associations succeeded in establishing centres: by 1960, 929 were known to exist. In 1981 the influential National Federation of Community Associations (established 1945), estimated the number of Associations and similar neighbourhood bodies as being well over 2,000 with more than 500,000 members. Two thirds of the organisations were responsible for some sort of community centre (Clarke, 1990).

In many places centres were greatly assisted by local authorities which often helped with salaries and running expenses as well as with erecting buildings. Capital grants however came mainly still from central government's education departments until 1975 when this duty was passed to the LEA's: new provision then slowed.

Central government grant had been restricted, with the strong support of the NFCA, to Associations which adopted a model constitution to ensure that they were concerned with overall neighbourhood welfare and could bring together all reputable local organisations, and run a multi-purpose centre. The imposition of such a rigid pattern was of doubtful wisdom. The effective running of an umbrella organisation proved to be most difficult in relatively deprived areas. Here narrower based organisations, often campaigning for tenants' rights, or to reduce social inequalities, had been established, particularly after 1965, and seemed more likely to meet local needs. The Home Office provided considerable finance towards four such Community Development Projects in that year as a possible alternative to Community Associations. (See Chapter 5.)

In 1980, partly in response to all these changes, and hoping to broaden its membership to a wider range of generalist neighbourhood associations, the NFCA became a National Federation of Community Organisations. After 1982 it gained independence of the National Council of Voluntary Organisations, which was dropping all its direct provision activities and concentrating on representing and servicing the range of voluntary organisations.

The NFCO, now under a popular title of 'Community Matters' and mainly financially supported by the Voluntary Services Unit of the Home Office rather than the Department for Education, had rather more than 800 member organisations in 1995. Far more were known to exist. Some new groups of this type were still being established but new community centre provision had become unusual, with financial help now restricted to District Councils.

The concerns of community associations widened after the mid 70's to include problems stemming particularly from unemployment. As well as helping neighbourhood associations to meet new demands, Community Matters, with the decline of LEA expenditure on all forms of liberal adult education, had to help its members threatened in their continuance principally from changes in charity and taxation law and requirements for higher physical standards in premises.

The Board of Education had set community centre development at the heart of its hopes for post-war expansion, particularly through more informal provision, of adult education. They were not fully realised. More informal adult education might have developed had government support been accorded to a variety of bodies which had this as a primary purpose. A number of community centres, generally in middle class rather than old working class or municipal estate areas, did however prove very successful as providers of informal and formal adult education. Associations acted as active partners helping the local education authorities in carrying out their duties to provide adult education under the 1944 Education Act. The difficulty of raising enough money to meet running costs frequently led Associations in less affluent areas to concentrate on the most popular social activities together with physical recreation provision. Social welfare needs also claimed more of their energy. However, from their inception very many community centres provided some informal education. A pamphlet of 1949 describes the scope of activity, together with some of the possibilities (Marks, 1949). They included the educational effects deriving from participation in the organisation and running of a neighbourhood social association. This proved to be a more significant aspect of the community association contribution to adult education in general than the organisation of specific educational activities, formal or informal.

## Other Voluntary Organisations as Adult Auxiliaries

The twentieth century has witnessed the establishment of a great number of voluntary organisations with many different specialist concerns. In 1928 the NCSS listed 180 such organisations in its first Directory. From 1948 to 1978 the count remained static at about 400; it then rose steadily to 2,500 by 1995, mostly of a national character. A minority only of those organisations regarded themselves as having an adult educational purpose. Many more, including the largest and most significant, may however be regarded as major adult auxiliaries.

Williams (1934) drew attention to the importance of a few such organisations to adult education, and Kelly (1993) considered them further. Their role lay first in raising consciousness on very many specialised issues of public importance and as major sources of information in regard to them. In this they may well have exercised a greater influence than the traditional adult education agencies, even if few of them attempted to provide the unbiased treatment, taking all sides and arguments into account in the accepted mode of adult tutors' handling of controversial issues.

The validity of a claim to adult educational importance of any particular voluntary organisation depends in part on the relative weight it accords to a genuinely informational as compared with a propagandist or campaigning role, and the means adopted as most likely to be effective in pursuit of it.

NACRO (The National Association for the Care and Resettlement of Offenders) is an example of an organisation which adopted a strongly educational role. It was formed in 1966 from an established amalgamation of groups endeavouring to give charitable help to discharged prisoners. Among the purposes set out in its new constitution were 'developing public awareness of the problems of offenders' and being a 'centre from which interested persons can obtain details of existing or proposed projects, current or proposed research ... (and) other information'. A budget of £35 million 30 years later, much of it derived from government grants, is largely spent on a wide variety of projects and experiments and research concerned with the treatment of offenders and particularly their problems with finding housing and employment after release. It includes also a number in the area of adult education. NACRO has been an important influence on the development of prison education and on relating it to public educational provision.

Impartial regular briefings on all penal policy and developments are a major source of information to 2,200 members and subscribers. These include some generally interested as well as a larger number of persons concerned professionally, if often voluntarily, as magistrates or otherwise. Press briefings serve a still wider constituency. These reflect an informative and educational rather than a campaigning style and tone. A separate consortium was established in 1994 of NACRO in association with other organisations concerned with penal policy, to pursue campaigning purposes.

Williams (1934) recognised the adult education contribution of the Council for the Protection (then Preservation) of Rural England. Founded in 1926 as an association of affiliated groups, it moved to an individual membership basis with 45,000 members by 1993. CPRE was a more specifically campaigning body than some other specialised organisations, but it rightly claimed to have as its principal weapons 'careful research, constructive ideas, reasoned argument, as well as a knowledge of how to get things done and effective lobbying'. For its members and others, through the circulation of a periodical, publication of large numbers of books and pamphlets and its public relations work, its claim to be an adult educational force remained clear.

At the other end of the spectrum of voluntary national, and in this case international organisations, Greenpeace may be cited as an example of one primarily campaigning through action for change which nevertheless also served an adult educational function.

The National Trust is of importance in an adult educational context not only because of its dominating size as the largest essentially voluntary organisation, although it has a statutory basis. It was established in 1895 as an organisation for the preservation of the amenity of the countryside, later developing its interest in historic houses. Its membership in 1969 was 177,000 rising to two and a quarter of a million by 1995. Its expansion illustrates the significance of the motorcar as an agent of change in adult education as in other aspects of life. By 1975 the Trust's purpose of preservation of the countryside and later extension to a museum function in relation to houses and their contents, developed to include the presentation of the historical significance of the country house as an agent of social history. If this function is sometimes alleged to involve a somewhat distorted historical perspective, the same accusation cannot be substantiated in relation to its educative efforts in the area of environmental studies. Guidebooks, catalogues and other informative publications together with a quarterly journal with a circulation of 1.1 millions were supplemented, after the appointment of an education officer in 1979, by increasing organisation of educational activities mainly for young people and children but also sometimes for adult visitors. One of its historians comments 'In the end what really matters in the life of the National Trust is the preservation of its properties and their enjoyment' (Gaze, 1988: 253). Clarke, L. in a final chapter adds 'Education had once been considered a word of doubtful taste at (National Trust headquarter offices). It is now fully embraced as a means of realising what the Trust has to offer the nation rather than as a didactic exercise' (ibid.: 312), though its contribution to the education of adults remains incidental to its major purpose and its possibilities are largely unrealised. In 1995 it launched a lifelong learning project, Minerva, followed by the appointment of an adult education officer.

The National Association of Decorative and Fine Arts Societies is an example of a group reflecting the growing interest in the arts. It grew from the enthusiasm and organisational skills of Patricia Fay who formed a first local society in 1965. The National Association came into existence in 1968. It included 80 local societies by 1976; by 1993 there were 69,000 members, largely but not exclusively women in 276 groups in the United Kingdom, together with further groups in Europe.

The aims of NADFAS, which became a democratically organised charitable trust, were 'the promotion and advancement of the aesthetic education of the public, the cultivation, appreciation and study of the decorative and fine arts, and the giving of aid to the preservation of our national artistic heritage for the benefit of the public'. The basic activity of local groups lay in a monthly lecture programme. Tutors were drawn from a panel approved by the national organisation, which also organised more concentrated and demanding study courses, including a foundation course in arts appreciation. Much of the teaching generally was based upon visits to collections. From 1973 onwards the Association also trained a growing number of volunteers to help with the conservation of art objects. Other volunteers recorded the contents of churches. A 'Young NADFAS' was also established. An associated trading company organised foreign holiday travel with cultural content. Local societies were responsible for paying their own way and the central organisation relied for its finance mainly on their contributions together with profits from its trading enterprise.

By 1995 there were few subjects of interest to adult students not also the concern of some voluntary organisation. The situation in a wide variety of social concerns was similar. Many of the voluntary organisations were highly specialised in subject interest; they included national learned societies whose connection with liberal adult education as well as their continued professional concerns varied greatly.

Interest in archaeology may serve as an example of provision in a subject area. Possibly responding to a growing national tendency to retrospection, but more certainly because of the impact of television, and publicity in relation to property development and road building, its remarkable growth since 1946 has been reflected also in the changes in adult education study subjects. In 1995 between 400 and 500 voluntary organisations concerned with archaeology were known to exist (excluding museums). The number grew steadily after the war to a peak in 1975, after which they stabilised, perhaps partly due to the growth of professional employment and the public funding of digs. The steady growth in the circulation of the publication *Current Archaeology*, since it was established in 1967, reflects the interest in the subject. It is one example of a rapid growth in the number and circulation of specialised magazines dealing with an enormous variety of subjects aimed at the general public. Their development is in itself a significant contribution to adult education provision so far unevaluated. The Writers' and Artists' Yearbook for 1994 included 84 pages listing magazines published in the UK.

Developments in other subject areas have also been considerable. At the other end of a broad organisational spectrum there were many spontaneous local groupings of adults interested in books or creative writing, music making, and recorded music, crafts, model engineering and a variety of leisure time interests together with aspects of parenting and other personal concerns, which together make a contribution to adult education provision of great, if uncharted, importance.

## Education Through Active Voluntary Body Membership

A minority of the many voluntary organisations in any locality had any formal adult educational objectives. The variety of their purposes and styles has been analysed most recently for the town of Retford in Nottinghamshire (Reynolds *et al.*, 1994) as part of a wider study of adult learning through voluntary organisations (Elsdon, 1991 and 1995; Stewart, 1992). The research suggests that local voluntary organisations in Great Britain number at least 800,000 and possibly 1.3 million. Overall membership, of individuals, may be as high as 30 millions.

Organisations' objectives variously included social, sporting, and leisure occupation, and service to the general public or special community activity, among other purposes. Some were generalist organisations: others highly specialised, but all contributed to the education of their members far beyond their particular objectives.

An understanding of this form of adult learning, which in part inspired the community association movement, has been developed by, among others, Brookfield (1993), who draws upon North American as well as British sources, as well as Elsdon and his colleagues. Their research shows that in the 90 per cent of local voluntary organisations which were democratic in structure, the adult educational dividend for members, though inevitably variable, went far beyond the acquisition of skills, competences and knowledge linked with the particular objectives the organisation pursued. Unpremeditated educational dividends for participants included a widening of interests and knowledge, especially in generalist organisations, and more importantly and very widely, individual member development, growth and empowerment. Some of the most significant educational effects stemmed in particular from active participation in the running of a small voluntary organisation. Progression was reflected in a wide variety of relationships and activities, even including some labelled as of vocational importance. Social effects were widespread and active membership of voluntary organisations was an essential contribution to civil society and the quality of life.

The research shows that participants benefited in these respects from participation in every kind of voluntary organisation, whatever their previous educational experience. Those with least formal education were active members of a wide variety of groups, beyond those pursuing traditional working class leisure pursuits. Local voluntary organisations overall were therefore particularly important in the contribution they made to the education of social groups increasingly excluded by cost and other factors from participating in many of the auxiliary adult agencies considered in this chapter, and indeed from taking part in mainstream adult education provision.

## Commercial Provision

In the 1940s commercial provision of adult education was to a great extent confined to vocational training, including examination preparation through correspondence courses. Summer courses, particularly in the practice and appreciation of the arts developed in the 1950s, following pioneer efforts by the Educational Centres Association in association in the late 40s with the Holiday Fellowship and Co-operative Holidays Association. Educational travel also boomed when currency restrictions were lifted in 1958 and much relatively expensive summer school provision developed.

The rapid rise in cost to the student of public adult education provision speeded a growth of commercially run day courses from the 1980s onwards. The breakdown of unjustifiable distinctions between liberal and growing vocational demands for education in such subjects as languages and computer studies further stimulated commercial provision.

## Women's Groups

Significant contributions to the history of British adult education have stemmed from efforts to secure a more satisfactory position for women in society and to meet their educational needs.

## Co-operative Women's Guilds

The Consumer Co-operative Movement, as an element in the Labour movement, had a long-standing active concern to improve educational provision. As part of this, the first Co-operative Women's Guild was established in 1883. The founders recognised a need to enable women, and in this case working class women, to take a proper role in the running of the male dominated retail societies. In fostering this on a socio-educational club base, they developed a trend pioneered by the Adult School movement.

In the early 1930s Guild membership numbered 60,000, mainly working class, and widely distributed throughout the country. In addition to continuing study and discussion needed to enable them to participate in running cooperative enterprises, they were studying and campaigning in regard to abortion as well as divorce law problems. 2,000 delegates attended their conference in 1933. By 1939 membership peaked at 87,000. Concern for women's issues extended to averting war. There was much co-operation with the WEA in the study of international relations and economics, if at a relatively low level.

With the reorganisation forced on to the retail societies by changing trade practice, society numbers and their prosperity reduced steadily; 85 only remained by 1990. The educational efforts of the Guilds, like educational activity in the movement generally, became more concerned with the movement's own problems, though peace, the interests of young people, consumer education and women's particular concerns in the political arena continued to arouse Guild discussion and conference resolutions. The number of Guilds steadily declined to 246 with a membership of under 5,000 by 1993.

In 1983 it was claimed that the Guilds were a 'major force in support of a liberal and more enlightened society' (*Society for Cooperative Studies*, 1983: 34). Their decline left an important social group increasingly unrepresented among informal adult education providing bodies.

## The National Federation of Women's Institutes

Women's Institutes existed in Canada since 1897, and were introduced into the UK during the First World War. Within two years of the establishment in 1915 in Wales of the UK's first WI, a hundred had been formed, and the first Annual General Meeting of the movement's National Federation was held in London in 1917, with 60 delegates representing 137 WIs. By 1919, 1405 WIs had a total membership of 52,000, and in 1933, 5,111 WIs recorded a membership of 299,000. Growth continued, although there was a slight dip during the Second World War, but recovery was swift, and by 1950, 7,450 WIs had a total membership of 440,000. (Women's Institutes,1951) Although the number of Institutes recorded in the 1993 Annual Report had risen to 8,590, individual membership had dropped to 295,000, and it was proving difficult to offset the ageing membership with younger recruits. However, the Federation remained a powerful body with considerable financial assets and an influential voice in public affairs.

From its beginning the movement had seen its role as a dual one, providing both social and educational opportunities for women and acting as a campaigning body. As with the Townswomen's Guilds, 'many former suffragettes became active members if WIs and contributed to its immediate success' (Women's Institutes, 1994) and the Federation and its constituent Institutes pressed for measures making for social betterment. Educational activities had a predominantly practical bias, but after the Second World War efforts were made to discard the 'jam and Jerusalem image', and there was a liberalising generally of the educational programme of regions and individual Institutes.

This was especially noticeable after 1971. Prior to that, a WI rule required a strictly 'non-party political and non-sectarian' stance. It was then changed, 'enabling Institutes to discuss all matters of political and religious significance provided that minority views were respected and WIs were not used for party political purposes' (Women's Institutes, 1994).

The extent to which the original rule was a reality, especially in the inter-war years, has been questioned, and a study of the Lancashire Federation of WIs during that time produced evidence of considerable

Establishment and pro-Imperialist bias. '... there were ... times when the Lancashire Federation, if not the NFWI itself, promoted establishment propaganda within educational programmes' (Thompson, 1996).

In 1970, Lowe was critical of the educational standards of many WIs, describing their programmes as being: '... very uneven, there is rarely continuity, and members themselves often describe them as "snippety"; the standards of many lectures are also low. The subjects discussed are overwhelmingly concerned with domestic skill ... though technical standards are very high' (Lowe, 1970: 141).

Also in 1970, Kelly commented:

It is difficult to exaggerate the effect of the women's institutes on village life. Hitherto the lives of the womenfolk had been almost entirely circumscribed by the narrow and unceasing round of domestic duties ... The monthly meeting... now became for many women the highlight in their otherwise restricted lives ... They discovered that they had opinions on ... matters and that their opinions were respected ... All this was citizenship education at its best and most practical (Kelly, 1993: 302).

However, there is little indication of the evidence on which Lowe's and Kelly's somewhat conflicting assessments were based.

A 1980 survey on attitudes to the WI of women in membership and outside the movement led to a further updating of the image of WIs, resulting in a three year promotion of three themes: women and education; women and health; and women in public life (Strathclyde University, 1980).

The establishment of a WI residential college – Denman – in 1948 illustrates the WIs ability to respond to new ideas. It was made possible by members' contributions as well as a Carnegie grant and Ministry of Education help towards running expenses. By 1969, despite financial difficulties, it had developed an impressive range of 170 courses annually, including some for mothers with toddlers, and later family weeks. In the anniversary history Kaye concluded: 'Looking ahead into the 70s there seems to be no reason why more advanced studies shouldn't be offered to those who want to go more deeply into a subject ... educational circles now regard (the college's) four-day lecture courses as the equivalent of a term's course in the average sixth form' (Kaye, 1970: 123). By 1995 Denman College had seen over 215,000 WI members attending its courses, and it was equipped to provide for over 6,000 each year. Some courses were week-long, most lasted a weekend, and beyond the WI staples of practical courses, the syllabus included varied subjects.

All courses open up opportunities to progress in the subject. Some enable members to work towards a WI certificate and/or another nationally recognised qualification – often in conjunction with distance learning, federation schools and courses at their local colleges. An increasing number of courses can provide students with the opportunity to gain nationally transferable credits from the Oxfordshire Open College Network in recognition of the work achieved on the courses (Women's Institutes, 1994–5).

During the quarter century after Lowe and Kelly wrote, the educational activities of the WIs deepened and broadened and much more attention was given to andragogical issues (Stamper, 1986). The Women's Institutes may be recognised as a more important contributor to auxiliary adult education than in the 1930s, as well as a major campaigning force.

## Townswomen's Guilds

Guilds, in some respects similar to the WIs and other women's organisations with a social and educational base, were established in urban areas with 4,000 or more inhabitants, from 1928 onwards. Many developed from Suffrage Societies which, after women achieved the vote, formed The National Union for Societies for Equal Citizenship. Its leadership, mainly of committed and well-to-do academic women, worked to develop a movement which would improve the status of women through adult education in handicraft, music and drama, but particularly through social studies.

By 1932, 142 Guilds had been established, and a campaigning organisation for equal citizenship separated itself from what in the next year became the National Union of Townswomen's Guilds. It adopted a rather formal structure designed to ensure that members developed their capacities beyond the requirements of domesticity (Merz, 1988).

Growth of Guild numbers was stimulated by a desire to see some remedy for the economic troubles of the thirties, as well as by the growing recognition of the continuing legal and economic disabilities from which women still suffered. By September 1939 there were 544 Guilds. Activities meeting defence needs, and later postwar planning enthusiasms, led to some increase in members of Guilds even during the war.

In 1948 the TWG was reorganised into a national and regional democratic structure of Guilds meeting monthly. Its constitutional objects were 'to advance the education of women irrespective of race, creed and party, so as to enable them to make the best possible contribution towards the common good; to educate such women in the principles of good citizenship; to provide or assist in the provision of facilities for recreation or other leisure time occupation ... in the interests of social welfare and with a view to improving their conditions of life'. With the aid of central government education grants, staff were employed and educational activity developed strongly. Work in drama, music and the crafts continued, and after 1953 social studies were strengthened by the introduction for consideration by every Guild, of specific questions planned to lead to political pressure over matters of particular social concern to women.

Membership peaked at about a quarter of a million in 2,400 Guilds in 1964. The ageing of the membership and the concentration on specific social studies issues were identified as possible causes of a subsequent decline in numbers. A comprehensive study commissioned from the Tavistock Institute in 1970 noted a paramount local member interest in social and recreational occupation and suggested that these were not easily reconciled with the TWG's educational and public service purposes, particularly in a society which was offering improved general adult education facilities as well as pressing women into employment.

Though membership further declined to 100,000 by 1993, of whom only 27 per cent were under the age of 60, and in spite of continuing financial problems, the Townswomen's Guilds organisation adhered to its adult educational purpose. However, local Guild programmes became more generally recreational in content, showing a considerable increase in a sporting component. Lectures and discussion continued to figure, together with craft activities. The standards achieved in these have been criticised (Adkins, 1980) and the TWG was cited as an example of the unfortunate gulf between professional and amateur standards. Efforts were made to improve them through regional and nationally based courses and other provision; drama and music festivals were similarly used to foster local activity and improve its quality. In the social studies field, techniques were developed to encourage active local participation in national surveys of opinion and provision in relation to environmental issues and those affecting the welfare of children.

## The National Association of Women's Clubs

A further social/educational women's movement developed from the Social Service Clubs in the Special Areas of the 1920s where unemployment was highest. These provided some specific educational activity as well as social and self help facilities, primarily for men, in 1,150 clubs with 160,000 members in 1937. Women's participation was at first generally restricted to a meeting one afternoon a week, though much of the burden of unemployment could only be mitigated by their domestic management skills, including their ability to 'make do and mend' and to create 'new from old'. These accomplishments presented educational possibilities, which together with social needs and those stemming from a doubly disadvantaged situation as the wives of the unemployed, led to a rapid development of separately organised women's clubs. Their progress owed much to an organiser, Lucy Butcher, appointed by the NCSS in 1933. Until her retirement in 1958, and using the usual NCSS device of a Standing Conference, she was secretary of what she turned into a national democratic association of independent women's clubs.

The men's clubs vanished with the drop in unemployment and the 1939–45 War. The women's clubs expanded to meet a fundamental need as well as in response to the changing demands on women of a war-time situation. They developed particularly strongly on municipal housing estates. Even before the war the clubs' educational activity included drama and, in Wales particularly, a good deal of music, as well as art and domestic crafts. Visiting speakers were invited; film shows and WEA classes were arranged. Social work was undertaken among refugees in particular. In 1958 between 400 and 500 women's clubs still had about 15,000 members, though numbers had declined from an immediate post-war high (Brasnett, 1969).

The following 15 years saw another expansion masterminded by a second gifted organiser, Norah (later Baroness) Phillips, and given continued help by many local Councils of Social Service. Some of these also provided professional organising assistance. Efforts to associate the clubs with the growing movement towards consumer education were unsuccessful.

The growth in women's employment, television, and possibly the expansion of more specialised adult education facilities, were blamed for a subsequent decline in number (Nicholas, 1995). Contraction accelerated after 1976 when 'hiving off' from the National Council of Voluntary Organisations left the movement dependent on a small central government education grant together with greatly increased demands on members for financial support. The central organisation was much reduced.

Though temporarily boosted with an effort to bring in clubs for wives in Service establishments, numbers of clubs declined to 220 with 12,000 plus members by 1993. Fundraising to keep clubs and the movement going, and demand for social rather than educational activities, tended increasingly to dominate club programmes. Craft activities continued and resolutions for the annual conference continued to stimulate some local public policy discussion.

A 1990 survey, required for continuation of central education grant, showed that 19 per cent of members had engaged in some FE activity during the preceding five years, often stimulated by club activity; 26 per cent of members were making some sort of social service contribution, and 7 per cent attributed a return to paid work to an increase in personal self-confidence stemming from membership (Nicholas, 1995).

## The National Women's Register

In 1960 an article by Betty Jerman appeared in *The Guardian* newspaper. The gist was that 'home and child-minding can have a blunting effect on a woman's mind'. This led Maureen Nicol to write to the paper suggesting that 'perhaps housebound wives with liberal interests and a desire to remain individuals, could form a national register, so that whenever one moves one can contact like-minded friends.' Within a week Maureen Nicol had received 400 responses and found herself the first National Organiser of a body which, by 1980, had 1,000 local groups and 21,000 members (Jerman, 1981). By 1995 the number of groups had fallen to 800, and the national membership was 10,500–11,000, but despite this decline in numbers, the National Women's Register (the name was changed from the original National Housewives' Register in 1987) remained both a significant body in the field of self-education and personal fulfilment, and an outstanding example of organisational self help and determination.

The aims of NWR were 'to offer to all women the opportunity to take part in informal discussion of a wide range of topics, both serious and light-hearted. NWR hopes to promote friendship, self-education, confidence and a better understanding of others' points of view, and, by means of the Register, to enable members to find friends quickly on moving to a new area' (*The Register*, 1994).

The NWR acquired charitable status, appointed paid officers, sought outside advice on a Strategic Plan, and, probably inevitably, moved to some extent away from the non-hierarchical body that Maureen Nicol had (by accident) set up. Nevertheless it remained essentially a grassroots organisation whose activities were determined by the interests of its members. The self-programming local groups generally consisted of between 10 and 25 women, although there was no rule for a maximum or minimum membership. Another group tended to be set up when size became unwieldy.

A survey conducted in 1970 found that over 60 per cent were aged between 30 and 39 but the age-range subsequently widened. Practically all local groups (94 per cent in 1970) met in each others' homes and, to avoid competitive catering, refreshments at local group meetings were restricted to coffee and biscuits. Discussion of purely domestic matters was discouraged. Members paid an annual subscription to the national body (£9 in 1995) and received copies of the magazine, as well as the advice and help of the National Group and Regional and Local Organisers. After the founder's pioneering stint of three years, until 1975 the business of running the national office was in the hands of teams of volunteers, but under a constitution agreed in 1976–7, a National Group was formed, elected bi-annually by postal ballot, and assisted by Regional Organisers.

Most groups met fortnightly or monthly. Outside speakers were sometimes invited, and Brookfield reports a scheme whereby he provided a local group with resource packs (Brookfield, 1983), but usually a member would lead discussion on a variety of topics. A weekend National Conference and one day regional conferences were held, with outside speakers on varied subjects. Activities were extended to include inter-group activities, a Research Bank, Correspondence Magazines, a Postal Book Group, a Penfriend Scheme, a House Exchange Scheme, and a Student Accommodation register of members offering 'B and B' to students going for interviews. Members going to live abroad set up their own groups in Australia, Canada, South Africa, Zimbabwe, Holland and elsewhere.

Jerman speculated on the likely effect on the National Women's Register of cutbacks in educational budgets and increasing unemployment which could 'send women back to the kitchen' (Jerman, 1981: 201). The increase in part-time work for women and the other changes in life style offered additional challenges. But the organisation survived, together with what one member called the 'cosy, middle class, slightly scatty, vaguely intellectual; but very aware, very interested, very involved' image (ibid.: 202).

In 1970, 58 per cent of the membership had had professional training, and 21 per cent had university qualifications. Though the Register made few inroads into the education of women on inner city housing estates, it probably assisted very considerably in the mental, emotional and social enrichment of those for whom it was intended.

## The University of the Third Age

The University of the Third Age (U3A) came to Britain from France following the publication of relevant research (Laslett, 1979). Discussions about principles, attended (inter alia) by Peter Laslett, Michael Young (Lord Young of Dartington), Eric Midwinter and Dianne Norton were held during 1980–1, and they played a vital part in the development of the British U3A (Cloet and Norton, 1992).

In France, L'Universite du Troisieme Age had started in 1972–3 and by 1981 was reported to have a total of 170 U3As there and elsewhere in the world. The first U3As in Britain started in 1982 in Cambridge, Sutton Coldfield, Stevenage and Harpenden (Cloet and Norton, 1992).

An early 'Prospectus' laid out the principles to be followed:

The U3A shall consist of a body of persons who undertake to learn and to help others to learn. Those who teach will be encouraged to learn, and those who learn shall also teach, or in other ways assist in the functioning of the institution

... the curriculum of the U3A shall be as wide as its human and financial resources permit ... No salary shall be paid to any member of the University for teaching or otherwise helping others.

Members should pay a small fee, and although the U3A should be seen to be making provision primarily for the retired, no bar was to be placed on members' age, sex or previous educational achievements.

Development was rapid. In 1983 a national body – The Third Age Trust – was set up with financial help from the Nuffield Foundation, and registered as a charity, with Dianne Norton working from her home as Executive Secretary. The brief of the Trust was to act as an 'umbrella' organisation for any groups who wished to establish a local U3A. It levied a per capita fee on member U3As and held annual conferences; issued a newspaper subsequently in co-operation with Saga; encouraged and maintained contacts with and between local groups; advised nascent groups on constitutions, programmes and other matters; ran an international travel service for member groups, and generally acted as a liaison body and a national voice. It had no controlling or inspectorial function as far as local U3As were concerned.

In 1986 grant was obtained from the Department of Education and Science, and 1988 saw the establishment of an office and the employment of a part-time Administrative Assistant. A part-time Chief Executive was appointed in 1989, and with money from the Rank Foundation, a three-year Fellowship was inaugurated to assist in developing new U3As (Cloet and Norton, 1992). By 1993, 257 local U3As were affiliated to the Trust, and growth continued.

It was possible for local U3As to be set up anywhere, by anyone, and of any size; they varied greatly, from large and flourishing metropolitan groups to those with a handful of members in small country places. Especially in the larger U3As it was usual to find a balanced provision between academic and esoteric subject matter and practical or socially based groups, but programmes depended upon the readiness of local people prepared to work on U3A principles, and the wishes of the local membership.

Some U3As met in free or rented premises; others in members' houses. Daytime, rather than evening, provision was usual, as this suited the elderly and largely female and middle class (Cloet and Norton, 1992) membership. The 'ageism' and separation of provision from the young had educational and possible social disadvantages, which could be partly overcome where U3As were accommodated in educational institutions.

Initially, British U3As were not recognised by the International Association of U3As, set up in 1975. The original French model required groups claiming the name to be established with backing from a 'proper' university. By 1993 the relevant statutes had been amended to allow for 'national differences', the British model legitimised, and a representative elected on to the governing board of AIUTA.

The movement met with considerable success in this country but it was also subject to criticisms. It was questioned whether the title 'University' should be used, either because the majority of local groups did not attempt to meet the academic standards or provision of a 'proper' university, or, conversely, because the term was seen to be off-putting to potential members who wished for a less academically rigorous or more socially based type of organisation. For those who preferred the 'academic' stance it was pointed out that some programmes contained very demanding subject matter, and a limited amount of research was even undertaken. For those with more modest academic standards, the fact that learning took place in a pleasant social milieu was justification in itself.

A more insidious point may be made. In an atmosphere of financial stringencies and ever more restrictions on the provision of liberal adult education by LEAs, 'proper' universities and voluntary bodies, a temptation existed for LEA and other organisers to get groups of adult students to affiliate themselves to the local U3A. It has been argued that this should be resisted as U3As should not become substitutes for professionally led adult education (Rogers, 1993: 7).

The significant difference between the French and British models of a U3A was that in the former a committee of local retired people negotiated with the university for the use of their facilities and expertise, so that Thirdagers in France were generally taught by university staff who had considerable say over the courses offered (Cloet and Norton, 1992). Although some British U3As established beneficial relationships with local universities, they rarely received teaching: indeed, the emphasis on self-help and mutually reciprocal education in the founding principles (Laslett, 1979) tended to discourage closer relationships. In the UK, the imported concept was regarded by some as a cuckoo's egg, laid in a well-founded, if diminishingly well-lined, nest. Some advocated a move towards the French position. However, as Morris conceded (Morris, 1984: 135), France had little resembling the British 'night school' or adult education tradition (Titmus, 1981: 135).

In 1994 the University of the Third Age Trust initiated a Review (Brodie, 1994). The researcher called for 'a greater measure of coherence in its purposes and priorities, and in its organisation and resourcing.' The movement needed more administrative support. The wide ranging nature of U3A activities involved 'ambiguities and inconsistencies. For many people it is an adult education movement imbued with intellectual and social purpose. Others might characterise it as a somewhat pretentious leisure club. This review is guided by the former interpretation ...' There was a need to mediate between local autonomy and 'obligation to the larger movement ... The self-help philosophy is to be applauded, but it can be read as self-serving, unless the evidence is to the contrary' (ibid., 1994). But the dichotomy was built into the system, and unless the Trust was prepared to take a more *dirigiste* line with its constituent U3As it was difficult to see how they could be persuaded or required to do other than follow paths determined by local members.

## Prison Education

Of other efforts to develop adult education to meet the needs of particular social groups, those in relation to the penal system have been one of the most significant. Education for those in penal establishments had its roots in late eighteenth and nineteenth century literacy work supplementing a continuing concern for religious education. The development of initiatives towards giving prisons some sort of positive training purpose beyond mere incarceration was later generally supported by penal administrators, notably Alexander Patterson. Educational activities developed in the years before 1939 but all depended on voluntary tutors. By the outbreak of war every prison had a voluntary education adviser and by 1937 400 teachers were providing some education for about 10,000 inmates. Provision included a variety of classes and lectures of 'liberal adult education' interest, as well as continuing literacy work.

The 1944 Education Act inspired the Prison Commissioners, with the active assistance of the Education Ministry and members concerned with adult education in H M Inspectorate of Schools, to set up provision based in cooperation with the LEAs. After 1953 LEAs were reimbursed by the Home Office for their expenditure which grew from £3,900 in 1946–7, two-thirds of it on correspondence courses, to nearly half a million pounds by 1964–5. There were then full-time and remarkably dedicated education officers in 29 establishments. All the teachers and other organisers were part-time and classes were restricted to the evenings. In spite of crises over prison security in the 60s and some departure from an optimistic philosophy of prison as treatment, educational provision grew. It was coupled with limited vocational training of prisoners initiated as a contribution to wartime industrial efforts in 1941.

The Prison Department appointed a full time Director of Education from the FE service in 1961 with, later, regional supporting staff. The scale of the provision grew to expenditure of £5.7 million in 1970 and this had nearly doubled at constant prices by 1980 and again by 1991–2 (House of Commons Select Committee Report, 1991–2: passim).

In spite of increasing recourse to imprisonment and a consequent rapidly increasing penal population, recognition of the value of education and training activity continued. It was widely seen as an important element in prison regimes, valuable in helping to provide constructive occupation as well as 'skills which they need to survive in the world outside after release' in contrast to a context in which 'the physical conditions and pattern of daily life bore, impoverish and degrade' (House of Commons Select Committee Report, 1990: v, vi).

With 15 per cent of prison inmates having a reading age of 10 years or less, basic education remained a major element in provision. RSA, C and G, NVQ, GCSE and A-level classes and Open University studies were also by the 1990s available in many establishments, together with a range of studies comparable to those available as liberal adult education outside. Day as well as evening classes became common and day release to FE institutions not unknown. A total of 7.57 million student hours achieved in 1992–3 represented a remarkable development of adult education over 48 years.

However, provision was very patchy, and subject to reduction and dislocation because of the varying pressures of prison life. It was also inadequate to meet demand. A survey in 1991 showed that 47 per cent of prisoners were attending some educational classes: half the remainder wanted to do so.

The 1992 Further and Higher Education Act caused a dislocation of prison education. With the removal from LEA control of the further education colleges with which it was linked, the provision was put out to competitive tendering. Forty-five contractors, mainly still colleges of further education, were engaged. The change involved serious administrative and legal problems. It was claimed that the change would provide a more uniform and systematic service, but there was widespread unease about its likely effect on the prison educational service.

## Arts Provision

The great development of arts provision after the 1939–45 war was foreshadowed and influenced by experimental work by the British Institute of Adult Education. It then grew from the related war time success of the Council for the Encouragement of Music and the Arts in providing high quality musical, theatre and opera performances and art exhibitions (see Kelly, 1993; Lowe, 1970). CEMA also supported and helped voluntary arts bodies in large numbers, including arts clubs and societies for musical, including amateur, performance.

The charter which set up the Arts Council of Great Britain in 1947 laid down its objectives as securing a greater knowledge, understanding and practice of the fine arts and in particular to increase the accessibility of the fine arts to the public and to improve the standards of execution. When revised in 1967 a new charter deleted the limiting word 'fine' and included responsibility for advising and co-operating with government departments, local authorities, etc.

To a considerable extent as a result of the demand which it was responsible for spreading, but which also derived from the general post-war expansion of secondary and higher education, public arts expenditure rose greatly over the next 50 years. In 1945–6 Arts Council expenditure from public sources was £235,000. By 1965–6 it was nearly £4m; it reached £225m by 1994 in spite of periods of stasis. Taking account of inflation, expenditure trebled from 1965 to 1975 and almost doubled again from 1975 to 1994. Total expenditure on the arts was later further increased with the development of industrial sponsorship. Local government bodies had been allowed to spend limited money on the arts since the Local Government Act of 1948. While most authorities spent nothing, others devoted considerable sums, including some building of performance areas, the lack of which had been early noted by the Arts Council as a hindrance comparable in importance to the lack of public funding, to the wider spread of arts appreciation. Expenditure on arts provision was transformed compared with the pre-war dependence on market forces, even if the arts in Great Britain were still poorly financed compared with the European pattern.

The ACGB has been subject to much and varied criticism. Some stemmed from its emphasis on support for what were judged by its professional advisers to be the most important creative talents of the day, and consequently also of a limited number of largely metropolitan based arts providers (Bick, 1991). Bick, like others, heavily criticised the Council's failure to assist provision tainted by commerce, its elitism generally, and its failure to support more popular art forms. Kahn castigated its neglect of the ethnic arts particularly (Kahn, 1976). Its policy of restricting aid to professional performance can also be criticised. There has been considerable criticism too of the Council's apparent lack of concern for its Charter duty to spread appreciation of the arts as well as to devote its resources to its preferred objectives of encouraging high standards particularly in 'static centres' (ACGB, 1956). As early as 1950 the Select Committee on Estimates, in its nineteenth report, urged the Council to turn its attention to making the arts more widely accessible, 'being content with less ambitious standards', and to develop work in the provinces. Throughout its life the Council maintained its duty, arguably rightly, to make no concessions on standards and to concentrate on increasing good quality provision. But it later took regularly increasing steps towards developing arts in the provinces and then towards assisting a wider variety of art forms including more popular and ethnic minority arts. However, direct effort to extend the population to whom the arts are of significance, and even to deepen the understanding of those who already appreciated them, continued to be largely neglected.

In 1976 the new ACGB general secretary turned to the Gulbenkian Foundation, which was already giving much help to the community arts movement, for funding for an education officer. Powerful arguments for more activity to be directed to extending enjoyment of the arts through educational work, contained in his reports for 1976–7 and 1982–3, culminated in a policy statement in February 1983 which stressed the importance of breaking down 'barriers to the arts sometimes created by such factors as social class and lack of educational opportunity'. The Council's educational functions were chosen as one of five areas for particular development (ACGB, 1983).

The Council's own educational activity in connection with the arts subsequently increased. As importantly, the educational activity of organisations receiving assistance became a consideration in assessing their grants. Most recipients tended to concentrate on the easier cooperation with schools rather than with those concerned with the education of adults. They looked to work with schoolchildren in time to increase the size of the adult audience. The lectures and workshops related to their presentations which most arts providers came to offer became an important contribution towards the education of the relatively initiated, helping to undermine the old undesirable gap between appreciation and practice in adult education.

In 1984 a major reorganisation imposed by the Department of National Heritage abolished the Arts Council of Great Britain, replacing it with separate councils for England, Scotland and Wales. However policy may change, the achievement of the ACGB in making arts performances increasingly available in the years following the war, compared with the situation in the 30s, are clear. Although repertory theatres had been initiated in 1908, building-based theatrical companies, never widespread, numbered only about six in the 1970s (White, 1975). Sixty such companies enjoyed Arts Council support by 1980 together with forty touring companies and there were additionally 150 fringe and alternative theatre groups (Adkins, 1980). Classical music performance, opera and exhibitions also showed comparable if not such widespread growth.

An important development paralleling the growth in the provision of performance was that of arts centres which were promoted and assisted by the Arts Council as well as local authorities. Unknown before the 1939–45 war, their numbers listed by the Arts Council had grown to around 300 by 1989. A tenth of them had links with adult education providers. A few were only performance bases; most however encouraged different modes of participation. Forster (1983) notes however a continuing fear that an 'academic approach' would discourage the often youthful clientele.

In 1993 the Arts Council reported the percentage of the adult population attending performances of different arts:

| | |
|---|---|
| Opera | 6.6% |
| Ballet | 6.8% |
| Classical Music | 12.2% |
| Plays | 23.8% |
| Jazz | 6.2% |
| Contemporary Dance | 3.4% |
| Art Galleries | 21.6% |

Overall 37 per cent of the adult population attended some form of arts provision. The accuracy of such percentages is open to question and they should be treated with caution. Whatever their shortcomings however, they show the scale of the continuing development of this auxiliary of adult education. The contrast between the substantial public expenditure it has attracted compared with other mainstream or auxiliary adult education is also striking.

## Museums and Art Galleries

Museums, like libraries, were often established to provide 'non-formal' education, although their founders may not have recognised the term. Gladstone spoke for many of his generation when he said: 'The libraries, these gymnasia, these museums, this system of public education, they are all instruments with which a war is carried on. War against what? War against ignorance, war against brutality' (Miller, 1976). That war has continued, uncertainly on some fronts, with perhaps an increased appreciation of conservation issues, and with diminished resources generally.

Often established with financial help from benefactors or by voluntary effort, museums and galleries vary greatly in size, scope and attractiveness. Staffed entirely by local volunteers, rehoused in 1993 in a building acquired for a peppercorn rent from the local Council and funded by voluntary contributions, the lively and well-designed museum at St Agnes in Cornwall attracted 4,000 visitors in its first year. It is one example among many similar enterprises.

At the national level, the National Portrait Gallery provided a good example of a clearly stated policy and effective practice. The 'Mission Statement' of its Education Department (NPG, 1994–5) stated its objectives as:

enhancing visitors' understanding and enjoyment of the collection and related subject areas through stimulating and imaginative interpretation;

providing a range of curriculum-related learning opportunities to formal education groups;
providing a range of leisure-learning opportunities to the various sections of NPG's audience;
encouraging the considered use of the NPG's collection by individual students and group leaders.

Its Education Department had in 1995 a permanent staff of five, with an annual budget of £70,000 from National Heritage and £20,000 from sponsorship. It provided a series of day schools, lunch-time and evening lectures and symposia, with an annual attendance of between 12,000 and 15,000. The lunch-time lecture audience consisted mainly of retired people (80 per cent), while for other events age ranges varied considerably. Some events were free although charges had been introduced for many. Saturday schools were provided for Open University students, and the gallery accommodated Birkbeck College (University of London) study days and sessional courses for part-time adult students. Staffing included an Education Officer (New Audiences) to develop an 'outreach' programme, with a series of mainly practical activities for all ages of visitor, in particular young adults, the disabled, returners to learning and people from ethnic minorities. There was a far-reaching programme of events based on a variety of subject matter linked to portraits.

The National Maritime Museum at Greenwich had always included lectures and other educational events, but in 1990 it developed its 'Open Museum' programme in cooperation with neighbouring Goldsmiths College. A College staff member, and the Head of Research at the Museum, each had a part-commitment to the work. They jointly worked out a programme for the year including lectures covering aspects of the museum's exhibits, day schools, and special events. Signed talks were given for deaf people, and 'touch talks' for the visually impaired. The programme was very varied. The sea and its ways, wars, and workers covered most interests, but since the Museum also included the old Royal Observatory and the Queen's House, astronomy, history, architecture and related subjects were also included. Unfortunately the new funding arrangements for university adult education, including Goldsmiths College, which favoured accredited courses (see Chapter 8) threatened this provision by the mid-90s. The *Museums Journal* (September 1994: 40) outlined the difficulties: 'The Open Museum programme attracts ... people who are interested in the museum's collections and related objects. Many students are well-qualified already and have no need or wish to obtain additional qualifications. Others are retired people with a similar outlook.' The Open Museum hoped for continued funding for this type of provision on a non-accreditation basis.

The National Portrait Gallery's Education Department, receiving its funding from National Heritage, was spared this particular dilemma. But all museums and galleries in the 1990s were forced to consider charging. This met less public disapproval than in 1974, when a questionnaire in three Midland towns found about 80 per cent disagreeing with admission charges (Chadwick, 1980: 39), but it was plainly at odds with the intentions of many museums' founders, and unlikely to increase attendance by the less well-off. Fortunately, Sir William Flinders Petrie's view of museums as 'charnel houses of murdered evidence' (*ibid.*: 63) had become out-of-date. '... They have become increasingly aware of the need to ... involve their institutions with the outside world ...' (*ibid.*: 71); and 'Museum education officers must be included among those who plan adult education' (Museums Association, 1971: 2; see also Chadwick and Stannett, 1995). A report by HM Inspectors in 1988 concluded that: 'Adult and community education is part of all museums' work ... in that the very act of opening displays to the public performs an educational function. Most of the museums seen in this survey offered more than this ...' (Department of Education, 1988: 8).

## The Public Library Services

The 1850 Public Libraries Act and several later nineteenth century acts stimulated the spread of municipal library services (see Chapter 2), so that by 1900 libraries were being established at a rate of 16 or 17 a year. The years 1899–1909 saw rapid development, despite continuing objections to the use of public money for such 'frivolous' purposes. Thereafter there was a falling off 'because practically every local authority which could afford to run a library on a 1d rate had now got one' (Kelly, 1977: 122). Even during the first world war, however, some libraries were established, and by 1918 there was a total of 602 in Britain. Following the optimistic third Interim Report of the Adult Education Committee of the Ministry of Reconstruction, the Public Libraries Act of 1919 enabled County Councils to adopt the Public Libraries Acts by resolution, and although county libraries 'could hardly have been born in less auspicious circumstances' (*ibid.*: 217), progress was made, especially after 1933, and by 1939 local government expenditure in England and Wales on libraries and museums had reached £3.2 million compared with £1.8 million in 1928. Manchester had set up the first Travelling Library in 1931, and by 1928 gramophone records were available on loan, followed in the thirties by paintings, photographs and slides (*ibid.*: 288).

The McColvin Report of the Library Association, published in 1942, followed by the Roberts Committee report in 1959 and the Bourdillon and Baker Reports for the Education Department (1962), were all concerned with the question of optimum size and efficient operation of the public library service, and led eventually to the Public Libraries and Museums Act of 1964, which placed on the Secretary of State for Education and Science the duty 'to superintend, and promote the improvement of, the public library service' and transferred more powers of provision from the smaller authorities to the counties (*Ibid.*: 359).

Nevertheless, library development was delayed by building controls and financial stringency, and even after the Act of 1964, 'upgrading of the library service ... was rendered impossible ... by the severe restrictions placed by the government on all forms of public expenditure' (Kelly, 1993: 346). Despite difficulties, and the Local Government Act of 1972 (1973 for Scotland) which reduced the number of library authorities in Great Britain from 460 to 161, and led to amalgamation with 'Leisure Services', librarians continued to meet new challenges, especially in the adult literacy campaign, in assisting the thousands of students in the Open University, and in the increasing provision of non-book materials (Kelly, 1977: 437).

Eventually, and erratically, restrictions on capital expenditure were eased, and new buildings appeared. This did not prevent a 'Libraries in Crisis Day' in 1992, when 'The Minister ... asserted that expenditure on Public Libraries in the UK over the decade had risen in real terms' (Sumsion, 1993: 77), while a Library Association canvass of a number of authorities had revealed drastic cuts in book funds, shorter opening hours, fewer staff, and branch closures. As John Sumsion, Director of the Library and Information Statistics Unit at Loughborough University implies, both statements are correct: 'the Library Crisis was more to be found in particular authorities' current plans than in historical statistics across the nation' (*ibid.*). In fact, per capita spending in real terms on books by public libraries during the 80s rose from £1.85 in 1981–2 to £1.97 in 1989–90 and then declined to £1.78 in 1992–3 (*ibid.*). Statistics must be used with caution, especially where money is concerned, but (possibly more significantly) other figures compiled by LISU indicated an overall decline in public library lending between 1982–3 and 1992–3, and a decline in the number of 'service points open 45 hours or more' from 934 in 1987–8 to 797 in 1992–3. Although an overall decline in lending is shown, the proportion of loans of audio-visual material compared with books markedly increased (LISU, 1994). All this suggests that public libraries were no more than holding their own in a harsh climate.

Over the years, if most librarians still concentrated on the supply of books on demand in what was described as a 'stereotyped supermarket model' (Bacon, 1980: 55), they had generally moved to provide a more open and accessible service. Further provision was patchy; Lowe (1970) lists a variety of extension services of adult educational import available in 1962, and states that 236 of 585 library services were engaged in some of them. Bacon (1980: 52) quotes research by Reid Smith that even as late as 1968 all librarians did not acknowledge that they should have an actively educational role, however deeply involved they were in local cultural activities. With some, that attitude persisted: a 1993 survey revealed that of 1,670 branch librarians, 1,281 thought 'My library is there mainly to *lend* things' (Walker, 1993). Generally, however, the needs of users were progressively met by extending loan services to include pictures, maps, CDs, and other audio-visual material. Displays and exhibitions – 39,000 in 1992–3 (CIPFA, 1994) – individual lectures and lecture series, accommodation for 'cultural' meetings, and cooperation in adult literacy schemes were added by many libraries to traditional book supply functions.

Individual public libraries could house only a fraction of the available material. The inter-library lending service became of increasing importance to scholarly readers, with a total of 1,370,797 requests received in 1992–3 and 93.1 per cent of them supplied (LISU, 1994).

Most public libraries became the main source of information on local adult educational facilities, including local as well as national voluntary organisations. In some places this provision was extended to brokering, advice and counselling (Gains, 1980). Help extended to cooperation in the devising and support of open learning programmes (Allred and Heeks, 1992). A report in 1978 suggested that the public library was more frequently visited by a wider range of people than adult education centres, and likely to appeal more to some as a 'neutral area' (Dadswell, 1978: 5; Brookfield, 1983:

159). The need to develop librarians' views of their role, and their training in relation to these new library uses, became widely recognised.

Increased individual study, related also to improved general educational standards, together with the surge in the publication of books and their often increased cost, with 15,257 adult non-fiction titles published in 1988 and 21,653 in 1993 (LISU, 1994) inevitably greatly enhanced the importance of libraries as adult education auxiliaries. So did the greatly increased volume of serious informative periodical publication.

*13*

# Learning for Work: Vocational Education and Training

## *John Field*

The history of workplace training in Britain is often portrayed as one of sorry neglect. A number of authors claim that Britain's failure to invest adequately in the skills and ingenuity of the workforce bears much responsibility for the fact that British capitalism has spent most of the twentieth century in trouble (Ashcroft, 1992; Finegold and Soskice, 1988; Sheldrake and Vickerstaffe, 1987). For the most part, the debate on the so-called 'failure of training in Britain' has tended to take the past for granted. Today's failings are presented as the inevitable outcome of a long process of under-investment in human resources, and examples of past policy weaknesses are certainly easy to identify. Plausible though such accounts may be, they have led to a one-sided and teleological history of training policy and practice, which are seen as little more than a prelude to contemporary discord.

This chapter considers the development of both policy and practice in respect of work-based training for adults in twentieth century Britain. For most of the century, most men and women were expected to acquire new skills and knowledge at work by relatively informal means; by and large, they picked up new tricks of the trade by experience, by watching and talking to others, by experiment, or under the guidance of senior colleagues. If the long-term consequences are as damaging as conventional wisdom insists, for the most part informal development was a reasonably rational response to the types of change that characterised the British economy during peace time, at least until the 1960s. In sharp crises, during both the First and Second World Wars, training policies developed that were designed to meet clear and urgent needs. Following both conflicts, government withdrew from the field, leaving it for employers to decide how they might manage the development of their own workforces. While political factors were crucial in changing this situation, it is impossible fully to understand how and why it changed without knowing something of the theories and practices adopted by those professionals charged with delivering training to adult men and women. As well as examining the policy context of work-based adult training in Britain, this chapter therefore also examines the rise of the specialist trainer. Like general managers, training professionals were a rare breed before the 1940s, and the theory and practice of training as a specialist craft only really took shape from the 1960s onwards, strongly influenced by the ideas and precepts of behaviourist social psychology. It is important to grasp this relatively unknown story, as well as the much more familiar pattern of changing government policy.

Modern training policy has its origins in the series of challenges faced by British capitalism in the late nineteenth century. As the first industrial nation found itself surrounded by a growing number of competitors, public concern over Britain's competivity was voiced in the 1880s and 1890s. Politically, the growth of labour organisation combined with continued urbanisation to generate new political forces, which in turn evoked a range of policy responses including the creation within the Board of Trade of a Labour Department specialising in such matters as conditions of employment, trade unionism and industrial remuneration (Davidson, 1985: 92–8). Important though these challenges were, they did little to puncture the dominant ideology of *laissez-faire* liberalism. State intervention in what were deemed the private affairs of employers remained minimal.

So far as training was concerned, most employers regarded informal instruction as sufficient. Following an initial training, any new production methods could be learned and taught by word of mouth and by example within the enterprise. In many respects, this was a rational response. Large parts of the industrial workforce were effectively self-regulating, in that skilled workers could be expected to supervise semi- and unskilled colleagues (Burgess, 1975; McClelland, 1990). Although most manufacturing industries experienced technical innovations, changes often came in a piecemeal fashion, and groups of semi-skilled and skilled workers adjusted relatively easily to the new methods. Where there were sudden transformations, resistance from workers tended to be fierce, as in the move from wood to metal in ship-building. Even here, where the reputation for rigid demarcation lines was at its strongest, the outcome was characteristically a compromise: new grades of skilled men emerged from the engineering trades to take on innovative processes (e.g. boilermaking), while other craftsmen adapted their skills to new materials and techniques (e.g. the shipwrights).

Government remained largely outside this process. For the most part, policy responses were aimed at the young. For example, the 1889 Technical Instruction Act allowed local authorities to levy a rate to support technical education – the so-called 'whisky money', which, as chapter two has shown, stimulated an expansion of publicly-provided technical education. Similarly, some of the larger state enterprises such as the arsenals and dockyards started to invest more systematically in the general education and training of apprentices.

At that stage, there was no question of giving the Labour Department any general responsibility for adult training. Established in 1893 as a section of the Board of Trade, the Department's main role was to collect statistics on such matters as wages and unemployment (Davidson, 1985: 85–97). While it carried out an investigation of labour colonies in the 1890s, with a view to establishing what role they might play in reducing unemployment and remedying 'urban degeneration', it saw these attempts at adult training as remedial measures aimed at reducing social marginalisation. Insofar as the Department was able to consider questions of 'national efficiency', its attention shifted after 1900 to matters such as working class consumption patterns and the cost structure of British industry (Davidson, 1985: 106).

Before 1914, then, most adults developed new skills and knowledge through informal means – 'sitting by Nelly', as it was called. Outside the workplace, a handful of experimental projects were established in the 1880s and 1890s to help the unemployed acquire practical skills, but these were marginal. Formal adult education had next to no role in British workplaces until the war generated an extraordinary explosion of adult training and retraining.

## 1914–1945

War, with its sudden demands for specialists of all kinds, marked a watershed. In and after the First World War, the state undertook to train both servicemen and women and then veterans; in doing so, it developed an operational theory of adult learning, and created an administrative infrastructure to implement and oversee policy. A number of the instruments created in this period were then applied to the training of unemployed men and women during the protacted crisis of the inter-war years. During the Second World War, the Ministry of Labour's role expanded still further, and a more sophisticated understanding of adult learning was applied. Often described as the first 'total war', the First World War directly involved the majority of Britain's adult population. As well as servicemen and women (though even here the scale was extraordinary) it brought new roles for civilians, including of course women recruited into engineering and other trades as essential war workers.

By 1917, the Ministry of Reconstruction was considering the role of training in the transition to a peacetime economy. Although the Ministry of Reconstruction's committee on adult education was explicitly limited to considering 'provision for, and possibilities of, Adult Education (other than technical or vocational)', its Final Report included a chapter on 'Technical Education and Humane Studies' which called for the development of 'opportunities for personal development and for the realisation of a higher standard of citizenship' through the broadening of vocational training to incorporate 'the intellectual and spiritual treasures of the race' (Ministry of Reconstruction, 1919: 153).

Following the war, government policy focused on more immediate matters. Those groups who had already been identified as likely losers from peace – women wartime workers displaced by men, disabled ex-servicemen, and other veterans who for one reason or another might find it hard to find employment – were priorities (Field, 1992: 31–41). In training these groups, government mainly used the resources of the Ministry of Labour. Other than for basic training for young unemployed boys and girls, relatively little use was made of local authority resources.

Women's training was largely concerned with returning them to the domestic sphere (as in local government adult education, where over one-third of provision was in domestic instruction; see Chapter 4). Ministry of Labour courses were operated by a quango; originally established in 1915 to encourage the movement of women into industry, the Central Committee on Women's Training and Employment was asked to consider, devise and carry out special schemes of work and training for women unemployed, or women whose capacities or opportunities have been injuriously affected as a result of conditions arising out of the war (quoted in Field, 1992: 34).

In practical terms, this involved two main types of course. Homemaker courses were for skilled workers who were at home for the time being, pending an opening in their old trade; Homecraft courses prepared women to enter domestic service. Eligibility was restricted to unemployed women aged between 16 and 35 (later extended to 45). Courses were sometimes run in the Committee's own centres and sometimes in association with local education authorities, but always in premises 'approximating as closely as possible those in typical middle class British homes', where trainees could be 'instructed in cooking, table service, laundrying and other duties of a capable housewife or servant' (Hill and Lubin, 1934: 147). Opened as a short term expediency, the Homecraft and Homemaker courses expanded in the face of persistent large scale unemployment among women, closing in 1939 with the onset of the Second World War.

Initially under the War Office, responsibility for training ex-servicemen was handed over to the Ministry of Labour in May 1919 (a decision made by Order in Council, precluding parliamentary discussion of the issue).Two categories were involved. First in terms of priority were those disabled at the time of their discharge; second were those who by enlisting had missed an apprenticeship or other initial training. Though it was hoped that private industry would train the majority, most were eventually placed either in technical institutes or government instructional factories (created originally to turn out semi-skilled machinists for munitions work, and taken over by the Ministry of Labour in 1919). Starting with five training factories, by the end of 1920 there were 52. As unemployment rose, so the training centres turned towards training unemployed veterans generally, switching in the process from a focus on engineering skills towards 'handyman training, designed to enable men to work largely on their own account or to obtain jobbing work with small employers' (quoted in Field, 1992: 37).

Adult training after the war, though intended as short term, had profound consequences. Whereas the dominant educational view of the adult had previously been that she or he was more or less fully formed, experiences in 1914–25 suggested otherwise. In government training factories as in the armed forces, instructors repeatedly discovered that the adult human was far more adaptable than supposed. One Ministry official saw this as an important and surprising breakthrough:

it was conclusively proved that men and women, past the age of apprenticeship, could be fitted for ordinary production work by training, not in the factory, but in special training institutions, whether State or private (Davison, 1929: 221).

The Ministry of Labour reported in 1924 that, although those involved included 'men broken by the war', they had demonstrated an aptitude for learning:

One feature which impressed itself upon all concerned with the Training Scheme was the marked improvement both moral and physical which took place in the great majority of the men (Ministry of Labour, 1923–4: 207).

Much of the training was, in fact, congruent with what later became widely known as behaviourism: emerging from army drill, it involved repetition and instruction in a sheltered environment. The emphasis on 'special training institutions' was reflected throughout the interwar years, as the government developed training strategies in response to persistently high levels of unemployment and sharp increases in the number of long term unemployed, both among young workers and adults.

Within the workplace, the situation of adult workers attracted little or no attention. There was some interest in whether or not technical changes were tending to deskill the (male manual) worker; mechanisation combined with scientific management were seen by some critics as combining to dehumanise the workforce, subordinating human interests to those of the machine. Whether such developments amounted in Britain to a full-blown system of 'Fordism' is doubtful, as is the deskilling hypothesis (Cronin, 1984: 61–9). Certainly enthusiasts of modern management believed that their approach required greater investment in human resources. The ideas of the American F. W. Taylor were applied not only in production line industries like motor manufacture, where Taylor's idea of scientific management originated, but also in 'batch production' industries such as shipbuilding (Hodges, 1946–7). Such arguments won few listeners among British managers before 1945, however. There is evidence of attempts to retrain a few sub-groups such as utilities employees in the 1930s (*Transactions of the Institute of Marine Engineers*, December 1934: 257), but these were few and far between. More common were attempts to provide training for supervisory grades, and particularly foremen. In reports issued in 1922 and 1928, the Association for Education in Industry and Commerce emphasised that 'specific training for foremanship is essential under modern factory conditions' – conditions which included, the Association noted, protracted exposure to the ideas and practices of trades unionism.[1] Even then, the preferred instrument was the senior staff of the firm concerned, rather than dedicated training specialists. If on a smaller scale than for supervisors, management development also expanded. Given the family-based nature of company ownership in Britain, and the limited nature of initial management education, management development remained rudimentary; most managers acquired highly specific skills through experience, but lacked wider general skills (Mass and Lazonick, 1990: 57).

Such developments had little impact on the demand for training specialists. This changed dramatically, though, in the Second World War. The war's impact on industrial training in Britain was profound. First, government was required to provide training, both for men and women who entered the armed services (including civil defence and the home guard) and for those who were employed in essential industries. Government also became increasingly concerned to influence practice in industry, to the point where the Ministry of Labour and National Service started to intervene in what had previously been the employer's domain. Finally, although there were few longer-term consequences, some aspects of vocational training found their way into the wider debate about post-war reconstruction – a debate which assumed however that the primary issues of concern were, and would remain, apprenticeship training and university education.

Government's direct role as a provider of training expanded dramatically during the war. First, it was faced with the massive challenge of training, at speed, those who entered the armed services, including the Home Guard and civil defence workers. Overwhelmingly this challenge was met by the armed services themselves, and as the war continued so the role of the training and education agencies of the armed services widened. By the end of the war, the Army in particular had developed an elaborate training and education system, largely delivered by commissioned officers, working with tutors' manuals that were often prepared by peacetime adult educators (see Chapter 3). Government also greatly expanded its civilian trades training. Between 1939 and 1945, the Ministry of Labour's training centres processed some 250,000 people, often somewhat hastily; perhaps a similar number were trained in other institutions, including the workplace (Select Committee on Estimates, 1951-2: 68). The number of men entering government training centres rose rapidly; by 1942, women were also being accepted onto courses in the training centres. At one stage, the Ministry tried to train skilled part-time women workers; plans were abandoned when it was discovered that employers 'generally found it more advantageous to employ part-time women workers on routine or unskilled work'. Short courses were developed for instructional staff, leading to the creation of what was effectively Britain's first specialist training workforce (Ministry of Labour, 1947: 101-6).

New entrants were important, but for most employers the existing workforce still provided the largest source of labour. To maintain output levels, training had to be combined with continued production. Training within the workplace increasingly replaced the earlier emphasis on specialist training institutions. Initially, the Ministry contended itself with establishing an advisory service and publishing a handbook for employers. As the conflict continued, the Ministry intervened directly, particularly in the training of workplace supervisors. Drawing on the application in the USA of behaviourist psychology, the Ministry in 1944 introduced its Training Within Industry (TWI) programme. TWI was aimed at helping foremen and other supervisors to develop their skills in 'instructing others, handling workers and improving methods', through short workplace-based courses in Job Instruction, Job Relations and Job Methods respectively. By mid-1945, the Ministry claimed to have trained over 10,000 supervisors in Job Instruction, 813 in Job Relations and 20 in Job Methods. The Ministry also offered residential courses at four universities for a new category of managers, defined as 'special officers who might be called personnel managers or welfare supervisors', many appointed as a result of government insistence on proper provision of workplace canteens, entertainment and other facilities (Ministry of Labour, 1947: 107-15). The longer term influence of this development can be seen in the creation in 1946 of the Ministry's Personnel Management Section, attached to its Factory Department, to provide an advice service to employers on a range of personnel issues.

Finally, vocational training entered the Ministry's plans for the post-war period. In the discussions over reconstruction, as in many other areas, politicians and civil servants alike looked as much to the past as to the future. So far as women were concerned, for example, there was much interest in the re-establishment of domestic service (despite its proven unpopularity with women workers during the inter-war years). Thus in 1944, 'In view of the importance of private domestic employment as a positive contribution to the health and welfare of the nation', Miss Violet Markham and Miss Florence Hancock were asked to investigate the post-war need for schemes for domestic service. Their report, published as a White Paper, subsequently led to the appointment by the Attlee government of an Advisory Council on domestic service, chaired by Miss Markham, followed by the launch of a National Institute of Houseworkers – largely financed by the Ministry – 'to raise the prestige of domestic work and to attract more women into the profession' (Ministry of Labour, 1947: 99, 210). Training courses were offered in centres and technical colleges, but the scheme was predictably short-lived.

Elsewhere, government policy was dominated by the short term needs of demobilisation, the drive for increased production, and the need to reduce the time needed to bring new employees to active production. If this led to a short-term focus on training delivery (training centres were turned over wholesale to meet immediate skills needs in construction and other hard-pressed sectors), it also concentrated the minds of training professionals. Because of its concern with short-term results, TWI was expanded with the onset of peace, with an active publicity drive aimed at selling its benefits to companies. Regional TWI associations were established, and in 1946 the Ministry launched the bi-monthly magazine, *TWI Topics*.

By 1945, then, a significant pattern had emerged. Short-termism predominated over long-term strategy. The Ministry's training service was strengthened in its inclination towards behaviourist training methods. Although state intervention was still limited, the Ministry was a well-established player in adult training, with a growing body of professional expertise at its disposal, and a wide network of contacts in companies. The Ministry had acquired new responsibilities during the war, entering the post-war years at the peak of its powers.

## 1945–79

Given the constellation of forces favouring a more interventionist approach in 1945, it is striking that little was done to promote more active training policies. In the longer run, the period between the election of the first majority Labour government and the return of the Conservatives under Mrs Thatcher in 1979 saw a number of significant shifts. At the level of policy, voluntarism was replaced by regulation, within corporatist structures. Under the 1964 Industrial Training Act, most employers had to pay a training levy, which was distributed through a network of industrial training boards; government expanded its own training programmes for adults from 1966 onwards, with a marked surge in activity in response to the protracted growth in unemployment from the mid-1970s onwards. This in turn created an explosion in the size, nature and practices of the training profession. This, indeed, constitutes the second major shift, and combined with a quantum leap in the size and role of management in firms, it produced a revolution in training. The theory and practice of work-based training, which had already started to become more complex and sophisticated during the war, were increasingly developed in response to technical and organisational change. With the rapid growth in numbers and higher profile which followed the 1964 legislation, this essentially pedagogic process became intertwined with attempts to turn training from a partly casualised occupation into a profession.

At first sight, the years after 1945 appear to represent a return to normality. Certainly this was the view of Sheldrake and Vickerstaff (1987), who devoted a chapter to the period 1946 to 1960 under the title, 'The limitations of voluntarism'. After a phase of wartime interventionism, government undoubtedly reverted to the view that training issues were for employers to resolve. Government's own role in demobilisation was focused on the unemployed and 'hard to resettle', who were encouraged to enter accelerated skills courses in the government training centres. The dominant view was reflected in the proceedings of a conference on Human Relations in 1952:

It is generally accepted in this country that, with or without the help of the educational institutions, voluntary organisations and government, employers themselves bear the major responsibility for the training of their own employees (Ministry of Labour and National Service, 1952: 97).

Although a government enquiry was established under Robert Carr MP in 1956, its report (*Training for Skill*, 1958) is generally seen as firmly restating the principles of voluntarism (Page, 1967: 37–8; Sheldrake and Vickerstaff, 1987: 35).

If policy trends were indeed somewhat retrogressive in the 1950s, training practice continued to evolve. First, there was some evidence that the demand for qualifications, generated by the needs of the armed services and industry during the war, had acquired its own momentum. This included a healthy number of adults, including those entering for handicraft teachers' certificates, for example (Foden, 1992: 57). Secondly, state intervention did not disappear; rather, the training methods introduced by the Ministry of Labour during the war were consolidated. If the Ministry GTCs declined in numbers and capacity, the TWI programme continued to be available to staff from the private and nationalised sectors through the 1940s, and it increasingly incorporated new training techniques as they became available. Third, there were important if limited achievements in the field of management development. While wartime proposals for a national 'Industrial Staff College' came to nought, new initiatives flourished in the early 1950s, such as the four-week executive development courses mounted by the British Institute of Management.[2] Fourth, Carr's report produced some results, including the creation of an advisory Industrial Training Council, whose members promptly lobbied for more power. As a tripartite body, the Council's members included nominees from the British Employers' Confederation and the TUC as well as from the nationalised industries, three government ministries and CGLI (Page, 1967: 38). Finally, government remained a provider, conducting a limited amount of training for unemployed adults, disabled people and ex-servicemen and women of good character. By 1962, the Ministry of Labour still had 13 government training centres, and ran two centres for trainer-training, at Letchworth in

Hertfordshire and Hillington outside Glasgow (*Ministry of Labour Gazette*, May 1964). Developments during the 50s, then, show more continuity with previous and subsequent decades than sometimes asserted.

Why, though, was more not done between 1945 and 1964? It was sometimes said that trade union resistance to the introduction of adult trainees was a problem (Royal Commission on Trade Unions and Employers' Associations, 1968: paras 345–8; Lee: 229–41). This can be discounted. Some unions were reluctant to accept that adult trainees should be treated as fully-skilled workers, but outright exclusion was rare. McCarthy's survey of the closed shop in the early 60s found only three industries where ex-trainees without a craft qualification were excluded from union membership and therefore employment: printing, private shipbuilding, and some minor iron and steel occupations (McCarthy, 1964: 45–8). Many industries – especially in the fast-growing service sectors – were only partially unionised if at all. Trade union conservatism, though a popular scapegoat (Aldcroft, 1992: 55–7), does not explain slow development of adult training in Britain.

Part of the answer must lie in the almost exclusive focus of government and employers on recruiting and training the young (Fieldhouse, 1993). So far as government was concerned, adult training remained mainly a concern for employers; the provision of focused training for the disabled and other vulnerable groups was accepted as a government obligation; training for those in work was not. That it was not an issue can be traced back to the structure of the labour market. At a time of relatively full employment, much of it in the public services and nationalised industries, labour shortages were rarely conceived of as skills shortages. New employees tended to pick up their skills 'sitting by Nelly'. Nor was the industrial context – dramatic economic growth fuelled by rising consumer demand – likely to generate a sense of crisis about training. The question thus concerns the quality and depth, rather than the existence, of training for adults.

Certainly, formal training for adult workers remained limited by the mid-60s. One 1965 survey of 203 engineering firms – a sector more active than the average – reported that 34 per cent claimed to train apprentices only and 18 per cent trained apprentices and craft workers only. Just 5 per cent said they gave some form of training to all categories of hourly-paid workers. Almost half of the firms surveyed employed no training staff at all, full- or part-time (Page, 1967, 36). Yet as shown earlier, movement was discernable before the 1964 Industrial Training Act was drafted. An early assessment of the Act's impact concluded that 'government intervention did give an added impetus' to what had previously been the rather 'sluggish' development of employment-based training (Giles, 1969: 24).

The 1964 Industrial Training Act (ITA) nevertheless marked a turning point. It unambiguously furthered the degree of state intervention in what had previously been regarded primarily as a concern of employers and managers: namely, training within employment. It took place in the context of a decisive turning point for the British economy: though in some respects it only became evident in the aftermath of the 1973 crisis, restructuring and early symptoms of deindustrialisation can certainly be discerned a decade before. The Act stimulated a number of key developments in the professionalisation of trainers, thanks to the higher profile given to training by legislation, and the massive expansion in training activity which it prompted.

Enacted in March 1964, the ITA established a tripartite Central Training Council of 34 members. Seven were employers, six came from the TUC, and others from a variety of educational, training and professional backgrounds. It required the Ministry of Labour to set up similarly representative training boards in separate industries, each empowered to subsidise employers who provided adequate training by raising a levy on firms in that sector. By 1966 there were thirteen boards in Britain, covering nearly eight million workers; by 1972, 27 boards had been created, covering some 15 million workers (Aldcroft, 1992: 59; Page, 1967).

Criticisms of the Act abounded from its origins. Trades unions, together with the emerging training lobby, argued that the Central Training Council had insufficient power (TUC, 1969). Employers denounced what they saw as an intrusive and costly bureaucracy; training standards required by the boards were seen as particularly unrealistic for small firms (Sheldrake and Vickerstaff, 1987: 37). Subsequently, the boards were criticised both for their failure to undermine what many employers saw as a restrictive apprenticeship system, then – contradictorily – to shore it up under the impact of recession and deindustrialisation (Aldcroft, 1992: 57–9). The system created under ITA has generally had a bad press. Is this justified?

What is certain is that the Act increased the volume of training activity, and raised its profile as a managerial and industrial issue. If primarily concerned with new employees, ITA also affected adult workers. An increase in overall training activity brought in its train an increase in training for adults. Admittedly, the growth of company-based training benefited men more than women, and young workers – new entrants above all – more than adults. W. John Giles' survey did, though, show that the proportion of firms training the over-21s in their workforce (both men and women) had increased markedly as a consequence of legislation (1969: 21). More indirectly, ITA influenced Ministry of Labour provision in its own adult centres. While the number trained in the last quarter of 1962 had dwindled to 1,921 (45 per cent of whom were disabled), the number twelve months later had risen to 2,421; by winter 1964, the total had reached 3,473; by winter 1966 it had climbed to 5,706 (13 per cent disabled). The volume of government-provided training for adults, while remaining small, grew steadily throughout the five years after ITA.

In 1966, the Labour government turned its attention specifically to adult training. Its chief concern was to secure an immediate increase in the number of skilled workers. Although accepting that industry retained major responsibility for its own training under ITA, and that the Act itself would improve the flow of qualified labour in time, the Ministry also believed that there was an urgent need for

an early increase in the numbers of skilled men, particularly in the engineering and construction industries, to meet persistent shortages (*Ministry of Labour Gazette*, May 1964).

It therefore decided to double the facilities in GTCs, and increase the numbers able to take part in other vocational training courses at colleges, or on employers' premises.

From the mid-1960s, trade union attitudes towards training tended to combine practical caution with rather vague good will. Union representatives were routinely courted by training professionals: in 1975, for example, speakers at the annual conference of the Institute of Training Officers included Patricia Turner of the General and Municipal Workers' Union (*Training*, March 1975, 15). In practice, trade union involvement tended towards the ceremonial: officials sat on boards and sub-committees, while the shop floor continued to regard training issues as largely remote from the day-to-day issues of trades union activism. If overt hostility towards the recruitment of semi-skilled workers from GTCs was rare, so was enthusiasm for training as a positive bargaining good (Rees, 1973). One result was that access to training was at best patchy. In particular, the new and growing categories of worker – above all women workers – were no more likely to benefit from workbased training than (mostly male) manual manufacturing employees. One 1969 survey of 165 midlands firms showed that office clerical staff – young women above all – received considerably less training than other categories of employee (Giles, 1969: 21). It was precisely the untrained who became the most vulnerable during the period of recession which followed.

In 1973 the UK – along with Denmark and the Republic of Ireland – joined what was then the European Economic Community. Membership of the EEC had a marked impact, albeit largely an unplanned one, on Britain's training policy, for since its inception the Community had set up a Social Fund targeted on inter-state transfers for the relief of unemployment. In its second phase, set to run from 1972 to 1977, the Social Fund was transformed into an active instrument of labour market policy. In response to rising unemployment among young adults in particular, the ESF was targeted on vocational training and retraining. The UK's Employment Department proved unexpectedly adept at coordinating proposals to the Social Fund; by 1975, the UK was receiving almost a quarter of the total budget, much of it going to underpin government programmes for unemployed people. For example, Training Opportunities Programme (TOPS) courses were developed on the basis of Social Fund grants, with significant consequences for the training market (Elliott, 1976: 10). Increased funding may have done little to raise the status and prestige of trainers – indeed, by associating the occupation with unemployment, it may have had the reverse effect. Nevertheless, it steadily raised the numbers and profile of those working in training and development occupations, and coming on top of the 1964 Act this was bound to create pressures towards professionalisation.

Trainer professionalisation was one of the most profound consequences of the 1964 Act. Even in the early 1960s, the number of people employed primarily in training roles was relatively small. Giles, in his survey of Midlands companies, confined himself to firms employing 500 or above; before the ITA, over three-quarters did not have a full-time training officer, and the same proportion lacked even a full-time instructor. He concluded that

One of the greatest handicaps to the swift implementation of the Industrial Training Act was the very small number of training specialists existing within British industry in 1964 (Giles, 1969: 23–4).

By 1966, he was able to report that 64 per cent of firms covered by the ITBs had a full-time training officer, and 58 per cent had at least one full-time instructor (*ibid.*: 24). The number of trainers employed in the training boards themselves was far from negligible. The Engineering Industry Training Board started by recruiting 150 training officers and advisers once it started work, and proposed to take on another 50 in the near future (Page, 1967: 91).

The vast majority of the new training staff were employed as instructors, and were recruited from the ranks of craft, clerical and operative employees whom they were to go on to train. Many, according to the Ministry, were selected for their craft skills, but 'some are chosen because they are getting too old for production work' (*Ministry of Labour Gazette*, March 1965). Perhaps one in ten, mostly employed in the larger organisations, had a more managerial (if rarely strategic) role; some had previously worked in analogous occupations, such as work study offices; many came from the armed forces. According to Terry Page, a consultant himself, the Act also 'greatly increased' the demand for training consultants, one of whom in fact served on the Central Training Council (1967: 141). Academic specialists also found their services in demand. A number of social psychologists such as John Annett, Peter Warr and Eunice Belbin (also a member of the CTC) won research grants from the Ministry, the CTC or individual ITBs to study aspects of training, including adult training.

In terms of numbers alone, then, the training community expanded rapidly. With only limited success, training officers and consultants started to develop some of the outward signs of professional status, including a professional body. Founded in 1964, the Institute of Training Officers a decade later had 4,987 members (*Training*, March 1976: 15). Presidential speeches were frequently occasions for reflection upon the standing and ethics of the training professional. However, the ITO was a rather weak body, with little clout and little external standing.

Training for trainers also developed patchily. In the immediate post-war period, opportunities for professional development were limited. Some courses were offered by the Ministry of Labour, which had trained its own instructors since 1940. Its open courses were intended chiefly to disseminate TWI. Others were offered by the British Association for Commercial and Industrial Education (BACIE), and by private institutions of various kinds. Demand, however, was limited, at least until the mid-1960s, when the effects of the Act started to make themselves known. BACIE's first course, in mid-1963, met with what one observer called an 'insultingly poor response' (Page, 1967: 69). Its second, later in the same year, had to be cancelled for 'lack of support', persuading the Ministry to meet half the fees of further approved courses (*Ministry of Labour Gazette*, February 1964). By the late 60s, a range of introductory courses was available in the management departments of some technical colleges. In the following decade, the range of courses also expanded, with the entry into the field of the universities (Brunel's Institute of Industrial Training was one major player) and some private institutions. The Employment Department's Training Services

Agency secured an ESF grant towards the cost of its own programme of twelve week modular sandwich courses, mostly held at polytchnics, colleges and private agencies (*Training*, August 1976: 23, and November 1976: 26).

Trainer-training went hand in hand with a strong interest in pedagogic issues. By now, the influence of behaviourism was well-entrenched. By the 1950s, a small but growing number of professional trainers had introduced TWI methods, along with audio-visual aids and other new techniques. TWI's influence was further widened as trainers moved from the armed services and Ministry of Labour to positions – often influential – in civilian industries. Frank Perkins, who had introduced TWI to Britain when he returned to the Ministry of Labour from a secondment to Washington, was among them, spending the next twenty years as chief education officer with ICI (Page, 1967: 135). TWI in turn helped stimulate interest among trainers in other, more sophisticated methods when they reached Britain in the 1960s.

Some trainers, of course, still used crude and highly didactic methods with their charges; little had changed since the simple-minded pedagogy of labour utilised for the long-term unemployed in the 1930s (Field, 1992: 69–70). However, particularly in the more senior levels of the training community there was widespread interest in developing more effective methods of teaching and learning. The TWI legacy lingered until well into the 1960s; the early TWI missionary Frank Perkins in 1966 left his post in ICI to become the Ministry of Labour's chief adviser on industrial training (Page, 1967: 135). By the late 1950s, the relatively blunt 'job breakdown' associated with TWI was giving way to post-Taylorist approaches such as skills analysis training (also known as the skills development method). Mainly practised in operative training, this was

a method of analysing the precise skills used at every minute phase in a job and then setting up training techniques and schedules to develop those precise skills in the operative. It was, in fact, the essence of the setting of realistic and economic training standards and of the flexibility that were missing from craft training (Page, 1967: 33).

Skills analysis training was actively promoted by the Central Training Council, as a means of focusing training effort more precisely and increasing its effectiveness.

The programmed instruction movement also emerged from behaviourist psychology. Programmed instruction (PI) reached Britain from the USA in the early 1960s. Initially treated by many as, in the words of one 1960s commentator, 'rather far-out' (Page, 1967: 32), by 1966 it had won sufficient acceptance for the CTC to promote its use as a means of improving the 'quality and efficiency of industrial training' (CTC, 1966: 1). PI was derived directly from behaviourist social psychology; its goal was to involve the learner actively in the learning process by means of (often self-) paced inputs, offered in small readily-assimilated units, with immediate rewards (or correction) for performance. It relied heavily on resource-based learning. At its plainest, this might involve a 'simple linear programme ... compiled in booklet form with one frame per page', with answers on the following page, as used in an experimental course for adult trainee bus conductors in London. At the other extreme was something called the 'Autotutor Mark II teaching machine', used to teach more complex skills like map-reading (Neale and others, 1968: 24–7).

Programmed instruction rapidly became something of a missionary movement. By the early 1960s, supporters had created an Association for Programmed Instruction, with a scholarly journal (*Programmed Learning and Educational Technology*), edited by the psychologist John Annett. A number of the larger firms signed on, including the GPO and British Empire Airways. The British Institute of Management was also an early convert. For its part, the Ministry grant-aided two publishers to produce textbooks in PI; subsequently Pergamon published case studies of PI in operation in an impressively large number of companies. While the results achieved could be impressive, the problem was cost; the initial outlay on a simulator for training process control operators ran to over £5,000, for example. Since most training officers had to struggle with personnel managers for access to what was still sometimes called the 'welfare budget', the role of evaluation and cost-effectiveness assessments became increasingly important to the trainer (Annett, 1968: 22).

Perhaps PI remained 'rather far-out' for most professional training officers and instructors. Nevertheless, it undoubtedly helped legitimate a turn towards active learning, and stimulated interest in resource-based learning. Active pedagogies rapidly replaced more passive and didactic models. In 1976, 90 per cent of ITO members claimed to use audio-visual aids in delivering training (Cook, 1976: 6). New information technologies were snapped up. Video met with immediate enthusiasm: *Meetings Bloody Meetings* (starring John Cleese, and in widespread use a decade later) was one of three summer 1976 releases from the newly-formed, highly successful company Video Arts Ltd.

By the late 1970s, voluntarism appeared to be dead. State intervention through ITA had greatly increased the volume and status of training within industry, and had created a body of high specialised training professionals. As a matter of domestic policy, and within the wider framework of the EEC, government was providing direct training to a growing number of unemployed adults. Overall responsibility for implementation lay with the increasingly influential Department of Employment, which administered UK applications under the ESF. Yet training matters were bound to be affected by the so-called 'great debate' on the relationship between education and work, sparked by Prime Minister James Callaghan's 1976 speech at Ruskin College. Following Callaghan, a number of political and business leaders criticised schools for being anti-industry, with the school-to-work transition attracting growing policy attention; by the late 1980s, the government had consolidated its direct control over the further education system, and achieved a tight grip over the transition points between school and employment (Gleeson, 1989: 22–4).

## 1979–95

By the late 1970s, work-based training practice was developing rapidly. The advent of the 1979 Conservative government, committed intellectually to the principles of radical liberalism (minimal state intervention, individual initiative, regulation through the market and so on), was bound to produce dramatic shifts in training policy, particularly after the Conservatives were re-elected with substantial majorities in 1983, 1987 and 1992. Unemployment, though, far from falling to its pre-1974 level of around 2.5 per cent, continued to present a major policy threat, to which training solutions were regularly attempted. Policy innovation (including a major restructuring of administrative responsibilities) was matched by further developments in professional training practice, with a significant increase in the self-confidence and status of what was now a sizeable occupation.

In the face of growing and persistent unemployment, the first and most consistent response of the Conservative governments of the 1980s and 90s was to raise public spending on training. Total government spending on training activities between 1979 and 1991 rose threefold. While much of the expansion of the early 1980s was concerned to manage youth unemployment, government also periodically addressed itself to the question of adult training (see Chapter 3 for discussion of MSC schemes, as well as the Department of Education and Science's REPLAN programme). When the Manpower Services Commission (MSC) launched the New Training Initiative in 1981, government committed itself to three objectives for the coming decade:

- to reform and increase skill training in order to end the reliance on time-serving and introduce training to standards;
- to equip all young people for work; and
- to widen opportunities for adults to train and re-train throughout their working lives.

While the third was in practice limited by MSC's lack of influence over employer-based training, adult training was also bound to be affected by the development of standards-based approaches.

As well as increasing spending on training in response to unemployment, government policy also aimed at increasing employers' involvement in training and development. In 1985, the government set up a review of Britain's vocational qualifications. Published in 1986, the report called for the creation of a national framework of standards-based qualifications, which were to reflect ability to perform the occupation ('competence') rather than completion of a course of training ('time-serving'). A year later, the National Council for Vocational Qualifications (NCVQ) introduced the elements of what subsequently became a new framework of vocational qualifications for England, Northern Ireland and Wales (Scotland had already embarked on an earlier but parallel reform of vocational qualifications). At every stage, government had sought to ensure that the new system was led by employers. NCVQ enjoyed strong representation from the business community, and was designed to operate as a business itself; the plan was for NCVQ to become self-financing by 1992. In setting the standards, a key role was played by Industry Lead Bodies; believing that employers knew best what skills and abilities they required, government argued that they should dominate the Lead Bodies. At least in rhetoric, the theme of employer leadership dominated the entire system.

Employers were also expected to take increasing responsibility for the training and enterprise programmes previously operated by the MSC. As a tripartite organisation, the MSC was something of an anomaly; its renaming as the Training Commission in 1988 was followed by its abolition when the TUC refused to co-operate in a new training programme for unemployed adults. In December 1988, the government announced proposals for new local bodies to administer training schemes, to be known as Training and Enterprise Councils in England and Wales and Local Enterprise Companies in Scotland. Administered by boards drawn from local business communities, the 104 TECs and LECs were invited to contract with government to deliver training for unemployed people and administer small business support programmes. Government's intention, according to the 1989 prospectus, was that in every area

the TEC will be a catalyst for change within its community. It will serve as a forum for local leaders ... And it will play a vital role in promoting the importance of training as a business strategy (quoted in Bennett, Wicks and McCoshan, 1994: 1–2).

In practice, the TECs have been driven by the simple financial imperative of delivering government's training schemes. Six years after their introduction, TEC/LEC leaders were complaining that their attempts to develop a training agenda independent of government schemes for the unemployed had produced few if any results (*Financial Times*, 7 June 1995). In particular, they failed to develop their role in respect of adult training (Bennett, Wick and McCoshan, 1994: 160–66). TEC/LEC budgets gave virtually no scope for pursuing this mission, and there was little encouragement from the Employment Department (and even fewer concrete suggestions) to promote the idea of lifetime learning. A partial exception to this general situation was the Investors in People programme, a system of kitemarking of local employers that enabled TEC/LECs to invest in companies with an established training culture. Companies were slow to take up the scheme, though it proved popular with further education colleges and some other training providers anxious to build closer links with their local TEC/LEC.

Were the government's attempts to raise the status and profile of training among firms successful? Certainly by the mid-1990s, it seemed that government policy had done little to involve companies more actively in training issues. If we consider the first decade of the NVQ experiment (Field, 1995), it is clear that the main market for the new qualifications was constructed, not by private sector employers, but by government itself (acting as an indirect purchaser through its fiscal controls over TEC/LECs and the Further Education Funding Council, as well as a direct purchaser for its own employees in the armed services and elsewhere). Furthermore, the setting of national standards took place with very little involvement by employers; rather the standards were researched and drawn up by training consultants, working with specialists in the Employment Department. NCVQ was not self-financing by 1992, still requiring continued government support in the mid-90s. A similar balance sheet could be drawn up for other areas of training policy, where measures designed to involve employers actively in training issues may unintentionally have had the reverse effect. In

1995, government announced that most of the functions of the Employment Department were to be absorbed into the Department for Education, with the declared intention of encouraging closer relations between vocational and academic education and training.

Much innovation in workplace training during the 1980s and 90s was not government-inspired, however. In developing opportunities for the workforce at large, far more significant was the transfer to UK firms of employer-led tuition aid schemes developed in the 1970s by the American car industry. First to cross the Atlantic was the Ford Employee Development Assistance Programme (EDAP). Ford's EDAP scheme required employees to give up their own time, while the company met fees and materials costs (see Chapter 3). Similar aid schemes were adopted by a number of larger manufacturing employers as well as some local authorities; significantly, such schemes usually enjoyed active trade union support (Forrester, Payne and Ward, 1995). Other key developments of the 1980s included efforts by a number of firms to identify themselves as a 'learning company', again inspired by US examples such as ICL, aiming to secure continuous employee development throughout working life. Generally speaking, such activities represented a broader approach to employee development than had been common among training professionals. While NVQs were rooted in Britain's well-established behaviourist and individualist training culture, the learning company approach tended to draw on humanistic social psychology and sought to change company culture and structures as much as the individual. However, this development was entirely unconnected with government policy initiatives.

The most significant consequence of Convervative government activity was probably the transformation of the training industry. With the growth of government spending on training in the 1970s, a trend which simply accelerated in the 1980s, the training market expanded considerably. So did the organisation of its professionals, with growth in the membership of the Institute of Training and Development (which dominated the thinking of the Training and Development Lead Body, responsible for the framework of NVQs for the profession), which in 1993 achieved a long-anticipated merger with the Institute of Personnel Management. As well as growth, the profession became increasingly specialised. Whereas previous periods of growth had resulted in expansion either in the public vocational training system or in the internal training departments of firms, the growth of the 1980s and 1990s led to an explosion in the private sector specialist training market. Increasing numbers of trainers worked either for small firms specialising in training, or they were self-employed. Forming tactical alliances with training professionals in the TECs and training specialists in the Employment Department, the early 1980s witnessed the emergence of a classic professional interest group in the training field (Shackleton, 1992: 79). Equally, the growth of private sector provision – ranging from consultancy to learning materials production – led to a significant fragmentation of activity. Despite the significant purchasing power of government, these developments may have helped place work-based training well beyond the boundaries of traditional state influence.

Desmond King has argued that Conservative training policy from 1979 to 1992 consisted of four elements (1993: 215). First, the government sought to weaken trade union influence over training, particularly as expressed in the apprenticeship system. Second, training was linked to the management of unemployment, especially by linking benefit payments to participation in training. (I would add that training also became government's preferred way of managing political tensions arising from mass unemployment and rapid deindustrialisation.) Third, government aimed at maximising employer preference and influence over training programmes. Fourth, government intervention was reduced to the minimum consistent with the Conservatives' political beliefs: by and large it was concerned with managing unemployment, and intervention in industry's own policies and practices was reduced. As a general account, this picture needs to be adapted to allow for the gap between conception and implementation. Whatever the intentions of government, training policy under the Conservatives in the 80s and 90s did little to enhance employer interest in, or even control over, training practice. What it did do was raise the profile of training in policy circles, and help create a critical coalition of interests who were able to press through and subsequently benefit from a number of highly significant reforms, such as the introduction of a standards-based qualifications system.

Like many of the advanced capitalist nations, Britain in the mid-1990s was in something of a quandary. Its policy-makers, like those of the European Union more broadly, shared a recognition of the vital importance of lifelong learning to future economic success. In a period of intensified global competition, according to the European Union White Paper on growth and employment, competitiveness depended on the speed with which innovation and know-how were brought to the market place; this itself depended upon the creativity, adaptability and quality of the workforce. In determining policies for education and training, it concluded that:

All measures must therefore necessarily be based on the concept of developing, generalizing and systematizing lifelong learning and continuing training. This means that education and training systems must be reworked in order to take account of the need – which is already growing and is set to grow even more in the future – for the permanent recomposition and redevelopment of knowledge and know-how (CEC, 1994: 136).

Such outspoken recognition of the urgency of lifelong learning in the abstract was pervasive by the mid-1990s, but it was nowhere matched by the identification of concrete measures to achieve this desirable goal.

In Britain, as elsewhere in Europe, the scale of investment required to encourage lifelong learning on any scale was a major deterrent to public provision. At a time when voters repeatedly indicated a desire for lower taxation levels, the only way in which state intervention could be financed was through a switch of resources away from initial education – a prospect that, when aired by the EU, met with no sympathy whatever from member states (CEC, 1991). Yet changing economic structures operated in such a way as to deter either employers or individuals from investing at the desired levels. With decreasing levels of employment in large organisations, and increasing insecurity of employment in small and large ones alike, it was increasingly unclear that it was either in the interests of individuals or of employers to invest in continuous lifelong learning. From the employers' point of view, the diminishing importance of internal labour markets meant that investment in development of the workforce could be focused on the decreasing number whose long-term career lay with the firm. From the individual's point of view, the increasing anarchy of the labour market meant that long term investments in education and training, of a kind which might have been appropriate for mobility up an established workplace ladder, were somewhat risky. Given the importance of credentials for employers as a screening mechanism, individuals continued to pursue qualifications in order to access the internal labour market, but the relationship between the levels and numbers of credentials and the qualitative ownership of enhanced skills remained – despite the attempts of NCVQ to introduce greater transparency – opaque. On the supply side, meanwhile, providers of vocational training responded by becoming increasingly short-term in outlook, following patterns of demand rather than attempting to identify shortages of key skills and meet them. The supply side of the market became increasingly complex, a development intensified by the rapid adaptation of new technologies to employee development. In this context decisions about training and development at enterprise level became increasingly complex and the outcomes more unpredictable.

## Conclusions

For most of the past century, training for adults was handled by employers, usually on a fairly casual basis. To the extent that this has changed – and the changes may be more apparent than real – this may be more because of internal political and organisational pressures than as the outcome of a concerted attempt to restructure British capitalism. A number of governments sought to reform training systems as part of a wider attempt to restructure the economy and enhance Britain's competitivity in world markets – notably the Wilson government of the 1960s, and the Thatcher government of the 1980s – but the training solutions implemented seemed to fall far short of these ambitious objectives. The development of semi-punitive training schemes to manage high levels of unemployment was, by contrast, a consistent pattern of British social and labour market policy. Attempts to toughen soft human capital by semi-punitive training schemes, and to be seen to be doing something about the unemployment problem, appeared in the interwar years and again following the economic crises of the 1970s onwards. Most such schemes were devoted to younger adults, though, and much policy attention continued to centre on the problems of the transition from school to employment.

Adult retraining became a major priority during the Second World War. While adult retraining played a significant role in the labour market policies of the First World War, and again during the depression of the 1930s, it only rose to prominence as a means of delivering the workforce needed once the war had entered its most critical phase. Although adult retraining lost much of its importance after 1945, the wartime crisis had lasting effects. In particular it helped generate a significant body of professional trainers, who had themselves been given at least a basic grounding in the theories and methods appropriate to training large numbers of adults to agreed standards of performance in a short timescale. It also helped generate a small group of 'organic intellectuals' – that is, of specialists in training theory and policy, initially confined to the civil service, but some of whom subsequently became academics and consultants, working in higher education and industry.

In wider policy circles, lifelong learning has been a major preoccupation only since the early 1980s. Earlier discussions of recurrent education and lifelong learning were confined largely to the somewhat rarefied atmosphere of transnational governmental think tanks, such as the OECD or UNESCO. Although they had some influence in stimulating governments to investigate current policies and practice, outside Scandinavia and some parts of the third world they had relatively few practical results in the short term. Indeed, the preoccupation with young people and the school–work transition was reinforced through the 1970s, as rising unemployment levels started to impact upon the young, and deindustrialisation led to sharp declines in traditional forms of socialisation such as apprenticeship. By the late 1970s, it had become clear that unemployment was affecting adults as well as new entrants to the labour market. Policymakers' attentions were further drawn towards adult retraining by the highly visible effects of deindustrialisation combined with the spectacular productivity gains achieved by new technologies. So dramatic were the consequences for traditional forms of work organisation that training solutions were widely canvassed, not solely by government and other public agencies, but also by trades unions, employers' organisations and local government.

By the 1990s, then, there was a widespread public consensus on the desirability of lifelong learning. Despite the lack of convincing evidence that any specific measures would actually have the consequences claimed (Shackleton, 1992), it had become conventional wisdom across western Europe that continuous lifelong learning was the single most important means of remaining competitive in a global economy. Inevitably, a sharpened emphasis on the capacity to learn throughout the working life had consequences for social exclusion, as those who did not belong to well-organised internal labour markets and lacked a strong initial education found themselves increasingly judged to be not only uneducated but untrainable. With growing numbers of individuals willing and able to devote their own resources to continuous lifelong learning, acute policy challenges emerged. Could the learning society be fostered without further damage to social cohesion? Could a socially divided society function efficiently and effectively in an increasingly competitive world? To these difficult questions was added a third, whose implications were potentially far-reaching: can the demand for growth and competitiveness at the global level be reconciled with ecological realities? While the third question remained too uncomfortable and difficult for most policymakers, the first and second questions were raised primarily in the context of European social policy discussions. As in so many other respects, UK training policies continued to be subordinated to political considerations rather than serving wider social and economic policy goals.

## Notes

1.  AEIC, Report on Education for Foremanship, 1928, Modern Records Centre, Mss 200/F/3/T2/2/2.
2.  British Institute of Management, Report by Chairman of Education and Training Committee, 7 April 1954, Modern Records Centre, Mss 200/F/3/T1/286.

## 14

# Broadcasting

## *Brian Groombridge*

### *Adult Education on Radio and Television*

Early in January 1927, a few days after the British Broadcasting Company had become the British Broadcasting Corporation, and 'the wireless' was still a novelty, the *Glasgow Evening Citizen* was provoked to declare:

We can imagine no more unsuitable medium for adult education than a state-owned service which enters the homes of people of every age, sex, political colour, standard of intelligence and rank in society (12 January 1927, quoted in Briggs, 1965, p. 226).

A year later, a Committee of Inquiry chaired by one of the most respected names in education at the time, Sir Henry Hadow, Vice-Chancellor of Sheffield University and editor of the *Oxford History of Music*, came to a more positive conclusion:

In the fifteenth century, when the embers of Greek culture were borne by wandering scholars through Europe to light anew the imaginations of men, the invention of the printing press came to the aid of the new learning. Again in the last hundred years new knowledge has revolutionized life and thought, and the universities, awakened to new needs, are sending out their teachers beyond their own walls. It may be that broadcasting will help this modern revival of learning as the printing press helped the Renaissance in an earlier age (Hadow, 1928: xv).

The appeal of broadcasting to the idealistic Hadow Committee, which knew very well that the BBC was not and never had been 'state-owned', lay precisely in its power to reach everyone, as its report (*New Ventures in Broadcasting: A study in adult education*) made clear:

The adult education movement, vigorous as it is, touches as yet only a small proportion of the population. Broadcasting, which is the latest agency to place itself at the disposal of this movement, can fill many of the existing gaps; it can widen the field from which students are drawn; it can provide a means of education for those beyond the reach of other agencies; it can put listeners in touch with the leaders of thought and the chief experts in many subjects; and it can lead on to more formal or more intensive study. There is little danger that it will supplant other educational facilities, especially if the educational bodies take their share in its development (*ibid.*: 87).

By 1973, broadcasting, in particular 'the general television output of the BBC and Independent Television', could be identified by another committee of enquiry as 'the principal adult education force in Britain'. The Russell Committee used the phrase on the very first page of its Report. Yet, principal force or not, the committee went straight on to regret that it could 'do no more than note this in passing'. The report deals only with the broadcasters' 'expressly educational work' (DES, 1973: 1–2).

How should the contributions of broadcasting, both mainstream and specialised, be assessed, being just to the past with an eye on prospects for the future? Was *New Ventures in Broadcasting*, a still readable, far-seeing and 'cultivated' document, over-optimistic about the promise of broadcasting in nourishing a new renaissance? And did the robust *Glasgow Evening Citizen* broach at least one real problem – the extraordinary heterogeneity of the audience – intrinsic to communication through what a later generation would call 'the mass media'?

This chapter will attempt to explain how and why broadcasting has had such a strong commitment to adult education; delineate the various adult educational roles that broadcasting has played; and examine the ambiguity (as evinced by the Russell Committee) of its position in relation to other agencies. In so doing, it may throw some light on broadcasting's position as a main instrument, and constitutive part, of a democratic culture.

## Education and the Origins of British Broadcasting

The roots of British broadcasting's strong commitment to adult education are to be found in the origins of the BBC itself, both Company and chartered Corporation; in the post-war reforming aspirations of many leaders of opinion at the time, who helped shape emerging policies on broadcasting; most famously in the firmly held beliefs and strong personality of John Reith, the first Managing Director and first Director General, who led it until 1938; and finally in the ability and vision of some of the first people whom Reith appointed to senior posts.

The 200 or so companies that made up the pioneering radio industry in Britain had a commercial interest in manufacturing and selling wireless equipment for domestic use. It served that interest to create an organisation capable of making a wide variety of programmes for people to listen to. The Government (through the Postmaster General) hammered out with the industry (comprising major players such as Marconi and a host of small enterprises), the means for achieving that end, which raised the capital for so doing by a listeners' hypothecated tax called the licence fee – the people who wanted something to hear on their wireless sets paid an annual subscription out of which the programmes (and the essential transmission systems) could be financed.

The body to be supported by the licence fee owed its existence to a creative intervention by the state, working in conjunction with the industry but it was not a part of the state apparatus, and it was not for long a commercial company either. The Company, created in 1922, became the Corporation in 1927, operating autonomously day to day under a royal charter, with government having to learn to keep its distance.

No one doubted that entertainment would be one of the main appeals of the new technology. However, it was not supposed that the medium would only be for entertainment. It could provide up to date information, notably for farmers and fishermen, it could provide opportunities for Christian religious worship on a daily basis, and it could provide education of all kinds.

Other countries gave different answers to the question: What is broadcasting for and how should it be organised? In some, both democratic and totalitarian, it became the voice of the state, controlled by ministries of communications. In the United States it was soon the voice of the market, delivering audiences to advertisers, and profits to shareholders. In Britain (and in the many countries which adopted the British model), it was from the start (and increasingly it grew into) something different – for many years the voice of a liberal establishment, in recent decades becoming also the voice of a culturally pluralistic society. As I write (1995), the situation is much less clear, through a combination of technological progress, changes in the global economy of mass communications, and controversial (even perverse) legislation.

Those responsible for laying the foundations of broadcasting in this country were also affected by the positive attitudes to social renewal and democracy that inspired the '1919 Report'. The key pioneers were quick to claim not only that audiences wanted benefits other than entertainment; they also saw that there was no reason why, with talent and imagination, education and information could not be made entertaining. The medium had to be treated seriously enough to attract into it people with such talent and imagination.

These aspirations were embodied in the strong social conscience and forceful personality of John Reith. In his book *Broadcast Over Britain* , published in 1924, the year that educational broadcasting formally began, Reith devoted a chapter to education. He called it 'The Best of Everything'. He foresaw that 'educational activity' could take three different forms – 'talks of general information in the course of evening programmes; ... lectures for reception in schools; and ... systematic series of lectures for adults at some convenient hour which will not interfere with the normal work'. These distinctions have remained more or less valid over the years. The first, general talks, has become part of 'general (*educative*) output', and the last constitutes the 'adult' aspect of *Educational* Broadcasting (the administrative labels in the BBC changed over the years, from Adult to Further to Continuing Education).

The Best of Everything was a concept soon demonstrated. It meant, for example, that talks on music could be given by the most outstanding specialists in the land – even by the Master of the King's Musick. Older adults still alive can recall their earliest introduction to music through the talks of Sir Walford Davies. The music itself could be made available on a scale never possible before in history. The sound was thin, but the BBC could give access to Promenade Concerts only enjoyed previously by people within reach of the Queen's Hall.

There was (as there has been almost ever since), a tension and some mistrust between the worlds of education and broadcasting, but Education was soon given a department to itself at the BBC, as were Music and Drama. It was headed by J.C. Stobart, who gave the new department some credibility. He had joined the staff in 1924, having been a former Inspector from the Board of Education. As a respected classical scholar, well known to the reading public as the author of *The Glory that was Greece* and *The Grandeur that was Rome*, he was able to build support for Reith's vision, within the BBC and in the outside world. He was himself something of a visionary: *The Radio Times* for June 13 1924 had on its front page a story announcing his appointment and already outlining his plans. He envisaged A Broadcasting University, to be free to all and innovatory: 'No one need be prevented from learning science by inability to pass in Latin' (Briggs, 1965: 187–8; Robinson, 1982: 32–3).

Stobart managed to get a two-page insert for adult education in *The Radio Times*, a joint commercial venture in those days with the publishing company George Newnes Ltd., and edited by the editor of *Titbits* (the BBC took it over in 1926). This did not satisfy him. In 1929 the BBC launched *The Listener*, expressly conceived as a weekly journal of adult education. It was edited by R.S. Lambert, well known in adult education circles (he had WEA and extra-mural experience in Sheffield and London), who had run the new BBC adult education section since 1927. Then, as now, whenever the BBC launches a project which is not broadcasting, objections were raised by the commercial interests involved, who resented what they saw as the BBC's unfair advantage. *The Listener* evolved into an educative journal, including the scripts of outstanding talks, with a circulation by 1939 of nearly 50,000. It survived as a successful and distinctive publication until 1991.

Meanwhile Reith had begun to win support from educators by setting up Education Advisory Committees as part of the formal BBC structure. Such arrangements have been a feature of educational broadcasting ever since, the broadcasting organisations recognising that they needed the goodwill of the educational establishment, and often needed its actual help, especially as educational broadcasting became involved in partnerships of various kinds with formal and non-formal bodies in the field.

The Education Department was allotted 40 minutes each evening, five days a week, for serial and topical talks. The first adult education series were on 'Insects in Relation to Men', 'The British Government', 'Everyday Life in Early Times', together with talks on health and music. By 1928, the time had come to develop closer relations with the audience and promote the better use of the output, through related publications, associated group work and active association with the established agencies of adult education.

In 1926, in an article in the first issue of the *Journal of Adult Education*, Stobart distinguished three forms of contact with listeners – the general cultural effect in nearly four million homes; contact – yet to be developed – with the organised body of adult students; and 'a mass of would-be students ... whose interest has still to be aroused'. 'Wireless must flow', he wrote, 'into the vacant spaces of continuing education.' He summed up the functions of radio programmes for these categories in these terms: 'For the first they are providing a stimulus, for the second an auxiliary, but for the third category they must try to provide something complete, however imperfect'. He advocated study guides as an extra and welcomed the interest being shown in the new medium by public librarians (Robinson, 1982). The first 'aid to study pamphlet', *One Hundred Years of Working Class Progress*, was published in May 1927.

One subsequent task for historians consists of discovering the implications in policy and practice for these distinct functions – stimulus, auxiliary, or something complete in itself. Kelly's *History of Adult Education in Great Britain* features it, along with cheap books, newspapers, public libraries, art galleries and museums, in a miscellaneous chapter entitled 'The Auxiliaries of Adult Education'. By opting for one of its functions, Kelly did not do justice to the actual scope of educational broadcasting, and his emphasis is quite different in the updating Prologue to the third edition (Kelly, 1992).

Right from the start, the bodies responsible for 'the organised body of adult students' showed (albeit ambivalent) interest. As early as 1923, the World Association of Adult Education asked the newly formed British Institute of Adult Education to explore the position of education in broadcasting, and as already noted in Chapter 3, one of the BIAE's first undertakings was to organise a conference on the topic. The journals of the WEA, the National Council of Labour Colleges, and the Tutors' Association subsequently expressed contrasting attitudes. *The Highway* (WEA) gave generous attention to radio, while *Plebs* (NCLC) took a much more suspicious view:

Our rulers have not been slow to profit by the lesson they learned during the General Strike as to the usefulness of broadcasting. An Adult Education Section of the BBC has now been set up, and a prominent WEA-er put in charge (Robinson, 1982: 43–4).

H.L. Beales, in the *Tutors' Bulletin*, recognised that many tutors regarded broadcasting as a soft option, a rival and a menace, but reckoned that 'Broadcasting does not queer our pitch; on the contrary we can co-operate with it to our mutual advantage'. Briggs quotes an article by Lambert in *The Highway* (October 1927): 'The WEA has long experience and knowledge of what is wanted educationally: the BBC has an instrument of unparalleled range and power for reaching the mass of the people' (Briggs, 1965: 218).

*New Ventures in Broadcasting: A study in adult education*, the report already quoted, was a product of this debate and the work of the influential Hadow committee. It was set up jointly by the BBC and the British Institute of Adult Education, to explore further the use to which this 'range and power' could be put. Its members belonged to the National Council of Social Service, London County Council, the Carnegie UK Trust, the Workers' Educational Association and the National Federation of Women's Institutes, plus the Board of Education. Hadow and his colleagues took broadcasting seriously, both as an educational force, and as an instrument of a democratic culture, and recommended developments which, as we shall see, were soon implemented by creating a movement of active listeners.

*New Ventures* was important in a more general way. It appeared at a time when the BBC was locked in one of its earliest disputes with Government. It had been forbidden to treat of matters which were or had become controversial. The Hadow Committee, arguing from educational premises, overtly backed Reith against the Government by justifying the broadcasting of controversy: 'To cut out controversial subjects is to cut out all that is most stimulating and most important to men and women, both as individuals and as citizens'. In the month its report was published, the Postmaster General lifted the ban.

## Trials, Errors and Growth 1929–39

Broadcasting was a success with the public. More and more people bought 'wireless sets' and the BBC's licence income increased. Three and a half million licence holders provided nearly £1 million in 1930, enough money to sustain regional as well as national services during increased hours of transmission.

Reith and Stobart had identified a role for broadcasting in the schools and their plans for this sector led to steady progress. There were inevitably problems to be resolved, material and curricular – where was the money to come from to buy wireless sets for schools, were the programmes meant to support, complement, or as some feared, displace the teachers? Were they meant to teach directly or to enrich the curriculum, to provide an audio-visual equivalent to the civilised habit of 'reading round' a subject? Since at that time a national curriculum was a centralising, foreign abomination, how was that to be organised, and how was the relevance of the output to be assured?

On the whole, these difficulties were overcome – over time, the schools were equipped; teachers were impressed by the sheer quality of the programmes; the BBC appointed Education Officers to work with the schools; an HMI was appointed to foster collaboration, and Schools Broadcasting gradually became securely established. The adult education story was not so straightforward. The education of adults is always and everywhere a more complex, amorphous domain than the schooling of children, involving a multiplicity of agencies (Stobart is said to have called it 'addled education'). There were, as expected, choices to be made between providing a general stimulus, reinforcement of an educational process for which other bodies were responsible, or a self-contained educational experience. The advantages and disadvantages of these alternative modes had to be discovered (and, with changing circumstances and the turnover of generations, they were not discovered once and for all, so that the arguments have been recycled at intervals). Adult education had won a place in broadcasting in part because of influential support from the BIAE, the WEA and other major bodies in the field. It was sometimes to find itself an object of envy, suspicion and discouragement from some of those same bodies.

The decade up to the second world war is dominated by a project which grew out of the *New Ventures* report. Soon after its publication (1928), the BBC set up the Central Council for Broadcast Adult Education, chaired first by Lord Sankey (later Lord Chancellor), then by William Temple, Archbishop of York (later Archbishop of Canterbury) – another keen 'WEA-er' who had been the WEA's National President between 1903–24. The following year the CCBAE announced a five-year Plan. The BBC's Adult Education Section would promote Listening Group Activities. This would, it was hoped, overcome a weakness diagnosed by the Hadow Committee. *New Ventures* had warned of the dangers of one-way communication and urged the promotion of listeners' discussion groups, supported by study-guides in print related to the programmes. In two years there were 664 listening groups, with leaders trained by the first BBC education officers. By the year 1932-3 there were 1,738 groups organised in four areas of the country. Registered groups received a syllabus, so that they could prepare for and follow up the programmes, broadcast mid-evening, Monday to Friday. The groups varied in size – from six people to a hundred.

Not a lot is known about the value of the project to listeners. Many wrote in to declare their interest. And they certainly grew in numbers. As well as booklets for each series, there was a handbook (also available in braille) called *Discusssion Groups and How to Run Them*. The wide range of subjects for group (or home) study included foreign languages, child rearing, the British Empire, the national character, and trade unionism. 'The Changing World' (1931) and 'The Way of Peace' (programmes and booklets) (1938) addressed social and political issues in some depth.

A series called 'The Citizen and his Government' caused such a furore that not all of it was broadcast. The 12 programmes were planned to include talks by Harry Pollitt, leader of the Communist Party, and Oswald Mosley, founder of the British Union of Fascists. The Foreign Office was much put out by the prospect of such contributors, and pressure was put on the BBC to drop them. Listening Group members wrote to complain that the first part of the series had been tame, and was to be cut just as it looked like getting interesting. The Adult Education Advisory Committee (successor to the CCBAE) backed the producers against what they saw as censorship. The BBC Governors and management wavered, and the Government had its way.

In 1933-4, the Listening Groups project faltered, and the optimism generated by their early rapid growth faded. Hadow had wanted an infrastructure of 14 regions, but money could only be found for four. Historians give quite different figures, but all agree that the numbers of participants was not growing significantly It seemed that many of those who had enrolled were already active in the WEA or elsewhere. They were not new recruits to learning as often as had been hoped. Even R.S Lambert, one of the founders of the 'movement', conceded:

It was an odd idea that listeners would be eager to leave their comfortable firesides on wintry nights and go out to some hall or schoolroom to sit round a loudspeaker and discuss the words of wisdom let fall by the invisible broadcaster in their midst (Robinson, 1982: 62–3).

The sympathetic but objective W.E. Williams evaluated the project and concluded: 'It is an auxiliary or supplementary service rather than a pioneering activity.' (*ibid.*, 1982: 56). The adult education bodies in the field and BBC staff themselves began to feel that the effort was a drain and a distraction. The adult education slots were cut from five to three a week and the BBC increasingly regarded the training of groupleaders as a responsibility for the field, not for the broadcasters.

The home listening audience for adult education talks was huge, five to seven million by now, compared with the numbers in the listening groups, so the latter's interest should, it was felt by Williams and others, not have too much influence on programme policy. The field bodies knew more about group study than the BBC, and should use broadcasting as a resource in their own way. So a corresponding division of responsibility was built into arrangements for production, advice and liaison. Once again there was a gap between production and use, between stimulus (public, professional, well resourced) and response (domestic, individual, haphazard). Group listening had not solved the problem – how to combine the reach of broadcasting with the depth considered essential by exponents of face-to-face forms of adult education. Many groups persisted nonetheless right through the war, and the scheme itself formally ended in 1947.

From the mid-thirties adult education listeners were treated as an element within the general audience, and it was the main audience's educational needs that prevailed. The techniques of broadcasting were evolving. Later generations remember that television used to transmit pictures of blackboards, but grew out of it, developing more sophisticated styles of presentation, so at this time broadcasters (producers and speakers) began to discover that the radio did not exist to take the lecture hall into the home. It called for its own styles. Advice was still taken about Talks policy from senior academics such as Principal J.H. Nicholson of University College, Hull, and Sir Walter Moberly, but the talks themselves were given by increasingly well known and popular speakers such as C.H. Middleton (gardening), Christopher Stone (gramophone records), Alistair Cooke (films) and J.B. Priestley, Harold Nicolson and William Beveridge (current affairs). Other genres began to provide information, entertainment and education blended together. The formal debate of the 1920s gave way to the skilfully edited feature programme, with recorded interviews and snatches of conversation; the lecture on social history gave way to Leslie Baily's 'Scrapbooks'. Drama' could include historical reconstructions such as D.G. Bridson's account of the Jacobite Rising, 'The March of the '45'.

By the end of the 1930s, the essential character of the BBC had become clear. It was neither the voice of the market, nor of the state (though the state often covertly pressed it into a narrowly defined political conformity). It was a public service, providing education, as well as entertainment and information. Broadcasting was already a force for adult education, though it had not yet discovered its main roles, nor achieved the most effective forms of co-operation with 'the field'. While not wanting to exacerbate or express too explicitly the nation's political conflicts, it treated its growing audience of serious listeners with respect. As the voice of a middle-of-the-road intellectual and cultural establishment, it was inevitably criticised for being stuffy, and on Sundays audiences were attracted away from it by commercial stations on the continent, but it succeeded nonetheless in being popular as well, with audiences for the wireless running into millions.

The BBC had become a culturally unifying force of a kind that Britain had never had before. That accounts in part for its essential role during the Second World War and, more particularly, for the forms and content of its adult education work during that period.

## The War and After, 1939–55

During the war, 1939–45, the BBC's three fundamental aims, to entertain, inform and educate acquired a sharper focus: through such legendary shows as 'ITMA', entertainment helped maintain civilian and military morale. Light music became 'Music while you Work' for transmission in factories as well as homes, offsetting the production line monotony of making equipment and munitions. Variety, as in 'Workers' Playtime', could come from a works canteen during the lunchbreak. Information about the progress of the war, as reliable as wartime circumstances permitted, was essential. It became the basis for trust, worldwide, but especially in occupied Europe, in the BBC's integrity. Education, disguised and overt, became increasingly popular, and the BBC made significant contributions to the national debate about, and understanding of, the peacetime reconstruction tasks that lay ahead.

The experience of group listening, never likely to succeed on a vast scale as a movement because always at variance with the way most people actually listened to radio, became relevant for men and women living in barracks and service camps. The BBC worked with the newly set up Central Advisory Council for Adult Education in HM Forces and with the Army Bureau of Current Affairs (see Chapters 3 and 8). The War Office found money for the Council to buy wireless sets. The broadcasts were accompanied by illustrated booklets on a wide range of subjects – arts, sciences and current affairs. A series on post-war plans, including the Beveridge Report, virtually the foundation document of the welfare state, predictably ran into trouble. The BBC and ABCA were charged with disloyalty by some right-wing politicians, who saw discussion of alternative ways of organising society as subversive. The BBC's main intention was summed up in the title of a 1943 series for adult and youth groups: 'Talking to Some Purpose'.

The public at large was stimulated to talk to an extraordinary degree by one of the most famous, long-running programmes in radio history: 'The Brains Trust'. In its format and content it was pioneering. A large and growing audience responded enthusiastically to a weekly panel discussion between four people answering topical questions, including Julian Huxley, world-renowned scientist and later the first Director General of UNESCO, and C.E.M. Joad, reader in philosophy at Birkbeck College, with a gift for popularisation. The success of this innovative programme in part encouraged planners in due course to create the Third Programme, forerunner of Radio 3.

When the war ended in 1945, the Government was determined that the demobilisation of men and women from the services would be better organised than after the First World War. The BBC for its part was keen to make a major educational contribution to the processes of resettlement and adaptation involved. Hence the setting up, early in 1945, of the Services Educational Unit (under the general aegis of the School Broadcasting Department because they were accustomed to the institutionalised use of the output at the listening end). A team of producers and presenters was recruited specially. It included Richmond Postgate, later to become Controller, Educational Broadcasting; one of the first political scientists to become well known later through television, Robert McKenzie; and the social historian Asa Briggs, still serving as a Regimental Sergeant Major. Publicity for the scheme used the slogan 'Brush Up for Civvy Street'. The Light Programme and the General Overseas Service on short wave carried 18 broadcasts a week on a wide variety of topics – not only on the practicalities of home-making, and job hunting, but also on the workings of central and local government, on music, science – and Samuel Pepys.

Forces Educational Broadcasts were a precursor of other major educational campaigns by the BBC (and later ITV) in association with non-broadcasting partners, including the Literacy Campaign (1975 and later) and the Computer Literacy Project (1983). Cain (1994: 35) calls them 'the second great experiment in broadcast education' (the first being the Listening Group movement). It was certainly the BBC's second major, dedicated educational enterprise on a substantial scale, but it was by no means the first time that the radio had made an educational contribution to the well-being of a particular section of the public.

The equally long tradition of charitable appeal broadcasting also had educative effects. During the 1920s, when unemployment affected two and then three million people, Reith and his associates wanted (as Cain himself reminds us elsewhere) 'to inform the community about the problem [and] also to alleviate the difficulties of those trapped by it' (Groombridge, 1994: 27). The resulting programmes provoked floods of letters, which were answered by the BBC's first outside, independent partner, the National Council of Social Service. The project was so successful that it came to an end. There was too much correspondence for the money available.

The BBC, encouraged by one of the recurrent official commissions of enquiry to which broadcasting is subjected (1949–51, chaired by Sir William Beveridge), was ready to make a new attempt at finding the right structure for broadcast adult education. A Further Education Experiment became a Further Education Unit, which then evolved into a Further Education Department, headed by Jean Rowntree. The Department produced series for the general public or of particular interest to specific occupational groups (such as coalminers or youth workers). They were widely publicised in a new way: a free leaflet, *Listen and Learn* was available through adult education organisations and libraries, and through the BBC's Education Officers in the field.

Considerable progress was made, but Beveridge set a high standard for it to be measured against: 'If the ideal of an informed democracy is to materialise, it will be necessary for the BBC to study and reach the audiences beyond'. There was certainly no prospect of a return to the notion that broadcasting's main role was to provide fuel for a study circle movement of active listeners. The pedagogical challenge created by the need in principle to communicate often with the whole audience and sometimes with segments of it, led not only to experimentation in programme planning and production, but to a body of sophisticated theoretical research on intelligibility and comprehension from such academics as Professor Philip Vernon and from the highly original scholar on the BBC Further Education Department's own staff, Joseph Trenaman (Briggs, 1979: 807–14; Trenaman, 1961, 1967).

The experience and reputation being acquired by the Department, the quality of the work being done, were laying the foundations for what, some 20 years later, was to be the BBC's most important ever joint venture with the educational world – the convergence of adult and higher education, and the democratisation of higher education, brought about through the Open University (see Chapter 11). Before that was to happen, the output for adult education was to be enlarged by two fundamental developments: the breaking of the broadcasting monopolies – of radio by television; then of the BBC by ITV.

## Diversification and Development: Media and systems, 1955–82

Broadcasting began to ramify. The radio channels were reorganised in 1967, creating Radios 1,2,3, and 4. Local radio came into existence. BBC Television re-opened in 1946. Independent Television came on air in 1955; BBC2 was inaugurated in 1964; Channel 4 in 1982.

Each of these reformed or new channels meant more opportunities for educative and adult educational programmes. This applied as much to ITV (and, 27 years later, to Channel 4) as to the BBC. Though commonly known as 'commercial television', these channels were not fully commercial in the American sense. A fierce debate in Parliament and the country led to an ingenious and creative compromise: public service broadcasting would in future be financed in two ways – by licence fee and by raising advertising revenue. Competition was between two forms of public service broadcasting, not between a public service system and a fully commercial one. Despite competition between channels, educational broadcasters came to regard themselves not as competitors, but rather as collaborative rivals in a shared enterprise. It had not started that way. When Associated Rediffusion, one of the first commercial contractors, started a service for schools in 1967, some months ahead of the BBC, the company was widely regarded as an impertinent interloper. However, the common ground and interest between the BBC and ITV was soon acknowledged. It was celebrated on the tenth anniversary of Schools Television in a 'Progress Report', *Teaching and Television: ETV explained,* edited by Guthrie Moir, an executive producer with Rediffusion, who proclaimed AETV (Adult Education Television) 'an important new branch' of ETV (Educational Television) (Moir, 1967: 2).

There was an enthusiasm for educational development in the 1960s, fuelled by a series of reports (Crowther, Albemarle, Beloe, Robbins, Newsom, Plowden), which the broadcasting organisations shared. The adventurous Director-General of the BBC (Hugh Carlton Greene) described the period as 'the educational decade'; one of his chairmen was the headmaster of Rugby School (Sir Arthur fforde); education was regarded as important enough to have its own Controller (John Scupham). There had been debate in educational and broadcasting circles about a channel dedicated to education. Those in favour stressed the scale and diversity of the need; those against resisted 'ghettoisation'.

Trenaman's research influenced the debate and subsequent practice. It had shown conclusively the enormous extent to which attitudes to education in the population varied. Everyone had things they wanted to learn, but only a quarter of the public had confidence in the value of education with a capital E. A huge proportion – 45 per cent – was in fact suspicious of, indifferent, or hostile to, the very idea of education (Trenaman, 1961, 1967). 'Education by stealth' on radio and television was justified as the analogue in broadcasting of outreach and community development work in the field, promoting learning by avoiding the outward forms and rhetoric of educational institutions, especially schools. Struck by the need and demand for education, however delivered, the Pilkington Committee (another enquiry into the state and future of broadcasting, 1962) recommended that the BBC be awarded a second general television channel, intending it to complement BBC1, by being intellectually adventurous, educative, and educational.

The Independent Television Authority (later, with arrival of 'commercial' radio, the Independent Broadcasting Authority) used Adult Education as a mandatory programme requirement. Some companies were keener and better at it than others, but all complied. Television transmission time was severely rationed to 50 hours per week per channel, but the Government (through the Postmaster General) made extra hours available on all channels for certain categories of output, of which adult education was one (religious programmes and programmes in Welsh were the others). The acknowledged difficulty of making a clear distinction between educational and educative output led to discussions among the professionals which were an odd blend of philosophical and administrative elements. John Scupham, with Edward Hutchinson (Secretary of the National Institute of Adult Education), ITA staff and others, finally produced a formula, accepted by Government, which stressed intentionality by providers and serial experience for the audience:

Educational television programmes for adults are programmes (other than school broadcasts) arranged in series and planned in consultation with appropriate educational bodies to help viewers towards a progressive mastery or understanding of some skill or body of knowledge.

Not unnaturally, the debate about the cogency and usefulness of this definition continued for years afterwards, but the BBC found it administratively helpful and applied it also to radio, even though radio transmission hours were not restricted. As television grew in credibility and popularity, fast becoming the dominant medium and for nearly everyone the main source of information about what was going on in the world, there were different pressures within the competing systems. ITV welcomed (or tolerated) adult education because extra hours brought proportionately more advertising time. In the BBC, Scupham and his immediate successors, Richmond Postgate and Donald Grattan, had to battle consistently against other BBC departments which resented resources going to 'minority' interests. The antagonism of the educational world to the proposed Open University ('University of the Air' as it was first called), remarked on in Chapter 11, was matched inside the Corporation.

The progress of what Moir had called 'an important new branch' was reviewed halfway through this period in the Russell Report (DES, 1973: 85–8). Though not concerned with mainstream broadcasting as a dominant form, Russell had serious observations and recommendations to make about 'AETV'. Significantly, the chapter is headed 'Media: Partners and Supporters', giving broadcasting a more central role alongside other more formally recognised agencies of adult education. It is enthusiastic in tone:

None of the other agencies with which we are concerned is ever likely to rival the ability of broadcasting to make education available to people who cannot or will not have recourse to it outside the home. And accessibility, we must emphasise again, is one of the criteria by which a well-developed system of adult education must be judged ... Certain kinds of teaching or demonstration ... can be accomplished more effectively through broadcasting than in any other way (*ibid.*: 86).

It looks to a phase of experimentation in which different combinations of media and educational providers are explored. It is impressed by 'the Open University, a permanent multi-media system of higher education for adults' and, in a much-quoted paragraph predicts:

The example of the Open University is likely to bring into prominence the need for similar forms of provision at other levels and in non-academic fields which would benefit from being serviced by modest analogues of the Open University (*ibid.*: 87).

As noted in Chapter 3, one of the main concerns of the Russell Report was the needs of people who were variously disadvantaged. By focusing on this issue, it had a permanent influence on the priorities of many field agencies and of educational broadcasters.

Russell also voiced a topical worry, noting that in 1972 the Government had lifted restrictions on transmission time, so that the broadcasting organisations could decide for themselves how long to be on the air. Adult education was no longer a protected category of output. There is always competition for airtime by programme controllers and makers, and whereas audiences for adult education were enormous by educational standards, they were, as Russell fairly acknowledged, small by broadcasting ones: 'We note that so far neither the BBC nor the IBA has felt it necessary to say that they would not *reduce* the amount of adult education in the new situation' (*ibid.*: 87). In the event, though the security of AETV (its presence, and almost as important, its scheduling) was and remains a recurrent theme, adult education was to maintain and improve its position at least until 1990.

The history of broadcast adult education must be more however than the history of its politics. The political equation at the time included the quality and creativity of the output, on which reputation depended. During these decades, the BBC was consolidating its position among broadcasters internationally – in both media, but especially in television – as one of the world's most impressive educational broadcasting organisations (NHK in Japan was another such, but internationally less influential). This was evident at meetings of the European Broadcasting Union, and recognised over the years by an abundance of international awards and prizes. There were institutions in other countries that compared favourably in their professionalism, but the scale, range and scope of the BBC's work, as well as its quality, in radio and in television, enhanced by publications and the field staff of education officers; and its relevance to the main educational and training developments within the society, all contributed to the BBC's prestige.

It was not always possible for ITV to do as consistently well, comprising as it did 15 separate companies, located in different parts of the country, all with small education staffs, and none with the critical mass of the BBC. Some of its output was networked, some was local or regional. At its best, ITV, series for series, was also recognised in EBU circles, and in educational circles at home, as a major contributor. It was noted for pioneering new veins of work – in relation to teacher training, unemployment, and other fields, which were then sometimes developed by the BBC on a national basis. Harlech Television produced 'Heading for Change', written and presented from Bristol by William Taylor (later Director of the Institute of Education in London) for teachers preparing for the raising of the school leaving age (ROSLA) to 16 in 1973. The BBC tackled the same theme on a national scale with a notable project called 'Rosla and After'. The education system itself, using conventional methods, could not possibly have provided such resources for this urgent professional development in the time available.

In 1976, Westward Television, then the franchise-holder for the south-west, based in Plymouth, was concerned over the problems of unemployment facing young people in the area. Westward formed a partnership with the National Extension College (NEC) and designed an information and advice project, comprising a series of television programmes ('Just the Job'), information of a practical kind in The Jobhunter Kit, and a telephone counselling service using trained volunteers. A grant from the Manpower Services Commission financed the additional NEC services. This form of collaboration, encouraged by Geoffrey Holland, Head of Special Projects at the MSC, set a useful precedent for the BBC. It was adopted for example by 'Action Special', an annual collaboration about employment and training opportunities between the BBC's Radio 1FM and the Department of Employment. Scottish and Ulster Television developed schemes similar to Westward's, tailored to the specific problems of their areas.

A decade or so earlier, the decentralised structure of ITV had facilitated seminal collaborative projects between television and higher education. Ulster Television and Queen's University Belfast created 'Midnight Oil', 42 half-hour programmes on medicine, law, literature, music, physics, history and economics (six programmes per subject), to give viewers some idea of what the university had to offer. The audience's response, according to the ITA's Annual Report 1962–3, 'exceeded all expectations'. The following year, Michael Young, who was about to set up the NEC in Cambridge and had already mooted the idea of an open university, inspired Anglia Television and the University to work together on a series at the other end of the day from Ulster's, called 'Dawn University'. The ITA ensured the series was networked; checklists in the programme journal *TV Times* enabled viewers to take part in three experiments in a lecture on 'Concentration and Attention'.

The most significant such project, 'Standard of Living' (1964), a joint venture between the Department of Adult Education, University of Nottingham and ATV (Associated Television), came closest as a model for the Open University itself. On offer for this experiment, grant-aided by the Leverhulme Trust, were 13 20-minute programmes on economics, plus, for those that enrolled on the related course, a handbook and an assigned tutor. The extra-mural and broadcasting staff planning the course together were in effect a prototype course team. Tutors, recruited from a wide range of educational bodies, formed a nationwide network. They worked at a distance and set up tutorial meetings with the students. The enterprise was carefully evaluated by Harold Wiltshire and his colleague Fred Bayliss (Wiltshire and Bayliss, 1965; Wiltshire, 1976). The size of the total audience is not known, but over 3,000 handbooks were bought, and 1,656 students enrolled for the correspondence course. Using a DES measure of 'effectiveness' current at the time (for attendance at university extramural courses), 77 per cent were effective. Though by definition mostly taught at a distance, 717 students applied for and were awarded a Certificate of 'Attendance'.

Professor Wiltshire believed somewhat austerely that television on its own could not teach effectively. It was better to use it as the lead-medium in a teaching system. Not everyone accepted his premise, but the conclusion was more persuasive. 'Standard of Living' gave impetus to the view that grew in strength throughout these two decades, that educational broadcasting belonged to the broader domain of educational technology (the National Council for Educational Technology was set up in 1967) and to the more comprehensive concept of distance education. Terms such as 'composite courses', even 'multi-media systems', were used increasingly, the latter obviously not in its modern sense, but as descriptions of teaching-learning packages. Broadcasting was normally seen as the principal medium, print and other media being routinely referred to as 'support'.

In Britain such systems were used to teach foreign languages, explore the arts, spread an understanding of science, family life and citizenship. In addition to 'support publications', books and pamphlets were produced about these experimental projects. Though commonly written by the producers themselves, they were not publicity documents. They catered for ongoing interest either in the subject matter (among listeners and viewers), or in the process (among broadcasters and adult educators). Michael Stephens (not to be confused with the Robert Peers Professor of Adult Education, University of Nottingham of the same name at the same time), wrote an assessment of an 'experimental "open learning" project' – mainly on BBC radio – about making better decisions, in the family or the community; Tony Matthews reported on an adult education partnership between the BBC, the TUC and the WEA; John Radcliffe and Robert Salkeld edited a many-sided account of the influential BBC Computer Literacy Project (Stephens, 1976; Matthews, 1978; Radcliffe and Salkeld, 1983).

Reading them in a more cynical climate, it is refreshing to find in these publications a sense that to work in broadcast adult education at that time was to engage through a creative medium in work that was directly and humanely in the public interest and to the benefit of countless individual viewers and listeners. Typical of this spirit was a speech made by Tony Matthews about partnerships between broadcasters and other bodies. The occasion was not a public relations one, but a European Broadcasting Union seminar, one of a regular annual series held in Basle at which producers and directors from different countries learned from one another. Having candidly analysed the frustrations and irritations – for all partners – of collaborative work, he said:

We don't always want to be on an ego trip, doing programmes that we like doing just for their own sake. We'd like to go further and get something done, and genuinely to help people learn and genuinely to help people who have problems ... So, if partnerships will help people in need to get some kind of social action, some kind of support ... well for God's sake, let's have partnerships (Tappolet, F., 1977).

The same idealistic but practical mood and belief was conveyed by David Hargreaves, the BBC Project Leader, in two detailed and substantial accounts of the most significant and elaborate collaboration of all: the Adult Literacy Campaign of the mid-1970s. (Hargreaves, 1977, 1980). This joint project, involved broadcasting with the British Association of Residential Settlements, every local education authority and many voluntary organisations. The BBC made use of both radio and television, and the whole campaign had the strong support of the Independent Broadcasting Authority, which encouraged the ITV companies to publicise it in their areas. The BBC programmes ('On the Move' and its sequels, featuring the then unknown actor Bob Hoskins) were supported by tutors' handbooks and students' workbooks, for personal use and for classes run all over the country by the statutory and voluntary bodies in the field. The campaign had been carefully researched and piloted. It made an immediate difference to thousands in the adult population (estimated at the time at about 2 million people) who were not literate. It had lasting outcomes (examined in detail in Chapter 6) in that the hitherto submerged problems of illiteracy and innumeracy stayed visible on the educational and political agenda; the Adult Learning and Basic Skills Unit (ALBSU) grew out of the Adult Literacy Resource Agency, originally set up with £1m from the government under the aegis of the National Institute of Adult Education; the liaison machinery created for the campaign became Broadcasting Support Services, co-ordinating the broadcasters with telephone helplines, field agencies and others, for various kinds of co-operation for educational social action and charitable purposes.

A similar ethos pervaded much of the work of ITV companies and of the IBA. To take two examples: As early as 1964–5 Thames Television (with Professor Frank Jessup, director of the Extra-Mural Delegacy, University of Oxford, as consultant), mounted an ambitiously farsighted series – 30 years before it became commonplace to speculate about the millennium – 'Towards the Year 2000'. A scholarly anticipation of the issues facing society enabled viewers to register for supporting literature and scripts, enrol for a correspondence course, attend conferences at Television House, and compete in a special essay competition. Yorkshire Television's initiative, 'Make it Count' (in association with the National Extension College) helped make the country aware that innumeracy was as big a problem as illiteracy. The IBA undertook research into the audience's educational needs and interests, just as the BBC did (BBC/ITA and Independent Television, 1969; Haldane, 1969), and successfully persuaded the ITV companies to appoint community education officers, liaising in the field alongside their well-established BBC counterparts.

Throughout its history, educational broadcasters have regularly sought advice on policy from experts and distinguished people from the field who served on a panoply of advisory bodies. Recognised authorities and other expert subject specialists were involved in the making of courses and programmes. In terms of personal knowledgeability, the distinction between the two groups was not clear-cut. Many educational broadcasters were in any case recruited from the formal system, and in this period the corps of broadcasting professionals, especially but not exclusively from the BBC, were increasingly recognised as educational authorities in their own right. Jennifer Rogers, for example, first produced her classic, *Adults Learning* (now in its third edition), in 1971, when she was a BBC education officer (Rogers, 1989). Broadcasting and research staff co-operating at the Open University had begun considerably to extend and deepen knowledge about learning and the media. In a submission to the 1977 (Annan) Committee of Enquiry 'On the Future of Broadcasting', including the question of a fourth channel, the Open University listed 24 different teaching roles for television and another nine for radio (Groombridge, in Roderick and Stephens, 1978).

In broader terms, broadcast adult education in Britain had by 1982 developed at least five main functions, identified that year by the Advisory Council for Adult and Continuing Education (ACACE). Paraphrasing its summary in *Continuing Education: From policies to practice*, these functions were:

(1) Educative programmes;
(2) Programmes, in principle from any part of the output, general or specifically educational, whose educational value is enhanced by publications (sometimes major texts in their own right);
(3) Programmes that spread awareness of adult education, publicise learning opportunities, encourage the use of locally available facilities;
(4) Programme and other materials, used as resources by tutors in face-to-face settings, a service much facilitated by appropriate off-air recording and copyright arrangements; and
(5) Broadcast and recorded programmes as an element in an integrated teaching scheme – whether devoted to one subject, one issue, or a complete curriculum (ACACE, 1982).

The relevant section of the report is headed 'New Technology and Open Learning', a title that marks a further level of the clarification achieved in the 1970s, moving on from Russell. For decades, while the term 'adult education' had by tradition been co-terminous with the face-to-face activities of a small set of specific agencies (in some formulations the WEA, university extra-mural departments, local education authorities, and few others), the relationship between adult education and broadcasting, both conceptually and in practice, was uneasy. The concept of 'Open Learning' now showed that there was a domain to which both sets of institutions clearly and equally belonged (Mackenzie, N., Postgate, R., and Scupham, J., 1975).

## Public Service Expanded – and Threatened, 1982–95

The chief author of that ACACE report was Naomi McIntosh, Convenor of its Committee on Continuing Education, and Professor of Applied Social Research and Pro-Vice-Chancellor at the Open University. As Naomi Sargant, she became first Senior Commissioning Editor, Educational Programming of the new Channel 4 in 1981.

The essential character of broadcasting in Britain was continuing to develop. With Channel 4 added to the other three television channels, British public service broadcasting came close to being the voice – more precisely the voices – of a pluralistic civil society, in Anthony Smith's phrase, 'the cockpit of culture'. (Smith, 1995). The name of Jeremy Isaacs, first Chief Executive of the new channel, should be added to Hugh Greene's as men largely responsible for the creative daring to harness broadcasting for a democratic culture, itself in process of confusing evolution. The same trend was manifested, albeit less clearly, with the proliferation of radio stations serving different localities, demographic segments of the population, ethnic groups, tastes in music, and other communities of interest. The BBC created Radio 5, dedicated to education and sport, including much continuing education, popularly presented.

Annan had been lobbied from all directions, but a vast amount of evidence came from people and organisations who advocated more airtime for education. Parliament decided in the 1980 Broadcasting Act (and reaffirmed in the 1990 Act) that Channel 4 should be a national network with 'a distinctive character of its own', based on 'innovation in form and content of programmes' meant to 'appeal to tastes and interests not catered for elsewhere'. 'A suitable proportion' of the output had to be educational (not including schools broadcasts, until the 1990 Act, still the responsibility of ITV). William Whitelaw was the Home Secretary responsible for this legislation, which not everyone had expected of a Conservative administration. The IBA (chaired then by Lady Plowden, still associated in the public mind with the primary school report bearing her name), gave the channel a target for education of 15 per cent of transmission time, wisely leaving the channel itself to define what 'education' meant. The emphasis was to be on the use to which the programmes were put. Fifteen per cent, it was calculated, would mean an extra hour a day, so there would be 700 hours a year in all for education (BBC and IBA), and more for adults than for schools (Sargant, 1992: 17).

Sargant has described 'this large and generous educational and social role' as 'extremely important to the social and cultural cohesion of the country'. One might add: the more pluralistic the society becomes, the more it needs resources for cohesion. In implementing the remit, she took the pragmatic view that people could learn as well from educative as from educational programmes, especially if they were reinforced by 'well-produced support materials'. This did not mean however that there was no need for programmes deliberately designed to encourage learning. They were to have an important place in Channel 4's schedules, and – in due course – at times when most people were watching. Editorial control was quite separate from advertising sales, but Isaacs had to be convinced that the programmes would be attractive enough to justify peak-time slots, and the IBA that broadening the educational agenda did not mean diluting it. (ibid.: 18–19).

Evidently, the paradigm shift in British politics since 1979 did not make a great difference to Channel 4, whereas the educational world at large, and adult education in particular, endured fully the rigours, some stimulating, some debilitating, of Thatcherism and its aftermath. So did the rest of broadcasting. In the 1990s, the central question became: Is broadcasting an industry just like any other, or does the public interest require it to be treated differently? The very concept of public service broadcasting was at risk. A political struggle developed round that question, complicated by technological advances marking an end to spectrum scarcity, and by the commercial internationalisation of the media industries as a whole, including satellite channels and cable. This struggle inevitably had implications for educational programming and activity. The Broadcasting Act 1990 removed from ITV any obligation to educate. Educative programmes remained, but its schools output was transferred to Channel 4. It became in principle and increasingly in appearance a commercial channel. Thames Television, which had a considerable commitment to education, lost its franchise. The IBA, which had been in law 'the broadcaster', was replaced by the Independent Television Commission (ITC), which became the regulator of commercial companies in a competitive industry.

Clearly the BBC was at risk from a series of Conservative Governments showing revolutionary zeal for privatization. Selling off Radios 1 and 2 was a seriously considered policy option. In this situation, it was appropriate for the BBC to play from its strengths, and to play up achievements which the commercial sector could not possibly afford. As part of this strategy, the tradition and the undoubted achievements of BBC education in the 1980s were given pride of place in such policy documents as *Extending Choice* , and in the BBC's many-sided, often wounding, efforts to protect itself from being dismantled for profit (BBC, 1992). In 1992 all the BBC's educational activities, with exception of the OU centre, were consolidated into one Directorate, embracing both radio and television and multi-media publishing, with its own ring-fenced budget. When a new Director was appointed in 1994, Jane Drabble, the head of education, became for the first time a member of the BBC's Board of Management. A lesson had also been learned from Channel 4 – BBC Education could buy programmes from independent companies, commission them from general output departments, and produce support material in print and other media for their programmes. An informative booklet about the serial adaptation of *Middlemarch* was one of the first fruits.

Channel 4 and the BBC prudently maintained the tradition of avoiding wasteful competition. Channel 4 kept clear of modern languages, at which the BBC had excelled for generations, but developed new ways of addressing old interests or new strands altogether, some deliberately popular, some addressing key minorities. Just as the BBC's computer project, including as it did the Acorn computer supplied to schools, had made Britain an exceptionally computer-minded nation, so Channel 4 and ITV's Central Television can claim to have helped put environmentalism high on the public's agenda. Channel 4 worked with ALBSU (numeracy programmes), NEC and BTEC ('Making sense of Marketing', 'Making sense of Economics'). BBC, ITV and Channel 4 co-operated with each other and with the field, at the level of specific projects, but also through the annual all-channel Adult Learners' Week. This was a high profile, promotional campaign, national, regional and local, for participation in adult education, planned in association with the National Institute of Adult Continuing Education and its members.

Seasons of educational programmes, not always billed as such, improved impact and penetration, so that they could reach exceptionally large audiences. Strands and long-running series on the other hand, fostered a more abiding contact with audiences. Thus people over 60 found much to interest them in 'Years Ahead', which ran from 1982–8 (Willcocks, 1984), and was later followed for a further two years by 'Third Wave'. 'Same Difference', a current affairs programme for disabled people with signing and subtitles, ran from 1987–91. In her own history of education on Channel 4, Sargant exemplifies such diverse content areas as 'Programmes for people with more time than money', Science and Technology, Basic Education, Disability, Consumer Education, for older people, Social Studies, and Health. Her highlights include 'Plants for Free' (which proved that gardening programmes could be genuinely educational and get impressive ratings); 'The Heart of the Dragon', an authoritative documentary series about modern China; and 'Write On', programmes to encourage people to develop their literacy skills (Sargant, 1992).

Channel 4 developed what it called 'Life After Programmes' through an impressive list of publications, some free, some for sale, and through these generated new forms of face-to-face activity. The editor responsible for this off-air enterprise, Derek Jones, had pioneered new uses of television in the 1970s, as an instrument of social development (Griffiths and Collingwood, 1970; Jones, 1976).

In 1993, for example, Channel 4 invested £450,000 in programme support activities. These included two major projects, one 'a guide to many of the issues around homelessness' ('Gimme Shelter'), requested by 5,000 viewers, to reinforce the programme season, 'Raising the Roof'; the other, a booklet, written by leading academic experts and journalists, to accompany the season of programmes on 'Bloody Bosnia'. This booklet was bought by 6,000 viewers. The project included a charitable appeal, managed by Broadcasting Support Services and the Refugee Council, which raised £200,000 (Channel 4, 1994). The authors of the 1928 report, *New Ventures in Learning*, would no doubt approve the existence of the Talking Heads Club and Gardening Club, with branches all over the country (22 Talking Heads branches were listed by the autumn of 1995) for viewers sharing common interests and a desire to discuss them seriously (Broadcasting Support Services, 1995).

At the BBC, despite considerable turmoil within the Corporation, educational broadcasters continued to develop what they called 'needs-related not news-related programming', as exemplified by the Computer Literacy Project already mentioned. The 'needs' were often those widely stressed in political circles at the time, and most programmes and support materials reflected five main priority areas: training and business; basic education; social and community education; foreign languages; and science, technology and the environment. There was increased investment in self-standing and self-financing educational packages, similar to those developed for the OU's non-degree work. In July 1995, the Director of Education assured Voice of the Listener and Viewer, the broadcasting consumer body, that 'the BBC is committed to continuing to place factual and educational programmes in peaktime'. It would also develop a network

('The BBC Learning Link)' with Further Education colleges, community schools, libraries, workplace centres, and Open University regional centres, 'to ensure the maximum use of ... programmes in an educational context and to increase the amount of two-way communications with audiences'. 'We will build', Drabble wrote, 'on the success of initiatives such as ... *Read and Write Together*'. This week-long campaign to encourage parents and children to work together on their reading and writing, had provoked 314,000 telephone calls (Drabble, to Mrs Jocelyn Hay, Chair of Voice of the Listener and Viewer, 1995).

As history shades into current affairs, many of the old tensions are resurfacing, between educational and general departments within broadcasting; over scheduling and resources; between transmission over the air and off-air technologies; and, at a deeper level, with implications for a democratic culture based on mutual learning: between a politically inspired commercial philosophy of broadcasting, which sees public service as a quaint anachronism, and a public service philosophy to which education in all senses is integral. Professor Jay Blumler, contributing in 1994 to an international survey on 'Television and Social Responsibility' judged that in Britain 'Competitive populism is advancing everywhere but social responsibility is nowhere denied' (Bertelsmann Foundation and European Institute for the Media, eds, 1995). A commitment to education remains a strategic component, especially for the BBC and Channel 4, internationally recognised. Channel 4 won the 1994 Carl Bertelsmann-Prize for Social Responsibility (sponsored by the German Bertelsmann Foundation). The BBC had its Charter renewed for another five years (from 1995), its UK output still to be financed by licence revenue. But 'BBC' has also become a 'brand name' and as such must become a commercially successful, global 'player'. In September 1995, BBC Worldwide Television set up a commercial division, BBC Worldwide Learning, to sell educational programmes, CD-Roms and language course materials. The commitment continues; its motivation is inevitably more mixed; the outcomes are not yet clear. There may be opportunities as well as risks for the future of adult education in these transformations, but the historical record is impressive.

As Reith foresaw, public service broadcasting can provide access, free at the point of use, to some of the finest scholars of the age, to historical archive, to landscapes beyond reach, to experiments too dangerous or expensive to perform locally. It has attracted outstanding educators to work in it and make use of it. There are some matters that it deals with better than print – let two random examples serve: Peter Montagnon's series, 'The Long Search', concretely illuminated the place of religion in the culture of 13 different societies in ways not possible through the printed word; more famously, print could not match the ecological vision shared with audiences in many countries through the collected works of Sir David Attenborough. Broadcasting reaches everybody. Small audiences for educational programmes are enormous audiences by the standards of face-to-face adult education. Broadcasting has increasingly raised awareness of those more intimate, local forms of education, not merely through factual programmes, but also through the storylines of soap operas. It has introduced or promoted significant innovations to the adult curriculum (literacy, numeracy, computers, third age studies, even Yoga, and many others). It became more valuable as broadcast programmes were reinforced by print and other audio-visual resources. It became more useful in practice when video recording in the home and educational centres, combined with enlightened copyright arrangements, overcame problems of scheduling and timetabling. It is almost as standard a resource in colleges of further education as it is in the home (Capron, 1994). It is now part of the world of open learning, as well as the world of the international media. To an extent that Reith could not possibly have envisaged, broadcasting has been a major force, probably the major adult educational force in contemporary British society, both through much of the general output and through the range and quality of its specialised provision in radio and television.

*15*

# Women and Adult Education

## *Roseanne Benn*

This chapter concentrates on provision for women, and women as students. The story of women as tutors and organisers waits to be told elsewhere. The history is like a plait interwoven with the political and economic history of Britain in the nineteenth and twentieth centuries, the evolving position of women in society and the development of adult education provision for women. But the strands are class as well as gender constructs, consisting of middle class liberal provision of education for its own members especially women denied conventional openings, e.g. extension; middle class provision for the working class, e.g. the Mechanics' Institutes and compensatory Sunday schools for literacy; and working class for working class, e.g. the trade unions and the co-operative movements (Coats, 1994). It could alternatively be categorised as relativist, where women are only seen in relation to others particularly their husbands and children; compensatory, where women's disadvantage can be overcome by incorporating them into existing structures and norms; liberal, with its emphasis on individual development and limited social reform; or radical, where education is seen as a site for collective action and social change. The form and content of adult education provision for women has varied over time, place, class and in relation to women's position in society. What has not varied is women's hunger for learning which survived even when the ethos and structures were against them.

## *The First Half of the Nineteenth Century*

Most nineteenth century adult education was developed primarily for men but there were notable exceptions and increasingly women found ways of accessing it and adapting it to their needs. However, to do so they needed to overcome both structural and cultural barriers. They had to struggle for adult education. Patriarchy was predominant, with women allocated the private sphere of the home and men the public sphere of work. This domestic ideology dominated bourgeois society for the whole century and the working classes more as the century progressed. It resulted in formal and informal barriers to access to education, a curriculum linked to domestic and child rearing roles and basic literacy and hence a reinforcement of the restriction on women's life chances (Purvis, 1980). Early provision for women was for salvation and domestic vocation and was frequently a process of normalisation and socialisation to male norms. The higher illiteracy rate for women restricted access to much adult education until the advent of compulsory state schooling (see Chapter 6).

All adult education at this time was through voluntary rather than state provision and attendance was also voluntary. Religious salvation was often a triggering force. The very first Sunday School exclusively for adults was a school established for young working class women in the lace and hosiery factories in Nottingham in 1798 teaching bible reading, writing and arithmetic (see Chapter 2). The adult Sunday School movement, however, developed in 1812 out of Bristol with a curriculum mainly limited to reading. This movement developed from middle class initiatives with the involvement of Nonconformist religious groups, especially the Quakers. There was normally separate provision for men and women with equal access for both, and a narrow curriculum with emphasis on literacy and religious reading. The number of such schools expanded over the years with more women participating than men. By 1816, there were 31 schools for women and 24 for men with the numbers admitted since commencement being 1,887 women and 1,434 men. This was probably because of their openness to women, the higher illiteracy rate amongst women and the attraction that their children were also being taught to read. The Nonconformist churches were unusual in arguing for full educational opportunity for girls and women, deriving from their belief that the intellectual capacity of women was equal to that of males. However, with the development of other forms of adult education such as the Mechanics Institutes, the Sunday schools began to decline (see Chapter 2; Purvis, 1980; Watts, 1980).

The Mechanics' Institutes, which began in the 1820s and are regarded as the major adult education movement of the nineteenth century, were founded to provide useful knowledge for working class men. Women had to struggle to be admitted and were allowed in reluctantly. When enrolled, they did not enjoy equality of membership or equality of treatment, typically not being allowed to vote or hold office. The statistics do not always exist to give a comprehensive picture of women's involvement in the Mechanics Institutes but the proportion of women members varied considerably over time and by geographical region. In the 1840s, in the large northern Institutes, almost a fifth of membership was female. In the south, around that time proportions could be as high as half to two-thirds. It is likely that they attracted middle class rather than working class women. The curriculum for women, when offered, was located in a domestic ideology enabling women to become good wives and mothers and to run a household and ignored the fact that large numbers of working class women were also wage earners. The Lyceums attempted to offer a more popular and cheaper education for working class men and women than the Mechanics' Institutes but without great success. There was equal access for women but again differentiation in the curriculum and treatment (see Chapter 2; Purvis, 1980).

The literary, philosophical and scientific societies of the nineteenth century were reluctant to admit either women or the working class though the Cornwall Philosophical Institution did decide in 1839 to allow ladies to attend every other monthly meeting. The mutual improvement societies which existed throughout the nineteenth century but were especially popular in the 1840s and 1850s, admitted women as well as men but their main contribution was to literacy rather than broader philosophical or political issues (see Chapter 2).

Education for females was summed up at the time as 'a mere blank, or worse, a tissue of laboured frivolities under a solemn name; a patchwork begun without aim, fashioned without method, and flung aside, when half finished, as carelessly as it was begun' (Grey and Sherreff, 1856).

## The Later Nineteenth Century

During the first part of the century, pressure was building for a change in women's roles. Economic pressures were acting on women both pushing them into the labour market and depriving them of a satisfactory economic function in their own homes. The 1851 census showed that not only were there more women than men but that many men either did not marry or emigrated (Watts, 1980). So there was a need for women, even middle class women, to be able to earn a living since marriage was not a possibility for all of them in a society which proclaimed this as their only role. At the same time women shared the same ethos as men that happiness was to be found in work and that idleness was intolerable (Bryant, 1979). Add to this the romantic idealisation of womanhood and the Victorian conception of the family and home and it can be seen that many women experienced tensions and frustrations and looked partly to education for an acceptable way out. Educators such as Emily Davies (1866) and philosophers such as John Stuart Mill (1869) were arguing for women to be seen as human beings first and foremost. It is arguable that the women's movement of the nineteenth century neither attempted nor wished to alter the framework of society or its system of shared values but did want women to be educated and to participate in the advantages of better schooling and higher education. Women started to campaign for particular reforms, not because they saw themselves as 'feminist', but because of the circumstances and restrictions of their lives (Rowbotham, 1973). Even those who campaigned for more radical reform were caught in a dilemma of wishing for education on equal terms but not wishing to appear unfeminine (see Delamont, 1978 for an interesting discussion of this bind of 'double conformity'). By 1870 women were still not citizens with educational rights, voting rights, property rights or union rights.

In the 1850s and 1860s, a number of Working Men's Colleges were founded across the country to provide 'useful' studies (see Chapter 2). Women were either formally or, more usually, effectively excluded on the grounds that their presence would disrupt any feelings of fellowship or brotherhood. When they were admitted, as with the Mechanics Institutes, they did not enjoy an equal status and were often offered a limited curriculum of basic education and practical subjects but not the more conceptual and enlightening disciplines offered to men. The number of women was usually much smaller than the number of men. By 1860, classes for women had disappeared. Because of this, Elisabeth Malleson founded the London Working Women's College in Queen's Square, London in 1864 more for expediency than from a belief in separate women's education. Many of the women involved would have preferred mixed provision. By 1874, the

College began to admit men and changed its name to the College for Men and Women. A separate women-only college, The College for Working Women, was formed in 1874 in Fitzroy Street, London, by a group unhappy with the move to co-education led by Frances Martin, to cater for the improvement and culture of working women with a wider and partially academic curriculum. The foundation of the College expressed the dichotomy that women-only provision could be tailored to women's circumstances and needs, moving away from the 'deficit' model but could also lead to marginalisation. The double bind that women were invisible in the mainstream and underfunded in their own separate provision continues today (see Chapter 2; Purvis, 1980).

From the 1830s onwards, an increasing number of elementary day schools, mostly private, opened in the evenings for adult students. Whilst at first this provision was *ad hoc* and voluntary, it moved towards more organised government grant aided provision by the end of the century. Both men and women could study basic education but women were encouraged to do practical tasks such as sewing whilst men were more likely to learn shorthand and bookkeeping. Some classes were aimed specifically at working class women.

The co-operative societies had been set up in the 1830s and 1840s to implement Owenite ideals though the radical socialist dimension gradually disappeared. The founding of the Women's Co-operative Guild in 1883 was for married women whose 'homes were their workshops' (Davies, 1904: 148). Though at first much of the curriculum was located in domesticity and women were defined primarily as customers, nevertheless the Guild was organised by the women themselves. Gradually the Guild expanded its activities into campaigns for social reform against the desperate condition of life of many of its members. It was also instrumental in training women to fill leading roles in the Co-operative society and other social and political organisations (education for participation) through training in public speaking, committee work and publicity formation. This fulfilled the co-operative society's aim to allow men and women to 'take part in industrial and social reforms and municipal life generally'. (see Chapter 2; Purvis, 1980).

In the 1830s, the Unitarians foreshadowed the university extension classes by providing lectures (with essays set) for women on subjects such as mental and moral philosophy and logic. By the 1850s and 1860s, the universities of Oxford and Cambridge were looking for ways of meeting educational needs in the wider world but needed local organisational help. At the same time ladies' educational associations in the large provincial cities of the North were looking for lecturers. As a consequence, James Stuart, a fellow of Trinity College, Cambridge, instigated a programme of lectures. This led to the foundation of the North of England Council for Promoting the Higher Education of Women, which sought to organise lectures in literary, historical and scientific subjects and promote higher examinations for women. Their proposals then led in 1873 to the birth of university extension in Cambridge, London and Oxford. The aims of this movement, although directed primarily at the education of all who had not had access to university scholarship but especially working class men, included the provision of courses to satisfy the growing demand for better education for women. In practice, this provision in the late nineteenth century was particularly popular with middle class women. Probably two-thirds of the participants were then women and of these few were working class. This was not a result of any formal restriction but rather the curriculum offered, the level of literacy demanded, the middle class ethos, fear of the male middle class academics, domestic responsibilities and the cost of attendance. It is also probable that the patriarchal structure of working class society permitted attendance at adult schools and Mechanics' Institutes but drew the line at university education.

In parallel with the extension movement, the university settlement movement developed with similar aims but a stronger commitment to social reform. This movement, which contributed to the more radical egalitarian strand of adult education, often opened their provision to women and several settlements such as the Women's University Settlement established in Southwark in 1887 were organised by women. However, the attitude of higher education to women can be summed up in this quote from the July 1887 edition of the *Durham University Journal* during the debate in Durham about the education of the 'gentle sex'. 'The intellectual inferiority of women as a class to man seems clear. It is also probable that this inferiority is inherent, and cannot altogether be eliminated' (see Chapter 2; Purvis, 1980; Watts, 1980).

## 1900–19

By 1901, there were over a million more women than men in England and Wales. Opportunities for employment needed to grow for women but these were hindered by poor education. The educational process was still made difficult for women by their domestic circumstances, the lack of attention paid to their needs and current ideology. Motherhood was reconstructed at the turn of the century as a result of concern over the falling birthrate, a high infant mortality rate, the growth in importance of the Empire and a perceived lack of morality. 'Schools for Mothers' were established by middle class women to give advice and guidance on maternal and domestic skills to working class women. Adult education began to develop the 'women's interest' curriculum which was to encompass an aesthetic focus as well as practical skills, centring women's development in the cultural as well as manual skills of the home. The Women's Industrial Council ran citizenship classes for women from 1909 for some years (Coats, 1994; Davin, 1978; Westwood, 1988; Hughes, 1992).

In 1908, the Joint Committee of the University of Oxford and Working Class Representatives met to consider the relation of the university to the higher education of workpeople. None of the members of the 14 strong committee were women. Their report *Oxford and the Working Class* was concerned to make higher education more available to working class people and one outcome was the tutorial class provision. Pre-First World War, men outnumbered women in tutorial classes by four or five to one. The Note to the second edition (1909) affirmed that 'the Tutorial Classes are of course open to women on the same terms as to men' and that the scheme is to benefit the education of working women as much as the education of working men (p v). However references to women were almost totally absent from the Report and no note was taken of their specific requirements. The political, social and economic needs of women were ignored. A case study on a tutorial class in the Report illustrates this marginalisation. It notes that 'men and women alike, showed a keen and intelligent interest' but, when examining recruitment figures, comments 'how difficult it is to get the working *man* to attend classes of this kind'. When discussing student fees, 'workpeople' are identified as '*men* whose income frequently does not exceed thirty shilling per week' (p 106, author's emphasis). Working class women would have earned considerably less than these men.

This invisibility of women also occurred initially in the newly formed Workers Educational Association (WEA) (1903). Mansbridge's vision of education for the betterment of the working class did not exclude women but did not recognise women as workers in their own right. The overwhelming majority of participants in the early days were male but in 1909 the organisation decided to move into education for women by setting up a Women's Department whose role was to make 'a special effort' on behalf of women (WEA, 1995: 16). By 1916, this initiative for women-only classes had lapsed due to the non-replacement of the National Women's Officer and the collapse of the Women's Advisory Committee (Jones, 1985). Westwood (1988) suggests that women were integrated into the WEA not as equal workers with men, but as people whose lives were located in domestic circumstances and hence as a case of special need. Mrs Bridge Adams clashed with Mansbridge over this and the issue of working women and their role in relation to knowledge and power (Mansbridge, 1944; Stocks, 1953). She also tried unsuccessfully between 1909 and 1912 to establish a Women's Labour College. The Women's Labour League had been calling on women since 1906 to 'educate themselves on political and social questions, work in social work, promote full citizenship rights of men and women' (Rendell, 1977) but the Women's League of the Central Labour College, when founded, was seen as subordinate and ancillary. Only about five per cent of those who attended classes were women but women answered the call (as they always seem to do) to support the social and domestic side of the College (see Chapter 10; Westwood, 1988).

Other forms of adult education were gradually being introduced. In 1899, Ruskin Hall was established as the first long term residential College. Although its articles of Association stated that it was open to both men and women, no women were admitted until 1919. Fircroft College, founded by Quakers, was sensitive to the issue of women but at the time it was impossible to consider a mixed residential college. Six one week summer courses were run for women in 1911 and were heavily oversubscribed. By 1913, the year was divided between two term courses for men and a one term course for women. In 1920, the Trustees resolved the problem by founding Hillcroft College as a women-only college to give working class women who had done so much in the war an opportunity for full time study and a springboard for a new life. The courses were one year residential and the curriculum non-vocational. In 1920–11 women were enrolled (see Chapter 9).

New voluntary bodies for women called Women's Institutes were established in 1913 and their numbers grew rapidly to 1405 centres by 1919. Though the curriculum was heavily concentrated on domestic issues, as with the Women's Co-operative Guild, involvement in the organisation of the local and national group gave some women members a practical training in participation, democracy, committee work and public speaking (see Chapter 12).

In 1918, women over 30, married women and graduates were given the parliamentary vote. In 1919 the Sex Disqualification (Removal) Act admitted women to the legal profession, higher grades of the Civil Service and the magistrature and women were admitted to Oxford as full members in 1920. Women had been given full degrees at London University from 1878 and from the beginning in the new city redbricks. Women had to wait until 1948 to receive the same privilege at Cambridge.

In 1919, the Adult Education Committee of the Ministry of Reconstruction surveyed provision for women (Ministry of Reconstruction 1919). The Committee's Final Report (the '1919 Report') provided a vision for the role of adult education in British post-war reconstruction which included women. There were two women members of the committee of 19: Mrs Davies of the Women's Labour League and Dr Marion Phillips, Women's Officer of the Labour Party. They wrote a separate section on Women and Adult Education which found that 'a minute fraction' of all adult students were women but the proportion of women attending extension lectures was estimated to be between a half and three-quarters (p 256). It noted that these lectures have often been the only means of humane education open to women and occasionally classes had adapted to the special needs of women, perhaps by providing a nursery or by making women-only classes available as 'the men were so much more advanced' (p 256). Local Education Authority provision was open to men and women but the women's courses were located in 'the domestic arts' and the classes in cookery, dressmaking, needlework and home nursing were attended by a considerable number of girls and women (p 257). The Adult School movement had 721 schools for women and 67 mixed schools with a curriculum of basic skills and bible reading. By 1919, the WEA was attracting women as a high proportion of students, organisers and even teachers, having special women's classes, sections and committees. The Report identified the Women's Co-operative Guild with its emphasis on public questions, as being one of the most important movements for women's education of the day (p 258).

The Report clearly noted the needs of women for more knowledge in their new roles as citizens and condemned the constraints of poor housing which demanded all their time (p 255). It avoided the trap of assuming equality of availability meant equality of opportunity and noted that men formed the great majority of students in classes as 'women have far less opportunity than men for continuing their education, owing to an unceasing round of household duties and care of children' (p 255). It recognised that the increased involvement of women in public life as a result of the war and the extension of the franchise to women over 30 years of age meant 'a greater advance towards full citizenship and the need for increased educational facilities adapted to the peculiar difficulties and special circumstances of women' which would allow women 'to advance abreast with men along the educational highway'(p 255). To enable this, the report suggested childcare facilities would be necessary. As well as recognising the needs of women at home, the Committee also valued the educational needs of working women. They distinguished three types of women – one coming to education to satisfy their own immediate desire for self-development, another whose interest was aroused in education for the sake of her husband and children, and, very interestingly, a third type who desired knowledge because 'her concern for the solution of the social problems with which she is surrounded has been quickened by the work of some political or propagandist society to which she belongs'(p 261). This classification was perceptive and forward looking. Interestingly, the Report commented that, in their opinion, the interest in education where it existed amongst working women was frequently of the latter public kind. The Report thus fragmented the concept of 'woman' and validated an emancipatory form of adult education for women as well as the domesticatory version which was so frequently provided. Its call for classes to have a large measure of self-government and to be relevant to women's experiences foretold the developments in women's education later on in the century (p 261). The Report was liberal rather than radical and did not attempt to upset the *status quo* or separate women from their domestic sphere but it did recognise the hardships of women's lives and the need for adult education to see women's special circumstances and not subsume them in the category of men. Unfortunately these particular recommendations did not have a major impact on subsequent adult education provision in the inter-war years nor in the immediate post-Second World War period.

## *1920–39*

The end of the war, combined with the 1919 Report, had created a need for new approaches to adult education for demobilised ex-service men and women and women wartime workers displaced by men. Women's training was promoted for industrial and domestic work. This was organised from 1920 to 1939 by the Central Committee on Women's Training and Employment who had the limited vision of training women as homemakers or domestic servants and instructing women in 'the duties of a capable housewife or servant' (Chapter 13).

The Townswomen's Guild was established in 1928, the year that women were given the vote on the same terms as men. This Guild, which grew out of the suffrage movement, was centred in urban areas. It was led by well-to-do academic women who aimed to improve the status of women through education in handicraft, music, drama and social studies. The Guild continued to grow through the middle of the twentieth century campaigning for women's legal and economic rights. Meanwhile, the Women's Co-operative Guild membership peaked in 1939 and in response to changes in retail societies gradually became a less active force in women's adult education (see Chapter 12).

Hillcroft College's expansion to 34 students by 1939 was very slow due to financial restraints. In 1926, it moved to Surbiton, where it developed reading, writing, thinking and speaking skills and provided other courses for unemployed women or wives of unemployed men to stimulate and refresh. By the end of this period, it was facing recruitment problems as few women were able to take up residential places so, against its founding ethos, it became more vocational. This move towards preparing women for teaching, social work and management jobs, in practice reflected the exit routes of many of the earlier students (see Chapter 9).

By 1936–7, one-third of all LEA enrolments were in women's subjects and recreational activities and 56 per cent of students were women (NIAE, 1951: 7, 9).

## 1940–54

The rhetoric of the 1944 Act was that of equality of access. However, this concentration on access rather than equality of outcome allowed women's secondary status and subordination to still remain invisible and women were silenced by the ideology of equal opportunities (Wilson, 1980). Certainly the concept of education for domesticity continued to be hugely influential. The Norwood Report in 1943 stressed the importance of relating boy's education to the labour market, but emphasised that girls' schooling must relate to their eventual place in the family. In the pamphlet 'Further Education: The Scope and Content of its Opportunities under the Education Act 1944', referred to as the post-war 'bible' in Chapter 4, LEAs were exhorted to encourage 'women's specialised interests', i.e. 'those which centre around the home' so that 'young women contemplating marriage, as well as those already married, can increase their skills in housecraft'. The pamphlet took its tone from current social policy which continued to emphasise the importance of motherhood and the family. Women were to be educated for the well-being of their family through a wider curriculum, still based on domestic skills but to be made more attractive by, for example, the inclusion in cookery classes of discussion on 'the planning of a balanced diet' and classes in housecraft and home management to include 'repair and decoration to fabric and furniture, planning good colour schemes, the best organisation of domestic equipment'. Women should be educated about broader interests such as education, housing, town planning, etc. through short courses entitled 'The Child under Five' or 'Housing for the Aged'. The section in the pamphlet on vocational activities tellingly talks of the student as 'he' but that on leisure and learning as 'men and women' (Ministry of Education, 1947).

At this time, more married women were entering the world of work but in low paid unskilled jobs. However, by the 1950s, upskilling meant that more jobs required educational qualifications and technical skills. This, together with better contraception and the need for a larger labour force, meant that improved education was needed for the middle class girls to cope with their dual role. However, working class girls were still educated for domesticity (Deem, 1981).

In 1951, the NIAE statistical survey showed that enrolments of women in evening classes in evening institutes and major establishments between 1930 to 1950 had risen to 60 per cent of all students.

The Ashby Report (1954), set up to review the organisation and finance of adult education, has been judged kindly as enabling the view of the 1919 Report to continue almost unchanged for a further quarter of a century (Stephens, nd: 11). A more critical reaction would be that the recommendations of the 1919 Report had not been carried out and throughout, the Ashby Report saw the student body as a homogeneous group and was totally insensitive to the particular needs of women. There were no women on the Committee.

## 1955–late 60s

In the 1950s and early 1960s, an increasing number of women entered the labour market encouraged by the economic growth, an increase in educational opportunities for girls and women, contraception and the consequent reduction in family size, and the growth of the welfare state which released women from some of their obligations (Deem, 1981). Nevertheless, the notion that women's place was in the home was still strong. The emphasis in educational change and development of this period, from primary to adult, concentrated on class rather than gender but there were improved educational opportunities for women in the establishment of the Open University (see Chapter 11) and the provision of special training or refresher courses for married women taking up or returning to teaching. Work place training was developing during this period but Chapter 13 shows that women were receiving considerably less training opportunities than men.

The proportion of women in the student body continued to grow. The expansion of LEA adult education in the 1960s meant that by 1968–9 there were 1,701,070 students of whom 69 per cent were women (Chapter 4). The background of students was changing as well. For example, by the 1950s, WEA students included less manual workers and more technical and supervisory workers as well as more housewives. Many of the WEA's married women students were from higher social categories (Chapter 7).

As recently as the Plowden Report of 1967, official ideology for girls education assumed a homogeneity of female interests, notably with regard to domestic interests. Women were ignored in the political arithmetic. However, during the 1960s, the tensions between women's position in the home and the demands of the labour market surfaced in the second wave of women's liberation. Demands began to be made over such issues as the sexual division of labour, the unequal power balance between the sexes, the construction of knowledge and women-centred learning. So women's educational studies evolved, focusing initially on making women's education visible and hunting out obstacles to the development of their full potential. These challenges to women's role in the family and the labour market were linked to other social liberation movements, the literacy and community education developments as well as to the passage of the Equal Pay Act in 1970 (Arnot, 1995).

## The 1970s

The 1944 Education Act and the expansion of the universities in the 1960s led to a growing discontent amongst women about their lack of career opportunities, their exclusion from institutions and skills at all levels and the nature of knowledge. The Women's Liberation Movement grew through consciousness-raising groups, a very powerful example of informal adult education, where women-only groups shared their experiences and began to understand that 'the personal is political'. The Women's Liberation Movement was a real focus of adult learning in the 1970s but its supporters, being suspicious of experts, generated their own counter knowledge and spread this mainly through non-formal self-directed learning, campaigning groups and the agency of adult education. The WEA and university extramural/continuing education departments responded and led the way, followed by the Inner London Education Authority (Thompson, 1983; Taking Liberties Collective, 1989; Hughes and Kennedy, 1985). The Sex Discrimination Act was passed in 1975 but without resources and real political commitment, its impact was questionable.

In 1973, the Russell Report *Adult Education: A plan for development* located its response in a class rather than a gender framework with its emphasis on provision for the working class, the socially and culturally deprived, and on trade union and political education (DES, 1973). There were very few references to women and none to the emerging women's movement. When women were mentioned, it was in their roles of wives, mothers and working mothers. It is a curiously worded document which appeared to self-consciously avoid discussion of women or women's issues, using expressions such as 'those who seek adult education related to the home and family' (p 9). Changing patterns of work and leisure and other changes in society were mentioned but with no acknowledgement of the very differing positions and hence requirements of the two sexes (p 12). The Report noted the significant number of women in adult education but neither sought to explain this phenomenon nor to actively improve provision for this majority of the client group. Its discussion on unmet needs focused on class rather than gender (p 8). Compensatory education opportunity for adults such as the Fresh Horizons course at City Lit in London (started in 1966) had already shown a demand for second chance provision especially from women, and the Universities' Council for Adult Education, in its statement to the Russell Committee, called for an appreciation of the change in careers and marriage patterns and for fresh start provision for middle aged women particularly through part-time study (UCAE, 1970). The Committee devoted a long section to Second Chance provision but never acknowledged the particular need by women for this type of provision (pp 96–99). The Report was influential in subsequent adult education policy initiatives, and did strongly assert the need for lifelong learning and adult education for personal development. However, its individualistic philosophy was the very antithesis to the ideas of collective endeavour developing in the women's movement and in the community education ethos of the time. There were fourteen Committee members, only two of whom were women.

The Alexander Report (1975) noted that adult education in Scotland attracted 'the older, the better-educated and the more affluent' and that more than two-thirds were women (Scottish Education Department, 1975: 15). Apart from this the Report was gender blind. There were two women on the committee of 21.

Similarly, the ACACE Discussion Paper (1979) on continuing education and the social context in which it must develop and to which it should contribute, was fundamentally unaware of gender issues, failed to examine the structural causes of social and economic disadvantage and located blame for educational shortcomings on the individual rather than society.

In this same decade, Hillcroft College was becoming increasingly a preparatory college for higher education and offering qualifications that would ensure entry. Northern College, founded in 1978, aimed to provide education for men and women taking into account their separate experiences and ideologies. The college actively wished to attract women into the male-dominated world of residential colleges (only one quarter of long-term students in all colleges were women in 1969–70). Northern exercised positive discrimination in selection, provided creches and were flexible about residential requirements but still found it only possible to fill one third of the places with women (see Chapter 9).

In trade union education, women played a marginal role until the 1970s when courses began to appear on equal pay, health and safety, and sex discrimination to reflect the new legislation. Increased participation of women and courses for women specifically developed later (see Chapter 10).

## 1980–95

The ACACE Discussion Paper (1980) on current trends in adult education and the issues to be met, described the world as though women did not exist or associated women simply with domesticity and child care. This slowly began to be rectified by the setting up of a Women's Education Policy Committee as well as an Ethnic Minorities Policy Group in the mid 1980s.

However, a reaction was building up against the continued emphasis on education for women consisting of parenting and domestic skills. 1981 saw the opening of the first feminist-influenced Women's Education Centre in Southampton with funding and provision shared by the University, the LEA, the WEA and the Equal Opportunities Commission. This was part of a growing movement in the 1970s and 1980s for a widening of the curriculum as well as the development of women-only provision influenced by feminism and economic changes. Coats (1994: 17) identified five major strands in this provision. Firstly, there were the re-orientation courses for women returning to study or work after a period of domestic responsibility to compensate for initial underachievement or to allow for a change in direction, updating and preparation. These were centred round a curriculum of confidence building, counselling, self-defence, study skills and academic content. An early example was the New Opportunities for Women Course at Hatfield Polytechnic in 1971. The Manpower Services Commission and LEAs offered Wider Opportunities for Women courses from 1978. Secondly, there were courses, usually taught by women, in areas where women were traditionally under-represented such as manual trades, electronics, computing etc. An example of this was the Women's Technology Scheme in

Liverpool which was set up in 1983 to offer vocational and educational training for women in areas such as micro-electronics. Thirdly there were the positive action courses such Women into Management. Fourthly, courses such as Professional Updating for Women provided updating courses for professional or qualified women for return to their career. Lastly, there were the feminist Women's Studies courses with their radical questioning of what is 'really useful knowledge' for women.

This provision of women-only courses in adult education has been challenged on the grounds that if institutions were constantly reminded that women were different from ordinary students, then they might reasonably assume that ordinary students were not women. It was also open to the accusation of marginalising women's issues with the consequent lack of impact on mainstream provision (Malcolm, 1992). However, the history of women's education shows continuous marginalisation, lack of resources and little policy support. Within this context, women-only provision represented a real advance.

The influence of feminism and Women's Studies from the mid-1970s helped to broaden out women's education and the curriculum because of the inter-disciplinary approach, the concern to change the way knowledge is constructed and the emphasis on student-centred, participatory learning.

One of the major initiatives of this period was the provision of Access to Higher Education courses. In 1978, the Department of Education and Science invited seven LEAs to participate in pilot preparatory courses leading to higher education and in particular teaching and social work. From the start, these courses attracted mainly women and approximately two-thirds of the 30,000 students on over 1,000 courses in 1995 were women (Benn and Burton, 1995). These courses were often timetabled in school hours and school terms with creche facilities and sometimes supported by discretionary grants in order to attract women who had missed out on higher education the first time around.

The TUC developed women-only bridging courses whilst attempting to both involve more women in mainstream courses and ensure that these courses dealt with the role of women and the role of sexism in the unions. The first TUC women's summer school was in 1988. Progress was real but limited (see Chapter 10).

The Women's Institute's residential college, Denman founded in 1948, continued to attract large number of participants and by 1995 over 215,000 members had attended its courses. Meanwhile, alternative national women's bodies emerged in the 1970s and 80s. One of the most significant bodies in self-education and personal fulfilment was the National Housewives Register, later changed to the National Women's Register (see Chapter 12).

In the 1990s, worrying indications occurred in adult education's provision for women. The Government continually emphasised the importance of the family and that a woman's place was in the home. Social policy supported these sentiments and welfare support was gradually eroded. The period of rapid growth of interest in education for women coincided with severe funding cuts and many women's courses were developed with short term funding which remained marginal to institutional provision and were the first to disappear in the various round of cuts of the late 1980s and 1990s (Malcolm, 1992). This was reflected by developments in the WEA. In the later 1980s, the WEA had employed a full-time woman National Officer to develop women's education and published an excellent range of materials to support women's education. However, when in 1993, the Women's Education Committee analysed the state of women's education in the WEA it revealed that the early 1990s saw a significant decline in provision for women and such provision that there was focused on individual development (Women Returner courses) rather than collective issues (Women's Studies provision). The Committee developed a strategic plan to mainstream women's education in WEA provision to counteract these tendencies (WEA, 1995).

This trend was also illustrated in the educational and career guidance services. Women had predominantly used these services for adults established in the mid-seventies. A review of this service in 1993 showed that since the late 1980s, women were encouraged into vocational training to meet the needs of industry rather than education to meet their own needs and that the recession led to a greater concentration on men (Rivis and Haughton, 1993). This changing balance of participation also occurred in LEA provision. Participation of men increased more than for women between 1982 and 1990 particularly in accredited courses although the proportion of women was still much higher in non-accredited adult education (Sargant, 1991). This is worrying in the light of the trend towards accredited adult education instigated both by funding bodies such as the Higher Education and the Further Education Funding Councils and by practitioner bodies such as the Open College Networks. In addition, it appeared that 'the structure of the adult education movement still remains firmly in the control of men ... men tend to be the fund raisers and power brokers of the movement' (International Council for Adult Education, 1990).

Even in 1995, women experienced constraints in adult education, whether these were from earlier experiences in school and work, lack of confidence, inappropriate provision or were cultural in origin. Much provision tailored to women's needs was threatened by student and institutional funding problems, inadequate child care facilities and a lack of political support for women's education and training (McGivney, 1994). Most of the advances achieved by women have occurred in periods of full employment and in the context of social democratic policies and ideologies (Deem, 1981). Women's education can be seen as cyclic. Periods of raised awareness, action and some gains are followed by periods of reaction, backlash and lost ground (WEA, 1995). The early 1990s saw a backlash against equal opportunities and were dominated by an ideology premised on individualism, the free market and the sanctity of the family. The Thatcher years permeated this period with an anti-feminist return to Victorian family ideology, yet at the same time the functionalist approach of the Conservatives acknowledged the need for a well educated workforce. This formed a complex framework within which education for women operated. The reduction in the Welfare State reimposed domestic burdens on women. The employment situation with the massive increase in part-time women's work increased the need for education and training for women whilst lack of financial subsidies put it out of the reach of more and more

(Coats, 1993). The increased emphasis on continuing education and training may have excluded from social participation as many women as it included.

This brief overview has shown that women were present in adult education in the nineteenth and early twentieth centuries but not treated equally, with a curriculum restricted to the division of labour in the home and the demands for a cheap workforce. Independence, where it existed, was located in the separatist bodies such as the Women's Co-operative Guild and the Suffrage Movement. In the middle and late twentieth century, women were in the majority in much adult education, and gradually at least some provision was developed to meet their particular requirements. By the mid-1990s, the situation appeared to be reverting. The story of adult education for women is rather like that of an arduous journey with one step back for every two steps forward.

## 16

# British Adult Education: Past, Present and Future

*Roger Fieldhouse*

We laid out in the Preface the three underlying aims of this book: to set the historical development of British adult education in its wider policy and ideological context; to examine its various forms and formulations; and to identify what purpose or purposes (if any) it has served. The attempts to answer these questions have been interwoven into all the chapters: it is not the intention to address them again in detail in this final chapter but rather to draw out some of the major developments of the last 200 hundred years of British adult education, and relate these to likely future trends.

The first three chapters provided an overview of the nineteenth and twentieth centuries during which time Britain evolved from an industrialising into an industrialised and then into a post-industrial or post-modernist society; and from an early nineteenth century *laissez-faire* state into a mixed-economy welfare state. More recently, attempts have been made by ideologically 'New Right' governments to roll back the interventionist structures of the welfare state in order to create an enterprise culture and replace dependency by self-help. Adult education has been caught up in these ideological shifts because at different times it has been expected both to contribute to the support structures of a welfare state and to equip people to survive in a self-help culture. It has been regarded as a means of enhancing both collectivism and individualism. This has frequently led to a confusion of roles and purpose.

Much of nineteenth century British adult education was aimed at the working classes, for a variety of reasons: to incorporate them into bourgeois society, to produce a more efficient work force, to alleviate the alienating effects of industrialisation, or to assist them in their struggles for social justice. But it very often ended up being colonised by the middle class, either because it reflected bourgeois culture rather than working class interests and needs, or because the educated middle class was better equipped to take advantage of further educational opportunities. Despite this, it developed a strong tradition of social purpose and a belief that adult education could and should contribute to social and political action. It also demonstrated a strongly liberal, non-vocational bias and male ethos, reflecting the culture of the nineteenth century educated class; and was predominantly voluntaryist, although the limitations of depending solely on voluntaryism became more apparent as the century progressed, and state support increasingly was sought and provided to rescue adult education from permanent impermanence.

The twentieth century has seen the publication of a series of influential reports and papers (in 1908, 1919, 1943, 1954, 1973, 1975 and 1991); the passing of important educational legislation (1902, 1944, 1988 and 1992); and the rise and fall of a plethora of independent bodies and government agencies or, more recently, semi-government quangos, concerned with adult education. All in their different ways have attempted to plan, promote, develop, direct, re-direct, or co-ordinate adult education. One of the consequences of all this activity has been to secure adult education as a permanent phenomenon, but it has also led to much closer incorporation within the state and to much more state intervention. More recently it has resulted in the gradual conversion of the adult education *movement* with a distinctive social purpose into a *service* (although whether this is a service to the participants or to the state is unresolved). This state involvement has been both a cause and a consequence of increased state funding of adult education, which became a very important means of support and influential factor during the twentieth century. We shall first review those sectors of the totality of British adult education which became significantly dependent on public funding.

The contribution of the local education authorities (LEAs) to British adult education since their formation has been mixed. Initially they inherited the responsibility for technical education from the technical education committees. This set them on a semi-vocational path, supplemented later by expanding recreational provision. The more prestigious non-vocational adult education was left, for much of the century, to the 'responsible bodies' (RBs). This division of labour fostered a notion of partnership between the LEAs and RBs which was sometimes fruitful but at other times more honoured in the breach. More seriously it contributed to the continuing separation of vocational from non-vocational provision, and for a long time condemned the LEAs to a perceived lower status in the field of adult education. The expansion of LEA adult education during the three decades after the Second World War was real if sporadic and uneven: by the time of the Russell and Alexander Reports the LEAs were undoubtedly the major players in the partnership with the RBs.

From the mid-1970s, many LEAs did respond to the Russell and Alexander recommendations to give greater emphasis on provision for disadvantaged groups, but their increasing financial difficulties forced them either to cut back on much innovative work, paradoxically making adult education less accessible to the 'disadvantaged'; or to introduce a two-tier service with provision for the well-off who could afford to pay the steeply rising fees, and for the 'conspicuously deprived' who were targeted by a compensation service. There was a widening gap between these two extremes, and an increasing number of people were unable to benefit from the restricted provision. The abolition of ILEA in 1988 was a totally negative message for all LEAs attempting innovative work for disadvantaged groups. The financial pressures also put a growing strain on the partnership with the RBs, as the LEAs were less and less able to offer either financial support or shared facilities.

The 1988 Education Reform Act reduced the powers of the LEAs, contributing to the growing fragmentation and destruction of a comprehensive adult education service. The 1992 Further and Higher Education Act further reduced the significance of the LEAs, leaving them with no more than residual adult education responsibilities unprotected by earmarked funding. The result was a declining resource base, cuts in professional staffing, higher fees, reduced programmes and a loss of much of the flexibility and variety which many LEAs had fostered in the previous half century. Some local authorities abandoned direct provision almost entirely: in other areas the better-off were still catered for but there was a decline in participation by the poor and elderly.

Conversely, after 1992, the further education sector was able to expand its provision of Schedule 2 work. There was a greater emphasis on vocational and utilitarian values at the expense of the broader liberal approach which had encompassed recreational and leisure courses, personal development and, in some local authority areas, a social and political aspect of adult education. After 1992 the changes in the balance of provision and funding mechanisms actually increased the opportunities for some categories of learners while excluding others (particularly older learners and many women) who did not want basic education or utilitarian further education or certification and progression. The long-term future role of the LEAs in this new world is far from clear.

Community education as a concept (going back to Henry Morris and the 1920s) obviously covered a wider field than the LEAs, but a number of LEAs adopted community education as a model after the Second World War and in the later 1970s and 1980s many attempted to implement the Russell and Alexander recommendations by adopting notions of 'community', defined in terms of locality, shared interests and social purpose. This community education attempted to develop a locally delivered public service in contrast to the increasingly competitive and market-orientated adult and continuing education of the 1980s, and to engage policy development with the local context in a systematic way. These efforts were greatly undermined by the 1988 and 1992 legislation which centralised power and emasculated the LEAs. However, the fragmenting tendency of post-modernism possibly offers new opportunities for community adult education to work with progressive social movements in order to develop a new radical agenda, forge more genuinely popular and democratic forms of education, and give a voice to groups which had become marginalised, or even silenced, by previous forms of adult education. (This theme is further examined later in the chapter.)

The adult literacy campaign which sprang up in the 1970s had its origins in earlier schemes, but was also part of the Russell and Alexander inspired 'new-direction' adult education. It enjoyed initial success in changing the agenda and approach of adult basic education (ABE), distancing it, at least to some extent, from earlier schools-based remedial models. However it failed to destroy altogether the 'deficit model' carried over to ABE from remedial or special needs education and from the selective educational tradition which equated educational 'failure' almost exclusively with individual deficiency. In practice, ABE was squeezed between two versions of social control: the discourse of disadvantage and compensatory education and the discourse of economic efficiency. The latter became more powerful in the

later 1980s, culminating in ABE's official recognition as part of Schedule 2 of
the 1992 Education Act. One of the new further education sector's objectives
became the reduction of adult illiteracy in order to improve the
employability of the adult population. Thus ABE became incorporated into
the mainstream which is arguably a better situation than the alternative
'ghettoisation' within the low-status non-vocational adult education sector.
However, it means that ABE is less well positioned to fulfil its potential as an
innovator of lifelong learning and even less likely than in the past to adopt
the alternative notion of an independent, emancipatory ABE serving a
collective movement for social and political change. This counter-discourse
was never strong, but it did flourish for a time in the voluntary sector and
the metropolitan LEAs. It does not appear to have any future in the further
education sector: its only hope is probably within the informal, voluntary
sector.

The WEA has undergone a considerable metamorphosis during the
course of the twentieth century. Starting out as an organising body to
promote university extension lectures for working class people, it soon
became that strangely British phenomenon, a publicly-funded voluntary
body. It increasingly provided adult education in its own right as well as
organising university courses. Gradually its own provision became more
important, its recruitment of working class people (however defined)
declined, and its voluntary basis was undermined by public funding and
growing professionalisation.    Whilst still enjoying a powerful, even
privileged, position within the world of British adult education, the WEA's
early aims – to promote university education for working people through a
voluntary organisation – became somewhat fudged if not altogether
invisible.

After 1992, the location of the WEA within the further education sector
gave the Association a new lease of life.  At least for some areas of work
funding actually improved, enabling the WEA to undertake some of the
work with the 'disadvantaged' that it had been rather unsuccessfully
struggling to do for many years. This was optimistically viewed in some
quarters as providing new opportunities for the Association. The WEA
General Secretary claimed that it had considered the FEFC criteria very
carefully and concluded that they would allow the WEA to pursue its aims
and objectives. 'We are at present in the situation where we have gone
through the necessary structural changes although there is still much to be
done in order to meet the new goals' he declared in 1995 (Lochrie, R.,
address to the Eric Bellchamber memorial meeting, Rochester, 8 July 1995).
But an alternative assessment would be that the WEA has become wedded to
an alien ethos which may coincide with the Association's aims for now, but
which might prove more uncomfortable in the future; and that there is a fatal
mismatch between the growing centralisation of the WEA and its
subservience to the FEFCs on the one hand, and voluntary member
autonomy on the other.

The WEA's future still depends, as it has done ever since its foundation
in 1903, upon its maintaining a unique and radical role for itself, based on
voluntaryism. It does not have to be the same role as in 1903 because the
world has changed out of all recognition since then. But 'what it must do is

abandon its neutrality in favour of a partnership which will see it actively assisting under-privileged groups in their struggle for social justice' and provide 'practical help to achieve responsible social action' (Gott, 1990: 72–3). Whether this will be possible within the further education sector in the future remains an open question.

The universities' partnership with the WEA at the beginning of the twentieth century accelerated the decline of the university extension movement inherited from the previous century. It was displaced by the very successful tutorial class movement initially organised by the WEA. But with the WEA's increasing concentration on promoting its own provision, coupled with the establishment of university extramural departments and growing professionalisation between the wars, the universities gradually established themselves as independent adult education bodies. After the Second World War they used their joint funding (from the UGC and the Ministry of Education) to consolidate their position and to some extent cut the ties with the WEA. University extension re-emerged as an alternative to the joint tutorial classes. This represented a move away from the historic values of the tutorial class movement, particularly its targeting of the working class and also its commitment to 'social purpose' adult education. This was seen by many as the demise of a 'great tradition' but by others as a necessary adaption to the needs of a different age. Whichever was true, it did result in a period of rather unfocused, *ad hoc* expansion during the 1950s and 60s. Part of this change of direction was a growing predominance of more vocationally orientated continuing education – a trend which was accelerated with government approval and funding incentives during the 1980s. This was followed by the abolition of the universities' RB status and termination of direct funding by the DES when responsibility for funding university adult education was transferred to the Universities Funding Council (UFC), and later the Higher Education Funding Councils (HEFCs). Whilst this brought academic respectability for university adult education by finally bringing it into line with other forms of higher education, it probably marked its end as a member of a separate and distinctive social movement. It had become just part of the mainstream of higher education.

This process was cemented in the early 1990s when the HEFCs for England, Wales and Scotland, following government directions, announced that in future there would be very little funding for university liberal adult education unless it was accredited and leading to recognised university awards. In practice this meant that there was no longer any distinction between university adult education students and other part-time higher education students studying for university awards. University adult education had become in effect a modular, part-time mode of lifelong learning within higher education. Whereas this could be considered a crowning victory for mature students, it is less obviously beneficial to the many adult students who want serious, university-level courses but are not interested in accreditation or progression. Nor is it clear what future there is within 'the mainstream' for specialist university departments of adult continuing education (some of which have already begun to disappear or be dispersed into the mainstream); or whether the very concept of 'university continuing adult education' will have any meaning in the future.

The appearance of the polytechnics and the Open University (OU) on the scene in the late 1960s and early 70s presaged significant changes in the world of adult education. The new polytechnics created increased opportunities for mature students to enter higher education on a part-time basis, although arguably this development (and the establishment of the OU in 1971) enabled the existing universities to ignore this sector for another 20 years. The OU not only opened up significant new higher education opportunities for adult students but also had a major effect on the introduction of a more flexible credit system throughout higher education, to the benefit of adult students. But it crucially diverted funding away from other fields of adult education in the 1970s and 80s, to their detriment. And despite its openness to students without qualifications, it has not yet resolved the problem of a significantly higher drop out rate amongst its less well qualified entrants. Moreover, its more recent determination to keep in the forefront of technological developments in distance learning threatens to reduce its accessibility to those poorer potential recruits who cannot afford the necessary hardware. There is a danger that it will reinforce rather than reduce the divisions between the educationally 'haves' and 'have-nots'.

The long-term residential colleges shared many of the same early twentieth century aims and values as university adult education and the WEA, with the obvious addition of the residential experience. More recently they have concentrated on an increasingly utilitarian preparation for work or for higher education, although the latter has been to some extent undermined by the very successful Access movement in further education and the Open Colleges. The long-term residential colleges have been more successful than many forms of adult education in the twentieth century in attracting working class or underprivileged students, but they remain an expensive mode of adult education with an uncertain future.

The short-term residential colleges, which very largely grew up after the Second World War, also face an uncertain future (those that have not already closed). They always existed on a financial knife edge, but their position has been rendered more precarious with the emasculation of the LEAs, many of which are no longer in a position to continue their support. This also applies to the non-residential centres. They have been very largely cast adrift to fend for themselves in the uncertain world of full-cost fees and commercial ventures. If they do survive they are likely to be serving a rather different clientele than in the past, when partnerships with the LEAs, the RBs and numerous voluntary groups sustained a rich variety of adult education in both the short-term residential colleges and the non-residential centres.

Still within the publicly-funded arena, it is arguable that broadcasting has been the major adult education agency of the twentieth century. Seventy years of educational broadcasting have very largely reflected Reith's early vision: a mixture of general talks, schools broadcasting and specially targeted programmes for adult learners. Obviously it took new forms and embraced new dimensions over time. These included the use of other media, particularly printed materials, in support of broadcasting; the advent of television; the abolition of the BBC's monopoly; and, in the early 1970s, the establishment of the OU and the adult literacy campaign. But in 1982 the

ACACE Report, *Continuing Education: From policies to practice* still reflected a recognisable version of Reith's 1924 plan.

Between the 1920s and 1990s broadcasting became increasingly dominant as 'the cockpit of culture' – a culturally unifying force representing middle brow, middle England. It fluctuated between its three roles as stimulant of adult learning; reinforcement of the work of the adult education bodies; and a self-contained adult education provider. But more recently greater emphasis has been put on the general educative role, extensively reinforced by support materials, rather than educational programmes *per se*. However in 1995 the BBC launched an ambitious new scheme which attempted to combine all three roles by broadcasting programmes on BBC2 throughout the night so that 'you can record while you sleep and learn at your leisure'. The broadcasts included extracts from frequently requested BBC series combined with on-screen learning and exercises; professional up-dating for people at work; a further and adult education strand (FETV) with two weekly slots; and special seasons on subject themes (*Adults Learning*, 1995, 7, 2: 30).

Despite such developments, the notion of public service broadcasting has been increasingly questioned, and with it the broadcasters' obligation to educate. The 1990 Broadcasting Act removed this obligation from ITV. Commercialism has become more dominant and there is ever increasing pressure on resources and scheduling for educational purposes. Educational broadcasting (like the OU) has also become partially subsumed into the burgeoning 'industry' of educational technology and multi-medium systems and into the more comprehensive concepts of open and distance learning.

Independent working class education (IWCE) was an attempt to escape from the controls associated with state funding. The Plebs League, the Labour Colleges, and their later subsumption in the National Council of Labour Colleges (NCLC), aimed to provide adult education for the working class which did not have to pull its punches or confine itself to the ideological middle ground. In its early days IWCE taught mainly politically 'relevant' subjects intended to equip the leaders of the working class movements to challenge the capitalist State. It was emancipatory, revolutionary education. But its chronic lack of funding had two fatal consequences. Firstly, enforced dependence on unpaid voluntary tutors resulted in some excellent teaching, but also in a lack of professional expertise. In time this undermined the pedagogical standard of much IWCE. And secondly, financial difficulties eventually forced IWCE into dependence on the trade union movement, and this proved just as illiberal and restrictive as dependence on the State. The trade unions and TUC became more and more prescriptive with the result that after the Second World War IWCE had no real purpose and fell into terminal decline.

For all their limitations, the trade unions were the major social movement to become involved in adult education in Britain. Initially this was largely in collaboration with IWCE and the WEA, and later in partnership with the universities. But gradually the trade unions embarked on organising their own adult education and with the election of 'their' Government in 1945, they and the TUC began to take very seriously the task of educating their membership to fulfil its responsibilities in the new, supposedly egalitarian, welfare society. Reflecting the view that their time had come, and that they now constituted a major part of the Establishment, the trade unions increasingly favoured essentially practical instruction which concentrated on skills acquisition and how to participate at various levels of society rather than the development of critical consciousness of economic and political forces which might lead to awkward questions about the nature of the new society. In this incorporated rather than oppositional role, the trade unions attracted state funding for their educational activities during the 1960s and 70s. But with the advent of Thatcherism in 1979 this state funding began to be used for a different purpose: to exercise control over the form and content of trade union education courses and even to manipulate the trade unions into a subservient role. With the more recent reduction and eventual termination of this state funding, the trade unions are faced with the challenging but potentially more rewarding task of promoting adult education as a function of a voluntary social movement rather than as an agency of the State.

There are, as indicated in Chapter 12, many voluntary organisations which provide opportunities for adult learning outside the formal, state-aided system. Indeed, as suggested in the Preface, and in a recent review of self directed learning among adults, participation in formal classes, courses and programmes may not be as popular or as significant a mode of adult learning as more informal approaches. (Percy, Burton and Withnall, 1994.) These may involve the concept of 'learning projects' identified by Allen Tough (1983), or less rationalistic and planned modes of learning activity, some of which are difficult to label as educational at all, but many taking place formally or informally in voluntary organisations (Percy, Burton and Withnall, 1994: 37). Their great strength is that they reflect where the students really are rather than where professionals think they are or ought to be. Consequently these forms of learning are popular and the learners are highly motivated. Their weakness is that they can be patchy in quality, lacking coherence, unchallenging or, at best, as 'good' as the organisation's membership happens to be. Although very little is known about the real quality of this informal learning 'there are hints in the North American research literature of frustration among learners, resources not available, intellectual wild-goose chases, misunderstandings and misconceptions' (ibid.: 38.)

Vocational education and training has also fallen mainly within the non-funded category of adult education: most training for adults has been promoted by employers rather than the State, albeit on a somewhat random basis. However, 'voluntary' may be an inappropriate term for much of this training especially as, more recently, it has attracted some state funding and direction. Particularly since the 1960s, both Labour and Conservative Governments have sought to stimulate and reform adult training as part of a wider strategy of restructuring the economy and improving Britain's world competitiveness although the training solutions implemented have fallen well short of these ambitious objectives. Much effort was also put into training schemes intended primarily to reduce unemployment in the 1930s and again following the economic crises of the 1970s onwards. These schemes were often semi-punitive in nature and mostly aimed at younger adults.

In the later 1970s, as it became clear that unemployment was affecting adults as well as young people, and that deindustrialisation was causing major employment problems for all ages, there was a shift away from the concentration on youth training. By the 1990s there was a widespread consensus that continuous lifelong education and training was the single most important means of remaining competitive in a global economy. This greatly influenced training policies despite the lack of hard evidence to support this notion, and the real risk of a deterioration in social cohesion caused by the exclusion from this training of those who did not belong to well organised internal labour markets and lacked substantial initial educational achievements.

The artificial division between vocational and non-vocational adult education and the identification of adult education as 'public' (i.e. state-funded) or 'voluntary' (non-funded) are two themes that thread their way through most of the chapters. Another is the tension between the social concern to put 'really useful knowledge' to practical use in social action, and the liberal emphasis on individual, personal development and fulfilment. From the early debates in the WEA, the tutorial class movement and IWCE to the more recent divisions between adult and community education, this tension has been a consistent intrusion. All three of these themes have sometimes been seen as simple dichotomies determining the curricula, pedagogy, organisation and resourcing of adult education. In reality they might more usefully have been treated as different but not opposite positions along the continuum of adult education.

Another prevalent theme has been the limitation of adult education's capability in eradicating all the inequalities and oppressions of society. Realistically it can only operate within the existing cultural and ideological parameters of society. It can contribute to changing the hegemonic culture and ideology but in practice it is much more likely to be incorporated into the oppressive structures of society and used to divert people's attention away from the causes towards the symptoms of inequality; or to identify oppression within a narrow, paternalistic and reductionist social class paradigm. It will then offer 'solutions' within that paradigm. In the past, these were predominantly identified as part of the class struggle. More recently adult education has reflected the more fragmentary ideology of post-modernism in locating most problems in the individual rather than in the nature of society and attempting to resolve them by meeting individual 'needs' or correcting their deficiencies. This was particularly apparent in Chapters 5 and 6 describing recent developments in community education and adult basic education.

For many years social class was a major preoccupation of British adult education. Much effort has been expended in trying to recruit working class or 'educationally disadvantaged' students to many forms of adult education. Indeed, for much of the two hundred years surveyed in this book, it can be said that this was the single most consistent purpose underpinning much of British adult education. But in pursuit of this purpose, practice very frequently fell far short of intention. Most adult education organisations have been thwarted in this aim by the educated middle class consistently gobbling up many of the opportunities provided, and by the working class or 'disadvantaged' showing a stubborn lack of interest in much of what was offered to them. More recently, there has been a marked decline even in the intention of targeting the educationally deprived sectors of society.

There have been fewer attempts to target women: indeed for considerable periods there was a feeling that women were over represented in adult education. For much of the nineteenth and earlier twentieth century women were represented in reasonable proportions in the student body, but curricula often tended to reinforce their unequal position in society. In the mid and later twentieth century women have become the majority in much adult education and there have been some attempts to meet their needs and interests more effectively. But by the 1990s there was a worrying indication that these improvements were being reversed.

As far as ethnic minorities are concerned, there is very little evidence of widespread attempts to recruit them or cater for their particular interests or shape the curricula to their requirements. Adult education has done very little to challenge their deprived position in society (Gidley, 1996).

It is arguable that in the fragmented, post-modernist 'New Times', adult education should be tackling its old preoccupations about equality, democracy, participation and social justice in new ways, engaging with 'the 'new social movements' for peace, women's liberation, racial justice, gay liberation and green issues'. And that it should address the crucial concept of citizenship in a less restricted way which gives proper recognition to different identities, and which confronts the 'New Right' re-definition of 'citizenship' with its greater emphasis on social duties rather than rights (Westwood, 1991: 49–51; Foley, 1994: 125; Roche, 1992).

History suggests that this new approach is more likely to emerge from an alliance between the less formal voluntary sector of adult education and the new social movements. Institutionalised adult education has, in the past, been more of a barrier than a facilitator to the involvement of social movements, with the partial exception of the trade union movement. This institutionalised adult education, closely related to the institutionalised structures of the modern industrialised state, would seem to have as doubtful a future as modernity itself. But history also suggests that voluntary effort unsupported by public funding and professional expertise experiences great difficulties in sustaining itself or preventing its standards of learning opportunities from declining to a low level.

The recent suggestion that the LEAs should turn themselves into professional support systems and facilitators providing neutral information, advice and guidance has already been referred to in Chapter 4 (Foster, 1992: 10). However, it is questionable how effective such support would be from an agency cut off from direct provision. Moreover, it does not meet the other major deficiency – financial support.

In the British adult education context, the WEA is the organisation which has had most experience in attempting to combine voluntaryism with professionalism and public funding. As indicated above and more fully in Chapter 7, this has caused major tensions and conflicts in the past and more recently given rise to a crisis of identity for the Association. Nevertheless, a reformed model of the WEA, attuned to the fragmentary post-modernist culture of the twenty-first century, is perhaps what is required, not just for the WEA but as a general model for adult education organisations, for the future. They will need to be popular and informal but also professionally knowledgable and supported by access to public funding which is not too closely tied to immediate political whims and fancies. They should 'build ... on adult education's tradition of people's knowledge as opposed to expert knowledge, of participation as opposed to instruction, and of collective and collaborative learning as opposed to individual education and training' (Finger, Asun and Volpe, 1995). And they must engage with a wide variety of social movements and ultimately be committed to a democratic social purpose embracing equality and social justice.

# Bibliography

Abell, S. (1992) *Effective Approaches in Adult Literacy*, ALBSU.

Ablett, N. (1909) 'The relation of Ruskin College to the Labour Movement', *Plebs*, 1, 1.

Ablett, N. (1915) 'The need for a policy', *Plebs*, 7, 4.

Action for Community in Rural England (1993) *Report, 1993*, ACRE, Cirencester.

Advisory Council for Adult Continuing Education (ACACE) (1979a) *A Strategy for the Basic Education of Adults*, ACACE, Leicester.

ACACE (1979b) *Towards Continuing Education*, ACACE, Leicester.

ACACE (1980) *Present Imperfect*, ACACE, Leicester.

ACACE (1981) *Protecting the Future for Adult Education*, ACACE, Leicester.

ACACE (1982) *Continuing Education: From Policies to Practice*, ACACE, London.

Adkins, G. (1980) *The Arts and Adult Education*, NIACE, Leicester.

Adult Literacy and Basic Skills Unit (ALBSU) (1987) *Annual Report 1986–7*, ALBSU, London.

ALBSU (1989) *ESOL: A Nation's Neglect: Research into the Need for English amongst Speakers of Other Languages*, ALBSU.

ALBSU (1992) 'ESOL: time to start afresh?', *ALBSU Newsletter*, 45, pp.2–3.

ALBSU (1993) *The Cost to Industry: Basic Skills and the UK Workforce*, ALBSU.

Aird, E. (1993) 'Keeping women on the agenda in education and training,' *Adults Learning*, 5, 3.

Aldcroft, D.H. (1992) *Education, Training and Economic Performance, 1944–1990*, Manchester University Press.

Aldred, C. (1981) 'Men and the unions – just a side issue?', *Union Studies Journal*, 4.

Alexander, D., Leach, T. & Steward, T. (1984) 'Adult education in the context of community education: progress and regress in the Tayside, Central and Fife regions of Scotland in the nine years since the Alexander Report', *Studies in Adult Education*, 16, pp.39–57.

Alexander, D. & Martin, I. (1995) 'Competence, curriculum and democracy', in Mayo, M. and Thompson, J. (eds) *Adult Education, Critical Intelligence and Social Change*, NIACE, Leicester.

Alexander, K. (1993) 'Critical reflections', *Edinburgh Review*, 90, pp.29–40.

Allaway, A.J. (1959) 'The Ashby Report and afterwards – A rejoinder', *Adult Education*, 32, pp.23–9.

Allen, G. and Martin, I. (eds) (1992) *Education and Community: The Politics of Practice*, Cassell, London.

Allen, V. (1957) *Trade Union Leadership*, Longmans.

Allred, J. & Heeks, P. (1992) *Open Learning in Public Libraries*, Library Association.

Ambrose, P., Holloway, G. & Mayhew, G. (nd) *All Change! Accreditation as a Challenge to Liberal Adult Education*, University of Sussex.

Annett, J. (1969) 'A systems approach', *Planning Industrial Training*, NIAE, pp.22–7.

Armstrong, M. (1982) 'The "needs-meeting" ideology of liberal adult education', *International Journal of Lifelong Education*, 1, 4.

Arnot, M. (1995) 'Feminism, education and the New Right', in Dawtrey, L. *et al.* (eds) *Equality and Inequality in Educational Policy*, Multilingual Matters/Open University, Clevedon.

Arnove, R.F. and Graff, H.J. (1987) (eds) *National Literacy Campaigns: Historical and Comparative Perspectives*, Plenum Press, New York and London.

Arts Council of Great Britain (1956) *The First Ten Years: 1946/56*, ACGB.

Arts Council of Great Britain (1983) *The Glory of the Garden*, ACGB.

Ashmore, O. (1990) 'University adult education', in Costello, N. & Richardson, M. (eds) *Continuing Education for the Post-industrial Society*, Open University Press.

Association of Metropolitan Authorities/Community Education Development Centre (AMA/CEDC) (1991) *Looking at Community Education*, CEDC, Coventry.

Atkins, J. (1981) *Neither Crumbs nor Condescension: The Central Labour College 1909–1915*, Aberdeen People's Press/WEA, Aberdeen.

Bacon, A. (1980) 'The role of a public library in a continuing education service', in *Adult Education and Public Libraries in the 1980s*, The Library Association.

Ball, J. & Watterson, A. (1981) 'Trade union education and race relations: the GMWU experience', *The Industrial Tutor* (Autumn).

Ball, S. (1990) *Politics and Policy Making in Education*, Routledge.

Banks, F. (1958) *Teach Them to Live*, Parrish.

Barker, R. (1972) *Education and Politics 1900–1951: A Study of the Labour Party*, Oxford University Press.

Baron, S. (1988) 'Community and the limits of social democracy', in Green, G. and Ball, S. (eds) *Progress and Inequality in Comprehensive Education*, Routledge, pp.82–101.

Baron, S. (1989) 'Community education: from the Cam to the Rea', in Walker, S. and Barton, L. (eds) *Politics and the Processes of Schooling*, Open University Press, pp.82–99.

Barr, J. (1987) 'Keeping a low profile: adult education in Scotland', *Adult Education*, 59, 4, pp.329–34.

Barton, D. (1988) 'Exploring the historical basis of contemporary literacy', *Quarterly Newsletter of the Laboratory of Comparative Human Cognition*, 10, 3, pp.70–6.

Barton, D. (1994) *Literacy: An Introduction to the Ecology of Written Language*, Blackwell.

Barton, D. and Ivanic, R. (eds) (1991) *Writing in the Community*, Sage.

Bayliss, F. (1991) 'Day release at Nottingham', *The Industrial Tutor* (Autumn).

Baynes, P. (1975) 'Adult education: The Russell Report in retrospect', *Ideas*, 30, pp.227–9.

Baynham, M. (ed.) (1986) *Doing Research*, Lee Centre, Problems of Representation Series, Goldsmiths College, London.

BBC (1992) *Extending Choice: The BBC's Role in the New Broadcasting Age*, BBC.

BBC/ITA (1969) 'Needs and Interests of the Adult Community in the United Kingdom': Report for the EBU conference.

Beale, J. (1980) 'A woman's place is in her union', *The Industrial Tutor* (Spring).

Beecham, D. (1984) 'How far has shop floor organisation been weakened and incorporated?', *International Socialism*, 23.

Bell, T. (1941) *Pioneering Days*, Lawrence and Wishart.

Benington, J. (1974) 'Strategies for change at the local level; some reflections', in Jones, D. and Mayo, M. (eds) *Community Work One*, Routledge & Kegan Paul, pp.260–77.

Benn, R. (1994) 'Access provision and mass higher education in Britain', in Lenz, W. (ed.) *Modernisierung der Erwachsenenbildung*, Bohlau, Vienna.

Benn, R. & Burton, R. (1995a) 'Access and targeting: an exploration of a contradiction', *International Journal of Lifelong Education*, 14, 6, pp.444–58.

Benn, R. & Burton, R. (1995b) 'Targeting: is Access hitting the bull's-eye?', *Journal of Access Studies*, 10, 1, pp.7–19.

Benn, R. & Fieldhouse, R. (1991) 'Adult education to the rescue in Thatcherite Britain', in Poggeler, F. & Kalman, Y. (eds) *Adult Education in Crisis Situations*, Magnes Press, Jerusalem.

Benn, R. & Fieldhouse, R. (1994) 'Raybouldism, Russell and New Realism', in Armstrong, P., Bright, B. & Zukas, M. (eds) *Reflecting on Changing Practices, Contexts and Identitites*, SCUTREA, Hull.

Bennett, R.J., Wicks, P. & McCoshan, A. (1994) *Local Empowerment and Business Services: Britain's Experiment with Training and Enterprise Councils*, UCL Press.

Bertelsmann Foundation and European Institute for the Media (eds) (1995) *Television Requires Responsibility, Vol. 2: International Studies*, Bertelsmann Foundation, Gutersloh.

Bick, J. (1991) *Vile Jelly: The Birth, Life and Lingering Death of the Arts Council of Great Britain*, Brynmell Press.

Bird, E. (1991) 'Gender and class in the adult education curriculum 1865–1900 in Bristol', *Gender and Education*, 3, 2, pp.183–97.

Blackburn, F. (1954) *George Tomlinson*, Heinemann.

Blaxter, L. (1992) 'Issues in Cross-sectoral Collaboration: the case of REPLAN' (unpublished report available from Dept of Continuing Education, University of Warwick).

Blumler, J. (1962) 'The Effects of Long-term Residential Adult Education in Post-War Britain, with Particular Reference to Ruskin College, Oxford', unpublished dissertation, University of Oxford.

Blyth, J.A. (1983) *English University Adult Education*, Manchester University Press.

Boaden, W. (1988) 'Adult education', in Morris, M. & Griggs, C. (eds) *Education: The Wasted Years? 1973–1986*, Falmer Press.

Board of Education (1943) *The Youth Service After the War* (The Wolfenden Report), HMSO.

Board of Education (1944; republished 1946 and 1950) *Community Centres*, HMSO.

Bogdanor, V. (1994) *Local Government and the Constitution*, Society of Local Authority Chief Executives.

Bonner, A. (1970) *British Co-operation: the History, Principles and Organisation of the British Co-operative Movement*, Co-operative Union Ltd, Manchester.

Bonnerjea, L. (1987) *Workbase Trades Union Education and Skills Project*, ALBSU.

Boswell, T. (1995) 'Lifelong learning: a framework for discussion', *Adults Learning*, 6, 9, pp.258–63.

Bowl, R. (1992) 'University adult education: backwards or forwards?', *Studies in the Education of Adults*, 24, 2, pp.199–216.

Bown, L. (1995) 'Learning, Liberty and Social Purpose', *Fifteenth Albert Mansbridge Memorial Lecture*, University of Leeds.

Boyden, J. (1970) 'Crisis in the adult colleges', *Times Educational Supplement*, 2865 (17 April), p.2.

Branson, N. (1985) *History of the Communist Party of Great Britain, 1927–41*, Lawrence and Wishart.

Brasnett, M.(1969) *Voluntary Action: a History of the NCSS, 1919–1969*, NCSS.

Brew, J.M. (1946) *Informal Education, Adventures and Reflections*, Faber and Faber.

Bridge Adams, M. (1912) 'New college scheme for training working women', *Plebs*, 4, 7.

Briggs, A. (1961) *The History of Broadcasting in the United Kingdom, Vol. 1: The Birth of Broadcasting*, Oxford University Press.

Briggs, A. (1965) *The History of Broadcasting in the United Kingdom, Vol. 2: The Golden Age of Wireless*, Oxford University Press.

Briggs, A. (1970) *The History of Broadcasting in the United Kingdom, Vol. 3: The War of Words*, Oxford University Press.

Briggs, A. (1979) *The History of Broadcasting in the United Kingdom, Vol. 4: Sound and Vision*, Oxford University Press.

Briggs, A. (1995) *The History of Broadcasting in the United Kingdom, Vol. 5: Competition*, Oxford University Press.

Briggs, A. & Macartney, A. (1984) *Toynbee Hall*, Routledge & Kegan Paul.

British Association of Settlements (1974) *A Right to Read: Action for a Literate Britain*, BAS, London.

British Institute of Adult Education (BIAE) (1934–5) *14th Annual Report*.

BIAE (1945) *Adult Education After the War*, Oxford University Press.

Broadcasting Support Services (1995) *Talking Heads: Information Mailout*, BSS, Manchester.

Brodie, M. (1994) *University of the Third Age: A Review*, U3A.

Brookfield, S. (1983) *Adult Learners, Adult Education, and the Community*, Open University Press.

Broome, V. & Brown, J. (1987) 'What about the members? Some thoughts on education as a union activity', *The Industrial Tutor* (Autumn).

Brown, C. (1975) Literacy in 30 hours: Paulo Freire's Process in North East Brazil, Writers and Readers Publishing Co-operative.

Brown, F. (1915) 'Women's League campaign in Bristol', *Plebs*, 7, 2.

Brown, G.F. (1980) 'Independence and incorporation: the Labour College Movement and the Workers' Educational Association before the Second World War', in Thompson, J. (ed.) *Adult Education for a Change*, Hutchinson, pp.109–25.

Brown, G.F. (1981) *Robert Peers and the Department of Adult Education*, University of Nottingham.

Brown, J. (1992) 'What about the members?' in Cox, D. (ed.) *Facing the Future*, University of Nottingham Department of Adult Education.

Browning, D. (1991a) 'Are Open Colleges too bureaucratic?', *Journal of Access Studies*, 6, 1, pp.72–9.

Browning, D. (1991b) 'Third Generation Open Colleges', *Adults Learning*, 2, 8, pp.238–9.

Bruce, M. (1974) 'A Fair Field Full of Folks', *David Crowther Memorial Lecture*, University of Sheffield.

Brumfit, C. (1985) *English as a Second Language*, Pergamon Press.

Bryant, I. (1984) *Radicals and Respectables: The Adult Education Experience in Scotland*, Scottish Institute of Adult Education, Edinburgh.

Bryant, M. (1979) *The Unexpected Revolution*, Institute of Education, University of London.

Bureau of Current Affairs (1950) *Discussion Method*, BCA.

Burgess, K. (1975) *The Origins of British Industrial Relations: the Nineteenth Century Experience*, Croom Helm.

Burke, C. (1987) 'Take ten: Sheffield', in Mace, J. & Yarnit, M. (eds) *Time Off to Learn*, Methuen.

Burrows, J. (1976) *University Adult Education in London: A Century of Achievement*, University of London.

Cain, J.T. (1992) *The BBC: 70 Years of Broadcasting*, BBC.

Cain, J.T. & Wright, B. (1994) *In a Class of its Own: BBC Education, 1924–1994*, BBC.

Calder, J. (1983) 'The Open University community education programme', in Tight, M. (ed.) *Opportunities for Adult Education*, Routledge/Open University, pp.173–87.

Caldwell, P., Gerhardt, P. & Kohn, R. (1975) 'Policies for the future: from above or from below?', *WEA News*, 16.

Calouste Gulbenkian Foundation (1968) *Community Work and Social Change* (Gulbenkian Report), Longman.

Cameron, D. (1995) *Verbal Hygiene*, Routledge.

Camfield, B. & Fisher, J. (1987) 'Missing link in trade union education?', *The Industrial Tutor* (Spring).

Campbell, J. (1987) *Nye Bevan and the Mirage of British Socialism*, Weidenfeld and Nicolson.

Cann, R. & Mannings, B. (1987) 'Incidental learning: a positive experience', *Adult Education*, 60, 2.

Cantor, M. & Roberts, I.F. (2nd edn, 1983) *Further Education in England and Wales*, Routledge & Kegan Paul.

Capron, J. (1994) *Broadcasting and Further Education*, Further Education Unit.

Carby, H.V. (1982) 'Schooling in Babylon', in *The Empire Strikes Back*, Centre for Contemporary Cultural Studies/Hutchinson.

Carroll, J.C. (1976) 'The role of the trainer in today's society', *Training*, 2, 4, pp.14–15.

Carter, P. (1983) 'For whom the block votes? A roundtable discussion', *Marxism Today*, September.

Casey, F. (1920) 'Beginning with the beginner', *Plebs*, 12, 4.

CDP Information and Intelligence Unit (1974) *The National Community Development Project: Inter-Project Report 1973*, London.

Central Advisory Council for Education (1959) *15 to 18* (The Crowther Report) 1, HMSO.

Central Advisory Council for Education (1967) *Children and their Primary Schools* (The Plowden Report), HMSO.

Central Joint Advisory Committee on Tutorial Classes (CJAC) (1910) *1st Annual Report*.

CJAC (1910–27) *Annual Reports*, 1–17.

CJAC (1930) *Annual Report*, 20.

Central Labour College (CLC) (1913) 'Appeal of the Central Labour College', NCLC Collection, National Library of Scotland, Acc. 5120, Box 2.

Central Training Council (1996) *The Use of Programmed Instruction in Industrial Training*, Memorandum no. 3, HMSO.

Chadwick, A. (1980) *The Role of the Museum and Art Gallery in Adult Education*, University of Nottinghamm.

Chadwick, A. & Stannett, A. (1995) *Museums and the Education of Adults*, NIACE.

Challinor, R. (1977) *The Origins of British Bolshevism*, Croom Helm.

Champion, A. (1976) 'Adult centres to-day' in Rogers, A. (ed.) *The Spirit and the Form*, University of Nottingham.

Channel Four Television Corporation (1994) *Report and Financial Statements, 1993*, Channel Four.

Charlton, C. (1985) 'Introduction', in Rowntree, J.W & Binns, H.B. (1902) *A History of the Adult School Movement*, University of Nottingham.

Charnley, A. & Jones, H.A. (1981) *The Concept of Success in Adult Literacy*, ALBSU.

Charnley, A. & Withnall, A. (1989) *Developments in Basic Education: Special Development Projects 1978–85*, ALBSU.

Chartered Institute of Public Finance and Accountancy (1994) *Library Statistics for the UK.*

Chief Education Officers and the UCAE (1964) 'The universities and adult education: a joint statement', *Adult Education*, 37, pp.129–32.

Childs, D. (2nd edn, 1986) *Britain Since 1945*, Methuen

Citrine, W. (1967) *Two Careers – A Second Volume of Autobiography*, Hutchinson.

City and Guilds of London Institute (1993) *A Short History 1878–1992*, CGLI.

Clapp, B.W. (1982) *The University of Exeter: A History*, University of Exeter.

Clarke, R. (ed.) (1990) *Enterprising Neighbours: The Development of the Community Association Movement in Britain*, National Fededation of Community Organisations and Community Projects Foundation.

Clegg, H. (1964) *General Union in a Changing Society: A Short History of the National Union of General and Municipal Workers 1889–1964*, Blackwell, Oxford.

Clegg, H. & Adams, R. (1959) *Trade Union Education – A Report for the WEA*, WEA.

Cliff, T. (1970) *The Employers' Offensive – Productivity Deals and How to Fight Them*, Pluto Press.

Clinton, A. (1977) *The Trade Union Rank and File: Trades Councils in Britain 1900–1940*, Manchester University Press.

Clissold, J. (1987) 'Liberal adult education – the decline of a myth', *Adult Education*, 60, 3, pp.236–39.

Cloet, A. & Norton, D. (1992) *Rank Fellowship Final Report*, U3A.

Clyne, P. (1972) *The Disadvantaged Adult*, Longman.

Coates, K. & Topham, T. (1974) *The New Unionism*, Peter Owen.

Coates, K., Topham, T. & Barratt Brown, M. (1969) *Trade Union Register*, Spokesman, Nottingham.

Coats, M. (1993) 'Women's education: a cause for concern?' *Adults Learning*, 5, 3, pp.60–63.

Coats, M. (1994) *Women's Education*, SRHE & Open University Press.

Cockburn, C. (1977) *The Local State*, Pluto Press.

Cockerill, J. (nd) *Second Chance: The Story of Hillcroft*, Hillcroft College, Surbiton.

Cohen, M. (1990) 'The Labour College Movement between the wars: national and north west developments', in Simon, B. (ed.) *The Search for Enlightenment: The Working Class and Adult Education in the Twentieth Century*, NIACE.

Coker, C. & Stuttard, G. (eds) (1975) *Industrial Studies 1: The Key Skills*, Arrow Books.

Cole, G.D.H. (1916) 'What Labour wants from education', *Plebs*, 8, 10.

Cole, G.D.H. (1925) 'The task ahead', *Yorkshire Bulletin*, 20, Leeds.

Cole, G.D.H. (1952) 'What workers' education means', *The Highway*, 44.

Cole, M. (ed.) (1952) *Beatrice Webb's Diaries, 1, 1912–24*, Longmans, Green.

Collins, P.A.W. (1956) 'Mr Wiltshire's Great Tradition: some disagreements', *Adult Education*, 29, 3, pp.167–74.

Commission of Enquiry into Industrial Unrest (1917) *No. 7 Division: Report of the Commissioners for Wales ...; No. 8 Division: Report of the Commissioners for Scotland*, Cmnd. 8668–9, HMSO.

Commission of the Eurorean Communities (1991) *Memorandum on Higher Education in the European Community*, Office for Official Publications, Luxembourg.

Commission of the European Communities (1994) *Growth, Competitiveness, Employment: The Challenge and Ways Forward into the 21st Century*, Office for Official Publications, Luxembourg.

Commission on Industrial Relations (1972) *Industrial Relations Training*, Report No. 33, HMSO.

Cook, E.R. (1976) 'Readership survey', *Training*, 2, 6, p.6.

Corlett, J. (1994) 'Lifelong learning at work: the Oxfordshire experience', *Adults Learning*, 5, 9, pp.232–3.

Cosgrove, F. (1983) 'Re-shaping trade union education: TGWU proposals for government support', *The Industrial Tutor* (Autumn).

Cosgrove, F. (1992) 'Distance learning in the TGWU', in Cox, D. (ed.) *Facing the Future*, University of Nottingham Department of Adult Education.

Cowan, I.R. (1968) 'Mechanics' Institutes and science and art classes in Salford in the nineteenth century', *Vocational Aspects*, 20, 47, pp.201–10.

Cowburn, W. (1986) *Class, Ideology and Community Education*, Croom Helm.

Cox, D. (ed.) (1992) *Facing the Future*, University of Nottingham Department of Adult Education.

Craik, W.W. (1964) *Central Labour College*, Lawrence and Wishart.

Craven, J. and Jackson, F. (1986) *Whose Language? A Teaching Approach for Caribbean Heritage Students*, Central Manchester Caribbean English Project, Manchester Education Committee.

Crombie, A.D & Harries-Jenkins, G. (1983) *The Demise of the Liberal Tradition*, University of Leeds.

Cronin, J. (1984) *Labour and Society in Britain, 1918–1979*, Batsford.

Crowther, G. (1969) A speech by Baron Crowther on the occasion of the Charter Ceremony, Open University.

Cunliffe, G. (1969) *Analysis of Social Work Courses in Universities*, University of Bristol.

Dadswell, G. (1978) 'The adult independent learner and the public library', *Adult Education*, 51, 1.

Dana, H.W. (1925) 'The place of literature in workers' education', *Plebs*, 17, 11.

Daniel, J. (1994) 'Address to Council Weekend' (September 23) Open University, mimeograph.

Daniel, W. & Millward, N. (1983) *Workplace Industrial Relations in Britain*, Heinemann.

Davidson, R. (1985) *Whitehall and the Labour Problem in Late Victorian and Edwardian Britain*, Croom Helm.

Davies, D. & Robertson, D. (1986) 'Open college: towards a new view of adult education', *Adult Education*, 59, 2.

Davies, E. (1866) *Higher Education for Women*, London.

Davies, L.J. (1904) *The Working Men's College 1854–1904*, Macmillan.

Davies, M. (1904) *The Women's Co-operative Guild 1883–1904*.

Davies, P. & Parry, G. (1993) *Recognising Access*, NIACE.

Davin, A. (1978) 'Imperialism and motherhood', *History Workshop Journal*, 5 (Spring), pp.9–65.

Davison, R.C. (1929) *The Unemployed: Old Policies and New*, Longman.

Day, K. (1988) *Public Attitudes Towards Back-up Literature, Research Report*, BBC Broadcasting Research for the BBC, BSS, Channel Four Television and the IBA, BBC.

De Bear Nicol, W.B. (1959) 'Growing points in adult education', *Education*, 113, pp.60–3.

Dean, D. (1971) 'Conservatism and the national education system 1922–40', *The Journal of Contemporary History*, 6, 2.

Dean, D.W (1986) 'Planning for a postwar generation: Ellen Wilkinson and George Tomlinson at the Ministry of Education, 1945–51', *History of Education*, 15, 2.

Deem, R. (1981) 'State policy and ideology in the education of women, 1944–1980', *British Journal of Sociology of Education*, 2, 2, pp.131–43.

Dees, N. (1981) 'Reflections on adult education', *Scottish Journal of Adult Education*, 15, 3, pp.5–11.

Delamont, S. (1978) 'The contradictions in ladies' education', in Delamont, S. & Duffin, L. (eds) *The Nineteenth Century Woman: Her Cultural and Physical World*, Croom Helm.

Dent, H.C. (4th edn, 1952) *The Education Act, 1944*, University of London Press.

Department of Education and Science (DES) (1966) *A University of the Air*, Cmnd 2922, HMSO.

DES (1969) *Report of the Planning Committee*, HMSO.

DES (1973) *Adult Education: A Plan for Development* (The Russell Report), HMSO.

DES (1978) *Higher Education into the 1990s*, HMSO.

DES (1980) *A Survey of Shop Steward Courses in England and Wales*.

DES (1988) *Survey by HM Inspectors on the Use of Museums in Adult and Community Education*, DES.

DES (1991a) *Education and Training for the 21st Century*, 2 vols, HMSO.

DES (1991b) *Higher Education: A New Framework*, HMSO.

DES & Welsh Office (1991) *Education and Training for the 21st Century*, 2, HMSO.

Devereux, W.A. (1982) *Adult Education in Inner London 1870–1980*, Shepheard-Walwyn and the Inner London Education Authority.

Dixon, R. (1965) 'The Hull University Extension Society', in Styler, W.E. (ed.) *Adult Education in East Yorkshire 1875–1960*, University of Hull.

Dobb, M. (1921) 'Colonial and imperialist exploitation: a Marxist analysis', *Plebs*, 13, 9.

Doyle, M (1980) 'Reform and reaction: the WEA post-Russell', in Thompson, J. (ed.) *Adult Education for a Change*, Hutchinson.

Doyle, M. (1986) 'Social purpose in adult education', *Adult Education*, 59, 2.

Drews, W. (1995) 'The British Short-Term Residential Colleges for Adult Education 1945–1995', unpublished PhD thesis, University of Ulster.

Duke, C. (1986) 'Continuing education trends and policy implications', *Journal of Education Policy*, 1, 3, pp.255–70.

Duke, C. (1995) 'Footprints in the Sand? – The Legacy of the University Funding Council's Support for Research in Continuing Education', unpublished paper presented to a UACE conference at the University of Lancaster (University of Warwick).

Duncan, R. (1992) 'Independent working class education and the formation of the Labour College Movement in Glasgow and the west of Scotland 1915–1922', in Duncan, R. & McIvor, A. (eds) *loc. cit.*

Duncan, R. & McIvor, A. (eds) (1992) *Militant Workers – Labour and Class Conflict on the Clyde 1900–1950*, John Donald, Edinburgh.

Durucan, C. (1986) *Continuing Education in British Universities*, University of Nottingham.

Dyson, R. (1978) *Determining Priorities for University Extra-Mural Education*, University of Keele.

Eckinsmyth, C. & Bynner, J. (1994) *The Basic Skills of Young Adults: Some Findings from the 1970 British Cohort Study*, ALBSU.

Education Digest (1982) 'Continuing education: the next 20 years', *Education*, 159, 14.

Edwards, J. (1986) *Working Class Adult Education in Liverpool: A Radical Approach*, Centre for Adult and Higher Education, University of Manchester.

Elliott, R. (1976) 'Training opportunities in the EEC Social Fund', *Training*, 1, 4, pp.10–11.

Elliott, R. (1982) 'Something is stirring – women and TUC education', *The Industrial Tutor* (Spring).

Ellis, A. (1937) *The Secret History of the NCLC*, Birmingham.

Ellis, E.L. (1992) *T.J.: A Life of Dr. Thomas Jones*, University of Wales Press, Cardiff.

Elsdon, K.T. (1991) *Adult Learning in Voluntary Organisations*, vol. 1, University of Nottingham Department of Adult Education.

Elsdon, K.T. (1994) 'Systems of adult education: can we learn from the past?', *International Journal of Lifelong Education*, 13, 4, pp.321–9.

Elsdon, K.T. (1995) *Voluntary Organisations: Citizenship, Learning and Change*, NIACE.

Elsdon, K.T. *et al.* (1993) *Adult Learning in Voluntary Organisations* vol. 3, University of Nottingham Department of Adult Education.

Elsey, B. (1974) 'Voluntary organisations and informal adult education', *Adult Education*, 46, 6, pp.391–6.

Entwistle, H. (1978) *Class, Culture and Education*, Methuen.

Eraut, M. (1985) 'Programmed learning' in Husen, T. & Postlethwaite, T.N. (eds) *The International Encyclopedia of Education*, 7, Pergamon, Oxford.

European Bureau of Adult Education (1983) 'Adult basic education', *EBAE Newsletter*, 1, Edinburgh.

Evans, B. (1982) 'Further education pressure groups: the campaign for continued and technical education in 1944', *History of Education*, 11, 1, pp.45–55.

Evans, B. (1983) 'Further education pressure groups: the campaign for adult education in 1944', *Studies in Adult Education*, 15, pp.92–101.

Evans, B. (1987) *Radical Adult Education: A Political Critique*, Croom Helm.

Evans, B. (1992) *The Politics of the Training Market: From MSC to TECs*, Routledge.

Fairbairn, A. (1979) *The Leicestershire Community Colleges and Centres*, University of Nottingham Department of Adult Education.

Farnes, N. (1988) 'Open University community education: emancipation or domestication?', *Open Learning*, 3, 1, pp.35–40.

Farnes, N. (1993) 'A distance education contribution to a social strategy to combat poverty: Open University community education courses in Glasgow', *International Journal of Lifelong Education*, 12, 3, pp.191–204.

Field, B. (1980) 'The southern counties adult education society: some 19th century views on workers' education', *Studies in Adult Education*, 12, 2, pp.101–8.

Field, J. (1984) 'A new approach to Second Chance Learning: South Yorkshire's Northern College', *Convergence*, 17, 1, pp.9–18.

Field, J. (1986) 'Expanding educational opportunities for the adult unemployed: a REPLAN initiative', *Journal of Further and Higher Education*, 10, 3, pp.3–8.

Field, J. (1988) 'Further and adult education after the Act', *Forum*, 31, 1, pp.17–18.

Field, J. (1989) 'Citizens, enterprise and community', *Journal of Community Education*, 7, 3, pp.23–6.

Field, J. (1991) 'Social movements: the cutting edge of European adult education', *International Journal of University Adult Education*, 30, 1, pp.1–12.

Field, J. (1992) *Learning Through Labour: Training, Unemployment and the State 1890–1939*, Leeds University.

Field, J. (1995) 'Reality testing in the workplace: are NVQs "Employment Led"?', in Hodkinson, P. & Issitt, M. (eds) *The Challenge of Competence: Professionalism through Vocational Education and Training*, Cassell, pp.28–43.

Field, J. & Taylor, R. (1995) 'The funding and organisation of adult continuing education research in Britain: trends and prospects', *International Journal of Lifelong Education*, 14, 3, pp.247–60.

Fieldhouse, R. (1967) 'Branch Organisation and WEA Democracy', unpublished discussion paper for the WEA.

Fieldhouse, R. (1977) *The WEA: Aims and Achievments 1903–1977*, University of Syracuse, New York.

Fieldhouse, R. (1981) 'Voluntaryism and the state in adult education: the WEA and the 1925 TUC Education Scheme', *History of Education*, 10, 1, pp.45–63.

Fieldhouse, R. (1983) 'The ideology of English adult education teaching 1925–50', *Studies in Adult Education*, 15, 1, pp.11–35.

Fieldhouse, R. (1984) 'The Ideology of English Responsible Body Adult Education 1925–50', unpublished PhD thesis, University of Leeds.

Fieldhouse, R. (1985a) 'Conformity and contradiction in English Responsible Body adult education 1925–50', Studies in the Education of Adults, 17, 2, pp.121–34.

Fieldhouse, R. (1985b) *Adult Education and the Cold War*, University of Leeds.

Fieldhouse, R. (1987a) 'Insecurity of tenure and academic freedom in adult education: an historical perspective', *Journal of Educational Administration and History*, 19, 1, pp.36–46.

Fieldhouse, R. (1987b) 'The 1908 Report: antidote to class struggle', in Harrop, S. (ed.) *Oxford and Working Class Education*, new edn, University of Nottingham, pp.30–47.

Fieldhouse, R. (1988a) *The Political Education of Servants of the State*, Manchester University Press.

Fieldhouse, R. (1988b) 'The ideology of adult education for HM forces during the Second World War', in *The Political Education of Servants of the State*, pp.99–123.

Fieldhouse, R. (1989) 'The Workers' Educational Association', in Charters, A.N. & Hilton, R.J. (eds) *Landmarks in International Adult Education*, Routledge.

Fieldhouse, R. (1989/90) 'The WEA and the universities since the war', *Workers' Education*, 3, 6.

Fieldhouse, R. (1990) 'Bouts of suspicion: political controversies in adult education 1925–1950', in Simon, B. (ed.) *The Search for Enlightenment: The Working Class and Adult Education in the Twentieth Century*, NIACE, pp.153–72.

Fieldhouse, R. (1993a) *Optimism and Joyful Irreverence: The Sixties Culture and its Influence on British University Adult Education and the WEA*, NIACE.

Fieldhouse, R. (1993b) 'Education and training for the workforce', in Fyrth, J. (ed.) *Labour's High Noon*, Lawrence & Wishart, pp.96–111.

Fieldhouse, R. (1994) 'The Labour government's further education policy 1945–51', *History of Education*, 23, 3, pp.287–99.

Fieldhouse, R. (ed.) (1991) 'The organisation of continuing education within universities', *UCACE Occasional Paper*, 7.

Fieldhouse, R. & Forrester, K. (1984) 'The WEA and trade union education', *The Industrial Tutor*, 3, 9.

Finch, J. (1984) *Education as Social Policy*, Longman.

Finegold, D. & Soskice, S. (1988) 'The failure of training in Britain: analysis and prescription', *Oxford Review of Economic Policy*, 4, 3, pp.21–53.

Finger, M., Asun, J.M. & Volpe, M. (1995) 'Learning our way out', paper presented to 1995 ESREA Conference, Strobl, Austria.

Fletcher, C. (1984) *The Challenges of Community Education*, University of Nottingham Department of Adult Education.

Flude, R. & Parrott, A. (1979) *Education and the Challenge of Change*, Open University Press.

Foden, F. (1992) *The Education of Part-time Teachers in Further and Adult Education,* University of Leeds.

Foley, G. (1994) 'Adult education and capitalist reorganisation', *Studies in the Education of Adults,* 26, 2, pp.121–43.

Follett, M.P. (1929) *The New State,* Longmans, Green.

Foote, G. (1986) *The Labour Party's Political Thought, A History,* Croom Helm.

Ford, B. (ND ?1951) *The Bureau of Current Affairs: 1946 to 1951,* BCA.

Fordham, P. (1991) 'The REPLAN programme in England and Wales', in Forrester, K. & Ward, K. (eds) *Unemployment, Education and Training: Case Studies from North America and Europe,* Caddo Gap Press, Sacremento, pp.151–77.

Fordham, P. (1992) 'REPLAN 1984–1991', *Studies in the Education of Adults,* 24, 2, pp.225–8.

Fordham, P., Poulton, G. & Randle, L. (1979) *Learning Networks in Adult Education,* Routledge & Kegan Paul.

Forrester, K., Payne, J. & Ward, K. (1995) 'Lifelong education and the workplace: a critical analysis', *International Journal of Lifelong Education,* 14, 4, pp.292–305.

Forster, W. (1983) *Arts Centres and Adult Education,* ACGB.

Forster, W. (1989) 'The Department of Education and Science and the university Responsible Bodies, 1983–7', *Studies in the Education of Adults,* 21, 1, pp.3–19.

Forster, W. (1990) 'Comment', *Studies in the Education of Adults,* 22, 1, pp.107–12.

Foster, P. (1992) 'The future of LEA adult education', *Adults Learning,* 4, 1, p.10.

Fowler, G. (1988) 'On the nature of political progress,' in Molyneaux, F., Low, G. & Fowler, G., *Learning for Life: Politics and Progress in Recurrent Education,* Croom Helm.

Frank, F. & Hamilton, M. (1993) 'Not Just a Number: The Role of Adult Basic Education in the Changing Workplace: Final Report to Leverhulme Trust', *Centre for the Study of Education and Training Working Paper,* 37, University of Lancaster.

Fraser, L. and Ward, K. (1988) *Education for Everyday Living,* NIACE.

Freeborn, S. (1986) 'A History of the Royal Institute of Cornwall and Its Role in Adult Education During the 19th Century', unpublished MPhil thesis, University of Exeter.

Freeman, M. (1984) *Taking Control: A Handbook for Trade Unionists,* Jurius Publications.

Freire, P. (1972) *The Pedagogy of the Oppressed,* Penguin Books, Harmondsworth.

Frow, E. & Frow, R. (1990) 'The spark of independent working class education: Lancashire 1909–1930', in Simon, B. (ed.) *The Search for Enlightenment: The Working Class and Adult Education in the Twentieth Century,* NIACE, pp.71–104.

Fryer, B. (1989) 'Some limitations of community adult education', *Journal of Community Education,* 7, 3, pp.26–8.

Fryer, B. (1990) 'The challenge to working class education', in Simon, B. (ed.) *The Search for Enlightenment: The Working Class and Adult Education in the Twentieth Century,* NIACE, pp.276–319.

Further Education Funding Council (FEFC) (1995) *Report from the Inspectorate: Workers' Educational Association.*

Gaffin, J. & Thomas, D. (1993) *Caring and Sharing,* CWS.

Gains, D. (1980) 'The cooperation of continuing advisory services with libraries', in *Adult Education and the Public Libraries in the 1980s,* The Library Association.

Galloway, V. (1993) 'Democracy and the community education curriculum: a time to review?', *Edinburgh Review,* 90, pp.45–55.

Gardener, S. (1991) 'Basic education and the Further and Higher Education Bill', *RaPAL Bulletin*, 16 (Autumn).

Garman, D. (1948) 'Trade union education', *Labour Monthly* (September).

Gatehouse Books (1985) *Where Do We Go From Here? Adult Lives Without Literacy*, Gatehouse Publishing, Manchester.

Gatehouse Books (1992) *Telling Tales: A Collection of Short Stories, Poetry and Drama*, Gatehouse Publishing, Manchester.

Gaze, J. (1988) *Figures in a Landscape: A History of the National Trust*, Barrie & Jackson with the National Trust.

Gee, R. (1994) quoted in 'Ambridge offers listeners lessons', *The Guardian*, 16 November.

Gerver, E. (1990) 'Adult education in Scotland: open? learning?', in Corner, T. (ed.) *Learning Opportunities for Adults*, Routledge, pp.27–41.

Gerver, E. (1992) 'Scotland', in Jarvis, P. (ed.) *Perspectives on Adult Education and Training in Europe*, NIACE, pp.389–404.

Gerver, E. (ed.) (1985) *Alexander Ten Years On*, Scottish Institute of Adult Education.

Gibson, G.G. (1986) 'Thoughts and action in the life of F.D.Maurice, with particular reference to London's Working Men's College', *International Journal of Lifelong Education*, 5, 4, pp.297–314.

Gibson, P. (1994) 'Participation and achiement: a different approach for Kent', *Adults Learning*, 5, 9, pp.237–9.

Gidley, N. (1996) 'Multicultural Perspectives on Adult Education: Putting Policy into Practice', Centre for Research in Continuing Education, *Occassional Paper*, 2, University of Exeter.

Giles, W.J. (1969) 'Training after the Act', *Personnel Management*, 1, 2, pp.20–6.

Gilroy, P. (1987) *There Ain't No Black in the Union Jack*, Hutchinson.

Glatter, R. & Wedell, E.G. (1971) *Study by Correspondence*, Longman.

Gleeson, D. (1989) *The Pardox of Training: Making Progress out of Crisis*, Open University Press.

Glyn Evans, A. (1927) 'Researching companies', *Plebs*, 19, 3.

Goldman, L. (1995) *Dons and Workers: Oxford and adult education since 1850*, Clarendon Press, Oxford.

Goodwin, H. (1983) 'Continuing education: from policies to practice', *Adult Education*, 56, 2, pp.98–104.

Gordon, P., Aldrich, R. & Dean, D. (1991) *Education and Policy in England in the Twentieth Century*, Woburn Press, London.

Gott, F. (1990) 'Towards 2003: an investigation into the relevance of the WEA today', *Studies in the Education of Adults*, 22, 1.

Government Social Survey (1968) *Workplace Industrial Relations*, HMSO.

Gowan, D. (1982) 'Student centred approaches revisited', *Trade Union Studies Journal*, 6.

Graff, H. (1987) *The Legacies of Literacy: Continuities and Contradictions in Western Culture and Society*, Indiana University Press.

Graham, R. (1983) *19th Century Self-help in Education: Mutual Improvement Societies*, University of Nottingham.

Grant, A. (1990) 'Trade union education: a TUC perspective', *The Industrial Tutor* (Spring).

Gravell, C. (1983) 'Trade union education: will state funding lead to state control?', *Trade Union Studies Journal*, 8.

Green, A. (1994) 'The Role of the State and Social Partners in Vocational Education and Training Systems', draft paper presented to the Spring Conference of the History of Education Society (Birmingham, 7 May).

Greenaway, J.R. (1988) 'The political education of the Civil Service mandarin elite', in Fieldhouse, R. (ed.) *The Political Education of Servants of the State*, Manchester University Press, pp.19–46.

Gregory, G. (1991) 'Community publishing as self-education', in Barton, D. & Ivanic, R. (eds) *Writing in the Community*, Sage.

Gregory, W.C.E. (1958) 'Aspects of the WETUC', *Adult Education*, 31.

Grey, M. & Sherreff, E. (1856) *Thoughts on Self-Culture*, London.

Griffiths, T. & Collingwood, W. (eds) (1970) *Adult Education and Television*, report of a conference at Dartington Hall, Independent Television Authority.

Griggs, C. (1983) *The TUC and the Struggle for Education 1868–1925*, Falmer Press, Brighton.

Groombridge, B. (1964) *The Londoner and his Library*, Research Institute for Consumer Affairs.

Groombridge, B. (1967) 'Adult education – the formative phase', in Moir, G. (ed.) *Teaching and Television*, Pergamon, Oxford.

Groombridge, B. (1976) 'Adult education and broadcasting: open education', in Rogers, A. (ed.) *The Spirit and the Form: Essays in Adult Education in Honour of Professor Harold Wiltshire*, University of Nottingham.

Groombridge, B. (1978) 'The mass media and higher education', in Roderick, G. & Stephens, M. (eds) *Higher Education Alternatives*, Longman.

Groombridge, B. (1979) 'Big bangs and bifocals', in Holloway, L. (ed.) *The First Ten Years*, Open University Press.

Groombridge, B. (1994) *Real Voices: Social Action on BBC Radio 1FM*, BBC.

Groombridge, B. (1995) *Enid Hutchinson: Perspectives on a Pioneer*, NEC/NIACE.

Groombridge, B. & Rogers, J. (1973) 'Using adult education programmes', *EBU Review*, 24 (March), Geneva.

Hadow, H. (1928) *New Ventures in Broadcasting: A Study in Adult Education*, BBC.

Haldane, I. (1969) 'The educational preferences of the viewer', in *Teaching by Television: Adult Education*, European Broadcasting Union, Geneva.

Hall, A.W. (1985) *The Adult School Movement in the Twentieth Century*, University of Nottingham Department of Adult Education.

Hall, S. & Jacques, M. (eds) (1989) *New Times*, Lawrence & Wishart.

Halsey, A.H. (1972) *Educational Priority: EPA Problems and Policies*, Vol. 1, HMSO.

Hamilton, M. (1989) 'The development of adult basic education in Britain', in Entwhistle, N. (ed.) *Handbook of Educational Ideas and Practice*, Croom Helm.

Hamilton, M. (1992) 'The development of adult basic education in the UK: a cautionary tale', *International Yearbook of Adult Education*, 19/20, Bohlau Verlag, Köln.

Hamilton, M. (1994) 'Who owns research?', in *Proceedings of the Conference on Adult Literacy: An International Urban Perspective*, City University, NY; Literacy Assistance Center; Unesco.

Hamilton, M. & Barton, D. (2nd edn, 1989) *Research and Practice in Adult Literacy*, Association for Recurrent Education, Sheffield.

Hamilton, M., Ivanic, R. & Barton, D. (1992) 'Knowing where we are: participatory research in adult literacy', in Hautecoeur, J.H. (ed.) *Current Research in Literacy*, ALPHA 92, Unesco, Hamburg.

Hamilton, M. & Stasinopoulos, M. (1987) *Literacy, Numeracy and Adults: Findings from the National Child Development Survey*, ALBSU.

Hamilton, R. (1991) 'Professionalisation: meeting the needs of the community educators?', *Scottish Journal of Adult Education*, 10, 1, pp.34–41.

Hannam, W.G. (1982) 'A foot behind the door: an historical analysis of adult education in prisons', *International Journal of Lifelong Education*, 1, 4, pp.361–372.

Hansard (1993) *House of Lords Debate, Adult Education: Funding*, 176–214 (23 Feb).

Hargreaves, D. (1977) *On the Move*, BBC.

Hargreaves, D. (1980) *Adult Literacy and Broadcasting: The BBC's Experience*, Report to the Ford Foundation, Frances Pinter Publishers.

Harris, R. (1984) *The Making of Neil Kinnock*, Faber and Faber.

Harrish-Worthington, P. (1987) *Back to the Future: A Study of Short-Term Adult Residential Education*, The Hill Residential College.

Harrison, J.F.C. (1959) 'The WEA in the welfare state', in Raybould, S.G. (ed.) *Trends in English Adult Education*, Heinemann, Oxford.

Harrison, J.F.C. (1961) *Learning and Living 1790–1960: A Study in the History of the English Adult Education Movement*, Routledge & Kegan Paul.

Harrison, J.F.C. (1971) *Underground Education in the 19th Century*, University of Leeds.

Harrop, S. (ed.) (new edn, 1987) *Oxford and Working Class Education*, University of Nottingham.

Hartley, T. (1992) 'The Tip of the Iceberg: State Funding and English Language Provision for Bilingual Adults in the UK: A Critical Review', MA dissertation, Lancaster University.

Haviland, R.M. (1973) Abstract of 'Provision for adult literacy in England', in Charnley, A.H. (1974) *Research in Adult Education in the British Isles*, NIAE.

Hawkins, T.H. & Brimble, L.J.F. (1947) *Adult Education: The Record of the British Army*, Macmillan.

Hennessy, P. (1973) 'The Co-operative College: looking up after the lean years', *Times Higher Education Supplement*, 76, 3 March, p.6.

Her Majesty's Inspectorate (HMI) (1991) *Education for Adults*, DES.

HMI (1992) *A Survey of the Provision for Adults in Schools: Strathclyde Region*, Scottish Office Education Department, Edinburgh.

Herrington, M. (1995) 'Dyslexia: old dilemmas and new policies: research and practice', *Adult Literacy Bulletin*, 27, special issue on Dyslexia (Summer).

Herrington, M. & Moss, W. (1991) 'ABE in England: how protected is it?', *RaPAL Bulletin*, 14 (Spring).

Higher Education Funding Council (England) (HEFCE) (1992) circular 1/92, 'The Funding of Teaching by the HEFCE in 1993–94'.

HEFCE (1993a) 'Continuing Education Advisory Group 93/1', Agenda Paper, 19 March.

HEFCE (1993b) circular 18/93, 'Continuing Education'.

HEFCE (1994a) circular 3/94, 'Continuing Education'.

HEFCE (1994b) circular 28/94, 'Continuing Vocational Education (CVE) Development Funding'.

HEFCE (1994c) consultation paper 3/94, *Funding of Teaching: Part-Time Study*.

HEFCE (1995a) circular 4/95, 'Funds for Non-Award Bearing Continuing Education'.

HEFCE (1995b) circular 11/95, *ibid*: 'The Outcome'.

HEFCE (1995c) *Higher Education in Further Education Colleges: Funding the Relationship*.

Higher Education Funding Councils (England & Wales) (HEFCE/HEFCW) (1992) *Continuing Education Policy Review*.

Higher Education Funding Council (Wales) (HEFCW) (1993) circular W93/10HE, 'Continuing Education Future Funding'.

HEFCW (1994) circular W94/1HE, 'Continuing Education Mainstream Survey'.

Highet, G. (1991) 'Gender and education: a study of the ideology and practice of community based women's education', in Westwood, S. and Thomas, J. (eds) *Radical Agendas?: The Politics of Adult Education*, NIACE, pp.153–66.

Hill, A.C.C. & Lubin, I. (1934) *The British Attack on Unemployment*, Brooking Institution, Washington DC.

Hinton, J. & Hyman, R. (1975) *Trade Unions and Revolution: The Industrial Politics of the Early British Communist Party*, Pluto Press.

HMI, see Her Majesty's Inspectorate.

Hodges, F.A.J. (1946–47) 'The application of modern management to the ship-building industry', *Transactions of the Northeast Coast Institution of Engineers and Shipbuilders*, 63, pp.141–68.

Hogan, J.M. (1957) 'The last refuge', *Adult Education*, 29, pp.246–9.

Holford, J. (1994) *Union Education in Britain – A TUC Activity*, University of Nottingham Department of Adult Education.

Holton, B. (1976) *British Syndicalism 1900–1914: Myths and Realities*, Pluto Press.

Hooper-Greenhill, E. (1992) *Museums and the Shaping of Knowledge*, Routledge.

Hooper-Greenhill, E. (1994) *Museums and their Visitors*, Routledge.

Hopkins, A. (1978) 'What about the workers?', *Times Educational Supplement*, 3302 (13 Oct).

Horobin, J. (1983) 'Adult education in Scotland from 1976 to 1981', *Scottish Journal of Adult Education*, 6, 1, pp.5–10.

Horrabin, J.F. (1921) 'Our point of view', *Plebs*, 13, 1.

Horrabin, J.F. (1929) 'The bookshelf', *Plebs*, 21, 3.

Horrabin, J.F. & W. (1924) *Working Class Education*, The Labour Publishing Company.

Horrabin, W. (1926) 'Do we still need a Plebs League?', *Plebs*, 18, 9.

Horsman, J. (1990) *Something in My Mind Besides the Everyday: Women and Literacy*, Women's Press, Toronto.

Hostler, J. (1973) 'The education of adults', *Studies in Adult Education*, 9, pp.58–64.

Houlton, R. (ed.) (1978) *Residential Adult Education: Values, Policies and Problems*, Society of Industrial Tutors.

House of Commons, *Debates 1987–8*, 123.

House of Commons Select Committee on Education, Science and Arts (1990 and 1991/2) *Reports on Prison Education*, HMSO.

Howard, U. (1991) 'Self, education and writing in nineteenth-century English communities', in Barton, D. & Ivanic, R. (eds) *Writing in the Community*, Sage.

Hughes, B. (1979) 'In defence of Ellen Wilkinson' *History Workshop*, 7.

Hughes, H.D. (1961) 'The pattern of recruitment to Ruskin', *Adult Education*, 34, 4, pp.201–5.

Hughes, H.D. (1977) 'Adult education: Russell and after', *Oxford Review of Education*, 3, 3, pp.283–90.

Hughes, H.D. (1981) 'Roles and functions in adult continuing education: statutory and voluntary bodies', *Educational Analysis*, 3, 3, pp.55–65.

Hughes, M. (1990) 'Rediscovering women adult educators', *Adults Learning*, 2, 4, pp.107–9.

Hughes, M. (1992) 'London took the lead', *Studies in the Education of Adults*, 24, 1, pp.41–55.

Hughes, M. & Kennedy, M. (1985) *New Futures: Changing Women's Education*, Routledge.

Hughes, V. (1995) 'Scottish college to fight its own battle', *Times Higher Educational Supplement*, 1195 (29 Sept).

Hunter, G. (1953) *Residential Colleges: Some New Developments in British Adult Education*, The Fund for Adult Education.

Hunter, G. (1959) 'Residential colleges for adult education', in Raybould, S. (ed.) *Trends in English Adult Education*, Heinemann, Oxford, pp.120–37.

Hutchison, R. & Forrester, S. (1987) *Arts Centres in the United Kingdom*, Policy Studies Institute.

Hyman, R. (1979) 'The politics of workplace trade unionism', *Capital and Class*, 8.

Illich, I. (1973) *Deschooling Society*, Penguin Books, Harmondsworth.

ILP Guild of Youth (1931) 'A socialist education policy', *Plebs*, 23, 4.

Inkster, I. (1985) *The Steam Intellect Societies*, University of Nottingham.

International Council for Adult Education (1990) *Voices Rising: A Bulletin about Women and Popular Education*, 4, 2.

Internationalist (1929) 'The colour line', *Plebs*, 21, 4.

Iphofen, R. (1993) 'The hidden costs of open learning', *Adults Learning*, 5, 2.

Jackson, J. (1964) 'Progress report on the National Extension College', *Where?*, 18, pp.22–4.

Jackson, K. (1970) 'Adult education and community development', *Studies in Adult Education*, 2, pp.165–72.

Jackson, K. (1980) 'Some fallacies in community education and their consequences in working-class areas', in Fletcher, C. & Thompson, N. (eds) *Issues in Community Education*, Falmer Press, Lewes, pp.39–46.

Jackson, K. (1989) 'A residential college in every community?', *Journal of Community Education*, 7, 3, pp.32–8.

Jackson, K. & Lovett, T. (1971) 'Universities and the WEA: an alternative approach', *Adult Education*, 44, 2.

Jeffs, T. (1983) 'Hands up for community education', *Youth and Policy*, 2, 2, pp.12–16.

Jeffs, T. (1992) 'The state, ideology and the community school movement', in Allen, G. & Martin, I. (eds) *Education and Community: The Politics of Practice*, Cassell, pp.17–27.

Jeffs, T. & Smith, M. (1991) 'Fallacy: the school is a poor base for youth work', in O'Hagan, B. (ed.) *The Charnwood Papers: Fallacies in Community Education*, Education Now, Ticknall, Derbyshire, pp.55–73.

Jennings, B. (1973) 'Albert Mansbridge', *Eighth Mansbridge Memorial Lecture*, University of Leeds.

Jennings, B. (1975) 'The Oxford Report reconsidered', *Studies in Adult Education*, 7, 1.

Jennings, B. (1976) information from research into WEA branch records.

Jennings, B. (1977) 'Revolting students – The Ruskin College dispute 1908–9', *Studies in Adult Education*, 9, 1, pp.1–16.

Jennings, B. (1978) 'Looking backwards and forwards', *WEA News*, ns, 15.

Jennings, B. (1979) *Knowledge is Power: A Short History of the WEA 1903–78*, University of Hull.

Jennings, B. (1983) 'The open-door university', *Studies in Adult Education*, 15, pp.47–59.

Jennings, B. (ed.) (1980) *Community Colleges in England and Wales*, NIACE.

Jepson, N.A. (1959) 'The local authorities and adult education' in Raybould, S.G. (ed.) *Trends in English Adult Education*, Heinemann, Oxford, pp.83–119.

Jepson, N.A. (1972) 'University adult education – 99 years old', *University of Leeds Review*, 15, 2, pp.275–304.

Jepson, N.A. (1973) *The Beginnings of English University Adult Education*, Michael Joseph.

Jerman, B. (1981) *The Lively Minded Women*, Heinemann.

Johnson, R. (1979) '"Really useful knowledge": radical education and working-class culture, 1790–1848', in Clarke, J., Crichter, C. & Johnson, R. (eds) *Working-class Culture: Studies in History and Theory*, Hutchinson, pp.75–102.

Johnson, R. (1983) 'Really useful knowledge: radical education and working class culture 1790–1848', in Tight, M. (ed.) *Educational Opportunities for Adults*, Routledge/Open University.

Johnson, R. (1988) 'Really useful knowledge 1790–1850: memories for education in the 1980s', in Lovett, T. (ed.) *Radical Approaches to Adult Education*, Routledge.

Johnston, R. (1992) 'Education and unwaged adults: relevance, social control and empowerment', in Allen, G. and Martin, I. (eds) *Education and Community: The Politics of Practice*, Cassell, pp.66–76.

Joint Committee of University of Oxford and Working Class Representatives (2nd edn, 1909, new edn, 1951) *Oxford and Working Class Education*, Oxford University Press.

Jones, D. (1976) *The North Devon Project*, Independent Broadcasting Authority.

Jones, H.A. (1974) 'The Russell Report on adult education in England and Wales', *Paedagogica Europea*, 9, 2, pp.65–75.

Jones, H.A. (1975) 'An outside view of adult education in Scotland', *Scottish Journal of Adult Education*, 1, 4, pp.30–32.

Jones, H.A. (1978) 'A view of adult education in the 1980s', *Adult Education*, 51, 3, pp.137–43.

Jones, H.A. & Charnley, A. (1978) *The Adult Literacy Campaign: A Study of Its Impact*, NIACE.

Jones, H.A. & Charnley, A. (1983) 'The adult literacy initiative 1974–79', in Tight, M. (ed.) *Educational Opportunities for Adults*, Routledge/Open University.

Jones, J. (1984) 'A Liverpool socialist education', *History Workshop Journal*, 18.

Jones, J. (1986) *Union Man – An Autobiography*, Collins.

Jones, P. (1978) *Community Education in Practice: A Review*, Social Evaluation Unit, University of Oxford.

Jones, P. (1990) 'Unesco and the politics of global literacy', *Comparative Education Review*, 34, 1, pp.41–60.

Joseph, K. (1989) Correspondence with John McIlroy.

Kahn, N. (1976) *Arts Britain Ignores*, Community Relations Council.

Kallen, D. (1979) 'Recurrent education and lifelong learning: definitions and distinctions', *World Yearbook of Education*, Kogan Page, London, pp.44–54

Kambouri, M. & Francis, H. (1994) *Time to Leave? Progression and Drop Out in Basic Skills Programmes*, ALBSU.

Kapitzke, C. (1995) *Literacy and Religion: The Textual Politics and Practice of Seventh-Day Adventism*, John Benjamins, Amsterdam/Philadelphia.

Kaye, B. (1970) *Live and Learn: The Story of Denman College 1948–70*, National Federation of Women's Institutes.

Kean, H. (1990) *Challenging the State: The Socialist and Feminist Experience 1900–1930*, Falmer Press, Brighton.

Keane, P. (1975) 'A study in early problems and policies in adult education: the Halifax Mechanics' Institute', *Social History* (Ottawa) , 8, 16, pp.255–74.

Keane, P. (1982) 'Early workers' education in Britain', *International Journal of Lifelong Education*, 1, 4, pp.353–61.

Keane, P. (1988) 'The state, laissez-faire and the education of adults in Britain', *International Journal of Lifelong Education*, 7, 1, pp.13–31.

Keddie, N. (1980) 'Adult education: an ideology of individualism', in Thompson, J. (ed.) *Adult Education for a Change*, Hutchinson, pp.45–64.

Keegan, D. (1994) *Otto Peters on Distance Education*, Routledge.

Keithley, G.R. (1982) 'Industrial Relations Training for Shop Stewards: Workplace Perception of its Objectives, Impact and Consequence', unpublished PhD thesis, University of Durham.

Kelly, J. & Grooms, C. (1986) 'TUC basic course: participants' views', *The Industrial Tutor* (Spring).

Kelly, T. (1956) 'The new approach to university adult education', *Adult Education*, 29, 3, pp.174–77.

Kelly, T. (1957) *George Birkbeck: Pioneer of Adult Education*, University of Liverpool.

Kelly, T. (1973) 'Two reports: 1919 and 1973', *Studies in Adult Education*, 5, 2, pp.113–23.

Kelly, T. (1977) *A History of Public Libraries in Great Britain 1845–1975*, The Library Association.

Kelly, T. (3rd edn, 1992) *A History of Adult Education in Great Britain*, Liverpool University Press.

Kendall, W. (1969) *The Revolutionary Movement in Britain 1900–21*, Weidenfeld and Nicolson.

Kibel, R. (1984) 'Education in NALGO', *The Industrial Tutor* (Spring).

King, D.S. (1993) 'The Conservatives and training policy 1979–1992: from a tripartite to a neo-liberal regime', *Political Studies*, 61, pp.214–35.

King, E.J. (1955) 'The Relationship between Adult Education and Social Attitudes in English Industrial Society', unpublished PhD thesis, University of London.

Kirkwood, C. (1978) 'Adult education and the concept of community', *Adult Education*, 51, pp.145–51.

Kirkwood, C. (1990) *Vulgar Eloquence*, Polygon Press, Edinburgh.

Kirkwood, G. (1991) 'Fallacy: the community educator should be a non-directive facilitator', in O'Hagan, B. (ed.) *The Charnwood Papers: Fallacies in Community Education*, Education Now, Ticknall, Derbyshire, pp.40–54.

Kirkwood, G. & C. (1989) *Living Adult Education: Freire in Scotland*, Open University Press.

Kunzel, K. (1975) 'The missionary dons: prelude to university extension', *Studies in Adult Education*, 7, pp.34–52.

Labour Party (1952) *Annual Conference Report*.

Lane, T. (1974) *The Union Makes Us Strong*, Arrow Books.

Langham, J. (1990) *Teachers and Television: A History of the IBA's Educational Fellowship Scheme*, John Libbey.

Laslett, P. (1979) *The Education of the Elderly in Britain*, Elmgrant Trust/National Extension College.

Laurent, J. (1984) 'Science, society and politics in late nineteenth century England: a further look at Mechanics' Institutes', *Social Studies of Science*, 14, 4, pp.585–619.

Lawson, J. & Silver, H. (1973) *A Social History of Education in England*, Methuen.

Lawson, K. (1977) 'Community education: a critical assessment', *Adult Education*, 50, pp.6–13.

Legge, D. (1977) 'Rewards and scars of a period of radical change', *Times Higher Education Supplement*, 293, p.13.

Legge, D. (1982) *The Education of Adults in Britain*, Open University Press.

Lewenhak, S. (1977) *Women and Trade Unions – An Outline History of Women in the British Trade Union Movement*, Ernest Benn.

Lewis, J. (?1992) *Inner London Report: The Future of the WEA in Inner London*, WEA London District.

Lewis, M.M. (1953) *The Importance of Illiteracy*, Harrap.

Lewis, R. (1984) 'The Central Labour College: its decline and fall 1919–29', *Welsh History Review*, 12, 2.

Lewis, R. (1993) *Leaders and Teachers: Adult Education and the Challenge of Labour in South Wales 1906–1940*, University of Wales Press, Cardiff.

Lewis, R. (1994) 'Speaking up for open learning', *Adults Learning*, 5, 7.

Library and Information Statistics Unit (LISU) (1994) *Library and Information Statistics*, Loughborough University for the British Library Research and Development Department.

Lieven, M. (1987) 'Adult liberal education', *Adult Education*, 60, 3, pp.225–30.

Lieven, M. (1988) 'Arguments for residential colleges', *Journal of Further and Higher Education*, 12, 2, pp.80–5.

Lieven, M. (1989) 'Access courses after 10 years: a review', *Higher Education Quarterly*, 43, 2, pp.160–74.

Lieven, M. (1991) 'State influence on adult education in Britain and Denmark: the case of the residential colleges', *Studies in Higher Education*, 16, 1, pp.29–40.

Limage, L. (1986) 'Adult literacy policy in industrialised countries', *Comparative Education Review*, 30, pp.50–72.

Limage, L. (1990) 'Adult literacy and basic education in Europe and North America: from recognition to provision', *Comparative Education*, 26, 1, pp.125–40.

Lloyd, B. (1991) *Discovering the Strength of our Voices: Women and Literacy Programs*, Canadian Congress for Learning Opportunities for Women, Toronto.

Lloyd, J. (1983) 'Unions accept employers' right to ratify courses', *The Financial Times*, 15 March.

Lloyd, W. (1950) *How to Run Discussion Groups*, WEA.

Lobley, G. & Moss, W. (1990) 'ILEA Goodbye!', *RaPAL Bulletin*, 11 (Spring).

London Borough of Newham (1985) *Going Community: Community Education in Newham*, London Borough of Newham Education Committee.

Loney, M. (1983) *Community Against Government*, Heinemann.

Longley, C. (ed.) (1975) *BBC Adult Literacy Handbook*, BBC.

Lovett, T. (1975) *Adult Education, Community Development and the Working Class*, Ward Lock Education.

Lovett, T. (1994) 'Bridging the sectarian divide in Northern Ireland: the Ulster People's College', *Adults Learning*, 5, 6, pp.155–57.

Lovett, T. (ed.) (1988) *Radical Approaches to Adult Education*, Routledge.

Lovett, T., Clarke, C. & Kilmurray, A. (1983) *Adult Education and Community Action*, Croom Helm.

Low, G. (1988) 'The MSC: a failure of democracy', in Morris, M. & Griggs, C. (eds) *Education – The Wasted Years? 1973–1988*, Falmer Press, Lewes.

Lowe, J. (1970) *Adult Education in England and Wales: A Critical Study*, Michael Joseph.

Lowe, R.A. (1972) 'Some forerunners of R.H.Tawney's Longton tutorial class', *History of Education*, 1, pp.43–57.

Lyddon, D. (1984) 'Demythologising the downturn', *International Socialism*, 25.

McCaffery, J. (1985) 'Women in adult basic education: barriers to access', in Hughes, M. & Kennedy, M. (eds) *New Futures: Changing Women's Education*, Routledge.

McCarthy, W. (1964) *The Closed Shop in Britain*, Blackwell, Oxford.

McCarthy, W. (1966) 'The Role of Shop Stewards in British Industrial Relations', *Research Paper 1, Royal Commission on Trade Unions*, HMSO.

McClelland, K. (1990) 'The transmission of collective knowledge: apprenticeship in engineering and shipbuilding, 1850–1914', in Summerfield, P. & Evans, E. (eds) *Technical Education and the State since 1850*, Manchester University Press.

Mace, J. (1979) *Working with Words*, Writers and Readers Publishing Co-operative.

Mace, J. (1992) *Talking About Literacy*, Routledge.

Mace, J. (ed.) (1993) *Women's Lives, Women's Literacy*, Papers from the 1993 Women and Literacy Conference, Literacy Research Group, Goldsmiths College, University of London.

Mace, J., Moss, W., Pidgeon, S. & Plackett, E. (1993) *Literacy and Gender*, Papers from the Women and Literacy Conference, Literacy Research Group, Goldsmiths College, University of London.

Mace, J. & Yarnit, M. (eds) (1987) *Time Off to Learn: Paid Educational Leave and Low Paid Workers*, Methuen.

McGivney, V. (1990) *Education's for Other People: Access to Education for Non-participant Adults*, NIACE.

McGivney, V. (1994) 'Women, education and training: a research report', *Adults Learning*, 5, 5.

McIlroy, J. (1980) 'Education for the Labour movement: UK experience past and present, *Labour Studies Journal*, 4, 3.

McIlroy, J. (1981) 'Fighting racism in the classroom – Part 1', *The Industrial Tutor* (Spring).

McIlroy, J. (1982a) 'TUC Stage 2 – an opportunity to change course?', *The Industrial Tutor* (Spring).

McIlroy, J. (1982b) 'Sexism and trade union education', *Trade Union Studies Journal*, 5.

McIlroy, J. (1983) 'Race relations and the traditions of adult education', in Tight, M. (ed.) *Opportunities for Adult Education*, Croom Helm.

McIlroy, J. (1985a) 'Adult education and the role of the client – the TUC Education Scheme 1929–1980', *Studies in the Education of Adults*, 16, 2.

McIlroy, J. (1985b) 'Goodbye Mr Chips?', *The Industrial Tutor* (Autumn).

McIlroy, J. (1987) 'Continuing education and the universities in Britain: the political context', *International Journal of Lifelong Education*, 6, 1, pp.27–59.

McIlroy, J. (1988) 'A turning point in university adult continuing education', *Adult Education*, 61, 1, pp.7–14.

McIlroy, J. (1989) 'The funding of adult and continuing education in Britain: the acid test', *International Journal of Lifelong Education*, 8, 4, pp.315–44.

McIlroy, J. (1990a) 'J.P.M. Millar 1893–1989', *Labour History Review*, 55, 1.

McIlroy, J. (1990b) 'J.P.M. Millar: an appreciation', *Studies in the Education of Adults*, 22, 1.

McIlroy, J. (1990c) 'The demise of the National Council of Labour Colleges', in Simon, B. (ed.) *The Search for Enlightenment: The Working Class and Adult Education in the Twentieth Century*, NIACE.

McIlroy, J. (1990d) 'The triumph of technical training', in Simon, B. (ed.) *loc. cit.*

McIlroy, J. (1992) 'The rise and fall of IWCE in the UK', in McIlroy, J., Spencer, B. & Welton, M., 'Symposium: beyond workplace learning', *Proceedings of the 11th Annual conference of the Canadian Association for the Study of Adult Education*, CASAE, Saskatchewan.

McIlroy, J. (1993) 'Tales from smoke-filled rooms', *Studies in the Education of Adults*, 25, 1.

McIlroy, J. (2nd edn, 1995a) *Trade Unions in Britain Today*, Manchester University Press.

McIlroy, J. (1995b) 'The dying of the light: a radical look at trade union education', in Mayo, M. & Thompson, J. (eds) *Adult Learning, Critical Intelligence and Social Change*, NIACE.

McIlroy, J. & Brown, J. (1980) 'Giving the workers what they want: the WEA and industrial education', *Adult Education*, 53, 2.

McIlroy, J. & Simon, B. (1991) 'Once again: J.P.M. Millar and independent working class education', *Labour History Review*, 56, 1.

McIlroy, J. & Spencer, B. (1988) *University Adult Education in Crisis*, University of Leeds.

McIlroy, J., Spencer, B. & Welton, M. (1992) 'Symposium: beyond workplace learning', *Proceedings of the 11th Annual conference of the Canadian Association for the Study of Adult Education*, CASAE, Saskatchewan.

McIntosh, N.E. (1975) 'Open admission: an open or revolving door?', *Universities Quarterly* (Spring), pp.171–81.

McIntosh, N.E., Calder, J.A. & Swift, B. (1976) *A Degree of Difference*, SRHE.

McIntosh, N.E. & Woodley, A. (1974) 'The Open University and second chance education', *Paedagogica Europaea*, 2, pp.85–100.

McIntyre, S. (1980) *A Proletarian Science – Marxism in Britain 1917–33*, Cambridge University Press.

Mack, J.A. (1938) 'Newbattle Abbey College and what it is accomplishing', *Life and Leisure Pamphlets*, 9, British Institute of Adult Education.

Mackenzie, N., Postgate, R., & Scupham, J. (1975) *Open Learning: Systems and Problems in Post-Secondary Education*, Unesco Press, Paris.

Mackenzie, R. (1989) *Partnership in Continuing Education: A Review of the Issues*, FEU.

McKibbin, R. (1990) *The Ideologies of Class: Social Relations in Britain 1880–1950*, Oxford University Press.

McLean, J. (1917) 'Independence in working class education', in Milton, N. (ed.) (1978) *John McLean: In the Rapids of Revolution*, Allison & Busby.

Maclure, J.S. (ed.) (5th edn, 1986) *Educational Documents*, Methuen.

McNair, S. (1992) *The Work of UDACE*, NIACE.

McNay, I. (1993) 'Marginalised or mainstreamed: future scenarios for education for adults', *Adults Learning*, 5, 1, pp.23–4.

Macrae, I. (1984) 'The making of a university, the breakdown of a movement: Reading University Extension College to the University of Reading, 1892–1925', *International Journal of Lifelong Education*, 13, 1, pp.3–18.

Mactavish, J.M. (1918, reprinted 1981) 'The WEA: its propaganda, organisation and method', in *The WEA Education Year Book 1918*, University of Nottingham.

Mahon, P. & Stirling, J. (1988) '"I can do that": the impact of trade union education', *The Industrial Tutor* (Spring).

Malcolm, J. (1992) 'The culture of difference: women's education re-examined', in Miller, N. and West, L. (eds) *Changing Culture and Adult Learning*, SCUTREA, pp.52–5.

Malone, E.W.F. (1960) 'The WEA – a new phase', *Adult Education*, 33, 3.

Mannion-Brunt, J. (1994) 'Derbyshire employee development initiatives', *Adults Learning*, 5, 9, pp.229–31.

Mansbridge, A. (1913) *University Tutorial Classes*, Longmans, Green.

Mansbridge, A. (1920) *An Adventure in Working Class Education*, Longmans, Green.

Mansbridge, A. (1944) *A Kingdom of the Mind*, Dent.

Marcy, M. (1922) 'Our teaching methods', *Plebs*, 14, 9.

Marks, H. (1949) *Community Associations and Adult Education*, NCSS.

Marks, H. (1982) 'Unemployment and adult education in the 1930s', *Studies in Adult Education*, 14, pp.1–15.

Marriott, S. (1981a) *A Backstairs to a Degree: Demand for an Open University in Late Victorian England*, University of Leeds.

Marriott, S. (1981b) 'State aid – the earliest demands for government support of university extra-mural education', *Studies in Adult Education*, 13, 1, pp.28–43.

Marriott, S. (1983a) 'Oxford and working-class adult education: a foundation myth re-examined', *History of Education*, 12, 4, pp.285–99.

Marriott, S. (1983b) 'The Whisky Money and the University Extension Movement: golden opportunity or artificial stimulus?', *Journal of Educational Administration and History*, 15, 2, pp.7–15.

Marriott, S. (1984) *Extramural Empires: Service and Self-interest in English University Adult Education 1873–1983*, University of Nottingham.

Marriott, S. (1985) *University Extension Lecturers: The Organisation of Extramural Employers in England 1873–1914*, Educational Administration and History Monograph no. 15, University of Leeds.

Marsh, A. (1966) *A Collection of Teaching Documents and Case Studies*, Pergamon Press, Oxford.

Martin, G.C. (1924) *The Adult School Movement*, National Adult School Union.

Martin, I. (1986) 'Education and community: reconstructing the relationship', *Journal of Community Education*, 5, 3, pp.17–23.

Martin, I. (1992) 'Education, community and policy', *Community Education Network*, 12, 1, pp.15–16.

Martin, I. (1993) '"New Times": new directions?', *Adults Learning*, 4, 6, pp.143–45.

Martindall, R. (1964) 'Trade union education – the end of a chapter', *Labour Monthly* (October).

Marwick, A. (1982) *British Society Since 1945*, Penguin Books, Harmondsworth.

Mass, W. & Lazonick, W. (1990) 'The British cotton industry and international competitive advantage: the state of the debates', *Business History*, 32, 4, pp.9–65.

Mathers, A (1995) 'Community education and local government reforms', *Concept*, 5, 2, pp.4–9.

Matthews, T. (1977) in Tappolet, F. (ed.) *Adult Education by Television*, European Broadcasting Union.

Matthews, T. (1978) *Trade Union Studies: A Partnership in Adult Education Between the BBC, the TUC and the WEA*, BBC.

Mayfield, G.E.T. (1965) 'The University of Hull Department of Adult Education 1928–1960', in Styler, W.E. (ed.) *Adult Education in East Yorkshire 1875–1960*, University of Hull.

Mayo, M. (1974) 'Community development: a radical alternative?', in Bailey, R. and Brake, M. (eds) *Radical Social Work*, Edward Arnold, pp.129–43.

Mayo, M. & Thompson, J. (eds) (1995) *Adult Learning, Critical Intelligence and Social Change*, NIACE.

Meacham, S. (1987) *Toynbee Hall and Social Reform 1880–1914*, Yale University.

Mee, G. (1980) *Organisation for Adult Education*, Longman.

Mee, G. & Wiltshire, H. (1978) *Structure and Performance in Adult Education*, Longman.

Mellor, W. (1920) *Direct Action*, Leonard Parsons.

Merz, C. (1988) *After the Vote: The Story of the Townswomen's Guilds*, TWG.

Michaels, M.I. (1938) 'Revolt in economics', *The Highway*, 30.

Middlemas, K. (1979) *Politics in Industrial Society*, Andre Deutsch.

Midwinter, E. (1972) *Projections: An Educational Priority Area at Work*, Ward Lock Education.

Midwinter, E. (1973) *Patterns of Community Education*, Ward Lock Education.

Midwinter, E. (1975) *Education and the Community*, George Allen & Unwin.

Midwinter, E. (ed.) (1984) *Mutual Aid Universities*, Croom Helm.

Miles, A. (1984) 'Workers' education: the Communist Party and the Plebs League in the 1920s', *History Workshop*, 18.

Miles, T. & Gilroy, D. (1986) *Dyslexia at College*, Methuen.

Mill, J.S. (1869) *The Subjection of Women*, London.

Millar, J.P.M. (1922) 'American teachers on the best teaching methods', *Plebs*, 14, 2.

Millar, J.P.M. (1929) 'The BBC and bias', *Plebs*, 21, 3.

Millar, J.P.M. (1930) 'The NCLC at work', *Plebs*, 22, 11.

Millar, J.P.M. (1931a) 'We are taken to task', *Plebs*, 23, 7.

Millar, J.P.M. (1931b) 'Our rejoinder', *Plebs*, 23, 9.

Millar, J.P.M. (1943) *Post-war Education*, NCLC, Tillicoultry.

Millar, J.P.M. (1948) 'Reply to Horace Green', *Plebs*, 40, 5.

Millar, J.P.M. (1951) *Education and Power*, NCLC, Tillicoultry.

Millar, J.P.M. (1979) *The Labour College Movement*, NCLC Publishing Society.

Millar, J.P.M. & Woodburn, A. (1936) *Bias in the Schools*, NCLC, Tillicoultry.

Miller, H. (1976) *Leisure and the Changing City*, Routledge.

Millward, N. & Stevens, M. (1986) *British Workplace Industrial Relations 1980–1984*, Gower, Aldershot.

Millward, N., Stevens, M., Smart, D. & Hawes, W. (1992) *Workplace Industrial Relations in Transition*, Dartmouth Publishing, Aldershot.

Milton, N. (1978) (ed.) *John McLean: In the Rapids of Revolution*, Allison & Busby.

Ministry of Education (1947a) Circular 133, 'Schemes of Further Education and Plans for County Colleges'.

Ministry of Education (1947b) *Pamphlet Number 8, Further Education: The Scope and Content of its Opportunities under the Education Act of 1944*, HMSO.

Ministry of Education (1954) *The Organisation and Finance of Adult Education in England and Wales* (The Ashby Report), HMSO.

Ministry of Labour (1923/24) *Annual Report*, HMSO

Ministry of Labour and National Service (1947) *Report for the Years 1939–1946*, HMSO.

Ministry of Reconstruction (1919) *Final Report of the Adult Education Committee*, Cmd. 321, HMSO.

Mitch, D.F. (1992) *The Rise of Popular Literacy in Victorian England: The Influence of Private Choice and Public Policy*, University of Pennsylvania Press.

Mitchell, D.G. (1964) 'An LEA blueprint', *Adult Education*, 37, pp.6–13.

Mitchell, G. & Field, J. (1980) 'Liberal education in a residential college', *Liberal Education*, 41, pp.15–21.

Moir, G. (ed.) (1967) 'Progress report', in *Teaching and Television: ETV Explained*, Pergamon Press, Oxford.

Moore, R. (1981) 'Political education in practice', *The Industrial Tutor* (Autumn).

Moore, R. (1994) 'Ford EDAP: breaking through the barriers', *Adults Learning*, 5, 9, pp.225–6.

Moore Smith, G.C. (1912) *The Story of the People's College, Sheffield, 1842–1878*.

Moran, M. (1985) *Politics and Society in Britain*, Macmillan.

Morgan, K.O. (1985) *Labour in Power 1945–51*, Oxford University Press.

Morley, D. & Worpole, K. (1982) *The Republic of Letters*, London.

Morris, C. (1984) 'Universities of the Third Age', *Adult Education*, 57, 2.

Morris, C. & Nwenmely, H. (1994) 'The Kweyol language and literacy project', in Hamilton, M., Barton, D. & Ivanic, R. (eds) *Worlds of Literacy*, Multilingual Matters, Clevedon.

Morris, H. (1924) *The Village College*, quoted in Ree, H. (1981) 'The origins of community education', *Outlines*, Community Education Development Centre, Coventry.

Munn, P. & MacDonald, C. (1988) *Adult Participation in Education and Training*, Scottish Council for Research in Education, Edinburgh.

Munns, R. & Strutt, P. (1981) 'Adult education in the workplace: values and conflicts in industrial language training', *Adult Education*, 53, 2, pp.79–84.

Murie, A. (1946) 'The discussion method', *Plebs*, 28, 12.

Murphy, R. (1985) 'Two working class educational institutions in mid-19th century Manchester', *History of Education Society Bulletin* (Spring), pp.8–13.

Murray, A. (1981) 'Race relations in shop steward courses – some recent initiatives', *The Industrial Tutor* (Autumn).

Museums Association (1971) 'Museums in education', *Report*, 1.

National Association of Teachers in Further and Higher Education (1993) *Adult Education*, NATFHE.

National Council of Labour Colleges (NCLC) (1923) 'Submission to TUC Education Sub-Committee'.

NCLC (1930) *Education for Emancipation.*

NCLC (1952) *Annual Conference Report.*

National Federation of Voluntary Literacy Schemes/ALBSU (1983) Action and Words: Sharing Literacy Skills in Community Groups, ALBSU.

National Institute of Adult Continuing Education (NIACE) (1989–90, 1992–3 & 1994–5) *Annual Reports.*

NIACE (1991) Director's Report to Council, June 1991.

NIACE (1994a) *Yearbook 1994–5.*

NIACE (1994b) *What Price the Learning Society?*

NIACE Archive:
(a) British Institute of Adult Education, Inaugration Committee Minutes, 1921.
(b) *ibid.*, Executive Committee Minutes, 1921–9.
(c) *ibid.*, AGM Minutes, 1922–8.
(d) *ibid.*, Agenda Committee (Unemployment) Minutes, 1933.
(e) *ibid.*, 14th Annual Report, 1934–5.
(f) National Foundation of Adult Education, Council Minutes, 1946–9.
(g) *ibid.*, Executive Committee Minutes, 1946–9.
(h) National Institute of Adult Education, Council Minutes, 1949–52.
(j) *ibid.*, Executive Committee Minutes, 1949–52.
(k) *ibid.*, Report and Financial Statement, 1950–1.
(l) *ibid.*, Annual Report, 1951–2.
(m) *ibid.*, Report and Fiancial Statement, 1959–60.
(n) World Association of Adult Education Minute Book, 1918–25.
(p) *ibid.*, Constitution, 1919.

National Institute of Adult Education (NIAE) Executive Committee, 26 June 1951, Appendix III, 'Relations between Adult Education and other forms of Further Education'.

Neale, J.G., Nye, M. & Belbin, E. (1968) 'Adult training: the use of programmed instruction', *Occupational Psychology*, 42, 1, pp.23–31.

Nicholas, S. (1995) *Education, Friendship and Fun: A History of the National Association of Women's Clubs*, NAWC.

Northern College (1983) 'A New Approach to Adult Education', paper presented to the Academic Board to the Council of Management of Northern College.

Northern College (1990/91) *Prospectus*.

Northern Ireland Textiles Industry Training Board (1969) *Report, 1 April 1968 – 31 March 1969*, HMSO, Belfast.

Norwood Report (1943) *Curriculum and Examinations in Secondary Schools: A Report of the Secondary Schools Examination Council*, HMSO.

Nottingham University College (1926) *Adult Education in the East Midlands 1920–26*.

OECD (1971) *Equal Educational Opportunity: A Statement of the Problem with Special Reference to Recurrent Education*, OECD, Paris.

OECD/CERI (1973) *Recurrent Education: A Strategy for Lifelong Learning*, OEDC, Paris.

O'Hare, B. (1981) 'LEA provision for adult education in the UK', *Irish Journal of Education*, 15, 1 & 2, pp.53–69.

Open University (1979) 'The first ten years', *Sesame* special edition.

Open University (1983) *Racism in the Workplace and Community*, Open University.

Open University (1994) 'Technology strategy for academic advantage', Senate Paper S/110/3.

Open University (1995) *Report of the Vice-Chancellor 1994*.

O'Rourke, P. (ed.) (1992) *Working with UDACE*, NIACE.

O'Rourke, R. & Mace, J. (1992) *Versions and Variety: A Report on Student Writing and Publishing in Adult Literacy Education*, Avanti Books, Stevenage.

O'Rourke, R., Pearse, J. & Tinman, A. (1992) 'WordPower and the publishing of student writing', *RaPAL Bulletin* 19 (Autumn).

Orwell, G. (1943) 'Poetry and the microscope', quoted in Orwell, S. & Angus, I. (eds) (1968) *The Collected Essays, Journalism and Letters of George Orwell*, 2, Secker and Warburg.

Owens, B. (1989) 'Paid educational leave and educational advance', *The Industrial Tutor* (Spring).

Owens, E.E.L. (1969) 'The size, efficiency and effectiveness of Local Education Authorities', *Journal of Educational Administration and History*, 1, 2, pp.30–39.

Page, G.T. (1967) *The Industrial Training Act and After*, Andre Deutsch.

Paine, T. (1969 edn) *Rights of Man*, ed. Collins, H. Penguin Books, Harmondsworth.

Palme Dutt, R. (1963) 'Notes of the month', *Labour Monthly* (September).

Park, T. (1969) 'Trade union education', in Coates, K., Topham, T. & Barratt Brown, M. (eds) *Trade Union Register*, Spokesman, Nottingham.

Patterson, R. (1973) 'Social change as an educational aim', *Adult Education*, 45, pp.353–59.

Paul, E. & C. (1918) *Independent Working Class Education*, Workers' Socialist Federation.

Paul, E. & C. (1921) *Proletcult*, Leonard Parsons.

Paul, E. & C. (1927) 'Research work – the use of public libraries', *Plebs*, 19, 2.

Payne, J. (nd) 'Active Citizenship and Adult Learning in Inner London', *Research Paper in Continuing Education*, 2, University of Warwick.

Peers, R. (1958) *Adult Education: A Comparative Study*, Routledge & Kegan Paul.

Pelling, H. (1984) *The Labour Governments 1945–51*, Macmillan.

Pentz, M. (1991) 'It can't be done', *The Second Ritchie Calder Memorial Lecture*, Open University (21 March).

Percy, K. (1989) 'An Evaluation of the FEU REPLAN project', FEU.

Percy, K., Burton, D. and Withnall, A. (1994) *Self-directed Learning among Adults: The Challenge for Continuing Education*, ALL, University of Lancaster.

Perry, W. (1976) *Open University*, Open University.

Peters, A. (1967) *British Further Education: A Critical Textbook*, Pergamon, Oxford.

Phillips, A. & Putnam, T. (1980) 'Education for emancipation: the movement for independent working class education 1908–1928', *Capital and Class*, 10, pp.18–42.

Phippen, F. (1921) 'Teaching methods', *Plebs*, 13, 7.

Pimlott, J.A.R. (1970) 'Continuing education', *Trends in Education*, DES, pp.50–55.

*Plebs* (1909a) 1, 3,'Editorial'.

*Plebs* (1909b) 1, 9, 'Editorial'.

*Plebs* (1914) 6, 8, 'Central Labour College'.

*Plebs* (1923) 15, 5, 'Our point of view'.

*Plebs* (1924) 16, 10, 'The Plebs Annual Meet'.

*Plebs* (1925) 17, 10, 'The NCLC Conference'.

*Plebs* (1928) 20, 8, 'The Annual Meeting of the NCLC'.

*Plebs* (1929) 21, 5, 'Report – Division 10'.

Pollins, H. (1984) *The History of Ruskin College*, Ruskin College Library.

Poster, C. (1971) *The School and the Community*, Macmillan.

Poster, C. (1982) *Community Education: Its Development and Management*, Heinemann.

Postgate, R. (1926) 'Research work – what it is and how to set about it', *Plebs*, 18, 11.

Postgate, R. (1931) 'History and "The News of the World"', *Plebs*, 22, 1.

Poulantza, N. (1978) *State, Power, Socialism*, Verso.

Powell, B. (1992a) *Securing Adult Learning* NIACE.

Powell, B. (1992b) *Adult Learners and the Further and Higher Education Act*, NIACE.

Powell, M.J. (1964) *The Story of Hillcroft College: The First Forty Years 1920–1960*, Langham Herald Press, Farnham.

Pratt, J. (1971) 'Open, University!', *Higher Education Review* (Spring) pp.6–24.

Pratt, J. (1973) 'Notes', *Higher Education Review* (Spring) pp.66–68.

Price, R. (1986) *Labour in British Society*, Routledge.

Principal Community Education Officers/Scottish Community Education Council (1991) *Adult Education in the Community Education Service*, Scottish Community Education Council, Edinburgh.

Pritt, D.N (1963) *The Labour Government 1945–51*, Lawrence & Wishart.

Pumfrey, P.D. & Reason, R. (1991) *Specific Learning Difficulties: Challenges and Responses*, NFER-Routledge.

Purvis, J. (1980) 'Working class women and adult education in nineteenth-century Britain', *History of Education*, 9, 3, pp.193–212.

Purvis, J. (1981) 'Inequality in the education of working class women, 1854–1900', *History of Education*, 10, 4, pp.227–43.

Purvis, J. (1989) *Hard Lessons*, Polity Press.

Radcliffe, C.J. (1986) 'Mutual improvement societies in the West Riding 1835–1900', *Journal of Educational Administration and History*, 18, 2, pp.1–16.

Radcliffe, J. & Salkeld, R. (eds) (1983) *Towards Computer Literacy*, BBC.

Raybould, S.G. (1949) *The WEA: The Next Phase*, WEA.

Raybould, S.G. (1951) *The English Universities and Adult Education*, WEA.

Raybould, S.G. (1957) 'Adult education in transition', *Political Education Quarterly*, 28, 3, pp.243–54.

Raybould, S.G. (1959) 'The Ashby Report and afterwards', in Raybould, S.G. (ed.) *Trends in English Adult Education*, Heinemann, Oxford.

Raybould, S.G. (1964) *University Extra-Mural Education in England 1945–62: A Study in Finance and Policy*, Michael Joseph.

Raybould, S.G. (ed.) (1959) *Trends in English Adult Education*, Heinemann, Oxford.

Ree, H. (1973) *Educator Extraordinary*, Longman.

Ree, H. (1981) 'The origins of community education', *Outlines*, Community Education Development Centre, Coventry.

Ree, H. (ed.) (1984) *The Henry Morris Collection*, Cambridge University Press.

Ree, J. (1984) *Proletarian Philosophers: Problems in Socialist Culture in Britain 1900–1940*, Clarendon Press, Oxford.

Rees, A.M. (1973) 'Trade union officials and government training centres', *British Journal of Industrial Relations*, 11, 2, pp.229–41.

Rees, D. (1982) *Preparation for Crisis: Adult Education 1945–1980*, G.W. & A. Hesketh, Ormskirk.

Reid Smith, E.R. (1968) 'The Attitudes of Chartered Librarians in NW England Towards Adult Education', unpublished MA thesis (Manchester University), quoted in Bacon, A. (ed.) (1980) *Adult Education and Public Libraries in the 1980s*, Library Association.

Rendell, M. (1977) 'The contribution of the women's labour movement to the winning of the franchise', in Middleton, L. (ed.) *Women in the Labour Movement*, Croom Helm.

Research and Practice in Adult Literacy (1994) *RaPAL Bulletin*, special issue on bilingual literacy, Avanti Books, Stevenage.

Rex, J. (1981) 'A note on trade union education and racism', *The Industrial Tutor* (Autumn).

Reynolds, A. (1931) 'The WEAer replies', *Plebs*, 23, 9.

Reynolds, J. *et al.* (1994) *A Town in Action: Voluntary Networks in Retford*, University of Nottingham Department of Adult Education.

Richards, D. (1958) *Offspring of the Old Vic: A History of Morley College*, Routledge & Kegan Paul.

Rivis, V. & Haughton, L. (1993) 'Positive guidance strategies for women', *Adults Learning*, 3, 5.

Roberts, C., Davies, E. & Jupp, T. (1992) *Language and Discrimination*, Longman.

Roberts, J.H. (1970) 'The NCLC: an Experiment in Workers' Education,' unpublished MSc thesis, University of Edinburgh.

Robinson, B. (1985) 'Bilingualism and mother-tongue maintenance in Britain', in Brumfit, C. (ed.) *English as a Second Language*, Pergamon Press, Oxford.

Robinson, J. (1982) *Learning Over the Air: 60 Years of Partnership in Adult Learning*, BBC.

Robinson, J. (1983) 'Broadcasting and adult learning in the UK 1922–1982', in Tight, M. (ed.) *Education for Adults*, Open University Press.

Robinson, J. & Barnes, N. (eds) (1968) *New Media and Methods in Industrial Training*, BBC.

Roche, M. (1992) *Rethinking Citizenship*, Polity Press.

Rockhill, K. (1987) 'Gender, language and the politics of literacy', *British Journal of the Sociology of Education*, 8, 2, pp.153–67.

Roderick, G. & Stephens, M. (1973a) 'The role of 19th century literary and philosophical societies in fostering adult education', *Journal of Educational Administration and History*, 5, 1, pp.28–33.

Roderick, G. & Stephens, M. (1973b) 'Middle class adult education and training: the Royal Institute in the 19th century', *Vocational Aspect*, 25, pp.39–48.

Roderick, G. & Stephens, M. (1985) 'Steam intellect created: the educational roles of the Mechanics' Institutes', and 'Mechanics' Institutes and the state', in Inkster, I. (1985) *The Steam Intellect Societies*, University of Nottingham, pp.20–32, 60–72.

Rogers, B. (1984) 'The trend of reading standards reassessed', *Educational Research*, 26, 3, pp.153–66.

Rogers, J. (1989) *Adults Learning*, Open University Press.

Rogers, J. (1993) *Report Back*, 1, 6, WEA.

Rogers, V. (1994) 'Feminist work and community education', in Jacobs, S. & Popple, K. (eds) *Community Work in the 1990s*, Spokesman, Nottingham, pp.65–77.

Rose, J. (1993) 'Willingly to school: the working class response to elementary education in Britain 1875–1918', *Journal of British Studies*, 32, pp.114–38.

Rowbotham, S. (1969) 'The call of university extension teaching 1873–1900', *University of Birmingham History Journal*, 12, 1, pp.57–71.

Rowbotham, S. (1973) *Hidden from History: Three Hundred Years of Women's Oppression and the Fight Against It*, Pluto Press.

Rowbotham, S. (1981) 'Travellers in a strange country: responses of working class students to the University Extension Movement 1873–1910', *History Workshop Journal*, 12, pp.62–95.

Rowntree, J.W. & Binns, H.B. (1985) *A History of the Adult School Movement*, University of Nottingham Department of Adult Education.

Royal Commission on Trade Unions and Employers Association (1968) *Report* (The Donovan Report), HMSO.

Royle, E. (1971) 'Mechanics' Institutes and the working classes 1840–1860', *The Historical Journal*, 14, 2, pp.305–21.

Rubenstein, D. (1979) 'Ellen Wilkinson reconsidered', *History Workshop*, 7.

Russell, L. see DES (1973).

Sadler, M.E. (1907) *Continuation Schools in England and Elsewhere*, University of Manchester.

Salkeld, R. (1979) *What Right Have You Got?: The First Two Years*, BBC.

Sargant, N. (1991) *Learning and Leisure*, NIACE.

Sargant, N. (1992) *Adult Learners, Broadcasting and Channel 4*, Channel 4 Telelvision.

Scarlyn Wilson, N. (1948) *Education in H.M. Forces 1939–46*, Evans Brothers.

Schuller, T. & Robertson, D. (1984) 'The impact of union education: a framework for evaluation', *Labour Studies Journal*, 9, 1.

Schwab, I. & Stone, J. (1987) *Language, Writing and Publishing*, Afro-Caribbean Language and Literacy Project, Inner London Education Authority.

Scott, P. (1984) *The Crisis of the University*, Croom Helm.

Scottish Community Education Council (1984) *Training for Change*, Edinburgh.

Scottish Community Education Council (1988) *Adult Education: Now ... and Then*, Edinburgh.

Scottish Community Education Council (1994) *Open All Hours?*, Edinburgh.

Scottish Education Department (1975) *Adult Education: The Challenge of Change* (The Alexander Report), HMSO, Edinburgh.

Scottish Education Department (1977) *Professional Education and Training for Community Education* (The Carnegy Report), HMSO, Edinburgh.

Scottish Higher Education Funding Council (SHEFC) (1993a) Consultation Paper 10/93, *Funding of Continuing Education*.

SHEFC (1993b) circular letter 16/93.

SHEFC (1994) circular letter 53/94.

Scottish Office (1991) *Access and Opportunity; A Strategy for Education and Training*, HMSO, Edinburgh.

Scottish Office Education Department (1992) *Costs and Benefits of Adult Basic Education*, Scottish Council for Research in Education, Edinburgh.

Sedgwick, G.F. & Winnard, D. (1971) 'Trade union education – is it a dead end?', *WEA News*, 1, 4.

Select Committee on Estimates (1951–52) *Fourth Report: Training, Rehabilitation and Resettlement*, HMSO.

Shackleton, J. (1992) *Training Too Much? A Sceptical Look at the Economics of Skill Provision in the UK*, Institute of Economic Affairs.

Sharp, P.R. (1971) 'Whisky money and the development of technical and secondary education in the 1890s', *Journal of Educational Administration and History*, 4, 1, pp.31–6.

Shaw, M. & Crowther, J. (1995) 'Beyond subversion', in Mayo, M. & Thompson, J. (eds) *Adult Learning, Critical Intelligence and Social Change*, NIACE.

Shaw, R. (1959) 'Controversies', in Raybould, S.G. (ed.) *Trends in English Adult Education*, Heinemann, Oxford.

Shaw, R. (1971) 'Universities and the WEA: myths and reality'. *Adult Education*, 44, 1.

Shearer, J.G.S. (1976) 'Town and gown together: 250 years of extra-mural teaching at the University of Glasgow', reprint from the *College Courant*, University of Glasgow.

Sheldrake, J. & Vickerstaff, S. (1987) *The History of Industrial Training in Britain*, Avebury, Aldershot.

Sheridan, D. & Calder, J. (eds) (1985) *Speak for Yourself: A Mass Observation Anthology, 1937–49*. OUP.

Shrapnell, S. (1974) 'They look normal but ....', in Bentovim, M. & Kedney, R. (eds) *Aspects of Adult Literacy*, Merseyside and District Institute of Adult Education.

Shrimpton, T (1985) 'Is further education providing for the unemployed?', *Journal of Further and Higher Education*, 9, 3, pp.3–8.

Simon, B. (1965) *Education and the Labour Movement 1870–1920*, Lawrence & Wishart.

Simon, B. (1974) *The Two Nations and the Educational Structure 1780–1870*.

Simon, B. (1980) 'The 1944 Education Act: a conservative measure' *History of Education*, 15, 1.

Simon, B. (1985) *Does Education Matter?*, Lawrence & Wishart.

Simon, B. (ed.) (1990) *The Search for Enlightenment: The Working Class and Adult Education in the Twentieth Century*, NIACE.

Simon, B. (ed.) (1991) *Education and the Social Order 1940–1990*, Lawrence & Wishart.

Small, N.J. (1975) 'Policy and structure in English adult education', *Studies in Adult Education*, 7, 2, pp.150–67.

Small, N.J. (1976) 'Two British adult education reports', *Comparative Education*, 12, 3, pp.255–65.

Small, N.J. (1982) 'LEA adult education: is there life to come?', *Studies in Adult Education*, 14, pp.85–94.

Smith, A. (1915) 'Women in industry: a reply to critics', *Plebs*, 7, 12.

Smith, A. (1995) 'The cockpit of culture', review of Briggs, A. *The History of Broadcasting in the United Kingdom 1955–1974*, *New Statesman & Society*, 2 June.

Smith, T. (1984) 'Trade union education: its past and future', *Industrial Relations Journal*, 15, 2.

Smith, V. (1980) 'Aspects of policy in Scottish adult education', *Continuing Education* (March), pp.11–13.

Snape, R. (1995) *Leisure and the Rise of the Public Library*, The Library Association.

Society for Cooperative Studies (1983) 'Women in cooperation', *Bulletin*, 47.

Society of Industrial Tutors/TGWU (1988) *The Impossible Dream: The Future of Paid Educational Leave in Britain*.

Spencer, B. (1987) 'University adult education under attack', *Higher Education Review*, 19, 2, pp.42–51.

Spencer, B. (1989) 'Making the difference: the two year TGWU distance learning course', *The Industrial Tutor* (Autumn).

Stamper, A. (1986) 'Education in Women's Institutes', *Adult Education*, 59, 1.

Standing Conference of Rural Community Councils (1977) *The Story of Rural Community Councils*, NCSS.

Standing Conference on University Teaching and Research in the Education of Adults (SCUTREA) (nd) *Victorian Learning and Leisure: Mechanics' Institutes*, Stockport.

Standing Consultative Council on Youth and Community Service (SCCYCS) (1969) *Community of Interests*, HMSO, Edinburgh.

Starr, M. (1917a) 'Why not?', *Plebs*, 9, 10.

Starr, M. (1917b) *How to Start a Social Science Class*, Plebs League.

Starr, M. (1924) quoted in 'The Plebs Annual Meet', *Plebs*, 16, 10.

Starr, M. (1929) *Lies and Hate in Education*, Hogarth Press.

Start, K.B. & Wells, B.K. (1972) *The Trend of Reading Standards*, NFER, Windsor.

Stead, P. (1977) *Coleg Harlech: The First Fifty Years*, University of Wales Press.

Steele, T. (1987) 'From class consciousness to cultural studies: George Thompson and the WEA in Yorkshire', *Studies in the Education of Adults*, 19, 2.

Stephens, M. (1976) *Living Decisions in Family and Community: A Retrospective Impression of an Experimental 'Open Learning' Project for Adults*, BBC.

Stephens, M.D. (1985) 'Extra-mural studies in England', *Education To-day*, 35, 2, pp.46–52.

Stephens, M.D. (1990) *Adult Education*, Cassell.

Stephens, M.D. (ed.) (nd) *The Ashby Report* (1954) University of Nottingham Department of Adult Education.

Stephens, M.D. & Lawson, D. (1979) 'An elegy on the loss of adult learning', *Education*, 154, 19 (9 Nov.).

Stephens, M.D. & Roderick, G. (1973) 'The Royal Institute of Cornwall: initiatives in 19th century adult education', *Paedagogica Historica*, 13, pp.85–106.

Stephens, M.D. & Roderick, G. (1983) *Samuel Smiles and 19th Century Self-help in Education*, University of Nottingham.

Stephens, M.D. & Roderick, G. (nd) *The Royal Cornwall Polytechnic Society*, University of Liverpool.

Stephens, W.B. (1958) *The Development of Adult Education in Warrington during the Nineteenth Century*, University of Exeter.

Stephens, W.B. (1987) *Education, Literacy and Society 1830–70*, University of Manchester.

Stephens, W.B. (1990) 'Literacy in England, Scotland and Wales, 1500–1900', *History of Education Quarterly*, 30, 4, special issue on history of literacy, pp.545–71.

Stevenson, C. (1985) *Challenging Adult Illiteracy: Reading and Writing Disabilities in the British Army*, Teachers College Press.

Steward, T. & Alexander, D. (1988) *Information and Guidance on Adult Learning Opportunities in Scotland,* Scottish Academic Press, Edinburgh.

Stewart, S., Reynolds, J. & Elsdon, K.T. (1992) *Adult Learning in Voluntary Organisations,* 2, University of Nottingham.

Stewart, W.A.C. (1974) 'The University's Commitment to Adult Education', *Ninth Mansbridge Memorial Lecture,* University of Leeds.

Stock, A. (1992) 'Looking back and looking forward', *Convergence,* 25, 4.

Stocks, M. (1953) *The Workers' Educational Association: The First Fifty Years,* Allen and Unwin.

Strathclyde Regional Council Policy Review Group on Community Development Services (1978) *Report* (The Worthington Report), Strathclyde Regional Council.

Strathclyde University (1980) 'Survey of Attitudes to the Women's Institutes', NFWI.

Street, B. (1994) *Adult Literacy in the UK: A History of Research and Practice,* National Centre for Adult Literacy Policy Paper Series, University of Pennsylvania, Philadelphia.

Stuttard, G. (1975) 'Studying together in an industrial context', in Coker, E. & Stuttard, G. (eds) *Industrial Studies, 1: The Key Skills,* Arrow Books.

Styler, W.E. (1951) *Questions and Discussion,* WEA.

Styler, W.E. (1965) *Adult Education in East Yorkshire 1875–1960,* University of Hull.

Styler, W.E. (1973) *A Bibliographical Guide to Adult Education in Rural Areas 1918–1972,* Department of Adult Education, University of Hull.

Sumsion, J. (1993) 'Seeking the whole truth: library and information statistics', *Public Library Journal,* 8, 3.

Sutherland, J. (1983) 'The political fund ballot and trade union education', *Trade Union Studies Journal,* 12.

Sylvester, D.W. (ed.) (1970) *Educational Documents 800–1816,* Methuen.

Taking Liberties Collective (1989) *Learning the Hard Way,* Macmillan.

Tawney, R.H. (1943) 'Education: The Task Before Us', Presidential address to the WEA Annual Conference, *WEA Education Pamphlet,* 6, WEA.

Tawney, R.H. (29 September 1948) Letter to S.G. Raybould, quoted in Fieldhouse, R. (1977) *The WEA: Aims and Achievements 1903–77,* University of Syracuse, pp.26–7.

Tawney, R.H. (1956) 'Design for democracy', *The Manchester Guardian,* 19 October.

Taylor, B. (1983) *Eve and the New Jerusalem,* Virago.

Taylor, F.J (1976) 'The making of the 1919 Report', *Studies in Adult Education,* 8, pp.134–48.

Taylor, J. (1978) 'The Advisory Council for Adult and Continuing Education', *Adult Education,* 51, 4, pp.209–15.

Taylor, J. & Warburton, M. (1981) 'Local Development Councils for adult education', *Adult Education,* 25, 1, pp.42–5.

Taylor, R., Rockhill, K. & Fieldhouse, R. (1985) *University Adult Education in England and the USA,* Croom Helm.

Taylor, R. & Ward, K (1981) 'Extra-mural work: different settings, common themes', *Adult Education,* 54, 1, pp.12–18.

Taylor, R. & Ward, K. (1988) 'Adult education with unemployed people', in Lovett, T. (ed.) *Radical Approaches to Adult Education,* Routledge, pp.242–62.

Tebbit, Lord (1989) Correspondence with John McIlroy.

Tett, L. (1994) 'Where have all the men gone? Adult participation in community education', *Scottish Journal of Adult and Continuing Education,* 1, 2, pp.41–49.

Tett, L. (1995) 'Community education', in Kirk, G. (ed.) *Moray House and Change in Higher Education*, Scottish Academic Press, Edinburgh, pp.59–68.

Thomas, J. (1982) *Radical Adult Education, Theory and Practice*, University of Nottingham.

Thompson, A. (1992) 'Sustaining the cutting edge: non-traditional partners in adult education', *Adults Learning*, 3, 6.

Thompson, E.P. (1965) 'The peculiarities of the English', in Miliband, R. & Saville, J. (eds) *The Socialist Register*, 2, pp.311–62.

Thompson, E.P. (1968 edn) *The Making of the English Working Class*, Pelican.

Thompson, G.H. (1938) *The Field of Study for WEA Classes*, WEA.

Thompson, J. (1983) *Learning Liberation: Women's Response to Men's Education*, Croom Helm.

Thompson, J. (ed.) (1980) *Adult Education for a Change*, Hutchinson.

Thompson, L. (1996) 'The golden thread of empire: women's popular education in Lancashire Federation of Womens' Institutes; 1920 to 1939', *Journal of Educational Administration and History*, 28, 1, pp.42–57.

Thompson, P. (1978) *The Voice of the Past*, Oxford University Press.

Thoms, D.W. (1974) 'The Education Act of 1918 and the development of central government control of education', *Journal of Educational Administration and History*, 6, 2, pp.26–30.

Thomson, C. (1991) 'A community work approach in adult education', *International Journal of Lifelong Education*, 10, 3, pp.181–96.

Thomson, D. (1964) 'Some implications of expansion', *Adult Education*, 36, pp.232–41.

Tight, M. (ed.) (1983) *Opportunities for Adult Education*, Croom Helm.

Tight, M. & Sidhu, K. (1992) 'Provision and productivity in university continuing education', *Adults Learning*, 4, 4, pp.101–2.

Titmus, C. (1981) *Strategies for Adult Education*, Open University Press.

Titmus, C. & Steele, T. (1995) *Adult Education for Independence*, University of Leeds.

Tomlinson, S. (1982) *A Sociology of Special Education*, Routledge & Kegan Paul.

Topham, A.J. (1979) *Teaching Trade Unionists*, University of Hull.

Topham, A.J. (1981) 'The need for political education', *The Industrial Tutor* (Autumn).

Topham, A.J. (1992) 'Education policy in the TGWU 1922–44: a tribute to John Price', *The Industrial Tutor* (Spring).

Tough, A. (1983) 'Self-planned learning and major personal change', in Tight, M. (ed.) *Education for Adults*, vol. 1, *Adult Learning and Education*, Routledge, pp.141–52.

Toyne, P. (1979) *Educational Credit Transfer: Feasibility Study. Final Report*.

Trenaman, J.M. (1961) 'An Investigation, by Statistical Methods, of the Effective Communication of Educative Material and an Assessment of the Factors Making for Such Communication, with Special Reference to Broadcasting', unpublished PhD thesis, University of Oxford.

Trenaman, J.M. (1967) *Communication and Comprehension*, an edited version of his 1961 PhD thesis with preface by Hutchinson, E.M., Longmans.

*Tribune* (1983) 'TUC to let employers vet training courses', 19 August.

TUC (1922) (1946) (1951) (1960) (1975) (1990) (1991a) (1993) *Report*.

TUC (1966) *Considerations Affecting Regional Facilities and Regional Organisation*.

TUC (1968) *Training Shop Stewards*.

TUC (1969) *Industrial Training Since the 1964 Act: A Report of a Conference of Trade Union Members of Industrial Training Boards*.

TUC (1970) *Supplementary Evidence to the Russell Committee on Adult Education. Organisation.*

TUC (1975) (1976) *General Council Report.*

TUC (1983) *Workbook on Racism.*

TUC (1986a) 'Trade Unions and the Economy': notes for Tutors.

TUC (1986b) *Tackling Racism.*

TUC (1987) *Review of the TUC's Education Service.*

TUC (1991b) *Report of Annual Meeting of Chairs and Secretaries of TUC Advisory Committees.*

TUC (1991c) Women's Committee: Minutes.

TUC/BEC (1963) 'Statement by the Trade Union Congress and the British Employers Confederation on the Training of Shop Stewards.'

TUC/CBI (1967) 'Statement by TUC and Confederation of British Industry endorsed by the Central Training Council.'

Turner, C.M. (1968) 'Political, religious and occupational support for the early Mechanics' Institutes', *Vocational Aspects*, 20, 45, pp.65–70.

Tylecote, M. (1957) *The Mechanics' Institutes of Lancashire and Yorkshire before 1851*, University of Manchester.

Uden, T. (1987) 'The REPLAN experience: a view from the centre', *Adult Education*, 60, 1, pp.7–14.

Unesco (1972) *Learning To Be* (The Faure Report), Unesco, Paris.

Unesco (1976) *The Experimental World Literacy Programme: A Critical Assessment*, Unesco/UNDP, Paris, New York.

Unit for the Development of Adult Continuing Education (UDACE) (1991) Report to NIACE Council (December).

Universities Association for Continuing Education (UACE) External Relations Sub-Commitee (2nd Dec. 1993), unpublished minute 2.

Universities Council for Adult and Continuing Education (Scotland) (UCACE(S)) (1993) 'Continuing Education in Scottish Universities', a briefing document for The Scottish Higher Education Funding Council.

Universities Council for Adult Education (UCAE) (1948) *The Universities in Adult Education: A Statement of Principles.*

UCAE (1961) *The Universities and Adult Education.*

UCAE (1962) *Memorandum to the Committee of Vice-Chancellors and Principals.*

UCAE (1970) *University Adult Education in the Late Twentieth Century: A Statement Submitted to the Committee on Adult Education.*

Van Straubenzee, W.R. (1976) 'Whither the Open University?', Lecture to Open University Students' Association, Bristol University (April 9).

Venables, P. (1976) *Report of the Committee on Continuing Education*, Open University

Venables, P.F.R. (1955) *Technical Education*, Bell.

Vernon, B. (1982) *Ellen Wilkinson 1891–1947*, Croom Helm.

Vincent, D. (1989) *Literacy and Popular Culture*, Cambridge University Press.

Wagner, L. (1995) 'The New Agenda for Continuing Education', *Occasional Paper*, 1, Forum for the Advancement of Continuing Education.

Walker, J.R.A. (1993) *Information Matters*, Information Services Group.

Waller, R.D. (1967) 'A philosophy of adult education', *International Review of Community Development*, 17–18, pp.1–8.

Wallis, J. & Mee, G. (1983) *Community Schools: Claims and Performance*, University of Nottingham Department of Adult Education.

Ward, K. (1983) 'A university adult education project with the unemployed', *Studies in Adult Education*, 15, pp.74–84.

Ward, K. & Taylor, R. (eds) (1986) *Adult Education and the Working Class: Education for the Missing Millions,* Croom Helm.

Wardle, P. (1994) 'Section 11 funding crisis', *Language Issues,* 6, 1, National Association for Teaching English and Other Community Languages to Adults, Birmingham.

Warren, A. (1971) 'The aims and methods of the education and training of shop stewards: a case study', *Industrial Relations Journal,* 2, 1.

Watson, M. (1987) 'The origins of the Mechanics' Institutes of North Lancashire', *Journal of Educational Administration and History,* 19, 2, pp.12–25.

Watts, R. (1980) 'The Unitarian contribution to the development of female education, 1790–1850', *History of Education,* 9, 4, pp.273–86.

WEA (1938) *The Adult Student as Citizen.*

WEA (1943) *Workers' Education in Great Britain.*

WEA (1945) *Handbook for Branch Officers.*

WEA (1947) *The Future in Adult Education: A Programme.*

WEA (1953a) *The Workers' Educational Association 1946–1952: A Review.*

WEA (1953b) *Trade Union Education: Report of a WEA Working Party.*

WEA (1954) *Implications of the Ashby Report ... (for) the Association.*

WEA (1958) *Education for a Changing Society.*

WEA (1960) *Aspects of Adult Education.*

WEA (1966a) *Report of Working Party on Structure, Organisation, Finance and Staffing.*

WEA (1966b) *Report for Branches of Special National Conference Decisions.*

WEA (1967) *Education for a Changing Society,* part 2.

WEA (1969) *Unfinished Businesss.*

WEA (1970) *Summary and Short Statement of Evidence to the Russell Committee.*

WEA (1973) *Report of the National Committee 1971–73.*

WEA (1975) *Report of the National Committee 1973–75.*

WEA (1976a) *Report of Survey of WEA Branches.*

WEA (1976b) *Work in the Priority Areas: 11 Future Developments.*

WEA (1991a) 'National Development Plan 1991–1994' adopted by the National Executive Committee (March).

WEA (1991b) 'National Executive Committee Report to Biennial Conference for 1989/91'.

WEA (1991c) *WEA Response to the Government White Papers.*

WEA (1991d) 'Around the Districts', *Reportback,* 1, 1.

WEA (1991e) National Executive Committee discussion paper (20 April).

WEA (1992a) National Executive Committee working paper on 'Constitutional and Organisational Matters' (15 Feb.).

WEA (1992b) 'Update United Kingdom', *Reportback,* 1, 4.

WEA (1992?) Discussion papers relating to 'An Association of Four Nations' and 'Relations between the National WEA and the Celtic Districts'.

WEA (1993a) 'National Executive Committee Report for 1991/93'.

WEA (1993b) 'Around the Districts', *Reportback,* 1, 5.

WEA (1994) *Reportback,* 1, 8.

WEA (1995) *Annual Report.*

Webb, R.K. (1971) *The British Working-class Reader 1790–1848: Literacy and Social Tension,* Augustus M. Kelley, New York.

Webb, S. & B. (1921) *The Consumers' Co-operative Movement,* Longmans, Green & Co.

Welch, E. (1976) 'The pre-history of the university tutorial class', *History of Education Society Bulletin,* 17, pp.39–44.

Westwood, S. (1988) 'Domesticity and its discontents: feminism and adult education in past times (1870–1920)', in Lovett, T. (ed.) *Radical Approaches to Adult Education*, Routledge.

Westwood, S. (1991) 'Constructing the future: a postmodern agenda for adult education', in Westwood, S. & Thomas, J. (eds) *Radical Agendas?: The Politics of Adult Education*, NIACE, pp.44–56.

Westwood, S. (1992) 'When class became community: radicalism in adult education', in Rattansi, A. & Reeder, D. (eds) *Rethinking Radical Education*, Lawrence & Wishart, pp.222–48.

White, A. (1963) *The Story of Army Education 1643–1963*, Harrap.

White, E.W. (1975) *The Arts Council of Great Britain*, Davis Paynter.

Whitston, K. (1982) 'Breaking fresh ground? The new TUC introductory course', *The Industrial Tutor* (Spring).

Whittam, F. (1929) 'Class consciousness runs riot', *Plebs*, 21, 5.

Wicks, H. (1992) *Keeping My Head*, Socialist Platform.

Wilderspin, E. (1968) 'Adult Education and Development', *R.H.Tawney Memorial Lecture*, Rochester.

Wilkinson, E. (1928) 'Should women wash-up?', *Plebs*, 20, 1.

Willcocks, J. (1984) *Years Ahead: Broadcasting and the Educational Needs of the Elderly*, Independent Broadcasting Authority.

Williams, D. (1973) 'Where will adult education stand after local government reorganisation?', *Adult Education*, 45, pp.348–52.

Williams, D. (1977) 'Adult and continuing education and the institutions of higher education' *Studies in Adult Education*, 9, 2, pp.165–76.

Williams, D.J. (1915) 'Letter', *Plebs*, 7, 1.

Williams, D.J. (1924) 'The standard of our education', *Plebs*, 16, 12.

Williams, J.E. (1954) 'An experiment in trade union education', *Adult Education*, 27, 2.

Williams, S. & Nicola, R. (1982) 'Education in NUPE', *Trade Union Studies Journal*, 6.

Williams, W.E. (1934) *The Auxiliaries of Adult Education*, British Institute of Adult Education.

Williams, W.E. & Heath, A.E. (1936) *Live and Learn*, Methuen.

Wilson, E. (1980) *Only Half Way to Paradise*, Tavistock.

Wilson, H. (1969) A speech by the Rt Hon Harold Wilson on the occasion of the [Open University] Charter Ceremony, 23 July.

Wiltshire, H.C. (1956) 'The Great Tradition in university adult education', *Adult Education*, 29, pp.88–97.

Wiltshire, H.C. (1957) 'The Great Tradition: a reply', *Adult Education*, 30, pp.6–19.

Wiltshire, H.C. (1963) 'Towards co-operation: Responsible Bodies and the LEA', *Adult Education*, 36, pp.184–92.

Wiltshire, H.C. (1976) 'Educative into educational: TV's transformation', and 'Teaching through television', in Rogers, A. (ed.) *The Spirit and the Form: Essays in Adult Education in Honour of Professor Harold Wiltshire*, University of Nottingham.

Wiltshire, H.C. (1983) 'The role of university adult education departments', *Studies in Adult Education*, 15, 1, pp.3–10.

Wiltshire, H.C. & Bayliss, F. (1965) *Teaching through Television*, National Institute of Adult Education/University of Nottingham Department of Adult Education.

Withnall, A. (1986) *The Christian Churches and Adult Education*, NIACE.

Withnall, A. (1994) 'Literacy on the agenda: the origins of the Adult Literacy Campaign in the United Kingdom', *Studies in the Education of Adults*, 26, 1, pp.67–85.

Women's Institutes, Nat. Fed. of, (1951) *Introducing Women's Institutes*, Gryphon Press.

Women's Institutes, Nat. Fed. of, (1994) 'Home and Country' video script, NFWI.

Women's Institutes, Nat. Fed. of, (1994/5) *Denman College Brochure*, NFWI.

Woodley, A. (1987) 'Has the Open University been an unqualified success?', *Journal of Access Studies*, 2, 2 (Autumn).

Woodley, A. (1989) 'Early undergraduate drop-out', Open University committee paper.

Woodley, A. & McIntosh, N.E. (1980) *The Door Stood Open*, Falmer Press, Lewes.

Woolf, B. (1922) 'The London Labour College curriculum', *Plebs*, 14, 8.

Workers' Education Trade Union Committee (WETUC) (1944) *Report of Workers' Education and the Trade Union Movement*.

Yarnit, M. (1980) 'Second Chance to Learn, Liverpool: class and adult education', in Thompson, J. (ed.) *Adult Education for a Change*, Hutchinson, pp.174–91.

Yeo, E. & S. (1981) *Popular Culture and Class Conflict 1590–1914*, Harvester.

Yorke, P. (1977) 'Education and the working class: Ruskin College 1899–1909', *Ruskin Students' Labour History Pamphlet*, 1.

Young, M. (1962) 'Is your child in the unlucky generation?', *Where?*, 10 (Autumn), pp.3–5.

Yow, V. (1993) 'In the classroom and not at the sink; women in the National Council of Labour Colleges', *History of Education*, 22, 2.

# Notes on Contributors

**Peter Baynes**  After the Second World War Peter Baynes commenced a career in post-compulsory education which continued throughout his working life. He taught at Hertford College of FE, where he was responsible for the evening class programme; was appointed FE adviser in Leicestershire, where he was involved in the development of Community Colleges; and retired as Dean of the School of Adult and Social Studies at Goldsmiths College in 1980. He served on the Executive Committees of NIACE and the Educational Centres Association. Since retiring he has taken an OU degree, is involved in the University of the Third Age, and writes.

**Roseanne Benn**  Roseanne Benn is a senior lecturer in the Department of Continuing and Adult Education at the University of Exeter. Previously she taught at Kingston Polytechnic and Hillcroft College. She has always been interested in the position of women in continuing education and is currently chair of the UACE Women and Continuing Education Professional Network and co-chair of the ESREA Gender Network. She has written widely on adult education issues and is co-editing a book on 'Women and Continuing Education'.

**Walter Drews**  Walter Drews is a product of adult education. His formal education was ended abruptly at the age of 11 by the outbreak of war in Europe. It was made good by many years attendance at 'night school' classes. He became an adult education tutor organiser and for 20 years was Principal of Wansfell Residential College in Essex. His recently completed PhD thesis was on the British short-term residential colleges 1945–95. His current teaching interests are German culture and educational gerontology.

**John Field**  Since 1994 John Field has been Professor of Continuing Education at the University of Ulster. Previously he was Director of Continuing Education at the University of Bradford and before that he worked at Northern College and in the Department of Continuing Education at the University of Warwick. Recent publications include *Learning through Labour: Education, unemployment and the state, 1890–1939* (1992) and *Education and Vocational Training Policy* (1994).

**Roger Fieldhouse**  In 1964 Roger Fieldhouse became tutor organiser for the WEA in North Yorkshire and, six years later, joined the staff of the Extramural Department at the University of Leeds. After some 12 years of researching Yorkshire history he turned his attention to the history of adult education, completing his PhD thesis on 'The ideology of English Responsible Body adult education 1925–1950' in 1984. Two years later he moved to the University of Exeter as Professor of Adult Education and Director of

Continuing Education. He has written extensively on Yorkshire history and the history and politics of British adult education.

**Brian Groombridge** Brian Groombridge, Professor Emeritus of Adult Education, the University of London, and honorary doctor of the University of Helsinki and the Open University, is a former Director of the Department of Extramural Studies in London, and Deputy Secretary of NIACE. His professional experience as a broadcaster includes writing and presenting adult education series for BBC Further Education Radio and for Independent Television. From 1968–76 he was the Independent Broadcasting Authority's Head of Educational Programmes, and more recently co-founder of EUROSTEP, an experiment in satellite communications with the European Space Agency. He was a member of the OU Planning Committee and the Russell Committee and has written widely on adult education and broadcasting.

**Mary Hamilton** Mary Hamilton is senior research fellow in the department of Educational Research, Lancaster University. She has worked for a number of years researching, teaching and publishing in the field of Adult Basic Education and literacy. Her interests are in processes of adult learning in formal and informal settings; developing collaborative research methodologies; policy and comparative perspectives on basic education for adults. She belongs to the interdisciplinary Lancaster Literacy Research Group and is a founder member of the national network, Research and Practice in Adult Literacy (RaPAL).

**John McIlroy** Currently reader in the Department of Sociology at the University of Manchester, John McIlroy has previously worked in the Extramural departments at Oxford and Manchester, particularly involved in access courses and work with trade union representatives. He has written widely on politics, industrial relations and the education of adults. Recent publications include *Going to University: The student guide* (Manchester University Press, 1993); *Trade Unions in Britain Today* (2nd edn, Manchester University Press, 1995); and, with Sally Westwood, *Border Country: Raymond Williams in adult education* (NIACE, 1993).

**Harold Marks** Harold Marks joined the Oxford University Delegacy for Extramural Studies as a full time tutor working for the WEA in North Staffordshire from 1936–42. After war service mainly in the Army Educational Corps, he became education secretary of the Educational Centres Association and adviser to the National Federation of Community Associations from 1946–50. He was then appointed an HMI concerned mainly with adult education. Since retirement as Staff Inspector in 1979 he has researched and written on aspects of adult education including education in penal institutions and FE Colleges, and the history of the Community Association movement.

**Ian Martin** Ian Martin is lecturer in Community Education at Moray House Institute of Education, Heriot Watt University. He has taken an interest in community education since being introduced to community-based approaches to adult education while working in Zambia in the 1970s. He has a particular interest in the potential relationship between popular education and progressive social movements. He is co-editor of *Community Education: An agenda for educational reform* (1987) and *Education and Community: The politics of practice* (1992).

**Naomi Sargant**  Naomi Sargant has combined a professional life as an educator and social researcher with a commitment to extending educational opportunities for adults. Starting working life as a market researcher, she became a founder-member of the Open University, running its Survey Research Department and subsequently becoming Professor of Applied Social Research and a pro-Vice-Chancellor. From 1981–9 she was Channel 4's Senior Commissioning Editor for Educational Programming. She currently works as a writer, researcher and consultant in the fields of the education of adults, evaluation and the media. She is a Visiting Professor at the OU, a Vice-Chair of NCVO and a trustee of the National Extension college and Open College of the Arts. As Naomi McIntosh she has published widely in the field of educational research. Recent books include *Learning and 'Leisure'* (1991), *Adult Learners, Broadcasting and Channel 4* (1992), and *Learning for a Purpose* (1993).

# INDEX

*(See page 454 for a list of abbreviations not included in the index.)*

# Other Abbreviations not in the Index

ACRE        Action for the Community in Rural England
ACSTT       Advisory Committee on the Supply of Training for Teachers
AETV        Adult Education Television
AIUTA       Association Internationale des Universités de Troisième Age
ALU         Adult Literacy Unit
BWP         (Army) British Way and Purpose
CTC         Central Training Council
ESA         Employment Services Agency
FETV        Further and Adult Education Television
FTE         Full-time equivalent
GCSE        General Certificate of Education
ITC         Independent Television Commission
NCILT       National Centre for Industrial Language Training
PEVE        Post-experience Vocational Education
PRO         Public Record Office London
SCCYCS      Standing Consultative Council on Youth and Community Serv-
            ices (Scotland)
SCEC        Scottish Community Education Council
SCUTREA     Standing Conference on University Teaching and Research in the
            Education of Adults
TSA         Training Services Agency